BISON
BOOKS

D0967126

Voices of Wounded Knee

By William S. E. Coleman

University of Nebraska Press
Lincoln & London

Manufactured in the United States of America
∞
First Bison Books printing: 2002
Library of Congress Cataloging-in-Publication Data
Coleman, William S. E., 1926–
Voices of wounded knee / by William S. E. Coleman,
[compiler]. p. cm. Includes bibliographical references
and index. ISBN 0-8032-1506-1 (cloth: alkaline paper)
ISBN 0-8032-6422-4 (paper: alkaline paper)
1. Wounded Knee Massacre, S.D., 1890—Personal
narratives. 2. Dakota Indians—Wars, 1890–1891.
3. Ghost dance—History. I. Title.
E83.89.C66 2000 973.8′6–dc21
99-087377

Listen now, you cannot sell the ground you walk on.—*Crazy Horse*

*

Our Pilgrim Fathers were a Godly people. When they landed that day on Plymouth Rock, from off the Mayflower, they fell upon their knees. They thanked Almighty God for the many blessings he had vouchsafed them that day in enabling them to reach the land of liberty and free thought. Later on they fell upon the aborigines.—*Mark Twain*

To: Commissioner of Indian Affairs

From: Daniel Royer
Indian Agent
Pine Ridge Agency, S.D.

December 29, 1890

On the Wounded Knee Creek this morning while the soldiers were disarming Big Foot and his band after their surrender, a fight took place, which resulted in the killing of about three hundred Indians and several soldiers, including Captain Wallace, with a number WOUNDED.

*

A beautiful dream, a wonderful dream, died there, there in the bloody snow.
—*Black Elk*

Contents

ILLUSTRATIONS *following page 198*

MAPS

Preface

In the summer of 1971 my sons and I drove west in search of information regarding William F. Cody (Buffalo Bill) and his career as a frontiersman and showman. At that time people were alive who had known Cody. We would interview an old-timer and be told of another a few miles ahead—and in this manner we moved across Nebraska and north to South Dakota. I did not expect that search to lead me to this project, one that would span more than twenty-five years of my life.

Several informants told us that Ben Black Elk, an Oglala Lakota who worked near Mount Rushmore, had memories of his father's accounts of a European tour with Cody in 1889 and 1890. This excited us since he was the son of Black Elk, the author of *Black Elk Speaks*, a book that had inspired a generation of readers.

It was early evening when my sons and I drove into the glade where the Lakotas camped while they worked around Mount Rushmore. The women and children of Black Elk's family lived in a simple wooden house, but the old chief and his son slept in a nearby tent. By the time we arrived, Black Elk had returned to camp after a day spent posing with tourists beneath the massive sculptures of former presidents.

A teenage grandchild directed me to the simple canvas tent. Sitting in it, chatting with his son, was the wizened but still vital Indian chief. Black Elk was a striking man. His hair was still black, his body lean and muscular; but his face, dominated by a prominent nose, was deeply wrinkled.

He immediately turned his attention to my two sons: Wim, seventeen, and Eric, twelve, and greeted them warmly. I knew enough about the Lakotas to understand that they believe that young boys, unlike white men, could be trusted and, more importantly, educated. They had not yet been corrupted by their white elders. I sensed that I was merely an escort.

The three of us were invited into Black Elk's tent. Only two bare mattresses were inside. With Black Elk's permission, Wim set up our tape recorder. Before I could ask a question, Black Elk began to speak, a severe cough punctuating his words. At first he merely recited things he had said many times before, but his eloquence grew as he talked. As he spoke, I interjected questions, but his answers were directed to my sons. He was addressing the future in the hope that the young would create a better world.

"Well, my name is Black Elk," he began, "Benjamin Black Elk. I'm the son of Black Elk. You've probably heard of him or probably read his book *Black Elk Speaks*, also *When a Tree Flowered*, also his last book *The Seven Rituals of the Sioux*."[1]

He began to tell of the Lakota past as it had been handed down to him. I asked fewer questions, and my sons listened, their eyes locked on this charismatic figure who told variations of stories they had read in history books, stories they now heard from within the Native American culture. As the day faded into twilight, history became new, illuminated, and alive.

Black Elk spoke of Buffalo Bill and of his father's appearances in Europe and return to Pine Ridge. It was the autumn of 1890, a time when there were rumors of the coming of a new Messiah, a Messiah that would save the Lakotas and bring back their way of life. Black Elk began to relate what had happened at Wounded Knee on December 29, 1890. Buffalo Bill Cody faded into the background as he talked.

"And the Indians were starving, see," he said. "At that time we were supposed to get rations, and we never got it, see. And we hate the guts of the white man for taking away their land away from us, and the buffalo—our only . . . cheap industry because we used the hides for our clothing and our tipi from the buffalo, and I can name three, four other items that we used from the buffalo.

"So there you are. My ancestors were desperate. They didn't like it all, what the white man was doing. And then somebody out in the West—says 'All right, brothers, I'm Christ, and you do this, you.' And they said, 'The white man will be wiped out of the face of the earth, and the buffalo will come back, and your dead will come back. But you must dance the Ghost Dance.'"

Wim asked, "What was this Ghost Dance?"

He had good reason to ask. It was rarely mentioned in high school or college history books then, and, when it was, it was treated like a minor incident, a footnote to the so-called Indian wars. As I listened, I looked back to my college days as a history major. I didn't remember any of my teachers mentioning the incident.

"Well, this was a religion. It was not warful," Black Elk continued. "But Wovoka told them you can't have no weapon, no nothing, not even a knife, when you dance.

"Well, naturally you know, us Indians, we believe in a Great Spirit, and we're supposed to be related to the four-leggeds and the wings of the universe. We are all one, see. The dirt. We also are dirt, see, and we go back to mother earth when we die.

"So they claimed that the Great Spirit established a relationship on this earth between man and the wings of the universe and the four-leggeds, which is anything that's movable. So when this man told them that you do this, . . . they took to it. They hated the guts of the white man because of all of this trouble they had. They were desperate. So they danced.

"And then Kicking Bear and Short Bull and Good Thunder, they were the ones that went to see the guy named Wovoka—supposed to be Christ—and they came back and they introduced the dance to the Sioux. But before that, all the tribes were dancing, see. We were desperate and in our last moments.

"It was religion. And the government says—the United States says—that [the] four greatest laws are the freedom of religion, the freedom of speech and so on. It was just religion. But the government feared it. At that time we were at war, you know. We had wiped Custer out, and Sitting Bull was still alive. My father was there when Custer was wiped out."

A more familiar page of western history suddenly entered Black Elk's tent: the defeat of Custer in 1876. I asked in amazement, "He was there?"

"Yeah, he was there. He was sixteen years old."

"Your father fought against Custer?"

"Yeah, he fought Custer. The teenagers, they were there, too."

"Did he ever say anything about it?"

"Yes, there was a book called *Black Elk Speaks*. You can buy that, you know—it's a dollar and a half—and it tells you the life story of my father, and I was interpreter for that book, see. And my father died in 1950 at the age of ninety-six. He told me all this. And he was there when that Wounded Knee happened, see."[2]

Black Elk digressed into details about the defeat of Custer that were not in *Black Elk Speaks*, but that is another story. Eventually Black Elk returned to his view of what had happened at Wounded Knee in 1890: "Oh, Big Foot was over to the north, near where Sitting Bull was. But the government was really, really afraid of us because they thought that we would make trouble. But it wasn't at all that way. We were just praying that the Great Spirit would help us out.

"Well, anyway, we'll say that we were in trouble, see, and we want the Great Spirit to help, but there's no way of getting help from nobody at all because we were subdued, and we were whipped, and, see, the white man was coming just like water. And all we could do was depend on the Great Spirit.

"So they danced the Ghost Dance. They claimed the Ghost Dance was introduced because when you die, your spirit goes away, but it'll come back. We sing to the Great Spirit, and we say, you know, just like that song that says . . . "

Black Elk began to sing in Lakota, a plaintive melody in a deep, resonant voice:

Ee-nah, hay coo-e-yay, Ee-nah, hay coo-e-yay.
Misunkala cheyaya omaniye,
Misunkala cheyaya omaniye.
Ee-nah, hay coo-e-yay, Ee-nah, hay coo-e-yay.

"That's what they sing. Then they hold hands. It's not a great big song, but it's sacred. [It] means: 'My Mother come back, mother come back. My brother is crying for you.'

"The mother had died and gone, see, and the little fella is looking for his mother and cries, see.

"So that's why they claim that when we dance that way, the buffalo will come back and the white man will be wiped out of the face of the earth, see, and that's the belief they had which is not right, see. It didn't happen that way. We got fooled.

"But the government was so afraid of us that Sitting Bull was killed. His own people killed him."

"His own people?" Wim asked.

"They couldn't arrest him. The white man, they was afraid of him, so policemen of his own tribe destroyed Sitting Bull and killed him. And they had a fight there, up at Grand River—and then they killed Sitting Bull.

"And Big Foot was there so he came back from the north over here. He was sick."

Black Elk's jump to Chief Big Foot, a Miniconjou Lakota, confused us. Then we realized that after Sitting Bull's death, Big Foot's people, who had been wandering away from their agency, took refuge in the Badlands.

"But when Big Foot came back to Porcupine Creek . . . when the soldiers went at him. And they escorted him to Wounded Knee. And that evening, they claim—the soldiers were pretty drunk, see. They claim, well, they drank all night, and they had a big time.

"Next morning, early morning, when the sun is up, Big Foot's gang and Big Foot—he was sick, see. And the soldiers, they took all the weapons away from him. They had the guns, everything, and they piled them in one place.

"And they claim what this one Indian said, 'No,' he said, 'we should die here. It's a good day to fight and a good day to die.' Just like Crazy Horse said when he wiped out Custer.

"So the soldiers try and take the gun away from him, and they claim they wrestled with that gun and that gun went off. When the gun went off, why, the soldiers were all thrown, and so they all fire. And the women and the children and everybody was right in the middle.

"Well, in this firing they killed almost three hundred women and children.

"About that time my father's not far off. He heard the gunfire so he went out there. He helped try and fight the soldiers, but they were outnumbered—didn't nobody have their weapon at all, see. So, we lost three hundred, about three hundred men, women, and children, which is not right, see.

"I always say that the government, this country, should study in history and in culture so we could know and understand each other better. But we haven't.

"I know the white man [because] I was a kid in Pennsylvania. I stayed six years over there. I graduated at Carlisle, Pennsylvania.[3] I'm a full-blood, but I know white man. But he doesn't know me yet.

"Anyway, my father described that fight. Most of the soldiers—the Seventh Cavalry . . . they're the cowards that came back and had revenge on us. My father said, 'A beautiful dream, a wonderful dream, died there, there in the bloody snow.'"

Later I discovered that a number of officers and noncommissioned officers at Wounded Knee had been with Reno's rear guard while Custer's troopers were being wiped out.

"[It] is up to us to make that dream come true," Black Elk resumed. "You know how Martin Luther King had a dream, but we hadn't. We didn't dream. We had a reality because before the white man came we were better off. We didn't know what the dollar was. We didn't know what whiskey was. We got along just fine. And our nation, our people nation's hoop was intact. It's a circle. We live in a circle. We believe that the Great Spirit has created us and all of the nature. The things that we see are part of the Great Spirit. That's what we believe. We were intact, but the white man came and broke that nation's hoop, and today, now, today, we Indians don't know what we are—whether we are going or coming back or what.

"We're a confused people. Not only us but the whole world is confused, you know, and if we do believe in our Indian religion there will be peace on this earth. Our pipe—it represents a portable altar that we use to pray to the Great Spirit. So that's how it happened.

"But that story, they say, that our people wanted to be like they used to be—wanted to migrate; they wanted nobody to bother them—today we have to change that. We have to keep our own culture. The white man's culture is being crammed down our throats so fast that we forget we're Indians. A lot of us Indians, we are ashamed that we are Indians. And the white man says, 'No, you take, go on reservations.' Why, all the little ones are getting away from our language. But we should be talking it."

"Do your grandchildren speak the language?"

"Yeah, my grandchildren speak it. I preach that, see, so all the little ones they talk the language."

By now we sat in the tent amidst dim shadows, listening to Black Elk's rich voice fill the small tent. He told more stories—fascinating stories about Custer's last stand, the Lakota religion, and Buffalo Bill—and he shared his views on education and tolerance.

As it darkened outside, we could see he was tiring. It was growing late, and Black Elk had to be at Mount Rushmore early the next morning to pose for pictures with tourists. The tips he received gave him money to support his family during the bitter Pine Ridge winters.

The conversation ended too soon. He and I shook hands, and he lightly touched my sons, smiling at them.

We drove away. It was a long time before we could say anything. There had been a magic in the old man's presence.

When we checked into our motel we played the interview again. It was then that I decided that the voices of the past must be allowed to speak.

A year later we read that Ben Black Elk was campaigning for George McGovern. A few months later, he died. There are many questions I could have asked him, but that evening in the gathering twilight was his time to speak to two young boys not yet white men. In the years that followed, his deep, rich-toned voice stayed with me as I began my search for the truth about Wounded Knee.

A few days later we stopped where Big Foot's band had camped in the Dakota Badlands. It was a bleak place in the summer, and I could only imagine how cold and windswept it must have been when the Ghost dancers camped there on that long-ago December day.

It was a short drive south to Wounded Knee through the fantastic landscape of the Badlands. At that time an old white church stood on the hill overlooking the Wounded Knee valley. Behind the church was the communal grave holding many of the slaughtered Lakotas. At its head stood an imposing gravestone. On it were carved the names of the Lakotas buried there. Other graves were nearby, some of Lakota soldiers who died in the service of their country during World War II. We wandered in the valley below. It was flat, but its flatness was intersected by gullies and a deep ravine. Here as many as three hundred Lakotas died. I would return again and again to study the terrain and trace the flow of the action. I was always disturbed by a sense of lives cut short. Indeed, as Black Elk said so many years ago, "A beautiful dream, a wonderful dream, died there, there in the bloody snow."

From Wounded Knee we drove through the Pine Ridge Reservation, stopping in the small town of the same name. I had been told that an old Lakota woman, whose name I have since forgotten, still lived there. She had been in the midst of the carnage that bloody morning of December 29, 1890. Perhaps I could record a first-person Lakota account of what had happened at Wounded Knee.

I left my sons in the car and knocked on the door of a small white house on a side street. An imposing middle-aged Lakota woman answered the door. She said the woman I wanted to interview was her mother, but she was too old and confused to speak with strangers. I asked if I could try. The daughter firmly refused, saying that when her mother spoke about the Wounded Knee Massacre, she was upset for days afterward.

Who was I to dredge up old horrors from a victim of my own government? I said I was sorry to have bothered her and left. I knew then that the living voices of the past were silent. The only voices left to me would have to be found in documents stored away in museums and family records: letters, journals, books, and newspaper clippings.

As time permitted, I began to create my mosaic. First I explored government documents and newspaper articles. Some were accurate, some biased, some intentionally warped. I ransacked dusty library stacks to find memoirs of soldiers and government officials. Most were self-serving. The task of writing about the Wounded Knee Massacre seemed hopeless.

In 1974, quite by accident, the first important document I needed to bring my book alive fell into my hands. I was living in London, researching the European tours of Buffalo Bill's "Wild West" exhibition and intermittently lecturing about the life and times of Cody at universities, museums, and film societies. After a lecture at the American Museum in Britain at Bath, J. M. Candler, then the curator, gave me a photocopy of a long letter written by someone identified only as W. R. C. I was asked if this might be a letter written by Buffalo Bill. I told him it was unlikely since Cody's initials were W. F. C.

As a courtesy, I took the letter back to my flat. The next day I found time to read it. It was an account of a young private's service with the Seventh Cavalry from November 1890 to January 1891. I called Candler and told him his museum possessed a remarkable document.

After checking further, Candler told me that the letter had been found in the effects of the Crickett family. In time I discovered that it had been written by Pvt. Walter R. Crickett and mailed from Pine Ridge to relatives near Bath.

In Crickett's first days at Pine Ridge, the youthful private was bivouacked near the "friendlies" living around the agency, but he soon found himself in the field. The climax of his letter was a harrowing description of the morning of December 29, 1890, at Wounded Knee.[4]

In the summer of 1977, my wife and fellow researcher, Linda, and I found an equally remarkable document. We were researching Cody's performance career at the Buffalo Bill Museum on Lookout Mountain in Golden, near Denver. In the museum's files I found a copy of a testimony given by Short Bull, one of the Lakotas who journeyed west to see the Paiute Messiah, Wovoka. The testimony had been mentioned by two other writers, but it had never been published or critically examined.

I studied Short Bull's account carefully, checking it against dates in other sources. At every point his testimony checked out. If there was a difference of any sort, it was one of perception between him and other Lakotas and especially between him and whites.

In the meantime, I began reading the literature about the Wounded Knee Massacre. I felt that most were too dependent upon white testimonies and remembered that someone once said that "History is written by the victors." I felt strongly that the victims needed to tell their story, too.

The two documents I had discovered and other firsthand accounts gathered dust in my files for several years. Then Linda persuaded me that I could write a book using these documents in a way that would let whites and Indians tell their versions of what had happened in 1890. If there were contradictions, perhaps readers could find their own truth or ponder deeper enigmas.

The method of putting it together came to me slowly. I did not want to write a conventional history in which snippets of documents were studded with the historian's commentary. The documents I assembled spoke eloquently and in great detail. I wanted to let those who were there speak with a minimum of interference. With this in mind I began a "collective autobiography." My job was to place the accounts in a historical sequence and link them with explanatory information.

I began my journey to Wounded Knee through the memories of those who were there. The search has been long and difficult, and it has involved no small amount of my time since 1974, but if the discoveries it has inspired will be useful to readers, that will be reward enough.

In some instances I have standardized spelling and capitalization, repunctuated, and clarified awkward passages that were taken down hastily by field researchers. I have tried to intuit the meaning of garbled sentences and fought through translations made through third parties. I trimmed repetitions and digressions common to conversation. Sometimes I worked from hurriedly written, virtually telegraphic transcriptions; other times I worked with typescripts whose errors were at least clear. In every instance, I tried to convey the meaning intended by each informant.

Some of the changes are slight. For example, the nineteenth-century custom of writing "to-day" has been changed to "today." Writers of the time wrote "Wounded Knee creek." or "Missouri river." I have changed these to "Wounded Knee Creek" and "Missouri River." I standardized the spelling of Oglala, on the advice of Oglalas who preferred this spelling to Ogallala. In my own commentary, I speak of the Lakotas rather than the Sioux, again on the advice of older Lakotas. These changes, I hope, will allow the reader's eye to move through the book without jarring departures from currently accepted practice.

I drew from numerous newspaper and magazine articles. In the latter I found the most factual errors, even though some were first-person interviews. I sensed the truth was in the raw material I gathered. I became aware that even in the sources I did use the truth had been stretched here and there; but, interestingly, I usually found Lakota testimony to be the most reliable.

By the time I began to write *Voices of Wounded Knee*, my files were bulging. Even as I wrote, I combed once more through libraries, collections, and my own files. Correspondence with those whom I met in the libraries resulted in further leads. The mass of material I assembled was intimidating; I faced an enormous jigsaw puzzle.

My task was to structure and focus the story I was telling. Fascinating but often repetitive material had to be edited. I had to resist piling proof upon proof. There are a number of detailed and accurate descriptions of the Ghost Dance, for example, but they are markedly similar. I excluded other documents as well. Even though they were intriguing, they were not pertinent to my central story.

I have made every effort to remain true to my sources; but truth is a perception filtered through our selves—it is an individual reality. Now I must stand aside and let the voices of the past speak for themselves. If my own opinions enter the narrative, as I fear they have, please accept or reject them as you wish.

Acknowledgments

Voices of Wounded Knee has been more than twenty-five years in the making. Much of the research was done at libraries and collections throughout the United States and Europe, but most was accomplished in the American West.

Before I give credit to anyone, I must recognize those who dictated, wrote, transcribed, and preserved the hundreds of documents that make up this book. For many, reliving the horrors of the massacre caused great pain. This book is written so they finally will have their word on what really happened at Wounded Knee on December 29, 1890.

For the last twenty-three years, my wife, Linda Robbins Coleman, has been my research associate and copyeditor. Working side by side with me in collections and libraries, she located valuable documents and hand-copied them when copying machines were not available, transcribed almost unreadable documents (often spending hours interpreting a blurred phrase or word) and field recordings, and made many editorial suggestions. While doing research at the Buffalo Bill Museum in Golden, Colorado, she spotted a dusty, half-forgotten file folder that held the testimony of Short Bull, and she recognized its importance. Her most important contribution, however, was giving me the idea and the belief that I could let those who were there speak fully by assembling their remembrances into a structured collage. I appreciate her patience and understanding when research superseded vacations and the more immediate realities of life.

There were many others who contributed to this book. Marjorie E. Robbins typed transcriptions onto disk and provided editorial assistance and proofreading through several drafts.

Kevin Brownlow took the time to read two drafts of this book and offer valuable comments. Early on in my research my two sons, Wim and Eric, worked with me as research assistants in several western and foreign collections.

I thank various grant agencies at Drake University, Des Moines, Iowa, especially the Center for the Humanities, the provost's office, and the Drake Friends of the Arts.

The individuals who assisted and guided me are too numerous to credit fully. Eli Paul, John Carter, and the always cooperative staff at the Nebraska State Historical Society were always there when I needed them, whether in person, by letter, or by telephone. I am especially grateful to Eli for taking the time to read and comment on the manuscript. He provided me with information that filled in glaring gaps in the narrative and offered valuable consultation on photographic sources.

I also thank J. M. Candler, then curator of the American Museum in Britain at Bath, for asking me to identify the letter written by Walter Crickett.

I thank attorney Mario Gonzalez for telling me about both the Alice Ghost Horse testimony and the testimony that a wagon of whiskey was delivered to Wounded Knee on the evening of December 28, 1890, and for verifying other details.

I express my gratitude to James Leonardo, the government documents librarian at Drake University, and his patient staff. My copy-editor, Kristin Harpster, must also be recognized for her great care and attention to detail.

Now to list just a few of the sources I utilized and to whom I owe my gratitude: the State Historical Society of Nebraska; the State Historical Society of South Dakota (with thanks especially to Laverra Rose); the Oklahoma University Library and its Western History Collections (with special thanks to John R. Lovett and Dr. Paul Sharp); the State Historical Society of Iowa; the Denver Public Library; the Buffalo Bill Historical Center in Cody, Wyoming; Scout's Rest Ranch in North Platte, Nebraska (thanks especially to former curator George LeRoy, who suggested that I interview Ben Black Elk); the Buffalo Bill Museum; the State Archives of Colorado; the Colindale Library of the British Museum; the Drake University Library; the Des Moines Public Library; the University of Iowa Library; the New York City Public Library; the American Museum in Bath, England; and the state libraries of Nebraska, Wyoming, North Dakota, and South Dakota. There are too many staff members to name. I have always been pleasantly surprised at the helpfulness of librarians and curators here and abroad. They are a very special breed, these keepers of the archives of our culture and our history.

I especially wish to thank the late Ben Black Elk for allowing me to interview him. His views on Wounded Knee inspired this project.

If I have omitted anyone, I ask for their understanding. The research and writing of this book has taken almost half my life. It has been a remarkable journey, filled with the amazement of discovery and the meeting of so many kind people who offered a hand along the way.

Chronology

June 25, 1876	Custer is defeated at the Battle of the Little Bighorn.
May 6, 1877	The main body of the Lakotas, led by Crazy Horse, surrenders.
July 19, 1881	Sitting Bull surrenders.
Summer 1885	Sitting Bull tours with Buffalo Bill's "Wild West" exhibition.
January 1, 1888	During a total solar eclipse, Wovoka has a vision.
May 10, 1889	Sitting Bull arrives at the Standing Rock Agency.
Midsummer 1889	Lakotas send their first emissaries to Nevada.
Midsummer 1889	The Crook Commission negotiates for Lakota land.
August 1889 to June 1890	Drought lingers in the Dakotas.
March 1890	Short Bull begins his pilgrimage to Nevada.
May 1890	The Ghost Dance begins in the Dakotas.
May 29, 1890	Secretary of the Interior John W. Noble is warned of the danger of the new religion by Charles A. Hyde.
June 1890	Rain falls in the Dakotas; the Ghost Dance is suspended while the Lakotas care for their crops.
June 18, 1890	Agent Maj. James McLaughlin recommends the arrest of Sitting Bull and other hereditary chiefs.
August 1890	The drought resumes as does the Ghost dancing.
August 22, 1890	Ghost dancing begins on White Clay Creek.
August 24, 1890	Agent Hugh D. Gallagher and Philip Wells visit White Clay Creek and stop the dancing.
Late summer 1890	Big Foot leaves the Cheyenne River Agency.
October 6, 1890	Kicking Bear visits Sitting Bull at Grand River Camp.
October 17, 1890	Dancing begins at Sitting Bull's Grand River Camp.
October 31, 1890	Short Bull preaches at Red Leaf Camp.

November 11, 1890	Agent Daniel F. Royer is confronted by Oglalas at Pine Ridge.
November 13, 1890	Harrison authorizes the War Department to suppress outbreaks in the Dakotas.
November 14, 1890	President Benjamin Harrison instructs R. V. Belt, acting commissioner of Indian Affairs, to use military strength to solve any problems at Dakota agencies.
November 15, 1890	Royer, hysterical, pleads with Washington for troop protection, then flees with his family to Rushville, Nebraska.
November 17, 1890	McLaughlin visits Sitting Bull at Grand River Camp for two days of conferences.
November 17, 1890	Maj. Gen. Nelson A. Miles commands Brig. Gen. John R. Brooke to dispatch troops to the Lakotas.
November 20, 1890	The Ninth Cavalry, under the command of Brooke, arrives at Pine Ridge; another detachment arrives at the Rosebud Agency.
November 22, 1890	Red Cloud makes a conciliatory speech at Pine Ridge. Short Bull is said to have preached a sermon on the Rosebud Reservation.
November 23, 1890	Royer, escorted by troops, returns to Pine Ridge with his family.
November 24, 1890	Over dinner in Chicago, William F. Cody and Miles agree on an attempt to persuade Sitting Bull to surrender.
November 26, 1890	Cody leaves Chicago to go to the Dakotas. The Seventh Cavalry arrives at Pine Ridge.
November 28, 1890	Cody arrives at Standing Rock Agency as Miles arrives in Washington.
November 29, 1890	Cody's mission is aborted by presidential order.
December 2, 1890	Special Agent A. T. Lea reports that the Lakotas have endured no hardships. Debate over the Indian issue begins in the U.S. Senate.
December 3, 1890	Zero-degree weather arrives in the Dakotas.
December 5, 1890	Snow begins to fall at Standing Rock. Father John Jutz and Lakota leaders visit the dancers in the Stronghold.

December 7, 1890	Ghost Dance leaders arrive at the Pine Ridge Agency for a parley.
December 12, 1890	McLaughlin is authorized to arrest Sitting Bull. An armed encounter occurs at Daly's ranch. Commissioner of Indian Affairs Thomas J. Morgan recommends Royer's dismissal, but no immediate action is taken.
December 13, 1890	Leaders disagree over surrendering at the Stronghold.
December 14, 1890	Miles leaves for the Dakotas. A detachment of the Eighth Cavalry under Capt. E. G. Fechet leaves Fort Yates at midnight to support the Indian police attempting to arrest Sitting Bull.
December 15, 1890	Sitting Bull is killed during the arrest attempt.
December 22, 1890	Big Foot escapes from Lt. Col. Edwin V. Sumner's Seventh Cavalry detachment. A fake Messiah appears at Pine Ridge.
December 28, 1890	Big Foot surrenders to a detachment of the Seventh Cavalry under the command of Maj. Samuel M. Whitside.
December 29, 1890	Massacre at Wounded Knee.
December 30, 1890	Col. James W. Forsyth attacked near the Holy Rosary Mission.
January 7, 1891	A military court of inquiry is convened to examine Forsyth's conduct at Wounded Knee. Royer is dismissed, and the military takes control.
January 15, 1891	The main body of Ghost dancers surrender at Pine Ridge.
January 21, 1891	Miles conducts a grand review near Pine Ridge.

VOICES OF WOUNDED KNEE

While bivouacking with fellow campaigners in the fall of 1913, Philip Wells, a veteran scout and interpreter, told friends what he heard about the origin of the name for Wounded Knee Creek:

Mr. Wells picked a chink out of the fire to light his pipe. Then he gazed across the flames to where the monument of Wounded Knee Battlefield showed in the moonlight.

"That's a way with names around here," he said at last. "They're all pretty long in the original Indian, and when the white man tries to say them he cuts them all down to the shortest possible extent. Wounded Knee Creek once was known as 'The Creek Where the Man with the Wounded Knee Was Buried.'"

"Some name that," came from another side of the campfire.

"But it's only Wounded Knee now," answered the old scout. "And it has its tradition, too. This time the Sioux and the Crows were fighting, as usual. They had met at where Fort Robinson stands now and had fought all the way along to a place about three miles from Pine Ridge. The Sioux had one great warrior, one who practically was doing all the fighting. The Crows had been getting the best of it and were pushing the Sioux mighty hard. And if it had not been for this warrior they might have annihilated them.

"But the warrior was a real fighter—one of those plungers, you know. Whenever he would see that the Crows were pushing his band too hard, he would break out, make a ride through the Crow lines, break up their ranks and then dash to cover again. The result was that gradually things changed and the Sioux were victorious.

"And it was about this time that an arrow went through the knee of the warrior and he fell off his horse, and with other braves, attempted to pull the arrow out. The poison began to eat into his being and the other warriors saw that there was little chance for him to live. And so they formed a cordon and fought beside him until he died. Then they buried him and went on.

"Therefore, as a result of his prowess, the Indians named the stream where he fell 'The Creek Where the Man Who Was Wounded in the Knee was Buried.'"

There came a few moments of quiet while Old Woman Dressed, Indian scout of the past, brought some wood to the blazing fire. (*Denver Post*, October 18, 1913)

This is just one of the stories telling how Wounded Knee Creek got its name.

1. Prologue to a Tragedy

New world coming soon—be prepared, good, and obedient—
all white people swept off earth—world as before, and Christ of red race
would return and rule world good—save it—everyone must be good.
—*Mrs. Wagonner*, a Lakota

✶

In 1889 the Oglala heard that the Son of God had come upon the earth
in the West. They said the Messiah was there, but he had come to help the
Indians and not the whites, and it made the Indians happy to hear this.
—*Capt. George Sword*, head of the Pine Ridge Indian police

A BEAUTIFUL DREAM IS BORN

During a solar eclipse on January 1, 1888, Wovoka, a Nevada Paiute living in Walker Valley, Nevada, had a vision of the coming of a new world. His experience transformed the history of the western tribes and led to the tragedy that occurred at Wounded Knee on December 29, 1890.

Wovoka was not alone in seeing such a vision. Alice Fletcher, a field ethnologist who studied the western tribes in the late nineteenth century, observed, The advent of a Messiah has been talked about among the Indians of the Missouri Valley for five or six years.

By and by people began to tell that the Messiah had been seen in the White Mountains near Mexico and others heard of him in the mountains of the Northwest. A year or more ago delegations of Sioux, of Cheyennes, and Arapahos and other tribes, went to find the Messiah and returned with wonderful stories. Some brought back bits of buffalo meat, and ornaments belonging to the dead. The manner of the destruction of the white race was described.

Those in the South said it was to be by cyclone; those in the West, that an earthquake would begin at the Atlantic coast, and, "rolling and gaping" across the continent, would swallow all the people. The northern Indians expected a landslide, and the Indians, by dancing when the earth began to move, would not be drawn under.[1]

In the autumn of 1890, Captain Dick, a Paiute, told war department fact finder Capt. J. M. Lee about an earlier Messiah. [A] long time ago—twenty years ago—*he said,* [an] Indian medicine man in Mason's Valley at Walker Lake talk same way, same as we hear now.[2] *The man Captain Dick spoke of was Tävibo, the father of Wovoka, the newest Messiah. Like those before him, Wovoka preached a pacifistic ritual whose dancing would destroy the white race and return the western tribes to their way of life. At no point in the new religion's development did its medicine men urge their followers to go to war.*

THE DAY THE SUN DIED

According to James Mooney, a Smithsonian Institution ethnologist, Tävibo died when Wovoka was about fourteen years old. When Wovoka became an adult, he, too, had visions of a new world. Inspired by his visions, Wovoka began to teach what would later be called the Ghost Dance.

After visiting Wovoka in Nevada in 1891, Mooney wrote, The prophetic claims and teachings of the father . . . must have made early and deep impression on the mind of the boy, who seems to have been by nature and deep impression of a solitary and contemplative disposition, one of those born to see visions and hear still voices.

The physical environment was favorable to the development of such a character. His native valley, from which he never wandered, is a narrow strip of level sage prairie some thirty miles in length, walled in by the giant Sierras, their sides torn and gashed by volcanic convulsions and dark with gloomy forests of pine, their towering summits white with everlasting snows, and roofed over by a cloudless sky whose blue infinitude the mind instinctively seeks to penetrate to far-off worlds beyond.

[In his youth] the young Wovoka became attached to the family of a ranchman in Mason Valley named David Wilson, who took an interest in him and bestowed on him the name Jack Wilson. . . . From his association with this family he gained some knowledge of English, together with a confused idea of the white man's theology. On growing up he married and still continued to work for Mr. Wilson, earning a reputation for industry and reliability, but attracting no special notice until nearly 30 years of age, when he announced the revelation that has made him famous among the tribes of the West.[3]

Wovoka began preaching his father's religion sometime in 1887. By all accounts he was a charismatic leader. John S. Mayhugh, former special census agent of Indians for Nevada, reported to his superiors, Wovoka is known among all Indians by the Indian names of We-vo-Kar and Co-We-Jo. He is an intelligent, fine looking Indian of about thirty-five years of age, who goes into trances, or seemingly so, for twelve to fourteen hours in [the] presence of large numbers of Indians, who come upon invitation of the prophet.[4]

According to Mooney, Wovoka's greatest revelation came during the 1888 solar eclipse, an event the tribes of the West called "the day the sun died." Mooney writes, Wovoka . . . had his most intense vision. What he saw confirmed what he had been preaching for at least a year.

An eclipse of the sun was a phenomenon which always excited great alarm among primitive peoples. In their system the sun is a living being, of great power and beneficence, and the temporary darkness is caused by an attack on him by some supernatural monster which endeavors to devour him, and will succeed, and thus plunge the world into eternal night unless driven off by incantations and loud noises.

On this occasion the Paiutes were frantic with excitement and the air was filled with the noise of shouts and wailings and the firing of guns, for the purpose of frightening off the monster that was threatening the life of their god. It was now as Wovoka stated: when the sun died . . . he went to sleep in the daytime and was taken up to heaven.

Mooney observes that at the time Wovoka was stricken by a fever, and he theorizes: The excitement and alarm produced by the eclipse, acting on a mind and body already enfeebled by sickness, resulted in delirium, in which he imagined himself to enter the portals of the spirit world. Constant dwelling on the subject in thought by day and in dreams by night would effect and perpetuate the exalted mental condition in which visions of the imagination would have all the seeming reality of the actual occurrences. To those acquainted with the spiritual nature of Indians and their implicit faith in dreams all this is perfectly intelligible. His frequent trances would indicate also that, like so many other religious ecstatics, he is subject to cataleptic attacks.[5]

To the Indian mind, writes ethnologist Fletcher, these visions were a form of reality: The continuity of life after death, of both men and animals, is undoubted. The reality of dreams and visions is unquestioned. When a man closes his eyes, or falls into a faint or trance among his living companions, the pictures he sees are considered to be reflections of actual persons and things, and are never attributed to freaks of memory or imagination.

The lost game, the dead friends, are frequently seen in dreams; therefore their continued existence is thought to be proven beyond doubt; and, as the living can thus enter the presence of the dead and return unchanged to this life, so the restoration of the dead to the living is comparatively a simple thing.[6]

After investigating the new religion, Hugh L. Scott, then an army lieutenant, reported, I saw Wovoka performing a series of gyrations that were most remarkable. At all hours of the day and night his cry could be heard all over camp, and when found he would be dancing in the ring, possibly on one foot, with his eyes closed and the forefingers of his right hand pointed upward, or in some other ridiculous posture. Upon being asked his reasons for assuming these attitudes he replied that he could not help it; that it came over him like cramps.[7]

During Scott's investigations, Wovoka accumulated a growing number of followers, some coming to learn the new religion's rituals, some asking for miraculous cures. Scott observed, John Wilson has progressed finely, and was now a full fledged doctor, a healer of diseases and a finder of stolen property through supernatural means. One day, while we were in his tent, a Wichita woman entered, led by the spirit. It was explained to us that she did not know who lived there, but some force she could not account for brought her. Having stated her case to John, he went off into a fit of jerks, in which his spirit went up and "saw his father" who directed him how to cure this woman. When he came to, he explained the nature of the cure to her and sent her away rejoicing. Soon afterward a Keechel man came in, who was blind in one eye, and who desired to have the vision restored. John again consulted his father, who informed him that nothing could be done for that eye because the man had held aloof from the dance.[8]

Even though Scott did not take Wovoka seriously, he reported to his superiors, Wovoka has given these people a better religion than they ever had before, taught them precepts which, if faithfully carried out, will bring them into better accord with their white neighbors, and has prepared the way for their final Christianization.[9]

Mooney, too, saw the new religion as beneficial. The moral code inculcated, *he wrote after studying the new rituals,* is as pure and comprehensive in its simplicity as anything found in religious systems from the days of Gautauma Buddha to the time of Jesus Christ. "Do no harm to any one. Do right always." Could anything be more simple, and yet more exacting? It inculcates honesty—"Do not tell lies." It preaches good will—"Do no harm to any one." It forbids extravagant mourning customs formerly common among the tribes—"When your friends die, you must not cry," which is interpreted by the prairie tribes as forbidding the killing of horses, the burning of tipis and the destruction of property, the cutting off of hair and the gashing of the body with knives, all of which were formerly the sickening rule at every death until forbidden by the new doctrine.[10]

After meeting Wovoka, Mooney wrote, When questioned directly, he said he believed it was better for the Indians to follow the white man's road and to adopt habits of civilization. If appearances are evident, he is sincere in this, for he was dressed in a good suit of white man's clothing, and works regularly on a ranch, although living in a wickiup.[11]

Even though there is a great deal of evidence that Wovoka's new religion was benign, it was soon characterized as a threat to peace in the West. That assertion was baseless, but it prevailed over the calming voices of firsthand observers.

Wovoka's message arrived at a time when the Lakotas living on the

Dakota reservations were especially vulnerable. In 1889 a great drought had spread across the plains, government rations promised in past treaties were not delivered, and the Lakotas were dying by the hundreds of starvation and disease. They were open to a dramatic vision of supernatural intervention. Wovoka's visions gave them hope of a better world. Indeed, it was their only hope for survival.

Thisba Hutson Morgan, a teacher at the government boarding school at the Pine Ridge Agency, observed, From the beginning of history, man has sought aid from mystical forces he recognizes outside himself when his own material sources fail him and he is clean forespent. So it was with the Sioux. They saw little in the future but hunger and despair for themselves and their children. They fell an easy prey to the rumors of a coming Messiah, and the Ghost Dance craze was the outcome.[12]

According to Fletcher, The story of the death of Christ had made a stronger impression upon some Indians than the story of his benefactions, and there are many Natives who regard the manner of his death as additional evidence of the white man's inhumanity, he not having hesitated to attack the Son of God. Such being the Indian's estimate of the white race, it is not to be wondered at that he has ventured to ally his treatment with that bestowed upon the Christ and to predicate the destruction of the common offenders.

The version making the earthquake the means of annihilation seems to have originated among the tribes of the Rocky Mountains; while the cyclone and landslide were suggested by those who live where the winds make havoc and quicksands render regions dangerous to dwell upon. Thus the forms of the catastrophes seem to have been suggested by the environment of the Indians framing the story.

Eight years ago, among the Oglala Sioux, *Fletcher continues,* I listened to men arguing the superiority of the Indian's reverence and sacrifice in the Sun Dance over the cruelty and cowardice of the Christians, who were not only guilty, by their own account, of murdering God's Son, but who sought to secure through this act their vicarious release from future suffering. This statement I have met many times in different tribes.[13]

THE FIRST PILGRIMAGE TO MEET THE MESSIAH

The Lakotas were excited by the rumors of the appearance of Christ in Nevada. Perhaps their own Messiah had returned to save them. The aged Chief Two Strike, who lived on the Rosebud Reservation, told a reporter in January 1891, We had come to fear that the government would let our wives and children starve, for rations were getting less and less all the time. Last spring we heard of a great medicine man out in the far West who had been sent from the Great Spirit to help the Indians. From what we could learn of him he was the white man's Christ.[14]

According to Capt. George Sword, a member of the Pine Ridge Indian police, the news of the Messiah came by way of the Shoshoni and Arapahos.[15] *Certainly, rumors were abroad of a Second Coming. On December 9, 1889, Father Aemilius Perrig, a Catholic missionary at the St. Francis Mission on the Pine Ridge Reservation, wrote in his diary,* Our neighbor, the Dakota medicine man, relates an apparition of our Lord to some Arapahos who being out hunting and having nothing to eat nor to drink prayed to the Great Spirit. Jesus is said to have appeared to them with his wounds, the crown of thorns, a piece of cloth around the loins and all covered with blood. Where Jesus stood the dust flew up and a spring of water sprang up to quench their thirst.[16]

The Oglalas at Pine Ridge Reservation, curious about whether there was a new Messiah or if Christ himself had returned, sent an elder, Good Thunder, along with four or five others, to visit the Messiah in Nevada.

Porcupine, a Cheyenne, says he made the pilgrimage because of his own inner vision. It appeared that Christ had sent for me to go there, *he told an informant*, and that was why unconsciously I took my journey. It had been foreordained. Christ had summoned myself and others . . . from fifteen or sixteen different tribes.

There were more different languages than I ever heard before, and I did not understand any of them. . . . The people assembled called a council, and the chief's son went to see the Great Father, the Messiah, who sent word to us to remain fourteen days in that camp and that he could come to see us.

He sent me a small package of something white to eat that I did not know the name of. There were a great many people in the council, and this white food was divided among them. The food was a big white nut.[17]

Morgan writes, It was believed that these first rumors came from the southern tribes close to the place where the chewing of the mescal bean gave them wonderful hallucinations, but they came also from the tribes of the northwest.[18]

Even though Fletcher had observed that among the Lakotas dreams and visions were considered reality, many Lakotas were dubious about the visions of a coming Messiah. A large minority, however, especially the more militant ones, accepted the visions that had been related to them and believed that the coming of the Messiah was inevitable. When the emissaries who had traveled to Nevada returned, they were ready to act.

The twenty-seven-year-old supervisor of Lakota Schools, Elaine Good-

ale, was probably the first white to meet the emissaries when they returned midsummer 1889. About that meeting, she writes, In the quest for fuller understanding of the unreconstructed Indian mind, I planned to accompany a party of my wilder neighbors upon an old-time antelope hunt. We set out on a wet midsummer afternoon for the Nebraska sandhills, a few us on pony-back, others packed with their goods into white-topped wagons. Our second night's camp in the wilderness found five families sleeping soundly after a hard day's travel. In my diary this item appears:

> July 23, 1889. So tired I fall asleep before supper. Later in the night a cry is raised, "A traveler comes!" Chasing Crane, on his way home from Rosebud is welcomed with supper and a smoke. He tells a strange story of the second appearing of Christ! God, he says, has appeared to the Crows! In the midst of the council he came from nowhere and announced himself as the Savior who came upon the earth once and was killed by white men. He had been grieved by the crying of parents for their dead children, and would let the sky down upon the earth and destroy the disobedient. He was beautiful to look upon, and bore pain as a sign of power. Men and women listen to this curious tale with apparent credence. A vapor bath is arranged, and I fall asleep to the monotonous rise and fall of the accompanying songs.

Goodale concludes, No intuition warned me of the bitter grief this self-proclaimed Messiah was soon to bring upon the Sioux.[19]

According to Two Strike, Good Thunder came back and told us that it was all true . . . , that he had seen the new Messiah and talked with him, and he said that He had come to restore the Indians to their former state. Some of us believed this good news and we began to hold meetings.[20]

The pilgrims invited Lakota leaders from several reservations to a council. There, Good Thunder and his traveling companions described their meeting with Wovoka.

Pine Ridge Indian Agent Hugh D. Gallagher, alarmed by the council, ordered the Indian police to arrest Good Thunder and two others. The pilgrims were asked by the agent and Captain Sword whether they had seen the Son of God and whether they held councils regarding the new religion, but Good Thunder refused to answer. Gallagher locked each in jail for two days. He released them when they promised to quit holding meetings.[21] *However, Good Thunder's message had made an impression on many Lakotas.*

A RELUCTANT PILGRIM

In the fall of 1889, Short Bull, a Brulé medicine man then in his midforties, was working at the Cheyenne River Agency. In months to come he would be described as a leader of Wovoka's new religion. A member of Chief Lip's Wazhaza band, he lived on the border of the Pine Ridge and Rosebud Reservations. Dr. J. R. Walker, an agency physician at Pine Ridge, described Short Bull as an open, generous and kind-hearted man who attends with diligence to his own business, frequenting public places only when necessity makes this necessary, and remaining quietly at home most of the time. . . . His face always wears a smile, telling unmistakably that nature made him gentle and benevolent.[22]

A far different picture of Short Bull would soon be painted by members of the press and the military.

That summer, *Short Bull says,* I went to carrying freight for the government between Valentine in Nebraska and the Rosebud Agency. I had made one trip and getting ready to make another, when a messenger handed me a letter. I asked for whom the letter was, his answer was, "Take it to the Council House."

I did as I was told to do. . . . When I came to the Council House, it was full of people, as they were dancing Omaha at the time. *At first Short Bull felt ignored.* No one came to me with a letter, *he says,* so I went again at night to the Council House, and saw two Brulés searching through the crowd as if looking for some one. One of the men was Eagle Pipe.

It may here be said that those present in the council room were all armed because Two Strike's son had choked one of the Indian police and a fight was going on outside.

When they saw me, they pulled off my blanket and placed me in the center of the circle. At this time I did not know what they meant. They then selected Scatter whom they said was to go with me on a great mission. Standing Bear, a Brulé, gave me a new blanket and leggings, saying: "We have a letter from the West saying the Father has come and we want you to go and see the Messiah."

Then the entire council told me what I must do: "You must try and get there, see him, recognize him, and tell us what he says and we will do it. Be there with a big heart. Do not fail."

I said nothing, *Short Bull remembered,* but I thought a good deal.

The next morning another council was held and here they told me what my mission was to be. Men and women were assembled and my Uncle spoke, saying, "I am not afraid to tell you what this letter contains."

The wind was blowing so furiously that the whole house was filled with dust, but as soon as the reading of the letter began the wind ceased. This gave me confidence.[23]

Then Wovoka's letter was read:

> I, Jack Wilson, love you all, and my heart is full of gladness for the gifts you have brought me. When you get home I shall give you a good cloud which will make you feel good. I give you a good spirit and give you all good paint. I want you to come again in three months, from each tribe in the Indian territory.
>
> When you get home you must make a dance to continue five days. Dance for four successive nights, and the last night keep up the dance until the morning of the fifth day, when all must bathe in the river, and then go to their homes. You must all do this dance in the same way.
>
> There will be a good deal of snow this year and some rain. In the fall there will be such a rain as I have never given you before.
>
> Grandfather says, when your friends die you must not cry. You must not hurt anybody or do harm to anyone. You must not fight. Do right always. It will give you satisfaction in life.
>
> Do not tell the white people about this. Jesus is now upon the earth. He appears like a cloud. The dead are all alive again. I do not know when they will be here; maybe this fall or in the spring. When the time comes there will be no sickness and everyone will be young again.
>
> Do not refuse to work for the whites, and do not make any trouble with them until you leave them. When the earth shakes (at the coming of the new world) do not be afraid. It will not hurt you.
>
> I want you to dance every six weeks. Make a feast at the dance and have food that everybody may eat. Then bathe in the water. That is all. You will receive good words again from me some time. Do not tell lies.[24]

Short Bull says that after he heard the prophet's message, I had faith to go. I had no belief in it before, but now my mind was made up. My people knew I was a man of truth and could be relied on.

I stood up and said, "My brothers—you are sitting here with your guns. This is not what the Messiah wants us to do, and when I leave here I ask you to drop your arms, follow my trail, watch my movements, and have no troubles with the whites or police. Be as one, drop no blood. If I have to stay two years I will try and see him myself and bring you his words."

Sore Back arose and said, "My boy, I select you to go West, You ask me to drop my arms and be peaceful and I will do it. I look to you to bring us the good word. Don't think we will shed any blood while you are gone. We will do right."[25]

The Lakotas picked eleven emissaries from three agencies to make a sec-

ond pilgrimage. Those chosen were Good Thunder, Yellow Breast, Flat Iron, Broken Arm, Cloud Horse, Yellow Knife, Elk Horn, and Kicks Back from the Pine Ridge Reservation; Short Bull and Mash-the-Kettle from Rosebud; and Kicking Bear from the Cheyenne River Reservation.[26]

They did not realize that their spiritual search for a lost past would bring disaster to their people; nor could they have known that their long journey marked the first step toward the tragedy that happened at Wounded Knee on December 29, 1890.

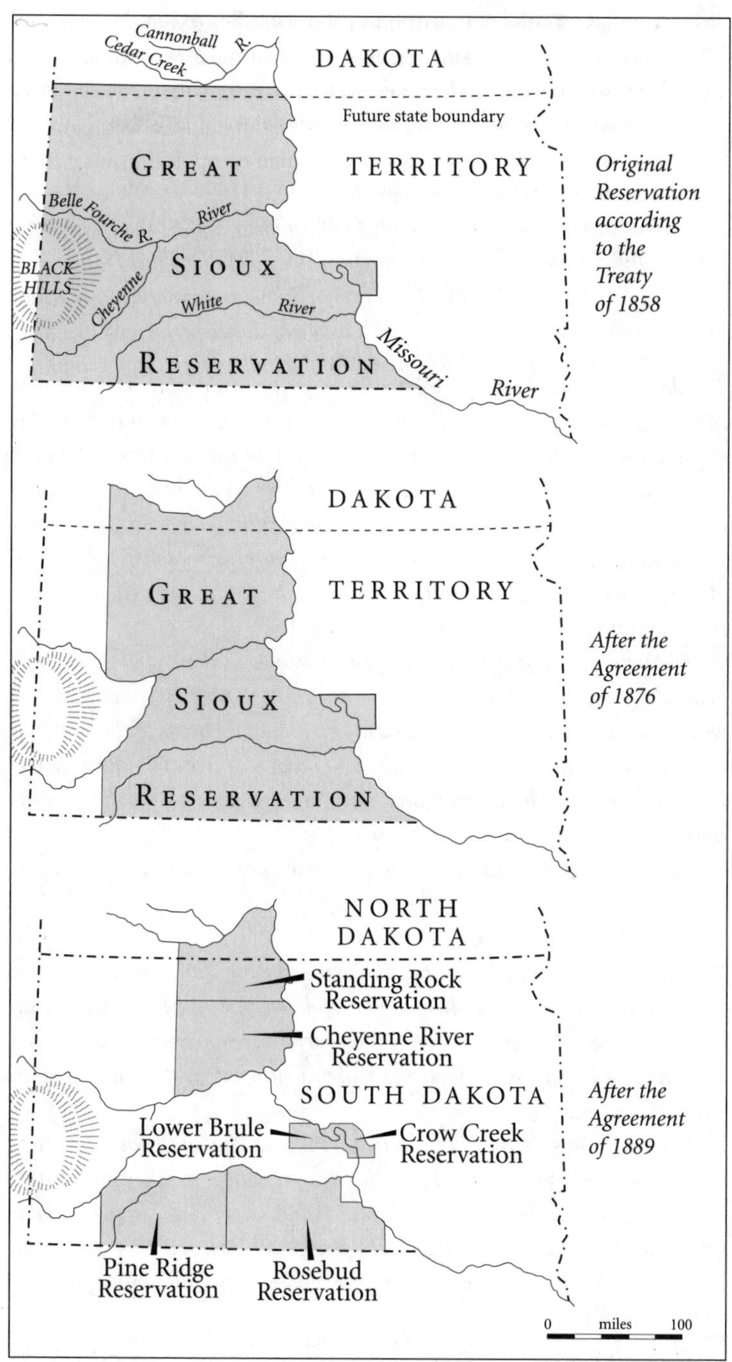

Map 1. Breaking up the Great Sioux Reservation. Redrawn from Smith, *Moon of Popping Trees*.

2. Broken Promises, Broken Treaties

Which God is our brother praying to now? Is it the same whom they have twice deceived, when they made the treaties with us which they afterward broke?—*Red Cloud*, Oglala chief at Pine Ridge

✶

The Indians . . . have at least one distinct impression regarding the government. They know that it never keeps its word. Any old chief will tell you that white men are all liars.—*Frederic Remington*, artist and war correspondent

AN IDYLLIC PAST LOST

The desperation that drove the Lakotas to send emissaries to meet the new Messiah in Nevada was deeply rooted in old conflicts between the Lakotas and the U.S. government. Perhaps it all began on June 25, 1876, when the Lakota and Cheyenne nations defeated Custer's command. In defending their camp on the Little Bighorn River, they outmaneuvered Custer and wiped out those directly under his command—approximately two hundred officers and men. Only the units in Custer's rear guard survived; although, they too suffered heavy casualties.

The magnitude of the Lakotas' victory exceeded their wildest dreams. Fearful of vengeance, they scattered, with the U.S. Army in pursuit. For a while they survived off the land, but the great buffalo herds of the past had been destroyed, and small game, too, had become scarce. The starving Lakotas were forced to accept that their only hope was to return to the reservations and surrender. There, government negotiators told them, they would again receive government rations they had been promised by an act of Congress on February 28, 1877.

The first mass surrender, led by Crazy Horse, was at Camp Robinson, Nebraska, on May 6, 1877. Others followed. Sitting Bull, who had fled to Canada with about twenty-five hundred followers, was the last to come in. On July 19, 1881, the aging medicine man surrendered at Fort Randall. Even though more blood would be shed, to all practical extent the Plains Indian wars had ended.

During the late 1870s and early 1880s, the seven Lakota tribes were confined to six Dakota reservations—Pine Ridge, Rosebud, Cheyenne River, Standing Rock, Crow Creek, and Lower Brulé. Chief Red Cloud's Oglalas settled at Pine Ridge, Spotted Tail's Brulés at Rosebud, Big Foot and Hump's Miniconjous at Cheyenne River, and Sitting Bull's Hunkpapas at Standing Rock.

These traditional chiefs had been brilliant field generals during the Indian wars of the 1870s, but they were also intelligent advocates for their

people's rights. In spite of their age and infirmities, many government officials feared the old chiefs' ability to rally their people and start a new Indian war. There was little basis for these apprehensions. Most of the Lakota leaders had visited the East and seen white power and wealth firsthand. They knew that armed resistance was futile.

Sitting Bull typified their attitude. While touring with Buffalo Bill's Wild West exhibition in 1885, he told eastern reporters, The white people are so many that if every Indian in the West killed one every step they took, the dead would not be missed among you. I go back and tell my people what I have seen. They will never go on the warpath again.[1]

Before their surrender, the Lakotas owned the western half of South Dakota. In the years following their surrender, they signed away a sizable fringe of the western section of their territory in return for annuities and rations. It was the best of their land. Even so, for most of the 1880s the Lakotas retained an area that extended continuously from the northern to the southern borders of South Dakota and westward from the Missouri River to the foothills of the Black Hills—roughly one-third of what is now South Dakota.

A generation earlier they could have survived in this vast area. Immense buffalo herds would have supplied most of their needs, and for variety, there would have been plenty of small game. But by 1884 the buffalo were nearly extinct, and small game had become scarce. The relentless slaughter of the buffalo by local farmers and hunters from the East had decimated the great herds that had roamed the Great Plains. No matter how much the Lakotas yearned for the past, the resources for such a life were irretrievably lost.

Seizing upon this grim reality, the government set about persuading and, when that did not work, coercing the Lakotas into taking up agricultural pursuits or ranching. There were two serious flaws in this policy. The Dakota reservation land was only marginally arable and barely suited for ranching, and many Lakota men refused to farm because they saw this as women's work.

Commissioner of Indian Affairs Thomas J. Morgan, who administered the government's demands for change, summed up the Lakota quandary when he reported, Prior to the agreement of 1876, buffalo and deer were the main support of the Sioux. Food, tents, [and] bedding were the direct outcome of hunting, and with furs and pelts as articles of barter or exchange it was easy for the Sioux to procure whatever constituted for them the necessities, the comforts, or even the luxuries of life. Within eight years from the agreement of 1876, the buffalo had gone and the Sioux had left to them alkali land and government rations.

It is hard to overestimate the magnitude of the calamity, as they viewed it, which happened to these people by the sudden disappearance of the buffalo and the large diminution in the numbers of deer and other wild animals. Suddenly, almost without warning, they were expected at once and without previous training to settle down to the pursuits of agriculture in a land largely unfitted for such use. The freedom of the chase was to be exchanged for the idleness of the camp. The boundless range was to be abandoned for the circumscribed reservation, and abundance of plenty to be supplanted by limited and decreasing government subsistence and supplies. Under these circumstances it is not in human nature not to be discontented and restless, even turbulent and violent.[2]

Charles E. McChesney, Indian agent at the Cheyenne River Agency, wrote to the commissioner of Indian Affairs on August 28, 1890, This is not a farming country, and until some means is found to overcome the hot, drying winds, it will never be; and time and money are wasted in attempting to farm here.[3]

Hugh D. Gallagher, veteran Pine Ridge Indian agent, believed, The lands are valuable for grazing purposes; but owing to the short summer season and lack of precipitation, agriculture can not be relied upon to make profitable returns even with the most experienced farmers.[4]

Frederic Remington, celebrated artist and war correspondent, flatly stated that even cattle raising had its limitations: Any stockman will tell you it is a question, and most of them will decide in the negative, when you ask if the high plains of the Northwest are a cattle country, to say nothing of agriculture.[5]

Maj. John Burke, a former scout who knew the Lakotas well, put the problem succinctly and sensibly: You cannot change the habits and customs of the Sioux Nation in thirteen years. Let us wait a generation or so before we begin to look for much in the way of results.[6]

Ethnologist Mooney sharply placed the Lakotas' problems in historical perspective when he wrote, It took our own Aryan ancestors untold centuries to develop from savagery to civilization. Was it reasonable to expect the Sioux to do the same in fourteen years?[7]

The older traditional chiefs were pragmatic men and knew an era had ended. Chief Red Cloud stated, When first we made treaties with the government, this was our position: Our old life and our customs were about to end; the game upon which we lived was disappearing; the whites were closing around us, and nothing remained for us but to adopt their ways and have the same rights with them if we wished to save ourselves. The government promised us all the means necessary to make our living out of the land, and to instruct us how to do it, and abundant food to support us until we could take care of ourselves. We looked forward with hope to the time when we could be as independent as the whites and have a voice in the government.[8]

Red Cloud's hopes were never realized. Retired Lt. Col. George P. Ahern bitterly wrote, Ever since 1882 there has been gross and continuous mismanagement of Indian affairs. . . . This able, brilliant people was crushed, held down, moved from place to place, cheated, lied to, given the lowest types of schools and teachers, and kept under the heel of a tyrannical Bureau.[9]

Gen. John R. Brooke, commander of the Department of the Platte in 1890, reported to his superior Gen. Nelson A. Miles that a congressional act in 1877 provides for a ration whose proportion of different articles of food are fixed for these Indians, and the act directs that such a ration shall be continued to them, or so much of said ration as may be necessary, until the Indians are able to support themselves.[10]

The Department of Interior ignored this act of Congress and continued to reduce the rations promised in past treaties. According to Brooke, In the year 1886 the annual authorized issue was 8,125,000 pounds; in 1889 it was 4,000,000 pounds, a reduction of 4,125,000 in three years, or an average annual reduction of 1,378,333 pounds; or, in other words, in that space of time, the beef issue has been reduced largely over one-half, and it is known that there has been no such corresponding reduction in the number of Indians or advancement in their ability to support themselves, as the land in the vicinity of this agency and adjacent to it is not sufficiently good for agricultural purposes, except by irrigation.[11]

Funds for irrigation were not forthcoming from a Congress that was intent on reducing the rations of the Lakotas.

ELOQUENT DISSENT

Of all the older Lakotas, Sitting Bull was the most militant and vocal in castigating the government for not keeping its word. This great chief was a charismatic spiritual leader whose eloquence and ironic humor often left government representatives in want of logical response. He was a medicine man, but that title indicates he was more than a healer; he was a spiritual leader who spoke out against those shrinking the world of his youth.

Sitting Bull's eloquence made him one of the great orators of his time. On August 21, 1883, during negotiations for a government purchase of Lakota land, Sitting Bull told members of a commission, Our reservation is not as large as we want it to be, and . . . the Great Father owes us money now for the land he has taken from us in the past. You white man advise us to follow your ways, and therefore I talk as I do. When you have a piece of land, and anyone trespasses on it, you catch it and keep it until you get damages, and I am doing the same thing now; and I want you to tell all this to the Great Father for me.

I am looking into the future for the benefits of my children, and that is what I mean when I say I want my country taken care of for me. My children will grow up, and I am looking ahead for their benefit, and for the benefit of my children's children, too, and even beyond that again.

I sit here and look around me now, and I see my people starving, and I want the Great Father to make an increase in the amount of land that is allowed us now, so that they may be able to live. We want cattle to butcher—I want to kill 300 head of cattle at a time. That is the way you live, and we want to live the same way. This is what I want you to tell the Great Father when you go back home. If we get the things we want, our children will be raised like the white children.

When the Great Father told me to live like his people, I told him to send me six teams of mules, because that is the way white people make a living, and I wanted my children to have these things to help them to make a living. I also told him to send me two spans of horses with wagons, and everything my children would need. I also asked for a horse and buggy for my children; I was advised to follow the ways of the white man, and that is why I asked for these things. I never ask for anything that is not needed. I also asked for a cow and a bull for each family, so that they can raise their own. I asked for four yokes of oxen and wagons with them. Also a yoke of oxen and a wagon for each of my children to haul wood with.

It is your own doing that I am here; you sent me here and advised me to live as you do, and it was not right for me to live in poverty. I asked the Great Father for hogs, male and female, and for male and female sheep for my children to raise from. I did not leave out anything in the way of animals that the white men have; I asked for every one of them. I want you to tell the Great Father to send me some agricultural implements, so that I will not be obliged to work bare-handed.

I want to tell you that our rations have been reduced to almost nothing, and many of the people have starved to death. Now I beg of you to have the amount of rations increased so that our children will not starve but will live better than they do now.

I want clothing too, and I will ask for that too. We want all kinds of clothing for our people. Look at the men around here, and see how poorly dressed they are. We want some clothing this month, and when it gets cold we want more of it to protect us from the weather. That is all I have to say.[12]

Sitting Bull's brilliant use of irony was perceived as ungrateful impertinence, and he was told to sit down and shut up. Government authorities recognized that Sitting Bull had the charisma and oratorical skill to rally his people. From that time onward, the government and its officials were intent on reducing his influence on his people.

Sitting Bull was not alone. The government, viewing the older chiefs as barriers to the future development of the Dakotas, set out to diminish their power. Red Cloud rightly complained that everything was done to break the power of the real chiefs, who really wished their people to improve; and little men, so-called chiefs, were made to act as disturbers and agitators. . . . I was abused and slandered to weaken my influence for good and make me seem like one who did not want to advance. This was done by the men paid by the government to teach us the ways of the whites. I have visited many other tribes, and find that the same things were done among them. All was done to discourage and nothing to encourage.[13]

THE POWER OF INDIAN AGENTS

The Lakotas who accepted government policy were labeled "friendlies" or "progressives." Those who questioned government policy were called "unfriendlies" or "nonprogressives." When a Lakota became too militant, he was labeled a "hostile."

There were severe penalties for dissension. According to Young-Man-Afraid-of-His-Horses, If a man had a trouble or dispute with the agent then the agent would take his ration ticket away from him, so he could not get food when it was issued. The man's wife and children suffered most. It was they who were punished and not the man.[14]

Elaine Goodale, supervisor of education in the Dakotas in 1890, acidly observed, A United States Indian agency is an absolute monarchy on a small scale,—a little Russia in the midst of Republican America.[15]

To back up his policies, each agent commanded a platoon of Lakota police. Dissidents were thrown in jail for indefinite periods of time at an agent's whim. Difficult leaders were deported to federal prisons or distant reservations. Ever paranoid about plots against their power, agents felt free to open their charges' mail. Civil rights as we know them were nonexistent on the Dakota reservations.

Even worse, some of the agents were corrupt and used their positions to misappropriate some of the supplies the Lakotas received. Red Cloud complained to a white friend, These men took care of themselves but not of us. It was made very hard for us to deal with the government except through them. It seems to me that they thought they could make more by keeping us back than by helping us forward.[16]

UNQUIET DESPERATION

The government sent commission after commission to the Dakotas. Each time they bargained for more Lakota land, land that could be developed by settlers, developers, and the railroads. Goodale observed, The period of the eighteen-eighties was marked by severe pressure for opening the thirty-thousand square miles of Sioux land to settlement—a drive engineered by the railroads and promoted by speculators in town sites, with the assistance of the frontier press.[17]

As the government pushed to purchase new land, Congress continued to cut appropriations for rations that had been promised to Indians in return for the land they had given up. Henry L. Dawes, a senator from Massachusetts, bluntly stated the government's rationale for this on the Senate floor: Heretofore for years it has been impressed upon Congress that the best way to treat the Indian was to starve him into self-support. "Root, hog, or die" has been a phrase put up over the door sometimes of those who have administered the affairs of the Indians. So a proposition was enacted into a law by the recommendation of the Indian Department that from year to year we should cut down the rations required by treaty and give notice to the Indian, "Next year you are only to have so much, and you must supplement it by the labor of your own hands."[18]

In his declaration, Dawes ignored the fact that the rations were not welfare. They were payment for land that had been sold. Rations were cut again and again, and the cash settlements promised in treaties were deferred until after whites purchased land—a process that could take years. The Lakotas found themselves in an impossible position, especially since disease and starvation had begun to take a heavy toll throughout the Dakota reservation system.

In 1891, Hump, a venerable Miniconjou chief, complained to a reporter, There was a great deal of discontent among the Indians at Cheyenne River Agency. Rations were issued once a month and they were very small. There was a little flour and beef every month. Sometimes there was a piece of bacon as big as my hand, but that was not regular. Sometimes there was baking powder and sometimes there was not. Annuity goods were not as much as promised and they never came until late in the winter. They ought to come in the fall. The agents kept on promising more and giving less all the time. The agent says, "Work hard and you get more." Indians work hard and get not so much.[19]

Red Cloud complained that a family got for two weeks what was not enough for one week. *He asked*, What did we eat when that was gone? The people were desperate from starvation—they had no hope. They did not think of fighting; what good would it do? They might die like men, but what would the women and children do?[20]

To add to the Lakotas' grim situation, an extended drought settled into the upper Great Plains. In 1890 Perain P. Palmer, newly appointed Indian agent at Cheyenne River, reported to the Indian commissioner, The raising of crops on this reserv[ation] has not been a success with the Indians; nor has it been a success with their white neighbors along the borders of the reserve. Year after year the Indians have prepared the ground in good shape and planted the seed in the right season, and in most cases cultivation has been well done, but very little or nothing has been harvested for the past four years.[21]

By early 1889 the situation was critical. At Standing Rock, Agent James McLaughlin reported, There were no rains in this locality from August 1889 to June 1, 1890, and very little snow; consequently the ground was very dry and much of the seed planted in the spring remained some weeks in the ground before germinating. About June 1 rains commenced, which were frequent and plentiful throughout the month of June and the early part of July, and all crops promised well until about the middle of July, when hot winds, blighted, or ruined all vegetation, according to the stage of its maturity when thus visited. In some localities oats and wheat were rendered worthless and not worth cutting, while to others from one-third to one-half a crop will be realized; the same applied to corn and vegetables, and even the grass was seriously injured, so that the hay crop is very scarce and it is difficult to procure a sufficient supply.[22]

At Pine Ridge, Gallagher painted an even grimmer picture: The present summer has been very dry in many localities, entirely destroying all the corn planted by the Indians. Potatoes, which have nearly always been a good crop here, will scarcely pay for the trouble of digging. This succeeding the drought of last year, when nearly all vegetation perished, will compel the Indians to depend for subsistence almost entirely upon what is issued to them by the government.[23]

In spite of protests by agents, the rations were cut even more. In 1876 there had been 30,000 Lakotas. In 1890 the agents reported a population of 18,812 Lakotas. In less than thirteen years, more than one-third of the Lakota Nation had perished. They were not decimated by war; they were dying of hunger and disease, a double plague forced upon the Lakotas by white mendacity and greed.

This population decrease may have been even more severe than these government statistics suggest. Agents sometimes inflated their populations so that more rations would be sent—some used the extra rations to assist their charges and others used them to sell for their own profit. Red Cloud, saddened, wrote to a white friend, The people were counted, and wrongly counted. Our rations were again reduced. The white men seized on the land we sold them through General Crook but our pay was as distant as ever. The man who counted us said we were feasting and wasting food. Where did he see this?

How can we eat or waste what we have not? We felt that we were mocked in our misery. We had no newspapers, and no one to speak for us. We had no redress. Our rations were again reduced. You, who eat three times a day and see your children well and happy around you, can't understand what starving Indians feel. We were faint with hunger and maddened by despair. We held our dying children and felt their little bodies tremble as their souls went out and left only a dead weight in our hands. They were not very heavy, but we ourselves were very faint, and the dead weighed us down. There was no hope on earth, and God seemed to have forgotten us.[24]

In June 1890, upon her return to the Lakotas, a horrified Goodale wrote, The Sioux country . . . was a veritable dust bowl, from the Missouri westward to the foot-hills and from the White river north to the Cannonball. I traversed every mile in my comfortable mountain wagon, with a Sioux couple of my choice as driver and chaperon. The pitiful little gardens curled up and died in the persistent hot winds. Even young men displayed gaunt limbs and lack-luster faces. Old folks lost their hold on life, and heart-broken mothers mourned the last of a series of dead babes.[25]

As the situation worsened, Bishop W. H. Hare, a veteran Episcopal missionary, urgently wrote to Secretary of the Interior John W. Noble, The Indian crops were a total failure. There is ample evidence that during this period, the rations issued lasted, even when carefully used, for only two-thirds the time intended. To add to their distress, this period 1889 and 1890, was marked by extraordinary misfortune. The measles prevailed with great virulence in 1889, the grippe in 1890. Whooping cough also attacked the children. The sick died from want. In this statement Inspector Gardiner, Dr. McGillycuddy, late agent, Miss Elaine Goodale, who has been in the camps a good deal, the missionary force, and many others whose testimony is of the highest value because of their character and their knowledge of the situation all agree.[26]

McLaughlin, who made few complaints to his superiors, felt compelled to report, A great deal of sickness prevailed throughout the winter and early spring, first from "la grippe," followed by "whooping cough," the latter being the more fatal, resulting in a large number of deaths in the camps. These epidemics carried off so many children that our records show 213 deaths while the births number but 208 for the fiscal year.[27]

Sword, captain of the Indian police and later a judge, noted that the death rate at Pine Ridge rose from 25 to 45 a month in a population of 5,500.[28] *A desperate situation was getting worse.*

ROOT, HOG, AND PATRONAGE

The disastrous situation in the Dakotas was intensified when the professional agents, whatever their merits, were replaced by local political appointees under a new policy of "home rule"—or, to put it bluntly—a patronage system. Few of these new agents were experienced. They were poorly equipped to cope with the growing tensions within the Dakota reservation system.

Late in 1890 Col. Richard I. Dodge, an army officer who had fought against the Lakotas, wrote a bitter indictment of government policy: [A] few years ago the Indian was wild, free, and independent. Now he is a prisoner of war, restrained of his liberty and confined on circumscribed areas. But a few years ago the Plains furnished him ample supply of food; now he is constantly on the verge of starvation. We leave our helpless prisoners to starve, and shoot without mercy the reckless few who, goaded to desperation by their sufferings, dare to cross the dead line of the reservation. In this horrid crime every voter of the United States is either actively or passively implicated, for it has its roots in the legislative branch of the government.[29]

Whites and Lakotas alike suffered from the drought. In his 1891 report Miles wrote, In fact, white settlers have been most unfortunate. . . . So serious have been their misfortunes that thousands have left that country within the last few years.

The Indians could not migrate from one part of the United States to another; neither could they obtain employment as readily as white people, either upon or beyond the Indian reservations. They must remain in comparative idleness and accept the results of the drought and insufficient supply of food. This created a feeling of discontent even among the loyal and well disposed and added to the feeling of hostility of the element opposed to every process of civilization.[30]

A HARD BARGAIN DRIVEN

The Lakotas had no other recourse than to sell more land. A commission headed by the venerable Maj. Gen. George A. Crook arrived in the Dakotas in midsummer 1889. The timing of the commission's arrival could not have been worse. According to Hare, The Indians were all called into the agency and kept there for a month by the Sioux Commission. During their absence their cattle broke into their fields and trod down, or ate up their crops. The Indians reaped practically nothing.[31]

Then, American Horse, a "friendly," declared, We lost considerable property by being here with the commissioners and have never got anything for it. Our chickens were stolen, our cattle some of them were stolen, our crops were entirely lost by us being absent here with the Sioux Commission, and we have never been benefited one bit by the bill; and, in fact, we are worse off than we were before we signed the bill. We are told if we do as white men, we will be better off, but we are getting worse off every year.[32]

Upon the arrival of the commission, Red Cloud pointed out that rations had been cut in open violation of past treaties. In response to this complaint, according to Brooke, the commission promised . . . to reestablish the amount of 5,000.000 pounds [of beef].[33]

A number of Lakota leaders distrusted the commission. From the first, *Gallagher would write,* the bill was opposed by a large and influential body of Indians. Among other opponents of the bill may be mentioned Red Cloud, Little Wound, Young-Man-Afraid-of-His-Horses, and Big Road. These chiefs all have large followings and succeeded in keeping their people from signing by telling them the whites were again trying to make dupes of them and that if the bill carried, all who signed it would regret their action when too late. They argued that the promises made by the commissioners were not in good faith, that when their lands were once secured, they would be laughed at when they called attention to these unfulfilled promises.[34]

In spite of previous broken treaties, many Lakotas trusted and respected Crook. While he had been an adversary in the field of combat, he had also been a man of honor. A majority listened when the general told them, It is certain you will never get any better terms than are offered in this bill, and the chances are you will not get so good.[35]

Red Cloud bitterly remembered, His words sounded well; but how could we know that a new treaty would be kept any better than the old one? For that reason we did not care to sign. He promised to see that his promise would be kept. He, at least, had never lied to us. His words gave the people hope. They signed. They hoped.[36] *Shortly after the commission completed its business, Crook died. Red Cloud tersely said,* Their hope died with him. Despair came again.[37]

What had happened before, happened again. According to the "Chadron (NE) Democrat," Father Craft, a Catholic missionary stationed at Pine

Ridge, complained in a December 20, 1890, letter to the "New York Freeman's Journal" that from the beginning of the treaties with the Indians, they have been disappointed, cheated, starved, deprived of both their own customs and those of the whites, which they had fondly hoped to assume with the aid of the government, and have been in every way abused, and more than discouraged. In their despair General Crook brought them hope. Their confidence in this led them to hope that he would be able to realize their hopes. His death was their death blow, and they so felt it. Their fears and despair after General Crook's death was increased by a further reduction of rations, and a delay, even of these.[38]

American Horse, who trusted Crook and signed the agreement, said, We were made many promises but have never heard from them since. The Great Father says if we do as he directs it will be to our benefit; but instead of this they are every year cutting down our rations, and we do not get enough to keep us from suffering. General Crook talked nice to us; and after we signed the bill they took our land and cut down our allowance of food. The commission made us believe that we would get full sacks if we signed the bill, but instead of that our sacks are empty.[39]

To Crook's credit, he did try to get the new agreement honored. Hare later wrote, Expectations and hopes ran high. The Indians understood little of the complex forms and delays of our government. Six months passed, and nothing came. Three months more, and nothing came. A bill was drawn up in the Senate under General Crook's eye and passed, providing the fulfillment of the promises of the commission, but it was pigeon-holed in the House. But in the midst of the winter's pinching cold the Indians learned that the transaction had been declared complete and half their land proclaimed as thrown open to the whites. Surveys were not promptly made; perhaps they could not be, and no one knew what land was theirs and what was not. The very earth seemed sliding from beneath their feet.[40]

As had happened with past commissions, promised rations were cut once again. Gallagher stated in his annual report, I must acknowledge it was a matter of some surprise when I learned shortly after the departure of the Sioux Commission that the allowance of beef for this agency had been reduced 1,000,000 pounds, or 20 percent, for the year.[41] *Now the Lakotas were receiving less than a third of the rations promised them in the 1877 treaty.*

Miles, commander of the Division of the Missouri, added another dimension to the betrayal of the Lakotas when he reported to his superiors in his annual report of 1890, An Indian inspector, in reporting to the secretary of the interior, under date of April 7, 1890, gives it as his opinion that it is a bad plan and a great injustice to receive beef in October at its full weight and issue it on that basis in January following, the Indians thereby losing over one-third, for which their money has been paid. He calls attention to the fact that the whites are now occupying Sioux lands secured under treaty made by the commissioners of 1889, and that the Indians do not get as much as they did before the land was taken.[42]

The cuts caused internal strife among the Lakotas. Gallagher reported, When it became generally known that the reduction was really going to be made, it caused an intense feeling against the Sioux Commission among those who had signed the bill. They were made targets for derision by the non-signers, who called them fools and dupes and told them they were now getting their pay in the same coin that had been received before whenever they were so foolish as to make contracts with the whites.[43]

American Horse flatly stated, I was speaker for the whole tribe. In a general council I signed the bill and 580 signed with me. The other members of my band drew out and it divided us, and ever since the two parties have been divided.[44]

The Lakotas were angered by the government's treachery, but they were deeply divided on what to do about it. Both factions, the "friendlies" and "unfriendlies," agreed that they were outnumbered and outgunned. They knew that starting a new Indian war would result in annihilation. They even feared annihilation might be the government's next form of aggression.

The Lakotas were ready to seize upon any escape from their desperate situation. Their best hope was Wovoka's new religion.

3. The Second Pilgrimage

Educate your children, send them to schools. You must not fight.
Do no harm to anyone. Do right.—*Wovoka*, the Messiah

THE JOURNEY WEST

Two days after Short Bull met with tribal leaders in March 1889, he began his pilgrimage to Nevada. At Pine Ridge, *he says*, Scatter and I found that Kicking Bear, He Dog, Flat Iron, Yellow Knife, Brave Bear, and Twist Back had left two days before for the West, and on the night previous Yellow Breast and Broken Arm had left.[1]

We were delayed one day at Pine Ridge to have the buggy repaired. We then started off and after hard traveling for two and one half days we caught up with the Oglalas at Sage Creek near the Caspar Mountains.

Here we also met Man and his two nephews, Louis and John Shangreau [two mixed-blood government scouts], who were returning to the agency from a trip to Fort Washakie. We told them we were traveling west to meet the Messiah.

We then traveled on to the Arapahos at Shoshone Agency where we stayed until one week after Christmas. Then we started on horseback to the end of Painted Rock. Here we boarded a railroad train and arrived at a point where only Chinamen were.

The agent at Fort Washakie gave us railroad passes. Little Sitting Bull of the Arapahos gave me 25 dollars, and I sold one of my beaded vests for 10 dollars.[2]

While we were at Shoshone Agency we danced the Omaha and got presents of money. We stayed three days at the Chinamen's town. We then boarded another train traveling one day and night, but owing to a "hot box" [box car] we had to get out at the forks of a large creek where we camped for the night. The next morning we walked about one and a half miles, reaching a small town.

Once more we began to travel by rail. The snow was so deep that plows were used to clear the road, which delayed us three days in a small town.

On the fourth night the road was open so that we could travel again. After spending the night on the train we came to a creek which was lined on either side by Lodges. A town was near so we got off the cars, traveling by foot to this Indian Village. The snow was very deep.

Two of the men of this camp had been to see the Messiah. The chief of the tribe was the brother of Old Washakie, who set up a tipi for us. We stayed nine days and nights, five of which were spent in Ghost Dancing—despite the snow, but a rainstorm came up and melted the snow shortly after the dancing began.[3]

Here, *Short Bull says*, ten Bannocks came over and took us with them. Horses were provided for us at an agency named Pocktella [Pocatello]. Here we met two big Indians, one with long black hair and the other with a black beard which looked so strange. They were both holding horses, the bearded man's name was Botee and the other Elk's Tusk Necklace.

At the request of the Washakie's brother, Yellow Breast and myself remained with him, while the others left. We went to his house, and here I saw a Lakota woman who was married to a white man.

Washakie's brother, speaking in sign language, told me, "Once I went to Washington and had a talk with Spotted Tail, Two Strike, and Red Cloud."

He told me that the Messiah would talk to me, but he wanted to say something to me first . . . , "Pay no attention to what some people say. The Messiah will tell you the truth."

I shook hands with all the Sioux chiefs and dropped my arms against them for good and am their friend. I said to them, "Don't be afraid, no one will harm you, here we are all friends. You will not die."

Here the Bannocks came in for their rations, and they gave us rations too, also horses, and took us with them to the other party who had gone on ahead, and we held a council at the house of Elk's Tusk Necklace who said, "My heart is glad to see all of you people to day. My people here always do as I ask of them. We shake your hands and are glad. What fighting we [have] done in the past is dropped. We are friends and hope we will always be so. Now we will go together to the Messiah. He sent for me three times and I went. He has now sent for me again and I will go with you."

After remaining here for ten days, over one hundred of us boarded the cars and traveled from the evening till the next night, where we changed cars to arrive at another agency of the Shoshones. From this point Sitting Bull of the Arapahos, Porcupine of the Cheyennes, several Bannocks, and I, Short Bull, started on our journey to see the Messiah by rail.

After traveling from town to town for two days we came to an Indian Village of the Rabbit Skin tribe whose tipis were made of bark and willows. They were named this because [of] their blankets and bedding being made of rabbit skins. The chief's name was Owns-the-People.

Their women were dressed like the white women, and they lived on fish. The Rabbit Skins have an agency. Their rations are small, but one beef suffices for the whole band. They are rich. They fish continually and sell it.

From this point we moved in wagons and other conveyances for one day to the Paiutes where we remained thirteen days and then began to travel west, camping on a large creek the first night, and then following the railroad to a station where some young men and women of the Rabbit Skin tribe met us. They told us to go to the right of the large house in the distance and there remain two days which was done.

After waiting two days my other companions started overland, all but one Gros Ventre, a chief of the Rabbit Skins, Two Bannocks, and me. We boarded a train at about three o'clock in the morning. At sundown we reached a white man's village where an agency was. This was the supposed home of the Messiah. There we met some Indians who told us the Messiah would come in three days.[4]

The pilgrimage was an intricate feat of coordination and communication between the tribes of the West, but they all managed to meet at an appointed time in Walker Valley.

Gen. Nelson A. Miles observed in his 1891 report, It is remarkable that by concerted action the delegations from the different tribes secretly left the various reservations, some starting from points a thousand miles apart from others, and some traveling 1,400 miles into a country entirely unknown to them, and in which they had never been before. The delegations from the Sioux, Cheyennes, and other tribes, secretly leaving their reservations, met at and traveled through the Arapaho and Shoshone Reservations in Wyoming, and thence via the Union Pacific they passed to Utah, and were joined by Gros Ventres, Utes, Snakes, Piegans, Bannocks, Paiutes, and others, until they came to a large conclave of whites and Indians, near Pyramid Lake in Nevada, where not less than sixteen prominent tribes of Indians were represented.[5]

THE MESSIAH SPEAKS

When he arrived in Walker Valley, Short Bull recalls, The Indians were like grass and flowers. The spot selected was a lovely one, a heavy growth of willow all around it and a circle had been cut down in the center with entrances north, south, east, and west. I was put in the west end with a Gros Ventre and Sitting Bull of the Arapahos.

In this circle were only a few Indian chiefs, all the rest camping outside. In two days the wagon party came. Besides every train bringing more and more people to this great gathering who had been sent for from all parts of the United States, there were Sioux, Cheyennes, Arapahos, Paiutes, Gros Ventres, Bannocks, Rabbit Skins, Indians with rings in their nose, and others whose names I did not know.

I was tired and I rested that day. The next day I got in a wagon and went out to a ridge which would be the spot where the Messiah would arrive. After looking for some time I could see no signs of him. Finally a messenger arrived asking for a wagon to bring the great Man in. It was given him. The crowds then mounted their horses to go and meet him, but in a short time the wagon appeared. From which direction it came, no one knew.

The wagon contained three persons—the driver, an Indian dressed in white man's clothing, and another man who had on a broad-brimmed brown hat with two eagle feathers in it, and a striped blanket. The person wearing the blanket was the Messiah.

Good Thunder, one of Short Bull's companions on the journey, gives a more dramatic account of the first meeting with the Messiah: The people said that the Messiah will come at a place in the woods where the place was prepared for him. When we went to the place a smoke descended from heaven to the place where he was to come. When the smoke disappeared, there was a man of about forty, which was the Son of God.[6]

When ethnologist James Mooney met Wovoka in 1891, the prophet was about thirty-five years old. Mooney saw that he was a young man, a dark full-blood, compactly built, and taller than the Paiute generally, being nearly six feet tall.[7]

Wovoka's commanding appearance inspired confidence and belief in his followers. He apparently bore stigmata that to his followers were proof of his divine nature. After his field interviews, Mooney wrote, All the delegates agreed that there was a man near the base of the Sierras who said he was the son of God, who had once been killed by the whites, and who bore on his body the scars of the crucifixion.[8]

Porcupine, a Cheyenne pilgrim, confirms this, stating, I had heard that Christ had been crucified, and I looked to see, and I saw a scar on his wrist and one on his face, and he seemed to be the man. I could see his feet.[9]

Short Bull says, I wanted to shake hands with him; but the chief told me not to, saying, "Wait till you go back. There he will shake hands with you."

At dusk I went out and told my people to come in. Inside the circle a small tipi was put up for the Messiah. He entered with his face toward the South. The tipi was opened, and we all stood before him. Everybody crowded to get a glimpse of him. He took off his hat, laying it on the ground with the crown down and brim up and said, "Hau."

An old man sat in front of him with his arms extended on his knees and another behind him in the same position. These were his interpreters. One of these interpreters talked in English to one of the Arapahos named Singing Grass, a son of old Chief Friday, who spoke to me in the sign language.

While the Messiah spoke, these men would stand up and interpret what he said. I sat directly in front of the Messiah and looked him all over from head to foot. He was dark-skinned, talked in a language similar to an Indian's, and I believe he was an Indian.

The Messiah said, "I have sent for you and you came to see me. I will talk with you tomorrow. Today I will talk to these people who have been here so long. We will now pray."

Here all who were assembled crowded in with their faces turned toward the west. The Messiah made a speech but they did not tell me what he said. I got a good look at him.

After he had ceased talking, dancing began in which he joined. Men, women, and all were singing and dancing with hands joined in a peculiar way, knuckle to knuckle going round and round, keeping it up for a long time.[10]

They were dancing what would soon be known as the Ghost Dance. The Lakotas preferred to call it the Spirit Dance.

THE MESSAGE

The next morning, *Short Bull says*, a crier called out for all to assemble as the Messiah was coming. The Inner Circle was spread over with white sheets for the people to sit on. Everything was quiet. The Messiah stood up and looked toward the west and began to talk through four interpreters.

The Messiah said to me, "I have sent for you to tell you certain things that you must do. There are two chiefs at your agencies, and I want you to help them all you can. Have your people work the ground so they do not get idle, help your agents, and get farms to live on. This is one chief.

"The other chief is the church," *Wovoka continued.* "I want you to help Him for he tells you of Me. When you get back, go to church. All these churches are mine. If you go to church when you get back, others will do the same. I have raised two bodies of men on this earth and have dropped one of them. That is the army.

"I want no more fighting. Take pity on one another, and whenever you do anything that is bad something will happen to you. I mean fights between Indians and whites. All over the world one should be like the other and no distinction made. Always sing and pray about me, for it is right.

"Two days from now all nations will talk one tongue."

I was puzzled by this, *Short Bull says*. I do not think he meant two days. It could have been two months, two years, or even two hundred years.

The Messiah continued to speak, "Then the sign talk will be no more. Educate your children, send them to schools. You must not fight. Do no harm to anyone. Do right always."

The Messiah prayed again and stopped. These are the words I got from him.[11]

Short Bull says the Messiah also told him, "Whiskey is bad. Who drinks, they cause murders and suicides. Across the ocean is a great church where he came from. That church belongs to me. You may go as you please. But the church is one belief, one faith.

"When you listen to me when I pray or teach from my church, all good people will come with me. The whole world will sing. The whole earth is now filthy and stenches. These murderers and suicides are that which now stink. You say, 'Father! Oh Father! Is that you?' All that [you] will say, say thus [and] the Father God will look at you. Those that have done wrong, he will shake the earth. This part of the earth will get it."[12]

Good Thunder gives a more hallucinatory account of the meeting. He says the Messiah said: "My grandchildren! I am glad you have come from far away to see your relatives. These are your people who have come back from your country."

Then he said he wanted us to go with him. We looked, and we saw a land created across the ocean on which all the nations of Indians were coming home; but after the Messiah looked at the land which was created and reached across the ocean, it disappeared. He said it was not time for that to take place.

The Messiah then gave to Good Thunder some paints—Indian paint, a white paint, and a green grass. He said, "My grandchildren, when you get home, go to farming and send all your children to school. And on way home if you kill any buffalo, cut the head, the tail, and the four feet and leave them, and that buffalo will come to live again.

"When the soldiers of the white people chief want to arrest me, I shall stretch out my arms, which will knock them to nothingness, or, if not that, the earth will open and swallow them in. My Father commanded me to visit the Indians on a purpose.

"I have come to the white people first, but they are not good. They killed me, and you can see the marks of my wounds on my feet, my hands, and on my back. My Father has given you life—your old life—and you have come to see your friends, but you will not take me home with you at this time.

"I want to tell you when you get home your people will follow my examples. Any Indian who does not obey me and tries to be on white's side will be covered over by a new land that is to come over this old one. You will, all the people, use the paints and grass I give you. In the spring when the green grass comes, your people who have gone before you will come back, and you shall see your friends then, for you have come to my call."

The people from many tipis sent for us to visit them. They are people who died many years ago. Chasing Hawk, who died not long ago, was there, and we went to his tipi. He was living with his wife, who was killed in a war long ago. They live in a buffalo skin tipi—a very large one—and he wanted all his friends to go there to live.

After his return to Pine Ridge, Good Thunder told Capt. George Sword, I was taken to a tipi where I saw a son who died in war long ago. When . . . we come to a herd of buffaloes, we killed one and took everything except for the four feet and tail, and when we came a little ways from it there was the buffaloes come to life again and went off.[13]

Porcupine told his informant, The Christ talked to all of us in our respective tongues. You can see this man in your sleep any time you want after you have seen him and shaken hands with him once. Through him you can go to heaven and meet your friends. Since my return I have seen him often in my sleep.[14]

Short Bull and his friends, led by the Messiah, then danced the Ghost Dance for the first time. At that time, Short Bull says, While we were dancing the Ghost Dance I saw white men, women, and girls joining in the dance.

I saw the Messiah daily for five days. It was then I saw that his name was tattooed on the back of his left hand.

On the fifth day I shook hands with him, and all he said was, "Soon there would be no world. After the end of the world those who went to church would see all of their relatives that had died. This will be the same all over the world, even across the big waters."

He asked us to return again in the fall of the following year. Then he would have more to tell us, but for reasons I will tell later, we did not go.[15]

Later, Wovoka would be accused of claiming he was Christ. Mooney, however, writes that during an 1891 interview, He makes no claim to be Christ, the Son of God, as has been so often asserted in print. He does claim to be a prophet who has received a divine revelation.[16]

THE JOURNEY HOME

Our party returned by the same route we came, only one accident occurring, *Short Bull says.* The train was overturned and fell over an embankment, but no one was hurt.[17]

Good Thunder offers a mystic account of their return journey: The Messiah said, "If you call upon me, I will shorten your journey when you feel tired of the long ways."

This we did when we were tired. The night came upon us, we stopped at a place, and we called upon the Messiah to help us, because we were tired of [the] long journey. We went to sleep and in the morning we found ourselves at a great distance from where we stopped. This was one of the Messiah's words came to truth.[18]

There seemed to be an awareness of the new religion at Pine Ridge even as the Lakota emissaries were meeting the Messiah in Walker Valley. On September 20, 1889, Father Aemilius Perrig wrote, Today Ohitica was here and explained why he did not come to school anymore. He said that God appeared to the Yutes [Paiutes] and told them to beware of the whites, not to believe them, nor to go to their schools or churches, else they would all perish. Therefore, Ohitica said he was afraid to come to our school. Rev. F. Superior's reasoning with him seemed to have little or no effect.[19]

By early April 1890, all of the emissaries to the Messiah returned to their tribes. Some began to preach Wovoka's message and taught their followers the Ghost Dance. According to ethnologist Warren K. Moorehead, the new religion spread like wildfire; and the Ghost Dance was organized and adopted by all the tribes from the Chinooks, far up in British Columbia, to the Shawnees and Kickapoos, in the Indian Territory. No other tribe entered into the dance with such spirit nor believed so firmly in the coming of the Savior as did the Sioux.[20]

Short Bull insists that he was not the first to preach the new religion: On the second day after my arrival, I went to the council house to tell them all about what I had seen and heard, but I was stopped by Indian police by order of the agent. They arrested and took me before the agent to whom I told my story.

Short Bull says he told Agent J. George Wright of the Rosebud Reservation, "I wanted to tell the Indians what I have told you, but the police stopped me."

He told me, "If you tell this story to the Indians, you will be a dead man."

I laughed and said it was a good story.

When the Ghost dancing began I did not go there. I went afterwards. It was not started by me but by Scatter.[21]

Luther Standing Bear, a "friendly" and a schoolteacher at the Rosebud Reservation who was educated at the Carlisle Training School in Pennsylvania, frequently served as Wright's translator. Standing Bear offers a less dramatic version of this encounter: I was called into the agent's office. There I saw an Indian called Short Bull and a young man known as Ce-re-aka-ruga-pi, or Breaks-the-Pot-on-Him. The agent started to question them in front of me, and I shall never forget what Short Bull said. The agent asked him to tell about the new religion which they were all getting so exited about, and why he believed in it.

In Short Bull's words: We heard there was a wonderful man in the Far West. He was a Messiah, so several tribes gathered together to go and see Him. We went to the place where the sun sets, and there we saw this man. He told us we were to have a new earth; that the old earth would be covered up, and while it was being covered we were to keep dancing so that we could remain on top of the dirt.

This man told us that all the white people would be covered up, because they did not believe; even the Indians who did not believe would also be covered. He showed us visions of the olden times when the buffalo were plenty; when the big camps were on the plains. All our people were dancing and having a big feast.

This man hit the ground and he made fire. He spoke to all of us at once, and all the different tribes understood him. He said that all the white people would be destroyed. He taught us a song to sing during this dance. He showed us where the sun dropped down into the ocean, and it boiled up and became hot.

At this point, *Luther Standing Bear says*, I spoke up and said to Short Bull, "That is not so; the ocean does not boil up with the setting of the sun."

Short Bull looked straight at me, but he had nothing further to say about the sun.

The agent spoke to both these men politely, and asked them not to stir up the Indians at Rosebud Agency. They both promised, and then left for home.[22]

Wright, in his 1891 report to the commissioner of Indian Affairs, wrote that Short Bull desisted until the following September [1890], at which time he renewed his preaching and started the dance in camps of the most non-progressive and disturbing element of Indians, which attracted the attention and curiosity of nearly all on the reserve.[23]

A few days later, *Short Bull says*, one of the Indian police and the interpreter Louis Rubadeau insulted me. I did not say much to them; but I said this to them, "The Messiah told me not to fight, and I will not. You may take a gun and kill me if you want to."

Louis Rubadeau said to me, "See if one of the dancers who are in a fit see the Messiah, If you can't do it, you will be lost."

His brother, who was nearby, grabbed him and dragged him away. Louis told Turning Bear, "If you will kill Short Bull, the agent will give you one hundred dollars, two horses, a cow, and a yoke of oxen."

Turning Bear said he had been told to rush into my tipi and grab me. Then other Indians would rush in to help him to finish the job. Turning Bear told this to me.

I laughed and said nothing.

This was in May, and the Ghost dancing had well begun.[24]

4. The Ghost Dance Sweeps across the Dakotas

The new dance among the Indians is worth going many miles to see.
—*Charles W. Allen*, editor of the *Chadron* (*NE*) *Democrat*

THE PILGRIMS RETURN

Educator Elaine Goodale, returning from visiting her family in the East, recollects, The five ambassadors sent across the Rocky Mountains by Red Cloud to investigate strange rumors of a Messiah for the Red Man had returned and reported shortly before I reached Pine Ridge in June 1890. The story they brought was the same as that we had heard from the lone traveler at our one-night camp eleven months before. Suddenly everyone seemed unable to talk of anything but the "new religion"! Some were merely curious; others were vaguely apprehensive of they knew not what. Only the more unsophisticated were ready to accept the notion of a miraculous intervention in their favor, at a moment when all hope failed and Heaven itself seemed to have turned against them.[1]

Shortly after the pilgrims returned, late spring rains cheered the Lakotas, and the initial enthusiasm for the Ghost Dance religion was replaced with planting activity. Even so, rumors spread that the new ritual was a war dance. The first murmur of danger came in a letter Charles A. Hyde of Pierre, South Dakota, wrote to Secretary of Interior John W. Noble on May 29, 1890. Hyde, having received a letter from a young Pine Ridge Lakota, felt compelled to write Noble, The information has come to me, confidentially, through a source that I have confidence in that the Sioux Indians or a portion of them are secretly planning and arranging for an outbreak in the near future probably tho' several weeks or months off.

I do not wish to cause any undue actions or alarm, but must suggest the advisability of keeping a careful watch on the different bands and using conservative judgment about allowing any of them to leave their respective agencies.[2]

In Noble's absence, Acting Indian Commissioner Robert V. Belt contacted his agents to ascertain if Hyde's suspicions had any basis in fact. In a June 18 reply to Belt, Standing Rock Agent James McLaughlin reported, As far as the Indians of this agency are concerned, there is nothing in either their words or actions that would justify this rumor, and I do not believe that such an imprudent step is seriously meditated by any of the Sioux.[3] *McLaughlin's reply was typical of those dispatched by the other Dakota agencies.*

Despite his lack of concern, McLaughlin did seize upon the opportunity to suggest cautionary measures. There are, however, *he wrote*, a few malcontents here, as at all the Sioux agencies who cling tenaciously to the old Indian ways and are slow to accept the better order of things, whose influence is exerted in the wrong direction; and this class of Indians are ever ready to circulate idle rumors and sow dissension, to discourage the more progressive; but only a few of the Sioux could now possibly be united in attempting any overt act against the government, and the removal from among them of a few individuals (the leaders of the disaffection) such as Sitting Bull, Circling Bear, Black Bird, and Circling Hawk of this agency, Spotted Elk (Big Foot) and his lieutenants of Cheyenne River, Crow Dog, and Low Dog of Rosebud, and any of like ilk of Pine Ridge, would end all trouble and uneasiness in the future.[4]

McLaughlin was most concerned with one of his charges at Standing Rock: Sitting Bull. In the months that followed, McLaughlin repeatedly sought permission to arrest the charismatic spiritual leader, but his requests were rejected again and again.

Washington officials, accepting the reassuring reports of the Dakota Indian agents, saw no reason for alarm or any need for such a drastic action as McLaughlin suggested.[5]

DANCING AT PINE RIDGE

By July the brief respite from the drought ended, and the Dakotas were parched. Crops were failing for the second year in a row. Again, the Lakotas felt a need to dance. The dances in the Pine Ridge area, especially, drew more and more devotees. Even then, Goodale says, Many groups were unaffected and only a small minority of the . . . Sioux gave full credence to the "new religion" [and] even these ignorant and unhappy souls preached no violence.[6] *The Ghost dancers were obeying the pacifistic precepts of Wovoka.*

Ethnologist Warren K. Moorehead, who visited Pine Ridge as the dancing reached its peak, described the ritual in great detail: The largest camp of dancers was located upon Wounded Knee Creek under the charge of Chiefs No Water, Short Bull and Little Wound. A large, level tract of prairie near the tipis was carefully prepared by the squaws. A pole or sapling some thirty-five feet in height was erected, to the topmost twigs of which was attached a white flag. The base of the tree, to a height of five or six feet, was covered with hundreds of rushes and reeds plaited together with the greatest of care. These gave the sapling the appearance of a tree which one frequently sees in a cultivated field in harvest time, with a shock of wheat or corn bound round it.

The squaws also built near the dance ground several lodges almost air tight, which were to be used as sweat houses, separate structures being provided for the women. Every person wishing to join in the dance was compelled to divest himself of his clothing and enter one of these tipis, some eight or ten persons being crowded into each house.

A fire was built near at hand in which stones were heated. These rocks were placed within the lodge and a bucket of water poured over them. Clouds of steam arose, completely filling the structure. This operation was continued as long as the subjects could bear confinement. When they issued from their baths attendants quickly threw blankets over the perspiring forms.

A priest or medicine man accompanied by four assistants and the village crier (whose business it was to announce all important events, speeches and councils) advanced to the sapling. Stationing themselves about the pole the crier called aloud to those who wished to participate in the dance to come forward at once. In obedience to the commands of the priest, several hundred men and women crowded up and, grasping hands, formed a circle fully two hundred feet in diameter.

While they delayed, the priests began a prayer to the Great Spirit. The following is a literal translation of one of the supplications: "Great Wakan Tanka: We are ready to begin the dance as you have commanded us. Our hearts are now good. We would do all that you ask. In return for our efforts we beg that you give us back our old hunting grounds, and our game. Oh, transport such of the dancers as are really in earnest to the Spirit Land far away and let them see their dead relatives. Show them what good things you have prepared for us and return the visitors safely to earth again. Hear us, we implore."

At the conclusion of the prayer the priests begin a doleful chant, which is taken up by the assembled multitude and loudly sung over and over again. The circle moves toward the left. For the first half hour the motion is a short step, not more than ten or twelve inches, accompanied by the bending of the knees. None of the dancers jump up or down until another prayer has been offered. The following words will acquaint the reader with the nature of the songs:

Ate he ye lo.
Canupa wan ci ci ca hu pi kte lo.
Ate he ye lo.
Ate he ye lo.

[My son, smoke and you will live.
Come to the sacred tree.
This the Father says.] [7]

After the space of half an hour the crier calls aloud and the participants pause.

"Weep for your sins," commands the high priest. Accordingly, the Indians set up a most horrible wail. They moan and cry, rolling upon the ground, apparently in great agony. Some of the more desperate ones crowd up to the sapling (which is called in their language a sacred tree) and thrust little gifts and tokens between the rushes.

Others cut their arms and wipe the blood upon the reeds, or detach small pieces of flesh from their sides, and stick these bloody tokens among the bindings. The scene is most impressive. Surely the Sioux are serious in their grief, for it is scarcely possible that men and women could feign in so natural a manner such sorrow, such repentance. Grim warriors, determined men to whose eyes tears had ever before been strange, will elbow their way through the crowd about the trees, and with heaving breasts and sobbing voices plead that Great Wakan Tanka forgive them for all their wickedness.

After these paroxysms of grief comes an intermission. The priests harangue the converts and exhort them to be of good heart, to hesitate not in the ceremonies. A new song is struck up for they have several Ghost Dance songs, and again the circle moves toward the left. The dancing becomes fast and furious. The men and women leap backward and forward. They seem possessed of the spirit of demons.

Frequently one or two, delirious with excitement, may break away from the dancers and go staggering across the plain. A woman reels against a tree near the creek, where she stands moaning and gasping. A youth throws himself headlong upon the ground with such violence as to cause great fears for his safety.

Meanwhile the priests are extremely active. They run from one excited dancer to another, gently compelling all to lie prone upon the earth. They wave an eagle feather (the symbol of holiness and purity) in the face of the subject, stare very fixedly at him and mutter incantations over his prostrate form. Undoubtedly the priests exercise an influence akin to mesmerism or hypnotism upon the distracted mind of the weary dancers. One Indian who had danced twenty-seven times told me: "The priest looked very fixedly at me. He stared into my eyes like a snake, and then I knew no more."

Of course the exhausted mind of the savage is in a fit condition to receive impressions of visions, to fall into trances or behold strange scenes in the spirit land.

The scene of a Ghost Dance at night makes a vivid impression upon the mind. The music in its strange wild key rings in the ears for days, while one can never forget the reeling figures, the earnest, expressive faces.

When the dance has been carried on for several hours, the priests arouse some of the sleepers and secure from them accounts of what they have beheld in the spirit land. This information is heralded by the crier, the chant being subdued almost to a whisper while he speaks. The visions are strongly alike in general character, although varying somewhat in detail.

Weasel, a dancer, told ethnologist Moorehead, When I fell to sleep, the music of the dance became fainter and fainter until it entirely disappeared. Then a great eagle came and, sticking his talons in my clothes, carried me away many miles into the skies. Suddenly we came upon a fair land and the bird halted by a stream, where there was a lodge made of rushes woven very tightly and neatly. In this lodge, the bird said, the Great Wakan Tanka was hidden, and that the Messiah would come forth at noon. I must wait, he said, until the Savior would appear. So I sat down upon the banks of this fine little valley and waited.

Presently there came forth a white man with a long beard. He showed me holes in His hands and feet, and said that the whites had made these wounds. He said that He would never appear to the whites again, that if the Indians would continue the Messiah dance He would appear to them the next summer, and that upon His appearance the world would come to an end.

Then he showed me a large village, larger than I ever saw in my life. The tipis were all constructed of buffalo hides, and resembled those we used to have in the happy years long since passed. Men and women, relatives of mine, rushed forward to greet me and embraced my neck, crying and sobbing, meanwhile, with joy at my coming.

The people conducted me to a large council house, where chokeberries and buffalo meat [were being] prepared and served. After eating I was shown great herds of elk and buffalo. The Good Man told me to return to my friends and relate what I had seen in his beautiful home. The earthly people must dance and pray and wait, He said, until His coming.

We were not to make use of guns nor were we to fight. The Messiah Himself would come to our aid and perform for us deeds that powder and ball could not. Then my relatives bade me farewell and I was born to earth again by the great eagle.

Day after day, *Moorehead wrote,* the faithful dancers dragged their weary bodies about the circle. They saw visions. They prayed as never man prayed before. With tears, fastings and self-inflicted tortures, they called in despair upon their Messiah. He answered them not.[8]

Charles W. Allen, editor of the "Chadron (NE) Democrat," commented, In the earlier stages of this peculiar craze the dances were held at points near the agency that were accessible to spectators from nearby towns and settlements across the line in Nebraska. Others from a distance also availed themselves of the opportunity to study the strange procedure. All kinds of conveyances could be seen moving to and from the camps where the ceremony was being performed.[9]

Sightseers continued to observe the dancing well into the fall. On September 25, 1890, Allen again reported, The new dance among the Indians is said to be worth going many miles to see.[10] *By now members of the press were calling the new ritual the Ghost Dance, and a few suggested that it was a war dance.*

Some settlers became apprehensive. Allen wrote, The emaciated condition of the dancers and the physical weakness of all the Pine Ridge Sioux for want of proper nourishment at the time was well known by the settlers of the surrounding country. This fact made war seem more probable to them and justified every move they made toward self-protection.[11] *In the several reports of the Ghost dancing there is no evidence of any warlike posturing by the celebrants.*

One of the dancing spectators that fall was an unnamed teacher at the day school on White Clay Creek. She painted a bucolic picture of the site of a ritual she attended on an October morning. There, she says, We came upon tents scattered here and there in low sheltered places long before reaching the dance ground. Large herds of ponies were feeding on the hillsides, watched over by numberless little urchins lazily sauntering in the sun, or gathered in merry groups.

The Indian always takes his ponies and dogs wherever he goes. Presently we saw over three hundred tents placed in a circle, with a large pine tree in the center, which was covered with strips of cloth of various colors, eagle feathers, stuffed birds, claws, and horns—all offerings to the Great Spirit.

The ritual the teacher visited had a new feature. That day, she says, I think they wore the Ghost shirt for the first time that day. I noticed that these were all new, and were worn by about seventy men and forty women. The wife of a man called Return-from-Scout had seen in a vision that her friends all wore a similar robe, and, on reviving from her trance, she called the women together and they made a great number of the sacred garments.

They were of white cotton cloth; the women's dress was cut like their ordinary dress, a loose robe with wide flowing sleeves, painted blue in the neck, in the shape of a three-cornered handkerchief, with moon, stars, birds, etc., interspersed with real feathers, painted on the waist and sleeves. While dancing they wound their shawls about their waists, letting them fall to within 3 inches of the ground, the fringe at the bottom.

Some wore beautiful brocades, others costly shawls given them by fathers, brothers, and husbands who had traveled with Buffalo Bill. In the hair, near the crown, a feather was tied. I noticed an absence of any manner of bead ornaments, and as I knew their vanity and fondness for them, wondered why it was. Upon making inquires I found they discarded everything they could which was made by white men.

The Ghost shirt for the men was made of the same material—shirt and leggings painted in red. Some of the leggings were painted in stripes running up and down, others running around. The shirt around the neck was painted blue, and the whole garment fantastically sprinkled with figures of birds, bow and arrows, sun, moon, and stars, and everything they saw in nature. Down the inside of the sleeve were rows of feathers tied by the quill ends and left to fly in the breeze, and also a row around the neck and up and down the outside of the leggings. I noticed that a number had stuffed birds, squirrel heads, etc., tied in their long hair. The faces of all were painted red with a black half moon on the forehead and on one cheek.

Slowly, the teacher says, the dancing grew in intensity. If one, more weak and frail, came near falling, he would be jerked up and into position until tired nature gave way. The ground had been worked and worn by many feet, until the fine flour-like dust lay light and loose to the depth of 2 or 3 inches. The wind, which had increased, would sometimes take it up, enveloping the dancers and hiding them from view.

In the ring there were men, women, and children; the strong and robust, the weak consumptive, and those near to death's door. They believed those who were sick would be cured by joining in the dance and losing consciousness. From the beginning they chanted to a monotonous tune the words—

Father, I come;
Mother, I come;
Brother I come;
Father, give us back our arrows.

All of which they would repeat over and over again, until first one and then another would break from the ring and stagger away to fall down. One woman fell a few feet from me; she came toward us, her hair flying over her face, which was purple, looking as if the blood must burst through; her hands and arms moving wildly; every breath a pant and a groan; and she fell on her back and went down like a log. I stepped up to her as she lay there motionless, but with every muscle twitching and quivering. She seemed to be perfectly unconscious.

At this point in the ritual, the teacher says hysteria seized many of the supplicants: Some of the men and a few of the women would run, stepping high and clawing the air in a frightful manner. Some told me afterwards that they had a sensation as if the ground were rising toward them and would strike them in the face. Others would drop where they stood. One woman fell directly in the ring, and her husband stepped out and stood over her to prevent them from trampling upon her. No one ever disturbed those who fell or took notice of them except to keep the crowd away.

They kept up their dancing until fully 100 persons were lying unconscious.

I asked one Indian, a tall, strong fellow, straight as an arrow, what his experience was. He said he saw an eagle coming toward him. It flew round and round, drawing nearer and nearer, until he put out his hand to take it, when it was gone. I asked him what he thought of it. "Big lie," he replied.

I found by talking to them that not one in twenty believed in it. After resting for a time, they would go through the same performance, perhaps three times in a day. They practiced fasting, and every morning those who joined in the dance were obliged to immerse themselves in the creek.[12]

The wearing of the Ghost shirt quickly spread. Indian Police Capt. George Sword says, All the men and women made holy shirts and dresses. . . . They said that the bullets will not go through these shirts and dresses, so they all have these dresses for war. Their enemies weapon will not go through these dresses.[13] *This belief, when reported, added to some settlers' fear that the new ritual was a war dance.*

By midautumn, accounts of the rituals became more fanciful. Mrs. James A. Finley, the wife of the post trader at Wounded Knee, told an eastern newspaper reporter, At a recent dance, one of the braves was to go into a trance and remain in this condition for four days. At the close of this period he was to come to life as a buffalo; he would still have the form of a man, but he would be a buffalo. They were then to kill the buffalo, and every Indian who did not eat a piece of him would become a dog.

The reporter writes, The man who was to turn into a buffalo was perfectly willing, and Mrs. Finley presumes they have killed and eaten him by this time. This lady is of the opinion that if the government lets them alone there will be no need of troops; they will kill themselves dancing. Seven or eight of them died as a result of one dance, near Wounded Knee.[14]

It is possible that a few of the older and more infirm dancers died from excitation and exhaustion during the rituals, but the suggestion of cannibalism among the Lakotas is absurd.

James H. Cook, a scout turned rancher who was visiting Pine Ridge in search of land, wryly observed, The effect of these messages was like that of the arrival and efforts of a great revivalist of the shouting Methodist school, who could soon have great numbers of blind followers under the influence of what he styled "the power."

When the news of the coming of the Indian Messiah was brought to me by some old Indian friends from Pine Ridge Agency, South Dakota, I went with them to the home of Little Bat at Fort Robinson and talked over the situation with him and with the Indians. I could see no harm, I told them, in dancing the Ghost Dance if they did not kill themselves while so doing; but I counseled against doing such deeds of violence against the white people, for such deeds could lead only to serious trouble. I told them that if the Great Spirit were going to bring about any such changes he would need no help in disposing of the whites; he could cause all of them—as such as he cared to remove—to die as suddenly as a flash of lightning.[15]

Cook remained at Pine Ridge and continued to mediate between the whites and the Lakota leaders.

Some aspects of the dance offended the Victorian sensibilities of the agents and missionaries. Rosebud Agent J. George Wright complained, The dancing among the Indians has its objectionable and demoralizing features. Among them are the men being clothed more in paint and feathers than in civilized dress, and their past exploits in time of hostility related to an appreciative audience of young people. While such dances can not be stopped entirely for some time to come, they are restricted to once a week, and prohibited in the working season.[16]

Charles A. Eastman, a thirty-two-year-old Santee Lakota medical doctor who came to Pine Ridge in the early autumn of 1890, observed, A religious craze such as that of 1890–1 was a thing foreign to the Indian philosophy. . . . It meant that the last hope of race entity had departed, and my people were groping blindly after spiritual relief in their bewilderment and misery. I believe the first prophets of the "Red Christ" were innocent enough and that the people generally were sincere, but there were doubtless some who went into it for self-advertisement, and who introduced new and fantastic features to attract the crowd.[17]

While it was generally held that the ritual was pagan, Father Perrig wrote in his diary on December 15, 1890 that Father Craft has seen last night the Ghost Dance performed at the Rosebud Indian camp. He found it to be all right, quite Catholic, and quite edifying.[18]

Even at this late date, there seemed to be no fear among the whites who observed the ritual. However, the sanguine views of the Ghost Dance were not shared by the growing number of reporters who arrived at Pine Ridge by midautumn 1890. They described it as a war dance performed by Lakotas who believed they were invulnerable to the bullets of the troops that defended the Dakotas. Anyone who had taken the time to observe and study the dancing knew better.

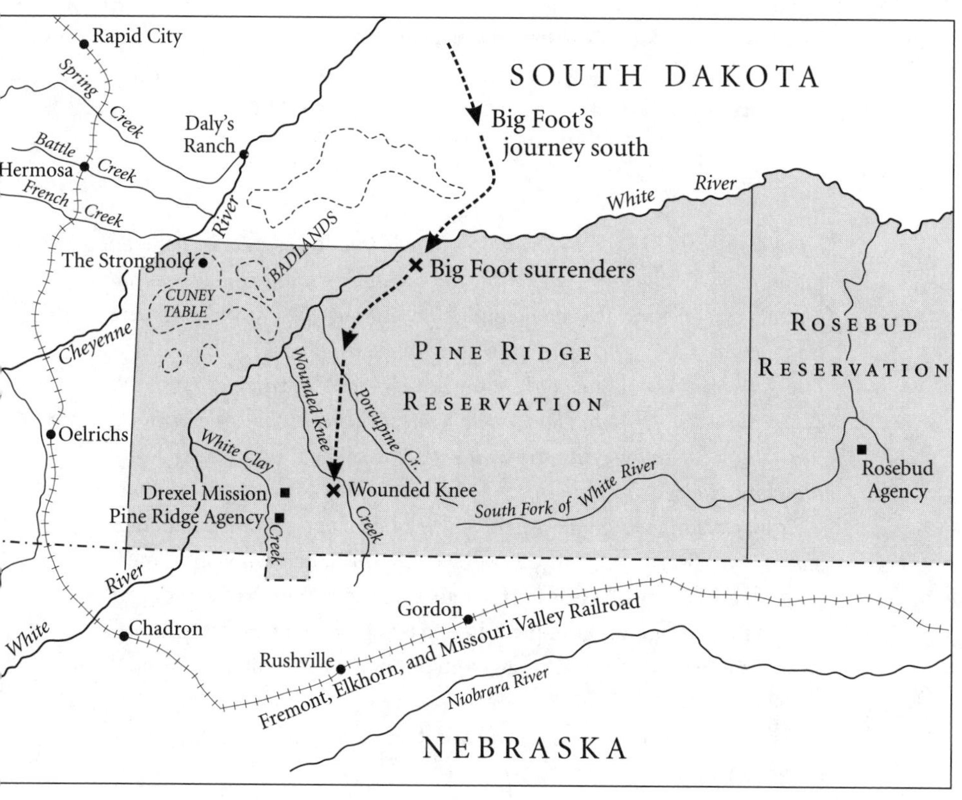

Map 2. Pine Ridge Reservation and surrounding area

5. A Failure in Communications

It was a pitiable, disgraceful affair forced on Indians and whites alike by politics, graft, and bad management.—*Dr. Valentine T. McGillycuddy*, Pine Ridge Indian agent, 1879–86

AFIELD

Small bands of Lakotas often wandered away from their agencies between ration days. Afield they could hunt the remaining small game and lead a semblance of their former nomadic life. Among these wanderers were Chief Horn Cloud, his wife, and their six sons—Joseph, White Lance, Frank, Sherman, William, and Dewey Beard (Waza Maza). Dewey, the eldest, was twenty-eight and had fought against Custer at the Little Bighorn. Traveling with him was his pregnant wife, White Face. Also traveling with the Horn Clouds was a grandson, Thomas, and a niece, Pretty Enemy.[1]

It was late in the summer when they first heard of the Ghost Dance religion. Dewey Beard says, One day as I sat with my father in his tipi, a messenger came saying a Savior for the Sioux had appeared to one in the far land of the setting-sun, who promised to bring again the buffalo and antelope and to send the white man from out of the land where we hunted in the old time.

This messenger was holy. He told us if we danced and prayed the Savior would appear.

"Does this mean that we shall fight again with the white man?" my father asked. "It is not good to speak so of war."

"No," said the messenger, "there is no talk of battles. When the Great One comes, the white people will go away, and in the land will be many things to eat."

"Let us see this thing," said my father to us. "The Great White Chief at Washington has broken his word, for he took our lands, saying we should have food as long as we lived. We are starving, while our families eat nothing but the wild turnips."

So we went to White Clay Creek, where the Indians danced the Ghost Dance, and we danced also, I, my father, and all my brothers.

When the spirit would not come to any of us, Chief Horn Cloud said, "My sons, it is strange that we do not see the Savior. I am told that they dance better at the Cheyenne Agency. We may see the Holy One there."

There, the Horn Clouds, interested in the new ritual, met Chief Big Foot's band. Dewey Beard says, We went to the tipis of Big Foot; but there it was the same, for the mystery came not to any of our family.[2] *In spite of the Horn Clouds' disillusionment with the new religion, they stayed with Big Foot's band. It proved to be a tragic choice.*

BIG FOOT'S ODYSSEY BEGINS

Big Foot, an aged but still feared Miniconjou Lakota chief, resided on the Cheyenne River Reservation. He and his people were known for their independence and dislike of government policies, a dislike they showed by staying away from their agency as much as possible.

As summer drew to an end, Big Foot and many of his followers accepted the Ghost Dance religion. When whites became aware that Big Foot and his people had joined the dancing, they labeled his people "hostiles." Some even speculated that Big Foot planned to lead his followers on the warpath. There was little reason for this fear. Big Foot was in bad health and had less than four hundred followers. Two-thirds of these were women and children. A little over one hundred could be classified as warriors, but many were older men and young boys. They were not a formidable fighting force.[3]

Some time in the spring of 1890, probably April, *Joseph Horn Cloud recollects,* Major Hennesey came with troops from Fort Meade and they camped close to Big Foot's camp, they on the south side and Big Foot on the north side about three miles away from Pass Creek and the Cheyenne River. *Joseph was speaking of Capt. A. G. Henissee, an officer who had brought three troops of cavalry and two companies of infantry to the area to observe the Ghost dancers' activities.*[4]

According to Joseph Horn Cloud, They remained friendly with the soldiers and had races and games and other amusements with the soldiers.[5] *By the end of the summer, Joseph says,* Some of the soldiers joined in the dance. Major Hennesey told the band they must dance only on Saturday, not all the week, so they obeyed.[6]

About this time, Joseph says, Some mixed bloods and loafers went to the agent with a bad report against Big Foot and that he had become hostile, but Big Foot was really friendly both to the whites and all Indians. He wanted peace all the time. Such was the condition of 1890.[7]

Big Foot, upset by these accusations, decided to move away from the agency. Frog, one of Big Foot's brothers, says, Big Foot and his band had been asked at different times during the summer by Red Cloud, Little Wound, Afraid-of-His-Horses and No Water to come to Pine Ridge Agency and join them.[8] *According to Joseph Horn Cloud,* We did not care for the news they brought us. Instead, Big Foot's band went hunting antelope in the Little Missouri River country in North Dakota. We had been out about six weeks hunting in that country and had killed many antelopes and had much dried meat for winter.

On returning to the camp again on Pass Creek, more messengers came from Pine Ridge bringing messages from Red Cloud, Little Wound, Big Road, Calico, No Water and several others saying, "Big Foot, we want you to come over with your band at once. We are having the Spirit Dance here, but many soldiers have come and we fear we are going to have trouble so we want you to come and make peace. If you can make peace we will give 100 horses to your band."

This was the third time such messages had come and now Big Foot's band began dancing.[9]

According to Dewey Beard, Big Foot told his followers, We have to go to the agency and get some annuities and some blankets and quilts; and when we come back, I will then see if we can go to the Pine Ridge Agency and make a peace.[10] *It is unclear whether Big Foot requested permission to go to Pine Ridge. If so, the request was denied. The last thing the army wanted was to have the legendary war chiefs who had defeated Custer gathered on the same reservation.*

Big Foot and his people, after receiving their rations, slipped away from their agency and returned to their nomadic life. As they wandered, Big Foot mulled Red Cloud's invitation to Pine Ridge.

DIFFERING FACTIONS AT PINE RIDGE

Many in the East believed that the venerable war chief Red Cloud was responsible for the growing religious fervor at Pine Ridge. Recently arrived eastern-educated Lakota medical doctor Charles A. Eastman disagrees, insisting, The leaders of the malcontents at this time were Jack Red Cloud, No Water, He Dog, Four Bears, Yellow Bear, and Kicking Bear. Friendly leaders included American Horse, Young Man Afraid of His Horses, Bad Wound, Three Stars.

There was another set whose attitude was not clearly defined, and among these men was Red Cloud, the greatest of them all. He, who had led his people so brilliantly and with such remarkable results, both in battle and diplomacy, was now an old man of over seventy years, living in a frame house which had been built for him within half a mile of the agency. He would come to council, but said little or nothing. No one knew exactly where he stood, but it seemed that he was broken in spirit as in body and convinced of the hopelessness of his people's cause.[11]

Philip Wells, a mixed-blood interpreter and scout, says the equally feared Little Wound had with perfect sincerity, bowed his proud spirit to what he knew was inevitable. . . . As an upright man he accepted the terms of advancing civilization. He was willing that his followers should adopt the new order as taught by the white conqueror. Upon this point his heart was unmistakably good. He placed reliance upon the good intentions of the Great Father as glowingly and emphatically pictured to him.

Imagine what must have been his disappointment when his people were deceived and victimized and subjected to wrongs which, from their long continuance, could not be excused or accounted for as accidental.[12]

As summer moved into fall, the nearly blind Red Cloud dictated despairing and conciliatory letters to white friends in the East and nearby towns. Even though these letters were published in newspapers throughout the nation, reporters repeatedly described Red Cloud as a militant.

After talking with some of the so-called war correspondents gathered at Pine Ridge, former scout James W. Cook says, Some of these gentlemen informed me that old Red Cloud was at the bottom of all the deviltry that was going on; that he was managing the hostiles who were out in the Badlands, making his headquarters at the fine house which Uncle Sam had so kindly given him in order to make him comfortable in his old age. It so happened that I was with Red Cloud every day and night at that time, and my associates every day and night were the headquarters Indian scouts, Little Bat, Woman's Dress, Yankton Charlie, Short Bull, and other Indian friends at the agency and at the hostile camp. Neither these men nor I could ever discover that old Red Cloud had anything to do with either directing the hostiles or giving them aid and encouragement.[13]

Why was there an attempt to bring the older chiefs and their people to Pine Ridge? Wells suggests Red Cloud's and Little Wound's attempt to gather the old chiefs together was a strategic ploy. Wells says, These first men whose highest duty was to secure the rights of the Indians to whom they belonged, may have planned to assemble a threatening force so that notice, and action based thereon, would be given to their demands for justice.[14]

Years later Wells repeated this view when he wrote, I talked with many Indian leaders during the Ghost Dance craze. A number of them said, "No, I do not believe it anymore than you do."

"Then," asked I, "why do you encourage it?"

The most frequent answer given was, "We have to arouse the white people or they will pay no attention to our petitions asking for better treatment. The white people have lied to us."

I said to the Indian leaders, "You would arouse the white people," and asked, "Will not that cause a war with them?"

They answered, "We prefer not to have war, but if we have to, we will."

I added, "And risk the danger of many getting killed?"

"Yes," they replied, "we will take the chance rather than endure the things we put up with now."

I asked them, "Do you expect to defeat the whites in a war?"

"No," they answered, "we do not expect to win a war with them, but there are other ways in which we stand to gain."

I asked them, "In what other ways do you stand to gain?"

They answered, "All white people are not bad. Many conscientious people in the East will work for us and help us win our point."[15]

What Wells described may have been the views of younger members of the Lakota tribes. While the older chiefs were capable of such subtle diplomatic maneuvering, they had traveled in the East as delegates representing their people and had seen the wealth and power of the white world. They knew that any act of war on their part could end in the annihilation of their people. While they did not object to their people's dancing, they did not encourage it.

It is not known why Red Cloud asked Big Foot's band to come to Pine Ridge, but it is likely the Pine Ridge chief wanted to have his people's leaders assembled in one place. There they could negotiate together and end the growing tensions in the Dakotas.

ATTEMPTS TO STOP THE DANCING

During a brief respite from the drought in spring and midsummer, the Ghost dancing subsided; however, after a dry August, the dancing resumed. Wells says, During the summer settlers living near the Reservation on the south and west were several times seized with alarms and false reports given out of an Indian uprising, and collected in assemblies for flight or protection, and Colonel Gallagher [Pine Ridge Indian Agent Hugh D. Gallagher] and I went out to assure them that their fears were groundless and to advise them to remain at their houses.[16]

Even though Gallagher felt the dancing was harmless, he was alarmed by its growing intensity. In his annual report to the Indian commission, the agent wrote: An Indian belonging to the Cheyenne River Agency who had lately visited the land where the new Christ is supposed to be sojourning temporarily came to this agency a few weeks since, and before I learned of his presence he had succeeded in exciting the Indians living upon Wounded Knee Creek to such a pitch that many of them swooned away during the performance of the ceremonies which attends the recital of the wondrous things soon to come to pass, and one of the men died of the effects of the excitement.

The visitor from Cheyenne River was Kicking Bear, the most ardent preacher of the Ghost Dance religion. Before Gallagher could stop the preaching of the new religion, Kicking Bear moved north to preach the new religion at the Cheyenne River and Standing Rock Reservations; but his enthusiasm for the religion remained behind.

On Friday, August 22, *Gallagher continues*, about two thousand Indians gathered on White Clay Creek about eighteen miles north of the agency to hold what they call the religious dance connected with the appearance of this wonderful thing. Noticing the demoralizing effect of these meetings I instructed the police to order the gathering to disperse, but found the police were unable to do anything with them.[17]

On August 24, Father Perrig, finding his congregation decimated by the growing enthusiasm for the Ghost Dance, complained, Only John Yellow Horse, Felix Tracy and Dick Big Head in Mass. *The reason for the absences, the priest wrote, was that* yesterday a large meeting of Indians took place about six miles from here down on the creek. The meeting was caused by that silly talk about the apparition of Jesus Christ.

In the absence of the agent, his representative sent a policeman with the order to return home to the Indians assembled. They refused to obey the order and did not comply with it. So a despatch was sent from Pine Ridge to Agent Gallagher in Chadron, informing him and summoning him home. He traveled all night and arrived at the agency this morning.[18]

Gallagher, in his annual report, described his encounter with the Ghost dancers: I visited the locality where the Indians had assembled on Sunday, the 24th instant, accompanied by twenty of the police. The Indians probably heard of our coming for they had dispersed before we arrived at the grounds, several of the bucks, however, were standing around in the neighborhood of where the dance had been held. These men were stripped for fight, having removed their leggings and such other superfluous apparel as is usually worn by them and stood with Winchesters in their hands and a good storing of cartridges belted around their waists prepared to do or die in defense of the new faith.

They were quieted after a time by being made to understand that we had no desire to harm them but had come to order the people to their homes, who, it had been reported, were gathered here in violation of orders. While nothing serious may result from this new religion . . . I would greatly fear the consequences should there be no restriction placed upon it.[19]

According to Wells, Gallagher was modest concerning his own bravery during the tense encounter. In an October 19, 1890, letter to Standing Rock Agent James McLaughlin, Wells wrote, Some time ago Colonel Gallagher, myself, and a lot of police went to the place of dancing to stop it, but they had stopped before we got there, but the Indians were laying in ambush for us, all armed and stripped for fighting, and as we rode up they drew their guns on us, but the colonel told the police to stand back in readiness and walked into their midst and ordered them to lay down their guns. A few of the leaders who were in sight did not; we found out before we left there that the woods was full of armed Indians. I am telling you this that you can see the magnitude the craze has taken if it will be of any service to you to know.[20]

McLaughlin would soon have reason to take Wells's advice. Kicking Bear was headed in his direction, intent on seeking new converts at Sitting Bull's camp on the Grand River.

Gallagher managed to stop the dancing for only a day. On August 25, 1890, Father Perrig wrote, It is reported that the Indians are meeting in different other places for the same pow-wow. *On September 14, he wrote,* All our Indians went to the Ghost Dances except six families. *On September 21, the priest added,* All our Indians except Calico off to Ghost Dance. *His congregation had virtually disappeared.*

By September 26, the priest was apprehensive: Father Jutz brought the news of some kind of uprising among the Rosebud Indians and that they had come to St. Francis in warpaint and was armed, and had taken their children from the school. . . . It gets more and more the appearance of deviltry. The appearing ghosts are said to express dislike for baptized persons. The apparition of him, who pretends to be our Lord (with the five wounds), forbids the Indians to call him Jesus, but only wants to be called Father. The entranced Indians pretend to have seen the happy hunting grounds. All the apparitions are inspiring the Indians with distrust, dislike, contempt or even hatred of the whites.[21]

As autumn began, newsman Charles W. Allen reported, There were no hostilities other than minor stock thefts from neighboring ranches. The element opposing the dance was the most influential in the tribe. The principal chiefs overshadowed the medicine men; and the latter, well aware of this fact, used much caution in their warlike interpolations in the newly acquired creed.[22] *Allen, too, believed that the older chiefs were intent on preserving the peace.*

Allen, however, was an alarmist when he accused the Ghost Dance leaders of adding "warlike interpolations" to Wovoka's pacifistic religion. They had no reason to. They believed that all they had to do was dance and wait until spring. Then the old world, the buffalo, and their ancestors would return.

By now the growing fervor of the Ghost dancers was beginning to alarm the settlers near the reservations. Many were panicking and a few fled the area.

Commissioner of Indian Affairs Thomas J. Morgan spent several weeks touring the western reservations that autumn. In his annual report to the secretary of the interior, Morgan described the white panic as an economic problem: Visiting the localities outside the reservation, I was astounded at the stories of timidity, alarm, and hurried flight everywhere related; the vacating of homes, in many cases permanently, and the enormous decline reported in real estate. It was freely declared by prominent gentlemen that "real estate in this region will not recover from the Indian scare in fifteen years."

Some white settlers fled to the cities, making great ado; but when the excitement was over and anything was said about returning to the ranches, these refugees replied: "What have I got to go back to?" Not that the Indians "had cleaned them out," for no Indians had been within 50 or 75 miles of these homes. Successive failures of crops and general shiftlessness had left little in hand.[23]

As the seasons changed, local officials, merchants, and state officials began to demand army protection and weapons. Some made these demands to assure their safety, others to bring an influx of troops and new business into the Dakotas. The military, eager to secure increased appropriations, was all too ready to move into the area and appear a preserver of the peace, especially when little risk of war was involved.

The most vocal advocate for this was the new commander of the Division of the Missouri, Gen. Nelson A. Miles. The flamboyant Miles, a veteran Indian fighter and an adroit politician, was the darling of the press. He was always available for press conferences, and, as tensions grew in the West, he skillfully manipulated the press by selecting his most pessimistic intelligence reports. Reporters, impressed with his confident manner, relayed his demands for a greater military presence in the Dakotas to their readers.

A few of Miles's fellow officers thought the general was creating a high profile to launch a political career. Whatever his personal ambitions were, Miles was intent on securing a stronger position for the military in the Dakotas. First, he believed that the army could administer the reservations better than the agents appointed under the patronage system. He was probably right. Second, calling up more forces would justify the army's request for increased appropriations. The army, which had declined in power in the years following the Civil War, felt it was overlooked by Congress in recent sessions. Now it had a reason for requesting larger appropriations.

Miles knew the Lakotas well and was respected by them. They even nick-

named him "Bear Coat" in reference to his favored winter field attire. The Lakotas were also aware that in the past Miles urged his superiors in Washington to honor the treaties they signed. On the national scene, he was indeed one of the strongest advocates for honoring old treaties.

DANCING AT ROSEBUD RESERVATION

As autumn began, Short Bull, now living on the Rosebud Reservation, says, My funds were getting low; so I applied to the agent for an order to get some freight at Valentine. This was refused me; I was somewhat angered but said nothing. I then went to live with my Uncle Hawk Eagle. I lived with him some time, occasionally visiting the dancing and finally participating in them. Becoming in time a "regular" dancer—day and night—I kept telling my people of the Messiah and they had faith in him—this was good.[24] *Within weeks Short Bull became one of the new religion's most eloquent advocates.*

In September the youthful and newly appointed Rosebud agent, J. George Wright, reported, After visiting the scene and studying the nature of the proceedings, the Indians were informed that such dances must cease, causing, as they did, a general demoralization among them, attracting Indians from all parts, interfering with schools, and causing a total neglect of stock and all belongings.

Criticism has been made by alleged friends of the Indians that no interference should have been permitted in this "religious exercise"; but no reasonable intelligent person, with the welfare of the Indians at heart, would indorse it, after having been a witness to the superstitious proceedings.[25]

Luther Standing Bear, a schoolteacher at Rosebud, recollected that the Ghost Dance was being held about eight miles west of the agency on a flat, on the west side of Little White River. We could plainly locate the dancers from the dust they raised and . . . the beat of the tom-toms. They would keep up the dancing until they fell from exhaustion. The Indians were really serious about it. . . . They felt that this new religion was going to rid them of the hated pale-faces who had antagonized them so long.

My father's band had not joined the dancers yet. Two of his brothers-in-law were in charge of them. High Pipe . . . was one of the men, and Black Horn was the other. Father had already moved over to Pine Ridge with his family, but had left his two brothers-in-law in charge of the balance of the Indians.

The dust was flying high in the sky every day from the dancing. As the enthusiasm grew, more dancers joined. George Wright, the agent, sent for me to see if I would go to my father's band with a message from him. This band was located about five miles west of the agency on the east side of Little White River, so they were only about three miles from the dancers across the river. They could both hear and see the dancers easier than ourselves.

I agreed to go, and Mr. Wright furnished me with a team and driver. He was a white man, and when we reached the camp I instructed him to drive into the center of it before he stopped. The tipis were all in a circle. It was quite a camp—about a quarter of a mile across it. When the wagon stopped, the Indians came out and stood around to listen to what I had to say. There was no excitement, but every one was curious as to the cause of my visit.

I told my people that I wanted to help them, and that was the reason I had come. I said it would not be right for them to join the Ghost dancers, as the government was going to stop it, and it would not be best for them to be found there. I told them the government would use soldiers to enforce the order if it became necessary.

The thought that the soldiers were coming disturbed them, but I told them if they felt afraid they could move their tipis in and put them around my house and camp there. My house was only about a half-mile from the agency. They all agreed to come there the following morning. This pleased me immensely to think that my visit and talk had been a success. When I returned and told the agent, he, too, was very happy.[26]

Agent Wright had a harsh solution to his problem. The following day, *he says,* [the Indians] were informed that rations would be withheld until they had returned to their homes and ceased dancing, which had the desired effect and the dance was confirmed to the few originators, to be more gradually suppressed.[27] *When such a choice was presented to the Lakotas, many chose food over religion.*

Wright was called to Washington early in the fall, after it was discovered that he had overstated the census for his reservation by two thousand Lakotas. Because of this discrepancy, Wright was accused of stealing the excess rations. In the meantime he was replaced by the inexperienced E. B. Reynolds. After a few weeks, Wright was exonerated and returned to his job. During his absence, Wright complained, The Indians taking advantage of the change in authority, soon again started the dance with renewed vigor, receiving encouragement from the adjoining agency, killing stock for feasts and defying all control.[28]

Mooney wrote that under the Harrison administration, fifty of the fifty-eight agents on reservations throughout the United States were replaced according to the plans of a new patronage system.[29] *Agent Gallagher at Pine*

Ridge was about to be replaced, and Charles McChesney at the Cheyenne River Agency was replaced by the inexperienced Perain P. Palmer. Palmer was faced with the formidable task of coping with Kicking Bear, Hump, and Big Foot. He, like the other new agents, was unable to suppress the dancing.

In reaction to the changes, the "New York Times" editorialized: Two of the most critical points in the Indian country are the agencies at Pine Ridge and Cheyenne River. The agents at these points were men of experience and generally acknowledged to be fit for their work, who knew the Indians and how to handle them—a knowledge only gained by time and practice. They have been displaced, and two entirely green men have been put in. Why? Simply and solely to give "patronage" to politicians. We denounced this sort of thing when it was done under the last Administration as monstrous; it is monstrous now, and the consequences are likely to be even more serious. If there shall be bloodshed and lives lost, a good part will be the price paid for our servitude to the vulgar, sordid, cruel, wicked spoils system, which its advocates like to call "American."[30]

The few experienced agents who remained tried to limit the dancing, and for the moment they were successful. They believed that the rigors of a Dakota winter would dull their charges' enthusiasm for the new religion and that when spring came the drought would be over. They and the commissioner of Indian Affairs asked the government for additional rations. They had seen religious crazes come and go over the years and saw no danger in the Ghost Dance. Food was the best solution.

THE "NEWSPAPER WAR" BEGINS

As the dancing spread, the eastern press dispatched reporters to the Dakotas. Describing the Ghost Dance as a war dance made good copy. Some of the dispatches were inaccurate due to the ignorance and ineptitude of the correspondents, but a few were intentionally exaggerated if not blatantly untrue.[31] *Rev. Thomas L. Riggs, a missionary at Pine Ridge, correctly observed,* The fact is that not one in a hundred of our western Sioux had any thought of making war against the whites. It was in very truth a newspaper war.[32]

As late as December 6, 1890, at the height of what the press declared a crisis verging on open warfare, the "Custer (SD) Chronicle" complained, The Indian scare continues unabated, having been intensified rather than diminished by the startling and [in] many instances highly exaggerated reports emanating from newspaper correspondents at the front who seem inclined to report the situation in its most alarming possible phrase. . . . So far as the people of the Hills are concerned, there does not appear to be any reasonable grounds for alarm, hence we would deem it advisable, for the present, and until danger presents itself, to dismiss fear and await further developments."[33]

Eastern readers were rarely presented with this point of view. Instead, they were bombarded with reports of Lakota outrages, all of which had little basis in fact. Much later—on January 15, 1891—former Pine Ridge agent Dr. Valentine T. McGillycuddy wrote Gen. L. W. Colby, the commander of the Nebraska National Guard: Up to this date there has been neither a Sioux outbreak nor war. No citizen of Nebraska or Dakota has been killed, molested or can show the scratch of a pin and no property has been destroyed off the reservation.[34]

McGillycuddy went on to say, As for the "Ghost Dance," too much attention has been paid to it. It was only the symptom or surface indication of a deep-rooted, long persisting difficulty; it would be as well [to] treat the eruption of small pox as the disease and ignore the constitutional disease.[35]

Big Road, a minor Lakota chief, put the Lakota point of view succinctly when he said, This dance was like religion; it was religious. Those who brought the dance here from the West said that to dance was the same as going to church.

White people pray because they want to go to Heaven. Indians want to go to Heaven, too, so they prayed, and they also prayed for food enough to keep them out of Heaven until it was time to go. Heaven must be a nice place, or the white man would not want to go there. That was why the Indians would like to go.

We danced and prayed that we might live forever; that everything we planted might grow up to give us plenty and happiness. There was no harm in the dance. The Messiah told us to send our children to school, to work our farms all the time, and to do the best we could. He also told us not to drop our church. We and our children could dance and go to church, too; that would be like going to two churches.

I never heard that the Messiah had promised that the Indians should be supreme or that the white man should be destroyed. We never prayed for anything but happiness. We did not pray that the white people should be all killed. The shirts we wore were made for us to go to Heaven. The dance was not a war dance, for none that went to it were allowed to have one scrap of metal on his body.[36]

Commissioner Morgan, during his visits to the western reservations, found little danger in the Ghost Dance. In his annual report in 1891 he wrote: During my absence from the office last fall on a tour of observation among the Indian agencies and schools, which lasted from September 5 to early in December, I had occasion to notice the effect of this craze among the several tribes, and it was brought up prominently in a council with the Kiowas, Comanches, etc., of Oklahoma.

I found that among the tribes which I visited the excitement was comparatively harmless; and although it had seriously retarded progress in civilization for the time being, it had been readily controlled and had furnished no occasion for alarm; and I added: "The only danger to be apprehended is that influence from without, emanating from those who in some manner might be benefited by the Indian uprising or the movement of troops or by the excitement growing out of 'wars and rumors of wars,' may precipitate a needless conflict and bring on a disastrous and costly war." *Morgan adds,* I have not been among the Sioux of the Dakotas.[37]

Such positive reports were overshadowed by more alarming news stories. In a "Washington Evening Star" interview, South Dakota Sen. Richard F. Pettigrew blamed these inflammatory press reports on what were called "space writers." Pettigrew complained, "Today he sends three columns of gore to any paper that will buy it and tomorrow he will contradict what he sends today, that his reward may be greater. All he wants is money, and he will write anything to get it."[38]

As the Ghost Dance spread, a large contingent of war correspondents settled into Pine Ridge. As Allen wrote in his memoirs, The reportorial staff by this time had increased to fourteen members. Two or three were free-lance space writers, so most of the dailies between St. Paul and St. Louis and from New York to Omaha, if they did not have their own representatives actually on the ground, at least had a look-in on the daily proceedings.[39]

These reporters rarely ventured into the field. Most stayed close to the telegraph office, seeking news from settlers who came into the agency or from handouts from the agent and the military. In their search for stories, they treated anyone coming into the agency as an expert. More than a few of these "experts" fed gullible reporters stories that were patently untrue. The headlines for one day were often based on events that never happened. In many ways, the press created what came to be called the Ghost Dance war.

CHANGES AT PINE RIDGE

In September Gallagher was serving his final days as agent at Pine Ridge. J. R. Walker, a Pine Ridge physician, says, Gallagher's personal excellence was beyond dispute, but he was so hampered by those above him in authority that the best he could do was to hold together and maintain what had been built up for him.

Gallagher found himself meanly assailed by two artificial defects—his politics and his religion. Commissioner Morgan was a narrow partisan and still narrower sectarian. He was a Republican and a Protestant. Gallagher was a Democrat and Catholic. This ought to have caused no friction and would not if the commissioner had been capable of statesmanlike views. Gallagher being of an opposite political faith, Morgan had no desire to allow him to make much reputation, and he being a Catholic, Morgan was careful not to encourage that church in its aspirations if he was not hopeful to thwart them altogether. Therefore the agent was remarkably successful where he was able to hold his own.

The commissioner cut down the rations and the allowances of beef which had been promised by the commission which has negotiated the Treaty of 1889. These arbitrary and demoralizing acts fomented the disturbances which harassed Gallagher's closing months of duty, for the reason that it put the Indians on a starvation basis. Suffering from hunger created widespread discontent. This state of unavoidable feeling was the soil in which the Messiah craze took root.

It enabled the leaders with designs and wrongs, urging them to harangue and influence the others and to work up a formidable cohesion and organization, and finally to upset all order and bring civil government to an end.[40]

Pine Ridge issue clerk Robert O. Pugh, an admirer of Gallagher, was more blunt about Morgan's religious bias: Commissioner Morgan was a Baptist preacher, filled with more religious zeal than sound judgment. He did not realize the importance of creature comforts as a foundation of religious conversion. Instead of meat, he gave them tracts. Told that the Indians were hungry, he inquired what kind of religious reading would be best for them. He acted as though a diminishing ration would create a spiritual appetite. He was zealous for God, expecting the Indian to take care of his own stomach before the time of enthrallment.[41]

Gallagher's son, Bernard, who was at Pine Ridge from 1886 to 1890, says, Colonel Gallagher had succeeded in closing all dances over the reservation, excepting one dance located on White Clay Creek, about four miles north of the agency; and in a personal call at this dance, he peacefully induced them to move their dance site back into the hill and out of sight of the main highway to preclude new sympathizers joining their movement. The craze was definitely dying out in the summer of 1890 with every evidence that another winter's season would make it a memory of the past.

It was just at this time that the new agent, Dr. Royer, appeared on the scene.[42]

Gallagher's replacement, thirty-six-year-old Dr. Daniel F. Royer, had been educated at Waynesburg Normal School in Pennsylvania and received a medical degree from Jefferson Medical School in Philadelphia. For several years he lived in Alpena, South Dakota. There he had diverse careers as a physician, druggist, journalist, and banker. As a loyal Republican he served two terms in the territorial legislature; because of his politics, he was appointed agent under the patronage system by the first governor of South Dakota, Andrew Mellete. Royer had no experience with the Lakotas, and, as time proved, he was emotionally and temperamentally unsuited to the pressures of being an Indian agent.

According to Bernard Gallagher, When the doctor arrived at Pine Ridge in the later summer of 1890 to take over the affairs from the incumbent Col. Hugh D. Gallagher, it was discovered that he was just about four months early, as Colonel Gallagher's four year term had yet some four months to run, as dated from the confirmation by the U.S. Senate of his presidential appointment.

Not wishing to start a controversy with Washington where the political complexion had changed from Democratic to Republican during his incumbency, Colonel Gallagher readily and without protest turned affairs over to the new agent promptly and moved his family to Chadron, Nebraska, some thirty-five miles southwest of Pine Ridge.[43]

Royer botched his job from the start.

McGillycuddy, a Republican and the agent at Pine Ridge before Gallagher, flatly stated, Royer was a gentleman totally ignorant of Indians and their peculiarities; a gentleman with not a qualification in his make-up calculated to fit him for the position of agent at one of the largest and most difficult agencies in the service to manage; a man selected solely as a reward for political services.

He might possibly have been an average success as an Indian agent at a small, well-regulated agency. He endeavored to strengthen up matters, but the chiefs and leaders who could have assisted him in so doing had been alienated by the former agent. They virtually said among themselves, "We, after incurring the enmity of the bad element among our people by sustaining the government, have been ignored and ill-treated by that government, hence it is not our affair."[44]

On December 20, 1890, the "Pioneer Press" condemned Royer's appointment in a scathing editorial: Consider the atrocious folly of our practical politics. Here is an agency, where many thousands of Indians are gathered, where an agent who knows his duty and does it has been established for many years, and where the Indians have come to like him and to trust him. To them, he is the government. To him, they are a lot of undeveloped, full-grown children whose individual peculiarities he understands, and can use to control them at pleasure.

Now comes a change of administration. For no reason in the world except to give a place to some political worker, this experienced man is removed and a green hand put in his place. Every time that this happens, the government deliberately invites a disturbance that may cost many lives and is sure to cost many dollars.[45]

The editorial proved prophetic.

A FAILURE OF LEADERSHIP

Shortly after his arrival, Royer, alarmed by the Ghost dancers and fearing for his and his family's safety, wrote to Morgan: I am satisfied that over half of our Indians have joined the dance and many more will follow. Over 600 were seen last week in one circle dancing, and they kept it up for nearly a week, and I am informed that after the next beef issue they are going to have the largest dance of the season. I am here to carry out your orders as far as I am able to do so and I shall do my utmost to handle these people to bring about the best results, but in doing so I have one request to make: "Give me a good police force to back me up."[46]

To Royer's credit, he did attempt to confront the Ghost dancers. Cook says the agent went out armed to order a Ghost Dance at Pine Ridge to cease. He was met by one Indian who was not afraid of a white man. The Indians who were present told me that this lone red man replied to Royer that white people danced when they wished to, and so did the Sioux. He asked the agent what he intended to do with the pistol which he was carrying, and whether he had ever killed an Indian. Then he bared his breast to the agent and said, "Here, kill me, for I am going to dance!"[47]

Royer backed down from this challenge of his authority. That was his first mistake. The scornful Lakotas immediately gave him a new name, Lakota Kokipa-Koshkala, or Young-Man-Afraid-of-Indians.[48]

On December 27, 1890, Perrig acknowledged how the problems at Pine Ridge were intensified by Royer's shortcomings. Special Agent Cooper, *the priest wrote,* asked F. Jutz in a letter for his opinion about the causes of the Indian troubles. We agreed to answer as follows . . . omitting . . . everything blameworthy of the agent. *Perrig also noted,* A part of the Indians here were dissatisfied with the cession of the land made last year. When the promises made by the commissioner were not fulfilled also those that had signed began to grow dissatisfied. Then the rations were curtailed against the express assurance of the commissioner to the contrary.

Into these already dissatisfied persons the Messiah revelations were thrown. Every day almost brought new revelations which all aimed at filling the Indians with distrust or hatred of the whites and with the hope of soon getting free from the rule and control of the whites and becoming their own Masters.—All this contributed to make the Indians less manageable, more insolent.

He continued, These were no excuses of insubordination heard of as long as Colonel Gallagher was agent. But as soon as the new agent, Royer, arrived, Colonel Gallagher was too busy with his papers to pay any more attention to the Messiah craze and the Ghost Dances.

The new agent is said to have forbidden the dance and threatened punishment to the trespassers. Nobody heeded his words and he did not make his threats good and that settled his authority. Agent Royer made other threats to parents who would keep their children from school. He never made his threats good, and nobody cares what the agent says in this regard. Even the police force grew very negligent in the performance of their duty, because they know that it matters little whether they perform their duty or not. They are not blamed nor punished.[49]

Pugh, a native of Great Britain married to a mixed-blood woman, painted an even darker picture of Royer. The outspoken clerk flatly accused Royer of using the spoils system to line his own pockets: When Gallagher went out of office, the wood, of which there was about 300 cords, and the hay, of which there was about 150 tons, and the grain—corn and oats—of which there was some 600,000 pounds in store at the agency.

After Royer came with his Chief Clerk, Bishop J. Gleason, they received 6000 head of cattle at 1200 lbs. per head when they actually weighed less than a thousand lbs. There were about 250 lbs., which at two and three quarter cents a pound, gave these grafters the snug sum of $40,000 (exactly $41,250). A good profit for a single dishonest transaction.

But this was not all the stealing. The wood, hay and grain [left from Gallagher's tenure] were stolen remorselessly—stolen clean. The wood went with such dispatch that the Boarding School had to burn tree tops and such inferior fuel. The school children did not leave the Boarding School. They were kept. This is positive.

Agent Royer and Chief Clerk Gleason, *Pugh continued*, were broken-down small politicians of South Dakota. Senator Pettigrew was their patron. They were overwhelmingly in debt. They came to this reservation as political adventurers in search of fortunes—of which they were much in need. From the day of their arrival to the day of Royer's departure, stealing went on at a galloping rate. Rations (sugar, coffee, etc.,) went as though they were blessed with animated life and were on a stampede.

The only thing that escaped the cyclone of robbery was the annuities which could not be disposed of without leaving tracks of easy detection. Assistant wise heads, who were beneficiaries of the transactions, counseled the bringing of the Army. The Army is a mammoth consumer—a safe destroyer.

The "wise" ones borrowed these supplies from the agent. The "wise" ones then sold the borrowings to the military. Vouchers, which were signed by an Indian, whose mark was witnessed by the clerk, were forged. The "wise" ones said if the troops came there would be a large demand for forage, fuel and other supplies, and that the opportunity for a harvest was at hand. The agent was advised that the need for troops was wholly wanting, but he insisted that he had private advices, which settled the matter in his mind. He went away and came back with the troops. He had previously disposed of Pugh by telling him that he must have a man in his place that he could depend on, so Pugh was put out to look after the beef here.[50]

A number of Lakota chiefs also complained about Royer's dishonesty; they criticized the dishonesty of other agents as well. Young-Man-Afraid-of-His-Horses flatly stated, Our agent was a very bad man.

Little Wound scorned all government agents, complaining, They have stolen from us and made themselves rich. We do not get the pound and a half of meat or beef promised us. We do not get our coffee, sugar and flour. The agents lie to us and lie to the Great Father.

Kicking Bear asserted, The Great Father promised us plenty, He sends us bad agents, who rob us.

Little Chief elaborated, The government took away our good land, promised us money and plenty to eat; they said they would bring us to a good country and teach our people to farm and be like white men. They brought us to this country where nothing grows. The agent steals our beef.

The agents lie about us after they rob us, *Rocky Bear said, and even "friendly" American Horse agreed, saying,* Many agents are bad and rob Indians. Let the Great Father turn out the bad agents and keep the promises which were made and there will be no more trouble.

Big Road, a Wafagas chief, condemned agents in general, telling Colby, The Great Father should have good agents, and he should not lie to us. His agents rob us and starve us, and do not give us anything they agreed to. They promise us good things—money, clothes, tools, and plenty of food for our good lands, and they said they would teach us to farm, but they lied. I do not lie like the white man. The Great Father should not let his agents steal.[51]

SHORT BULL PREACHES A SERMON

On October 31, 1890, Short Bull preached a sermon to his people at the Red Leaf Camp. There he told his followers, My friends and relatives: I will soon start this thing in running order. I have told you that this would come to pass in two seasons, but since the whites are interfering so much, I will advance the time from what my Father above told me to do. The time will be shorter. Therefore you must not be afraid of anything.

Some of my relations have no ears, so I will have them blown away. Now there will be a tree sprout up, and there all the members of our religion and the tribe must gather together. That will be the place where we will see our relations. But, before this time, we must dance the balance of this moon, at the end of which time the earth will shiver very hard. Whenever this thing occurs I will start the wind to blow. We are the ones who will then see our fathers, mothers, and everybody.

We, the tribe of Indians, are the ones who are living a sacred life. God, our Father, Himself has told and commanded and shown me to do these things. Our Father in Heaven has placed a mark at each point of the four winds; first, a clay pipe, which lies at the setting of the sun and represents the Sioux tribe; second, there is a holy arrow lying at the north, which represents the Cheyenne tribe; third, at the rising of the sun lies hail, representing the Arapaho tribe; and fourth, there lies a pipe and nice feather at the south, which represents the Crow tribe.

My Father has shown me these things, therefore we must continue this dance. If the soldiers surround you four deep, three of you on whom I have put holy shirts will sing a song, which I have taught you, around them, when some of them will drop dead, then the rest will start to run, but their horses will sink into the earth also; then you can do as you desire with them. Now you must know this, that all the soldiers and that race will be dead; there will be only five thousand of them left living on the earth. My friends and relations, this is straight and true.

Now we must gather at Pass Creek, where the tree is sprouting. There we will go among our dead relations. You must not take any earthly things with you. Then the men must take off all their clothing, and the women must do the same. No one shall be ashamed of exposing their persons. My Father above has told me to do this, and we must do as he says. You must not be afraid of anything. The guns are the only things we are afraid of, but they belong to our Father in Heaven. He will see they do no harm. Whatever white men may tell you, do not listen to them. My relations, this is all. I will now raise my hand up to my Father and close what he has said to you through me.[52]

GENERAL MILES STEPS IN

There was no call to war in Short Bull's sermon, yet Royer and many settlers continued to be alarmed. In his 1891 report, Miles wrote, So general was the alarm of the citizens, the officials, of the general government, the governors of the States, and the press of that part of the country, that all earnestly appealed for aid and protection for the settlements.[53]

In a letter dated October 29, from P. P. Palmer, Indian agent, Cheyenne River Agency to the Interior Department, he says of Hump and his following that the best means of preventing an outbreak among the Indians would be to take these leaders entirely out of the reach of their followers.

In a letter dated October 30, 1890, D. F. Royer, Indian agent at Pine Ridge Agency, informs the commissioner of Indian Affairs that—

> Some of the disadvantages originating from the Ghost Dance is the believers in it defy the law, threaten the police, take their children out of school, and if the police are sent after the children, they simply stand ready to fight before they will give them up. When an Indian violates any law the first thing they do is to join the Ghost Dance, and then they feel safe to defy the police, the law, and the agent.

And further—

> I have carefully studied the matter for nearly six weeks and have brought all the persuasion through the chiefs to bear on the leaders that was possible, but without effect, and the only remedy for this matter is the use of the military, and until this is done, you need not expect any progress from these people; on the other hand, you will be made to realize that they are tearing down more in a day than the government can build up in a month.[54]

Miles was carefully selecting his sources of information.

During a fact-finding trip west it was reported, When General Miles visited the Cheyennes in early November, he was asked if he would send troops if the Messiah appeared. Miles replied, "The Great Father will send soldiers."

"Heap soldiers?" was the aboriginal inquiry.

"Yes, heap soldiers," said the general. More soldiers than any of you ever saw, and when they come, I'll whale the hell out of you."[55]

Miles was all too willing to provide Royer with military protection.

6. Standoff at Standing Rock

Indians! There are no Indians left but me!—*Sitting Bull*

✶

There was not one white man who loved an Indian and not an Indian but who hated a white man.—*Gen. Nelson A. Miles, Serving the Republic*

✶

I was not born to eat out of the white man's hand.—*Sitting Bull (Ta-ton-ka-i-yo-ton-ka)*

OLD ANTAGONISTS

James McLaughlin, the Indian agent at the Standing Rock Agency, had twenty years of experience in the reservation system. He was adept in dealing with his superiors in Washington and had survived the recent political changes of administrations. A Roman Catholic whose wife was half Lakota, McLaughlin's longevity in a system run by Protestants was remarkable.[1]

McLaughlin's prime objective was to turn the Standing Rock Hunkpapas to agricultural pursuits, even though he admitted in his annual reports to the commissioner of Indian Affairs that farming was at best a marginal pursuit on his reservation. Most of his charges accepted his directives; but, one man—the charismatic medicine man, Sitting Bull—stood between the agent and the realization of his goals. McLaughlin was not adverse to taking strong actions against anyone who questioned his authority; he considered any Lakota who questioned him a candidate for military prison. Sitting Bull was well aware of the agent's ruthlessness and cleverly sidestepped confrontation. This infuriated McLaughlin, whose superiors told him not to arrest Sitting Bull.

In 1890 Sitting Bull, then in his late fifties, resided near his birthplace in a peaceful valley on a bend of the Grand River some forty miles south of the Standing Rock Agency. There, he and approximately 250 of his followers lived in log cabins strung out along the riverbanks. They plowed their fields with oxen issued by the government, raised livestock, and hunted small game. They supplemented their own efforts with meager biweekly government rations.

Sitting Bull had chickens, horses, and over twenty head of cattle, and he lived in a solid log cabin.[2] *At Grand River he and his followers enjoyed more freedom and led an easier and healthier life than the Hunkpapas living closer to the Standing Rock Agency. Their independence and near self-sufficiency were protests against the government's agricultural policies.*

Sitting Bull and McLaughlin had been at odds since the day after Sitting Bull's arrival at Standing Rock on May 10, 1883. On May 11 Sitting Bull and his followers requested that Sitting Bull be placed in charge of distributing rations to their tribe. Sitting Bull also asserted that he should be the "big chief" at the agency. Both requests were denied. Sitting Bull added one other request, however, stating that he wanted to delay his entry into agricultural life for a year. This request, too, was denied.[3]

Their mutual animosity may have been intensified over a personal issue involving Mrs. McLaughlin. In 1884 Mrs. McLaughlin and her son had accompanied Sitting Bull on a fifteen-city platform tour of a Wild West exhibition. The medicine man was billed as the slayer of Custer, and his friendly greetings to his audiences were interpreted by the show's manager, Col. Alvarez Allen, as a "lurid account of the Battle of the Little Big Horn."[4] *Sitting Bull could not speak English and may not have known how his words were being interpreted.*

In 1885 Sitting Bull was invited to tour the United States and Canada with Buffalo Bill's "Wild West," an elaborate and popular outdoor exhibition. Touring with Cody was popular with the Lakotas and other Plains tribes for good reason. They received good pay and other benefits, and most enjoyed seeing the world for the first time.

As the star attraction for the 1885 season, Sitting Bull was especially well paid; he earned more than some of Cody's white stars.[5] *After his return, Sitting Bull tersely described his view of the white world*: "The white man knows how to make everything, but he does not know how to distribute it."[6]

Sitting Bull did not rejoin the "Wild West" for the 1886 season. Instead, he resumed his peaceful life on Grand River.[7] *In 1887 Cody planned to take his exhibition to England as part of Queen Victoria's Jubilee celebration. According to Standing Rock interpreter Frank Zahn*, Cody . . . took for granted that Sitting Bull would go. Mrs. McLaughlin was engaged as interpreter. The trip was planned . . . [but] when Cody came to Standing Rock, Sitting Bull refused to go. No coaxing, no persuasion, nothing would budge him. "I have seen enough," he said, "let someone else go. I am not going."

So, *Zahn says*, that ended Mrs. McLaughlin's brilliant dreams of traveling in Europe. She could not forgive Sitting Bull for this disappointment. She was bitter against him and influenced her husband. Mr. McLaughlin denied Sitting Bull all privileges after this. Bitterness grew on both sides that never ended.[8]

Mrs. McLaughlin had good reason to be disappointed. Cody's tour started in London and resulted in a command performance before Queen Victoria. It was one of the most celebrated and successful entertainments of the century.

According to Zahn, Two friendlies, Gall and John Grass were the pets after this. They were lauded and extolled and made much of by the agent and his wife. Sitting Bull was belittled. Stories were told of what a coward he was. Indians that wanted to get into the good graces of the agent packed stories back and forth.[9]

Sitting Bull complained to his friend Grasping Bear, "White Hair [McLaughlin] wanted me to travel around with Buffalo Bill and across the sea, so that he could make a lot of money. Once was enough; I would not go again. Then I would not join his church, and ever since he has had it in for me."

Sitting Bull smiled scornfully, "Long ago I had two women in my lodge. One of them was jealous. White Hair reminds me of that jealous woman."[10]

According to Zahn, When Sitting Bull . . . likened the agent to a pretty jealous woman, it got back to the agent, which made matters worse, of course.[11]

In 1888 Sitting Bull embarrassed McLaughlin before a government commission. The medicine man opposed the commission's offer to buy eleven million acres of reservation land at the absurdly low price of fifty cents an acre. It was an arrangement McLaughlin supported and encouraged.[12]

McLaughlin later boasted that he had saved the Lakotas from being underpaid for their land during these negotiations.[13] *This claim does not bear close examination. Sitting Bull's first serious biographer, Stanley Vestal, aptly observed,* The official minutes of the council prove beyond a doubt that [McLaughlin] strongly urged the Indians to sell their land for a song, and that they took him at his word and refused to do so. It was Sitting Bull, *Vestal concludes,* not the agent, who saved those millions of acres and dollars for his people.[14]

To save face, the humiliated agent resigned from the commission. From that time, McLaughlin's hostility toward Sitting Bull was open and virulent.

In 1889 the two men were in opposition again when Gen. George A. Crook arrived with another land-buying commission. This time McLaughlin outmaneuvered Sitting Bull. The medicine man, his influence diminished, returned to Grand River and withdrew from further tribal politics.

Near that time Sitting Bull said, "I don't want a white man over me. I don't want an agent. I want to have the white man with me, but not to be my chief. I ask this because I want to do right by my people, and cannot trust anyone else to trade with them or talk with them."[15]

Sitting Bull, fearful that he might be arrested or assassinated, asked Grasping Bear, "Why should the Indian police come against me? We are of the same blood, we are all Sioux, we are relatives. It will disgrace the nation, it will be murder, it will defile our race. If the white men want me to die, they ought not to put up the Indians to kill me. I don't want confusion among my people. Let the soldiers come and take me away and kill me, wherever they like. I am not afraid. I was born a warrior. I followed the warpath ever since I was able to draw a bow."[16]

Grasping Bear says, "Thereafter, Sitting Bull believed that his days were numbered. He went no more to the agency, but asked others to bring his rations. As early as the summer of 1889, he had told his nephew Chief Joseph White Bull, 'Great men are generally destroyed by those who are jealous of them.'"[17]

A QUESTION OF CHARACTER

McLaughlin frequently expressed a low opinion of Sitting Bull. In his autobiography he described Sitting Bull as a stocky man, with an evil face and shifty eyes.[18] *In a letter to the Indian commissioner on October 17, 1890, the agent wrote*, Sitting Bull is a man of low cunning, devoid of a single manly principle in his nature, or an honorable trait of character, but on the contrary is capable of instigating and inciting others (those who believe in his promise) to do any amount of mischief. He is a coward and lacks moral courage; he will never lead where there is danger, but is adept in influencing his ignorant henchmen and followers, and there is no knowing what he may direct them to attempt.

Sitting Bull is a polygamist, a libertine, habitual liar, active obstructionist, and a great obstacle in the civilization of these people, and he is totally devoid of any of the nobler traits of character, and so wedded to the old Indian ways and superstitions that it is doubtful if any change for the better will ever come over him at his present age of fifty-six years.[19]

McLaughlin was also irked because Sitting Bull held to his own religion. One Bull, Sitting Bull's nephew and one of McLaughlin's policemen, said, "Bishop Hare of South Dakota visited Sitting Bull in the fall of 1890 and wanted Sitting Bull to join the Catholic Church but he absolutely refused—saying the Indian had his own religion."[20]

Others defended Sitting Bull's character and bravery. Pine Ridge physician Eastman insists, He was no coward, and I do not agree with Major McLaughlin in his estimate of Sitting Bull's character. He was no medicine-man, but a statesman, one of the most far-sighted we have had.[21]

Wooden Leg, a Cheyenne, agrees, I have no ears for hearing anybody say he was not a brave man. He had a big brain and a good one, a strong heart and a generous one. In the old times I never heard any Indian having spoken otherwise of him.[22]

Scout Frank Grouard wrote, The name of Sitting Bull was a "tipi word" for all that was generous and great. The bucks admired him, the squaws respected him highly, and the children loved him and were taught to emulate his example. He would have proved a mighty power among our present day politicians—a great vote-getter with the people—had he been a white man with a congressional ambition. He might, then, in truth, have been renowned as a political economist; but in his savage economy he utterly and persistently refused to celebrate ration day at an agency, or exchange his wild freedom for the bondage of civilization.[23]

Mary Collins, for ten years a resident at Standing Rock and part of the Congregational missionary at Little Eagle on the Grand River, realized Sitting Bull opposed her efforts to convert him and his followers. Even so, she wrote, I learned many things about Sitting Bull's individuality. He had some very indefinable power which could not be resisted by his own people or even others who came in contact with him. When I become a more thorough student of psychology, I shall understand him better; but even with the knowledge I did have, I comprehended more easily the character of the Indian chief who was always so tender, gracious and invariably sweet.

About this time, *Collins observes*, the people were much concerned about the dry year; there had been no rain for months. The Indians went to Fort Yates for their rations, and one day at this period they were gathered together and Sitting Bull announced that it would rain. He took a buffalo skin, waved it around in the air, made some signs, placed it upon the ground and—IT RAINED. . . . This is only one incident which shows why people had such faith in him.[24]

SUSPICIONS AND SPIES

During the summer and early autumn of 1890, Sitting Bull wisely refused to come into the Standing Rock Agency to receive his rations. Instead, he sent his family. Again and again he offered excuses for his absence. He probably was aware that McLaughlin was plotting his arrest; thus he kept his distance and remained at his Grand River Camp.

If Sitting Bull made such an assumption, his apprehension was justified. McLaughlin later wrote, I had made arrangements to put up a station, consisting of a house for wayfarers and shelter for teams . . . twenty-two miles from the agency and eighteen miles from Sitting Bull's camp on the Grand River. . . . A detail of police was sent to the station, ostensibly to work on the structure, actually to be within reach when the order was given for the arrest of the medicine man.[25]

These police also served as spies and kept McLaughlin informed of activities in Sitting Bull's camp. It was here the agent felt trouble could begin;

or, worse still, Sitting Bull might leave the reservation and become a general threat to the Dakotas. During the summer, *the agent recalled*, I was repeatedly compelled to refuse Sitting Bull permission to visit the Cheyenne River Reservation. Some reports had come to us of the introduction of the Ghost dancing religion in the southern reservations, and I declined to allow Sitting Bull to leave his home.[26] *Sitting Bull obeyed and remained at Grand River.*

There was good reason for the dancing. While McLaughlin does not mention the privation and illness in his annual report, Capt. E. G. Fechet, commander at Fort Yates, does. The months of October and November, *Fechet recollected*, were trying and full of anxiety to me as commanding officer of the fort. The fort might well have been considered in a state of siege. Epidemics of measles, grippe, and whooping cough threatened it from north, west and south; while to the east across the Missouri River scarlet fever was raging. This, of course, necessitated a rigid quarantine.

We were further menaced from the south by hundreds, possibly thousands, of Indian warriors, desperate from hunger and half crazed by religious excitement. Fortunately Major McLaughlin, aided by his wife, and ably seconded by the well known war chief of the Sioux, Gall, and other loyally disposed chiefs, was able to stem the tide of fanaticism to the extent of confining it to the settlements on the upper Grand River, which was largely composed of Sitting Bull's followers.[27]

The situation was not as dangerous as Fechet writes, but it was this sort of report that General Miles took seriously. Miles, in his 1891 report, expressed his concerns: The runners of Sitting Bull, who for years had been the great war chief and the head center of the hostile element, traveled in various directions, but more especially to the tribes in the Northwest, carrying his messages to get ready for war and to get all the arms and ammunition possible, and for all the warriors to meet near the Black Hills in the spring of 1891.[28]

Miles's assessment of the situation had little basis. Many who knew Sitting Bull say he was a medicine man and spiritual leader, not a warrior, especially as he aged. Miles, who knew Sitting Bull well, should have known this. Either Miles's intelligence sources had failed him, or he was creating a convenient fiction that would aid the army in its lobbying during the appropriations hearings in Congress.

KICKING BEAR VISITS GRAND RIVER

Sometime in the early fall, McLaughlin observes, Sitting Bull sent six of his young men to Cherry Creek, on the Cheyenne River reservation, with an invitation to Kicking Bear to make him, Sitting Bull, a visit.[29] *Invited or not, Kicking Bear, the main Lakota apostle of the Messiah, arrived at Sitting Bull's camp on October 6, 1890, and began preaching the new religion.*

One Bull told the agent that Kicking Bear preached to his followers, "My brothers, I bring to you the promise of a day in which there will be no white man to lay his hand on the bridle of the Indian's horse; when the red men of the prairie will rule the world and not be turned from the hunting-grounds by any man. I bring you word from your fathers, the ghosts, that they are now marching to join you, led by the Messiah who came once to live on earth with the white men, but was cast out and killed by them. I have seen the wonders of the spirit-land, and have talked with the ghosts. I traveled far and am sent back with a message to tell you to make ready for the coming of the Messiah and return of the ghosts in the spring."[30]

This was hardly a call to arms. Instead, it was a call for dancing—dancing that would eliminate whites from the Dakotas by supernatural means.

The many visitors to Sitting Bull's camp in October and November were not endangered. As part of her duties as supervisor of Indian schools, Elaine Goodale visited Standing Rock in the fall and met with Sitting Bull, even as his people were receiving instructions in the practice of the new religion from Kicking Bear. She writes, I sent my driver, Industrious by name, to invite his "uncle" to dinner in my tent on the golden October day of my visit to the Grand River day school, but the canny old man would say little beyond the conventional protestations of friendship for the "rich" (the white people), and a leaning toward the "White Robes" who were about to hold annual convocation a day's journey from his village. While representatives of Bishop Hare's seventeen hundred communicants were meeting on Oak Creek, however, a very different scene was being enacted forty miles distant, where Sitting Bull's people were learning strange rites from Kicking Bear, a high priest of the new Messiah.[31]

McLaughlin, afraid that the Ghost Dance would spread to Standing Rock, immediately set out to remove Kicking Bear from the Standing Rock Reservation. To accomplish this, he writes, I sent a party of thirteen policemen, under the command of Crazy Walking, a man in whom I had the most complete faith, with orders to arrest Kicking Bear and eject him from the reservation.

The policemen found Kicking Bear and Sitting Bull conducting a séance. . . . So impressed was the officer in charge of the police detachment with the dance and the wonderful stories told by the dancers about their visions, that he was turned from his purpose. Both officers, being in a dazed condition . . . returned without executing the order, fearing the powers of Kicking Bear's medicine. Several members of the force tried to induce the officers to permit them to make the arrest but the latter would not allow it, but simply told Sitting Bull that it was the agent's orders that Kicking Bear and his six companions should leave the following day. Sitting Bull was very insolent to the officers and made some threats against some members of the force, but said the visitors would leave the following day. This report was brought to me on October 14.[32]

Chief One Bull, who served in McLaughlin's Indian police, offers a somewhat different view of what happened: I, One Bull, in company with Crazy Walking and Chatka, were all serving on Indian police force. McLaughlin ordered us to stop the Ghost Dance. Crazy Walking told the dancers to stop. Sitting Bull answered him as follows: "The education of my children is uppermost. I have a school in my locality. This dance is not the most important undertaking. They will, eventually, stop."

This is what we reported to McLaughlin on our return.[33]

Somehow Sitting Bull's conciliatory words made McLaughlin more suspicious. The agent, never mentioning this positive report, later wrote, I immediately sent Chatka, a second lieutenant of the police force, to eject Kicking Bear. Lieutenant Chatka was a man of great firmness of character, and when he asked for only two men and said he would drive Kicking Bear out, I knew that the medicine of Kicking Bear would be wasted on him, whatever it might cost him mentally.

Chatka arrived at Sitting Bull's camp on the Grand River the next day. A very large party of Indians were dancing. The lieutenant pushed his way through the dancers, notified Kicking Bear and six men from Cheyenne River reservation who were with him, to leave the Standing Rock reservation forthwith. . . . I cannot imagine a performance requiring more courage, from an Indian standpoint, than that accomplished by Lieutenant Chatka that day.[34]

There is an interesting contradiction here. McLaughlin described Chatka in his 1891 report to the Indian commissioner as being in a dazed condition and fearing the powers of Kicking Bear's medicine.[35] *In spite of this statement, McLaughlin later cites Chatka for bravery. Thus it seems that McLaughlin's later autobiographical writing was colored with the passing of time.*

That night, *McLaughlin claims*, Sitting Bull broke the peace-pipe which he had kept sacredly since his surrender at Fort Buford in 1881. He deliberately broke it in the presence of the assemblage of Ghost dancers, saying that he was ready to fight and would die for this new religion if need be.[36]

The second wife of former Pine Ridge agent Valentine McGillycuddy,

Julia, says that when Sitting Bull broke his pipe, he declared in despair, "Now I want to die."[37]

In his report to Commissioner Thomas J. Morgan on October 17, two days after Kicking Bear left Sitting Bull's Grand River Camp, McLaughlin complained, The news comes in this morning that they are dancing again and it is participated in by a great many Indians who become silly and like men intoxicated over the excitement. The dance is demoralizing, indecent, and disgusting.[38]

In addition to his lengthy report, McLaughlin sent a telegram on October 17 to the commissioner asking, I . . . respectfully recommend the removal from the reservation and confinement in some military prison, some distance from the Sioux country, of Sitting Bull and the parties named in my letter of June 18 last, herein before referred to, sometime during the coming winter before next spring opens.[39]

In that earlier communication, McLaughlin had asked for the removal of "Sitting Bull, Circling Bear, Black Bird, and Circling Hawk of his agency; Big Foot and his lieutenants at Cheyenne River; Crow Dog, and Low Dog of Rosebud; and any of like ilk of Pine Ridge," *probably meaning Red Cloud and his son Jack.*[40]

Acting Indian Commissioner Robert V. Belt replied:

Office of Indian Affairs,
October 29, 1890.

James McLaughlin,
United States Indian Agent.

SIR:

Your report of October 17, concerning the present attitude of some of the Sioux Indians on the Standing Rock Reservation has been submitted to the honorable secretary of interior, who directs me to instruct you to inform Sitting Bull and the other Indians named by you as engaged in encouraging the Ghost Dance and other like demoralizing conduct, and inciting and fomenting dissatisfaction and discontent among the peaceably disposed Indians that he is greatly displeased with their conduct, and that he will hold Sitting Bull to a strict personal responsibility for the misconduct, acts of violence, or any threats, actions, or movements to which any of the Sioux Indians may be guided, influenced, or encouraged by him or as a result of his bad advice and evil councils, [and] that any misconduct by him personally or by others through his inducement or encouragement will be visited by severe punishment. And further, that he must show his good intentions and his submission to the authority of the Indian service, and by doing all in his power to restrain any of the Sioux Indians who may be disposed to acts of disobedience or violence, threats, etc., and that he shall exert whatever influence he may have over any of the Indians to turn their backs upon the medicine men who are seeking to divert the Indians from the ways of civilization.

Very respectfully,
R. V. Belt.
Acting Commissioner.[41]

In response to this directive, McLaughlin sent several emissaries to Sitting Bull's camp to persuade the medicine man to come into the agency. When one, Gray Eagle, arrived at Grand River, he lectured Sitting Bull, "Brother-in-law, we're settled on a reservation now; and we're under jurisdiction of government. We must do as they say. We must cut out roaming around, live as they say and must cut out this dancing."

Sitting Bull, who was not about to leave his lifelong home, replied, "Yes, you're right but I can not give up this place as it's seated in us. You go ahead and follow what white man says; but for my part, leave me alone."

"If you're not going to obey and not do as the whites say," *Gray Eagle argued,* "you are going to cause a lot of trouble and [it will] cost your life. I have sworn to stay by government. We have been friends a long time; but, if you are not going to do as whites say, we will not be together anymore."[42]

Lone Man, a member of McLaughlin's police, offers a similar view, stating, "I was sent to go and report what I could see or hear from Sitting Bull. I went down and found a house full. They had not treated me with much courtesy. Sitting Bull said, 'I suppose you have come on the same errand as the rest.'

"I said that I had come to advise him to drop the Ghost Dance as it would come to nothing and might deceive the people who were looking to him as chief. I said that if he wants to dance why not take one of the less attractive dances like a grass dance or scalp dance. Many of the people are old and cannot stand it. They are my friends. If you have anything to say, say it so that I can report. In the hostile days we young men followed you, etc.

"He replied, 'Yes, I depended on you then, but now you have turned with the whites against me. I have nothing to say to you. If these people wish to say anything they may, but I will not. You police have annoyed me. So far as I am concerned you may go home.'"[43]

It is uncertain whether Sitting Bull believed in the new religion or was refusing to place himself in McLaughlin's hands. Most reports indicate that he approached the new religion with caution and did not immediately accept it.

DOUBTS OR ACCEPTANCE?

Robert P. High Eagle, a young Lakota home from the Carlisle Indian School, accompanied Lone Man on his visit to Sitting Bull's camp. He found Sitting Bull less belligerent. I was curious about this Ghost Dance, so I went to see it, *High Eagle says*. We were camping near Sitting Bull's place on Grand River and there was a dance going on in the middle of the circle. There were guards all around the camp. Anybody not wearing Indian clothes was not allowed in camp. We took out our saddle blankets to wear, but they wouldn't let us in unless we also took off our store clothes. So we stayed back. They were dancing, holding hands. After a while one fell down and they also stopped to see what he would say. He would then tell his vision. Then they would continue dancing until some more fell down and were given a chance to tell what they had seen.

I had an uncle who was one of the main administrators of this ceremony. He came over and asked me if I wanted to join it. "Don't you want to be saved? All those who wear white men's clothes are going to die."

He gave me a feather to wear and wouldn't let me in unless I would discard my civilian clothes. Lone Man had a policeman's uniform. He called Sitting Bull over and interviewed him in his log house. He had some orders from the agent, I think.

Sitting Bull was all painted up when I saw him. He was dressed in his ordinary Indian way, but he wore no feather on his head. It didn't appear to me that he was the leader. He was merely a sort of advisor. He didn't wear a Ghost shirt when I saw him, but wore a blanket. He was very nice and invited Lone Man and me to supper.

We went into a tent alongside of his log house. He had some cattle and horses there, especially the white circus horse he had got from Buffalo Bill. He had a deep bass voice. He was very kind that day, as was his general custom. He was a little bit shorter than Black Prairie Dog, but heavier set. . . . He welcomed children to his home at any time but did not give them presents or anything like that.[44]

High Eagle was not alone in believing Sitting Bull had not accepted the Ghost Dance. Otter Robe told Vestal: Sitting Bull's people respected and didn't dance as much. At one time [there was a] Ghost Dance in and around Sitting Bull's house; Sitting Bull's wife and children took part. *Otter Robe attributed Sitting Bull's presence to the fact that it* wouldn't look right for Sitting Bull to be run out of his own house.[45]

Vestal, in his research with primary sources, was told that Sitting Bull said near this time, It is impossible for a dead man to return and live again.[46]

Miles, McLaughlin, and the eastern press proclaimed that Sitting Bull had embraced the Ghost Dance religion. However, according to Goodale, Stanley Vestal, biographer of Sitting Bull, points out that he was among the last of the old leaders to take up the craze, and that with no little doubt and hesitation. His attitude might be summed up in the saying attributed to Little Wound: "If this is something good, we ought to have it; if not, it will fall to the ground of itself."[47]

McLaughlin either was not aware of these statements or chose to ignore them. He reported to his superiors in Washington, Sitting Bull is high priest and leading apostle of this latest Indian absurdity; in a word he is the chief mischief-maker at this agency, and if he were not here, this craze, so general among the Sioux, would never have gotten a foothold at this agency.[48]

McLaughlin's spies gave him almost daily reports of what was happening in Sitting Bull's camp. One of these was John Carignan, the schoolmaster who taught near Sitting Bull's enclave on Grand River. Carignan later told an interviewer, Sitting Bull and many others of the prominent chiefs visited the school off and on, and at these visits I remonstrated them at the way in which they were going on, especially keeping their children out of school, etc., to all of which their replies was that they were keeping their children from school in order to prepare for the coming of the Messiah.

In October the attendance had fallen away to about fifteen scholars, I visited Sitting Bull's camp every chance I had to watch the Ghost Dance and report its progress to the agent. My presence was seldom noticed, but one time I remember being asked to remove my hat, when I got too close to the circle.[49]

By November, the schoolmaster said, My school attendance had got down to about eight or nine students, and the Ghost Dance was about in its prime.[50]

A NEW DIRECTIVE

McLaughlin's problems at Standing Rock were minimal compared to the dancing at the Pine Ridge, Rosebud, and Cheyenne River Reservations. The most agitated Lakotas were at the Pine Ridge and Cheyenne River Reservations. At Cheyenne River, Hump and Big Foot's followers were dancing—some six hundred people in all. The inexperienced Cheyenne River agent, Perain P. Palmer, sent his Indian police to break up the Ghost dancing, but they withdrew when met by Indians armed with repeating rifles.

On November 10 Palmer sent the commissioner an alarming telegraph: There is no doubt now that the hostile Indians at the dancing camps are preparing to defy the authority of the department.[51]

In spite of this eruption at Cheyenne River, the focus remained on Sitting Bull's camp on Grand River. On November 14 McLaughlin received a telegram from Belt that stated, The president has directed the secretary of war to assume a military responsibility for the suppression of any threatened outbreak among the Sioux Indians, and that an officer of high rank be sent to investigate the situation among them. He suggests that the agents separate the well-disposed from the ill-disposed Indians, and, while maintaining their control and discipline, so far as possible to avoid forcing any issue that will result in an outbreak. You will exercise wise discretion in carrying out the president's suggestion, carefully observing the caution he directs and avoiding publicity of these instructions.[52]

While McLaughlin wanted action taken against Sitting Bull, he did not want military intervention. Years later he wrote, At this late date I am frank to say that I feared military interference with the Indians, not that I doubted the capacity of the military, but because I was convinced that a military demonstration would precipitate a collision and bloodshed, which might be avoided.[53]

In an attempt to circumvent the new policy, McLaughlin visited Sitting Bull's camp on November 17 and 18 and tried to persuade Sitting Bull to change his ways.

MCLAUGHLIN MEETS WITH SITTING BULL

The only accounts of McLaughlin's visit to Sitting Bull's camp are in McLaughlin's autobiography and a letter he wrote to Morgan on November 19, 1890, immediately following his return to the Standing Rock Agency, and which was quoted in the "New York Times." In the latter, he reports, I proceeded, in company with Louis Primeau, a mixed-blood interpreter, to the Grand River, where I was informed a big dance was in progress.

I arrived at Sitting Bull's camp about three o'clock in the afternoon. It was Sunday, and I was not surprised to see a large gathering of people in front of the houses, six in number, in the center of the camp. . . . Having approached the camp by a road not usually traveled, and my coming being unexpected, I found the Ghost Dance at its full height. There were about two hundred people standing in a circle about the dancers, and except for a few men who endeavored to avoid being seen by me, I received no attention from the enthusiasts as I approached. . . . The madness of the dance demonstrated the height of distraction to which the dancers had attained.[54]

My eyes were drawn to a tipi which I had not noticed before but which commanded my attention now, for within the wide-open flaps of the wigwam, seated on a sort of throne, was my old friend, Sitting Bull.

He was very much thinner than a few weeks previous, but the look he gave me showed that his wits were not dulled or his hatred and envy lessened by the rigors of his life. By his side, fantastically dressed stood Bull Ghost, Sitting Bull's mouthpiece in the Ghost Dance exercises.

McLaughlin recalls a woman fainting while dancing and writes, The woman, still in a swoon, was laid at Sitting Bull's feet, and Bull Ghost announced in a loud voice that she was in a trance and communicating with the ghosts; upon the announcement the dance ceased, so that the dancers might hear the message from the spirit world.

Sitting Bull performed certain incantations, then leaned over and put his ear to the woman's lips. He spoke in a low voice to his herald, Bull Ghost, who repeated to the listening multitude the message which Sitting Bull pretended to receive from the unconscious woman.

The excitement was very intense, the people being brought to a pitch of high nervousness by the treatment prescribed by Sitting Bull for his followers. He required that each initiate, as well as those desiring to join the Ghost dancers, take a vapor-bath every morning.[55]

I did not attempt to stop the dance then going on, as, in their crazed condition under the excitement, it would have been useless to attempt it; but after remaining some time talking with a number of the spectators, I went on to the house of Henry Bull Head, three miles distant, where I remained over night.[56]

At daylight the next morning, I returned to Sitting Bull's camp. It was barely six o'clock when I arrived. . . . The camp was very quiet, but there were figures about the long rows of wickiups in which the Ghost dancers were taking their vapor-baths.

I entered Sitting Bull's house and found his two wives and four of his children within. The women, very much excited, said that Sitting Bull was taking a bath and offered to go and call him. They were told not to disturb him, as I would wait until he had finished his bath; and after conversing with the family a few minutes, I left the house. As I turned the corner of the building, I came face to face with the old medicine man, who had seen me entering his cabin and came to learn why I was so early abroad. He was naked, but for a breech-cloth and moccasins, and he looked very thin and more subdued than I had ever seen him. He stopped and said, "Hau."

"Hau," said I, and extended my hand, which he took; and I drew him toward the wagon and away from the cabin. He was handed a blanket, which he gathered about him, and stopped, sullen, but not fiercely insolent, as he had been with white people since the dancing had commenced. Other figures crept out of three wickiups in the early morning light and began to gather around us. Sitting Bull said nothing, and I made up my mind that I would proceed at once to tell him what I had to say before the entire encampment could congregate and disturb us.

"Look here, Sitting Bull," I began, "I want to know what you mean by your present conduct and utter disregard of department orders. Your preaching and practicing of this absurd Messiah doctrine is causing a great deal of uneasiness among the Indians of the reservation, and you should stop at once."

He was actually meek, and I thought perhaps he might be sincere in his religious fervor; but his crafty eye dispelled that idea. Without giving him time to talk, I recalled all my connection with him and showed him my friendly inclination.[57]

McLaughlin then addressed Sitting Bull's followers: I spoke very plainly to them, pointing out what had been done by the government for the Sioux people, and how this faction by their present conduct were abusing the confidence that had been reposed in them by the government in its magnanimity in granting them full amnesty for all past offenses, when from destitution and imminent starvation they were compelled to surrender as prisoners of war in 1880 and 1881; and I dwelt at length upon what was being done in the way of education of their children and for their own industrial advancement, and assured them of what this absurd craze would lead to, and the chastisement that would certainly follow if these demoralizing dances and disregard of departmental orders were not soon discontinued. I spoke with feeling and earnestness, and my talk was well received, and I am convinced that it had a good effect.

Sitting Bull, while being very obstinate and at first inclined to assume the role of "big chief" before his followers, finally admitted the truth of my reasoning and said that he believed me to be a friend to the Indians as a people, [and that even though] I did not like him personally, . . . when in doubt in any matter in following my advice he had always found it well, and that now he had a proposition to make to me which if I agreed to and would carry out would allay all further excitement among the Sioux over this Ghost Dance, or else convince me of the truth of the belief of the Indians in this new doctrine.

He then stated his proposition, which was that I should accompany him on a journey from this agency to each of the other tribes of Indians through which the story of the Indian Messiah had been brought, and when we reached the last tribe, or where it originated, if they could not produce the man who had started the story, and we did not find the new Messiah, as described, upon the earth, together with the dead Indians returning to reinhabit this country, he would return convinced that the Indians had been too credulous and imposed upon, which report from him would satisfy the Sioux, and all practices of the Ghost societies would cease; but that, if found to be as professed by the Indians, they be permitted to continue their medicine practices and organize as they are now endeavoring to do.

I told him that this proposition was a novel one, but that the attempt to carry it out would be similar to the attempt to catch up the wind that blew last year; that I wished him to come to my house, where I would give him a whole night or day and night, in which I thought I would convince him of the absurdity of this foolish craze, and the fact of his making me the proposition that he did was a convincing proof that he did not fully believe in what he was professing and endeavoring so hard to make others believe.[58]

This he would not do, but said: "My heart inclines to do what you request, but I must consult with my people. I would be willing to go with you now, but I cannot leave without consent of my people. I will talk with the men tonight, and if they think it is advisable I will go to the agency next Saturday."[59]

He did not, however, promise fully to come into the agency to discuss the matter, but said he would consider my talk and decide after deliberation.[60]

Goodale observed that Sitting Bull's offer to accompany Agent McLaughlin . . . to Mason Valley, in Nevada, and abide by what they should find there certainly indicates an open mind.[61] *Sitting Bull's suggestion, however, was possibly another example of his ironic humor, a humor that McLaughlin did not understand.*

I could get no further promise from him and drove away, *McLaughlin continues,* the crowd threatening and sneering, but held in check by the upraised arm of the old medicine man, standing almost naked in the bright but chilly morning sunlight. Our talk had lasted about an hour, and I said nothing to Primeau, who accompanied me, nor did Primeau make any remarks as we drove out of the camp, but I know that we both felt more comfortable when we got over the ridge of hills and out of rifle-range of the crazed throng of Ghost dancers.

That was the last time that I saw Sitting Bull alive, for he sent me word by Strikes-the-Kettle the following Saturday that he could not come to the agency.

I reported this visit to the department, and, being quite convinced that Sitting Bull would not come in, I wrote, under date of November 19, recommending that the Ghost dancers be attacked in their weakest point of their religious armor—through their stomachs.[62]

McLaughlin concluded his letter to the commissioner with a summation of his experiences in Sitting Bull's camp: I consumed three days in making this trip, and feel well repaid by what I accomplished, as my presence in their midst encouraged the weaker and doubting, and set those who are believers to thinking of the advisability of continuing the nonsensical practice they are now engaged in. I also found that the active members in the dance were not more than half the number of the earlier dancers and believe that it is losing ground among the Indians, and while there are many who are half-believers I am fully satisfied that I can keep the dance confined to the Grand River district.

From close observation, *he wrote*, I am convinced that the dance can be broken up, and after due reflection would respectfully suggest that in case my visit to Sitting Bull fails to bring him in to see me in regard to the matter, as invited to do, all Indians living on Grand River be notified that those wishing to be known as opposed to the Ghost doctrine, friendly to the government, and desiring the support provided in the treaty must report to the agency for such enrollment and be required to camp near the agency for a few weeks, and those selecting their medicine practices, in violation of departmental orders, to remain on Grand River, from whom subsistence will be withheld.

Something looking toward breaking up this craze must be done, and now, [with] cold weather approaching, is the proper time. Such a step as here suggested, would leave Sitting Bull with but a few followers, as all, or nearly all, would report for enrollment, and thus he would be forced in himself.

There are not many firearms among these Indians, *McLaughlin conceded*; still there are a few, and as a pledge of good faith on their part they should be required to turn in all their arms to the agent and get a memorandum receipt for the same. Knowing the Indians as I do, I am confident I can, by such a course, settle the Messiah craze at this agency, and also thus break up the power of Sitting Bull, without trouble and with but little excitement.[63]

The response to this request was not what McLaughlin expected. On November 20 Belt telegraphed McLaughlin and advised: If condition of affairs now and for future requires that leaders of excitement or fomenters of disturbance should be arrested and confined to insure quiet and good order among Indians, telegraph me names at once, so that assistance of military while operating to suppress any attempted outbreak may be had to make arrests.

Again McLaughlin was faced with military intervention. In compliance with Belt's instructions, he writes, I wired the names of the men whose arrest I had suggested the preceding June, adding the names of Iron White Man and Male Bear, but added that I thought it imprudent to attempt making the desired arrests at that time, and invited attention to my suggestion of the 19th.

At that time the situation was well in hand, and if I could have chosen the time, I could have arrested Sitting Bull without bloodshed. The plan was simple enough: it being the custom of the Indians of the entire reservation to congregate at the agency once every two weeks (every alternate Saturday), to receive their rations, and on these issue-days Sitting Bull was practically alone at his camp on Grand River, forty miles from the agency.[64]

McLaughlin, however, had orders not to make such an arrest, so be bided his time, waiting for another opportunity.

PEACE IN VIEW

On November 22 "Chicago Tribune"'s correspondent reported, Major McLaughlin's visit to Sitting Bull's camp had the effect of stopping the Ghost Dance for a time at least. McLaughlin received a letter from Bull yesterday, who says he has taken a friend's advice and stopped the dance. Bull's child is very sick, or he would have come to the agency today to draw rations. It is reported here that Bull's following is growing less because the Messiah has not appeared, and that discourages the chief.

The agent thinks there is no probability of trouble at present, and there may not be this winter or spring. He is working hard on the Indians with a corps of able assistants, and makes strong arguments against the craze. The people on the east side of the river are fleeing for their lives with no one in pursuit. The excitement is all unwarranted. The reports of the massacre forty miles south are believed to be unfounded.[65]

Despite the easing of tensions at Standing Rock, the first armed confrontation was less than a month away.

7. Confrontation at Pine Ridge

[I]f the Seventh-Day Adventists got up on the roofs of their houses in their ascension robes to welcome the Second Coming of Christ, the whole U.S. Army is not rushed into motion.—*Dr. Valentine T. McGillycuddy* to *Walter S. Campbell*, December 15, 1928

ROYER PANICS

On Monday, November 10—a ration day—newly arrived Pine Ridge agent Daniel F. Royer was confronted by angry Ghost dancers. According to Charles A. Eastman, An Indian called Little had been guilty of some minor offense on the reservation and had hitherto evaded arrest. Suddenly he appeared at the agency on an issue day, for the express purpose, as it seemed, of defying the authorities. The assembly room of the Indian police, used also as a council room, opened out of my dispensary, and on this particular morning a council was in progress. I heard some loud talking, but was too busy to pay particular attention, though my assistant had gone in to listen to the speeches.

Suddenly the place was in an uproar, and George Sword, *the captain of the Indian police*, burst into the inner office, crying excitedly "Look out for yourself, friend! They are going to fight!"

I went around to see what was going on. A crowd had gathered just outside the council room, and the police were surrounded by wild Indians with guns and drawn knives in their hands. "Hurry up with them!" one shouted, while another held his stone war-club over a policeman's head. The attempt to arrest Little had met with a stubborn resistance.

At this critical moment, a fine-looking Indian in citizen's clothes faced the excited throng and spoke in a clear, steady, almost sarcastic voice: "Stop! Think! What are you going to do? Kill all these helpless white men, women and children? And what then? What will these brave words, brave deeds lead to in the end? How long can you hold out? Your country is surrounded with a network of railroads; thousands of white soldiers will be here within three days. What ammunition have you? What provisions? What will become of your families? Think, think, my brothers! This is a child's madness."

It was the friendly chief American Horse, and it seems to me as I recall the incident that this man's voice had almost magic power. It is likely that he saved us all from massacre; for the murder of the police, who represented the authority of the government, would surely have been followed by a general massacre.

Jack Red Cloud, son of Red Cloud and a Ghost dancer, thrust the muzzle of a cocked revolver almost into the face of American Horse. "It is you and your kind," he shouted, "who have brought us to this pass!"

That brave man never flinched. Ignoring his rash accuser, he quietly reentered the office; the door closed behind him; the mob dispersed, and for the moment the danger seemed over.[1]

Issue clerk Robert O. Pugh says that when he came back from lunch, The front office was crowded with Indians and Indian police, and Dr. Royer was at the back door beckoning to me. The agent was in a great fright and could scarcely speak above a whisper.

I asked him what was the matter. "Don't you know?" asked the terrified man.

When I told him I did not, the agent replied, "We have almost been massacred," and much more of the same tenor betraying his agitation. He declared further that he was going to leave at once and take his family. I advised him not to do so [as] such a course would bring his official career as agent to an end speedily, and tried to calm his excitement with assurance that there was no danger and that no trouble would ensue.

But the agent was prostrated and could not regain his composure.[2]

Royer's panic created a volatile situation at Pine Ridge. The "friendlies" and "hostiles" now found themselves in opposition. If there was any danger, it was to the "friendlies," not the whites.

Eastman continues, That evening I was surprised by a late call from American Horse, the hero of the day. His wife entered close behind him. Scarcely were they seated when my door again opened softly, and Captain Sword came in, followed by Lieutenant Thunder Bear and most of the Indian police. My little room was crowded. I handed them some tobacco, which I had always at hand for my guests, although I did not smoke myself.

After a silence, the chief got up and shook hands with me ceremoniously. In a short speech, he asked my advice in the difficult situation that confronted them between the Ghost dancers, men of their own blood, and the government to which they had pledged their loyalty.

Thanks to Indian etiquette, I could allow myself two or three minutes to weigh my words before replying. I finally said, in substance: "There is only one thing for us to do and be just to both sides. We must use every means for a peaceful settlement of this difficulty. Let us be patient; let us continue to reason with the wilder element, even though some hotheads may threaten our lives. If the worst happens, however, it is our solemn duty to serve the United States government. Let no man ever say that we were disloyal! Following such a policy, dead or alive, we shall have no apology to make."

After the others had withdrawn, Sword informed me confidentially that certain young men had threatened to kill American Horse while asleep in his tent, and that his friends had prevailed upon him and his wife to ask my hospitality for a few days. I showed Mrs. American Horse to a small room that I had vacant, and soon afterward came three strokes of the office bell—the signal for me to report at the agent's office.

I found there the agent, his chief clerk, and a visiting inspector, all of whom obviously regarded the situation as serious. "You see, doctor," said the agent, "the occurrence of today was planned with remarkable accuracy, so that even our alert police were taken entirely by surprise and readily overpowered. What will be the sequel we can not tell, but we must be prepared for anything. I shall be glad to have your views."

I told him that I still did not believe there was any widespread plot or deliberate intention to make war upon the whites. In my own mind, I felt sure that the arrival of troops would be construed by the Ghost dancers as a threat or a challenge, and would put them at once on the defensive. I was not in favor of that step; neither was Mr. Cook [a Lakota clergyman], who was also called into conference. But the officials evidently feared a general uprising, and argued that it was their duty to safeguard the lives of the employees and others by calling for the soldiers without more delay.[3]

Sword, Thunder Bear, and American Horse were sent for, and their opinions appeared to be fully in accord with those of the agent and inspector, so the matter was given out as settled. As a matter of fact, the agent had telegraphed to Fort Robinson for troops before he made a pretense of consulting us Indians, and they were already on their way to Pine Ridge.[4]

On November 11, the day after the incident, Royer telegraphed Commissioner Morgan, pleading, The situation at this agency is such that I deem it for the best interest of the service that I be permitted to come to Washington DC, and explain to you personally. Please grant authority for me to come at once as the circumstances justifies it.[5]

Royer followed his telegram with a detailed letter. In a postscript he added, It is useless for me to try and make anything out of these people against such opposition, and it should be stopped at once.

Acting Commissioner R. V. Belt curtly replied, It is in the interests of the service . . . that you remain at agency at this time. Submit matters fully and prompt by letter, or if emergencies demand it, by telegram.

Royer fired off another telegram, telling Belt, Very important that I come to Washington at once. The agency affairs will not suffer during my absence at this time. Will leave good experienced men in charge.

Cannot explain matters satisfactorily by telegraph or letter. Indians will remain quiet during my absence. You will agree with me when you see me personally that it is important for me to come. Please grant me the authority to come at once. There is no immediate danger of any trouble with the Indians committing any depredations but I would be glad to have an opportunity to explain to you personally my ideas as to the proper course to pursue in managing the agency.

On the same day, the agent wrote a long letter repeating his plea that he be allowed to go to Washington. He also claimed, The craze has steadily increased until now it has assumed such proportions both in the number and the spirit of adherents that it is entirely beyond the control of the agent and the police force, who are openly defied by the dancers, and as a means of stopping the dances, the agent suggests sending a body of troops sufficient to arrest the leaders therein and imprison them and disarm the balance of the reservation.[6]

The Department of Interior was reluctant to request the assistance of the army since it was locked in a power struggle with the War Department over who should manage the reservations. Requesting troops would have been an admission that the Department of Interior was unable to cope with the growing tensions in the Dakotas. For the moment, Royer's request for troops was tabled.

As the commissioner of Indian Affairs put off Royer, the agent became even more frightened and desperate. Emma C. Sickels, who established the day school at Pine Ridge, aptly described Royer's behavior, saying, His whole attitude to the Indians has been, "Oh, please, be good and don't make any trouble." The friendly Indians ignored him after a few discouraging experiences, the treacherous ones used him as their tool, while all despise him.[7]

Thisba Hutson Morgan, a teacher at the boarding school at Pine Ridge, adds, Royer, . . . so nervous and so frightened by the situation in which he found himself, shut himself in the house the government provides for the home of the agent and refused to be interviewed, causing some of his immediate duties to fall upon the school superintendent.[8]

On November 15 Royer, now hysterical, telegraphed Washington: The Indians are dancing in the snow and are wild and crazy. I have fully informed you that employees and government property at this agency have no protection and are at the mercy of these dancers. Why delay further investigation? We need protection, and we need it now. The leaders should be arrested and confined in some military post until the matter is quieted, and this should be done at once.[9]

This alarming telegram gave General Miles a cue for action. Miles quickly secured permission to send troops to the Dakotas. Within hours he began dispatching troops to the areas where the Ghost dancing was most prevalent.

Fearful of his safety, Royer packed up his family and fled to Rushville, approximately twenty-five miles to the south. Pugh saw little reason for the agent's flight. There was a sharp scene between the Indians and the Indian police, *he admits*, but it was only a war of words.

I went among the Indians, most of whom I personally knew. Two of them were Sitting Bull's followers; these I was well acquainted with, and stepping up to one of them I took him by the collar and led him away to the issue office talking to him in a comprehensible way. After loading him with eatables, I turned to the crowd which had followed and threw out some boxes of crackers and other provisions and told them to go home as they were making it unpleasant at the agency. They went away satisfied and perfect quiet reigned.

By this time the affrighted agent had his team ready and his family in the buggy to leave. He told me to act as agent. I suggested that he appoint the chief clerk; but Royer said that since I had successfully quelled the disturbance, he would devolve the conduct of affairs to me.[10]

According to Judge Eli S. Ricker, After the agent quit the agency, the resident Presbyterian minister, Reverend Mr. Sterling, attempted to visit the boarding school and work up a high feeling among the teachers over the situation; but he was promptly stopped by Mr. Pugh who could not check his desperate intuition until he threatened, as the acting agent, to place him in the guardhouse if he did not desist. The minister went that night with his family to Rushville.[11] *Joining in the exodus were the wives and children of traders and other whites.*

On November 17 Royer sent Belt both a telegram and a letter. He reported, Today I received communication from the offender stating that the policeman who attempted to enforce my orders must be discharged or I could expect trouble and I was given four weeks to do it. The police force are overpowered and disheartened. We have no protection [and] are at the mercy of these crazy dancers.

Again Royer pled for permission to go to Washington; again his request was denied.

MILES TO THE RESCUE

By now, some of the news stories coming out of the Dakotas were bizarre and fanciful. On November 17 the "Omaha World Herald" reported that Joseph Buckley . . . came in today and says every Indian on the reservation will shortly go on the warpath and that they have got possession of

Custer's rifles, which the United States Army never found. . . . Local hardware men have in the last few days sold their entire stocks of ammunition to the Indians.[12] *This was not the last time that the ghost of Custer was invoked in the Dakotas.*

Erroneous reports of battles and massacres continued to pour in. The Nebraska National Guard commander, Gen. L. W. Colby, later complained, On the 20th, some of the newspapers had reports of an important battle with the Indians, the sole foundation of which, however, was the imaginative brain of the reporter.[13] *From Pierre, South Dakota, it was reported,* No one here credits the reports of a massacre.[14] *The newspaper war still raged, and it fueled Miles's efforts to send even more troops to the Dakotas.*

On November 20 the "Chadron (NE) Democrat" reported, Troops F, I, and K of the 9th Cavalry, and Company C of the 8th Infantry, stationed at Fort Robinson, passed through Chadron yesterday at noon, enroute to Rushville, at which point troops from Fort Omaha and Fort Niobrara have also massed, and seven companies from Fort D. A. Russell, Wyoming, are expected also.[15] *All these were from nearby forts; but, within days, Miles would be sending troops from throughout the United States.*

Belt had lost his battle with the War Department, but he still tried to retain some control of the situation. On November 20, the "Chadron Democrat" also reported: Commissioner Belt says that the troops should not interfere with the Indian Ghost Dance unless they commit some overt act, as the craze will die out of itself, when the Messiah fails to appear.

This is where Mr. Belt is mistaken, *the "Chadron Democrat" editorialized.* The [Lakotas] had a day set for [the Messiah's] miraculous appearance last August and he failed to come, so they immediately trotted out a new prophesy, and they will do the same thing again, and there is no telling where their craze may end. It should be stopped suddenly and permanently.[16]

The arrival of troops did little to allay the settlers' fears or stop the dancing, and the false rumors and unsubstantiated news reports that abounded only exacerbated fears. On November 22 South Dakota governor Arthur C. Mellette received a telegram stating that seven people had been massacred by Indians near Lebeau. Included in the telegram was a plea that the governor dispatch militia to the scene.[17] *Later it was learned that this report, too, was unfounded. Mellette, faced with a growing panic, decided to study the situation firsthand.*

The same day, it was reported, The settlers are becoming very much alarmed and are fleeing to the towns, leaving most of their possessions behind them. At Gettysburg there seems to be the most excitement, and

Governor Mellette has gone there tonight with a large supply of arms and ammunitions hoping to quiet the alarm. Telegrams were received by him this afternoon from several points asking assistance.[18]

In Rushville Royer helped fan the growing panic when he told a reporter: "I think it is just as well that people outside be placed in possession of exact facts in this case. It is not worthwhile to deny further that trouble is imminent. Everyone of these hostiles is heavily loaded with ammunition and they will use it. I have been among them before."

"What are you going to do?"

"We can do nothing yet until the Interior Department and the War Department give instructions. What we think most advisable to do is wait and let them play their part. They will do it, too. Bloodshed is all that will stop them."

"That applies to stopping the dances?"

"Yes sir; among the Oglalas, and soon."

The reporter added, Not a man in the agency who knows anything about Indian character does not predict trouble.[19]

Even though it was widely known that Royer had never worked on a reservation before his appointment to Pine Ridge, the reporter accepted without comment the agent's statement, "I have been among them before."

Some on the scene, including Dr. Melvin Gilmore, believed that Royer had motivations other than fear when he pleaded for troops. After interviewing many whites and Lakotas at Pine Ridge, Gilmore wrote, It was thought by many that Royer did this because the coming of the soldiers brought business for the storekeepers, saloon men, hotels, and he would profit by it.[20] *If that was Royer's intent, he succeeded. The Dakota agencies would soon be crowded with hundreds of troops.*

On November 23 rancher and former scout William D. McGaa told Royer that on the night of November 21, while staying in a Ghost dancer's lodge, midway between Pine Ridge and Buffalo Gap, He pretended to go to sleep. After he had been in bed about two hours, one of the Indians bent over him to discover whether he was still asleep. Then he heard them deliberately plotting to lead General Brooke and his soldiers into an ambush and shoot them down. Their plan as McGaa heard from their own lips, is to continue the Ghost Dance till the troops try to stop it.

The place selected to carry out their murderous design, *McGaa contended*, is a place sixteen miles and a half north of here, where the White Horse Creek empties into the Wounded Knee and lies in something of an amphitheater shape. The only practical way of leading to the spot is by a road that follows along the bank of White Horse Creek. Upon either side of the road are dense clumps of trees, so many as to almost form a wall on either side of the approach.

The plot is to have a Ghost Dance in the center of the amphitheater and have the woods on either side full of Indians when the military comes up to stop the dance, and they would easily be shot down by the Indians in ambush on either side.[21]

No attempt to assassinate Gen. John R. Brooke ever materialized.

MARCHING TO THE FRONT

On November 18, the "Omaha World Herald" vividly reported the evening departure of the largest contingent of troops to that date: In the shadows of the barracks at Fort Omaha last night, when the bugle sounded a call at 6 o'clock, four companies of the Twenty-fourth Regiment mustered, the clank of arms echoed across the moonlit parade ground and among the rickety quarters. The comrades left behind gave three cheers and the band played "Annie Laurie"—it really did. Half an hour later the troops marched to the railroad platform and an hour's wait brought along a special train, one a Pullman car.

Every woman and child within a mile came down to see the soldiers off. The comrades cheered and the troops ordered out marched into the train. They were laden with Merriam packs, a knapsack and haversacks, and carried canteens, blankets and guns. They were out for a week's marching, a winter's skirmish duty or perhaps an action. For they were ordered into the field against the restless Indians at Pine Ridge Agency.

The train was destined to Rushville, and thence the troops will march twenty-four miles to the agency. Following the troops' train was a train conveying six transport wagons and four mules for each, baggage, a wagon load of cartridges and fifteen days' rations. Some of the soldiers were old campaigners against the Sioux. Some have been out on six or seven similar expeditions without having a chance to fire a shot. They did not anticipate fighting, but they were ready for it. They had as soon stayed home, but took the march into the region of snow and blizzards with soldierly stoicism.

Some of the younger men playfully cut off a lock of their hair and gave them to comrades or the girls they left behind them, that as they said, the Sioux should not get all their hair. It was the first expedition sent out from Fort Omaha against the Indians since 1876, when General Crook operated against them in the Rosebud campaign and the Twenty-third Infantry was sent from the fort.[22]

On November 19 it was reported from the Rosebud Agency, When the Indians on this and the Pine Ridge Agency wake up tomorrow morning, they will find themselves surrounded by the strongest body of United States troops which has been mustered in the West since the defeat of Geronimo. It can be predicted that if some unfortunate act on the part of the soldiers does not add to the excitement of the redskins, the threatened uprising will never occur.[23]

An anxious Red Cloud, upon learning that more troops were coming, wrote a letter to L. J. F. Iaeger, a friend who lived in Chadron:

> Dear Friend:
>
> I will write a few lines to you this morning to show that I remember you as a friend. I have been a friend to the whites that live near the reserve, and I want to have peace all around. I hear something yesterday about 2 o'clock, so that is what I want to tell you. I hear that soldiers at Fort Robinson are coming here tomorrow. I tell you this because I do not want to have trouble with the soldiers and other good white people that are near me. I want you to publish my letter so the people of Chadron may know that I am a friend to them. If you can I want you to write to the Great Father in Washington.
>
> Your friend,
> Chief Red Cloud[24]

Red Cloud and other Lakota elders feared that the army was forcing the Lakotas into a war.

In spite of peaceful protestations by Lakota elders, Miles continued to send troops to the Dakotas. According to the secretary of the interior, Troops were entered to other agencies until finally nearly half of the infantry and cavalry of the U.S. Army were concentrated upon the Sioux reservations.[25] *Now it was the Lakotas' time to be fearful.*

TROOPS ARRIVE AT PINE RIDGE

On November 20, 1890, under Brooke's command, five companies of infantry, three troops of cavalry, one Hotchkiss gun, and one Gatling gun arrived at Pine Ridge. Two troops of cavalry and six companies of infantry simultaneously arrived at the nearby Rosebud Agency.

Thisba Hutson Morgan says, I was standing in the school yard talking with some of the Indian girls. They called my attention to a low cloud of dust along the road, and as they do, they pointed with their lips toward it and said, "See, the soldiers are coming." I could see little else but dust and had no information to confirm or deny their statement. They asked, "Why are the soldiers coming?"

Their keen eyes could tell the type of travelers causing the dust. They could possibly have had advance information via an Indian route that the soldiers were coming but they did not know why.[26]

Eastman writes, A friend rushed into my quarters and awakened me. "Come quick!" he shouted, "the soldiers are here!"

I looked along the White Clay Creek toward the little railroad town of Rushville, Nebraska, twenty-five miles away, and just as the sun rose above the knife-edged ridges black with stunted pine, I perceived a moving cloud of dust that marked the trail of the Ninth Cavalry.

There was instant commotion among the camps of friendly Indians. Many women and children were coming in to the agency for refuge, evidently fearing that the dreaded soldiers might attack their villages by mistake. Some who had not heard of their impending arrival hurried to the offices to ask what it meant. I assured those who appealed to me that the troops were here only to preserve order, but their suspicions were not easily allayed.

As the cavalry came nearer, we saw that they were colored troopers, wearing buffalo overcoats and muskrat caps; the Indians with their quick wit called them "buffalo soldiers."[27] *With the arrival of this crack unit, according to Eastman*, the wildest rumors were in circulation. Indian scouts might be seen upon every hill top, closely watching the military encampment.[28]

The Ninth Cavalry and its attached units made their camp near the Lakotas who had gone to Pine Ridge. Morgan observed that the Ninth Cavalry, one of the four black regiments of the time (but which was under the command of white major Guy V. Henry), was much feared by the Indians.[29] *According to Morgan*, They encamped about a half mile to the south of the school house on White Clay Creek, and from my classroom there was nothing to obstruct the view. I could look down upon their tents and the tipis of the friendly Indians who had moved into the agency to remain until the trouble could be settled.[30]

The Lakotas knew from past encounters that the Ninth Cavalry was better disciplined and more dedicated than many of the ragtag white regiments. Its arrival signaled to the Oglalas that the army meant business.

At the Rosebud Agency, Luther Standing Bear had visited some of his relatives who had become Ghost dancers. He persuaded them and other dancers to surrender. They did not remain at Rosebud long, however. Standing Bear wrote in his autobiography, When I awoke the next morning and looked out of my window in expectation of seeing their tipis pitched about my house, I was greatly disappointed. There was no sign of their camp. I looked up the road in the direction they would have come, but there was no one in sight. Then I knew something had frightened them from keeping their promise.[31]

Upon learning that troops were on their way to the Rosebud Agency, about eighteen hundred Upper Brulé men, women, and children stampeded toward Pine Ridge, destroying their own property before leaving and that of others' as they left.[32] *When they arrived at Pine Ridge, they found that troops had arrived there as well. Many turned and fled to join the Ghost dancers camped near the Badlands.*

The Lakotas were not the only refugees who fled from the agencies. By November 20 it was reported from Pine Ridge that the wives and children of all the traders and other whites about the agency have left for the safer points along the railroad, and the men here are prepared for the worst.[33]

MILITARY LAW PREVAILS

Three days after Pine Ridge was firmly under military control, Royer returned to his post. Ricker observes, Mr. Pugh heard the clear notes of a bugle, and going out a little way he espied the winding column of three troops of cavalry approaching with the redoubtable Agent Royer driving safely in the center.[34] *His return amidst the protection of hundreds of troops was greeted with considerable amusement. From this time on, Royer's days as an agent were limited.*

By then, Elaine Goodale writes, We were now practically under martial law, with General John R. Brooke in personal command. The infantry set up tents on the common, by degrees protecting them with trenches and crude breastworks. The streets were patrolled, and a buffalo-coated sentinel stood guard night and day around the Oglala boarding-school, whose doors were kept locked upon hundreds of children from all parts of the reservation—partly, no doubt, as hostages for the good behavior of their parents.

Old, sick and little ones were suffering from exposure in thin cotton tents; the grazing was soon gone and the ponies were starving. Worse still, police, mixed-bloods and even church members were threatened with reprisals from the excited Ghost dancers.

The Episcopal minister, Reverend Charles Smith Cook, and the newly appointed government physician, Dr. Charles A. Eastman, were college-trained Sioux, suffering from inner conflict between sympathy with their unhappy people and loyalty to government and civilization. This was a clash of cultures and not of races, for the great majority of Dakotas remained throughout loyal and sane.

However, the presence of troops was a scarcely veiled threat. Swarms of war correspondents from Omaha, Chicago and New York felt obliged to invent highly colored stories in default of authentic news. Some officers admitted that "the army doesn't know what it is here for," while at the same time we heard that the men were bored with long inaction and "spoiling for a fight."[35]

According to Gilmore, Old settlers told me that there were "dead soldiers" strewn from Rushville to Pine Ridge and that the 8,000 soldiers who streamed in indulged in carousing and drinking.[36] *Local merchants who demanded the army's presence in the belief it would bring them new business had been duly rewarded.*

In the East others planned to profit in a different way from the so-called Ghost Dance war. Miles and his superior, Maj. Gen. John M. Schofield, immediately began to lobby Congress for increased appropriations and a larger standing army.

RED CLOUD SPEAKS

On November 22, during a meeting at Pine Ridge between tribal chiefs and the military, Red Cloud made an eloquent and placating speech. According to the "New York World," he spoke with many gestures, but deliberately, as if weighing every word. *Again the old chief was conciliatory:* "I see some of my friends here this morning and want to tell them all something. I have some more friends in Washington. The Great Father's friends are all my friends. We are all friends of the agent and we are friends of the soldiers. I have been working under the direction of the Great Father at Washington for twenty years.

"I have been to Washington ten times to see my Great Father. We asked for churches and schools on these creeks about the reservation and we got them. My people have built houses about these churches and schools, and some of the places look like villages. I tell my people to take care of their stock and increase it, and they are doing it. . . . Then I send my children to the big schools in the East, where they learn something.

"I don't want to fight and I don't want my people to fight. We have lots of old women and lots of old men. We've got no guns and we can't fight, for we have nothing to eat and are too poor to do anything.

"On this reservation I am the head man, and they all look to me. I haven't been to see the dancing. My eyes are sore and I can't see very well, but when they get well I will go to see it. I will try to stop it. Those Indians are fools. The winter weather will stop it, I think. Anyway, it will all be over by spring. I don't think there will be any trouble. They say that I have been in the dance. That is not right. I have never seen it.

"When we made our treaty it was promised there would be no troops on the reservation, unless it was at the order of the Great Father. They are here, though, and I suppose it is all right.

"My name is Red Cloud. That is all I have to say about this question."[37]

Red Cloud continued to speak in this conciliatory manner throughout the crisis. Never once did he issue a threatening statement. Even so, the press and military continued to label him as a "hostile."

At the same meeting, Tornbelly, one of the minor chiefs, declared that he did not know what the troops were on the reservation for, but insisted that the dancing must not be stopped. "We don't want to fight," said he, "but this is our church. It's just like the white man's church, except that we don't pass around the hat."[38]

On the same day the "New York World" reported Red Cloud's conciliatory speech, it reported: Two of the most reliable scouts in the government employ reported to General Brooke at 9 o'clock last night that 150 lodges of the Wounded Knee fanatics, including some of the most desperate and treacherous redskins in this part of the country, had moved to White River, twenty miles north of here, and had begun the dance in a wilder manner than has been known before.

The scouts say they talked with several of the leaders, and the latter all declared that they had fully determined that they would shoot any government officials or soldiers who attempted to suppress the dance. This is considered by far the gravest news that has come to General Brooke since his arrival. All of these Indians are armed and they have large quantities of ammunition and provisions and are receiving heavy reinforcements hourly.[39]

Indeed, a number of Lakotas had repeating Winchesters, but they did not begin to match the firepower of the army's deadly Hotchkiss and Gatling guns.

ARMY INFIGHTING

Miles's tactics were not universally accepted by other army officers. On November 21, in an interview with a "Washington Evening Star" reporter, an unnamed top-ranking officer questioned Miles's motives. He dared to state that Miles is predicting a general Indian war and virtually asks that the command of the entire army be turned over to him. He wants to create a scare and pose as the savior of the country. In fact he is almost in the attitude of a political Messiah, such as the Indians themselves are looking for. I have no doubt in the world that he is honest in his candidacy. He has shrewdly enlisted the favor of nearly every newspaper man in California, and has by his agreeable manners and the expenditure of his means managed to make himself very popular in a certain way in the

West. He is one of the most ambitious men in the army and he is pulling his wires shrewdly.[40]

Miles, furious, telegraphed Schofield: I regard this as a malicious and unwarranted attack, and I send you this clipping with the recommendation that necessary steps be taken to ascertain the identity of the "prominent officer."[41] *The offending officer was never publicly identified, but it was probably Brig. Gen. Wesley Merritt, an experienced Indian fighter. He obliquely voiced similar views in the press a few weeks later, but he was not the only one within army circles to criticize Miles.*

Miles attempted to put a positive face on his actions when he told reporters on November 22, "I have received advices from Gen. Brooke which say that the turbulent Indians have evidently changed their minds, and instead of making an attack they are more submissive."

In reply to a question whether he considered the "evident submissiveness" as a good sign, the general said that the treachery which is natural to Indians was not to be underestimated. *Then Miles admitted*, "Of course the longer they refrain from hostilities the better it is for the army, for the reason that it gives us the advantage of valuable time to locate troops at available points."

There was another reason Miles was glad that time was on his side. As a veteran Indian fighter, he knew that the Lakotas avoided winter warfare. Perhaps he believed that when spring came and there was no cataclysm, the whole affair would end. By then the army would have received increased appropriations and be in the command of the reservations.

CONFLICTING REPORTS

Discrepant reports continued to pour out of the West. From Mandan, North Dakota, it was reported on November 23 that settlers have been coming into Simm, forty miles west of here, all day. Roving bands of Sioux scared them. More guns were shipped tonight. . . . The actions of the Indians satisfy everybody that grave danger exists of an outbreak in the spring if not before.[42]

The "Pioneer Press" reported from Pierre, South Dakota, that two Indian missionaries of the Episcopal Church, Ashley and Garrett, arrived in Pierre tonight from Pine Ridge Agency. They were warned by Indians it would not be safe for them to remain there. They report many families leaving the vicinity.[43]

On the same day the "Chicago Tribune" published a dispatch from Aberdeen, South Dakota, that stated, Reports indicate that the Indians are along the east side of the Missouri River, north of Pierre, to Mandan.

The settlers are becoming very much alarmed and are fleeing to the towns, leaving most of their possessions behind them.[44]

However, the day before, it was reported from Sioux Falls that Bishop Hare of the Episcopal church, who has had charge of the missionary work of this denomination for ten years among the Sioux Indians, arrived in this city yesterday after a visit of a month among the various missions of the reservation. He is probably the best posted man on the situation in the country, and has given special attention to the Messiah craze for months. In an interview with the *Omaha Bee* correspondent he said:

"So far as I am able to judge from the results of my trip, the Messiah craze is not gaining, but rather the reverse. I should fear the results of forcible interference with them in their present excitement. Time will reveal the deception practiced by the ringleaders of the movement, for the promised crisis will not come, and meanwhile the Indians will have danced themselves out. . . . This craze will take care of itself and run its course. It will indeed be an unfortunate thing if the troops are sent among them. It will precipitate war with absolute certainty."[45]

A news dispatch from Bismarck concurred with Hare's evaluation of the situation: The Indian scare in this section is subsiding. A dispatch from Governor Mellette, of South Dakota, to officials in Bismarck says there is no truth in the rumors of Indians crossing the river into Campbell County, nor rumors of an Indian outbreak in South Dakota. The danger is now believed to be over at Pine Ridge and other southern agencies.

On the same day it was reported from Washington, Major General Schofield told reporters that every hour that passed without an outbreak brightened the prospect of a peaceful settlement of the present difficulties. As he issued his optimistic words, Secretaries Proctor and Noble, in consultation with the president, decided that two regiments of cavalry should be sent to Pine Ridge from Arizona and New Mexico.[46] *Now Miles was deploying troops from throughout the United States.*

On the same day, a wire service reported to the "Chicago Tribune": Everything is quiet at Pine Ridge Agency, but the officers are apprehensive of trouble soon. The temper of the larger portion of the Indians is very ugly although some have abandoned the dance and come back to the post.[47]

Another service reported, Dispatches received by General Miles state [that] the separation of the friendly and turbulent Indians is proceeding rapidly at Pine Ridge. General Brooke, in a press conference, reported that he anticipated no immediate trouble and thought the separation will make easier the task of restraining the turbulent Indians from overt acts.[48]

Even as Brooke spoke, a ranchman named Scoville, who had left his place near Rosebud to take refuge here, *told the "New York World"'s Rosebud reporter that he had* talked recently with some of the Messiah Indians. They said that the Indian did not stop the white man from worshiping his Great Spirit, and that if the white man tried to stop the Indian he would fight and kill all the whites that came near. They only wanted to be left alone to dance, and no whites must come about. If the Great Father sent soldiers to stop them they would be served like Custer's soldiers were.[49]

On November 21, the same day, concerns arose about Chief Big Foot's wandering band of Miniconjous. It was reported from Chamberlain, South Dakota, that the troops stationed below the fork of the Bellefourche and Cheyenne rivers have been notified to make preparations to remain where they are until next spring. This military camp is in the vicinity of the belligerent Big Foot's village, and as Big Foot is one of the active spirits on the Messiah craze the soldiers will keep a watchful eye on him.[50]

As December approached, eastern newspaper readers must have been thoroughly confused.

SHORT BULL PREACHES A SERMON

The next day, November 22, it was reported from Chicago that General Miles was in receipt of a telegram from Rosebud from one of his officers. The officer gives a sermon delivered by Short Bull, the so-called prophet of the Messiah, at Rosebud Agency.

The sermon the unnamed officer sent Miles was nearly identical to the sermon reported on October 31. The main difference was that Short Bull had predicted the imminent demise of the white race: "There may be soldiers surround you but pay no attention to them. Continue to dance. If the soldiers surround you four deep three of you upon whom I have put my holy shirts will sing a song I have taught you and some soldiers will drop dead. The rest will run, but their horses will sink into the earth. The riders will jump but they will sink into the earth and you can do what you desire. Now, you must know this, that all the soldiers and the white race will be dead. There will be only 5,000 of them living on the earth."[51]

It is uncertain whether the officer was reporting the earlier sermon, a new one, or an embellished tale told by a scout or rancher.

The next afternoon, November 22, Miles told the press, The number of Indians going from the Rosebud Agency to the Pine Ridge Agency is increasing. Advices show this Messiah craze extending to our Indians near the mountain borders and between the home nations and Canada. *Newspaper reports from throughout the West and as far as Canada and Mexico tended to support Miles's assertion that the dancing was spreading rapidly throughout the western tribes. The spread of the dancing, rather than a war, was Miles's greatest concern.*

Miles backed away from a winter confrontation and began concentrating on the possibility of a spring uprising. He had good reason for this tactical change. The number of Ghost dancers hiding in the Badlands was rapidly decreasing.

On the same day, November 22, it was reported from Valentine, Nebraska, A Rosebud Indian named Short was the only Indian in town today. To an interpreter he said that the Rosebud and Pine Ridge Messiah Indians had concentrated on Pass Creek, near the mouth, and if any Indian went to that camp he had to become one of them or leave, in which event they confiscated his rifle and ammunition.

Pass Creek is on the edge of the Badlands, *the correspondent added,* and it is the purpose of these Indians when close pressed to fall back into these, from which it will be almost impossible to dislodge them.[52] *It would seem the remaining Ghost dancers were planning to take to a winter retreat in the Badlands.*

While all this was happening, conflicting reports continued to appear in eastern newspapers. On November 23 the "Iowa State Register" ran a reassuring headline:

> INDIAN SCARE ABOUT OVER
> Some of the Settlers in the Vicinity of the agencies Still Leaving Their Homes, But No Indians Are Pursuing Them and the Ghost Dances Have Been Stopped. Thought Now That No Further Trouble Will Occur and a Generally Easier Feeling Prevails.[53]

On the same day, the "New York World" trumpeted:

> THE BLOODSHED BEGUN
> Seven White Men Killed by Indians. Wounded Knee's Men Defiant. But No Indians Are Pursuing Them and the Ghost Dances Have Been Stopped. Red Cloud Says the Ghost dancers Are Fools—He Doesn't Want to Fight—Doesn't Want His People to Fight—An Enlightened View of the Duty of the Indians to Themselves.[54]

The report of the massacre of seven white men was false. It may have been a rehash by a reporter of the erroneous report of a massacre a few days earlier.

The day these headlines appeared, Miles appeared at his Chicago office on a Sunday morning, not a usual workday. He put in a long day. According to the "New York Times," It was after 2 o'clock this morning when the commanding general left the headquarters in the Pullman Building after he kept the wires hot with orders to the commanding officers with the troops in the Northwest now among the Indians.[55] *Miles chose to base his actions on the most alarming reports.*

By Monday, November 24, it was reported from Washington that the War Department is giving every assistance in its power to General Miles. In addition to the military force in his division, ten troops of cavalry stationed in Arizona and New Mexico and Texas, and a large force from Fort Riley, Kansas, including two light batteries of artillery, have been forwarded to Pine Ridge Agency to reinforce his command. All of these movements have been sanctioned by the president, who is deeply interested in the Indian situation.[56]

Though he was busy, Miles took time to scare the press by saying, "The disaffected camps, scattered over several, hundred miles of territory . . . number about six thousand, and not more than fifteen hundred of these are effective mounted troops."[57]

Miles was exaggerating. Little more than a thousand Lakota men of fighting age were involved in the Ghost dancing in the Badlands. At worst, the army and the Ghost dancers were evenly matched in manpower, but the army outmatched the Lakotas in firepower.

According to the "New York World," Miles had assembled the largest force that has been mustered in the West since 1876–77. . . . The troops at every fort and station in Missouri, Nebraska, Dakota, Minnesota, Montana, and Wyoming will be drawn upon; and other detachments of the army are under orders to hold themselves in readiness.

The correspondent went on to speculate that General Miles believes that if the Indians do go on the warpath, the campaign against them will be a protracted one for he is moving field artillery and large quantities of ammunition and supplies, as well as cavalry and infantry. The troops are under orders not to attack the Indians until they do something more warlike than dancing. Instructions are to prevent trouble if possible by persuading the Indians to return to the agency.[58]

At the moment the possibility of a winter Indian war seemed unlikely, but Miles continued to send troops to the Dakotas.

8. Rumors, Restive Troops, and a New Initiative

The Red Skin left their agency, the Soldiers left their Post,
All on the strength of an Indian tale about the Messiah's Ghost
Got up by savage chieftains to lead their tribes astray;
But Uncle Sam wouldn't have it so, for he ain't built that way.
They swore that this Messiah came to them in visions sleep,
And promised to restore their game and Buffalos a heap,
So they must start a big Ghost Dance, then all would join their band,
And may be so we lead the way into the great Bad Land.

CHORUS:

They claimed the shirt Messiah gave, no bullet could go through,
But when the Soldiers fired at them they saw this was not true.
The medicine man supplied them with their great Messiah's grace,
And he, too, pulled his freight and swore the 7th hard to face.

—Barracks ballad composed by *Pvt. W. H. Prather*,
Ninth Cavalry, I Company

A BELATED INVESTIGATION

On Monday, November 24, 1890, General Schofield instructed General Miles to find out if the cause of the present dissatisfaction among the Indians is due more to lack of rations than to their belief in the coming of the new Messiah.

There are plenty of reports on that subject already in the hands of the War Department, *the "New York World"'s correspondent commented*, and all of them declare that the Indians have been unpaid and underpaid and that their petitions for more rations have been disregarded by the Indian Bureau.

In accordance with the instructions, Colonel Heyl, inspector general, left for the West this afternoon, and will visit all the army posts and most of the agency stations. He is accompanied by an amanuensis who will take verbatim reports.[1]

This fact-finding mission was months and even years late. Since the appropriations deliberations were about to start in Congress, it is likely that the investigation was a War Department ploy to make deficiencies within the Department of the Interior and its Bureau of Indian Affairs public.

On the same day the mission was reported, a headline in the "New York World" proclaimed:

PLOTTING A MASSACRE

Scheme to Entrap and Slay Gen. Brooke's Command. Troops Hastily Dispatched from St. Louis to Pine Ridge. Sitting Bull Said to Have Ordered a General Outbreak at the Firing of the First Gun—Missionaries Warned to Leave Pine Ridge—A Girl Attacked by an Indian at Bismarck.[2]

According to the "New York World"'s reporter, Lakotas were leaving Pass Creek, the site of a major Ghost Dance, and were moving toward Pine Ridge. The warriors traveled with Short Bull, and the older men, women, and children moved on their own. Both, it was reported, were coming in to talk to the Commanding General Brooke on their behalf. *The correspondent further stated that* Chief Two Strike intends to stab the commanding officer as a signal for an attack by his band.[3]

Since Two Strike was not with Short Bull at this time, it would seem that the reporter was working from an unreliable source, and on the same day, the "New York Times" reported that General Miles attaches little importance to the reports of a plot to assassinate General Brooke.[4]

Other frightening dispatches were filed. At Standing Rock, it was reported that O. Stewart, the agency saddler, while out riding yesterday, visited the Indian camp four miles from town and saw the Indians perform the Messiah Dance. The Indians were all nearly naked and painted hideously.

They gathered around Stewart, who was badly frightened at their threats. One Indian pointed toward the blazing sun, shaking Stewart with the other hand, and saying, "See! See! There he is now. The Indian Messiah is coming now. See! See!"

Stewart was compelled to look at the sun, and when he acknowledged he saw the Messiah, the Indians seemed greatly pleased. He was then released and came to the agency as fast as his horses would bring him.[5]

As he mustered his forces, General Miles placed the Nebraska National Guard on alert. According to the "Chadron (NE) Democrat," the troops were becoming restive: The militia boys are sorely disappointed that they were not ordered to the front and given an opportunity to cover themselves with glory by cleaning out the rebellious Sioux. The boys wanted to go real bad and kill a nice mess of Indians apiece, but the authorities, dreading a war of extermination, were moved to compassion for the guileless children of the forest . . . so the boys had to content themselves with swooping down upon the boardinghouse tables and destroying the grub.[6]

At Pine Ridge General Brooke continued to display the power of his forces. On November 26 William Fitch Kelley reported to the "Nebraska State Journal," The sun came forth this morning upon as pretty a scene as it had ever shone upon before. All the troops were out early doing their daily drill work, the cavalry dashing over the hills, sometimes in company troop, officers at the head, suddenly careening about and forming huge squares, with a side nearly a mile in length, advancing, then retreating and doing numerous other military maneuvers with precision and promptitude. The infantry and artillery were also out in full force, cooperating with the cavalry in the clear cool air of the morning. They presented a spectacle worth going many miles to behold.[7]

The army's Gatling guns had the ability to pour rapid fire into a Lakota camp, and the Hotchkiss gun was described by Lakotas as "the gun that shoots today and kills tomorrow." The daily displays of firepower frightened the Lakotas who had stayed away from the Badlands or who had surrendered. Many wondered if Pine Ridge was safe. Miles's strategy of building up his forces was having a reverse effect. Instead of persuading the dancers to surrender, he was on the verge of driving those who had obeyed government policy to flee to the Badlands.

The "New York Times" reported, The constant maneuvering by the troops here, the rush of cavalry and infantry with cannons and pack mules, and the wild reports of the coming of regiments and battalions of soldiers have terrorized the Indians encamped about the agency to such an extent that there came very nearly being a stampede in their villages last night. The redskins, both the dancers and the friends of the whites, have got it into their heads that the massing of such a big force of men here means their extinction, and that they are going to be corralled and shot down like dogs.[8]

On November 25 Kelley reported, Today was beef issue day, and an order from General Brooke last evening, who has full command here by order of the War Department, was given that no beef should be given out. Thousands of Indians viewed the troops in their drill and then set out over the prairie for the beef pen, but they were quietly told that no beef was to be given out today. After many ominous looks, fierce words and sullen behavior in general, they gradually dispersed to their encampment, where again it was all talked over in, to say the least, a very animated fashion, and thus the poor Sioux have received the first in what is certain to be a wholesome lesson to all of them before the thing is settled.

It is said the beef will be issued tomorrow or next day, the delay being due to the general desire that all the troops be here. There will then be some conditions exacted. What they are no one can foretell. It is only surmise, for no one but the two agents and General Brooke know. The most skillful questioning of the newspaper men divulges nothing from them. Courteous and accommodating they are in many ways, their mouths are closed firm.[9]

Brooke seemed intent on breaking the spirit of an already demoralized people. From all reports he was successful.

Near this time Brooke asked issue clerk Robert O. Pugh what was being distributed to the Lakotas who had surrendered. "They are getting," replied Mr. Pugh, "ten pounds of bacon, one pound of baking powder, four pounds of coffee, fifty pounds of flour, two bushels of salt, two pounds of soap, seven pounds of sugar. This is the quantity allowed to 100 rations for 100 Indians per day for two weeks."

"Too little, entirely too little," exclaimed the general with much emphasis. "Who of us don't know that the people cannot be satisfied or contented or anything else if they don't have enough to eat, and the government should be finding it out pretty soon."

"For one thing," said Agent Royer, "they don't get the beef that's coming to them. A beef weighing 1,100 pounds when it gets to us shrinks to 700 before it gets to the Indians, and the Indians are the losers."

"But it is not the beef alone that is short," resumed the general. "It is about everything else except soap, and there seems to be plenty of that." [10]

OUTNUMBERED AT PINE RIDGE

The Lakota population at the agency had grown so large that the troops were outnumbered. Realizing this, Miles, reaffirming an earlier order, telegraphed General Brooke on November 23: Confidential. Do not allow your command to become mixed up with Indians, friendly or otherwise. Hold them all at a safe distance from your command. Guard against surprise or treachery.[11] *Disobedience of this order would lead to tragedy for the troops and Lakotas alike.*

The residents and newspaper reporters at Pine Ridge were uneasy about being outnumbered by the Lakotas that had surrendered there. On November 24 the "New York World"'s Pine Ridge correspondent reported, There is a feeling of dread here. Late on Saturday evening the authorities discovered that the agency was almost completely surrounded by the Indian camp. Yesterday morning an order was given for all the Indians to move off into the low lands upon the banks of Wolf Creek, that runs off to the southeast, and it was promptly obeyed. The decrepit coffee-coolers stood about and smoked, the elder boys gathered the ponies together from the surrounding knolls, and the squaws tore down the smoky tipis. Only a few Springfield rifles and Winchesters were noticed, but many of the old men carried about their waists belts filled with loaded cartridges.

There are seven thousand Indians all told in the reservation. About eight or nine hundred of them have come in to receive their rations, but of this number there are not a hundred and fifty able-bodied warriors. The young men, the hot bloods and discontented ones and the fanatical Ghost dancers, are not among them. The reports from the Indian teachers, squawmen and half-breeds agree that the disaffected Indians will send their squaws to draw their supplies: the bucks themselves will hold out and as soon as the rations and beef have been issued they will demand a council.[12]

However, at least one veteran frontiersmen did not see danger ahead. The "Omaha Bee" reported on November 24, Your correspondent interviewed a squawman now living on the Sioux reservation, and having an Indian wife and many children. He is called Big Bat by the Indians, has lived among them for thirty years, and is intelligent, wealthy, and of wide influence among them. He stated in substance that no outbreak or depredation of any nature would occur. "The Indians have been dancing," said Big Bat, "but that does not signify that they want to murder white settlers or fight soldiers."

"Are many of them armed?"

"Yes, about two-thirds of the males, but they do not want to fight. I attended a council of the dancers night before last when they discussed all these matters, and the leaders' speeches to the young bucks were all to the effect that while they could easily wipe out the troops now on hand, if they did so there would be ten soldiers there the next day where there had only been one the day before, and it would only be a question of days until the last Indian would die.

"'Besides,' they said, 'where would we all go to? We are surrounded on all sides by soldiers and settlers. We have no provisions for a campaign and would surely starve, and our squaws and children would perish before our eyes.'

"The whole council united in advising and agreeing to submit peacefully to whatever demands the government demanded."[13]

At the same time, the army devised a novel solution to its problems. The War Department, *the "New York World" reported,* has just authorized General Miles to increase the number of ["friendly" Lakota] scouts to twelve hundred. It is said at army headquarters that the payment of thirteen dollars per month to each Indian scout with the privilege of wearing a blue army blouse and an acknowledged connection with the United States government are inducements too powerful for the average Indian to resist. . . . The twelve hundred scouts enlisted will, it is hoped, exert a strong peaceful influence through their family and tribal relations.[14]

This mass enrollment of scouts would enlist nearly one-fifth of the Lakota warriors on the Dakota reservations and increase the army's forces by a similar ratio. If the scheme worked, the Ghost dancers would be outnumbered by a considerable margin, since by late November fewer than seven hundred warriors were in the Badlands, and many of these were surrendering.[15]

As fast as the Ghost dancers came to the agency, *it was reported*, they were separated from the friendly Indians and forced to pitch their tipis about old Red Cloud's house. His son, Jack Red Cloud, was the first of the dance leaders to come in. . . . There are nearly a hundred lodges of Ghost dancers in the village about Red Cloud's. If Little Wound comes in, the population will be increased to nearly fifteen hundred souls.[16] *It was believed that there were nearly eight hundred people with Little Wound.*

On November 25 the "New York World" reported that today Agent Cooper's spies brought him reliable information that Two Strike and his band were upon Porcupine Creek, killing cattle and robbing houses. He says about 800 people are with his band. Cooper had doubted the report before and sent his scouts out to confirm it, which they did. Indeed it is most surprising the way that Special Agent Cooper and Royer keep informed of what the Indians are doing within a radius of 200 miles from here. Their vigilance is ceaseless and rewarded by wonderful results. Considering this situation, General Brooke is also ever careful. He did not go to bed at all last night.

This morning Agent Cooper issued an order that every person who did not reside upon the reservation should at once leave, and his police are now sending them out. He was kind enough not to include the corps of newspaper men.[17]

THE SEVENTH CAVALRY ARRIVES

On November 26 the late George Armstrong Custer's famous Seventh Cavalry marched into Pine Ridge. The Seventh, under the command of Col. James W. Forsyth, included eight companies of about eight hundred men and a company of artillery that had a battery of four guns.[18] *Their arrival was greeted with alarm by the Lakotas. Many of the Seventh's senior officers and several of its noncommissioned officers had fought in Reno and Benteen's rear guard at the Little Bighorn in 1876. In weeks to come, there would be much speculation in the press about whether these survivors were seeking revenge.*

Serving in the Seventh was a green British recruit, Pvt. Walter R. Crickett.[19] *His long letter home is one of three surviving accounts of the Wounded Knee Massacre written by enlisted men. Crickett begins his detailed account by writing:* We got the order on the 23rd Nov, '90, that our regiment was for the front, the place being Pine Ridge S.D. where the Indians had broken out and gone on the war path and committing all sorts of outrages. It was morning when the order came and by four that afternoon we was all aboard the train [and] had all our horses and transportation along. That is what takes the time to load.

We traveled all night and next day until we got to a place in Nebraska called Lincoln about six P.M. where we took the stock off, watered and fed, started again about twelve, and got into Rushville at five the day following, that being the nearest point to Pine Ridge. There we unloaded every thing and left that afternoon for the agency.

Camped that night at White Clay Creek about twelve miles from Rushville. At five the next morning was up, had a cup of coffee, and a few biscuits, struck camp, and was in the saddle a little after six, and then made straight in. Got there about four and went into camp where we stayed until the 26th December when orders came for the first battalion to go to Wounded Knee Creek to stop Big Foot's band going into the Badlands. It took about two hours to strike tents and pack up all our things having to go on mules as wagons could not travel in the Badlands.

It was the Seventh Cavalry's first but not last trip to Wounded Knee Creek.

The more sensationalist members of the press seized upon the possibility that the Seventh's veterans were intent on seeking revenge for their Little Bighorn defeat. Kelley, after talking with members of the Seventh Cavalry, wrote, Although they give vent to their feelings very cautiously, fearful of infringing upon military etiquette, it is well known that the Seventh Cavalry is fairly itching, if it may be so expressed, to be away and pursue the poor Indian. These are the same Indians who mercilessly shot down the gallant Custer and 300 men of the Seventh Cavalry on that memorable day of June 25, 1876. Many of the present officers were with Reno on that day, only four miles distant, and it is safe to say the Sioux will receive no quarter from this famous regiment should an opportunity occur to wreak out vengeance for the blood taken at the battle of the Little Big Horn.

It is touching to notice how the memory and acts of that day are treasured in the hearts of the officers and men. To them they are of the most sacred character never to be forgotten, for they loved their dashing colonel, their brother officers, the daily companions of their life in the service for many years.[20]

According to some accounts, revenge was not sought by just the veterans of the Seventh Cavalry. E. M. Keith, a clergyman at Pine Ridge, told

Judge Eli S. Ricker, I myself talked with infantry soldiers marching to the agency from Chadron who expressed to me the sentiment that all they desired was to get to the Indians and they would do them up.[21]

While small units of the Seventh Cavalry were sent into the field, its main body remained at the camp outside Pine Ridge. Reconnaissance in force was delegated to the Ninth Cavalry.

According to an officer correspondent to the "Army and Navy Journal": The chilly November nights already give us a fair taste of what a winter campaign under canvas is like in this climate, and our only consolation is that the noble red man is probably as uncomfortable in his tipi as we are in a wall tent.[22]

There was one major difference. The wall tents were heated and had wooden floors. The Lakotas at Pine Ridge lived in cloth tipis and were hungry.

FABRICATIONS AND LIES

Local residents were becoming incensed by the alarmist stories being telegraphed to larger newspapers. On November 27 the "Chadron Democrat" complained, The sensational story which appeared in the [Lincoln (NE) State Journal] last week about an Indian killing a soldier at Rushville was totally unfounded and without a shadow of truth. The fellow that reported it here in Chadron and claimed to be an eye witness to the horrible butchery, was at the best a miserable apology of a first-class liar and could not get anybody but the *Lincoln (NE) State Journal* to credit his tale.

On the same day, the "Chadron Democrat" complained, "Surrounded by Reds" was the flaming headlines in one of the Omaha dailies the first of the week, but the body of the article disclosed the fact that the "Reds" consisted of aged men, squaws, and children. Those Omaha newspaper men are making themselves the laughing stock of everybody, not excepting Chief Red Cloud and his band of "bloodthirsty savages."

Local residents were incensed at this irresponsibility, the "Chadron Democrat" continued: On Monday [November 24] some of our citizens circulated for signature a protest to the *Omaha Bee* and *Omaha World Herald*, asking them to discontinue the publication of sensational reports of the Indian troubles which have filled the columns of the Omaha papers for the past few weeks. Although the protest will probably not do any good, it is no doubt a move in the right direction, as the wholesale publication of outlandish and improbable falsehoods as have appeared in the state papers cannot but prove detrimental to this part of the country, and will be the means of retarding settlement for years to come. Let it be stopped at once.[23] *The reporters in question were the "Omaha Bee"'s Will Cressey and the "Omaha World Herald"'s Carl Smith.*

In addition, it was reported, A meeting of citizens was held at the court house Tuesday evening, the object being to urge the War Department to immediately put a stop to "the Indian scare." Appropriate resolutions were passed and forwarded to the department.[24] *No action was taken against the offending reporters.*

S. B. Shirk, *the "Chadron Democrat" continues,* came over from his ranch on the reservation last Saturday and is spending the week with old acquaintances in the city. Mr. Shirk's ranch is situated on the White River about eighty miles from Chadron. The Indians are camped about fifteen miles from his place, but he knew nothing of an Indian scare until reaching here.[25]

The eastern press rarely printed stories about people like Shirk. Instead they published more alarming accounts. The newspaper war continued to rage even as Miles's troops remained on alert and waited for something to happen.

CHANGES AT ROSEBUD

On November 26 the "Omaha Bee"'s correspondent at the Rosebud reported, The beef issue passed quietly. No one was refused beef, even those coming from Two Strike's, Crow Dog's and White Horse's camps. No arrests were made.

Short Bull and the rebels have moved to Corn Creek, about seventy-eight miles from Rosebud and Pine Ridge. Some have taken their wives and children and are driving all the cattle they can pick up.

The correspondent speculated, No attack is anticipated at Rosebud. Pine Ridge Agency is a fort while Rosebud is just the place to ambush troops. The agency is situated in a hole having six deep winding canyons leading to it. Any one of these would hold 2,000 Indians and their approach could not be seen. Colonel Smith said: "If I picket and guard this agency as it should be, I have not sufficient men. Old Spotted Tail picked this place for the Indians, not for the convenience of anyone else."[26]

The correspondent added, Everyone at Rosebud is pleased with the reinstatement of Agent Wright.[27] *While in Washington, Wright had successfully defended himself against the accusation that he had inflated his census figures. He returned to find that many of his charges had left the agency.*

Among those who fled Rosebud was seventy-year-old Chief Two Strike. He and his followers seemed headed toward Pine Ridge, a move the gov-

ernment found threatening. Officials were afraid that Two Strike and Red Cloud would join forces.

According to Chief Two Strike, there was no basis for fear. In January, after the trouble had ended, he told a reporter, "We had not thought of going on the war path against the government or our white neighbors.

"One day a white man employed at a trader's store at the agency came to my camp and told me that the soldiers were coming to stop the dance. This scared us, so we put our women and children into wagons and got on our ponies and left our homes. We went to Pine Ridge and asked Red Cloud and his people to let us have a home on their reservation. They said we might stay, but in a short time we heard that the agent at Pine Ridge had sent for soldiers to come and make us stop dancing. Then we went to the Badlands, and some Oglalas, who had joined our dance went with us.

"We went there to keep away from the soldiers. We did not want to fight; we only wanted to be left alone and be allowed to worship the Great Spirit in our own way. We did not go off the reservation, nor rob any white man of his property. We did take some cattle, which we knew belonged to the Indians, for they had been bought by the government with the Indian's money. We did not mean to fight, unless the soldiers came to the Badlands to break up our dance and take our guns away from us. If the soldiers had not come to our country there would have been no trouble between us and the government."[28]

DISAGREEMENTS IN THE BADLANDS

While Two Strike and his people began a leisurely journey toward Pine Ridge, Short Bull and his followers continued to dance in the Badlands. Indian police from Pine Ridge were dispatched to seek his surrender. While in the ring dancing one day, *Short Bull says*, one of the Indian police, a son of Rope Necklace, a Cut-Off, caught hold of my shoulder and turned me around, said "You have your ears."

The dancing stopped and White Horse told the policeman to go away, as the Messiah's words were right. He said, "He only wanted the people to do two things, farm and go to church. We should not fight but be friends. I do not see any wrong in that. It is right and true. Short Bull has told the agent all these things. We sent him to see the Messiah, and we believe the words he has brought. He speaks the truth. The Indian police are making trouble and soon plenty of whites will come here and make us trouble. That is all I have to say."

The policeman left and the dancing was resumed. The next day Sore Hip sent for me and I went to him. He told me that he had seen Red

Cloud sometime ago in reference to transferring a number of families to Pine Ridge Agency and that he was going to see him again and that he would be back in five days, but requested me to go to my home and stay there until he should return, which I done. But while en route from the agency to my home I was met by a band of Oglalas who had come over for the purpose of dancing.

So we camped with all the young men who were Brulés and Oglalas [and] danced the Ghost Dance. Among the young men was a brother of Iron Foot who took quite a lively interest. He said he had seen the Messiah and was much worked up over it.

On the 5th day after the dance I went to Black Pipe Creek and waited for Sore Hip, all of those who wanted to be transferred to Pine Ridge Agency going along. We met Sore Hip who told us that all had been arranged for our removal and that we were to start in four days. So on the night of the third day those who had no wagons moved to Pass Creek, and the main body was to move the next day, but before moving we had a great Ghost Dance that night.

In the middle of the night I was awakened by a friend who told me that many of my people were moving toward Pine Ridge Agency which surprised me, and some Indian freighters who had just returned from Valentine sent me word that soldiers were moving toward Rosebud Agency. I did not know why this should be, and it made me angry.

One of these freighters, Rescuer, son of Elk Road, told me that they were coming to arrest me and if I was not given up they would fire on us all. It was on account of many lies, spread by others that I was to be arrested for. Rescuer said all the freighters heard the same.

This was in November. I called my people together on Pass Creek and told them to move forward and I would stay here alone as I did not want them to have any trouble on my account.

I told my people, "I want nothing but what was right for myself and family. I had done as they wanted me to, and now have no rest day or night. My brother White Thunder and my cousin Thumb had been killed for jealousy and now they want me. Go on, I will stay here; if they want to kill me they are welcome."

That night they moved, all save myself and a few young men. My family who were on Pass Creek moved also. That night my brother came to me and said it was all lies that the freighters said, and the next morning some of the young men came back for me and I followed them camping that night on Corn Creek. We broke camp the next morning moving to Medicine Creek where we rested, camping that night at the forks of Medicine Root Creek.

The next morning an Oglala came to us telling us to move our camp to the crossing by American Horse's village which we done. Having settled our camp we went in a body to the home of Little Wound singing a song of treaty of friendship.

An old man known as Issowonie rode around our circle and stopped in the middle saying to us, "My boys, save your powder, guns, bows, arrows, and ammunition, for the agency is full of soldiers. Red Cloud says if they do anything we will fight them, and Little Wound says the same. Our own people have caused the soldiers to come here by telling lies. American Horse, Charging Thunder, Fast Thunder, Spotted Horse and Good Back told these lies. Tomorrow morning we will go to Wounded Knee Creek."

The agent had sent for Little Wound to bring me and my people to the agency, so Little Wound started with me and ten Brulés. We halted at the house of Cherry Cedar where we ate some dried meat, continuing afterward to the agency bluffs and resting, Little Wound going on ahead to the agency.

It was sundown when Cheyenne Creek was reached, and afterward going to the lodge of Twist Back on the agency. While in this lodge I was called out by some of my young men who told me the Indian soldiers were about to surround us. At this we remounted our horses and rode back to our camp on Wounded Knee Creek. Our people were surprised and feared something was wrong.

The old crier then told me to move my people who were poorly mounted to the Badlands, as his people had told him to bring me this word, and should anything happen Red Cloud and the rest would join us there with plenty of horses.

The Oglalas brought a large lot of horses to us, saying that they belonged to a white man, Big Bat, who lived up the creek. We went to him, and he told us that if there is going to be a fight he could not take his horses with him as he had so many all over the country and if we wanted to ride them we could, so some of the Brulés did take them.[29]

According to Short Bull, in spite of the teachings of their new religion, the two most powerful Lakota chiefs agreed that the Lakotas should defend themselves if they were attacked.

The Ghost dancers made their new camp on an isolated Badlands plateau directly north of Pine Ridge and about ten miles southeast of the mouth of Battle Creek. In time it became known as the Stronghold. In Miles's words, It would be impossible to describe that country. It appears to have been the result of volcanic action. It was a mass of barren hills, narrow valleys, ravines, canyons, mounds, and buttes, almost devoid of trees and with very little verdure. By following circuitous trails one could ride on horseback over portions of it, but it was wholly impracticable for wagons, and so extensive that it afforded an excellent rendezvous or refuge for hostile Indians. As the Indian supplies were exhausted they could send out in almost any direction and find some game—deer, elk, or domestic cattle—to supply them with food. They were abundantly supplied with horses and well equipped with arms and ammunition.[30]

On December 5 Father Perrig wrote in his diary, From their position they command a view of 10 miles around and have a safe retreat into almost inaccessible rocky recesses of the Badlands. 2000 soldiers could not do them any harm there.[31]

The Ghost dancers were well entrenched and prepared to stay away from the forces Miles continued to muster. It would not be easy, but they certainly were capable of holding out until the promised arrival of their Messiah in the spring.

Lakota "friendlies" from Pine Ridge, eager to end the standoff, entered the Stronghold and attempted to persuade Short Bull's followers to surrender. Short Bull, fearing arrest, ignored their overtures. He says, Sore Hip, High Hawk, and Chief of the Black Hills, a white man who is a judge, came out to us to have a talk. I did not go to the Council and don't know what was said.

The next morning we moved toward the Badlands and camped there that night. High Hawk and the others return[ed] to the agency, no good having been done by them.[32]

Short Bull was afraid and for good reason. More troops were arriving in the Dakotas daily. Eight hundred troops were dispatched from Forts Bayard and Wingate in New Mexico. Troops were moved from Fort Logan near Denver and ordered to join the troops coming from Fort Wingate. From Fort Leavenworth, Kansas, it was reported, Orders were received directing four troops of cavalry to be ready for marching orders.[33]

Miles's efforts to increase his forces were unrelenting, but he was quickly running out of options. The "Chicago Tribune" reported from St. Louis on November 29 that two hundred raw recruits have been ordered from Jefferson Barracks to fill vacancies in short regiments on the frontier. One hundred of the men go to Minneapolis and from there will be assigned to different regiments at Fort Snelling and Fort Meade. One hundred cavalrymen go to Omaha and from there to South Dakota. The men go to South Dakota immediately to join General Brooke's troops in the field.[34]

REPORTS OF DEPREDATIONS

As November ended, the fearful and starving Lakotas surrendered in increasing numbers. As they did, it was reported, Between one and two thousand of the Indians who refused to come into the Rosebud Agency in response to the agent's order started westward toward what is known as the Badlands. In their stampede, they have committed depredations on cabins and stock of friendly Indians who went into the agency. *It would later be discovered that these Rosebud escapees planned to surrender at Pine Ridge.*

The reports of hostile depredations, a euphemism for pillaging and living off the land, were true. When the Lakotas migrated, they sustained themselves on what they could find. A news story dated November 26 reported, Along the trail of the Indians, Red Eagle found the cabins broken open and rifled of all their contents, even the calico lining of the walls being stripped off. Trunks were on the floor with their heads and sides battered in and their contents stolen.

Even Little Wound's cabin had been broken into. The doors of the little log houses were split, and where padlocks and staples held them from within, the thieving savages shattered the windows and crawled into the buildings. Charley Tomahawk's store on Wounded Knee was entered in this way. Not a thing was left on the shelves. Red Eagle saw where the ponies of the marauders had been turned upon the haystacks. At the camping place, he also saw fresh beef, which shows that the Indians had been killing stock in the neighborhood. All the sufferers from the raid in progress are the Sioux and Cheyenne, who are practically held captives here by order of the army and agency officials.[35]

The damage was done to the properties of other Lakotas, not whites. While whites considered these thefts criminal, the Lakotas believed that if something had been abandoned, it should be put to good use. As Little Wound stated, much of what the Lakotas possessed, especially the cattle, had been given to them by the government and was considered common property in payment for land they had sold.

CHANGES AND EVALUATIONS

At this time the secretary of the interior, in an effort to pacify the Lakotas, directed the release of rations sufficient to conform to the Agreement made in 1877.[36] *The newly allotted rations did not arrive for nearly a month, but ironically, on the same day it was reported,* A rough draft of the regular army appropriation bill is now ready and will be submitted to the subcommittee tomorrow. A very significant feature of it is the appropriation of $600,000 to aid in carrying on the Indian campaign. An increase of $150,000 over last year is made in the purchase of horses for the cavalry; $300,000 is provided for the special transportation of troops, and $300,000 for the subsistence of the Indians captured. *The correspondent then editorialized,* This feature of the bill proves conclusively that the War Department is anticipating a lively and expensive campaign with the Indians.[37]

In early December Colonel Heyl, inspector general of the Division of the Missouri, returned to Chicago after an inspection tour in the Northwest just as the Senate was taking up the appropriations bill. In contrast to the dire newspaper reports being published daily, Heyl told reporters, "My opinion is that there is no imminent danger of any serious trouble. As a matter of fact, the danger has never been as serious as reported. Many settlers in Dakota and Nebraska became panic stricken. They sold their property for anything they could get, abandoned their homes and rushed to the nearest railway station, when they were in no more danger from the Indians than we are here in Chicago.

"I reached Pine Ridge on the twenty-seventh. The dance had ceased for three days before I got there, and it had not been resumed when I left. The Indians were quiet and peacefully disposed. Some of the young Oglala Sioux, particularly the younger bucks of that tribe, were anxious for trouble, but these were pretty much controlled by the older and wiser heads."[38]

Heyl's findings must have been in Miles's and Schofield's hands before Heyl returned to Chicago, but the troops kept moving into the Dakotas.

RUMORS OF AN ATTACK ON THE STRONGHOLD

Miles had delayed moving against the Stronghold, but as November ended, it seemed that the impatient Seventh Cavalry would see action. At eight o'clock last night [November 30], it was thought the hour to march was at hand, *reads a report from Pine Ridge.* The cavalry received orders not to remove any part of their uniform, to sleep on their arms, and hold themselves in readiness to move at a moment's notice. There was a heavy undercurrent of excitement, but official mouths, as usual, were closed tighter than clams.[39]

The "New York Herald" elaborated, A report gained circulation here last evening that the Ninth and Seventh Cavalry were under marching orders and would leave about midnight for the hostile camp on Porcupine Creek to put a stop to the depredations of the Indians and arrest the ring-leaders.

The report was credited, and as nothing to the contrary could be learned at army headquarters, a wild scramble ensued among the press representatives for horses and other equipment for an active campaign with the troops in the hostile country. The agency presented a decidedly active appearance: horses were saddled, pack horses were loaded with bedding and provisions, and everything was placed in readiness for a march to the front at a moment's notice.

The camp was astir until daylight but no forward movement being ordered, the troops remained in camp. The fact that word was received from the hostiles that they were coming to the agency today undoubtedly prevented the troops from being ordered out.

The hostiles will reach here late this evening, and it is believed that the action taken on their arrival will have considerable bearing on the present situation of affairs and some definite understanding may be arrived at.[40] *After so much waiting and press exaggeration, even a surrender was considered to be an hostile act.*

In the days to come it was reported again and again that the cavalry was about to ride into the Badlands. The orders never came.

These reports did not go unnoticed by the Lakotas. A report came from Pierre, South Dakota, on November 30 that the Lakotas were getting intelligence reports from the newspapers. According to the "Chadron Democrat," Ghost Horse, an Indian spy, who was sent to Big Foot and Hump's camps at the mouth of the Cherry Creek . . . said there were several educated Indians among the Cherry Creek "hostiles," who came to Pierre regularly every few days and bought copies of each daily newspaper on sale, which they took back and read to the chiefs and leading braves, thus informing them of what is occurring at other points.

The Indians all seemed to enjoy this, laughing heartily when they heard of the great alarm everywhere, and settlers gathering at towns, sometimes one hundred miles east of the Missouri River, for self-protection.

It seemed to strengthen their belief that the Messiah is coming, *Ghost Horse said*, and that the whites are becoming afraid and ready to die off or flee and leave the land to the Indians.[41]

How the Lakotas reconciled the inaccuracies and exaggerations in the news stories they read was not explained.

On November 29 it was reported from Washington that Colonel Thomas M. Vincent, assistant adjutant general, United States Army, now on duty at army headquarters in this city, *told reporters*, "For my part I was inclined to treat the matter pretty much as the usual scare until reports were received from Agent McLaughlin and then matters began to assume a more serious aspect, owing to his experience and long residence among them.

"McLaughlin is a pretty good judge of the Indian character, and when he sounded the alarm it was time to heed it. But he had a remedy as was shown by the appointment of 500 good Indians as scouts, for like his white brethren, an Indian is pretty apt to be impressed with a brief show or badge of authority. These new men will be invaluable not only in ferreting out and preventing any trouble, but will set a good example to the other Indians who have not been so fortunate as to be awarded a uniform and brass buttons by the government."[42]

The recruitment of Lakota scouts had begun.

ALARMIST REPORTS CONTINUE

Alarmist reports continued to appear with annoying regularity: Great excitement prevailed in Brewster, Blaine County, last Tuesday. A telegram, supposed to have been sent from Valentine by a special agent of the department, stated that the Indians from Rosebud were on their way south, and advised the settlers to arm themselves in order to resist the "red devils." After a whole lot of imaginary gore had been spilled, it was discovered that they had been frightened by a bogus telegram, and now the people of Brewster refuse to lay aside their guns, but persist in looking for the man who fooled them, and they promise him a red hot reception if found.

Ludicrous reports appeared as well: A lady residing in the mountains of Tennessee claims to be a sister to Red Cloud, the noted Sioux chief, and relates how he was stolen from his parents by the Indians at the tender age of three years, and when discovered had become so used to their ways that he refused to rejoin his almost heart-broken family, but preferred to stay with the last remnant of a once-mighty race.

The writer concluded, Probably Mr. R. Cloud has forgotten all about his early history, but we hope when he receives *the Democrat* and reads this paragraph, he will at once set about making amends for his past conduct, and during the remainder of his days devote his time and attention to cheering the declining years of his Tennessee relatives.

The "Chadron Democrat"—here from December 4, 1890—was maintaining its sense of humor at the growing desperation of the press for a sensational story.

FEARS OF THE GHOST SHIRT

Many whites persisted in believing that the hostilities would begin with the arrival of spring or with the appearance of the Messiah. Their fears were not allayed by reports from Pine Ridge regarding the Ghost dancers' growing faith in the magical protection of Ghost shirts: A government courier and a scout came in from Wounded Knee late last night and reported that the Ghost dancers had killed one of their number. The dancers had their medicine man concoct the old time preparation with which the braves of Custer's time always saturated their shirts preparatory to going to war. This concoction is supposed by the Indians to ward off bullets.

Yesterday, after the fluid of supposedly wonder charm had been mixed, a war shirt was dipped into it and then put on one of the braves. The wearer of the charmed raiment jumped into the midst of the dancers and called upon them to fire at him. They complied, and at the first shot Mr. Brave who had on the "bullet proof" shirt fell to the ground mortally wounded. When General Brooke heard of the affair he simply remarked dryly, "Probably the shirt was not long enough."[43]

A variation of this story was reported from Pine Ridge: Scouts last night brought information from the hostile camp of Red Dog on Wounded Knee Creek that aptly illustrates the depth of the fanatical belief among the Indians on the coming and power of the Messiah. Mrs. Eagle Horn, wife of a prominent Indian in the Messiah crazed band, had gained considerable reputation during the past few weeks as a powerful wakan, which, translated, means mysterious woman who can perform miracles. As a test of her abilities, she called the band together yesterday and told them she could make them impervious to the bullets of the soldiers and prevent them from being harmed in any manner.

Having a great faith in her mysterious power, Porcupine, a leading Indian, volunteered to offer himself as a subject on which to bestow her divine influence to prevent him from being harmed by the leaden messengers of the firearms. It was arranged among the Crows that Porcupine should mount his pony and fight single-handed against the balance of the band. After receiving the necessary blessing from the mysterious woman, Porcupine prepared to mount his pony, but while doing so his Winchester in some manner became discharged, the bullet taking effect in his leg below the knee and inflicting a serious wound.

Almost a panic immediately resulted and the Indians were loud in their derision of the prophetess, claiming that she was an impostor. They have now entirely lost faith in her and she has been relegated to the rear of the councils of the tribe. Such instances as this will do wonders toward rescuing the Indians from the fanatical belief that is now ingrained in them, and even if let alone it would be but a short time until they would clearly see the error of their ways and lose faith in the Messiah and the good things he has promised them when he comes to deliver them from the power of the white people.[44]

These colorful reports, including placing the Ghost shirt as far back as

1876, were probably fictions created by a reporter or his informant. Even in the face of mounting military forces, settlers were concerned that Ghost dancers who believed they were invulnerable could be dangerous.

As the situation at Pine Ridge stabilized, Miles turned his attention north and to Sitting Bull's camp on Grand River.

BUFFALO BILL'S LAST TRAIL

Col. William F. Cody's popular outdoor exhibition, Buffalo Bill's "Wild West" had completed the 1890 summer season of a triumphant European tour. Cody returned to the United States after putting his troop into winter headquarters in Germany. Miles, upon learning that Cody was back in the United States, summoned the scout to Chicago. They were old friends and mutual admirers, and Miles had a mission for Cody.

Miles outlined his reason for calling Cody to Chicago in his annual report to the secretary of war, stating, It . . . was deemed advisable to secure . . . Sitting Bull, and others, and remove them for a time from that country.

To this end, authority was given on November 25, 1890, to William F. Cody, a reliable frontiersman, who has had much experience as chief of scouts and who knew Sitting Bull very well and had perhaps as much influence on him as any living man, to proceed to Standing Rock Agency to induce Sitting Bull to come in with him, making such terms as he might deem necessary and if unsuccessful in this to arrest him quietly and to remove him quickly from his camp to the nearest military station.[45]

At first view, Buffalo Bill's assignment seems absurd. He was rich, famous, and one of the best known showmen in the Western world. His "Wild West" exhibition had toured the eastern United States and much of Europe, playing to hundreds of thousands and even millions each season. He was forty-four, and his last attempt at scouting for the army had been in the summer of 1876 in the days after Custer was defeated. Cody could have refused his assignment with good conscience, but buried within the international celebrity remained a patriotic frontiersman who missed the old days.

Debunkers have attacked Cody's penchant for elaborating on his frontier deeds in stage and arena performances. Certainly, Cody had done less than his press releases and performances would have the public believe; but he was no cardboard hero. His youthful years as a scout were filled with distinction, including a Medal of Honor.[46] *His bravery was admired; he was known as a man who kept his word, a quality the Lakotas believed was rare in white men. As early as 1872, Cody had spoken out for Indian rights and denounced the breaking of treaties in several newspaper interviews. Militant Lakotas trusted Cody more than they trusted most white men.*[47]

Miles was reasonably certain that Cody could enter Sitting Bull's camp and parlay with the medicine man and his followers. Persuading Sitting Bull to surrender seemed a peaceful course of action. After all, throughout the recent weeks whites freely visited Sitting Bull's village on the Grand River.

On November 24 the old friends enjoyed a convivial dinner at a prominent Chicago restaurant and discussed Cody's mission.

Having no standing as an army officer or as a government agent, *Cody said*, it was necessary for me to be supplied with some sort of credentials, in order to secure the assistance I should need on my mission. When I informed General Miles of this, he took out one of his visiting cards from a case and wrote the following on the back of it:

> CONFIDENTIAL
> HEADQUARTERS DIVISION OF THE MISSOURI
>
> Chicago, Ill., Nov. 24, 1890
>
> Col. Cody,
>
> You are hereby authorized to secure the person of Sitting Bull and deliver him to the nearest com'g officer of U.S., troops taking a receipt and reporting your action.
>
> Nelson A. Miles
> Major General
> Com'g

Miles added the following request:

> Com'd'g officers will please give Col. Cody transportation for himself and party and any protection he may need for a small party.
>
> Nelson A. Miles[48]

Two days later it was reported that Buffalo Bill packed up his collection of rifles and left the city with Frank Powell, known as White Beaver; R. H. Haslam, known as Pony Bob, and John Keith, of North Platte, Neb. With these companions Buffalo Bill intends to strike terror into the hearts of his old Sioux enemies, and the war whoop of the famous scout will drown the yell of the Indian fanatics.[49] *The satirical tone here suggests that some of the press neither took the mission seriously nor saw much danger in it. Even so, if Cody could persuade Sitting Bull to surrender, it would be a national publicity coup.*

Once the scout was on his way, Miles requested orders to go to Washing-

ton to confer with his superior General Schofield, General of the Army. His request was granted.

As Miles departed Chicago, he told reporters, "I go to Washington to confer with the General of the Army concerning the Indian situation. The situation is grave, and the necessity for a vigorous winter campaign is becoming more and more apparent. We are probably face to face with a winter campaign. The hostile Indians ought to be compelled to surrender and they ought to be dismounted and disarmed, and they will be. That is all I can say."[50]

In spite of the continuing mass surrenders of Ghost dancers, Miles insisted there would be a winter war. This contention ran counter to the experience of veteran Indian fighters. The Lakotas had never gone to war in winter, and Miles, a veteran of several campaigns in the Indian wars, certainly knew this.

RIDING INTO THE JAWS OF CONVIVIALITY

Buffalo Bill's arrival in Bismarck, North Dakota, was reported on November 27: His party will go directly to Sitting Bull's camp, on Grand River. It will be remembered that Sitting Bull did not come in on Saturday, the regular ration day, but sent word that his child was sick. It is believed Buffalo Bill was sent out to get at the bottom of the Messiah craze.[51]

Charles W. Allen commemorated the scout's appearance with a satirical piece written for the "Chadron Democrat": Beefalo Bill, the long haired unterrified western scout, has torn himself away from the pleasures of the Old World and the seductive company of kings, queens, jacks, and ten spots, and hastened to the scene of the bloody conflict to fearless aid in the demolition of commissary cigars and government whiskey. Bison William's long experience on the frontier of Omaha and North Platte will doubtless prove very beneficial to the curled darlings of West Point, who have been accustomed to take theirs with sugar and nutmeg.[52]

Allen apparently believed that Cody would join the troops in their leisure-time drinking and carousing rather than entering into any truly dangerous enterprise; indeed, what followed resembled a comic operetta.

Upon learning of Buffalo Bill's imminent arrival, McLaughlin wrote to schoolmaster and spy John Carignan and requested a status report on the situation at Grand River: Everything is reported quiet or rather quieting down at the other agencies, and I do not believe any trouble will grow out of this craze if prudence is used.

A telegram says that Colonel Cody (Buffalo Bill) and a special agent are in Mandan en route here, and will reach here tonight.

Write me a line and send by bearer as to what your observations have been since you returned to Grand River.

Is the dance going on, are the number of dancers increasing or decreasing, is their enthusiasm as great as it was, and do you believe that any Indians have gone to Pine Ridge or other agencies from here?[53]

Carignan replied by courier six hours later: I sent a courier back immediately as I do not wish Indians to know of his coming down. I have been out twice in the Camps since Tuesday and find everything quieter; dancing still at Sitting Bull's, but not in large number, owing to the fact that Male Bear has started a dance on Little Oak Creek.

At a council held at Iron Star's house today, I saw the principal men of the new dance, with the exception of Sitting Bull, if any one were to leave the reserve I am confident that some of those at council would have been amongst them. The Indians seem to be very peaceably inclined, and I do not apprehend any trouble.

The Indians have been told that the soldiers are coming down here, and are badly frightened. If they were assured different there would be no danger of any of them leaving. I have done all I could in telling them that the reports they have heard are all lies, and that no one would try to prevent them from dancing. I am positive that no trouble need be apprehended from Sitting Bull and his followers, unless they are forced to defend themselves and think it would be advisable to keep all strangers other than employees, who have business amongst the Indians away from here.[54]

McLaughlin, in spite of this reassuring report, did not want interference on his reservation, but he was powerless to stop Cody. He immediately set about rectifying the situation.

By then, Buffalo Bill was well on his way to his meeting with Sitting Bull. Frank Zahn told Walter S. Campbell, My father, William P. Zahn, [a translator and scout] had a log cabin at the mouth of the Cannon Ball River at that time. Cody stopped and asked my father to accompany him to Fort Yates. Said Cody, "Bill (meaning my father), I have enough stuff here in the buggy for every pound Bull weighs."

Cody then said, "Sitting Bull is blamed for this Ghost Dance craze and I am going to try and get him into the agency."

Said my father, "Bill (meaning Cody), if they leave Old Bull alone, he will stop this dance, cold weather will be coming on and the Indians will break camp and go to their homes."[55]

Cody and his entourage ignored Zahn's advice and proceeded to Standing Rock, arriving there sometime during the afternoon of November 28.

Lt. Matthew Forney Steele, a young officer stationed at Standing Rock, remembered: Colonel Cody announced to Colonel Drum that he had come to arrest Sitting Bull and he backed up his announcement by presenting General Miles's visiting card on which the officer, who was at the time the division commander with headquarters at Chicago, had written an order directing the commanding officer of Fort Yates to let Colonel Cody have such assistance as he demanded to enable him to make the arrest of Sitting Bull.

It was certainly a very extraordinary order for a division commander to send one of his best post commanders.

But Colonel Cody stated that he was going to arrest Sitting Bull, and that is what General Miles's note ordered our post commander to aid him in doing. All Colonel Cody asked of Colonel Drum was a team to take him down to Sitting Bull's camp. He did not want any soldiers; he was going to make the arrest single-handed.

Well, McLaughlin and Colonel Drum and all of us knew that if Colonel Cody made any such attempt he would be killed and it would be the beginning of war with Sitting Bull's band. So Buffalo Bill must be stopped if possible. He must be kept at Fort Yates until telegrams could be got through to Washington and replies received back. Meantime Buffalo Bill with his companions must be "entertained" at the officers' club to detain him,—and it took the Indian agent and the post trader and all the convivial officers of the garrison serving in relays to "entertain" them.[56]

Colonel Drum, the post commander, agreed, saying, A discussion was commenced in regard to the situation, but it was noticed that Colonel Cody who asked for whiskey was somewhat intoxicated and that the Colonel continued to drink and was in no condition to attend to business that afternoon and evening.

Had Colonel Cody been in condition to attend to business when he first arrived, it is possible, he might have got Sitting Bull; but I hardly think it probable, unless he bought him.[57] *The wagon load of gifts suggests that buying Sitting Bull was indeed Buffalo Bill's plan.*

According to A. R. Chapin, an assistant U.S. Army surgeon at Standing Rock, Cody made things easy. As he left the train to come to Yates he received word of the birth of a grandchild (I believe his first), and he had to celebrate. Of course, his idea of a celebration was one grand spree. The officers at the post were told of what was going on and requested to assist but his "capacity" was such that it took practically all in details of two or three at a time to keep him interested and busy through the day.[58]

While Buffalo Bill was otherwise occupied, McLaughlin sent a telegram to Washington, protesting Cody's mission: William F. Cody (Buffalo Bill) has arrived here with commission from General Miles to arrest Sitting Bull. Such a step at present is unnecessary and unwise, as it will precipitate a fight which cannot be averted. A few Indians still dancing, but it does not mean mischief at present. I have matters well in hand, and when proper time arrives can arrest Sitting Bull by Indian police without bloodshed. I ask attention to my letter of November 19. Request General Miles order to Cody be rescinded and request immediate answer.[59]

Earl A. Brininstool, after interviewing an unnamed participant in the drinking bout, wrote, Colonel Cody seemed quite willing to remain at the officers' club for the balance of that day and night, quite unconscious of the errand which brought him to Fort Yates, while the post officers by "relays" entertained him. During that afternoon and evening "all went merry as a marriage bell" at the officers' club, and Colonel Cody had apparently forgotten about Sitting Bull and the object of his visit to Fort Yates.[60]

What reporter Allen had anticipated had happened. Cody, reputed to be an accomplished drinker, seems to have suffered no ill effects from his afternoon and evening of conviviality. When he stumbled into his bed is unknown, but Lieutenant Steele says, Early next morning Cody demanded his team and set out for Sitting Bull's camp on Grand River. No message had arrived from Washington calling him back, but two Indian couriers were stationed on the door step of the adjutant's office with the reins of their ponies in hand, ready to mount and fly after Colonel Cody the instant such a message should come.[61]

Much has been made of Cody's half-day delay, but Miles had not set a deadline for Cody. A late afternoon or early evening departure from Standing Rock on November 28th would have achieved only another night of camping on the trail. If McLaughlin had not been plotting to stop the mission, Cody's afternoon and evening drinking bout would have merely been a convivial interlude with old friends.

In spite of the delays, the "Chicago Tribune" reported, At about eleven o'clock, accompanied by an interpreter and one or two others, Colonel Cody left the agency for Bull's camp, which they will doubtless reach sometime tonight. It appears that trouble is anticipated in case the arrest is attempted, and the military people at Fort Yates, adjoining this agency, are busily engaged making preparation for a campaign, although as quietly as possible. The two troops of the Eighth Cavalry, F and O, are getting in readiness to take the field at a moment's notice. Ammunition sufficient for an extended campaign and rations for ten days have been issued to the troops, and all preparations made for a movement at any moment, day or night. It really begins to look like war just now, but it is hoped and believed that such a calamity will be averted.

Couriers arrived from Bull's camp last night report dancing going on, but everything [is] quiet and orderly.[62]

With plenty of robes to keep out the intense cold, *Cody writes*, we started out on our journey a little apprehensive but fully determined to go through with it. Five or six miles from the post we met three men in a wagon driving toward the agency. They told us that Sitting Bull's camp had been lately moved, and that it was now further down the river. I knew that if the old man was really on the warpath he would be moving up the river, not down, so I felt considerably reassured.[63]

At this point, the plot against Cody's mission thickened. According to Steele, Another ruse had been arranged. Two roads ran from Yates to the Grand River villages. They were parallel to each other and four miles apart. It could not be sure which one Buffalo Bill would take. A man was thereby sent out on each of these roads several hours before Colonel Cody's departure, with confidential instructions. One of these men was met about twenty-two miles out by Cody's party. The man, a half-breed who spoke English, was apparently coming in from Sitting Bull's village on Grand River. He greeted the party and asked them casually which way they were bound.

"Oh, we are going down to see him," the half-breed replied, "Old Bull is on his way to the agency at this minute on the other road."

They parlayed a little now and Colonel Cody convinced himself that the half-breed knew what he was talking about, and then turned round and started back for Yates with his party.[64]

Mary Collins tells a similar story: Colonel McLaughlin, knowing the Indians and their ideas, sent a messenger to warn Buffalo Bill that Sitting Bull was coming to Fort Yates by another road. Buffalo Bill immediately turned back. This was only a ruse to dissuade Buffalo Bill from capturing Sitting Bull, but he was ignorant of the fact and returned. This gave Colonel Drum time to get Buffalo Bill sent away.[65]

DERRING-DO UNDONE

As Cody set out on his mission, Miles arrived in Washington.[66] Sometime on November 29 it was decided that Cody would be recalled. Whether Miles was involved in the decision is uncertain. The "New York Times" reported from Standing Rock while Miles was meeting with his superiors: Information is obtained tonight that the commanding officer of the post has received instructions from General Miles to take steps to postpone the arrest of Sitting Bull for the present.

Major McLaughlin this morning anticipated such an order and sent two couriers out on the road toward Bull's camp, one to take a station at a point ten miles and the other at twenty miles, so that when the news came a courier from here would be immediately dispatched with orders to Buffalo Bill not to attempt to make any arrest. The couriers are at this writing flying over the prairie as fast as their little ponies can carry them, in order, if possible, to catch Buffalo Bill, who has six hours' start of them, before he reaches Sitting Bull's camp. If they catch him all will be well.[67]

In the meantime, Steele writes, a message arrived which Colonel Drum and Major McLaughlin were hoping for and anxiously expecting from Washington, a message directing Colonel Cody be recalled. . . . He was met by an Indian courier riding at full speed and was handed a copy of the message.[68]

Cody, in his ghostwritten autobiography, writes that the courier gave him a telegram, which read: The order for the detention of Sitting Bull has been rescinded. You are hereby ordered to return to Chicago and report to General Miles. *According to Cody, it was signed by President Benjamin Harrison.*[69]

I returned to the Post, *the disappointed Cody writes*, turned back my presents at a loss to myself, and paid the interpreter fifty dollars for his day's work. He was very glad to have the fifty and a whole skin, for he could not figure how the five hundred would be of much help to him if he had been stretched out on the Plains with an Indian bullet through him.

I was supplied with conveyance back to Mandan . . . and took my departure the next morning. Afterward, in Indianapolis, President Harrison informed me that he had allowed himself to be persuaded against my mission in opposition to his own judgment, and said he was very sorry that he had not allowed me to proceed.[70]

Brininstool speculates, The Colonel was doubtless highly indignant, but he continued on to Fort Yates, and a few hours later departed for the railway station at Mandan, and the incident became a closed one.

Which is why was doubtless saved to the world, for a time, a royal good fellow and a most excellent showman.[71]

Whether Cody had been in any danger is questionable. No other white who visited Sitting Bull at Grand River had been attacked.

On December 1 the "New York Times" reported from Bismarck: Buffalo Bill arrived here tonight on his way East. His mission to Standing Rock failed, owing to the clash between the Interior and War Departments. He was on his way to Sitting Bull's camp when a courier overtook him, with dispatches from General Miles countermanding his previous orders. It transpires that the Interior Department, acting on the advice of Major McLaughlin, would not consent to the arrest of Sitting Bull.[72]

Miles quickly wrote Cody a letter of commendation. It included a not too subtle criticism of his superiors, and, inferentially, the president of the United States: I regret that you did not accomplish the object of your mission, but it was, however, not through any fault of yours. On the representation of Agent McLaughlin that in his opinion the arrest of a certain Indian would precipitate hostilities, the president gave the order to suspend arrest. I do not concur in the opinion of the agent.

I appreciate the energy, spirit, and fortitude of your undertaking and realize that you would enter into the work the same as you have in other hazardous service.[73]

Several days later, General Schofield bluntly repudiated Miles's plan. "I did not at all believe in the Buffalo Bill idea," *he told reporters*, "and that purpose was quickly abandoned."[74]

Miles had been publicly repudiated by his commander. Years later, still stinging from his failure, Miles would tersely write, I concluded that if the so-called Messiah was to appear in that country, Sitting Bull had better be out of it, and I considered it of the first importance to secure his arrest and removal from that country. My first effort in that direction proved a failure, owing to adverse influence that was used to defeat my purpose.[75]

A disappointed Buffalo Bill, still ready for action, returned to his home in North Platte to await further developments. Within weeks he would be back in action again, not as a colonel, but as a brigadier general in the Nebraska National Guard. As Cody waited, McLaughlin launched his own plan to end Sitting Bull's influence.

9. In the Corridors of Power

They made us many promises, more than I can remember, but they never kept but one; they promised to take our land and they took it.
—*An Old Lakota man* at Pine Ridge

DIFFERING POINTS OF VIEW

On December 2nd, an incredible letter was delivered to Acting Indian Commissioner Belt. In it Special Census Agent A. T. Lea reported from Pine Ridge, There is no suffering among the Indians for the want of food.[1] *Lea spent several weeks in the Dakotas before he arrived at this conclusion. In addition to this ridiculous conclusion, Lea had not endeared himself to the Lakotas at the Rosebud Agency. While there, he lopped two thousand people from the census roles, removing a proportionate amount from the limited rations that were available.*[2] *In the weeks to come Lea's findings and actions would remain a source of controversy and anger among the Lakota leaders; Lea's actions caused even more starvation than the starvation he denied existed.*

Upon hearing this, the "Chadron (NE) Democrat"'s editorial writer angrily asked, Who is this man Lea that speaks so glibly about the Indians of Pine Ridge Agency having a superabundance of rations? We venture to say he is a monumental fraud and prevaricator, and one of that class of persons whose appointments to the Indian service has precipitated the present Indian trouble upon the country.[3]

On the same day as this article, the U.S. Senate launched a fiery debate regarding what should be done about the situation in the Dakotas. Here, too, Lea became a focal point in the discussions about the plight of the Lakotas.

The debates mirrored the public's attitude toward the Lakotas in particular and Native Americans in general. The country was polarized in this issue, and the majority questioned the need for honoring the treaties by increasing rations to the Dakota reservation system. A minority insisted that all treaties be honored.

The debates began with a resolution to send arms to the state militias in the region:

COCKRELL: Let the joint resolution be read as it has been agreed to.
VICE PRESIDENT: The joint resolution will be read as amended.
The chief clerk read as follows:

Resolved, That the secretary of war, under such regulations as he may prescribe, be, and he is hereby, authorized to issue to the States of North and South Dakota and Nebraska, out of any ordinance stores which

> may belong to the United States and which have been superseded and are no longer issued to the army, 1,000 rifles each and ammunition for the same, not to exceed 50 ball cartridges for each arm, to enable the authorities of said States to assist the United States in protecting citizens and their property against depredations by Indians: *Provided*, That the said ordinance stores shall remain the property of the United States and that the governors of said States shall each furnish security satisfactory to the secretary of war for the care and return of same arms when the same shall be demanded: *And provided further*, That the quotas to said States under the act of February 12, 1887, for arming and equipping the militia shall not be hereby diminished.

The first to speak was the eloquent Senator Daniel Voorhees of Indiana. Democrat Voorhees, nicknamed the Tall Tree of the Wabash because of his leanness and height, was a proponent of honoring past treaties. He immediately expressed concern about reports issued by General Miles regarding starvation among the Sioux:

VOORHEES: Mr. President, I shall not oppose the passage of this resolution; I shall not vote against this supply of arms to that threatened people; but I cannot let it pass, with the feelings I entertain in regard to the administration of Indian Affairs, without a word.

If the provision of the resolution was to issue one hundred thousand rations and more to the starving Indians it would be more consistent with the Christian civilization than the policy we are now pursuing. When the major-general of that department publicly interviews and publishes the fact that the Indians are driven into revolt—rebellion, if you please to call it so—and to the savagery of Indian warfare by starvation, it becomes inexpiable crime, in my judgment, on the part of this government to stand silently by and do nothing except furnish arms which may kill them. General Miles has stated to the public, and he has so stated to me before the publication of his interview, that these Indians are being starved into hostility and that they prefer to die fighting to being starved to death.

I look upon the policy which has been pursued in the administration of Indian Affairs as a crime in the sight of God and man. I look upon the present outbreak, or threatened outbreak, which will bring not merely destruction of the Indian, but also bathe the snows of the Northwest with the blood of our own brave soldiers and officers, as something revolting in the extreme. Instead of sitting here debating election bills and force bills and providing the issuance of arms to the States of the Northwest for their protection, we should be hurrying anxiously, eagerly, to provide for feeding these starving people.

General Miles says they have been hungry for the past two years, that they are wretched and perfectly desperate, and would rather die with arms in their hands than die from pitiless starvation. They have no newspapers. Their privations and sufferings can not be made known. They have been suffering in silence for years while there is guilt, all the same, somewhere. There is deep blood guiltiness somewhere on this subject, and I have intended to introduce a resolution asking for an investigation, but, upon reflection, I have entire respect for the Committee on Indian Affairs personally and as a committee, and I have no right to assume to instruct them. And yet, sir, in some of the branches of the government, or perhaps in more than one, there is a blood guiltiness that will have to be answered for.

Somebody is responsible for starving these people into hostility, a hostility which, as I have said, will cost them not merely their lives, but cost the lives perhaps of thousands of American citizens and hundreds of American soldiers. A condition of things has been brought about by a penurious and parsimonious policy, or by dishonesty, I know not which, that jeopardizes the whole Northwest and causes a soldier like General Miles, with a grave and serious aspect, to speak of the situation in terms of the greatest apprehension.

Why sit we here idle and do nothing, when we know that by sending food to these people they will stop their frenzied meetings and Ghost dances? They are dancing the dance of death by starvation and the dance of desperation.

While I am willing that this resolution shall pass and that the white people shall arm themselves for protection against the impolicy of this government and its frightful consequences, still I could not refrain from emphasizing the occasion by these few words.

I dislike to talk, Mr. President; I dislike to criticize; I dislike to animadvert upon anybody; but I repeat there is a crime somewhere in the policy of this government towards the Indian people which somebody ought to be made to answer for and to answer for with swift severity. I do not know, sir, what the Committee on Indian Affairs propose; doubtless what is wise and best; but I have heard nothing. I have heard no endeavor to reach the real trouble that exists amongst these Indians. there may be some measures going on, although when I asked General Miles whether we could do something to avert a pending strife his answer was that he feared it was too late.

That was his answer. Whether it was good or not, I am glad my skirts are clear of any of the blood which will be shed growing out of a starvation policy, a policy of inequity and of crime against the Indians, a policy enough to keep them from starving to death when dispossessed of their homes.

After some discussion, the Republican senator from Massachusetts, Henry L. Dawes, rose to refute Voorhees's assertions. He had investigated Indian Affairs in the Dakotas with a select committee in 1885 and supported cutting the rations promised in past treaties. He held the view that privation would force the plains tribes into becoming self-sufficient.

DAWES: Mr. President, I am glad that the senator from Indiana (Mr. Voorhees) has discovered the real cause of the trouble among the Indians at this time, for those who live among them and those who have had a great deal to do with them in the past are now engaged—General Miles and others—are very much perplexed, and there is great diversity of opinion as to what is the cause and what is the best remedy for the evils which now threaten the peace and the life of the frontiersmen. Without doubt, a great deal that the senator from Indiana has said is true, that there is a large body of Indians who are starving, short of food, and that, that condition of things very much aggravates the evil which is prevalent among those Indians; but that it is the very origin of the evil or that a supply of food to them will be the cure is very much doubted by those most familiar with the Indian character and with the causes, so far as they are known, of this trouble.

The Indians who are starving are the Indians that have been led by this religious craze, if I may so call it, to abandon their homes and their places of residence and follow a fanatical chief upon the warpath and abandon all the sources of supply and means of support that they have hitherto enjoyed. Combined with that has been the drought which has prevailed for two or three years among the white people as well as among the Indians in that quarter, so that large sections of the country settled entirely by the white people have appealed to the charity of the United States to keep the inhabitants from starving.

Now, sir, I apprehend that very soon there will come here from the other body propositions which will render it necessary for us to go more fully into the causes and the best means of remedying these evils and protecting our people from the impending peril, which is great, and with which I, in conference with General Miles, was greatly impressed.

He sees only the Indians starving who are on the warpath. The difficulty with the Indian service all along in the past has been a constant change of policy. Heretofore for years it has been impressed upon Congress that the best way to treat the Indian was to starve him into self-support. "Root, hog, or die" has been a phrase put up over the door sometimes of those who have administered the affairs of the Indians. So a proposition was enacted into a law by the recommendation of the Indian department that from year to year we should cut down the rations required by treaty and give notice to the Indian, "Next year you are only to have so much, and you must supplement it by the labor of your own hands."

It is well to hold out every possible inducement to the Indian to turn from his dependence upon the rations of the government to his own supply, and it is well to resort to all the devices within the limits of justice and reason to induce him to do it. This was one of the courses followed out in the Indian appropriation bill by cutting down from year to year the amount appropriated for the rations of that large body of Sioux Indians where this difficulty seems to be most aggravating, and last year the Indian appropriation bill came to us with a reduction of $150,000 below the estimate of the department. The Senate put upon it $100,000 of the $150,000, so that it was finally reduced only $50,000.

Then, again, I see in the newspapers that it is suggested at the Interior department that in reference to these Indians—and I believe it is in the estimates of this year—we go back to the supply required by the Sioux treaty twenty years ago, when the number of Sioux at this time is not, at most, more than two-thirds the number when that treaty was made, and of that two-thirds I think it is fair to state that a quarter of that two-thirds are now self-supporting Indians. When you hold out to them the alternative of supplies furnished them without labor, toil, the white man would turn from work as I have seen many a brainy Indian turn around and with a smile on his face say, "What occasion have I to work when you have stipulated to supply all my wants until I do work?"

Dawes had clearly stated the government's rationale for breaking the old treaties. After Dawes continued in this manner, Voorhees pursued the issue of starvation:

VOORHEES: Does not General Miles say that these Indians have been hungry for two years? He says they have been hungry for two years; that they have not been properly fed for two years. That is what he says.

DAWES: Of course General Miles said that to the Senator———

VOORHEES: He said that in his interview.

DAWES: But General Miles did not say anything to me beyond that; the great difficulty in dealing with these six thousand Indians who were congregating under their leaders and on the warpath was that they are starving and they have nothing to eat. They are away from their tipis and their homes, wherever they are, and are that class of Indians who never did a day's work in their lives. The Indians that have worked, the Indians that have turned toward civilization and have a plow or a hoe or a rake or are under the severalty act, are not in this line. Peace among the Indians will come and come to stay when the Indian shall have it impressed upon him that the mode of life followed by him in the past, the chase and the fishing and all that, has not only gone, but with it has gone everything else that pertains to Indian life.

VOORHEES: If the senator will allow me, I will ask if he does not know that the white people out there are suffering because of the drought; that there have been short crops, and that the Indians, whom he now speaks of as having gone to cultivating the soil, and among whom he says there has been no want, the agricultural Indians, are suffering and in want now because of the failure of crops?

DAWES: I said it twice.

VOORHEES: On the contrary, you said there was no distress amongst them.

DAWES: I said, as to the Indians General Miles has trouble with and does not know what to do with, he finds the case aggravated and finds it next to impossible to treat it safely and avoid bloodshed without feeding them, and that is why $100,000 worth of provisions are on their way there to feed these people what are in arms; and I trust that these Indians who have not gone on the warpath, and have found themselves short in their own crops like the white people will not be left to suffer or to draw the contrast that the only Indian regarded by the government is the Indian who fights the government. The peaceable Indian, the Indian who looks toward civilization and the future may starve, he may go into war, he may have a disregard of the obligations of the government toward him, and nothing is said in the Halls of Congress or anywhere else about it; but when the Indian goes on the warpath then he gets something out of the government. That is a policy which I trust is gone forever.

The senator must know that the Indian tribes have resorted to violence for the very purpose of getting out of the government grants and donations, and have told those that they have tried to induce to join them, "So long as you are peaceable and quiet you will get nothing out of the government." That day I trust is past. I hope the government will meet the present exigency just as exigencies in perilous times have to be met, but that no precedent will be established of further treatment of the Indians after this peril has passed.

Dawes saw any increase of rations as a bribe that would encourage future revolts. At no point did he admit that the rations were payment for land appropriated by the government, not a dole. Instead, he argued that cutting rations—that is, breaking treaties—was a justifiable tactic that would force the starving Lakotas into agriculture. At no point in the debate did he or his supporters mention that an agricultural way of life was nearly impossible in the land left to the Lakotas. It is also evident that neither he nor Voorhees seemed to be aware of the pacifistic nature of the ghost dance. Both sides of the debate were acting on Miles's assertion that an Indian war was imminent.

Later in the proceedings, Pearce, a Republican senator from North Dakota, rose to join the attack on Voorhees:

PEARCE: Mr. President, I wonder sometime why the white people in the locality being mentioned now do not themselves go on the warpath because they are hungry. The Indian seems to get hungry as well as noble the further we get from him. I live within a few miles of the great Sioux reservation; I have been there for the last two months, and this is the first time that I have ever heard it asserted that the Indians are on the warpath, or in danger of going on the warpath, because they were hungry. I see them everyday in the town where I live, and they are sleeker and better fed apparently than even my distinguished friend from Indiana. (Laughter.)

VOORHEES: Does the senator suppose that General Miles knows what he is talking about or does he not? Who knows best about Indian matters, the officer in command or the senator from North Dakota?

PEARCE: I will come to that. I am nearer to them than General Miles is, but as I was saying, I will come to that in a moment. I have no doubt that there are Indians in some of the agencies who are complaining of insufficient food; but it has appeared in the newspapers that General Miles has stated that the Indians are in danger of starvation, have been hungry for two years, and are going on the warpath because of that. I question very much whether the general has made that statement. I understand the secretary of war has made arrangements by which the Indians who are complaining can be fed and relieved of their hunger as near as it is possible ever to relieve the Indian of his hunger. I never saw one yet who was satisfied.

The senator from Indiana tells us in one breath that these men are starving and the next instant he tells us they are armed with Winchester rifles, mounted in fine style, and are ready to stand off 6,000 soldiers of this Republic. Why, sir, if a man was starving, if the senator from Indiana was starving, and had a Winchester rifle, I venture to say he could get a barrel of flour with it without any trouble. (Laughter.)

Mr. President, I wish to be perfectly kind in my remarks, because I used to have this same sentimental feeling regarding the Indians, but I believe the trouble today is that these Indians are fed and clothed and allowed to live upon the bounty of the government, and therefore, as the old adage says, "the devil always finds mischief for idle hands to do," and they become dangerous men. I apprehend that you may take the same number of white men and place them on reservations, and feed them and clothe them, and they will have the devil in them in less than six months and go off on the warpath themselves.

Whenever the government has been called upon, it has treated the Indian with the greatest kindness. When the report came that the Devil's Lake Indians were starving last winter, I introduced here, and interrupted the proceedings of the Senate to do so, a bill appropriating $25,000 to feed them, and under the suspension of the rules the bill was passed, and at the same time the white settlers who had gone out there to reclaim that land, to build up their homes, were suffering for the lack of food and raiment, and the government made no offer to them.

I hope, sir, that this resolution will pass, because I have seen within the last three weeks men and women fleeing into the towns, not from starving savages, but from those who, for pure mischief, those who were regarded as friendly Indians, like the Arickarees and Mandans, were marching through the country and holding a war dance for the express purpose of frightening the poor settlers and their wives and children.

The senator from Massachusetts has given me this interview with General Miles:

> The causes of the difficulty are easy of discovery. Insufficient food supplies, religious delusion, and the innate disposition of the savage to go to war must be held responsible.

The beleaguered Voorhees, sensing a discrepancy, fought back.

VOORHEES: From what paper is that?

PEARCE: The *New York Tribune.*

VOORHEES: Let me see it.

HAWLEY: Substantially the same item has gone all over the country.

PEARCE: I have no doubt, sir, that this craze, this belief that the white men are to be wiped from the face of the earth, is at the bottom of this business, and that the Indians themselves do not attribute their disposition to any lack of food.

VOORHEES: Mr. President, "insufficient food" is the first phrase the senator reads as a part of the interview with General Miles. Then other things follow. "Insufficient food supplies," a people not well fed, then, as having some religious delusions and the natural disposition of an Indian to fight rather than to starve to death. Let us see what else

General Miles says before he gets through this interview. Towards the close of it he says:

> The Northern Indian is hardy and can suffer a great deal. Yes, he can take his Winchester rifle and fast until he gets into the neighborhoods and settlements, and then he may get a barrel of flour and several scalps besides.

PEARCE: He will go for the scalps first.

VOORHEES: Here is what the senator from North Dakota doubtless could not read even with very large magnifying glasses:

> These hostile Indians—Says General Miles—have been starved into fighting, and they will prefer to die fighting rather than starve peaceably.

Why did you not read that first?

Voorhees had found an opening. Now the tables were turned, and Pearce was at a disadvantage.

PEARCE: I did not see it, in the first place, and I stated—

VOORHEES: No, indeed; "these hostile Indians have been starved into fighting." I said so. I said that was the cause. The senator from Massachusetts said it was not, and stated that General Miles had not said it.

Now, I know General Miles. I know him to be one of the most brilliant, magnificent officers the American Army ever had in it. I know him as a man of ability aside from the profession of arms. He is a man with a high sense of justice, and I will take his statement far sooner than I would that of the senator who lives near the Sioux reservation, where he and his people long for the lands belonging to the Indians and will get them as soon as possible. The military officer is an impartial observer in the discharge of his duty; the senator is the fox near the pen where the geese are. Of the one—and I do not mean to be offensive—I would not take his testimony on this subject as outweighing anything; but in the case of General Miles, with dispatches coming to him to give him information, I am willing to risk what little reputation I have in standing where he stands. I repeat not merely for the senator from North Dakota—for I pass by what he says as very light; he is an interested party; he wants the land which lies next—but I say to the senator from Massachusetts, who has some humanities (laughter)—well, he has, Mr. President, however you might doubt it from his speech here this morning—that General Miles said with the crisp sentence of a soldier.

Miles had seemingly become an authority for both sides of the issue.

Perhaps in his interviews with senators from both parties he had managed to speak with sufficient ambiguity to win the confidence of each side.

Voorhees continued to make his case, quoting Miles further:

> These hostile Indians have been starved into fighting—You understand, "have been starved into fighting." Do you hear?—and they will prefer to die fighting rather than starve peaceably.

That is the dish furnished up by the administration of Indian Affairs at this present writing. If you like it, gentlemen, take it. I would rather have any other crime laid to me than a participation in a policy which starves those Indians into fighting.

Now Voorhees's attack, striking at the economic issues that created the purchase of Lakota land, becomes vicious, The senator—I will not say the senator from Massachusetts, but the senator from North Dakota living out there and looking on their lands with longing and lust which is unspeakable—may rail at the Indian and call his life of small account and think that "the only good Indian is a dead Indian," but there are other people who die in this matter. The screams of mothers are to be heard. The wail of children is to be borne on the gale. The senator saw fit to honor me with an association with the Indians in certain points of personal appearance. I will say to him that soldiers whose lives are as valuable as his, both privates and officers, will bite the dust in this miserable war, brought on by a starvation policy, the starving of Indians into fighting. "I thank thee, Jew," for furnishing me with the paper containing this interview with General Miles.[4]

At that point the vice president moved to other business. If headlines counted, it would seem that Senator Voorhees had won the first day's debate.

> STARVED INTO REVOLT
> Mr. Voorhees's Explanation of the Indian Troubles. He Approves Gen. Miles's Statement that the Indians Prefer to Die Fighting Rather Than Be Starved to Death—A Debate in the Senate Which may Lead to Good Results.[5]

During the next day's debate, Voorhees used the starvation issue to hammer his opponents. First, Voorhees introduced new evidence to support his contention that starvation had caused the dissension in the Dakotas—a letter from Charles Foster, former governor of Ohio, who had served on the 1889 Dawes Commission:

VOORHEES: Mr. President, I do not wish to delay for a single moment the passage of the joint resolution, but after what transpired yesterday I think it but just not only to myself but to the general commanding that department as well as to the country to submit some matter that has come to my hand since.

We are all acquainted with Governor Foster of Ohio. Many of us have served in the other House with him. We know him to be a man of high character and of great prudence both in action and in expression. He has recently served upon a most important Indian commission in the section of the country now in trouble, and his views therefore ought to have, and doubtless will have, great weight. I have an interview from him as published in the *Cincinnati Enquirer*, transferred to another paper. The editor of the paper himself prefacing the interview says:

> On the history of the Sioux Indians and the causes that have led to their present uprising no man in the country, perhaps, is better informed than Ex-Governor Charles Foster, who was one of the celebrated Indian commission whose labors were recently concluded, and who resided for months amid the scenes that are now pregnant with war. The distinguished ex-governor is intimately acquainted with the chief actors in the border drama now being enacted in the Dakotas. An *Enquirer* staff correspondent, after a journey of 200 miles, called upon Governor Foster yesterday at his home in Fostoria, Ohio, for the express purpose of ascertaining his views upon the Sioux troubles, and any other information which his long familiarity with the savage tribes might enable him to furnish. The visitor was not disappointed. Governor Foster not only received him affably, but delivered his opinions regarding the Sioux uprising in a decisive and emphatic manner that added much to the interest of his conversation.

In my opinion—
Now quoting Governor Foster—

> In my opinion all the present difficulties with the Indians might easily have been avoided. The whole matter has been brought about by a combination of bad policy and the incompetence of some officials. I do not want to reflect upon the Indian department, nor upon any one in particular; but I am thoroughly acquainted with the condition of things out there and feel strongly in the matter. My full views regarding the so-called uprising of the Sioux I would not care to have expressed in print, but I will relate a little history to you and then you will understand the case for yourself. In 1868 the government fixed the reservation for the Sioux, a tract of land 400 miles long and almost as large as the State of Indiana, and as time went on it was found very desirable to gain possession of their land, which cut South Dakota in two, leaving the Black Hills on the west and the territory east of the Missouri on the other side and extending into Nebraska and North Dakota.

I made some suggestions yesterday about the innate proclivity of a white man to steal an Indian's land. I find Governor Foster has the same view on the subject:

> But it is necessary to gain the consent of three-fourths of the Sioux before taking their land. Congress simplified matters by taking the lands first and getting the consent afterward, and a commission of three, of which I was a member, was appointed to gain these consents. Well, it had been provided in the bill that the Indians were getting certain rations, which would be diminished in quantity as the Sioux advanced in civilization and grew able to take care of themselves. Our commissioner told the Indians about this and of course gave them to understand that the government would furnish them with provisions as long as they needed them. But these promises have not been kept.
>
> The correspondent then asks: How do you mean?
>
> Governor Foster answers: Simply this. When we were out there the Sioux were suffering from the effects of a bad summer. Why, sir, we went up the river when the thermometer registered 110. The crops planted by the Indians were in fine condition. Ten days later we returned and found it all ruined. The grain was withered, everything growing blasted by the continued dryness and heat. Now, was it reasonable for the department to enforce the plan of gradually reducing the rations when such a calamity had fallen upon poor Lo? That would have been done, however, had we not presented the case at Washington and secured appropriation for the tail end of the winter.
>
> The correspondent asks: But this year?
>
> The governor answers: That is what I am coming to. My dear sir, bad as the summer of 1889 was, this summer was much worse. The Indians' crops were destroyed and they had nothing to live upon except what the government might give them. Why, the white settlers had to appeal for assistance from the East. The Sioux were in just as bad a condition, or worse. They were starving, sir, that is all, and that is what caused this talk of war. The Sioux are starving.

This is the language of Governor Charles Foster, not mine. I repeat it. He says:

> The Sioux are starving.
>
> The correspondent asks: Did they get no rations?
>
> He answered: Not enough; a miserable pittance of what they should have had. And even after the bad summer another cut was made in the rations.

I will repeat that:

> Even after the bad summer another cut was made in their rations. Give the Sioux plenty to eat and there will be no further trouble.

This comes from a man of large and long experience, the peer of anybody on this floor, recently connected with the administration of Indian Affairs in that department, and he tells this Senate, he tells the country, "Give the Sioux plenty to eat and there will be no further trouble." That is what I thought yesterday. That is the reason why I said I would rather vote for the issuance of 100,000 or 500,000 rations than for arms with which to kill them.

Governor Foster proceeds:

> I believe the trouble has been greatly exaggerated anyway, and in this belief I am corroborated in some things that I heard today. But I want to say right now that of the 5,600 Sioux Indians in the various tribes, 4,600 signed our treaty, and I have yet to see the name of one of these concerned in the present difficulties.

These are the "bad Indians" who were talked of here by the senator from North Dakota. They have kept faith, according to Governor Foster. Every man who has signed the treaty, he says, has kept the faith. The name of not one of the signers appears in these difficulties, and yet they are to be arraigned and denounced here as faithless. I do not mean by the senator from Massachusetts. I know the senator's feelings on this subject. He desires to be just. Whether he has had sufficient power or whether he had prescience sufficient to foresee these troubles that might have been avoided, is not for me to discuss. I do not enter upon that; but I have felt it my duty to lay these views of Governor Foster before this body in connection with the discussion which took place yesterday, and these views fully and emphatically uphold the views which General Miles expressed to the public.[6]

Foster's contention that three-fourths of the Lakota had signed the treaty was questionable. In any event, those who signed the treaty were labeled "progressives" and those who did not were called "nonprogressives" or "hostiles." This was even the view of the sympathetic Voorhees.

Later in the debate Voorhees returned to Governor Foster's letter:

VOORHEES: I will read a little further from Governor Foster's interview by way of answer to some things that have been said:

> There is Sitting Bull, about whom so much is said. He is only a feeble old man, hardly respected in his tribe.

The senator from Massachusetts seemed to want to lay the whole thing upon him, a bad Indian, of course.

DAWES: Now, see how these men differ. General Miles told me last thing before he took the cars here that Sitting Bull was the greatest Indian that had ever lived in this country since Tecumseh.

VOORHEES: Why not subpoena them? Why not send for them before your committee?

DAWES: I would say to the senator that General Miles has no personal knowledge of the condition of things there.

VOORHEES: He has gone out there.

DAWES: He has been on the Pacific coast for the last few years.

VOORHEES: I understand.

DAWES: And has come to his new assignment very lately. I do not understand that he has been on this ground at all. Governor Foster, as is said by the senator from Nebraska (Paddock), got all of his information of the condition of things a year and a half ago, and not now.

Here is this man, whom I tried to quote from memory this morning, who has been on the ground for fifteen or twenty years, and who has the confidence of all political parties and administration and kept through all of them as a pattern man, knowing more than anybody else about the condition of things there, and he does not put it on that ground. The fact is as I have stated.

VOORHEES: I understood the senator from Massachusetts to say yesterday that there was a large amount of rations now on the way and much needed. Why did not this good man you speak of call for them earlier to prevent this crisis?

DAWES: Because this good man I speak of thinks the crisis arises from some other reason.

VOORHEES: I will submit some other testimony. Governor Foster says:

> The Ghost Dance and the Messiah were new to me. I think, however, that neither is the origin of the present discontent among the Indians. It is just as I said at the beginning: lack of food is the prime cause of the trouble.

Mr. President, I said yesterday that I could not trace the administration of Indian Affairs through all its ramifications and channels so as to locate the trouble. I can diagnose the disease, though—it is some place—and here, as throwing a little light on that subject, I will read another paragraph from Governor Foster's most interesting interview and leave the senator from Iowa to attack him on that if he chooses. Governor Foster says:

> I also met George Wright, one of the best Indian agents in Dakota, and he told me all about the trouble out there, and how it originated, and his story only confirmed me in what I already believed.

Wright, the Rosebud agent, had recently been in Washington to defend his census figures and prove he had not inflated the number of Lakotas at the Rosebud Reservation. How his exoneration related to Lea's reduction of the population figures at Wright's reservation is not known.

DAWES: Who?

VOORHEES: Mr. Wright. There were several mistakes made by the department, and when I say this I do not mean to reflect upon the officials in charge. Perhaps I should say that the department has been unfortunate in some instances. One grave error was made in discharging Agent Gallagher from Pine Ridge and in putting Royer in his place. Gallagher, who lives in Decatur, Indiana, is a Democrat.

I know him well and was responsible for his appointment. Governor Foster continues and says:

> But when you have a good Indian agent you want to keep him, no matter what his politics. They are few enough, sir. They fired Gallagher, a man who has always kept his Indians in order, and replaced him with Royer, who is evidently unfit for the position, at least in times of trouble. There was discontent among the Indians, because of insufficient rations, and Royer, frightened, sent his wife to civilization and let the Sioux do pretty much as they pleased, resting satisfied with the fact they did not attack him. Wright, at Rosebud Agency, did differently. He told the Indians that they must stop the Ghost Dance, and they did it. He told me today all was quiet among the Sioux except at Pine Ridge.

With this contribution to the sum of knowledge, I will stop reading from the interview with Governor Foster. One other word, however, I wish to say.

The senator from Massachusetts broke out in a fierce and clamorous protest against newspaper men. Sir, I thank God for newspaper men, especially in dark places. Newspapers are not sufficient in that quarter of the world. I said yesterday in my remarks that there were no newspapers out there to proclaim the miseries of these Indians. They have suffered in silence for long years, and to every newspaper man who has thrown a single ray of light on this miserable business I return my heartfelt and profound thanks. Newspaper men may get things wrong sometimes, but in the main, in the great volume of what they do, they contribute to the light and knowledge of the world and to the triumph of the cause of justice. That I have to say in response to the criticism of the senator from Massachusetts.

After a brief interchange between other senators, Dawes rose and questioned the point of the entire discussion:

DAWES: In this peril perhaps it is unwise for us to take a moment's time to inquire what is the cause of it, except this habit of solving the Indian question once a fortnight by a column in a newspaper or an interview with somebody, and spreading it out, made up principally of charges of injustice and fraud upon the government of the United States. It seems to me people are being misled in that regard. With exceptions I have it to say that I believe that for the last twenty-five years, the government of the United States has been in the main dealing as fairly and as honestly with the Indians as has been the dealing of man with man in this country. There have been exceptions. There have been attempts to overreach him, but the condition of things, as the senator from Colorado has said, is not such that cheating the Indian in the dark and by devices and by tricks has passed away. The counting of cattle into five or six thousand by driving them around a hill can no longer be practiced upon Indians, as in days past.

The Indian has, in the main—certainly for the last ten or fifteen years—been treated fairly and squarely.[7]

On December 4, after further debate, the arms bill was amended to include weapons shipments to the states of North and South Dakota, Nebraska, and Wyoming. After it was passed, a joint resolution was introduced for an appropriation of five thousand dollars for a Senate-sponsored investigation "as to the causes of the trouble among the Indians."[8] *No one seemed prepared to believe that the Lakotas were starving.*

MILES MOVES AHEAD

Miles's maneuvering for a strengthened military was paying off, but he did not relent in pursuing his objective. To gain public support, he took his case to the press almost daily.

On December 2, as the Senate debate raged, Miles glumly told reporters, "The seriousness of the situation has not been exaggerated. The dissatisfaction is more widespread than it has been at any time for years. The conspiracy extends to more different tribes than have heretofore been hostile, but that are now in full sympathy with each other and are scattered over a larger area of country than in the whole history of Indian warfare. It is a more comprehensive plot than anything ever inspired by the prophet Tecumseh, or even Pontiac. A general uprising would be a most serious affair.

"Altogether there are in the Northwest about 30,000 who are affected by the Messiah craze; that means fully 6,000 fighting men. Of this number at least one-third would not go on the warpath, so that leaves us with about 4,000 adversaries. There are 6,000 other Indians in Indian Territory who will need to be watched if active operations take place. Four thousand Indians can make an immense amount of trouble, but the tithe of that number were concerned in the Minnesota massacre, yet they killed more than five hundred settlers in a very brief span of time. The Indians are better armed now than they ever were, and their supply of horses is all that could be desired. Every buck has a Winchester rifle and he knows how to use it. In the matter of subsistence they are taking little risk. They can live on cattle just as well as they used to on buffalo, and the numerous horse ranches will furnish them with fresh stock when cold and starvation ruin their mounts. The northern Indian is hardy and can suffer a great deal. I hope the problem may be solved without bloodshed, but such a happy ending to the trouble seems improbable."[9]

Other reports refute Miles's grim assessment of the situation. Certainly, his estimate of the number of Ghost dancers was inflated; and at no time did he mention the widely known pacifistic nature of the religion. Either he was acting upon faulty intelligence reports or he was positioning the army for the upcoming appropriations bill. Truly unconscionable, though, were his alarmist remarks, which added to the growing fears of a new Indian war.

As Miles was predicting an Indian war, Belt interpreted the Ghost Dance as a matter of tribal politics when he spoke to a group of reporters: "It seems to me that the whole trouble has been brought on by old bucks, who began to become restless, partly from idleness, partly from a desire to regain their influence over the people, and partly from undue influence of designing whites, but largely from inexplicable causes. (Parenthetically, I might add, pure cussedness.) The main leaders in the present trouble are men who have been recognized as big chiefs in days gone by, but not so recognized now. Yet they think they see in this movement an opportunity to regain their lost titles."[10]

Belt's evaluation of the situation had little basis in reality. Most of the older chiefs in the southern reservations still retained considerable influence and were working to calm the situation. Even Sitting Bull at Standing Rock, while permitting dancing at Grand River, had adopted a wait-and-see attitude toward the dance and its power. With the exception of Big Foot and his band of Miniconjous, the most fervent proponents of the Ghost Dance were led by younger Lakotas such as Short Bull and Kicking Bear. Both Belt and Miles had evaluated the situation incorrectly.

As Miles anticipated the worst, Colonel Heyl, inspector general of the Division of the Missouri, returned from a visit to the Dakotas. His findings were far from those supplied by Lea. During an interview on December 3 in Chicago, Heyl said: "My opinion is that there is no imminent danger of any serious trouble. The troops are concentrated and seem to have the situation perfectly in hand."

"Do you consider the movement of the Indians toward the Badlands as ominous?" he was asked.

The colonel smiled, "I'll tell you about the alarming retreat to the Badlands," he said. "In the Badlands there are many fertile spots on which the Indians live. When the exhorter went out calling the tribes into the agency, these Indians abandoned their homes. In their absence some bands of marauders have been committing petty depredations such as stealing chickens and household utensils. This came to the knowledge of the Indians at the agency, and numbers of them are slipping away whenever they can get an opportunity for the purpose of going back to protect their chattels.

"The principal cause of the Indian troubles is lack of proper provisions in the way of rations—principally meat rations. The latter were reduced 1,000,000 pounds for the Pine Ridge Reservation alone, and the authorities there have a practice of issuing a steer at the weight at which it is received. In the Spring it would not weigh more than 600 pounds, but it would be issued at 1,000 pounds all the same. Of course, the Indians would lose the difference. This is one great source of dissatisfaction.

"The Indians generally, I think, are inclined to accept any proposition made to them by the military authorities of a peaceful nature, but when I left there was a big snowstorm and a blizzard coming, which I think will cool the ardor of the young bucks."

Then Heyl ventured an opinion that contradicted the public statements of his commander: "I do not anticipate a Winter campaign in the Indian country in that sense of the word, but troops will be kept there as against any trouble that might happen this Winter or any attempt to go on the warpath in the Spring. The Indians are not properly fed, and there will be the probability of trouble until they are. In the Spring they may make a break—that is, the young bucks—but they can be controlled. Troops will be there to attend to them if they make trouble."[11]

Winter finally came to the Dakotas. On December 3, the "Omaha Bee" reported, Zero weather and a driving storm of cutting sleet prevail here. The troops are hugging their camp fires, while the Indians are freezing in their gauze like tipis just outside the agency precincts. Today Agent Royer will call in all the Indians at the agency and give them a big feed at the store house. Should the present storm continue, and particularly should there be a heavy fall of snow, the ponies of the Indians now here, and whose hay has been stolen by the hostiles, would die of starvation. At the best this Winter will inevitably be very tough.

Then "Omaha Bee" reporter Will Cressey editorialized, These copper faces who have bowed their heads to the government rule in the present instance are suffering, while their rebellious and thieving brothers are living on the fat of the land.[12]

PREPARING FOR A CAMPAIGN
The Military Appropriations Bill to Contain a Large Sum for the Indian Campaign. General Miles to Proceed at Once to the Scene of the Trouble—More Troops Ordered to the Front. To Fight the Indians Heavy Appropriations to Be Asked For[13]

On his return from Washington, Miles told Chicago reporters that he planned to travel to the Dakotas in a few days. There he intended to study the situation firsthand. Again he enhanced his image with the press and the general public. To them he was not an armchair general; he was a man of action.[14]

AN OLD CAMPAIGNER SPEAKS HIS MIND

On December 7, 1890, a retired veteran who had served on the frontier in the years after the Civil War voiced his views in a press conference held in his home in New York City: That grizzled old warrior, William Tecumseh Sherman, has very pronounced views upon Indians generally, and particularly upon the present excitement among the tribes. General Sherman sat Saturday among his pictures and books in his "den" in the basement of his house, No. 75 West Seventy-first Street, and talked in crisp, even gruff, sentences about Indians—talked with a terseness that would do credit to the most taciturn chief among them. General Sherman calls them "Injins," with an accent of mingled detestation and contempt. He settled the problem thus:

"Injins must either work or starve. They never have worked; they won't work now, and they never will work."

"But," ventured a reporter of the *World*, "should not the government supply them with enough to keep them from starvation?"

"Why should the government support 260,000 able-bodied campers?" returned the warhorse, with a snort. "No government that the world has ever seen has done such a thing.

"Who started this story about a Messiah?" asked the general, laying down his book which he had taken up as if in impatience at all the redskins. "Injins don't look for the coming of one Messiah. They look for the coming of a million Messiahs. Each buffalo is a messiah to them. They look for the return of the buffaloes. Then they can eat without working. But the buffaloes don't return. They have all been killed off."

"Do you think, General, there will be an Indian war this Winter?"

"Nonsense!" ejaculated the soldier. "You have to change the whole face of nature before an Injin will go on the warpath in November."

"But, General, it is stated that 13,000 troops have been passed around Pine Ridge Agency."

"That's mere nonsense. I don't believe there are 2,000 troops there. Another thing: why do intelligent men and intelligent newspapers speak, in this connection, of localities that are, in fact, hundreds, even thousands of miles away from each other as if they were within a stone's throw of each other? Is it to add to the scare? If a man raises a whoop, say in Georgia, is there any reason for you to hide in a cellar in New York?"

"Do you expect, sir, an Indian uprising in the Spring?"

"Uprising? There'll be a 'down' rising. If the Indians rise up they'll be thrashed. They're in good hands."

"What do you think, General, of Secretary of War Proctor's plan to raise the army to 30,000 men and to enlist two regiments of Indians?"

"After all," answered General Sherman, "these things are not my business now. They do not concern me. I care nothing about them. The 'Injins,' as I said, are in very good hands when in the hands of General Miles and of the men on the entire frontier."

Then the leader of the march to the sea went back to his book, sublimely indifferent to all the "Injins" this side of the happy hunting ground.[15]

While General Sherman's viewpoint differed somewhat from present government policy, he, too, agreed that "root, hog, or die" outweighed the treaties that had been made with the Plains Indians. Sadly, there was nothing to root for in the dry winter descending on the Dakotas. The Lakotas, in greater numbers, were giving up the Ghost Dance and returning to their agencies in hope of receiving sustenance—sustenance that would not be authorized until the morning of December 29, 1890.

As Sherman was holding forth in New York, it was written from Standing Rock Agency that official reports received at General Ruger's headquarters yesterday say that the Indians in Sitting Bull's camp, on Grand River, have at last stopped dancing. This stoppage is due, principally, to the cold weather, but partially to exhaustion and, possibly, in a measure, to the fact that steps have been taken towards the establishment of a cordon of troops around the camp of the recalcitrant reds. It is not probable that of all the Indians on the reserv[ation] and subject to the orders of Major McLaughlin there are more than a hundred effective warriors who would take up arms to resist the arrest of Sitting Bull. . . . If nothing were done before spring to show the power of the government this number would be largely augmented.[16]

On December 7, in spite of the reports that the dancing was on the decline, Miles again told the press: "Generals Ruger and Brooke have been doing all they could to put the small number of available troops in position to be useful and so far as possible stay the threatened cyclone, yet the end of the Indian troubles is by no means immediately at hand. No other civilized country would tolerate many thousands of armed savages scattered through different States and Territories. The people of Texas, Western Kansas, Nebraska, North and South Dakota, Montana, Wyoming, Utah, Eastern Washington, Idaho, Arizona, and New Mexico are seriously interested in this subject. While the fire may be suppressed in one place it will be smoldering and liable to break out at other places where least expected, under the present system."[17]

Was the present system Miles wanted to replace the reservation system? Did he want some further isolation of the Lakotas—perhaps under military rule?

THE SENATE DEBATE RESUMES

In the Senate, on December 8, the tenacious Voorhees continued to pursue his ideas when Dawes, after citing Lea as an expert, again refused to consider a need for food among the Sioux. Voorhees launched an eloquent attack on Dawes's indifference, affirming that Miles's statements were more authoritative then those of Lea:

VOORHEES: The witness who I call is known; his first name is known, and his second name. It is known where he is from, and it is known who appointed him. He is a major general in the United States Army, in charge of that whole department, and responsible for the truth of what he says—"responsible," as the saying is, "here and elsewhere." He says:

> We have overwhelming evidence—Not merely evidence, but "overwhelming evidence," not from one man, but—from officers, inspectors, and testimony of agents as well, and also from the Indians themselves, that they have been suffering for the want of food more or less for two years. One of the principal causes of dissatisfaction is this very matter.

He goes on further to say, which I call to the attention of the senator from Massachusetts:

> One of the principal objects—Says General Miles—of my recent visit to Washington was to urge the necessity of immediate relief—

The senator from Massachusetts says there is no need of any—and—General Miles says further—"I am happy to say that success has crowned my efforts."

He got that relief which is needed, which the senator from Massachusetts says is not needed; and reads Lea as witness, anonymous Lea.

> The secretary of the interior—Says General Miles—has ordered increase of rations, and has asked Congress to appropriate the necessary money. General Brooke telegraphs this morning from Pine Ridge, saying, "There has been an issue of rations, excepting beef. The orders to the agent at the agency from the secretary of the interior increase the Indian's rations but only slightly in meat.

Now, whom are we to take? I am not going to be unjust about this matter, nor exacting, nor out of temper, nor impatient; but whom are we to believe? Lea—Lea from nowhere, appointed perhaps by the commissioner of Indian Affairs to fix things—or a man like General Miles, who says he has overwhelming evidence? Does the senator from Massachusetts rise here and dispute General Miles's word? He says he has overwhelming evidence not only from officers, inspectors, agents, and Indians themselves, but from all sources, and it is his duty to have this kind of evidence for what he does. He says he came to Washington to have relief supplied, and he got supplied. If there was not need of it, certainly the department has been greatly imposed upon and General Miles has done a very improper thing if Lea is correct.[18]

Later in the debate, Pearce quoted a speech by Turning Bear that questioned the wisdom of making the Sioux come into their agencies:

PEARCE: General Brooke sent an agent to these Indians who were reported as going on the warpath and asked them to come in for a consultation yesterday or the day before, I believe yesterday, and they came into the camp at Pine Ridge, and in the course of the consultation held there Mr. Turning Bear made a speech, and this, among other things, is what he said: "It would be a bad thing," said Turning Bear,

> for them to come nearer the agency, because there was no water or grass for their horses here. He could not understand how their young men could be employed as scouts if there was no enemy to be watched. They would be glad to be employed and get paid for it. They might come in,

> but as the old men and old women have no horses, and as their people have nothing generally to pull their wagons, it would take them a long time to come. If they should come, they would want the Great Father to send horses and wagons out to the Badland camp and bring in the great quantities of beef, etc., they had there and take it anywhere to a new camp that would be agreed upon. In conclusion Turning Bear hoped they would be given something to eat before they started back.[19]

The Lakotas' reluctance to come closer to the agency was couched in practical terms, but they were apprehensive of the army's growing military presence. Turning Bear was driving his own bargain. If his people were to come closer to Pine Ridge, they would need help. The offer of help by the army might signal there were no other plans for those who surrendered.

Even though the debate extended past the authorization of sending arms to the states, the Senate came to no conclusion other than to further investigate the condition of the Lakotas, something that was already known and had been investigated more than once.

Shortly after the debate ended, Frederic Remington offered his own solution to the problem, if indeed there were a problem. After we regard Indians as children in their relation to us, *he wrote in "Harper's Weekly,"* we must understand another thing, and that is that they are only second to the Norsemen of old as savage warriors. They possess all the virtues and some of the weaknesses of that condition. About a year ago a Portuguese newspaper intimated that the English nation were simply Norse pirates, notwithstanding they were supposed to have progressed somewhat in a thousand years. Twenty-five years has not made a plodding, praying man out of the befeathered brave of the Great Plains, and twenty-five years more will not either.

Above wealth, wives, children, and civil renown, there is one thing an Indian holds next to his God, and around their mind is emblazoned the halo of him who can fight and die. A soldier—that is the man whose image fills an Indian's eye. The bow and the lance were the emblems of all that was noble in the old days, and a little man in a blue uniform is the only thing good about the white people which an Indian ever saw. He represents courage, justice, and truth; and while the civil agents sent from Washington to dole out bad and insufficient rations to a conquered race may receive the homage, they can never command the respect of the wild tribes.[20]

After reading about the Senate debate, Remington wryly observed: It was only through the statements of a general in the United States Army that the United States Senate learned that the Sioux were being starved.

If the Great Plains tribes could be pacified, Remington proposed, The War Department could then organize them into a semi-industrial military force, much after the fashion of the Cossacks, whose company chief is responsible for their operations in peace and their deeds in war. He is both the head of the village and the war chief. Four or five irregular cavalry regiments could be organized, at the discretion of the war-office officials, and then the separate troop formations could be 100 men each. We might say, for instance, that is A Troop of the First Irregular Cavalry—they are Crows, and that is K Troop of the same regiment—they are Cheyennes. Each company should have its own permanent village situated near its agricultural or stock-raising operations and let the captain of the company be the head of the village. He has judicial and administrative powers, and is responsible to his superior in a military way.

These officers should come from the regular army, *Remington continues,* and they may apply for the appointments after their experience and natural capacity are considered. Under this arrangement pride of company is inculcated, and emulation is natural between the troops and their commander. Each officer would then be given an opportunity to apply his theories, and by experience much might be developed. There can be issued the regular clothing and pay of a soldier, and a ration for themselves and families such as is sufficient. . . . This would cost a little more than under the Interior Department, but when we figure on the attendant Indian wars, it would be as nothing. In time the regiments of the regular army could be withdrawn from the small posts, and concentrated by brigades, with great good to themselves from every point of view.

All this has been suggested in times past, and found fault with by a certain class of politicians "who are not in with the deal," and by a good many estimable people belonging to Indian societies, who are in a habit of congregating with the purpose of harrowing up each other's feelings over the wrongs of the red men.[21]

This, in fact, was what the army was doing when it started recruiting Lakota scouts in large numbers.

10. On and Off the Reservation

We will not lay down our rifles because we are afraid of the consequences. We have done wrong; we know it. If we stop now we will be punished. The Great Father will send many of us to his big iron house to stay many moons. We would die. No, we will not go and give up. We know the Great Father better than he knows us, or cares to know us.
—*Unidentified Lakota chief*

WINTER COMES

The Lakotas who surrendered at Pine Ridge were bitterly disappointed. Winter weather had come, but increased rations had not. In a letter to a friend in the East, Red Cloud lamented, My people have no food, no warm skin tipis like they used to have, but those they have are made of thin cotton and were made two years ago. A few were made last year but they are most all worn out. The clothing and bed clothing is very scant also.

So my friend you will appreciate our suffering from cold, because I cannot allow my people to go to their comfortable homes while the government officials desire them to stay here.

I am not speaking for myself but for my people, as I live here in my own house. I hope the government will not detain my people here much longer as many of my old and very young people will perish.[1]

On December 10 Red Cloud wrote T. A. Bland, corresponding secretary of the National Indian Defence Association: In consequence of these hard times, many of my people got weak and sick from the want of proper quantities of food, 217 of them dying since the fall of last year from starvation.[2] *The situation was worsening as winter closed in.*

Years later Dr. Eastman would recollect: It may be imagined that I was more than busy, though I had not such long distances to cover, for since many Indians accustomed to comfortable log houses were compelled to pass the winter in tents, there was even more sickness than usual.[3]

In spite of these harsh conditions, the Lakota camps near Pine Ridge remained crowded, and more dancers surrendered daily—some, perhaps, out of hope that rations would eventually arrive and some out of fear of army firepower. Even though Census Agent Lea reported to the commissioner, There is no suffering among the Indians for the want of food. . . . The present trouble is not due to hunger, *there is no doubt these conditions existed.*[4]

LIFE IN THE FIELD

As temperatures dropped, the army settled in for a harsh winter. Corporal Guy Palmer, serving with Company H of the Eighth Infantry at the Rose-

bud Agency, reported his stern regimen: In conical wall tents, eleven of us in all; reveille at 5.45 A.M., well clad in overcoats, fur caps and gloves, field belts, gun, entrenching tool and canvas leggings; fatigue at 7 A.M.; drill, at 9 A.M.; dinner, at 12.30 P.M.; guard mount, at 3.30 P.M., and retreat at 3.45 P.M.; three circles of Doty's—the inner or camp guard, the intermediary pickets, posted on the surrounding peaks, and an exterior guard of cavalry.[5]

An unidentified officer at the nearby Rosebud Agency found his duty there frustrating. He wrote the "Army and Navy Journal," My bottle of ink has thawed out, and now I will write you a few lines to wish you a merry Christmas. In the first place, since this great Sioux War began Pine Ridge has been getting all the newspaper notoriety. Rosebud Agency is being left in the cold. Cold? I should say so. If you want to find out, come out and try some of these December mornings. Yes, left in the cold.

Someone in the *Omaha Bee* the other day said yes, but what are the soldiers doing at Rosebud? Well, we are doing enough. We were well equipped and armed and ready to march on and tackle the Sioux. The only reason that we didn't "tackle" was that our big chief had not ordered us to do so. We must wait for orders. If Short Bull or Mr. Two Strikes kick over the traces we will show them what we can do. Our camp here was established on November 19. At that time [it was] composed of three companies, A, B, and H, of the 8th Infantry and two troops, A and G of the 9th Cavalry.

After listing the officers in his command, the officer noted, There are not many Sioux about us and they stand around and watch with great interest the busy appearance of our camp as it moves along toward perfect readiness to march against the Sioux in the Badlands, or take up a winter campaign. . . . Everything runs along just as regularly as clockwork. Visit the corral of the Q. M. Dept. and you will find wagons, mules, and harness pack trains, with old Arizona and New Mexico packers in charge. Everything is in readiness to move at a moment's notice. If orders came right now the whole camp would be moving to the front in a couple of hours' time, just as though they had never stopped at Rosebud Agency.

As at Pine Ridge, the Rosebud officer noted, Our cavalry has Negroes for soldiers, and it is said that the two troops here are the best two of "buffalo soldiers" in the service. Capts. Cusack and Garrard take much pride in keeping these fellows up to the mark. They are good riders, are cheerful in the performance of their duty, and are good rifle shots.

Here, too, there were frequent artillery drills: Lieut. Geo. Ruthers, 8th

Inf., is our ordinance officer. He has a new 1½ inch Hotchkiss mountain gun. The gun is a beauty, and Mr. Ruthers has already done some fine work at practice since our arrival here finding the range. Yesterday I saw him fire live shells at a boulder about 6 feet square and 2,000 yards distant. Every shell struck the mark and exploded. The whole thing was a grand surprise to the body of Indian police, who were standing near looking on.

The gun will be most serviceable in running out the hostiles from rocky basins in the Badlands. I think we will stay close by the lieutenant.

Lieut. Butts, of the 21st, has the Gatling gun. This we will use in case we get in a tight place. It is said to have a scattering effect upon the Sioux, especially at 200 and 300 yards. We saw the lieutenant doing some fine work with it yesterday at 500 yards. We don't want to get in front of the piece.

The unit was also equipped with long-distance signaling equipment: These officers can be seen out daily with their fires and heliographs, and at night with torches, signaling from the different peaks and elevations. The country affords a fine opportunity for signaling. There are no trees in this country, not a tree to be seen as far as the eye can reach, nothing bigger than a blade of grass. The country is sandy and rolling.

With this then-sophisticated communications equipment, the army quickly sent dispatches from the field that were released to the press. After being edited, the stories were telegraphed to the East and appeared in the next day's newspapers.

Early in December the weather moderated, allowing the unidentified officer to conclude his account with a near idyllic description of an evening in bivouac. There, he wrote, A stroll through the camp in the evening will find the tents well lit up, the soldier boys sitting or lying about reading their papers and letters from home, or playing games. The officers have favorite tents in which they congregate and talk over the chances of a big Indian winter campaign.[6]

The daily drills were not without danger. In mid-December, Lt. Alexander R. Piper of the Eighth Infantry wrote his wife, from his camp at Pine Ridge, Yesterday at drill three 9th Cavalrymen were hurt, one had both forearms and collar bone broken and I should think Henry would come off his charging and wild riding pretty soon. This makes four men he has hurt and one horse had to be shot from its injuries.[7]

At Pine Ridge, Private Crickett had little reason to complain; he found his life enjoyable. There, the soldiers mixed freely with the Lakotas. After the dance, *Crickett wrote,* there was a feast of dog which they stewed in right good stile. I tasted it once and found it pretty good. These Indians was the friendliest. Next was the beef issue which was grand. The beasts would be all droven into a large pound. Then the bucks would all form round mounted on ponies and armed with fine Winchesters and speers.

Then so many names would be called, the slide lifted, and out would come the steer with his tail well up and away he would go [with] the Indians after it, and so on until the prairie was black with them all yelling at the top of their voices like so many devils let loose. They would chase them untill played out then would speer them to make them go faster. When done would shoot then. Then the squaws come up and skin them, then they are divided between the families, but not before they have a good feed as that is when they like it best. You could see them scoop the blood up with their hands and there is no doubt they enjoy it.[8]

An officer at Pine Ridge who signed as "Infantry" in a letter to the "Army and Navy Journal" proposed that to take and shackle Red Cloud, Sitting Bull or other fomenters of discord should be the first step to be taken. . . . Troops should not be concentrated at our expense without some action, and the cost should be taken out of the allowance of the Indians. . . . These Indians are children and need spanking, but the great father in Washington is treating them like men—which they cannot appreciate and never could.[9]

"Infantry" further reported, Providence is smiling on us now with most beautiful weather. It may be the Indian Messiah who is helping us.

According to "Infantry," the Lakotas were profiting from the influx of troops: The Ghost shirts now being brought in are spectral things. Some old hag has got on to it and is making imitations for sale, and not the original ones worn and hallowed by use.[10]

During the inaction Private Prather had time to add verses to his ballad:

About their tents the Soldiers stood, awaiting one and all,
That they might hear the trumpet clear when sounding General call
Or Boot and Saddles in a rush, that each and every man
Might mount in haste, ride soon and fast to stop this devilish band
But Generals great like Miles and Brooke don't do things up that way,
For they know the Indian like a book, and let him have his sway
Until they think him far enough and then to John they'll say,
"You had better stop your fooling or we'll bring our guns to play."[11]

A MISSION OF PEACE

As the troops drilled and waited at Pine Ridge, efforts were being made to persuade the remaining Ghost dancers to surrender. The leader in this efforts was Swiss-born John Jutz, a seventy-year-old Franciscan priest, who had spent seven years among the Lakotas. Four of the these had been at Rosary Mission and School, just north of Pine Ridge. According to Elaine Goodale, Jutz declined military protection, and not only cared for about a hundred children throughout the disturbance but fed and sheltered many fugitives. He also went freely among the Ghost dancers in an effort to mediate and bring about a voluntary surrender.[12]

At this time Father Perrig wrote in his diary on December 2, Rev. f. Jutz went to offer General Brooke his service in going to meet the Rosebud Indians and learn their intentions. *The reason for this offer, according to Perrig, was that three Rosebud Indians had just arrived at the agency. One was High Hawk, from Cutmeat Creek, and the other was Sorrel Horse, a son-in-law of Two Strike. It would seem that Two Strike wanted to explore the terms of a surrender.*

Afterwards, *Perrig continued,* High Hawk came down to the Mission. He is not very communicative, but he said that there were about 500 lodges down on the White River, mostly Licangas, but 20–30 lodges of Oglalas. He said their intention in coming over was to settle on this reservation and not to fight. This is probably an afterthought and surely not the first intention of all of them.

We supplied High Hawk and the other Indian with provisions and they struck out for the camp on the White River.[13]

On December 3 Perrig wrote, Today Rev. f. Jutz wanted to go with Red Cloud to the camping-place of the Rosebud Indians (near the mouth of Wounded Knee Creek across Big White River in the Badlands). At the last moment Red Cloud excused himself and sent his son Jack, a notorious dance-chief, with f. Jutz. Moreover, f. Jutz took along our servant, Frank Martinez, as interpreter. They started about 11 o'clock A.M.[14]

On Friday—two days later—the "New York World" reported that after a journey of great hardship, *Jutz and his companions* were halted by Indian pickets ten miles outside the hostiles' camp. Runners were dispatched back to the camp, and on their return the priest and young Red Cloud were conducted to it, closely guarded by Indians armed with Winchesters. It was eleven o'clock Saturday morning before the camp was reached, and two hours later the chiefs met with Father Jutz in council. There were present Two Strike, the head chief, Turning Bear, Short Bull, High Hawk, Crow Dog, Kicking Bear, Eagle Pipe, Big Turkey and High Pipe. The pipe of peace was conspicuous by its absence.

Father Jutz opened the council by asking the chiefs to state the particular cause of the grievance that had led them to assume so startling an attitude of war.

An unnamed chief said, "We object to the recent census returns made by Mr. Lea. His enumeration as he is now making it would not give us food sufficient for us to live on. Lea put us down many less for each tipi than the tipi contains. We are to receive food according to that enumeration. We shall starve if the Great Father chooses to lay a trap to cheat us; we will have one big eat before the starving time comes. After that we shall fight, and the white man shall see more blood and more dead from our guns than ever before. Then we will go to the last hunting-ground happy. If the white man did not mean to cheat us out of food, the Great Father never would have sent soldiers.

"There is no need for soldiers if the Great Father intended to be fair with us. . . . We know he intends cheating us by the way the census man is putting down figures that he has and by which we are to be fed. The Great Father has done another wrong. He put a new line—a new boundary line—between Rosebud and Pine Ridge Agency that makes many of us leave our homes and give them to others.

"The Great Father broke the old treaty when he did this. We can no longer believe the Great Father. He says to us: 'Children, you shall never be moved again unless you want to move,' and then he went right away and moved us. We are done with promises, and now we make a promise that we will fight, and the Great Father will find that we will not break our promise.

"We will now be very plain with you, Christian Father, and tell you another thing, something of which you may have already thought. . . . It is this: We will not lay down our rifles because we are afraid of the consequences. We have done wrong: we know it. If we stop now we will be punished. The Great Father will send many of us to his big iron house to stay many moons. We would die. No, we will not go and give up. We know the Great Father better than he knows us or cares to know us."[15]

The Lakotas' fear of annihilation by the massed troops emerged in this eloquent speech; but, by now, at least one leader, tired of starvation and disease, was ready to die fighting. The pacifism taught by Wovoka and his disciples were being put to the test. Jutz listened patiently and made no reply.

Others took a more moderate stance. After a long pause, *the "New York World" reporter wrote,* Crow Dog said that they might come in if the soldiers were taken away. Father Jutz then urged them with much fervor to be peaceable and give up their designs of war. He explained that the soldiers were not to harm the Indians but to protect the agency; that the rations had been increased at the agency; and that if they came, General Brooke would telegraph Washington and get permission for them to stay on this agency as they desired. So far as depredations were concerned, the Father told them they had better stop committing them, and they would be more easily forgiven. Finally he urged the chiefs that they all come back with him.

To this, some of the older ones made favorable answers, but the younger ones, who were heavily in the majority, said no; but the old men finally agreed that they would come on horseback to Father Jutz's house, which is about four miles northwest of the agency, this morning, and there meet General Brooke and tell him in person just what they had told Father Jutz.

This brought on a renewal of bitter opposition from the majority, which came near ending in a row. Finally the young chiefs cooled off, and Two Strike, addressing Father Jutz, said: "Hold your hands up to the Great Spirit and tell us, as though you were about to start on a journey to the last hunting-ground of the red man, whether what you say to us from General Brooke be true and that we will not be harmed if we come in simply to talk to General Brooke."

Father Jutz complied with the request, and all the chiefs then extended their hands towards the heavens, and with great solemnity promised that they would come.

This ended the council, and Father Jutz and Young Red Cloud withdrew, the former telling the chiefs that if they broke their word to him he would never again believe an Indian.

The "New York World" reporter also noted that in the Stronghold Father Jutz says he saw between 1,000 and 1,200 young braves all fully armed, and he supposes from the size of the camp and the great number of pickets out that the hostiles number over 2,000 fighting men. He saw a large number of cattle being driven in from all directions, slaughtered all about the camp and the meat being cured.

Jutz also told the authorities at Pine Ridge, The camp is remarkably well fortified with embankments and finely constructed rifle pits and is wholly inaccessible by military, otherwise than on foot and in single file, and as to using cannon or such pieces as Gatling or Hotchkiss guns, such a thing is entirely out of the question.[16] *Jutz greatly overestimated the number of warriors in the Stronghold.*

A few days later, General Miles admitted to reporters, There were not more than three hundred hostile Indians [warriors] in the Badlands; not enough to give the troops much trouble, but sufficient to cause havoc among the settlers if they break away and are on the warpath.[17] *It was most unlikely that this small force of Lakotas would abandon their families in the Badlands redoubt and go on the warpath.*

Jutz's mission had not been in vain. He returned to Pine Ridge on Sun-

day, December 7, followed by representatives of the Brulé. According to the "New York World," They came bearing a flag of truce and armed with Winchesters and Springfield rifles. The entrance of the novel procession produced the greatest excitement since the trouble began.

First came the chiefs Turning Bear, Big Turkey, High Pine, Big Bad Horse and Bull Dog, who was one of the leaders in the Custer Massacre. Next came Two Strikes, the head chief, seated in a buggy with Father Jutz. Surrounding these was a body guard of four young warriors. All the Indians were decorated with war paint and feathers, while many wore Ghost-dance leggings and the Ghost-dance shirt dangling at their saddles. Bunches of eagle feathers were tied on the manes and tails of most of the ponies, while the backs of the animals were streaked with paint. The luridly warlike Cavalcade proceeded at once to General Brooke's headquarters in the agency residence.

At a given signal all leaped to the ground, hitched their ponies to the fence, and, guided by Father Jutz, . . . entered the general's apartments, where the council was held, lasting two hours.

At the beginning of the pow-wow General Brooke explained that the Great Father, through him, had asked them to come in and have a talk regarding the situation. A great deal of misunderstanding and trouble had arisen by the reports taken to and fro between the camps by irresponsible parties, and it was therefore considered very necessary that they have a talk face to face.

General Brooke said the Father wanted to tell them if they could come in near the agency, where General Brooke could see them often, and not be compelled to depend on hearsay, that he would give them plenty to eat and would employ many of their young men as scouts, & c. He said he had heard they were hostile Indians, but he did not believe it. The soldiers did not come here to fight, but to protect the settlers and keep peace. He hoped they (the Indians) were all in favor of peace, as the Great Father did not want war. As to the feeling over the change in the boundary line between Pine Ridge and Rosebud Agencies, he said that and many other things would be settled satisfactorily after they had shown a disposition to come in. Wounded Knee was suggested as a place that would prove satisfactory to the Great Father to have them live.

The representatives of the hostiles listened with contracted brows, sidelong glances at one another and low grunts. When the general had concluded his remarks, Turning Bear came forward and spoke in reply. He is the finest specimen of the blanket-wrapped Indian that has been seen here, *the "New York World" reporter observed*. He has a face that is positively handsome, a form as erect as a flagstaff and a voice that would provoke favorable comment in legislative halls. He proved a most entertaining person.

Turning Bear, who would prove to be a clever and eloquent advocate for his people, was reported by the "New York World" as saying to Jutz and his representatives that it would be a bad thing for them to come nearer the agency, because there was no water or grass for their horses here. He could not understand how their young men could be employed as scouts if there was no enemy to be watched. They would be glad to be employed and get paid for it. They might come in, but as the old men and women have no horses and as their people have nothing to pull their wagons it would take them a long time to come. If they should come they would want the Great Father to send horses and wagons out to the Badlands camp and bring in the great quantities of beef, & c. they had there and take it to any new camp that might be agreed on.

General Brooke would not make any major concessions until his visitors were ready to surrender. As for the horses and wagons being sent after the beef, *according to the reporter*, the general said that and many other things would be considered after they had acceded to the Great Father's request to move into the agency.

After the pow-wow was over the band was conducted to the Commissary Department and given all they could eat. The squaws living here at the agency came in gala-day feathers and gave a squaw dance. The hostiles went back to their camp to report without making any promises.[18]

On December 8, the day after the conference with Brooke, Bishop Hare felt it necessary to reassure a reporter from the "New York World," stating, I have visited several Indian agencies recently, and have late news from all the Sioux Indian country, but I have yet to learn of a single case of insult, much less of violence, offered to any teacher or missionary in any of the fifty-odd stations scattered all over the disturbed districts in South Dakota. I have never feared a general uprising.[19]

Brooke, by now, had decided that an attack would be too costly; however, he believed he might bring the matter to a close by luring the Ghost dancers out of their redoubt. Reporter Kelley opined, General Brooke realizes that the very serious task on hand is . . . trying to withdraw the Indians from this place. He possibly thinks they will emerge from this place and nimbly tumble into a military trap.

Kelley believed this was not a valid plan and asked his readers, Why should they come out and leave their homes and supplies unprotected? It is well known in Indian warfare [that] Indians do not usually begin an attack upon their enemy. Certainly not unless they have overwhelming numbers and a superiority of position.

They know as well as General Brooke knows that troops are massed all about the edge of the Badlands, ready to advance in there if they can do so. Then why should they be tempted to leave them, giving them credit of a small degree of intelligence? If the Indian is ever cunning, he certainly is in time of war; and no one is better acquainted with the country, the number of his enemies . . . than he; and it seems folly to suppose he would abandon such a position as he possesses if fighting is to be done.

The Indians have every advantage they could ask in acting upon the defensive. Is it then reasonable to suppose he will leave all without consideration and take the field on the offensive?[20]

TAKEN TO TASK

Local newspapers were angered by the continued irresponsibility of some of the reporters stationed at Pine Ridge. The "Chadron (NE) Democrat" pointed an accusing finger at two reporters: The Indian excitement is accounting for one thing at least, that of having produced a crop of fine, large sensational mongers and liars of the first water, chief among which stand C. H. C. [Will Cressey], special correspondent of the *Omaha Bee*, and W. F. K. [William Fitch Kelley], of the *[Lincoln] State Journal.*

From the very beginning of the present trouble they have shown a marked proclivity to enlarge upon every trivial incident and distort the truth far beyond the bounds of reason, besides having at times manufactured stories of blood and rapine in order to pander to the depraved tastes of the lovers of the marvelous and create a sale for the papers which they represent. For a short time while the public mind is excited and ready to believe almost anything relating to Indians and Indian affairs, the unjournalistic and despicable methods of the above-named papers to increase the revenue at the price of honor and truth may be successful, but on the succession of calmer moments when the threatened battles and outbreaks fail to materialize, and the numerous tales of raids and war dances shall have been proven false, the people will be as free to condemn as they have been to applaud. They will demand the truth and feel chagrined at the imposition that has been practiced on them by the unscrupulous, unprincipled papers which they have been duped to believe.[21]

In spite of the transgressions of the press, Miles felt the situation was stabilizing. On December 11 he telegraphed his commander, General Schofield: Reports from General Ruger and General Brooke are quite favorable. The presence of the troops now in position has had a demoralizing influence upon the Indians and those that a week ago were defiant and warlike are now giving evidence of submission.[22]

If one report is to be believed, the Stronghold was proving to be less than an ideal refuge. White Swan, a member of the Indian Supreme Court at the Cheyenne Agency, told a reporter, Many of the Ghost dancers are suffering and even dying now from a form of la grippe induced by dancing outdoors during cold weather. As no agency physician is allowed to go among them, the disease is spreading rapidly.[23]

Problems were growing at lesser agencies as well. From Watertown, South Dakota, it was relayed, Reports have been coming into this city for several days past of great destitution among the Indians on the Sisseton and Wahpeton Reservations. It was learned today that unless assistance is speedily rendered the Indians will starve. Several settlers living along the borders of the reservation fear that the Indians will thus be compelled to steal from the whites to prevent starving. *The correspondent stressed,* These Indians are not given to Ghost Dances, but will be forced to steal or starve.[24]

In the midst of all this turmoil, a few reaped economic benefits. On December 11 the "Chadron Democrat" commented, The merchants are kept very busy here at this time as the soldiers have just been paid off. We notice that Chadron is coming in for a share of the business here, judging from the teams that have arrived from there loaded with merchandise.[25]

As mid-December approached, the weather remained mild, the merchants counted their profits, and the restive troops had time to seek recreation. Only the Lakotas were suffering.

DIFFERENCES OF OPINION IN THE BADLANDS

BLOODY INDIAN BATTLE
Fought by the Forces of Short Bull and Two Strike. Twenty to Fifty Killed. Both of the Belligerent Chiefs Claimed the Leadership. Useless to Talk of Peace. At Pine Ridge It Is Thought That War Is Inevitable. The Indians Running Off Cattle.[26]

The growing tranquility at Pine Ridge was broken by a new report of violence. On December 12 the "Chicago Tribune" featured the above headline and reported, Yankton Charlie, a full-blooded Sioux and government scout, came in at two o'clock this morning from the Indian camp in the Badlands and reports a bloody fight among the followers of the Indian chiefs Short Bull and Two Strike. Each claimed the leadership and each tried to secure it by force.

The result is from twenty to fifty dead Indians. This report is verified by several friendlies who have been waiting for some time to escape to the agency. As the spies took advantage of the fight to make their escape it is not known yet which chief conquered.

It is useless to talk of peace, *the "Chicago Tribune"'s correspondent decreed*. There has been no attempt made on the part of the hostiles to move out of their entrenchments since the peace council was held. None of the promises made then have been kept. There is great excitement here.

It is said that when the chiefs returned from the agency, a council was held. Two Strike and his followers favored peace, but Kicking Bear, Short Bull, and other chiefs, composing the majority of the camp, took decided ground on the other side. The council lasted several hours, during which the excitement reached its highest pitch and finally broke up in a fight. *It was further reported that* the troops have received orders to be in readiness by tomorrow to march to the Badlands.[27]

On December 13 the "Chicago Tribune" followed up on its story of the previous day, insisting, Reports of the fight between the Indians in the Badlands are confirmed. Two Strike and his party were victorious and left the Badlands for Pine Ridge Agency, encamping on White Earth River. The chief sent in to General Brooke asking for help to clean out Short Bull and his warriors.

The next day the "Chicago Tribune" printed still another account of a conflict in the Stronghold, this one filed in Rapid City: A soldier from Camp Wells reports that the Indians in the Badlands have begun fighting again among themselves. This news was brought by government scouts and friendly Indians. The battle took place in Grass Basin. Two Strike and his followers circled around Short Bull and his followers all the forenoon, actively skirmishing, each leader bound that his supremacy as chief of the whole band be acknowledged.[28]

Two Strike was headed into Pine Ridge, but there is no other record of him requesting an attack on Short Bull. It is doubtful that he and Short Bull had even seen each other. At the time these news stories were reported, Short Bull was entrenched in the Stronghold, and Two Strike was moving slowly toward Pine Ridge and surrender.

Short Bull offers a less lurid account of differences among the Ghost dancers in the Badlands. The day after he met with emissaries from Pine Ridge, he says, The next morning, we moved toward the Badlands and camped there that night. High Hawk and the others returning to the agency, no good having been done by them. After we went into camp some half-breed Indians came to us. No Ear was in charge asking us for stray horses. They looked through our herd, and, while picking some out, one of our Indians was kicked in the head, so we killed the horse that kicked him.

The shot caused an excitement in the camp which only proved to be some wrangling among the Indians. I called them together and bid them to stop, saying, "I wanted no trouble. You must stop. You should do right, have no fighting. You have taken and butchered other people's cattle and stolen horses.

"We will move back to the agency, sell our ponies, pay for these cattle, and have no more trouble. The Oglalas must listen to what I say as well as the Brulés. You have plenty of dried meat now, but do as I ask you."

They would not listen, but moved toward White River. I again asked them to listen. They had no ears. I told them to go to the agency and that as soon as I got over being mad I would come in too.

At this the young men surrounded me. I covered my head with my blanket so I could not see who would kill me for I heard their guns cock. One of them spoke up, bidding me to uncover my face so I done it. I told them that the reason I covered my face was that I did not care to see who would kill me, and wanted no trouble. The women then came in crying. The warriors left to recall the party who had started for the agency and brought them back to my camp which was on the hill by the Badlands.[29]

Short Bull does not mention any casualties during the quarrel or even Two Strike's presence in the Stronghold. In a December 14 entry, Perrig tends to support Short Bull's account: Afternoon: Big Turkey, Two Strike, Bull King and several others came on a visit. They said Short Bull was chief of the recusants, though he himself would rather have come up. But the dissatisfied ones did not let him go.[30]

While the struggle for power of some sort occurred in the Stronghold, on December 13 the "Chicago Tribune" trumpeted:

> INDIANS PUT TO ROUT
> Battle between the Troops and Kicking Bear's Band. Losses on Both Sides. Many Indians, Including Kicking Bear, Captured. The Fight in the Bad Lands. Two Strike Victorious Over his Enemy, Short Bull. Going Out After the Hostiles.[31]

Neither the headline nor the story that followed had any basis in truth: A special courier from the camp of two troops of the Sixth Cavalry stationed on the South Fork of the Cheyenne River says a squaw-man named Rider has brought a report to the commanding officer that there has been a bloody encounter four miles north of Pine Ridge Agency between the United States troops and some four or five hundred Indians under Kicking Bear, and that a number have been killed on both sides, [and] that the Indians have been put to rout and a large number captured, including Kicking Bear.[32]

While Two Strike was reported to be in a bitter power struggle, he was actually traveling toward Pine Ridge. This story, like many others published in the "Chicago Tribune," were untrue. On December 13 the "Tribune" accurately reported from Pine Ridge, Two Strike is keeping up his record as a slow traveler. He promised General Brooke to come in at once and has succeeded in marching seven miles in seven days. Black Fox, the scout, says that the wily leader is camped on White River waiting for provisions to be sent to him. *Brooke was not about to give Two Strike rations until he came into Pine Ridge and surrendered.*

Colonel Corbin in Chicago was more optimistic and commented to the press, "Two Strikes is an obstreperous fellow and has been one of the malcontents among the Sioux. The reports that he has started in to Pine Ridge augurs well."[33]

The "Chicago Tribune"'s reporter gave a likely reason for Two Strike's slow progress in coming into Pine Ridge. He observed, False rumors from Pine Ridge keep the peaceably disposed Indians from coming near the agency. It is rumored the cavalry will start in the morning.[34] *That possibility remained a rumor. With the exception of small patrols, Brooke's command remained at Pine Ridge. Miles remained reluctant to send his troops into the field, partly because he feared any encounter at the Stronghold would be bloody and partly because he knew his troops were outnumbered by the Lakotas. If Two Strike did come in, the number of Lakotas near Pine Ridge would increase drastically.*

Even though Brooke delayed taking action, the first armed encounter of the Ghost Dance war was about to take place.

FRACAS AT DALY'S RANCH

AMBUSHED BY COWBOYS

A Band of Indians Fired on While Raiding on Battle Creek. Three of the Redskins Are Killed and One White Man Is Wounded in the Skirmish—The Braves Put to Flight, but Their Reappearance with Reinforcements Feared—Two Strike Making Slow Progress Toward Pine Ridge—Sensational Rumors Denied.[35]

A correspondent for the "Chicago Tribune" who was stationed in Rapid City reported that on December 12, A courier from the camp on Spring Creek says a collision took place between a number of cowboys and a band of Indians at Daly's ranch, just above the mouth of Battle Creek, west of the Cheyenne [River]. *The reporter had been told that* the cowboys were looking for stolen horses, and knowing that Indians were in the vicinity hid behind a wood pile on the ranch and waited. Presently the Indians dashed up, whooping and yelling, and three of them started to ride through the gate, when a cowboy named Fred Thompson fired and one of them fell from his pony, dead. A volley was then fired by all the cowboys, and two more Indians fell from their horses, the horses running through the gate into Daly's yard riderless.

The firing then became general on both sides and one cowboy was shot through the right shoulder. He is still unconscious and will probably die. As darkness was coming on, the Indians withdrew, carrying their dead and wounded with them. Jack Daly, George Holden, and M. Day came up just as the Indians retreated and also exchanged a number of shots with them. Great anxiety is felt here as to whether the Indians will secure reinforcements and return.

As usual, accounts of the event varied widely from reporter to reporter and from participant to participant. J. B. McCloud, a member of the South Dakota Militia, remembered years later: The men inside were making coffee and preparing to eat breakfast when one of the boys chanced to look across the river and saw a body of horsemen riding at full speed for the ranch. They were quickly recognized as Indians by their long streaming hair and trappings.

The men whose horses were in the stable seized their guns and were wild to reach their horses, as the stables were about twenty-five rods from the house—right at the ford for which the Indians were riding—and this was, at that time, a bad country in which to use the cow-punchers phrase "to be left a-foot." Captain Akin commanded the boys to conceal themselves behind the trees and logs, etc. and wait until the Indians reached the enclosure, and as the stable doors were all in view of the house and exposed to our fire the horses could not be taken at least by the band of Indians as there were but 32 of them and there was 16 of us.

Well, on came the Indians and all the yelling and whooping ever heard; they could have done themselves proud as warriors if yelling were all that is necessary to whip a bunch of South Dakota cowboys and miners, but it isn't—as these Indians soon discovered. The Carlisle graduate (who for an Indian was exceptionally brave) appeared to be the leader. He rode through the river, past the stables to where a pair of bars or gateway led into the enclosure about the ranch. When halfway through the bars, he evidently took in the whole situation [and] raised his gun and fired. It was his last shot.

The fight was on, and now let me tell you something good about Indians. This Indian fell from his horse, his feet and legs lying across the bars which were down at one end only, and although the fallen Indian was in full view of several of our men who were pouring lead at them, two of the Indians rode to the fallen Indian, one on each side. Leaning from their horses [they] raised and swung him as though he had been a blanket between their horses and disappeared with him behind the hay-stacks and barns—only a few feet distant, it is true, but this was an act of bravery and daring which an Indian is equal to only in event of being able to rescue a fallen companion from an enemy.

I suppose they thought we would take his scalp, though out there are few white men who would do that, for while it's all right to talk about scalping an Indian, you know an Indian is a human being. You can't do it, at least you can't scalp one unless you are partially depraved—I think there was but one Indian scalped during the outbreak of '90 and '91, and there is no record of this one instance.

Well, these Indians adopted the usual Indian tactics and remained behind the stable and hay-stacks and corrals which were made of heavy logs and peppered lead at us for several minutes but their aim was poor. For every time an Indian showed his face there were several shots fired at him, and while they frequently struck near, they injured none of us.

Presently the firing ceased and then came an order to charge to the stables. Of course, we did not know where the Indians were and they might have been behind the barns etc., waiting for us to come out in the open but they were not—they were retreating. When we reached the stable several rose from them out of sight [covered by] the timber and bushes. [They were] crossing the river at a point enabling them to keep the barns between themselves and us until they were in the timber.

However, they covered their retreat in a masterly manner by leaving a few Indians behind who, from concealed positions, kept up a constant firing. Talk about running—when the firing first began an Indian just crossing the river was riding a fine looking horse, evidently a stolen one and not used to firing, for in stopping quickly in some manner the frightened horse fell on the rocky ford and ran back up Cedar Creek from whence they came. The Indian actually outran the horse, first seizing its tail then reaching the saddle and springing onto it while the horse was running at full speed. I would like to take that Indian out and challenge the world's most famous foot racer—a few South Dakota rangers with guns behind him would enable him to win. I saw something that day which induces me to believe an Indian, when going into battle frequently, ties one foot to the stirrup, for an Indian at whom shots were fired (at least one was) fell from his horse and was dragged by one foot for a considerable distance, in fact out of our sight. As the ground was sandy, he stirred up great clouds of it [for] as long as we could see him.

The Indians crossed a table after leaving the river in sight of us, and there were four saddles unoccupied. Have you ever heard an Indian death song? Well, no white man can produce anything like it, at least we could not. Rage—despair—sorrow—all combined seemed to be included in the awful wail those fellows set up when they finally gave up and left the field.[36]

Short Bull, who was on the other side of the action, gives a far different account of the fracas. He paints a picture of trigger-happy cowboys rather than a firefight that lasted most of a day, and he mentioned only one Lakota casualty. Five of our men were sent to Cheyenne River to buy sugar and other things for our use, *he says*, and as they neared a house, at the end of which was a haystack, they were fired upon by a party of whites. My nephew Circle Elk, a young boy who had been to school at Carlisle was killed. He could speak English and for that reason was sent with the party.[37]

The "New York World"'s correspondent arrived at Daly's ranch later in the day. Once there he found that the cowboys felt they had been involved in a full-scale attack and believed another attack would follow. The reporter grimly wrote, We found a number of settlers, all armed to the teeth. After leaving the ranch, and while crossing a table, we sighted a small band of Indians coming up. They discovered us at about the same time and at once turned back. They were without doubt intending to return to the Daly ranch, which, whatever may be the result of this trouble, is a doomed place.[38]

Short Bull says, When the four returned, all of the young men mounted their horses to bring back the body of my nephew. I could see them in the distance going backward and forward.[39]

The search party was not successful in finding the body, so Short Bull and his followers withdrew into the Badlands.

At the end of his report, the "New York World"'s correspondent editorialized, The importance which I have attached to the killing of this one Indian, who was the leader of the band, may seem strange to some, but not to any one acquainted with Indian warfare. Notwithstanding all the depredations which the Sioux have committed during the past thirty days, they had not killed one white man, nor had an Indian been killed, and until such an event occurred, there was a probability of this trouble ending peaceably and within a few days.

Now, even if the Indians do return to the agency, they will come back next Spring for revenge, and unless there is a general war, this neighborhood will be harassed for years on account of the killing of that one Indian.[40] *This prediction never came true.*

News of the encounter spread quickly. To the north, from Pierre, South Dakota, it was reported, Governor Mellette . . . thinks that the fight will probably result in bringing matters to a focus and cause the army to move and do something to protect that settlers and maintain the authority of the government.[41]

By now, many were becoming restive, wondering when Miles would take action. He was yet to show his hand.

There was another cause for alarm on the evening of the skirmish at Daly's ranch. The "New York World" reported, About 9 o'clock Friday night, a great light suddenly blazed up in the northwest in the direction of the Badlands and spread along the sky for a distance of a couple of miles. Men posted in Indian signals say this means that the Indians in the Badlands have determined to fight. The Indians in the camp of the friendlies say it means that their brothers in the Badlands will be on the warpath within one sun, and that all Indians who do not join them are dogs and enemies forever.

The Sixth, Seventh and Eighth Cavalry and 500 State militia have started for the Badlands, and it is the general opinion here that a fight with the hostiles is now inevitable.[42] *The predictions there would be warfare within a day and the report of an attack on the Stronghold proved to be false.*

Fearing an attack by the army, Short Bull's followers began to improve their fortifications. The next morning, *Short Bull says,* We all assembled on the dancing ground, and Knob Arrow said, "Let us ditch this hill and if anyone comes here they cannot get to us."

I told them to do as they pleased, but to first get my nephew's body, whereupon some of the young men started, the remainder digging the ditch. They found the body partly burned by prairie fire so it was wrapped up and left. We then went over to where the fire was and were met by white soldiers who fired on us, so we turned back.

I then told my people if these cowboys fire on you, fire back, and when we got close to them again they fled.[43]

Colonel Corbin, in charge of the Chicago command offices of the Division of the Missouri during Miles's absence, told reporters, The light which appeared in the sky on Friday night was undoubtedly made by some of the more hostile braves to bring on a fight with the troops. The troops stationed at the Badlands will be fully prepared if an attack should be made.[44]

AN ARMY AT THE READY?

ON THE VERGE OF WAR
Troops Closing in With the Hostiles in the Bad Lands. Ranchers Organized and Armed to Defend Their Homes.[45]

Nerves were fraying among the settlers and the troops. Patrols cautiously approached the Badlands but stayed away from the Stronghold. Villagers, frightened by the reports of the foray at Daly's ranch, began to take matters into their own hands and set up defenses in their towns.

On December 11 a dispatch from Fort Lincoln, North Dakota, stated, The people of Hebron, a few miles west of here, have just completed a formidable earthwork and are now prepared to stand off any number of redskins that may come against them. The fort is circular in form, about 100 yards across, and provided with interior embankments. The ground in front is covered with an entanglement made of barbed-wire stretched on short stakes.[46]

The next day it was reported, New Rockford people slept on their arms last night. A party of Sioux Indians camped near town and kept up the Ghost Dance all night. Their whoops could be plainly heard in the village. The Indians stole flour from the mill here until an armed guard was placed in the building. A few cattle were also killed. Settlers are coming in from all directions.[47]

On December 15 the "New York World"'s correspondent, riding with the Seventh Cavalry along the Cheyenne River, wrote, I can say from actual knowledge, however, that the ranchers in Spring Creek and Battle Creek Valleys have stood far more without retaliating than I supposed any white men would. Everyone we met had a gun, most of them swore that hereafter they would kill every Indian they found on this side of the Cheyenne. It has simply come to this: the Indians must be disarmed, even if it is necessary to kill them first, or else all these valleys will continue to be raided until the settlers kill them off. The women and children have been taken to the towns and the men have returned well armed and travel in crowds of four to a dozen.[48]

As matters remained on hold, the "Army and Navy Journal" complained, Owing to the Indian troubles, a number of officers on leaves of absence have had to relinquish them and start for the front, much to their personal discomfort and expense, but there has been no lack of cheerfulness in the acceptance of the situation.[49]

Brooke's troops in their winter quarters at Pine Ridge were becoming restless. In a letter dated December 14, Piper grumbled to his wife, The Indians have not come in yet and there is a rumor that the cavalry will soon (tomorrow or the next day) go after them. It certainly is time something was done; here we are pampering a lot of worthless loafing Indians. If they don't choose to come, then they ought to be made to come, and awfully fast too.

Now I am disgusted. Hayden has just come in with an order for me to turn over my Hotchkiss Gun to Captain Capron. That means we are to be left behind when the troops go out. I am not so sure they are going, however, and won't believe they are until I see them start.

From the way the wagons are moving around it is evident that something is in the air. But we have received no orders and are evidently to be left behind.[50]

Brooke realized that his men were chafing at the inaction and moved several units into the field. Kelley wrote on December 14, Orders have been given by General Brooke to have the Seventh, Eighth and Ninth Cavalry ready to march to the Badlands at sunrise tomorrow. The Seventh will start from Pine Ridge. Eight troops of the Sixth Cavalry are now at the junction of the Cheyenne River and Rapid Creek. They will close in from this place. The Eighth Cavalry is scattered along the line of the Elkhorn Road, at Buffalo Gap, Oelrichs and Smithfield. They will probably consolidate at some unknown place and advance from the west on the Indians.

It is now thought the troops will move promptly at break of day tomorrow. No attempt will be made to surprise the hostiles but a steady march will be made forward and a final closing up will be the line of action carried out.

The cavalry will be under the command of Colonel Forsyth, a man who has had large experience with Indians and Indian warfare.

The Seventh, no doubt, will add glory to the honorable name they have already won in the impending struggle.[51]

The anticipated move did not develop, and the Seventh remained in bivouac. General Miles, *according to Piper*, has ordered that all movements be suspended until he reaches Rapid City to personally direct the movement.[52]

By now the command at Pine Ridge was sizable. According to the "Chicago Tribune," The Sixth Cavalry consists of 500 to 600 men. Accompanying them will be 250 infantry under Captain Wells of Oelrichs, and

300 state militia under M. H. Day.[53] *The Seventh and Eighth Cavalries had an equal number ready to march. Together these military units grossly outnumbered the warriors who remained away from the agencies. The only advantage the Ghost dancers had was their remote and rugged Badlands location.*

The Stronghold, which had been thoroughly observed by the emissaries who had visited the Ghost dancers, was an intimidating defense position. According to J. B. McCloud, the Ghost dancers had fortified themselves on a table land or plateau in the Badlands at a point about ten miles southeast of the mouth of Battle River. *There, McCloud says,* This Stronghold was approached from one direction only and this approach was a narrow strip of table land which they were able to protect from having numerous rifle pits placed thereon. It was indeed a stronghold well adapted to their purposes.[54]

Piper attached to his letter a diagram of the Stronghold: This little drawing will give you an idea of the situation at the Badlands. The Indians are on a high mesa, the country around being sunk like that country we went through the day we went to get Ring. The enclosure where the letters are is the mesa, the dotted line shows route of troops from Pine Ridge. A. B, D, C are the only passes to the top of the mesa; B, C, and D are guarded by the 6th and 8th Cavalry and at A 9th and 7th are to make the advance. The Indians have put up earthworks across the pass at E and imagine themselves perfectly secure.[55]

Another reason for Brooke's delay may have been a lack of matériel. The "New York Herald" commented on this possibility: Nearly a year ago several light batteries were furnished with a new pattern gun—a very expensive one, but far better and more effective than the old pattern. One of the batteries so supplied is here, and its commanding officer says that up to the date of his being ordered on this duty sufficient ammunition had been furnished for only a very limited amount of target practice, and the order for field duty, caught them without a single round of ammunition.

Of course the telegraph was at once brought into play, securing assurances that necessary ammunition would be expressed to some point en route. This was about November 20, but up to the present time it has been impossible to get the ammunition, and we have the amusing spectacle of a battery of artillery shipped by rail over six hundred miles to the scene of supposed Indian hostilities, without a single round of ammunition after three weeks have passed.

Another business department of the army does queer things at times.

For the last few years nothing has been done to keep to the pack trains, an absolute necessity in all Indian warfare, and as a result of such short-sighted policy, when the occasion for the probable use arrives the mules have to be bought at any price, shipped at any season of the year, and put immediately at work, the nature of which is extremely hard and wearing on a well-seasoned mule. It is humiliating to add that 150 mules were received from the East for use as pack mules for field service, and not a halter or even a rope to prevent their roaming at will into the Indian camp. Of course a guard of soldiers is watching them.[56]

Brooke had good reason for delaying an attack on the Stronghold. An assault on it would probably result in heavy army casualties. Brooke chose to negotiate with the Ghost dancers rather than initiate a military action.

Brooke's delay did anger local residents. On December 19 an angry editor of the "Hermosa Pilot" fulminated, If there ever existed a state of affairs that exasperated American citizens with this government beyond all moderate expression, it is the manner in which the military authorities have neglected protecting the lives and property of the residents of the eastern portion of Custer County, along the borders of the reservation. For weeks . . . these blood-thirsty red-skins have succeeded in frightening people from their homes, causing them great hardship and expense that they are wholly unable to bear. And this, when we read daily of so many hundred soldiers lingering idly about the agency, and other points of quiet retreat, where the ugly warring savage is least likely to go. These troops have been seriously needed along Cheyenne River . . . for the past few weeks, and they were called for but came not, until last week. *Ye* Gods! Isn't it enough to boil the blood of a lover of home and country? . . . Last week the magnanimous military authorities ordered about 100 soldiers . . . while thousands of the blue-coated gentry were merrily engaged killing time, safely away from where the horny-handed citizens were driven to the desperate and painful past-time of killing Indians.[57]

11. A Scapegoat Is Selected

I have every confidence in the good intentions of the Sioux as a people. They will not be aggressors in any overt act against white settlers, and if justice is only done them, no uneasiness need be entertained.
—*Agent Maj. James McLaughlin*

DANCING AT GRAND RIVER

A wary Sitting Bull continued to remain at his camp on Grand River in spite of repeated efforts by Agent James McLaughlin to lure him into the Standing Rock Agency. According to Capt. E. G. Fechet, a former commander of Fort Yates, Rations were issued at the agency every second Saturday. Previous to October, Sitting Bull seldom failed to come in person and draw his share. From that time on he sent some member of his family to procure his rations, and no inducement of the agent could tempt him to appear at the agency. This determination of Sitting Bull frustrated one of the schemes to get him into safe-keeping. In the event of his coming in, Colonel Drum had intended quietly to surround the agency with the troops. Each company and troop had its position designated and on signal were to move up quickly. Sitting Bull, by remaining at home, declined to walk into the trap laid for him.[1]

Despite the intense suffering of the Lakotas at Standing Rock, on December 7, a ration day, Sitting Bull again did not come in. The "New York World"'s Standing Rock correspondent reported, The Indians of this reservation were here yesterday drawing rations, all families being represented. Sitting Bull's wife and boys were here also. Agent McLaughlin had arranged a plan to arrest Sitting Bull had he not received an order from the Interior Department suspending for the present any arrests whatsoever.

Sitting Bull may have been informed by Indians who read newspapers that he would be arrested if he went into Standing Rock Agency.[2] *Whatever the explanation for his not coming in, it is certain that the wary medicine man kept his distance.*

All seemed to be calm on Grand River. Official reports received at General Ruger's headquarters yesterday say that the Indians at Sitting Bull's camp on Grand River have at last stopped dancing, *the "World"'s reporter stated.* This stoppage is due, principally, to the cold weather, but partially to exhaustion and, possibly, in measure, to the fact that steps have been taken looking towards the establishing of a cordon of troops around the camp of the recalcitrant reds. . . . There are [not] more than a hundred effective warriors who would take up arms to resist the arrest of Bull.

Something will be done and speedily, and it is likely that by the first of the new year . . . Sitting Bull, Wounded Knee, Big Foot, The Hump, and Circling Bear . . . will be taken prisoners by the military and sent to join Geronimo in Dry Tortugas.

Sitting Bull deprecates, or pretends to deprecate, hostilities. In a recent letter to Colonel W. F. Drum, in command at Fort Yates, Bull said that while he was "constantly praying he never prayed to kill."

Probably he is shrewd enough to know a Winter campaign would end his career as that of 1880–81 should have done.[3]

Despite the decrease of dancing and Sitting Bull's statements, the military instructed fearful settlers to remain close to the agency.

One settler ignored the military's recommendations: Congregational missionary Mary Collins. Now that the Ghost Dance proceedings had gone so far, the government deemed it wise to order all the white people into the garrison, *she wrote.* All the white persons practically were gathered in except the Farm School people. I had gone to the garrison a day or so previous and when the government decided to order the people to come there they would not let me go out again. Word came that night that the Indians had come down from the reservation and that there was going to be a battle. The Indians had heard that I, too, had gone to the garrison and they said "If Wenonah [Collins's nickname] too has gone to the garrison then even she has deserted us and there will be war."

I wanted very much to leave the garrison and go back to my house and let the Indians still have faith in my loyalty to them at least for I was not afraid of them.

Colonel McLaughlin and Colonel Drum, who was in charge of the garrison, plainly saw the situation and asked me if I cared to go out, and I told them that I did. Consequently they allowed me to go; and as I rode over the prairie over each little butte, I could see an Indian looking at us. As they discovered it was "Wenonah" they spoke my name and dropped out of sight; we were not molested once. They were all delighted to think that I had returned to them.

On the Sunday following [December 8], *Collins continues,* I went to see Sitting Bull and found thousands of people gathered there. I held services with Mr. Grindstone and to this day I never hear "Nearer My God To Thee" but I think of that dreadful time. Our converts sang the song in a wild rough way and the music, screams, and shouting of the awful dance were mingled with our voices until you could scarcely hear anything.[4] *Collins exaggerated her estimate of "thousands" at the Ghost Dance; there were not thousands of Lakotas on the entire Standing Rock Reservation.*

On the same day, Doane Robinson writes, of Collins's ordinary congregation of more than one hundred, only three persons appeared; and then the noise of the nearby dance drowned their hymns of devotion. The people were possessed by a religious fervor bordering upon insanity.[5]

After our services, *Collins writes,* I went to the Holy tent of Sitting Bull and asked admittance. He sent out word that he could not see me at that time. I replied that I wished most earnestly to talk with him and after a while he sent out a message that he would speak with me. He directed that I must pass to the left and not step on certain places. I went in and sat down as he told me, and he continued performing other ceremonies. At length I explained to him that he must scatter the people who had gathered here in such a throng for this dance.

I said, "Sitting Bull, you know you do not believe these things that you are telling your people. You know that the Indians have not risen from the death out in the White Mountains and that the buffalo and deer and your favorite hunting dogs are not alive again. You know that you are deceiving your people who have always trusted you. The law orders you to go to Fort Yates and you must obey. You must go and talk with the officials there and tell them that you will have this dance cease. Otherwise the soldiers will come and kill all of your people. Your best warriors and men will be shot and the families will go unprovided for, and you, Sitting Bull, will be responsible for this terrible calamity. You must send the people home."

Here I mentioned the names of the leading chiefs and pictured to him how they would be killed without hesitation by the soldiers, and their families would die of starvation.

Sitting Bull listened gravely and replied: "Sister, I have gone too far; I cannot give it up; the people will laugh at me."

"It makes no difference how much they laugh," retorted the missionary, "this thing must be stopped at once. Go out to them and tell them to stop dancing and go home."

"Sister, I cannot," doggedly answered the old priest.

"You must do it; you must do it right now; the soldiers are coming," I exclaimed, almost hysterical by this time.

"Sister, I cannot," replied the old priest. "Go to the people, sister, and tell them to go home. Tell them that I, Sitting Bull, said it."

After this, I went out from the tent and looked at the people screaming, dancing, and wildly waving their arms in the air. One man whom I knew well fell upon the ground affecting that he was unconscious. I went up to him and said, "Louis, get up, you are not unconscious, you are not ill; get up and help me send these people home."

Louis rose and looked about him. All the people saw him obey me and of course lost their faith in the dance. Many of them turned to go home though some still stayed. I think we met at least a mile of wagons filled with Indians returning to their homes. At least many of them were convinced that it was useless to dance and that what Sitting Bull had told them was false. Many were sent from the dance and others returned before entering it at all.

This was the last occasion I had to see his people before the awful tragedy occurred which ended Sitting Bull's life. I think I was the last white person whom he saw before that time. Colonel McLaughlin and others were there shortly before but not at so late a date and when so many hundreds of people were gathered together when the dance was at its height.[6]

Collins's visit and her feisty behavior suggests there was little danger in Sitting Bull's camp. McLaughlin seemed to take this point of view as well. While he was in Bismarck on December 11, he told reporters, There is no danger of an outbreak and there never has been. Sitting Bull and his followers are still keeping up the Ghost Dance on Grand River, but their wild enthusiasm is rapidly abating.

A reporter added, The major thinks a week or more of cold weather will wind up the dancing. He says that he can arrest Sitting Bull without any trouble, but there is no occasion for taking him into custody.[7]

In spite of this pronouncement, McLaughlin continued to seek permission to arrest Sitting Bull. Permission was not forthcoming; instead, McLaughlin's initiatives were limited by government directives issued on November 14 and December 1. Both ordered that in any suppression of an outbreak by force, the agency should cooperate with and obey the orders of the military officers commanding on the reservation.

These orders practically placed the whole conduct of affairs in the hands of Colonel Drum, *observed Fechet,* [but] he and Major McLaughlin were at all times in perfect accord. Throughout the entire civil and military services, two men better fitted for the trying and delicate duty to come could not have been found.[8]

On December 12, as McLaughlin told reporters that all was calm at Standing Rock, interpreter Louis Primeau sent the following order to the Indian police stationed near Sitting Bull's camp: Tell Bull Head not to come in here. You will proceed to build the station I spoke of to you. . . . You must watch Sitting Bull closely. We learned sufficient news to lead us to believe that he is going to leave the reservation. If he should, you must stop him, and if he does not listen to you, do as you see fit. Use your own discretion in the matter, and it will be all right. I want you to assemble the police force and tell them for an excuse that you want them all together to build the station. This will be a good excuse to assemble them without suspicion. Bull Ghost brought a letter to me and it stated that Sitting Bull wanted to go on a visit, and if he should insist on going you can do as you think best, and it will be all right. Shave Head will meet you tomorrow. And should I think of anything else, he will instruct you.[9]

In spite of the relaxed situation at Standing Rock, McLaughlin and General Miles continued to insist that Sitting Bull planned to leave Standing Rock and go south. There is no evidence to support this belief. Mrs. One Bull, a member of Sitting Bull's band, later told an informant, We had no intention of leaving the place and going to any other reservation as people afterward said we had.[10] *Another informant told Walter S. Campbell,* The Reverend Reed says there was no foundation for the suspicion that Sitting Bull was going south except that he had been feeding up his horses and supervising oats.[11] *One Bull, a member of Sitting Bull's band, also says,* Sitting Bull had no intention to go to Pine Ridge. He had forty-five head of cattle, lots of hay, and a field of oats cut.[12]

Mrs. One Bull says, Bull Ghost had told Sitting Bull the evening before that they wanted him at the agency and he said: All right I will go in to the agency tomorrow and see what they want. If they put me in prison they may do so if they think that will do any good."[13]

Gray Eagle, Sitting Bull's alienated brother-in-law, differs. He told Campbell, The agent had me watch him [Sitting Bull]. It appeared he was getting ready to leave, as he was getting his horses into the corral and feeding them and repairing saddles, etc. It was therefore determined to arrest him and take him to the agency. We were also afraid that Big Foot and others might come up . . . and encourage him to go away. The day before the arrest I told Sitting Bull that he would be arrested within a few days and taken to the agency, not having taken my advice, and I expressed hope that he would act discreetly.[14]

Whatever Sitting Bull's intentions were, McLaughlin's informants continued to report that Sitting Bull planned to head south and join the Ghost dancers in the Badlands. With these reports in hand, McLaughlin felt the time had come to arrest Sitting Bull.

THE ORDER FOR ARREST

Miles, still chafing at Buffalo Bill's recall, wrote to Colonel Drum at Standing Rock and issued the following order:

HEADQUARTERS DEPARTMENT OF DAKOTA

St. Paul, Minn.
December 12, 1890.

To Commanding Officer, Fort Yates, N. Dak.,

The division commander has directed that you make it your especial duty to secure the person of Sitting Bull. Call on Indian agent to cooperate and render such assistance as will best promote the purpose in view. Acknowledge receipt and, if not perfectly clear, repeat back.

By command of General Ruger.
M. Barber
Assistant Adjutant General[15]

Colonel Drum, *McLaughlin later wrote*, furnished me with a copy of the order, and upon conferring with him in reference to the arrest, we fully agreed on the course of procedure. Colonel Drum was quite of the same mind that I was about the necessity for making the arrest while Sitting Bull's camp was practically deserted [and] that it should be made by the Indian police, with the military supporting at a convenient distance to aid the police in case of attempted rescue, and it was finally determined that the arrest should be made on the next ration day, December 20, unless it was precipitated by Sitting Bull trying to leave the reservation.[16]

For some reason, Drum sidestepped Miles's order and turned the attempted arrest over to McLaughlin and his police. Miles was again thwarted, this time by one of his own officers.

To lead his police McLaughlin chose Lieutenant Bull Head. A correspondent for the "New York World" claimed that Bull Head, one of the most trustworthy Indians of this reservation, has always bitterly hated Sitting Bull and regarded him as an arrant fraud, puffed up by his notoriety. No better man than Bull Head could have been selected to take charge of Sitting Bull's arrest.[17]

Others concur that Bull Head and Sitting Bull were enemies. An unnamed cavalry officer who had ridden with Fechet told a reporter for the "Pioneer Press," "Bull Head, who was in charge of the Indian police, was a bitter enemy of Sitting Bull."[18]

Interpreter Frank B. Zahn told Campbell, In the early days when Bull Head was a "hostile," a group of warriors were going on a buffalo hunt. Sitting Bull and Catch-the-Bear were among the warriors (twenty in all). Through jealousy, Bull Head accused Sitting Bull and Catch-the-Bear of being women.

At this time Sitting Bull and Catch-the-Bear rode up to Bull Head and, with small clubs, struck him until he fell off his horse. A feeling of enmity always existed between Bull Head and Sitting Bull after this trouble.[19]

Whether McLaughlin intentionally chose a leader who was antagonistic to Sitting Bull is uncertain, but it was well known that Bull Head resented Sitting Bull.

About six o'clock in the evening of December 13, *McLaughlin wrote in his memoir*, Bull Ghost came into the agency with a letter to me from Sitting Bull, his last utterance, full of defiance and implied threats, but so incoherent as to be difficult to understand. It was written by Andrew Fox, Sitting Bull's son-in-law, who could speak English and write a little. These portions I could decipher:

> I had a meeting with all my Indians and am writing this order to you.... God made the red race and the white, but the white higher.... I wish no one to come to me in my prayers with gun or knife.... And you, my friend, to-day you think I am fool and you tell some of the wise men among my people ... so you don't like me.
>
> I don't like myself, my friend, when some one is fool.... You think if I am not here the Indians is civilization.... Also will I let you know something. I got to go to Pine Ridge Agency, and to know this pray. So I let you know that and the policeman told me that you going to take all our ponies, guns too. So I want to let you know this. I want answer back soon.
>
> Sitting Bull[20]

Even in this short version, Sitting Bull's letter cannot be considered defiant or threatening. What he wrote are the words of a disillusioned man who is ready to travel to Pine Ridge to see firsthand how the Ghost Dance religion was practiced. The complete letter is an even deeper expression of the medicine man's despair:

> To the Major in the Indian Office:
>
> I want to write a few lines to day & let you know Some thing. I meeting with all my Indians to day & writing to you this order. God made you all the white race & and also made the Red race & and gave them both Might & Heart to know everything on the world; but white High then the Indians; but to say, our father is help us the Indians. So we all the Indians knowing. So I think this way. I wish no one to come to in my pray with they gun or knife: so all the Indians Pray to god for life & and try to find out goods road and do nothing wrong in they life: This is what we want & Pray: because we did not Say nothing about your pray because you pray to god: so we all Indians, while; we both to Pray only one god to make us: & you my friend to day. you thing I am fool; I you take some wise man among my people. & you let them know back

East. the white people. So I knowing that. but I think that is all right. because I am fool to pray to God. So you don't like me: My Friend. I don't like my self. when some one if fool; I like him; So you are the same, you don't like me because I am fool; & if I did not Here. then the Indians will be civilization: because I am Here. & all the Indians fool, & I know this is all you put down on newspapers back East. So I seeing the paper but I think it is all right: & when you are Here. in my camp. you was give me good word about. my pray. & to day you take all back from me: & also I will let you know some thing. I go to agency & to know this pray: So I let you know that & the police man. told me you going to take all our Poneys, gun, too; so I want you let me know that. I want answer back soon.

Sitting Bull[21]

It would seem that McLaughlin excerpted this letter to present Sitting Bull in the worst possible light.

The *"New York World"'s correspondent reported*, Meanwhile everything was done to throw Bull off his guard and to remove all his suspicions, while at the same time Bull Head, the lieutenant of police, who was to have charge of the work, was instructing his police, and every preparation was making against failure; but again events happened to change the date fixed for the arrest.[22]

When this report was dispatched Sitting Bull had only two more days to live.

THE NOOSE TIGHTENS

Early in the fall of 1890 Sitting Bull had a vision in which he saw himself being killed by Indian police. His friend One Bull said, From that time on Sitting Bull seemed to feel—really—he was to be killed by his own people.[23]

Sitting Bull's vision would soon come true.

Though he allowed McLaughlin's Indian police to attempt the arrest of Sitting Bull, Drum planned to send in supporting troops who would stand clear until the arrest was made. In many ways it was an ideal arrangement for the army. If anything went wrong, it would be McLaughlin's fault, but if things went seriously awry, the army would ride to the rescue; and, if there were any casualties, they would be among the police, not the army.

Finally, on December 14, McLaughlin began his preparations for Sitting Bull's arrest. That morning, the agent writes, former Ghost dancer Hawk Man No. 2 was engaged in bringing logs up from the Grand River . . . when he met Iron Star, another policeman, riding his horse, which was the best and fastest horse owned by any of the police. Iron Star had Carignan's letter. Hawk Man asked to be allowed to carry the letter to the agent; and, turning his team over to Iron Star, he took the horse and brought the letter here. The distance was forty miles.

Hawk Man did not know the nature of the message, but he was proud of the distinction that the service could give him, doubtless thinking that it would bring nearer to him the coveted honor of the blue uniform and a place on the permanent police roll.

He was nearly exhausted when he arrived at the agency, and I sent him to the police quarters giving instructions that he be taken care of and kept there all night. He was very anxious to be doing something, but I was not thinking of sending him back to the river. Moreover, I wanted to send Sergeant Red Tomahawk, whom I was certain could be trusted to carry through the important orders that were going to Lieutenant Bull Head and who was intelligent enough to properly convey the verbal directions.[24]

A letter from John M. Carignan arrived late in the afternoon. It was just what McLaughlin needed to set his plan in action:

Grand River, S.D.
Dec. 14, 1890.
12:30 A.M.

Major James McLaughlin
Standing Rock Agency, N.D.

Dear Sir:

Bull Head wishes to report what occurred at Sitting Bull's camp at a council held yesterday. It seems that Sitting Bull has received a letter from the Pine Ridge outfit asking him to come over there as God was to appear to them. Sitting Bull's people want him to go, but he has sent a letter to you asking permission, and if you do not do it, he is going to go anyway; he has been fitting up his horses to stand a long ride and will go on horseback in case he is pursued.

Bull Head would like to arrest him at once before he has a chance of giving them the slip, as he thinks that if he gets the start, it will be impossible to catch him. He says to send word to him by courier immediately, also to let him know what your plans are, if soldiers are to come—he says to send them by Sitting Bull's road.

He also mentions something about Shave Head coming down here, but as I am not good enough interpreter to understand, he has said that you can use your own judgment in regard to that one thing. I understand thoroughly and that is that the poor man is eat out of house and home—he says that with councils and couriers coming to his place that even the hay he has is nearly all gone. I sympathize with him, as I am nearly in the same boat.

If you send a dispatch to Bull Head through me, please send me some envelopes, as I am entirely out can't even find one to enclose this letter.

Yours very respectfully,
John M. Carignan[25]

McLaughlin later wrote, Colonel Drum . . . having seen the courier passing his quarters, and being anxious to learn the latest news from the Sitting Bull camp, came into my office while I was reading the letter and upon being informed of its contents concluded that the arrest should be made the next morning. I was anxious that the arrest should be made by the police, because otherwise it was not possible without bloodshed; and for the reason that the arrest . . . being made by the police would have a salutary effect upon the Indians in general.

Colonel Drum heartily agreed with me in this view of the case, and it was determined that two troops of the Eighth Cavalry, numbering one hundred men, with Captain E. G. Fechet in command, should leave Fort Yates at midnight in order to arrive at the Oak Creek crossing of the Sitting Bull road by 6:30 of the 15th, to support the police if necessary; and before Colonel Drum left my office, I wrote the following letter in English, with a translation of it in Sioux, ordering the arrest of Sitting Bull, which I sent to Lieutenant Bull Head by Second Sergeant Red Tomahawk.[26]

United States Indian Service
Standing Rock Agency
December 14, 1890

Lieut. Bull Head, (or Shave Head), Grand River,

From report brought by Scout "Hawk Indian" I believe that the time has arrived for the arrest of Sitting Bull and that it can be made by the Indian police without much risk.—I therefore want you to make the arrest before daylight tomorrow morning, and try and get back to the Sitting Bull road crossing of Oak Creek by daylight tomorrow morning or as soon after as possible. The cavalry will leave here tonight and will reach Sitting Bill crossing on Oak Creek before daylight tomorrow morning, where they will remain until they hear from you.

Louis Primeau will go with the cavalry command as guide and I want you to send a messenger to the cavalry command as soon as you can after you arrest him so that they may be able to know how to act in aiding you or preventing any attempt at his rescue.

I have ordered all the police at Oak Creek to proceed to Carignan's

School to await your orders. This gives you a force of 42 policemen for you to use in the arrest.

Very respectfully
James McLaughlin
U.S. Indian Agt.

P.S. You must not let him escape under any circumstances.[27]

This postscript would arouse suspicions about McLaughlin's intentions to arrest Sitting Bull. Had he devised a strategy that would force Sitting Bull and his followers to resist?

According to McLaughlin, These orders, in duplicate, were . . . given to Sergeant Red Tomahawk, a man who could be depended upon to get through with them, and who did so and signally distinguished himself the next morning. The verbal instructions given Red Tomahawk as to assembling the scattered detachments of Indian police were complete.[28] *McLaughlin does not specify what was included in his verbal instructions.*

McLaughlin also sent Carignan more specific instructions that suggest McLaughlin hoped to capture Sitting Bull alive.

Standing Rock Agency, N.D.
Dec. 14, 1890.
4:30 P.M.

J. M. Carignan, Esq.
Grand River, S.D.

Dear Sir:

I send a letter, by bearer of this to Bull Head, ordering him to arrest Sitting Bull tonight. It must be done without fail as the cavalry will start this evening and reach the Sitting Bull crossing of Oak Creek tomorrow morning to protect the police from that point into Post. Should by any chance Bull Head be away from Grand River having started into agency to fix upon a plan of arrest, let Shave Head carry out the orders and arrest him as directed in the letter to Bull Head, which you will find herewith. It will hardly be necessary for all the police to come in with Sitting Bull, unless they should be opposed by all the infected Indians following them after they reach Oak Creek, a number can return and keep watch of the other Indians that none attempt to leave the reservation. Have it announced in the plainest way possible that no Indians will be disturbed and all will be treated in a kindly manner, unless they should attempt to leave the reservation.

I trust that the whole police force can be concentrated promptly.

Very respectfully,
Jas. McLaughlin,
Ind. Agent.

> P.S. Be sure to see that they have a light wagon ready to bring Bull in, so that there will be no delay by such an oversight. You had better come in for a time. If Bull Head's wagon is not convenient and they need yours I will see that you are compensated for its use.
>
> J. McL. Agt.[29]

Now every eventuality was covered, and the plan to arrest Sitting Bull was complete.

In the meantime, McLaughlin writes, Hawk Man No. 2 was received at the police quarters with due honor as the bearer of important tidings, though what news he brought remained a problem to the Indians, no man knowing, except those concerned, that orders had been given for the arrest of Sitting Bull.

A good supper was prepared for the courier, but he ate little and talked less. He had the air of a man who was impressed by something that impended, but he knew nothing of the cause of his uneasiness and depression. It was observed by the policeman on duty at their headquarters that he could not rest. There being an air of expectancy about the agency at the time, no particular attention was paid to Hawk Man when, impelled by fate, he went out and got his horse that he had ridden from Grand River, forty miles that day, and mounted and started back on the trail [to Grand River] that led him home and then on.

Hawk Man got home during the night, but could not remain there. He got another mount and rode to Bull Head's house, which he found deserted by the police. They had gone on to Gray Eagle's—whose two sisters were married to Sitting Bull, and were presently to be reduced to widowhood. There he found the policemen had started for the camp of Sitting Bull, and full of the inspiration that was leading him to his death, he followed the trail and caught up with Bull Head's command as the detachment was entering Sitting Bull's camp.[30]

Hawk Man No. 2 rode more than 40 miles more that night and, if the 12 miles he drove his team between Oak Creek and Grand River earlier that morning is included, he rode a total of 120 miles in less than a day. It was an epic feat of horsemanship and human duration.

A CALL TO ARMS

As McLaughlin put his plan in action, Drum set up the army's part in the operation. Drum gave Fechet, who Miles would later describe as an experienced, judicious officer, the duty of backing up the Indian police.[31] *Fechet had commanded Fort Yates prior to Drum's arrival early in the fall.*

McLaughlin's police saw the backup force as a valid tactic. Red Toma-

hawk says, The original intention was that if we, the police force, should happen to be alone, Sitting Bull's people would not respect us; but if they should see the military power show themselves, perhaps they will pull down a little bit.[32]

According to Drum, the late-night departure was designed to prevent any attempt at rescue on the road—the cavalry did not start before midnight so that an Indian runner could not give the alarm before the police had acted.[33]

As evening approached, none of Drum's troops suspected that action was imminent. Lt. Matthew Steele was having Sunday dinner with his wife and Lt. David J. Baker of the Twelfth Infantry and his wife. Steele says, Darkness had settled down upon the valley of the Missouri and the officers at old Fort Yates were, most of them, in the midst of their dinners when the stillness of the evening was suddenly broken by the sharp notes of an infantry bugle. It was sounding "Officers' Call," that signal which makes every officer of the garrison spring to his feet and start for the commandant's office.

"That means we shall go out tonight," I remarked as Lieutenant Baker and I rose from the table. Mrs. Steele and I were taking Sunday dinner with the Bakers, and Baker and I hurried away leaving our wives to have their dessert and coffee by themselves.[34]

Fechet would also write about that evening. In his words, On the 14th, about 6 P.M., as we were enjoying our after dinner cigars beside our comfortable fireplaces, "Officers' Call" rang out loud and shrill on the clear frosty air. In a few minutes all the officers of the fort were assembled in Colonel Drum's office. He informed us briefly that the attempt to arrest Sitting Bull would be made that night. He then turned to me and said that the command of the troops going out would be given to me, that my orders would be made out in a short time, and that my command would move at midnight. Instructions were at once given to load the wagon and to serve a hot supper for all the men at 11 o'clock.[35]

According to Steele, it was a short walk to Drum's office since Fort Yates was a very compact little post built in the days when the Sioux were fresh from the warpath of 1876. A loopholed block-house, relic of those times, guarded it on one side. The commandant's office stood in the center of the little square parade-ground, which was surrounded on three sides by the barracks of the enlisted men and on the fourth by the line of officers' quarters.[36]

The "New York World"'s correspondent joined the officers during Drum's briefing. He was jubilant to find that he would be one of two journalists riding with the expedition. The other was an unnamed officer in

Fechet's command. In preparation for the night ride the "World"'s correspondent attended the officers' call at 6 P.M. He reported, On assembling in the colonel's office the officers were briefly told by him that he was charged by the division commander with the arrest of Sitting Bull.

"I am in hopes," said the colonel, "that the arrest may be made by the Indian police and without resistance. The arrest will be attempted by them at dawn tomorrow morning. At midnight tonight the two troops of cavalry will start on the road to Sitting Bull's camp, equipped in light marching order. A courier will meet you to inform you as to what success the police shall have. If they succeed in taking Bull they will turn him over to you. If a fight takes place you will go to their assistance and relief. If Bull succeeds in getting away you must follow."[37]

THE POLICE MOVE INTO POSITION

John Lone Man, a member of McLaughlin's police, described his part in the arrest in considerable detail. One morning, *he told Vestal,* the 14th day of December, 1890, while I was busily engaged in mending my police saddle at my home on the Grand River, about 36 miles south of Standing Rock Agency, policeman Charles Afraid of Hawk of Wakpala District came to me with the message that all of the members of the entire reservation Indian police had been ordered to report immediately to the Lieut. Henry Bull Head's place, about three miles south of Bull Head Sub-Issue-Station. This place was about 30 miles up the river, west from my home, and about 40 miles southwest of the Standing Rock Agency. Afraid of Hawk was sent to notify me in person.

I asked him what was up. "Oh," he said, "I have a hunch that we are going to be ordered to arrest Sitting Bull and his Ghost dancers, which I am very sorry to say."

"That is just what I had expected all the time—something unpleasant would be the outcome of this Messiah Craze," I said to him.

I invited him to dinner, fed his horse, and I got ready. I had an excellent saddle horse—an iron grey gelding—in the best condition for service. I had him shod all around on all fours with "Neverslip" horseshoes. I named him Wacinyanpi—Trusty—for he had proven himself a thoroughly reliable horse. My wife hearing the news became rather nervous and excited for she seemed to realize that there was a serious trouble coming.

Dinner being over, I bade my wife and children good-bye and we left for Bull Head's place.

On the way up we notified several police—Bad Horse, Armstrong, Little Eagle, Wakutemani, Brown Man, Hawk Man (No. 1), and Good

Voice Elk and others so that, by the time we arrived at Bull Head's place there were about 12 of us from our way and the rest of the 37 were all from different districts in the reservation.

Of course, we had quite a lot to say on the way among ourselves knowing full well that we were called to take a final action to suppress this Ghost Dance which was becoming a menace to the tribe. . . . I'm simply expressing my viewpoint as one who had reformed from all heathenish, hostile and barbarous ways, formerly one of the loyal followers of Chief Sitting Bull.

Major McLaughlin, then Indian agent, took a liking to my efforts trying the new way of living and at once appointed me assistant boss-farmer—a position I held for two years. . . . I had adopted new ways and had discarded all superstitions and other old time customs and practices.[38]

It was about six or seven o'clock in the evening when we reached our destination [Gray Eagle's home], . . . White Bird and Red Bear—police privates, were assigned to take care of the saddle horses belonging to the Indian police. These two were my relatives so I felt quite at home with them. Lieutenant Bull Head was likewise a relative to me and needless to say anything of his ever warm reception for me in his home.

While we were all assembling, two members of the force from what is now known as Kenil District arrived. They were Shave Head and High Eagle. Lieut. Bull Head went out to meet them. There Bull Head and High Eagle were standing with hands clasped and lock-arms. Bull Head said: "So, brother, you are going to be with me again."

High Eagle replied, "Wherever you go—I shall always follow you even unto death."

Bull Head said, "Good."

It was a well-known fact that these two comrades had been pals from childhood up "sharing each others sorrow, sharing each others joy."

After our supper, when all had arrived, Lieut. Bull Head called a meeting and we all got together on the very spot where Sitting Bull was born many years before.

Bull Head said, "Friends and relatives, I am sure you are all over anxious to know why you have been called here this evening and am quite positive that every one knows and expects that sooner or later we would be called to this serious order. I have this communication from Major McLaughlin, which will be read to you by our friend Charles De Rockbraine, who is serving as assistant farmer and interpreter in this District."

Here, Charley, popularly knows as Chaska among the Indians, came forward and read the order in Sioux language so that everyone understood what the order was about. I do not think any of the Indian police present could read or write in English or Dakota language.

We all felt sad to think that our chief with his followers had disobeyed orders—due to outside influences, and that drastic measures had to be resorted to in order to bring them to discipline.

Personally, I expected a big trouble ahead. During this time this Ghost Dance was indulged in, several times have the leaders made threats that if the policemen tried to interfere with the matter, they would get the worst of it for the Ghost dancers were well-equipped with "ogle wakan"—medicine shirts, which were supposed to be bulletproof, and for the further fact, several attempts were made by different officers of the police force [who] had attempted to break up the camp in a peaceable way, but failed.

The order being for us to act about daybreak and as the night was rather long, we tried to pass the intervening time in telling war stories. The Indian police who were on this campaign were a class of Dakotas who had enviable achievements and attainments and who [had] the highest estimation in the minds of government officials, missionaries, traders, as well as possessing good influence in their respective communities.[39]

SADDLE UP!

The Eighth Cavalry's detachment, ready to back up the police, readied for its departure. According to Fechet, The squadron moved out promptly at midnight. I had mounted after bidding Colonel Drum good-bye, when he stepped to the side of my horse, and putting his hand on mine, said, "Captain, after you leave here, use your own discretion. You know the object of the movement; do your best to make it a success."[40]

The "New York World"'s reporter wrote, The officers present were Captain Fechet and Lieuts. Crowder and Brooke, of G Troop; Lieuts. Slocum and Steele, of F Troop, and Assistant Surgeon Chapin. Louis Primeau, a half-breed and chief of the Indian scouts, went as guide and interpreter; Captain Fechet commanding the battalion. In addition to pistols and carbines F Troop carried the Hotchkiss gun, and G Troop took a Gatling gun. Two meals of hard bread, bacon and coffee and two feeds of grain were taken in G Troop's light wagon. No bedding or buffalo coats were carried.[41] *The artillery allowed the Eighth Cavalry to remain at a distance from any resistance the police might encounter. How they would protect the police with their guns in close combat would prove to be a problem in the hours ahead.*

There was one other problem for Fechet to solve. Drum, in his order wrote, If on arrival at Oak Creek, Captain Fechet learns that the police are fighting or need assistance, he will push on and if necessary follow Sitting Bull as long as possible with his supplies, keeping the post commander informed by courier of his movements.[42] *Fechet's troops were stripped down and ill-equipped for a lengthy pursuit. Their mission was limited.*

Maj. William G. Wilkerson, then a private with Troop G of the Eighth Cavalry, says, The ground was covered with deep snow, and a hard sleet storm had been raging all night. As we had already covered some 20-odd miles and had as many more to cover, we were then just a sheet of ice and chilled to the bone, the prospect ahead of us did not look very rosy.

After mounting we started off at a gallop, and as the horses were all smooth shod it was very difficult to keep them up on their feet. Several did go down but fortunately their riders were thrown clear and were not hurt. That ride was about the hardest that this writer ever experienced.[43]

According to Fechet, The command was to proceed only to the crossing of the Oak Creek, which was 18 miles from Bull's camp. After receiving this order, on consultation with Colonel Drum, commanding the post, it was decided that I should move as close to Bull's camp as possible without discovery, and there await the police.[44]

Halfway from Yates to Grand River, *Lieutenant Steele wrote,* our trail crossed Oak Creek where the command was halted, and Captain Fechet called the officers to him at the head of the column.

"Gentlemen," said he, "Colonel Drum told me an Indian courier would meet us here and tell me how the Indian police are getting on with their job and guide us to them. We have been here several minutes but there is no sign of the courier. My orders are to secure the person of Sitting Bull. What do you think we should do, wait here for the courier or go ahead?"

Our unanimous answer was "Go ahead."

"That is precisely what I had already made up my mind to do," he answered, "but I am glad you agree with me. You may return to your troops."

In a minute or two the command "Prepare to mount, mount" was given by word of mouth (trumpet signals carried too far on the still, crisp night air), and the troopers who had been dismounted to rest their horses swung themselves back into their saddles and the trot was resumed.[45]

Carignan, near Sitting Bull's camp, says that he, Lone Man, Hawk Man, Brownman and Looking Elk proceeded to Bull Head's house up the river about five miles from the school, and in order to reach there had to go through Sitting Bull's camp. The night was very dark and hazy and in passing by, some one called out of one of the tents and asked who it was. I replied in Indian, giving my name. I was best known as "Jack," which seemed to satisfy him.

I reached Bull Head's house about 2:30 A.M., but found no one at home excepting his wife, two children and an Indian woman. They informed me that Bull Head and a small force had proceeded over to Gray Eagle's house by a roundabout way in order to be closer to Sitting Bull's at day break, and that I was to send my instructions over by courier to him there, and to use my team and wagon in taking his family as far as Oak Creek, where he would meet me with his prisoner.

I cautioned the four policemen I had with me and told them to go on to where Bull Head was, and tell him to be sure and take a light wagon and team with him.[46]

The attempt to arrest Sitting Bull was under way.

MILES GOES TO THE FRONT

A news dispatch from Chicago reported that General Miles, accompanied by Captain [Marion P.] Maus, A.D.C., left Chicago last Sunday, December 14, for St. Paul, going thence to Pine Ridge Agency and other points. General Miles remarked that in all his experience with Indians he had never known any delusion to be so widespread and far-reaching as the Messiah craze had come to be. General Miles had spared no efforts to have the troops ready for any unforeseen emergency that may arise, no matter from which agency or quarter actual conflict with the Indians may occur.[47]

Simultaneous with the general stepping quietly aboard the train at the big railroad depot in Chicago, the expedition, which had been with equal quietude under preparation at Fort Yates [and] which forms part of the agency, was also ready to move. Almost at the same moment that General Miles's car glided out for the Northwest the members of his little command here silently took their departure and were quickly lost in the darkness that enveloped the wilderness stretching to the camp of Sitting Bull on the banks of the Grand River.[48]

Miles knew the extent to which Sitting Bull hated agency life. The first time they met, Miles said Sitting Bull declared: "God Almighty made me; God Almighty did not make me an agency Indian, and I'll fight and die fighting before any white man can make me an agency Indian."[49]

Would Sitting Bull resist? Would he be killed in an attempt to remain

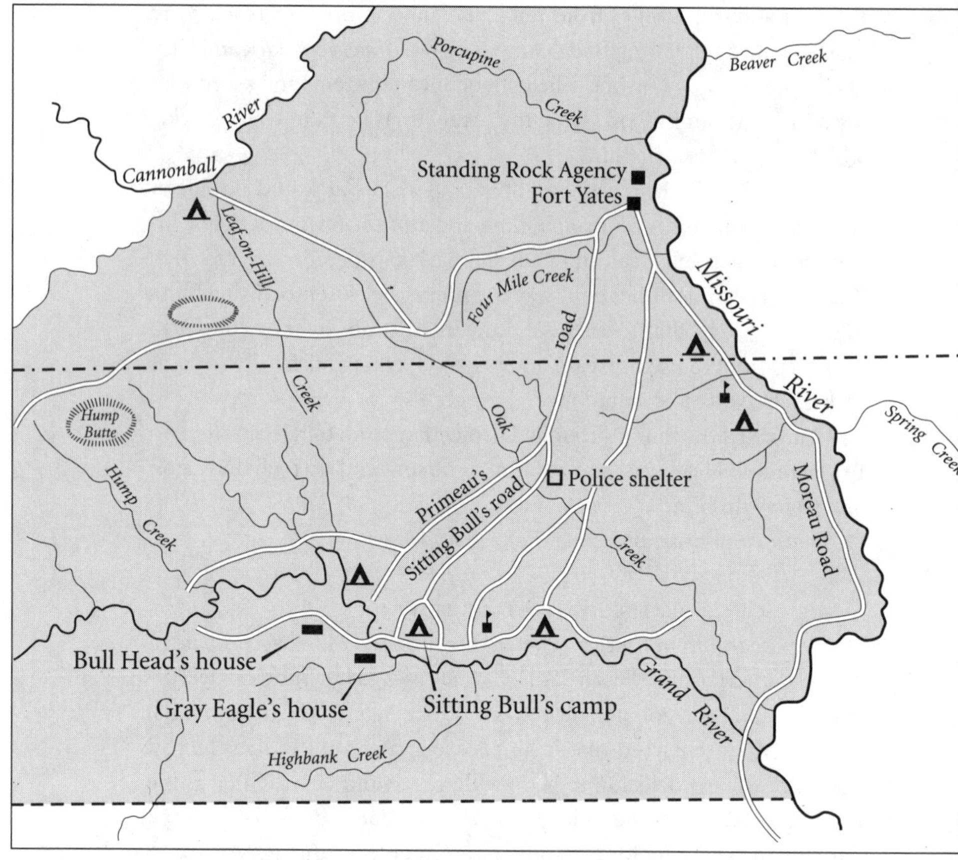

Map 3. Grand River Reservation and surrounding area

free? Certainly Miles knew there was a chance that Sitting Bull would die during the attempt to arrest him. Was that his intention?

The "New York World" 's correspondent, while writing admiringly of his fellow riders, harbored a suspicion that there was a plot to kill the medicine man. After the expedition, he reported, Sitting Bull's promise to die fighting had much to do in shaping the determination of a sudden decisive result, as well as the old chief's oft-expressed wish to be remembered as the last Indian on the continent to give up his rifle. When General Miles left Chicago headed in this direction it was the beginning of the end.

The expedition which started from this agency for Sitting Bull's camp, forty miles distant, to take him dead or alive, with the chances ten to one of his death, was no haphazard foray of semi-savage Indian police and ill-advised army subordinates.

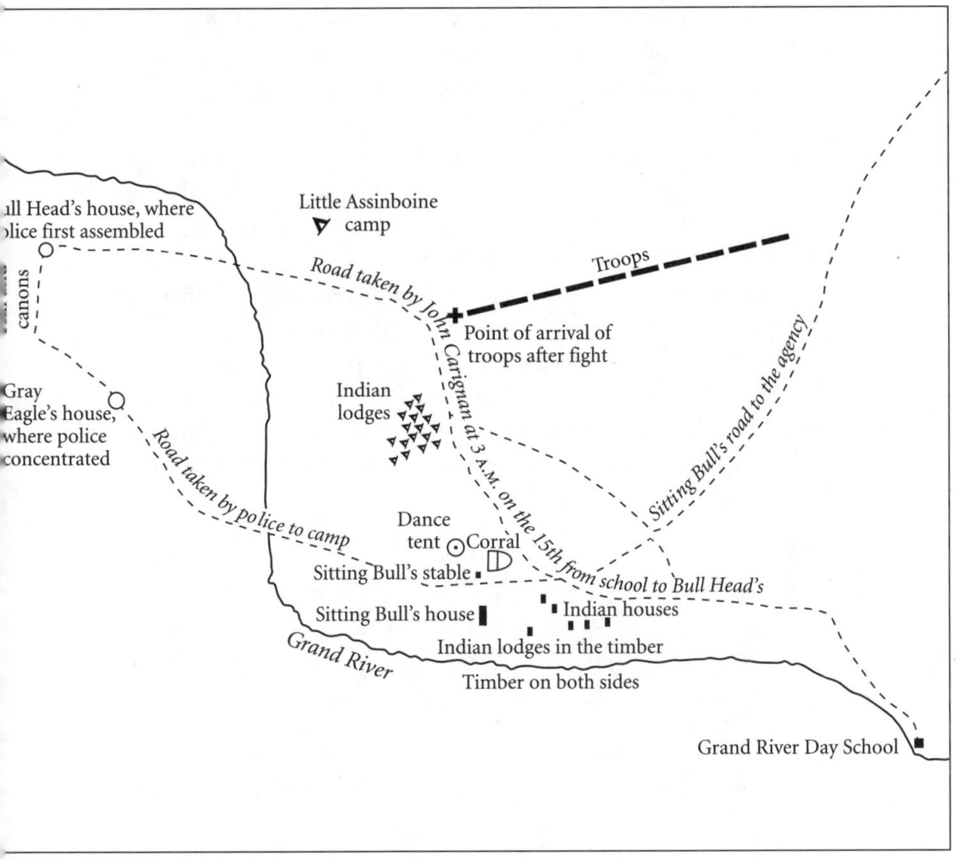

Detail of map 3 showing Sitting Bull's camp on the Grand River

The van was led by men of Sitting Bull's own blood. Superbly mounted and accoutered, every one wore the bright brazen buttons and showy blue cloth uniforms of Uncle Sam's service. This was no mere coincidence. It was to be part of the great object lesson to the Ghost dancers and a new method of solving the Indian problem, by turning the Indians wholesale into soldiers.

One thing is certain. The band of well-fed, warmly clad, copper-faced athletes that led the way for the white soldiers bent on a mission of utility, was a striking contrast to the starving, ragged, crazy wretches that formed such a menace in the Grand River Camp.

Close behind the blue-coated Indian horsemen's hardy ponies, but taking a slower pace on the frozen trail came Captain Fechet's cavalry command. The cavalry were encumbered with two pieces of modern light artillery, machine guns. . . . To the rear of Fechet's cavalry, and at times taking a double quick step forward, for the night was bitterly cold, the infantry command of Colonel Drum swung along in the darkness. A weary, difficult march it was.

The distance and the capabilities of the troops to withstand the fatigues of such a journey had been figured out nicely and when the first faint light of dawn appeared, the expedition was within easy distance of its destination. The broken order of a triple separation of forces had been carefully preserved, and the Indian police were the first to sight the huddled cluster of ugly looking tipis on the river bank.

The night was dark and the road in many places was covered with ice and snow and lay over a good deal of hilly country. Whenever it was practicable, the command marched at a trot and made quick time.[50]

It was a long, hard ride. At its end would be the first battle of the Ghost Dance war.

12. Dawn on Grand River

Sitting Bull as I knew him and studied him was I may say a very high grade man. A man may succeed in getting in the limelight as a "false alarm" for a limited time, but if he holds his own for years, as he did, he is way above the ordinary.—*Dr. Valentine T. McGillycuddy* to *Walter S. Campbell*, [July?] 20, 1929

THE LONG MARCH

Many years after the massacre at Wounded Knee Lone Man told Walter S. Campbell, Daybreak was drawing near and Lieutenant Bull Head asked that we offer up a prayer before starting out and without waiting or calling upon anyone else, led us in prayer. After this an order was issued to saddle up our horses. When everyone was ready we took our places by two and at the command "hopo" we started.

Black Hills, a member of the party, says Lieutenant Bull Head told him, "I am going to get killed. I will not run away from danger. Be brave, like the agent told us to be."[1]

We had to go through rough places, *Lone Man said*, and the roads were slippery as we went through the Grand River bottoms. It seemed as if the owls were hooting at us and the coyotes were howling all around us that one of the police remarked that the owls and the coyotes were giving us a warning—"so beware" he said.

Before we started, Bull Head assigned Red Bear and White Bird to have the favorite white horse of Sitting Bull's (which was always kept in the shed or in the corral at nights) caught and saddled up and be in readiness for the chief to ride to the agency upon his arrest. The rest of the force were ordered to station themselves all around Sitting Bull's cabin for the purpose of keeping order while the officers went into the cabin and cause the arrest. Bull Head said to me, "Now you used to belong to this outfit and was always on the good side of the chief. I wish you would use your influence to keep order among the leaders who are going to become hostile."[2]

Those who were there agree this white horse was given to Sitting Bull by Buffalo Bill at the end of the Wild West's 1885 season.[3]

Before the departure, a final coordination was established between Agent McLaughlin's police and the military. The "New York World"'s officer-correspondent reported, The distance [from Standing Rock to Grand River] was forty-three miles. The United States troops stopped and consulted with the police about five miles from the tipis on the Grand River. It was agreed at a consultation that the troops should move up to within two to three miles of the Indian camp and station themselves where they could easily be signaled.[4]

There is some evidence to support the accusations that McLaughlin's police had reinforced their courage with whiskey before they left. J. F. Waggoner, an enlisted man in Company H, Twelfth U.S. Infantry, later swore in an affidavit, I affirm that I saw a jug of whiskey in the possession of said Indian police and that I saw several of the police the worse for liquor shortly before they left the troops to arrest Sitting Bull on the morning of December 15, 1890.[5]

Joe Claymore, *another white man*, says Red Tomahawk told him that he was the last policeman to leave the agency and that when he left, McLaughlin sent by him [Red Tomahawk] a jug of whiskey to Lieutenant Bull Head. *Claymore adds*, Lieutenant Bull Head was drunk, as well as many other policemen.[6] *Mrs. One Bull also claimed that* Sam Bruguier said Jack McLaughlin had boasted to him that he gave liquor to the police just before they started to arrest Sitting Bull.[7]

Black Hills protested these charges, stating, The story that booze was given the police is positively not true.[8]

Drunk or sober, the police were on their own.

The strategy used to arrest Sitting Bull was questionable. Skirmishes and battles in the Indian wars often lasted a matter of minutes and rarely more than an hour or two. Keeping the cavalry in reserve two or three miles away meant that the small detachment of Indian police could be wiped out if they encountered resistance. McLaughlin was either an inept tactician, or he set up a battle between his police and Sitting Bull and his followers so he would receive all the glory if the police were successful. On the other hand, the army had shown an unwillingness to force an armed encounter with the Lakotas. Perhaps Colonel Drum and McLaughlin decided to let the Lakotas fight among themselves, therefore absolving themselves from any blame if their tactics were unsuccessful.

THE ARREST

Captain Fechet rode into dawn, certain that everything was in order and that his troops would not have to go into battle. After daybreak, *he later wrote*, I expected every minute to meet the Indian police with Sitting Bull as their prisoner, it having been arranged by Major McLaughlin, Indian agent, that they should make a descent upon Sitting Bull's camp about daybreak, arresting Bull and delivering him to me for conduct to this post.

From the best evidence obtainable, I am led to believe that the police under the command of Bull Head and Shave Head, about forty strong,

In 1887 Paiute medicine man Wovoka, then in his late thirties and living in Walker Valley, Nevada, began preaching what would eventually be called the Ghost Dance religion. During a total solar eclipse on January 1, 1889, he had his greatest vision. National Anthropological Archives, Smithsonian Institution, photo no. 1659-BB.

Short Bull, a Brulé medicine man who in 1889 was in his mid-forties, was working at the Cheyenne River Agency when he was asked to join the Lakotas who traveled to Nevada to visit Wovoka. National Anthropological Archives, Smithsonian Institution, photo no. 3151.

Kicking Bear, a friend of Crazy Horse and by birth an Oglala, became a Miniconjou chief when he married Woodpecker Woman. He had gained fame as a warrior and medicine man prior to joining the Lakota delegation to Nevada. National Anthropological Archives, Smithsonian Institution, photo no. 3192-B.

Above: Sitting Bull and Indian agent Maj. James McLaughlin pose during an 1886 ceremony at which the rock that gave Standing Rock Reservation its name was dedicated. Even then there was an enmity between the two men. National Anthropological Archives, Smithsonian Institution, photo no. 3117-D.

Top right: Red Cloud, nearly seventy years old and half-blind in 1890, was photographed with his wife, Pretty Owl, prior to his death in 1909. They were married more than half a century. Photo courtesy of the Nebraska State Historical Society.

Bottom right: Elaine Goodale, supervisor of education in the Dakota reservation system, married Lakota physician Charles A. Eastman in June 1891. Both cared for the wounded Miniconjous who survived the Wounded Knee Massacre. Photo courtesy of the Sophia Smith Collection, Smith College, Northhampton MA.

Above: Col. James W. Forsyth, front row center, seventh from the right, sits amidst the officers of the Seventh Cavalry who were at Wounded Knee on December 29, 1890. Several, including Forsyth, served with Custer at the Battle of the Little Bighorn. Photo courtesy of the Nebraska State Historical Society.

Left: Scout and interpreter Philip Wells, whose nose was almost severed at Wounded Knee, found himself in the midst of the firing and later persuaded a number of women and children to surrender. The scar from his wound is evident in this photograph, taken some time after the massacre. National Anthropological Archives, Smithsonian Institution, photo no. 3251-B.

Right: Brothers White Lance, Joseph Horn Cloud, and Dewey Beard posed for this picture, ca. 1907. All were involved in the fighting at Wounded Knee. Dewey Beard and White Lance were badly wounded but continued fighting until the women and children escaped through the ravine. Joseph Horn Cloud, then a teenager, helped Miniconjou women and children to flee. Photo courtesy of the Nebraska State Historical Society.

Big Foot, also known as Spotted Elk, sits at the center of a Lakota delegation that went to Washington in 1888. National Anthropological Archives, Smithsonian Institution, photo no. 55602.

Top: This photograph showing Big Foot's frozen body as it laid in front of the remnants of his burnt tent was taken at least one day after the massacre. His body was interred in the mass grave. Photo courtesy of the Nebraska State Historical Society.

Below: Unidentified members of a burial party headed by Paddy Starr load Lakota bodies into a wagon while troops watch. According to Starr, the mass burial of Lakotas began on December 30, 1890. Dr. Charles A. Eastman, however, places the burial date as three days after the massacre. Photo courtesy of the Nebraska State Historical Society.

No 49

Burial of the Dead
at the Battle of Wounded Knee S.D.
copy Righted Jan 1st 1891 by the
North Western Photo Co
Chadron Neb
No 1

Top left: A temporary hospital was set up in the Holy Cross Episcopal Church at Pine Ridge. Here, Elaine Goodale, Dr. Charles A. Eastman, Rev. Charles Cook, Bishop W. H. Hare, and other Pine Ridge residents attended the wounded Miniconjous. This item is reproduced by permission of the Huntington Library, San Marino CA.

Bottom left: Paddy Starr, standing in the grave on the left, was paid two dollars per body by Maj. Gen. Nelson A. Miles. He claimed that he placed 168 bodies in the mass grave located on the hill from which artillery was fired into Wounded Knee Valley. To Starr's right is local resident Bill McWilliams. Photo courtesy of the Nebraska State Historical Society.

Above: William F. Cody (Buffalo Bill) was photographed with Maj. Gen. Nelson A. Miles near Pine Ridge on January 16, 1891. Cody was then a general in the Nebraska National Guard. Photo courtesy of the Nebraska State Historical Society.

According to most firsthand accounts, Red Tomahawk (pictured) and Bull Head were the first to shoot Sitting Bull during the attempted arrest at Sitting Bull's Grand River Camp on December 15, 1890. Bull Head was mortally wounded; Red Tomahawk survived the encounter. Photo courtesy of the Nebraska State Historical Society.

entered Sitting Bull's camp about 5:50 A.M., on the 15th instant, for the purpose of making the arrest of Sitting Bull.[9] *The police arrived at Grand River at the appointed time.*

We waited, *Gray Eagle says*, across the river and finally went over to make the arrest. It was agreed that Bull Head, Shave Head and Red Tomahawk should go into the house and get Sitting Bull out and that Cook (Yellow Wolf) should go to the other house and see who was there.[10]

McLaughlin, reconstructing the event from accounts given him by his police, claimed that initially everything went according to plan: Thirty-nine regular policemen and four specials under Bull Head and Shave Head rode into the Sitting Bull camp at early dawn the next morning. Some of the men had traveled immense distances to rendezvous at the home of Lieutenant Bull Head, and all were firmly determined to make the arrest. Sitting Bull's band lived in houses stretching along the Grand River for a distance of four or five miles. Many of the houses were deserted, the Indians having engaged in dancing the greater part of the previous night.[11]

Mrs. One Bull does not mention any dancing the evening before the attempted arrest. Instead, she says, The night before we had visitors who stayed late, and we were sleeping soundly when the police came.[12] *Whether there had been dancing is not known. Newspapers had recently reported that the dancing at Sitting Bull's camp had ceased; but, in any event, the camp was asleep when the police arrived.*

We rode in a dogtrot gait, *Lone Man says*, till we got about a mile from the camp, then we galloped along and when we were about a quarter of a mile, we rode up as if we were going to attack the camp.

It was still dark and everybody was asleep and only dogs which were quite numerous, greeted us upon our arrival and no doubt by their greetings had aroused and awakened the Ghost dancers.[13]

According to McLaughlin, Sitting Bull had two log cabins a few rods distant from each other, the wagon road passing between, and the ten policemen entered one of the houses and eight entered the other, so as to make sure of finding him. They found him in the larger building of the two.[14]

Upon our arrival, *Lone Man continues*, we quickly dismounted and while the officers went inside we all scattered round the cabin. I followed the police officers and as per orders, I took my place at the door.

Bull Head, followed by Red Tomahawk and Shave Head, knocked at the door and the chief answered, "How, timahel hiyu wo," ("all right come in"). The door was opened and Bull Head said, "I come to arrest you to take you to the agency. You are under arrest."

Sitting Bull said, "How, Let me put on my clothes and go with you." He told one of his wives to get his clothes which was complied with. After he was dressed, he arose to go and ordered his son to saddle up his horse.[15]

Other accounts say the arrest was less than amiable. Lone Man, who was there, differs: When we took Sitting Bull, we rushed into house and five or six took hold of Sitting Bull striking matches in the dark. The old man said, "This is a great way to do things, not to give me a chance to put on my clothes in winter time."[16]

According to Mrs. One Bull, The police came into the house and grabbed Sitting Bull out of bed and told him they wanted him in a hurry. He said, "You seem to be very kind to me all of a sudden—much more so than ever before. If you will leave me alone I can go myself. I intended to go there anyhow this morning and have got my horse ready in the corral."

With his usual sense of irony, Sitting Bull added, "You church members have come here to do to me what is not right. I am defenseless, and you come around."

Mrs. One Bull accused the police of drinking during their mission. She told an informant, The police were intoxicated and used insulting language. They smelled of whiskey as though it had been spilled on the floor. I heard one of the police say, "Shoot these people—they belong to this bunch."

A member of Sitting Bull's camp, Little Assiniboine, replied, "Don't do that, they are women."

Gray Eagle, who had remained outside, says, As soon as the three police went into Sitting Bull's house, I warned the women who were crowding around to stay back; and as soon as I got to Sitting Bull's house the police had him outdoors naked and were trying to put a shirt over his head. He was angry and said he would not go and was calling on his friends to attack the police. Sitting Bull said, "What are you holding that gun to my head for? Do you think you can scare me into this?"

According to Mrs. One Bull, Bull Head followed behind with a revolver in his hand continually poking the chief, saying, "You got no ears." *She flatly states,* He made no resistance.

Members of the Indian police and Sitting Bull's band agree that Sitting Bull was naked when he was first brought out of his cabin but that he was taken back inside to dress.

It seems that his followers initially accepted that their leader was being arrested. One Bull says, The oldest wife of the chief called her sons, saying, "They have come after your father. Bring his white horse to ride. Saddle him up and bring him."

Mrs. One Bull says Sitting Bull, too, commanded his followers, "Saddle up my horse."

Sitting Bull was taken back into his cabin and allowed to dress. This gave the medicine man's followers time to organize an attempt to save their spiritual leader.

Inside the cabin, Little Soldier says, Eagle Man helped Sitting Bull put on leggings and moccasins and shirt and pantaloons, blue, government issue. Sitting Bull balked all the time and made the soldiers mad by not going.

The arrest was taking too much time. Worse still, John M. Carignan complained, The police did not follow out their instructions about taking a team, and when they got their prisoner, a delay was made in rigging up a horse or something to take him in, and as a consequence the camp was aroused.

By now, Lone Man says, Several leaders were rapidly making their way toward Sitting Bull's cabin making all sorts of complaints about the actions of the Indian police. Matt Wawoyuspa, Catch-the-Bear, came up close saying, "Now, here are the 'ceska maza'—'metal breasts,' [meaning police badges] just as we had expected all the time. You think you are going to take him. You shall not do it."

Catch-the-Bear, an elder, then shouted, "Come on now, let us protect our chief."

The police were still waiting for the arrival of Sitting Bull's horse; the situation was getting tenser by the minute. The police were outnumbered and in the midst of the camp. While they were gone after the horse over towards the stable, *Red Tomahawk says,* the hostile men were all surrounding us with their guns and told us to keep our hands off from him. So we advised them that we only came for this man, and if they left us alone everything would be all right, and we told them that other was a lot of children to be considered and also old women and old people that they must think about.[17]

Lone Man says that while Sitting Bull was dressing, his teenage son, Crow Foot, moved by his wailing mother and the complaining remarks of Catch-the-Bear, went inside, and said to Sitting Bull, "Well, you always called yourself a brave chief. Now you are allowing yourself to be taken by the Ceska maza."

Sitting Bull then changed his mind and in response to Crow Foot's remark said, "Ho ca mni kte sni yelo." "I will not go." *In another inter-*

view, Lone Man says that Crow Foot came in and said, "What are you going for? They are making a fool of you. You must be crazy."

Sitting Bull now said he would not go. He said he would die first.

However, Mrs. One Bull, who stood to one side, says, I did not hear Crow Foot say anything before Sitting Bull was shot.

The age of Crow Foot has been variously given. McLaughlin, in his annual report lists his age as seventeen, but he is described in newspaper articles as being a boy of but twelve.[18] *Mrs. One Bull remembers that* Crow Foot was 14 years old. He was one of the twins born in 1876, just before the Battle of the Little Big Horn. *One Bull, her husband and Sitting Bull's nephew, agrees, stating,* Crow Foot was a boy of school age, fourteen years, and was a school boy at the time.

According to Lone Man, after Crow Foot berated his father, Lieutenant Bull Head said to the chief: "Come, now, do not listen to any one."

Lone Man claims he was trying to persuade Sitting Bull to leave peacefully: "Uncle, nobody is going to harm you. The agent wants to see you and then you are to come back,—so please do not let others lead you into any trouble."

It was an empty promise but one probably given in good faith.

According to McLaughlin, They had been twenty minutes or more in Sitting Bull's house, and it was in the gray of the morning when they came out.

But the chief's mind was made up not to go, so the three head officers laid their hands on him. Lieutenant Bull Head got a hold on the chief's right arm, Shave Head on the left arm and Red Tomahawk back of the chief—pulling him outside.

Everyone agrees there was a commotion when Sitting Bull came out of the cabin. The "World"'s correspondent, who was riding with Fechet, was told, Sitting Bull's wife set up a howl on the outside, which seems to have been the signal for the assault.

Lone Man offers a different interpretation of this cry. When Sitting Bull started to go with the police, *he says*, according to the custom of Indian wives and other women relatives, instead of bidding him good-bye the way it was done by civilized people, one of Sitting Bull's wives burst into a loud cry which drew attention.

Hawk Man No. 2 was standing by the door as Sitting Bull and the police came out of the cabin. By this time, the "World"'s correspondent says, He had ridden not less—rather more—than 120 miles in 22 hours (18 miles of it by ox team) and was in at the death.

Red Tomahawk says, While I was standing there holding Sitting Bull, I saw some of the Indians were with big sticks trying to club me and some of them pointed guns at me, and at the same time this old man kept on saying, "Now, now, now" and "I don't want it."

At this moment, we heard some Indians coming along armed, repeating some angry words, so our lieutenant told the Indians that were coming towards us: "Brothers and sisters, cousins and uncles and nephews, don't do anything bad."

Gray Eagle, Sitting Bull's brother-in-law, says, I was told by the agent that if I would go, nothing would happen and that Sitting Bull would obey me.

After Sitting Bull was brought out, with an Indian policeman on each arm, I remembered the agent's words; and I goes up to Sitting Bull and said, "Brother-in-law, do as the agent says. Get in the buggy and go with the police."

Sitting Bull replied, "No, I'm not going. Get away, get away."

Gray Eagle angrily retorted, "All right, I'm through. I have tried to save you."

Then Gray Eagle raced over to Sitting Bull's wives, who were both his sisters, and said, "Go over to my house across the river—don't stick up for your husband. He is wrong."

She said, "Yes."

Lone Man says, The Ghost dancers were trying to get close to the chief in every possible manner, trying to protect him, and the police did their best, begging in their way, not to cause any trouble; but they would not listen. Instead they said, "You shall not take away our chief."

The whole camp was in commotion—women and children [were] crying while the men gathered all round us. [They] said everything mean imaginable but had not done anything to hurt us. The police tried to keep order but was useless—it was like trying to extinguish a treacherous prairie fire.

Shoots Walking says, Sitting Bull was brought out about forty yards from the house and was surrounded by a cordon of policemen with the officers in the middle of the enclosed space.

According to Little Soldier, They brought a white horse (gift of Buffalo Bill) held by White Bird and Warbonnet. Put cowboy saddles on horses between Shave Head, Bull Head, and Sitting Bull.

At this time, policeman Black Hills says Sitting Bull declared, "I will not go unless you kill me first!"

We urged him to go as the soldiers were coming; and if they began shooting, they would frighten the children; but if he went peaceably there would be no trouble.

Mrs. One Bull insists that Sitting Bull did not make resistance or call on any of his friends to shoot policemen. He said he was going with the policemen.

At this time, *Shooting Walking says*, Catch-the-Bear broke through the cordon of police and weeping and lamenting demanded that the police turn Sitting Bull loose. Closely following Catch-the-Bear, three other hostiles broke through the cordon of police wearing blankets with their rifles concealed under them. As they entered the ring they threw their blankets away and made for the group of officers surrounding Sitting Bull.

Little Soldier said, Dark when four hostiles broke through. Knew each by voice. Police afraid of the four hostiles who were Catch-the-Bear, Strikes-the-Kettle, Brave Thunder, and Spotted Horn Bull—old warriors. Crawler said, "Hopo, hopo, kill old police first. They have experience and young will flee."

Crawler had blanket and knife which Eagle Man took. He was spokesman.

The officer-correspondent, watching from a distant hillside, says, Suddenly there was a puff of smoke beside a tipi and the sharp crack of a Winchester. The shot was instantly answered by a volley from the police at their blanketed tribesmen, many of whom were already mounted and in frenzied pursuit. The police volley told with deadly effect, and the firing in a moment was general on both sides.

THE BATTLE IN THE DARK

Mrs. One Bull says, The police told me to get out and go to the other house. As I went out they were shooting.

In the heat of the excitement, *Lone Man says*, Catch-the-Bear pulled out a gun from under his blanket and fired into Lieutenant Bull Head and wounded him.

Little Soldier remembers the moment in the same way: Catch-the-Bear fired at and shot Bull Head. Red Tomahawk was turned but turned the pistol around and shot Sitting Bull. Shave Head and Bull Head in front and one shot at Sitting Bull came from their direction.

Catch-the-Bear reached the group of officers first and fired point blank at Captain Bull Head, *Shoots Walking says*, the bullet striking Bull Head at about the waistline and passing through his body.

Before Sitting Bull shot gave three brave grunts, *Little Soldier says*. Then [he] called, "Hopo, Hopo!" (I am in distress, help me, help me!)

Then Shoots Walking says, At the same time Strikes-the-Kettle shot Sergeant Shave Head. When Captain Bull Head was shot he immediately raised his rifle and shot Sitting Bull. The bullet struck Sitting Bull just above the sternum and passed upward and back through his body, breaking the spinal column where the neck and body join. Where the bullet left the body it tore a hole about two inches in diameter. Sitting Bull dropped dead. Neither Bull Head or Shave Head fell when shot, but Sitting Bull collapsed at once. I actually saw these things.

Lone Man, on the other hand, says, Lieutenant Bull Head fired into Sitting Bull while still holding him, and Red Tomahawk followed with another shot which finished the chief.

There is no question who killed Sitting Bull, *Shoots Walking asserts.* I saw the captain of the police kill him, saw him fall, and saw the terrible wound made by the heavy police rifle afterward. It literally tore the upper part of his chest to pieces.

Gray Eagle disagrees: Bull Head, Sitting Bull, and Shave Head fell down together. Bull Head never fired a shot. He did not shoot Sitting Bull. Red Tomahawk killed Sitting Bull.

Red Tomahawk says, When they fired at the lieutenant and the lieutenant was dropped, I took my gun out and fired at Sitting Bull a second fire, and at this next moment they fired in every direction, so before Sitting Bull could drop I fired a second shot again so he dropped.

Charging Bear agrees: At the same time, Red Tomahawk on his left shot Sitting Bull through the heart and, as he fell, he shot him through the head.

Mrs. One Bull insists that the shot that hit Sitting Bull was the first one fired. Immediately after this a lot of firing commenced. The police were closed in around Sitting Bull and fired into and killed each other. The friends of Sitting Bull had no chance to help him and could not have done so even if they had been well armed. Bull Head, *she says,* was shot by one of the police; *but she admits,* When the firing started I ran.

None of the police admitted that they fired at each other.

Lone Man, who was related to Sitting Bull and loyal to Bull Head, was torn by what had happened. Seeing that one of my dearest relatives and my superior was shot, I ran up toward where they were holding the chief, when Catch-the-Bear raised his gun—pointed and fired at me—but it snapped. Being so close to him, I scuffled with him and without any great effort overcame him, jerked the gun away from his hands and with the butt of the gun, I struck him somewhere and laid him out.

In another testimony, Lone Man says Catch-the-Bear tried to fire again, and I tried to stop him, and failing, I shot and killed him. *Little Bear confirms this, flatly stating,* Lone Man killed Catch-the-Bear.

Like many fire fights in the Indian wars, violence immediately exploded in several directions. Some shots may have even been fired simultaneously, as may have happened to Sitting Bull. Later observers would say he received multiple wounds.

According to a Lakota legend, Sitting Bull's prized horse, which was trained to perform during the gunfire of Buffalo Bill's "Wild West," sat down amidst the firing and raised its hoof in a solitary salute. Stanley Vestal, with no attribution, says several of the Indian police were frightened, fearing that the spirit of Sitting Bull had entered the horse.[19] *Benjamin Black Elk told me his relatives had told him a similar story.*

Among those who fell during the first flurry of gunfire was the brave rider, Hawk Man No. 2. Of the four elders who came to Sitting Bull's rescue, three died—Catch-the-Bear, Spotted Horn, and Black Bird. With them died the peacemaker, Little Assiniboine. Strikes-the-Kettle was wounded but got away.

McLaughlin told his superiors, A fact worth mentioning is that during the fight a number of women of the Sitting Bull faction attacked the police with knives and clubs, and the latter in every instance simply disarmed them and put them in one of the houses under guard until the troops arrived.[20] *There is no other report that the Hunkpapa women joined in the fight.*

Once Bull Head fell, Red Tomahawk took charge. So then they all commenced to scatter, so we chased them and told them that "You wanted to fight, so now we will fight. Don't run away, stand still."

So at my opportunity I went over to the stable and there I saw Sitting Bull's horse all ready to saddle up, so I told one of the policemen to get on the horse and go in to the agency and report this matter.

The messenger, Hawk Man No. 1, rode through the gunfire toward the approaching troops.

WITH THE REAR GUARD

The "World"'s correspondent, waiting with Fechet's command, reported that suddenly a scout came riding at full speed over the crest of a hill from the direction of Sitting Bull's camp. He was excited and breathless. He reported that Sitting Bull had been killed and all the police except himself.

A moment later another Indian came galloping down the road as fast as his pony could bring him. He was a little less excited and his report was not so discouraging. He said that most of the police were dead; that the rest were surrounded in Sitting Bull's house and stable by more than a hundred hostiles, and that the police were almost out of ammunition and would all be killed if we did not hurry to their relief.

This scout was sent on to Fort Yates and the agency with a short note to the commanding officer from Captain Fechet stating that the cavalry would hasten at once to relieve the policemen.

According to Fechet, This courier . . . was mounted on the famous white horse given Sitting Bull by Buffalo Bill.

I forwarded to the commanding officer the substance of the courier's report, with the additional statement that I would move in rapidly and endeavor to relieve any of the police who might be alive. The command was at once put into condition for immediate action.

The men at once prepared for action by removing and stowing away their overcoats and fur gloves. While they were doing this I rode along the line, taking a good look at each man. Their bearing was such as to inspire me with the greatest confidence that would do their full duty.

A light but extended line was thrown in advance, the main body disposed in two columns in column of fours, about three hundred yards apart, the artillery between the heads of columns.

Then, according to the "World," "Gallop! March!" was the order, and away the tired horses went, panting, over the rough, broken hills—the command was moved with all speed to a point on the high lands, overlooking the valley of Grand River, and immediately opposite Sitting Bull's house and the camp of the Ghost dancers, some distance of 1500 yards.

Fechet says, At this time we could hear some firing. In a few minutes we were in position on the highlands overlooking the valley of Grand River, with Sitting Bull's house surrounded by the camp of the Ghost dancers, immediately in front and some twelve hundred yards distant.

Back at Standing Rock, Drum says, At 12:30 P.M. 15th instant, I received word from Captain Fechet that at 7:30 A.M. he was within three miles of Sitting Bull's camp and was met by a policeman who informed him that the police and Indians were fighting, that Sitting Bull had been arrested and afterwards killed to prevent his escape, [and] that the cavalry would push on as rapidly as possible to the assistance of the police.

On receipt of this information and not knowing how large a force the hostiles might have, I moved out of the post for Grand River at 12:30 P.M., with 30 men of Company "H" and 37 men of Company "G" 12th Infantry, (as many men as I thought it safe to take from the post) 10 days rations, 10 days forage, and necessary camping equipage for both cavalry and infantry. To do this I was obliged to hire six two-horse wagons to haul forage.[21]

The crest of these hills, *the "World" reported,* was the point that cavalry made for and reached at about 7 o'clock. From there we saw a dense cloud of blue smoke hanging over and about Sitting Bull's house. The fight was still going on. Beyond this house is a small but dense cottonwood bottom, from which the firing on the house came.

Despite the attempts to coordinate the two forces, Fechet arrived too late to offer substantial support to McLaughlin's police. In fact, the troops were late, arriving on the hills above the valley as much as an hour and a half after the firing started. Lone Man felt they arrived too slowly: According to the instructions received, we were expecting them, but they did not show up in our critical moment. Maybe it was just as well they did not for they would have made things worse as heretofore they generally did this. *He and his comrades would have good reason to complain.*

As the troops came on the scene, the officer-correspondent says, F Troop dismounted and hastened down the slope to the next ledge, about a hundred yards from the woods. G Troop remained mounted and were moved around to find a position more to the right. The Hotchkiss gun was put in position at the highest crest, about twelve hundred yards from the woods. Indians were seen moving about in the woods and fire was opened upon them with carbines, the men being ordered to fire just one shot apiece, to see what effect it would have.

Sgt. George B. DuBois, commanding a squad in F Troop, does not mention the preliminary shots when he wrote a friend, Then I got the command to take my squad (No. 1) and move as skirmishers five hundred yards in front of the troops and move at a gallop. It was a rather ticklish job and none of the officers dared come up, so I moved off till I came to a bluff about a thousand yards from the camp and in plain view and then you should have heard the Red Devils yell. It was awful. I halted till the troops came up and then F Troop was dismounted and thrown out on a skirmish line and commenced firing and the Hotchkiss on the hill was firing over our heads and soon drove them out and they disappeared like magic.[22]

The officer-correspondent reported that the long-range carbine shots were answered by loud war-whoops and firing. The latter, of course, fell short. A second later a shell flew from the Hotchkiss down into the woods with a louder and more demoralizing sound than that of the carbines. Only a few of these shells were needed to cause a stir among the trees, and within a few minutes all fire from the woods ceased, and Indians were seen fleeing up the hills on the opposite side of the river.

Lone Man says, Immediately they fired a cannon toward where we were. *Other members of McLaughlin's Indian police agree that the troops fired indiscriminately into the valley.*

According to Fechet, he delayed advancing into the valley because he saw a party of Indians approaching, apparently 40 or 50, on a high point on our right front, some 900 yards distance; but whether a party of police and friends or Bull's people, could not be determined.

While trying to make out the position and identify the two parties, there were a few shots fired by the party on the hill and replied to from Sitting Bull's house. There was also firing from the woods beyond Bull's house, but on whom directed it was impossible to tell.

At first there was nothing to indicate the position of the police. Our approach apparently had not been noticed by either party, so intent were they on the business at hand. The prearranged signal (a white flag) was displayed, but was not answered.

I then ordered Brooks to drop a shell between the house and the clump of timber just beyond. It may be well stated here that the Hotchkiss gun would not have been up on the line at this time but for the courage and presence of mind of Hospital Steward August Nickel. In going into position over some very rough ground the gun was overturned and the harness broken, so that the animal drawing it became detached. Steward Nickel, a man of exceptional physical strength, coming up with his Red Cross ambulance and seeing the plight the gun was in, seated himself on the bottom of the ambulance, bracing his feet against the tail-gate, took a good grip with his hands on the shafts and told his driver to go ahead, and in this way dragged the gun up to the line.

Red Tomahawk confirms this: At that next minute there was a bomb bursting beyond us. I looked around and then I knew it was the cavalry that commenced to fire the cannon, so I took one of those holy shirts that was used in the Ghost Dance and I tied it to a stick and I commenced to wave the stick, but they still continuously fired the cannon, so I tried to send one of those policemen, but the policemen did not go, so I got on a horse myself and I went towards the cavalry.

Lone Man says, Being ordered to display a "flag of truce" I tore off a piece of the white curtain, tied it on a long pole, ran out where they could see me, thinking they would cease firing but all was of no avail. They continued firing and the cannon balls came very close to where I was so that at times I dodged.

According to Red Tomahawk, The cavalry were standing about a mile and a half from where we were. So I went up there and told the captain about it, but the captain didn't care about coming down, so I got the lieutenant and with his command we went down below. *Red Tomahawk did not identify the officers he contacted, but it would seem that Fechet was slow in leading his troops into the valley.*

In the meantime, Lone Man says, We drove the hostiles across the river and they charged back. One policeman was shot on the ice. We charged back and forth.

The officer-correspondent says Sitting Bull's people were fleeing, but he mentions no fight on the ice: It was at this critical juncture that Captain Fechet's men dashed up, and machine guns, which had been put in position, opened on the redskins. The latter were too dismayed at his unexpected onslaught to stand for a moment, and all bolted for the river.

Lone Man says, Finally, the soldiers stopped firing and made a beeline toward us.

IN THE VALLEY

In the valley, the officer-correspondent says, The firing from the Winchesters was now redoubled by both parties, the police using their ponies as protection. *There, as cousins and friends fought, McLaughlin later wrote*, Five other policemen besides Shave Head and Bull Head lay on the ground, their blood an atonement for the deeds of their people. And eight of Sitting Bull's band would dance no more. *His judgment of the event is harsh considering that he placed his police in a position where they would be forced to atone for the actions of the Ghost dancers.*

Before the battle ended at least eleven members of Sitting Bull's camp were dead.

According to the "World," not all of Sitting Bull's followers crossed the river: A part of the hostiles retired to a stable a hundred yards off, and the policemen pursued and drove them out. The policemen also got possession of the house and took in their dead and wounded. The hostiles then fell back into the woods, and the fight was kept up until the cavalry drove them out.

Lone Man, back from the river, says, The rest of the police, now seeing nothing else for them to do but to defend themselves, became engaged in a bitter encounter with the Ghost dancers. It was day-break and the Ghost dancers fled to the timber and some already started running away into the breaks south of the Grand River. The police took refuge behind the sheds and corrals adjoining the chief's residence, knocked the chinks out, firing in the direction of the fleeing Ghost dancers.

One of our police was lying on the ground behind a shed when some Ghost dancer shot him in the head and killed him instantly. This was my brother-in-law John Strong Arm, who came with me from our camp.

The "World" reported, The police were at that time almost out of ammunition, and were fighting hand to hand, but the sight of the soldiers and the roar of the machine guns alarmed the hostiles, and they fled up the Grand River.

RETRIBUTION

Finally, there was no more firing, *Lone Man says*, and we proceeded gathering up our dead and wounded.

We brought the wounded to the cabin and cared for them. While we were doing this, my friend, Running Hawk, said to the police: "Say, my friends, it seems there is something moving behind the curtain in the corner of the cabin."

The cabin, instead of being plastered, the walls were covered with strips of sheeting, sewed together and tacked on the walls making quite a bright appearance within. There stood Crow Foot and as soon as he was exposed to view, he cried out, "My uncles, do not kill me. I do not wish to die."

The police asked the officers what to do. Lieutenant Bull Head, seeing what was up, said, "Do what you like with him. He is one of them that has caused this trouble."

I do not remember who really fired the shot that killed Crow Foot—several fired at once.

One Bull says his wife told him, After the fighting, the police went inside Sitting Bull's house and looked behind a trunk for spoils. Under a bed they found Crow Foot. They pulled him out by foot and stood him up. Crow Foot said, "You killed my father, but I want to live. I'm only a school boy."

Lone Man shot him.[23]

After interviewing survivors, Mrs. Catherine Weldon, a white friend of Sitting Bull, says, Crowfoot, who had hid under the bed, was dragged out and killed though he was unarmed and begged for his life most piteously. His skull was crushed and four balls fired into his body.[24]

Gray Eagle, who was with the police, admits, Crow Foot was dragged out and killed by the police just to revenge the family for the wounded police, as he had done nothing.[25]

Shoots Walking says, After the battle we carried the dead and wounded into Sitting Bull's house. When we made the third trip for the body of Little Eagle we heard two shots following a commotion in the house and a voice pleading for mercy. As we came near the house a body was hurled through the door. It was Crow Foot. He had hidden under a pile of bedding in the corner of the hut and when found by the officers had been shot by Lone Man and One Feather.[26]

Lone Man candidly says, We dragged Bull Head into the house and as he lay dying he told us to kill Crow Foot, as he was the cause of all the trouble. I then struck Crow Foot across the forehead with my gun, knocking him down, and as he lay there we fired three shots into his body.

By all accounts, fourteen-year-old Crow Foot was summarily executed by McLaughlin's vengeful police.

While this was happening, a few of the policemen vented their rage on Sitting Bull's body. Mary Collins says the police stoned him and pounded him until he was horribly mangled into a jelly. *Shoots Walking confirms this, saying,* As the police came back to the point where the fighting started and saw their officers lying mortally wounded and their comrades dead, many of them shot into the body of Sitting Bull. His body was badly mutilated.

Swift Cloud, a half-brother of Little Eagle, was not a policeman, but as he came to the battleground and saw his brother lying dead, he seized a club and beat the head of Sitting Bull into a shapeless mass. Holy Medicine, who was not a policeman, but was a brother of Broken Arm, also came to the battleground and, seeing his brother dead, seized a club and beat the remains of Sitting Bull.[27]

Weldon, after interviewing Sitting Bull's family, also said that the police beat his head into a pulp, and then rifled his pockets.[28]

A BELATED RESCUE

When the cavalry arrived in the village the fighting had virtually ended. According to Fechet, As the dismounted line approached the house the police came out and joined the command.

Lieutenant Slocum, with his troop dismounted, was ordered to advance immediately upon the house. Lieutenant Crowder with "G" Troop mounted, moved rapidly to the right along the high lands, covering the flank of the dismounted line.

For a while the officers held back and ordered their enlisted men to advance toward the camp. Sgt. George DuBois later wrote, The police ran up a white flag and while they came up to us the Indians made their escape and then we went down in the camp on a skirmish line and hunted all around and found one buck in the brush and made short work of him. The Indian police had their blood up and one would have shot a kid about six years old only I knocked his pistol up and talked him out of it.

According to DuBois, the mutilation of Sitting Bull's body continued after the arrival of the troops: The scene around the camp was awful. I saw one fellow go up to Old Bull and cut him across the face with an ax and one went and struck him with a club and one cut him with a knife till his own wife couldn't know him and the dead looked horrible cut and shot and the blood and brains lay around in all shapes, broken guns and blood over everything.[29]

In a few seconds, *the officer-correspondent writes,* we saw a band of policemen as they came and formed in line. Most were in the dark blue uniform, but many of the twenty recently appointed have no uniforms. These had large white cloths about their necks and shoulders to distinguish them from hostiles. Troops had previously been advised as to these badges.

Once a semblance of order was restored, the "World"'s correspondent reported, The police presented a fine appearance standing in line to receive the soldiers, but the spectacle a few yards behind them was horrible in the extreme. Eight corpses lay about on the ground, riddled with bullets and mutilated. Sitting Bull was on his back and his face was hardly recognized, so shot up and battered it was.

In Lone Man's words, The troops arrived and upon learning what had happened the officer ranking highest proceeded to where Sitting Bull's corpse was and with a (branch [or] brush) took the third coup and said: "Sitting Bull—big chief, you brought this disaster upon yourself and your people." Louis Primeau was interpreting.

Whether it was Fechet or one of his officers who took the unearned coup is uncertain. What is clear, though, is that it was not a proper gesture to make in front of men who had just been in hand-to-hand combat with their own relatives.

There were further efforts to desecrate Sitting Bull's body. Black Hills says, After the soldiers came into camp, a soldier picked up a neck-yoke and pounded Sitting Bull's head until he was restrained by the Indian police.[30]

One of the officers assigned a man to guard the mutilated body. Enlisted soldier Albert L. Bloomer wrote years later, When we arrived and the Indian police left the cabin, one of them dropped a pole in an attempt to crush Sitting Bull's skull while another struck him in the face with his quirt, and that is the reason I was detailed as guard with orders to allow no one to molest the body.

I think Sitting Bull was about 5′10 to 5′11 and must have weighed from 250 to 300 pounds and after it was all over and I was ordered to move the body away from a large pool of blood. I took hold of his arm and tried to drag him away so his body would not freeze to the ground. I thought he weighed a ton.

He was dressed in trousers, shirt & moccasins. I think the trousers had fringes, clothing soiled and coarse black hair streaked with grey—just fine for watch chains.

He was lying on his back with head towards his cabin. There was no snow but the ground was froze. He was about 10 to 15 yards from the cabin.[31]

Bloomer overestimates Sitting Bull's height and weight; but, even so, this was far from the man McLaughlin described as being emaciated from Ghost dancing.

Fechet surveyed the battlefield: Upon arriving at this place I found evidences of a most desperate encounter between the agency police and Sitting Bull's followers.

In the vicinity of the house within a radius of fifty yards were found the dead bodies of eight hostiles including Sitting Bull; two horses were also killed. Within the house there were found four dead and three wounded policemen.

It was learned through the interpreter that the hostile Indians had carried away with them one of their dead and five or six of their wounded, making an approximate total of fifteen casualties in Sitting Bull's band.

That evening, the officer-correspondent wrote, Inside the house were the dead and wounded policemen. Little Eagle, Afraid-of-Soldier, Broken Arm and Hawk Man were dead. Shave Head was mortally wounded in the stomach. Another policeman was shot in the foot. Shave Head died the next morning. Clots of blood lay in trails leading into the wood, and there is no doubt several other hostiles were killed and wounded.

No other report mentions casualties being carried away, but it is possible that other members of Sitting Bull's band were killed in the random artillery fire and that these bodies were ritually buried elsewhere by their families.

Fechet said that intermittent firing from Sitting Bull's band continued: The Hotchkiss gun was then turned upon the party on our right front, this with some fire from a dismounted line of "F" Troop caused them to retreat rapidly from their position up the valley of the Grand River to the northwest.

The line was advanced through the timber dislodging a few hostiles who disappeared rapidly up the river through the willows.

The officer-correspondent reported that while the firing was in progress against the Indians in the wood, a dozen or more bucks were seen lying on a slope of wood about four hundred yards from the cavalry line. They were in full view and made a fine target.

One of the Indian scouts hastened down on the opposite side of the hilly land and when next we saw them they were out of range and running with all speed. The skirmish line of the police appeared, moved down the hill and through the camp to where they were examining the tipis on the way.

The line after advancing through the willows some six hundred yards, *Fechet states*, fell back to the immediate vicinity of Sitting Bull's house leaving pickets at the furthest points gained by the advance.

Lieutenant Crowder in the meantime observed the Indians gathering at houses up the river about two miles from Bull's camp [and we] moved in pursuit of them. The Indians fell back from every point upon the approach of the troops, not showing any desire to engage in hostile action against the soldiers.

After going a short distance up the river, *the "World" reported*, the fleeing redskins scattered and went off in all directions through the country toward the Badlands. Some of them may try to reach the Indians of Two Strike's band farther south, while others will seek escape to the north. However, there is little chance for them in any direction. The soldiers are located all around the Badlands, and the Indians will have little chance to get at the ranchers that are located in that district; even if they attempted to go on small raids, the soldiers are so placed as to head them off.

Fechet continued his search for Sitting Bull's followers: All three houses for a distance of about two miles were examined and all were found deserted, *he says*, but showed signs of recent occupation. Failing to come up with the Indians in this direction "G" Troop fell back and joined the main command at Sitting Bull's lodge.

Lt. Matthew Steele was detailed to search the cabins. In the cabin not occupied by the policemen, *he says*, we found Sitting Bull's two squaws and several other Indian women. I took a squad of soldiers into the cabin to examine it. I noticed that two or three of the squaws sat fast upon the bed which was very low. This aroused my suspicion and we pulled them off and lifted the heavy tick. There beneath it, flat on his stomach and face, lay Sitting Bull's son, a mute about eighteen years old.

In this room there hung an oil portrait of Sitting Bull in a deep gilt frame. It had been painted by a Mrs. Weldon, a woman from the East who had spent several weeks visiting Sitting Bull the summer before, I had forbidden the soldiers to touch anything in the room, but suddenly I saw one of the special Indian policemen snatch this picture from the wall and smash its frame with his rifle. He also punched a hole through the canvas, but I got the portrait away from him before he completed its destruction.

I carried it back to Yates with me and informed Major McLaughlin of the circumstances, and told him I should like very much to keep it, if the dead chief's squaws could be induced to let me do so. A day or two later McLaughlin told me the squaws said I might have it for two dollars.

I handed him the two dollars for them, and I still have the torn canvas which I keep as a valuable relic.[32]

As Sitting Bull's band fled, the "World"'s correspondent wrote, One Bull is about the only leader left of Sitting Bull's band. Nothing has been heard of him as yet, but if he is alive and among the hostiles the chances are that he will bring the scattered braves together and make a stand with the idea of revenging his dead chief and friends by killing a few soldiers.

Fechet justifies breaking off pursuit, saying, My orders were also explicit as to the arrest of Sitting Bull so I contemplated no pursuit of his band. I did not feel authorized to follow the Indians up the valley, especially as I felt satisfied from the report of Lieutenant Crowder that it would only result in unnecessarily fighting peaceful Indians away from their homes and that the withdrawal of the troops, together with the messages I communicated to the Indians to the effect that the capture of Sitting Bull only was desired, would tend to reassure those who were loyally disposed towards their agent.

The obedient Fechet drew his troops back to the village, There, Lone Man says, The soldiers having dismounted rushed to the camp—ransacking anything worth keeping.

Fechet does not mention any looting, but he does say he questioned the police about what had happened prior to the cavalry's arrival. While engaged in the investigation, *Fechet says,* breakfast had been prepared for the men and grain given the horses. Going to the cook's fire for a cup of coffee, which I had just raised to my lips, I was startled by the exclamation of the police, and on looking up the road to where they pointed, saw one of the Ghost dancers on horseback in full war array, including the Ghost shirt, not to exceed eighty yards away. In a flash the police opened fire on him, at which he turned his horse and in an instant was out of sight in the willows. Coming into view again some four hundred yards further on, another volley was sent after him. Still farther on he passed between two of my picket posts, both of which fired on him. From all of this fire he escaped unharmed, only to fall at Wounded Knee two weeks afterward.

It was ascertained that this Indian had deliberately ridden up to our line to draw fire, to test the invulnerability of the Ghost shirt, as he had been told by Sitting Bull that the Ghost shirt won in battle would be a perfect shield against the bullets of the white man. He, with some others of the most fanatical of the party, fled south, joining Big Foot's band. He was one of the most impetuous of those urging the chief not to surrender to Colonel Sumner, but to go south and unite with the Indians in the Badlands, backing up his arguments by the story of the trial of his shirt.

Who can tell but that the sanguinary conflict of Wounded Knee, December 28th, would have been averted if the Indian police had been better marksmen, and had brought down that daring Indian?

The excitement over the bold act of the Ghost dancer had scarcely died away when another commotion was raised by the discovery of two young boys concealed in the house where the squaws were. They were found under a pile of buffalo robes and blankets, on which several squaws were seated. These boys were taken to the agency and turned over to Major McLaughlin—not murdered before the eyes of the women, as one newspaper account of the time stated.[33]

Red Tomahawk took charge of the police force, *Lone Man says*, and after everything was prepared to take the dead and the wounded Indian police as well as Sitting Bull's corpse, discharged us from this campaign, and having complimented us for doing our duty as we did, asked us to attend the funeral of our comrades killed in the fight.

Some of the relatives of the police arrived, and such lamenting over the dead was seldom known in the history of my race. Taking a last look on my dead friends and relatives, I, in company with Charles Afraid of Hawk, started for home. On the way, we passed several deserted homes of the Ghost dancers and felt sorry that such a big mistake was made by listening to outsiders who generally cause us nothing but trouble.

THE NEWS SPREADS

Father Perrig wrote in his diary that in Pine Ridge on December 15, Corn Man came and told the children. 1) That Sitting Bull and other Indians were killed. 2) That they should go home—and when I told him to go home, he told the boys that 3) He would come again and kill us blackrobes. 4) That he would go now and roam about to see where he could kill a white man.[34]

How the news of Sitting Bull's death reached Corn Man before it reached the whites is unknown. The Lakota ability to know of happenings elsewhere was attributed, in at least one instance, to a heightened awareness. According to Judge Ricker, Mr. Pugh, the supply clerk at Pine Ridge, disdaining any spiritual or psychological knowledge or any opinions on these subjects . . . says that he has often observed that the Indians have a comprehensible mode of receiving impressions, that some have explained by saying, "that it is their flash light system."[35]

Rumors of Sitting Bull's death spread throughout the day. It was reported from St. Paul, Minnesota, that the report received here late this afternoon that Sitting Bull had been killed is apparently confirmed by advices received by General Miles . . . this evening . . . stating that Sitting Bull and his son were killed, but giving no further particulars. *General Miles received a second more detailed dispatch that evening from Standing Rock. McLaughlin reported the turn of events to the commissioner of Indian Affairs sometime in the evening.*[36]

Miles, realizing the situation was at its most volatile, kept his troops on the alert but took no action. On the evening of December 15, William Fitch Kelley reported, The troops will not leave tonight, but will tomorrow. All indications induce that belief. General Brooke will not be interviewed. The Seventh Cavalry, a Hotchkiss and Gatling guns accompany the infantry and the heavy artillery will guard Pine Ridge. Colonel Forsyth, who commands the field force, will not move today for fear of stampeding Two Strike's band, six miles from here, who came that far yesterday.[37]

That same evening, Miles, before embarking on a train to the Dakotas, spoke to reporters and defended his inaction, stating, "I have been criticized in some quarters for failing to order the military to make a direct attack upon the Indians. Naturally the troops who were assembled near Pine Ridge, Standing Rock, and other points could see no reason why a prompt and early movement on the hostiles should not be made. But while they were lying inactive other troops were being massed at various strategic points so as to completely surround the troublesome Indians. When the time is ripe a movement will be inaugurated."[38]

General Brooke, fearing that the Lakotas camped near the Pine Ridge Agency might seek revenge, delayed telling the reporters at Pine Ridge what had happened at Grand River until the next morning. The "New York Herald" 's correspondent at Pine Ridge reported on December 16 that the official report of Sitting Bull's death arrived in time to stop the advance of the cavalry this morning at 8 o'clock. It is not deemed safe for it to leave this agency until it is known how the Indians will receive the tidings of their loss. They may be quieted down by it, but more likely fear that they are to be arrested or killed, and will stampede for the Badlands. There are over 3,000 Indians here and the infantry could not protect the agency if the cavalry leaves. Everything is in confusion.

The "Herald" 's correspondent added, Two Strike is within five miles of this agency with one hundred-eighty-four lodges, principally old men, women, and children. He has sent word that he will arrive today and do whatever General Brooke says. This offer of Two Strike stopped the movement of the troops for a while. They are, however, having everything in readiness to start at a moment's notice.[39] *Hundreds of armed Rosebud Brulés were on their way to surrender at Pine Ridge. The army feared that Two Strike could change his mind about surrendering and avenge Sitting Bull's death by attacking Pine Ridge.*

During the day Brooke telegraphed his Chicago headquarters: All the Indians who can be brought in are now here, leaving about two hundred bucks in the Badlands who refuse to listen to anyone or anything.[40]

If the fewer than 40 refugees who had been with Sitting Bull and the 300 men, women, and children in Big Foot's wandering Miniconjou band are added to the 200 Ghost dancers in the Badlands, there were fewer than 400 Lakotas away from the reservations. Perhaps 150 of these could be counted as fighting men. This was hardly a significant force, especially when it is compared to Miles's thousands of troops. One of his cavalry regiments alone outnumbered the Lakotas.

Even so, Miles continued to post more troops to the Dakotas. The "New York Herald" reported, Today every available troop of cavalry . . . adjoining Indian country has been ordered to be in readiness, while every infantry corps and regiment within reach has been put under marching orders for guard duty. General Miles's orders were today sent to every post in the West from that of Sheridan on the banks of Lake Michigan to Snelling and Buford to be ready at a moment's notice to march for the scene of war. The command struck Fort Sheridan like a thunderbolt, but the boys welcomed the orders. . . . Similar scenes have been enacted at all the other posts and forts in the Northwest today. Every man is under orders, furloughs have been canceled, and the dreary round of post life has been supplanted by the more serious preparations for actual war.[41]

In a letter to his wife dated December 16, Lieutenant Piper wrote, I now know the true state of affairs. . . . General Miles has ordered that all movements be suspended until he reaches Rapid City to personally direct the movement. We are thinking this has been brought about by the killing of old Sitting Bull and six others at Standing Rock Agency by the Indian police. They were trying to arrest old Sitting Bull and he resisted and was assisted by a lot of his followers—seven dead is the result.

In the same letter Piper wrote that on December 15, Two Strikes with 184 lodges are in camp at the Catholic mission. They came in yesterday A.M.[42] *Two Strike had peacefully surrendered, but his band had added significantly to the Pine Ridge Lakota population.*

By now Miles's main concern was the hundreds of Lakotas camped around Pine Ridge, not those who remained in the Badlands. While the new residents were disarmed and without ponies, their sheer number was intimidating. Miles was not about to leave Pine Ridge defenseless while it was surrounded by three thousand Lakotas. Again he delayed sending troops into the Badlands, but he did have detachments looking for Big Foot's wandering Miniconjou band.

BIVOUAC AND LAMENTATION

Fechet's exhausted troops started their journey back to Standing Rock late in the day. He says, I gave orders for the command to withdraw to Oak Creek, . . . of which the commanding officer of Fort Yates was informed by courier, with the request that he communicate his further orders to me at the point. Previous to leaving, word was sent up and down the valley to the friendly Indians of this movement, in order that they might avail themselves of the protection of the troops in their withdrawal to the agency, which they did in considerable numbers. All the dead Indian police together with their wounded and the body of Sitting Bull were brought in by me. Upon reaching Oak Creek at 6:00 P.M., I was met by a courier who informed me that the commanding officer at Fort Yates with two companies of infantry and ten days supplies, would reach Oak Creek some time in the night.

On the march, *Drum reported,* I received more assuring dispatches from Captain Fechet, but thought it best to push on. Owing to the heavy loaded wagons I did not reach Oak Creek until 11:30 P.M.—distance 22 miles. I found the cavalry at Oak Creek, to which point Captain Fechet had returned.

The attention of the commanding officer, *Fechet proudly reported,* is invited to the celerity of this movement. In brief, the command marched from here to Sitting Bull's camp and back to Oak Creek in seventeen hours. This, with the ground covered in getting into position and the demonstration to the right by Lieutenant Crowder, made for a total distance of at least seventy miles.

It must be taken into consideration that the movement back to Oak Creek, eighteen miles, was made very slowly. Thus it will be seen that the march out, including the movement into position, was made at the rate of over six miles an hour. During the whole march the column moved steadily, without stretching out or closing up, a most satisfactory commentary upon the drill and discipline of the two troops composing my command.

Lieutenant Steele remembered, Along with us in Indian wagons, for we had no wagons of our own, we hauled the bodies of Sitting Bull and our dead policemen. We also took our wounded policemen and Sitting Bull's two squaws with us. That night we bivouacked at Oak Creek, twenty-five miles from Yates. It was the place where the Grand River Indians habitually camped on their way to and from the agency to draw their supplies. Not a stick of fire wood was to be had and we had no bedding except our saddle blankets; so it is needless to say that we were all too cold to sleep.[43]

At Sitting Bull's camp, the lament for the dead began. There, the "New York Herald" reported, The women and children of the dead savages made last night hideous with their wailing.

For the soldiers, the cold was intense and fuel so scarce, *Fechet says,* that only very small fires could be made. Our stomachs were in a state of collapse, as we had but one light meal since leaving the post, twenty-four hours before, during the first seventeen of which the entire command had ridden over sixty miles, and part of it nearly seventy miles. Supper was cooked in short order, and the infantry generously sharing their blankets with us, the balance of the night passed comfortably.[44]

Private Wilkerson also speaks of that night's discomfort: We camped at Oak Creek that night, and as we had no tents or blankets, except saddle blankets, there was nothing to do but sit around the fire on the snow. It was not safe to lie down, as we very likely would have frozen. It happened to be the writer's turn for guard duty, and as I had drawn third relief, my turn was from 11:00 P.M. to 1:00 A.M. About midnight I heard the tramp tramp of a large body of men, and immediately challenged; receiving the reply "an armed body," I called the corporal of the guard. The body proved to be Colonel Drum with two companies of the 12th U.S. Infantry.[45]

Fechet, relieved, says, Colonel Drum was both pleased and surprised to find that we were all right. He had brought extra blankets with him, and they were mighty welcome. The men could now roll up in a blanket and lie down to sleep, and they required no rocking to put them to sleep.

After a long and anxious conference with Colonel Drum as to further operations, it was decided that pursuit might possibly do much harm, by causing many Indians to flee into the Badlands. Accordingly Colonel Drum ordered the command to Fort Yates, the movement to commence at daylight.

Fechet wrote in 1898 of Drum's command to break off pursuit: Subsequent events proved the wisdom of Colonel Drum's decision, as, in response to the message sent by McLaughlin by runners to those who had left the reservation, one hundred and sixty returned in a few days, and two weeks later eighty-eight more were added to the one hundred and sixty.

Of those that had held their way to the south, one hundred and sixty-eight men, women, and children surrendered to Lieut. Harry E. Hale, Twelfth Infantry, on the 21st, near the mouth of Cherry Creek, a tributary of the Cheyenne River. Only about thirty-eight men, women, and children went to Big Foot's camp. Had pursuit been made, all the Indians of Sitting Bull's faction would undoubtedly have been forced into the band of Big Foot, thus swelling the force which met Colonel Forsyth at Wounded Knee.[46] *The army still insisted that Big Foot's band was a threat to peace in the Dakotas. Of all the Ghost Dance leaders, however, Big Foot was the least militant; he made his desire for peace clear to everyone he met.*

The next morning, before returning to Fort Yates, the troops traced the eighteen miles they had traveled the night before so they could check out Sitting Bull's camp. According to Drum, they found that the hostiles had scattered and that if I moved forward to Grand River, I would probably do more harm than good. I broke camp and returned with the whole force to this post.

Fechet saluted McLaughlin's police in his report: I cannot too strongly commend the splendid courage and ability which characterized the conduct of the Indian police, commanded by Bull Head and Shave Head throughout this encounter. After the fight no demoralization seemed to exist among the police and they were ready and willing to cooperate with the troops to any extent desired.

In Washington on December 16 General Schofield took time during an interview to praise the police, telling reporters, "Look at these police, faithful, true, and victorious and glorying in their victory. I believe that the North American Indian, with authorized enlistment, good pay, and good food, would be the finest soldier the world could ever see. Wherever he has been tried he has never failed."[47]

Drum had reason to be proud of his troops and mentions the police as well: The distance marched between 2:30 P.M. on the 15th and 5:00 P.M. on the 16th was forty-four miles. To do this with Troops just out of barracks, it was necessary to assist them by letting a few at a time ride in wagons. Both cavalry and infantry are in good condition, and ready for any future service. Too much cannot be said of the excellent conduct of the police, had they been better armed and been supplied with ammunition, I am of the opinion that many more of the hostiles would have fallen.

Drum concluded his lengthy report with a plea: I earnestly recommend that Congress be asked to provide for the wounded Indian police and for the families of those who were killed. No soldier could have rendered better service and it would greatly encourage other Indians. Agent

McLaughlin has rendered most valuable assistance by his advice, by furnishing information and by his able management of the police force, which is composed of picked men.

As Fechet began his march back to Standing Rock Agency, a reporter at Bismarck, North Dakota, complained, [L]ittle news is obtainable from Standing Rock today, as the iron-clad non-intercourse rules of the military hold a tight rein over the officials of the military telegraph. All newspapers are cut off from any communication by wire with the agency. The mail driver from Winoma this afternoon knew nothing more than was published by all the morning papers. A courier is expected from the post at any minute with information.[48] *Even though the army was secretive, the news of Sitting Bull's death spread quickly. By morning it made the headlines of newspapers across the United States.*

At Standing Rock, however, a jubilant McLaughlin wasted no time telegraphing Indian Commissioner Morgan in Washington: Indian police arrested Sitting Bull at his camp, forty miles northwest of the agency, this morning at daylight. His followers attempted his rescue and fighting commenced. Four policemen were killed and three wounded. Eight Indians were killed, including Sitting Bull and his son, Crowfoot, and several others were wounded. The police were surrounded for some time, but maintained their ground until relieved by the United States troops, who now have possession of Sitting Bull's camp, with all the women, children, and property. Sitting Bull's followers, probably one hundred men, deserted their families and fled west up the Grand River. The police behaved nobly and great credit is due them. Particulars by mail.[49]

The "New York Herald" reported, Indian Commissioner Morgan showed this telegram to the president late on the evening of December 15. The president said that he had regarded Sitting Bull as the great disturbing element in his tribe, and now that he was out of the way he hoped that a settlement of the difficulties could be reached without further bloodshed.[50]

The Commissioner and the president did not know that McLaughlin had exaggerated the number of Hunkpapas fleeing south almost three times over. By the agent's own count, Sitting Bull's camp had only 248 residents. This included women and children, so there could have been no more than 75 men of fighting age at Grand River. McLaughlin knew that most of these had remained in the area. Indeed, within a day many of these had surrendered.

McLaughlin's police fought bravely, but they were only slightly outnumbered and had the element of surprise on their side. Later, the agent tried to put the achievement of his police in the best light, writing, A total of 43 imperfectly armed police opposed about 150 of Sitting Bull's followers, whom the police routed, driving the Indians from the field and into the adjoining woods, holding the battleground . . . with great courage and coolness.[51]

McLaughlin was not alone in overestimating how many of Sitting Bull's followers had fled south. The "New York Herald" reported, The number of Indians who departed hastily for the Badlands is about one hundred and twenty. They are being followed cautiously by the troops who do not fancy getting pocketed in the hills, where there are from three hundred to five hundred Oglala bucks, under the command of Short Bull and Crow Dog.[52] *The "Herald"'s estimate of fighting men in the Badlands also was greatly exaggerated.*

Only thirty-eight men, women, and children fled south to join Big Foot's band. No more than a dozen of these were men of fighting age. Even so, reporters declared this small band of refugees was ready to go on the warpath.

Within a day, the few friends the Lakotas had in the press began to ask if Sitting Bull had been assassinated. Once again Miles had outmaneuvered McLaughlin. If Sitting Bull had been intentionally killed, the killing was carried out by McLaughlin's Indian police not Miles's troops.

Years later, McLaughlin was correct about one outcome of this tragic event when he wrote, Sitting Bull's medicine had not saved him, and the shot that killed him put a stop forever to the domination of the ancient regime among the Sioux of the Standing Rock Reservation.[53]

13. Aftermath and Repercussions

The policemen did not kill Sitting Bull. They murdered him in cold blood. . . . He was not armed. You might omit some of my wording—it is only my personal opinion.—*Chief One Bull*

✶

SITTING BULL AND SON SLAIN

A Great Disturbing Element Among the Sioux Indians Ends His Career.
A Conflict Between Indian Police Who Had Arrested
the Wily Old Chief And the Followers of the Latter, in Which
Sitting Bull and His Son and Others Are Killed.
More Than Probable, Now That Their Chief is Gone, That the
Troubles Will Be Settled Without Further Bloodshed.
—*Iowa State Register*, December 16, 1890

MILES'S MOTIVES QUESTIONED

As the news of Sitting Bull's death spread across the nation, veteran Indian fighter Brig. Gen. Wesley Merritt scoffed at the possibility of a winter Indian war. At a press conference in St. Louis, he said, "I sincerely trust that this is a final settlement of the threatened Indian outbreak. Not that calamity might not have been averted by other means, however, for I am not by any means clear, mind, that there would have been an uprising. I have maintained from the first that an Indian insurrection at the approach of winter, when the braves were in need of food and forage, was an improbable thing. These Indians, despite all reports to the contrary, are poorly armed. Again it is contrary to all precedent that the Indian awaits the massing of troops around his reservation before going on the warpath. His operations are conducted with the utmost secrecy.

"This prophet business has been overworked, and the Indian's confidence is now really waning as regards Heavenly interference. The Messiah has been too widely diffused, so to speak, for even the credence of the ignorant Sioux. The truth is that much more has been made of this threatened outbreak than the situation warranted. True, the Sioux Indians are armed with Winchester repeating rifles, more or less deadly as both muzzle and breach, but the Sioux is helpless without his horses. A man like General Crook would not have called all the troops from the South in an emergency of this kind, and he would have been pretty apt to have been master of the situation."

A reporter asked, "General, what does this concentration of troops from the South mean?"

Merritt's reply was oblique, but his target was certainly General Miles. "It is not for me to say; but it is pretty well understood in army circles that private ambitions have had more or less to do with the present Indian situation. Some officers have manifested a tendency to criticize the employment of troops from New Mexico, California, and Texas, men unacclimated, and therefore ill prepared for the rigors of Indian campaign in winter when there were three regiments, namely the 3d, 11th, and 19th Infantry, under General Howard, in Michigan, and around Lake Superior, men nearest the seat of the trouble and fully acclimated.

"Remember that I do not join in this criticism. I have no insinuations to make concerning that mischievous little insect sometimes termed the 'presidential bee'; nor do I compare present maneuvers to the darky's razor, which 'cuts a comin' and gwine,' as some army officers have done."

The general then turned to his evaluation of the situation as it stood in the Dakotas: "I think if the report be true that Sitting Bull has been killed there will be no further trouble. Sitting Bull dead is unquestionably a 'good Indian,' and certainly nothing he would do in life would become him as well as the leaving. He was always a troublesome factor, and he has remained a menace since the Custer massacre, far more so, in my estimation, than did Pontiac among the Illinois Indians after the thwarting of his schemes in colonial days."[1]

Even though Merritt was careful to make this criticism of Miles appear to be drawn from discussions he heard among other officers, rarely has a high-ranking officer spoken so bluntly about a colleague's actions. Miles, furious, demanded a retraction, and Merritt quickly complied.

A WAKE FOR THE DEAD

Old Sitting Bull has gone away,
Beyond the world of care
To join the Ghost Dance warriors
In the Badlands over there.[2]

By the afternoon of November 16, Captain Fechet and his command returned to the Standing Rock Agency, and the events at Grand River became a grim reality to the families of the Indian police who were killed and wounded. The "New York Herald" reported, The women and children of the dead savages made last night hideous with their wailing. . . . They are in charge of the troops and will be disposed of as Major McLaughlin directs. The bringing in of the dead bodies of Bull and his sons caused a great deal of excitement.

There is a great deal of bitterness among the squaws of the Indian policemen, who charge that they were sacrificed to save Uncle Sam's pale face soldiers. These Indian women will keep up death songs for weeks, cutting off their hair, chopping pieces from their fingers and slashing their bodies fearfully.

In some quarters, the cavalry are blamed for permitting the Indian police to ride off so far in advance when if the two bodies had come upon the hostile Indians together, the latter would have overwhelmed and Sitting Bull taken into custody without resistance.[3]

Lone Man, exhausted and sick at heart after his fight with members of his own tribe, recalled, I reached home and before our reunion I asked my wife, brothers, sisters and mother to prepare a sweat bath for me, that I may cleanse myself for participating in a bloody fight with my fellow men. After doing this, new or clean clothes were brought to me and the clothes I wore in the fight were burned up. I then was reunited with my family. God spared my life for their sake.

The next day I took my family into the agency. I reported to Major McLaughlin. He laid his hand on my shoulders, shook hands with me and said: "He Alone is a Man, I feel proud of you for the very brave way you carried out your part in the fight with the Ghost dancers."

His comment nearly set me a crying.[4]

Sgt. Shave Head was brought home mortally wounded. McLaughlin movingly described his death: After being brought forty miles in an ambulance, 1st Sergeant Shave Head was still alive when he was carried into the agency's hospital; from a frightful wound in the pelvis, his vitals protruding and his hours were numbered. But his mind was clear and he forgot neither friend nor foe. And his pain was forgotten when he saw the white men, doctors and agency officials, standing about his bedside and weeping, knowing that he would soon be dead. He beckoned to me to stoop over him.

"Did I do well, father?" said Shave Head, and I could only nod, for the tightening in my throat choked me.

"Then I will die in the faith of the white men and to which my five children already belong, and be with them. Send for my wife, that we may be married by the Black Gown before I die."

And a white man was put on a swift horse and sent for the wife of Shave Head, eighteen miles distant, that he might be married to her after the custom of the whites and die in peace. Shave Head had hitherto held to the faith of his fathers and, although he had given his children to the Black Gowns, he had all his life declined the invitation to become a member himself, for he was a man of strong heart and strong head, and no weakling to be moved by argument that he did not fully understand. But he saw the days of the Indian and his tribal customs of marriage were over and he would wed according to the white man's faith.

But death, riding a swifter steed than that given to the wife of Shave Head, came first to the side of the bed in the hospital. Day was breaking over the buttes east of the Missouri when Shave Head opened his eyes and asked if his wife had come and was told that she would arrive in a quarter of an hour.

"It will be too late," he said. Then to me, "Did I do my duty?" He was told that he had done well and that the whites would not forget him. "It is well," he said, and Shave Head turned his face to the wall and died.

Fifteen minutes later the wife of Shave Head wailed her lamentations at the door of the hospital and the whites, who owed much to her husband, solaced her. A granite shaft was erected at the head of Shave Head's grave to perpetuate the memory of this man who hated fiercely, loved well, and kept the faith to the death. And Shave Head's widow sits in her cabin on Standing Rock Reservation nursing the fragment of a hope that the Great Council of the whites will some day keep faith and give her a place on the pension rolls as the widow of a good soldier.[5]

McLaughlin would fight in vain for a pension for Shave Head's widow.

Two days later, on December 17, *McLaughlin wrote,* We buried Shave Head and four other Indian policemen with military honors in the cemetery at Standing Rock, and while Captain Miner's entire company of the Twenty-Second U.S. Infantry fired three volleys over the graves of these red heroes, . . . a great concourse of the Sioux of the reservation stood in the chill bright sunlight of a fair winter's day mourning aloud for their dead.

I quietly left the enclosure and joined a little burial party in the military cemetery at Fort Yates, situated about five hundred yards south of the agency cemetery. Four military prisoners dug the grave, and in the presence of A. R. Chapin, Assistant Surgeon, U.S.A., H. M. Deeble, acting assistant surgeon, U.S.A., Lieutenant P. G. Wood, U.S.A., post quartermaster, now brigadier general retired, and myself, the body of Sitting Bull, wrapped in canvas and placed in a coffin, was lowered into the grave.[6]

Lt. Matthew Steele elaborates on the burial procedures, The dead policemen were buried in a single grave at the agency with full military honors; and, at the same hour, in the cemetery at Fort Yates, the body of Sitting Bull was buried by the prisoners of the post guardhouse unaccompanied by any honors or ceremonies.[7] *Steele does not mention McLaughlin's presence at Sitting Bull's burial.*

Pvt. William G. Wilkerson offers a grimmer description of the medicine man's burial: Sitting Bull's body was put into a dump cart, a hole dug in the ground of the military cemetery, and the body dumped into the hole, the ground leveled over, with no mark whatever to show where the body of Sitting Bull, the last of the great Indian chiefs rested.[8] *Again, McLaughlin's presence is not mentioned.*

According to Fechet, Sitting Bull was buried in the military cemetery because the surviving Indian police and their friends objected so strenuously to the interment of Sitting Bull among their dead.[9]

Years later Sitting Bull's body was removed by his relatives to a burial place in the Grand River Valley, his last home and the place of his birth.

REASSURANCES, RUMORS, AND ACCUSATIONS

Military authorities quickly announced that Sitting Bull's death solved their problems at Standing Rock and perhaps throughout the Dakotas. In Chicago Adjutant General Corbin, meeting with reporters, predicted, "The Indians, who had great faith in him, would come into the agency within the next two or three days, when they hear of his death. If they do not, General Brooke has things in shape to make short work of them. They are penned up in the Badlands, where nobody lives and where they can do no harm.

"If the Indians should insist on fighting, it will only last a few days. There are very few ranches in the vicinity of the Badlands, so it will be impossible for the hostiles to make raids."[10]

As Sitting Bull's body was buried, Miles left St. Paul and was on his way to the Dakotas. There he could lay claim to engineering what seemed to be an army victory.

In spite of the military's assurances, local settlers remained apprehensive and feared retaliation. On December 16 it was reported that the country round about is terribly wrought up over the killing of Sitting Bull. Instead of creating an easy feeling, it has aroused much apprehension. It is feared many families of settlers will feel the vengeance of Sitting Bull's followers. It is expected that settlers will flock to Bismarck and Mandan by [the] hundreds as soon as the news of Sitting Bull's death is known.

The correspondent added, An enterprising Bismarck merchant this morning offered $1,000 for Sitting Bull's hide.[11]

The report of this grisly offer created a stir in the East. An indignant Dr. T. A. Bland, head of the Indian Defence Association, wrote an angry letter to the commissioner of Indian Affairs:

> Sir:
>
> I observe in the public press a statement to the effect that the body of Sitting Bull was removed from the coffin before it was buried and taken to a dissecting room. The reasonable supposition is that it is the

intention of the parties having the matter in charge to make his bones a subject of speculation and perhaps his skin also, as the papers state that a Bismarck merchant offered $1000 for it.

I beg to ask you if you do not hold it the duty of the government, as guardian of the Indians, to inquire into this matter and take measures to punish any parties, whether government or not, who may be found guilty of such desecration of the dead chief's body.

Respectfully,
T. A. Bland.[12]

The commissioner sent a copy of Bland's inquiry to McLaughlin, asking for an explanation. McLaughlin replied:

I saw Sitting Bull's remains upon arrival at agency and was present on the afternoon of Dec. 17, 1890, in the Military Cemetery and saw his grave which had been partly filled with soil before I got there, and feel confident that he was neither dissected or scalped before burial and also quite confident that his grave has not been disturbed since.

James McLaughlin
U.S. Indian Agent.[13]

H. M. Deeble, A.A. Surgeon, U.S.A., supported McLaughlin's statement:

I received the body of Sitting Bull about 4:30 P.M. on the 16th of December 1890 and it was in my custody until it was buried on the 17th. During that time it was not mutilated or disfigured in any manner. I saw the body sewed up in canvas put in a coffin and the lid screwed down and afterwards buried in a grave about 8 feet deep; in the presence of Capt. A. R. Chapin, asst. surgeon U.S.A., Lieut. P. G. Wood 12th Infantry, post quartermaster and myself.[14]

Neither McLaughlin or Deeble mention the previous mutilation of the body after the foray at Grand River, something that several observers on the scene described. It also should be remembered that one observer said that Sitting Bull's body was not placed in a coffin.

Once the bodies of the dead were laid to rest at Standing Rock, the threat of an Indian uprising faded. The members of Sitting Bull's band who had not fled south began to surrender. A less than honorable peace had come to Standing Rock. Now the action shifted south to Pine Ridge and Big Foot's camp on the Cheyenne River.

SUSPICIONS ARISE

Within hours of Sitting Bull's death, the country was polarized. Many newspapers, politicians, and public figures were cruelly jubilant, but a few suggested that the medicine man had been deliberately killed. Among those who accused the government of assassination was Sitting Bull's friend Mrs. Catherine Weldon. She angrily told reporters, "The whole affair was a deliberately planned and cruelly executed assassination."[15]

Reverend W. H. H. Murray, a friend of Sitting Bull, wrote a letter to the "New York World" on December 21, 1890, stating, His death is sad enough. It would have been sad to many of us who knew him as he was and admired him for what he was had he died in peace amid the remnants of his people and the mourning of his race. But killed as he has been in obedience to a conspiracy and as the outcome of a plot to make an end of him untried by process of law, proven guilty of no crime, unconvicted of any overt act, we pronounce his killing a crime and his sudden removal in the manner and substance of it an outrage and a murder.[16]

The "Chicago Tribune," too, hinted at the possibility of assassination, suggesting that officials in Washington had hoped for this outcome: All eye-witnesses agree, as to the acts that, every circumstance considered, make the final tragedy involving the extermination of the brainiest Indian that every lived one of the most picturesque and characteristic incidents of American history. That the government authorities, civil as well as military, from President Harrison and General Miles down, preferred the death of the famous old savage to capture whole-skinned, few persons here, Indian or white, have a doubt. It was felt that Sitting Bull's presence anywhere behind iron bars would have been the cause of endless troubles, while should he fall victim to the ready Winchester, the thousands of Messiah-crazed Ghost dancers would rudely realize that his "medicine," which was to make them bullet-proof, would be worthless after all and should be forsaken for the paths of peace.[17]

The "New York Herald" was more forthright, flatly stating, It is said there was a quiet understanding between the officers of the Indian and military departments that it would be impossible to bring Sitting Bull to Standing Rock alive, and that if brought in nobody would know precisely what to do with him.

Though under arrest he still would be a source of great annoyance, and his followers would continue their dances and threats against the neighboring white settlers. There was, therefore, a complete understanding between the commanding officer and the Indian police that the slightest attempt to rescue the old medicine man should be a signal to send Sitting Bull to the happy hunting ground.[18]

Years later, General Colby, Nebraska National Guard commander, included this allegation word for word in his memoirs.[19] *Was he quoting the "New York Herald," or was he the reporter's source? If the latter, it is pos-*

sible Colby was relating comments he had heard among officers while in the field late in 1890.

In his autobiography McLaughlin disclaimed any responsibility for the death of Sitting Bull: I regretted the death of Sitting Bull not only because that act that precipitated it brought about the killing of six Indian policemen, together with himself and seven of his staunchest supporters, and although the elimination of the old medicine man was necessary for the welfare of the community, I was exceedingly sorry over his demise at the time and the way it occurred. I stood for peace, the peace of the community and the welfare of the well-disposed Indians, and thought that the arrest would be made without bloodshed. It was not the shedding of Sitting Bull's blood I regretted so much as I did the killing of the loyal Indian policemen who were shot down by crazed fanatics on Sitting Bull's order. And he brought on the trouble which ended in his death and also the killing of much better men than he was.[20]

On the morning of December 16 General Schofield conceded to reporters, "Sitting Bull was a conspicuous man as an Indian. He was not a warrior. He was not a great battle chief. He never in his life wore the 'war bonnet' of the Indian. He was a 'medicine man,' what would be called in our civilization a preacher, a teacher. He was purely an Indian politician, and the effort to get him into our camp and endeavor to dissuade him from his wretched demagogue Ghost Dance were what led to his death."

When the reporters asked if there had been any scheme to lure Sitting Bull into a trap and kill him, General Schofield snapped, "Certainly not."[21]

Had Sitting Bull's death been engineered, and if so, had McLaughlin's police been sacrificed to this end? It is useful to remember Fechet's comment in his report: The attempt to arrest Sitting Bull was so managed as to place the responsibility for the fight that ensued upon Sitting Bull's band which began the firing.[22] *It also is worth remembering McLaughlin's postscript to his charge to Bull Head*: You must not let him escape under any circumstances.[23]

Indeed, the police had been placed in a dangerous situation, and Fechet's troops failed to ride to their rescue. Whatever the truth, McLaughlin and Miles, despite their differences, got what they wanted: Sitting Bull was removed from the scene.

The "New York World" raised the charge of assassination again on December 28, asserting, The impression here is growing stronger every day that Sitting Bull's death was brought about by deliberate assassination. He was undoubtedly killed without military jurisdiction. Were it not for the *World*'s correspondent's unearthing the real facts the country would still believe that Sitting Bull was shot by the Indian police while resisting arrest. There was no resistance whatsoever. It was a crime, cruel and cowardly.[24]

The "World"'s editorial writer, referring to Murray's comments, demanded that the affair receive a searching inquiry. As it stands now it was organized butchery, and one of the most shameful incidents in our "century of dishonor" towards the Indians.[25]

On December 22, 1890, U.S. Representative Blanchard of Louisiana, reacting to charges in the press, offered a resolution to the House of Representatives:

> *Whereas*: The recent killing of the Indian chief, Sitting Bull, appears to have been accomplished under circumstances recognized neither by the laws or war nor those of peace;
>
> *Resolved*, That a committee consisting of five members of this House, who are members-elect of the House of Representatives of the Fifty-second Congress, to be appointed by the Speaker of the present House, is directed to inquire into and investigate the killing of the said Indian chief, Sitting Bull, and the immediate causes leading thereto, and whether a state of war existed which justified his summary taking off, and, if not, what justification, if any, there was for his violent death at the hands of Indian police in the employ of the government.
>
> *Resolved*, That the committee is charged with the duty of investigating the threatened Indian outbreak in the West, and the causes thereof, whether neglect by the government of its treaty obligations with the Indians, or the tardy or inadequate fulfillment of such obligations on the part of the government had anything to do with the turbulent state of affairs existing among the Indians.
>
> *Resolved*, That the committee shall have power to appoint subcommittees and to travel from point to point, as may be necessary, and in doing so it is authorized to use government conveyances and means of transportation.
>
> *Resolved*, That the committee may sit during the present session and after the final adjournment of the present Congress, and shall make a report by the 1st of December next to the Fifty-second Congress.[26]

It was reported that Representative McAdoo of New Jersey also offered for reference a resolution reciting that it is charged in the public press (to the involving of the national honor) that certain Indian reservation police officers, acting under the authority of the civil and military powers of the United States, did unjustifiably kill the Sioux chief Sitting Bull and afterward barbarously mutilate his remains, and calling on the secretaries of War and of the Interior for all official correspondence relating to the matter, and more especially for the reports of those officers and agents directly concerned in the ordering and effecting of the arrest of Sitting Bull.[27]

Nothing came of these resolutions. McLaughlin and the military's explanations regarding the treatment of Sitting Bull's body were accepted.

EULOGIES FOR SITTING BULL

Many newspapers printed attacks on Sitting Bull's character in the days that followed. Some were tasteless and cruel. One of these was an editorial comment in the "Army and Navy Journal": Sitting Bull is now a "good Indian," and from his elevation to the happy hunting grounds doubtless looks back with pleasure on his earthly career. Still there are some cruel enough to say that he was a crafty, wily, sly, old fellow, always disgruntled, always an element of discord, to the last degree suspicious and superstitious, and altogether one of those Indians who insist upon their rights but never recognize their duties.[28]

The use of the term "good Indian" for a dead Indian was not confined to the "Army and Navy Journal." It appeared in many major newspapers, including the august "New York Times."

Senator Sanders of Montana jeered, "I am in great distress of mind; my heart is bowed down with woe because of the death of my fellow being. Mr. S. Bull, formerly a resident of my State, but recently a sojourner in a neighboring Territory, has gone the way of all flesh; and there is other copper-colored flesh that would not go far astray if it followed him. S. Bull was a man of some activity in the line of industry which he pursued. His vocal organs were always in good repair; his larynx never troubled him as much as it did other people; if he ever suffered from any pharyngeal difficulty I was not aware of it and his stomach was never satisfied.

"In justice to him I should say that most of the work he did was performed by somebody else. (If there's any bull in that it's all right, we're talking Bulls just now.) His fighting was universally by proxy, and the domestic labor pertaining to his home was entirely vicarious, as his squaws can testify. He was a newspaper Indian, craving notoriety and deadhead advertising. I knew him as a warrior and can say truthfully that, when he was not taking any risks, he expressed himself fearlessly. Vale, Bull."[29]

Bird Robinson, secretary to Agent McLaughlin, wrote some years later that Sitting Bull's death was gratifying to those parties in charge of Indian affairs. This satisfaction does not arise from the fear of any danger impending from him, but because he was arrogant, obstinate, and conceited.[30]

Not all the comments regarding Sitting Bull were negative. Lt. B. L. Handeford, a veteran Indian fighter, offered a positive view of Sitting Bull in a letter to the "World": He was a man of unusual strength of character. He had the misfortune to be on the losing side in a struggle between two races. He knew that his side was weak, but he would not for that reason desert. He was a man of brains, and under an elective system of government would have been chosen by the Indians as one who could be depended upon to look after their interests. No speech ever made in the halls of Congress in connection with the Indian question has had a more manly ring than that of Bull to Major Brotherton in 1876.

Placing his rifle in the hands of his six-year-old son, he said: "I surrender this rifle to you through my young son, whom I now desire to teach in this way that he has become a friend of the whites. I wish him to live as the whites do, and be taught in their schools. I wish to be remembered as the last man of my tribe who gave up his rifle. This boy has now given it to you, and he wants to know how he is going to make a living."[31]

Sitting Bull's bitter irony had irritated more than one public official. Certainly many government officials were relieved that the medicine man would not longer be a problem.

Perhaps the final irony in Sitting Bull's life was that he was killed by his own people. In regard to this, Stanley Vestal, who interviewed many of the survivors of the "Battle in the Dark," observed that though the killing of Sitting Bull was unnecessary and unjust, the men who went after him were certainly brave to the point of foolhardiness. For as you well know, it is strictly contrary to tribal law for members of one band to enter the camp of another bearing arms. Many of the police regret their part in that affair now, and confess they were misled. But they deserve honor for their courage, and when a Sioux has both courage and honor, his spirit must rest content.[32]

A MINORITY OF HOSTILES, A MAJORITY OF FEAR

At Pine Ridge, while the attempt to arrest Sitting Bull was under way, General Brooke readied his troops to advance on the Stronghold. Then, on December 16, William Fitch Kelley reported, Last night at 9:30 an order was received from General Miles delaying the day of marching which was to have been at 8 o'clock this morning.

The death of Sitting Bull at Standing Rock at this moment, it was thought, would greatly complicate matters with the friendly Indians six miles from this place. . . . It was doubtless thought by General Miles that his death while being arrested would have a strong tendency to stampede the friendly chiefs with Two Strike and also those who have been connected with this trouble in the past, but supposedly not at the present. They would foresee in Bull's death their own future fate.

Sitting Bull has a few warm friends here, prominent among whom is the old Chief Red Cloud, this past connection being cemented by mutual life-long hatred of the white man.[33]

The "New York Herald" correspondent from Pine Ridge reported that many local settlers anticipated revenge and mused that the runners will no doubt bring in distorted details of the trouble at Standing Rock and thereby undo all that has so far been done to pacify the crowd here.[34]

This was written while Red Cloud was attempting to calm the situation and persuade the Lakotas in the Stronghold to surrender. On December 16, the "Lincoln (NE) State Journal" reported that a council attended by Red Cloud, Little Wound, and about twenty-five others is now in session here for the purpose of advising General Brooke as to the best action to take with the hostiles in the Badlands. Two Strike and his followers have reached a point about eight miles from the agency and are expected in soon.[35]

At this juncture, *Charles A. Eastman writes,* We next heard that the remnant of [Sitting Bull's] band had fled in our direction, and soon afterward, that they had been joined by Big Foot's band from the western part of Cheyenne River Agency, which lay directly in their road.[36] *At the moment no one at Pine Ridge knew the size of the group that had fled Grand River.*

Elaine Goodale was similarly concerned, saying, Suddenly, into the midst of our wonted Christmas preparations—the weaving of cedar garlands, the singing of carols—crashed the breath-taking news of the seizure and death of Sitting Bull.[37]

The settlers panicked again, and their panic was again fed by exaggerated newspaper stories. The "New York Herald"'s correspondent reported, All sorts of rumors are afloat, and it is not a difficult matter to gain credence for almost any yarn, no matter how wild and unreasonable.

Another news item in the same newspaper read, Tonight's dispatch from Mandan, Bismarck, Dickinson, Medora, and Little Missouri say that farmers are bringing their families into towns until they find out where the bloodthirsty followers of Sitting Bull are headed. It is generally believed that they will kill cattle wherever they find them and massacre settlers who offer the slightest resistance.[38]

The settlers were panicking, as were the 38 equally frightened men, women, and children who had fled Sitting Bull's camp. The army would later count 14 of these as men of fighting age. McLaughlin reported that another 50 of Sitting Bull's band fled elsewhere, while 160 surrendered immediately.[39] *Those who fled from the Grand River Camp certainly were not the fearsome group described in many news stories of the day.*

In spite of the alarming reports, the Lakotas were surrendering in even greater numbers. On December 16, as the lamentation for the dead began at Standing Rock, Miles telegraphed Schofield, General Brooke reports that Two Strike and 184 lodges of about 800 Indians are now encamped at Pine Ridge Agency; and [with] these, [and] the other Indians at Pine Ridge and Rosebud, all the Indians are now on reservation. The 16,000 Sioux who have been restrained and professed loyalty would have positive reassurance, with the least possible delay, that the government will perform and fulfill its treaty obligations.[40]

Brooke's report is incorrect. Short Bull and Kicking Bear's Ghost dancers remained in the Stronghold, and Big Foot's band roamed nearby. Together the bands did not add up to a formidable fighting force. No more than 300 Lakota men, women, and children remained in the Badlands.[41] *Big Foot's wandering band contained less than 350 men, women, and children. Soon they were joined by the 38 Hunkpapas who had fled from Grand River.*

By now there were fewer than seven hundred "hostiles" away from the agencies. Less than a third could be classified as fighting men; in contrast Miles had mustered more than eight thousand troops in the Dakotas. The Ghost dancers still away from the agencies were even outnumbered by the five hundred Lakotas who had been recruited as scouts. The Ghost Dance war seemed to be ending just as Miles arrived on the scene.

On December 17 Kelley wrote, General Miles has at last come to the seat of war. He passed through Rushville last night with his staff in a special car and will go at once to Rapid City. The general expects to make this place his headquarters, and it is understood he will take command of the troops in the field on the northern border of the Badlands.[42]

For the moment, Miles chose to stay away from Pine Ridge and let Brooke handle matters there.

MILES'S DILEMMA

Despite his superior forces, Miles avoided an attack on the Stronghold. The last thing he wanted was an encounter with the Ghost dancers on their own ground. His greatest problem was at Pine Ridge, where the agency was virtually surrounded by the hundreds of Lakotas who had surrendered. Miles did not dare to go into the field in force. His only choice was to play a wait-

ing game in which he depended on hunger to persuade a total surrender of the Ghost dancers.

Still, Miles sent patrols into the field that were large enough to dissuade the Ghost dancers from coming out of the Stronghold. On December 16 units of the Seventh and Ninth Cavalries, under the command of Col. James Forsyth and Maj. Guy V. Henry, moved toward the Badlands and reconnoitered the area near the Stronghold.

The inaction irritated some of the soldiers. Some were afraid that those still in the Stronghold would slip away and go on the attack. An unnamed officer grumbled to the "Army and Navy Journal," Unless Indians have changed they will not "corral" well, and will not stay to be thus surrounded. If not attacked in this position, to waste the lives of soldiers, they will have to be corralled for months to surrender, when they should be disarmed, shackled, and sent east to jail.

The moral effect of this will be greater than a fight, a scattering, and a gradual return to agencies. This grand *coup d'etat* or strategic move may work, but I doubt it. The Indian will get outside and whack us and skip and scatter us as he chooses—*nous verrons*. The cavalry, representing over half the cavalry corps of the army, will do its part, and the battery of the fighting 1st Artillery will not be found wanting now, as it never has in the past.

In a postscript the officer wrote, The order for our move has been suspended. This whole matter is a farce. Someone has blundered, and the feeling here is that the great expense to the War Department, as well as for officers and their families, and annoyance to all, is due to the weakness, if not more, of an Indian agent and the disposition to give too ready an ear to Indian troubles. Let Congress investigate this matter, with Senator Pettigrew at the head.

All quiet. One day we are to move, the next we are not.[43]

At Pine Ridge Red Cloud was apprehensive. He sensed that the death of Sitting Bull was only a beginning. He expressed his fears in a despairing letter to a white friend:

> There was no hope on earth, and God seemed to have forgotten us. Some said they saw the Son of God; others did not see Him. If He had come, He would do some great things as He had done before. We doubted it because we had seen neither Him nor His works.
>
> The people did not know; they did not care. They snatched at the hope. They screamed like crazy men to Him for mercy. They caught at the promise they heard He had made.
>
> The white men were frightened and called for soldiers. We had begged for life, and the white men thought we wanted theirs. We heard

> that soldiers were coming. We did not fear. We hoped that we could tell them our troubles and get help. A white man said the soldiers meant to kill us. We did not believe it, but some were frightened and ran away to the Badlands.[44]

Near that time, Red Cloud also wrote General O'Beirne, I cannot imagine what all this was done for as my people had done nothing to create any alarm among the whites. My heart is sad, but I still have a little hope for my people.[45]

Amidst all this confusion and waiting, Miles and his staff emphasized their accomplishments to the nation. In Chicago, Miles's spokesman, Adj. Gen. Corbin, assured reporters that all was well, stating, "Of course it is impossible to forecast with accuracy just how it will affect his followers, but the probabilities are that it will discourage them. Sitting Bull was making 'big medicine' and giving them to understand that he 'stood in' with the Great Spirit, who would protect them against the bullets of the soldiers. Now, on learning that his 'medicine' is not powerful enough to protect himself, and that he has been the first to be toppled over by a bullet, his influence will be gone—their faith in him will be gone.

"They are now in a position to learn of his death about as soon as we are and I fancy they will all come into the agency within the next two or three days. If they do not, General Brooke has things in shape to make short work of them. They are penned up in the Badlands, where nobody lives and where they can do no damage. Of course, some of the young bucks may come out and raid a few ranches in the neighborhood, but they can't do much damage. It is probable that General Brooke moved against them this morning, and even if it comes to a fight I do not expect the war to last four or five days."[46]

No such move occurred.

STILL MORE RUMORS OF A MASSACRE

While the situation cooled, a few members of the press dredged up another rumor. On December 17 the "World"'s correspondent, riding with units of Col. Eugene A. Carr's Sixth Cavalry, sent an alarming dispatch via courier from a camp near Daly's Ranch: A rancher has just arrived at this camp with a report of a fight between a cavalry command and a large body of Indians. He says the fight was a desperate one, and two officers and fifty men of the cavalry were killed, while the Indians lost still more heavily. The redskins were finally repulsed, and when the rancher left they were in full retreat.

The messenger did not know whose command it was, but it is supposed to have been the three troops of the Sixth Cavalry under the command of Major Tupper.

Major Perry, in command of the Companies E and G at this camp, was preparing to march to the scene of the battle, when a courier arrived with orders from General Brooke, directing him to cover the Deadwood and Chamberlain road, to the east of the Cheyenne, to prevent the escape of any of the hostiles northward.

Soon afterwards a squaw man came in and reported 300 hostiles moving in our direction. We had previously had intimation that our camp would be attacked, and that the signal would be the firing of the grass. The grass had been fired in several places, and this leads us to believe that the squaw man's information is reliable.

We have been informed that four more troops, 250 strong, are on their way to reinforce us. We are weak as to numbers, only 125 all told, but with our Hotchkiss guns and a naturally strong position we can defy ten times our number of redskins.[47]

A report from Daly's ranch claimed, Things have about reached a crisis here. The Indians are seen in all directions, and we are prepared for an engagement at any moment. Pickets are thrown out and they report seeing a number of Indians. The scouts reported we would be attacked this morning, and the signal would be the setting fire to the grass. The grass has been set on fire and a number of ranches are seen burning. They may not attack our camp until tonight or tomorrow morning. A rancher reports that several white men were killed on the Cheyenne River.[48]

Army officials in Chicago correctly questioned the accuracy of these reports. There it was reported, Adjutant General Corbin is inclined to discredit the news. He says a conflict under the conditions mentioned and at this time was not on the programme. He feels assured that neither General Miles nor General Brooke has any knowledge of such a conflict, else he would have received intelligence of it before this. If it turns out that there was a fight he says it will probably prove to have been with a detachment of the Sixth Cavalry under Colonel Carr.[49]

Miles was quick to repudiate the story. From Rapid City, South Dakota, it was reported, General Miles . . . is in communication with General Carr by courier. He knows nothing of the reported engagement at Daly Ranch, the report seeming to be untrue. General Carr is encamped at the junction of Rapid and Cheyenne Rivers on the west borders of the late reservation forty miles east of this place with three battalions of the Sixth Cavalry, over 400 men.

The Indians in the vicinity, in small thieving bands, have been stealing horses from the ranchmen in the vicinity. Some skirmishing has occurred between the Indians and ranchmen, in which one Indian is known to have been killed by the ranchmen defending their stock, but no engagement of troops has occurred.

The troops will cross the Cheyenne River and proceed towards Pine Ridge when, it is believed, the trouble will begin. General Miles has but 1,500 troops here now. More will be required to support General Carr.[50]

The next day still another report describing encounters at Daly's ranch was reported: A courier just in states a party of fifty men are besieged fifty miles from here on Spring Creek, at Daly's ranch. The Indians have made three attempts to fire the ranch, but were not successful. One of the occupants is M. H. Day, aide-de-camp to the governor of the state. The courier who brings the news had to break through the Indians, firing both his pistols right and left. One of their bullets penetrated his coat.

General Carr has sent Major Tupper with 100 men to the rescue.[51] *Here, the careless reporter writes that the "massacred" command of Tupper had been sent to investigate its own demise.*

General Kelton chided some reporters, "We will get those bucks into a corral pretty soon, and then I guess the Indian war you newspaper men are waging will be over."[52]

Dr. Eastman bitterly observed in his memoir, United States troops continued to gather at strategic points, and of course the press seized upon the opportunity to enlarge the strained situation and predict an "Indian uprising." The reporters were among us, and managed to secure much "news" that no one else ever heard of.

Border towns were fortified and cowboys and militia gather in readiness to protect them against the "red devils." Certain classes of the frontier population industriously fomented the excitement for what there was in it for them, since much money is apt to be spent at such times. As for the poor Indians, they were quite as badly scared as the whites and perhaps with more reason.[53]

It was reported from Denver on December 17 that seven companies of the Seventeenth Infantry at Fort Russell, near Cheyenne, were today ordered to leave immediately for Pine Ridge.[54] *Despite the mass surrenders, Miles was calling in more troops.*

14. Surrender

All my people have houses which they built themselves like white men, and it is unreasonable to suppose such people as mine established as they are here, would go to war with the U.S. government to whom they have to look for the very necessities of life, to say nothing of the fact that my country is surrounded with railroads, . . . white farmers and towns. It must be apparent that there is no room for us to go to war.—*Red Cloud*

BIG FOOT'S ODYSSEY CONTINUES

Alice Ghost Horse, thirteen years old in 1890, left a remarkably detailed account of life in Big Foot's band during the fall and winter of 1890. After weeks of wandering, Alice writes, We were camped at the mouth of Cherry Creek the last part of December 1890.

There was my father, Ghost Horse, and my mother, Alice Her Shawl, and two younger brothers. The Wicasa Itancan (leader) was Spotted Elk (Big Foot). Up the creek was Hump and his followers.

At this time, my people were Ghost dancing above Plum Creek, straight east of Cherry Creek across the river. We went up there when they have the dances, but children were not allowed in so my brothers and I played near the wagons. The dances usually lasted for four days. Quite a few camped up there during that time. We usually went back to Cherry Creek when they got through.

The agent at Fort Bennett at the Cheyenne Agency was a military officer, and he would send Lakota scouts to the camp to ask questions about the Ghost Dance.[1]

Joseph Horn Cloud, who was a little older than Alice, says, After the rations were issued to us, we returned to Big Foot's camp, and after a few days we closed up our houses, fences and gates to make things solid and secure. We started to the agency where Fort Bennett then was, to draw our annuities.

When we got to a little store on Cheyenne River kept by one old and two young Germans, 20 miles above Cheyenne Creek, we went into camp. In the night an old Indian came into camp and told us that soldiers were coming up the river, and next day two young men came in a diagonal course across from Cherry Creek to Big Foot's camp bringing news of the killing of Sitting Bull.[2]

Big Foot feared that the killing of Sitting Bull was the beginning of a white war against the Lakotas and decided it was time to go into an agency and surrender. Of the agencies in the area, he preferred Pine Ridge, possibly because of Red Cloud's repeated invitations to come there.

Big Foot decided they should flee to Pine Ridge, *Alice Ghost Horse says.* On short notice, it was decided to move out the very next day, so they all staked out their horses close by, and all went to bed.

Next day, we packed up in a hurry that morning and we were ready to move out. I was on my horse and my two brothers rode in the wagon. My mother rode in the back with the youngest brother and the other one rode up front with my father. We had an extra horse tied to the team. This one could be rode or used as one of the team.

At the time, Chief Hump was traveling with Big Foot's band. Hump was also thinking about surrendering. Joseph Horn Cloud says, The next day [December 21] a number of Hump's men came up to Big Foot, there being some thirty wagons. That evening Indian scouts came into camp and reported that soldiers were coming up the river to where Big Foot was. The scouts advised him not to go to the agency for the annuities.

Before noon, some cavalry came and Big Foot was told to go up the river to his old camp to his old home.

These soldiers were led by Lt. Col. Edwin V. Sumner and included C and I Troops, Eighth Cavalry, and C Company, Third Infantry. They bivouacked on Narcisse Narcelle's ranch on the north bank of the Cheyenne River, approximately twelve miles from Big Foot's camp. The next morning they met Big Foot. Sumner told Big Foot he was angry that his band was harboring members of Sitting Bull's band and asked Big Foot to turn back and go home. Big Foot agreed to this.

Sumner escorted Big Foot to Narcelle's ranch, where Big Foot and his band camped for the night. Wary of an attempt to escape, the troops surrounded the Miniconjous. The troops counted 333 men, women, and children in the band. It is uncertain if this number included the refugees from Standing Rock.

Before sun up, *Joseph Horn Cloud continues,* the bugle sounded the call, and an interpreter told us to go to Big Foot's camp. An officer counted the young men and told us to march with the soldiers. The next section of wagons was one headed by two old women. They were passing through a gate, two wagons abreast when the wheels locked and the wagons got entangled so that they could not proceed.

An officer told them to "hurry up, hurry up, be quick."

A young man called Black Coyote, a relation to the women, spoke up and said, "I am still living; I don't want to see my relations abused by a white man."

He took off his coat and rushed to the officer. The interpreter Felix Benoit called out, "Hold on!"

The officer mounted, spurred his horse and rode away to the soldiers. He had been treating the Indians as though they were mere animals. He was very angry. As soon as this young man took off his coat all the Indians said, "Let us go ahead of the wagons."

We all mounted and rode up to the wagons in front and then all the wagons came together in a park. The soldiers had left us for a while. There was ice on both sides of the river. We cut this away, and both they and the soldiers went over.

Now we were near our old settlement. Black Coyote, a nephew of Big Foot, told the officer they would not go any further but would go to their old camp. The officer refused to let them stop. Then two Indians, Henry One Eye and Standing Elk, rose up to him and, seizing his horse by the bits, they led him to Big Foot. Then the officer said, "Let me go! I will let you go to your houses."

He was released and all the Indians repaired to their camp, the soldiers going to the forks of the Cheyenne River. We were not disturbed again for a long time.

Before they settled in for the night, Dewey Beard says Big Foot asked Sumner: "My friend, why do you camp so close?"

Sumner replied, "You are dancing the Ghost Dance, and I fear you will do wrong."

"No, we intend no harm. If we do nothing but dance, that cannot be any one's business but our own," said Big Foot.

"The agent at Pine Ridge is frightened and has called for many soldiers. He says you are bad, and I have come to stop this."

"I will go away from here," said Big Foot, "and my people will go with me; but we are good Indians and do not want you to follow us. We will dance to the holy spirit if we wish, but we will do no harm."

"You must have a pass if you leave the reservation," said the white man, at which my father, who had come to the soldier's tent with Big Foot, said:

"My friend, we are not on the warpath. We are praying to our Savior and doing no evil. Do you get a paper from the Great Father at Washington when you pray to the white man's God? I think perhaps the Great Spirit does not know you."

When the sun was down, Big Foot gave us orders to make ready in secret; so when the soldiers were asleep that night we slipped away quietly to Cherry Creek, camping in a circle.

The next day the soldiers came again and pitched their tipis near us, while the officer said to Big Foot: "You must move back to your old camp."

"We are not cattle to be put in a pen," said our old chief, speaking very slowly; and then in a great voice he cried, "We will pray where we please."

That day the soldiers left, *Dewey Beard continues.* Shortly after this, a band of old people and squaws and children from Sitting Bull's camp came riding by bareback and we knew there was trouble gathering in the tipis of that chief; so Big Foot called us together again, saying: "I fear disasters are coming, my people. We had best go back to our old place as the soldiers told us to do, so the Great Father will know we are not bad Indians."

Big Foot, realizing it was dangerous to shelter the refugees, had the choice of fleeing into the Badlands with them or moving closer to his agency. He chose flight, perhaps to protect Sitting Bull's followers, or out of fear that the soldiers would turn on his own band. Accordingly, we moved back to the Cheyenne, *Dewey Beard says,* but immediately many soldiers camped near us again. In the night time more came, so that when we arose in the morning they stood in a line all about us, with their guns in their hands. They pointed a cannon at us.

When we came out of our tipis to look at them, our women were greatly frightened. Then, as we watched, a half-breed advanced, announcing that the officer wished to speak with Big Foot. That one answered: "Let him come to our camp and talk. We mean no harm, but he should not point his guns at us, for we do not like it."

The officer arrived and through his interpreter commanded us to surrender.

"Why should we do that?" said Big Foot. "We are not hostiles, we are only hungry Indians beseeching the Great Spirit for food. When you took our lands you said we should have plenty to eat, but we are starving. Let us have food, so that we may think about it for a day or so; then perhaps we will go with you."

The soldier talked with our head men until afternoon, securing, at last, from Big Foot a promise that we would not go away before the next morning. The soldiers gave us no food.

At daybreak we found them standing in a line again, with their cannon pointing at our tents. It was very close by. The officer sent word that we could have but a little time to consider, and if we did not give up before the sun was as high as his hand, he would fire the big gun, killing our women and children.

"We must go with this man," the chief said to us.

So we did. The next day some of the soldiers marched before us, and some of them marched behind, while others were on both sides of our wagon; but Big Foot rode a pony near the front and said nothing, for he was very sad.

All day we watched him. As afternoon drew on, he announced quietly to one of his braves, "Get ready!"

The man rode back down the line, passing the word, whereupon our squaws threw out the tipi poles, one by one, and dropped every heavy thing, scattering the goods for a long way. When he saw this, the officer rode up to Big Foot.

"Why do your people throw away things?"

"The ponies are weak," said our chief.

When the sun was two fingers high, the old man spoke again, "Our horses can go not further. We will camp here where there is good water."

Giving the sign, we suddenly turned out in a body, leaving the soldiers, at which they looked foolish. By the time they had gotten together we were some distance up a narrow creek, and they had to follow after like a snake's tail in the grass. When we had gone a little way our leader said: "We will camp here, but do not allow one pony to get away."

So we unhitched and built fires as though to cook, while our guards came near and stopped; for it was dark. Word was passed to the braves who rode ponies to put blankets over their shoulders, so they would look like women, and then to build many small fires. While this was being done the squaws in the wagon farthest away from the soldiers were told to move on. When they had gone for a little time, the next wagon was told to follow, and so on, one by one, till their remained only the two nearest the whites. When these drove off, an under-officer came to Big Foot.

"Where are the wagons?"

"They have gone to the other side of our camp," the old man replied, but in a few moments the messenger came again and asked to see them.

"Come," said Big Foot, to us who had stayed about the fire, "let us show him where they are."

At which we rose up together. When he saw there were braves beneath the blankets, the man ran away, crying loudly:

"We are attacked!"

We leaped to our ponies and rode fast. Overtaking the wagons, we shouted to the women to drive hard, and in a body we went ahead all that night as rapidly as possible, and on the next day were in the Badlands.[3]

General Miles was furious. Sumner had allowed more than 350 Miniconjous to escape.

SHORT BULL WAVERS

At Pine Ridge the "friendlies" were eager to persuade the "hostiles" to come into the agency and surrender. They had seen hundreds of troops arriving and feared the army was there to start a war. Many volunteered to intercede with the Ghost dancers remaining in the Stronghold.

According to Judge Ricker, Man Above said, They was sent out to Short Bull's camp—the hostile camp at the Stronghold—to make a peace. . . . Fifty men went with them the first time; there were ten scouts and forty other Indians; these all went from the agency. "This," he says, "was about this time of the year—the leaves were all off the trees [and] there was a good many soldiers at the agency."

When they got over there to the Stronghold they stopped at Short Bull's camp. Short Bull's men were angry at the fifty men because they came from the agency to make a peace, and they shot their guns over the heads of the fifty men to express their indignation at their mission, and they told the fifty to back to the agency. The fifty men came back to the agency.

General Miles told these scouts every time to go.[4]

The "Army and Navy Journal" reported, Five days afterwards twenty scouts and one hundred thirty other Indians went over on a second trip to Short Bull's camp in the Stronghold. This party found Short Bull's people very angry and the conditions very dangerous. Their reception was a volley over their heads and ordered them to go back to the agency. And they went back, without accomplishing anything.

On the afternoon of Saturday, December 20, another delegation of all the prominent chiefs of the nation came to General Brooke and made such an urgent and earnest plea that they be allowed to go out and bring in the "hostiles" that he consented. They started the next morning with about two hundred carefully-selected men and expected to reach the camp of the disaffected about noon on Monday, December 22.

This was an effort of such strength and influence that it was believed to be almost impossible to resist it, as it was the wisdom and influence of all the head chiefs of the Brulé and Oglala Sioux, supported by a small but powerful body of warriors, who certainly would not hesitate to use force to bring the malcontents to their senses.[5]

Short Bull offers a different view of the situation and mentioned making no threats. A delegation of Oglalas, *he says,* came to us from Pine Ridge to make a treaty. Among the chiefs were No Neck, Yankton Charlie, Standing Bear, and Crow Dog. They brought us presents. We killed one of the stolen cattle and made a feast. I told these chiefs that if my people would be allowed to go to Pine Ridge to live and draw rations there they would all be satisfied to go in.

The next morning we held a council at which it was decided that we all move together toward the agency on the following day, but [with] some starting that same day. The next morning at daybreak the main camp moved, all but me and my uncle, Come-Away-from-the-Crowd. During all this time we were being watched by some Cheyenne Indian soldiers, watching all of our movements, but they could not get to us. That night my uncle and I started to reach our main body that had gone away in the morning, but we failed to reach them. We camped by ourselves on a large hill.[6]

Man Above confirms this, saying, The scouts went out on the third trip—thirty in all went this time, Short Bull gave up this time.[7]

Short Bull knew that if he returned to Pine Ridge Agency he could face a prison term or deportation to another reservation. He decided to enjoy a few more days of freedom, but other sources suggest he planned to come in and surrender when he felt he could do so safely.

A "MESSIAH" APPEARS AT PINE RIDGE

On December 22 the newsmen at Pine Ridge finally had something amusing to write. The "Chadron (NE) Democrat" laconically reported, From a description furnished the *Democrat*, we have been enabled to "locate" the new "Christ." His name is Hopkins, and he hails from Iowa. Last Friday we were favored with a visit from this gentleman, but during our conversation with him, we never once thought him other than a common seeker after news and bent on seeing the sights at Pine Ridge; neither did he hint that he was the Indian Messiah (he probably was silent for fear he might be crucified by the unbelievers in Chadron were the fact known) but quietly inquired the best way of reaching the front. We gave him all the needed information, and he departed, only to be ruthlessly scoffed at by the soldiers and newspaper correspondents upon his arrival at Pine Ridge.

Poor Hopkins; he would have fared better had he tried to pass himself off as Judas Iscariot.

But it was "Hopkins's choice."[8]

Indeed, Hopkins's next stop was Pine Ridge. There, the corps of reporters included fourteen resident correspondents. They led a pleasant and often convivial life. Their dispatches were largely drawn from reports the army released or from accounts of those who came into the agency, but on December 21 a story came directly to them. Charles W. Allen, still working for the "New York Herald," reported, About the middle of the forenoon

Buckskin Jack came in with his customary broad grin, remarking, "The Messiah has come."

Each of us shot him full of question marks at the same instant, then gave him a chance to unfold his news. He was talking with an Indian in front of one of the stores when he noticed a stranger eyeing him. Presently the Indian walked away and the stranger approached and inquired the way to Red Cloud's camp. The instruction was given him; then he told Jack confidentially that he was the Messiah and had come to council with the Indians but wished to consult Red Cloud first. He then went into the store and Jack came to the hotel.

This amusing recital was but finished when Jack, looking out the window, said, "There he goes now!"

We all rushed to the porch and saw what we took to be a middle-aged man, with a slight limp and cane, dressed in ordinary fashion, walking along the opposite side of the street toward Wolf Creek bridge. We watched him descend the hill and emerge, then take the left-hand trail leading to White Clay Creek and follow it up to Red Cloud's camp.[9]

During this time reporter William Fitch Kelley remembered that the would-be Messiah lived quietly, praying among the Indians constantly. The Indians treated him with consideration and respect, as is their custom with the demented. That he was not the Christ was best proven to them in that he was wholly ignorant of their language. The man was modest, genteel in bearing, an attractive man in person. In conversation he was singularly well versed in natural theology, philosophy, and the sciences. He modestly but firmly maintained that he was the Messiah.[10]

None of the traditional chiefs took any stock in their visitor's claim. Some say that Red Cloud walked up and spit on the Messiah, saying, "You go home. You are no son of God."[11]

Allen says, The next we heard of the would-be Messiah, General Brooke had sent a patrol to bring him to headquarters. There, after the usual questioning, he gave him a berth in the guard-house.[12]

At this point, "Omaha Bee" correspondent Will Cressey found out what had been happening. That evening, *Allen says,* we were taking our after-supper smoke, when one of the boys came in with an extraordinary grin spread over his face and was quickly asked what was up. Now we were aware of Cressey's habit of stuttering when unduly excited, and it was disclosed that Cressey had just returned and heard of the advent of the Messiah. Our amused friend was sitting in the office at headquarters when Cressey came rushing to the door and cried: "G-G-General, have y-y-you g-g-ot C-C-C-hrist in the g-guard-house?"

About ten o'clock the next morning the agency spring wagon drove up in front of the guard-house. "The Messiah" who gave his name as Hopkins, got in with two Indian policemen and was driven across the state line, placed on the trail that led south, and told to keep going.

All accounts described him as being a pleasant but ordinary person, aside from being obsessed with the idea that he had a call to fill the role of the Messiah to the Sioux.[13]

A bemused "Chadron Democrat" reported, Late advices from Pine Ridge state that the Messiah has made his appearance but was promptly taken in charge and deposited outside the corporate limits of the reservation.[14] *The would-be Messiah was given a train ticket back to Iowa and returned home after a brief moment of fame.*

BIG FOOT'S DECISION

To the northeast a now-ailing Big Foot began to edge out of the Badlands. At that time, Dewey Beard says, Big Foot was so bad that we camped two days at this spring. While waiting, White Lance and Bad Brave and Comes Lie Hard were dispatched back to White River to see if any soldiers were coming. They saw nobody. When Big Foot came to the spring, three messengers were sent forward to the agency to give notice that Big Foot was on his way to the agency and was very sick with pneumonia. It was told to the messengers to further report that Big Foot came not secretly, but openly and peaceably. Next day we moved to a point on Red Water about one mile below my present place.

In the night, one of the three men sent to the agency didn't get beyond Wounded Knee, but found soldiers camping over there. Two went on to the agency.

Next morning, we saw some looking glasses shining up on the hill southeast of them. We were going to move the camp, but we were waiting for those who were shining the glasses to get back into camp.

Those shining the glasses were Bear Comes and Lie and Shaggy Feather—the latter was an Oglala who had come back from Pine Ridge with Bear Comes and Lie. They brought news this way that Short Bull's whole camp is going to move to the next the day after tomorrow and they want us to move in the same day. They wanted Big Foot to hurry up to be in time; "they," meaning the Indians at Pine Ridge Agency, wanted Big Foot's company in on time because they wanted to make peace. They sent word to Big Foot that cavalry was out at Wounded Knee, and for him to go around these and avoid them and come to the agency. They sent this word by Bear Comes, Lie Down (this was Shaggy Feather).[15]

Big Foot's band was wending a cautious trek as their chief mulled the advantages of coming into Pine Ridge. Alice Ghost Horse says, We crossed Cherry Creek at the mouth where it empties in the river. We were to follow the wagon trails that went west all along the river on the north side. The old wagon trails lead to T'akini. We ran all the way to the bottom of the river and stopped half way to water the horses and cook something to eat. My mother had some pemmican which we all shared before we continue on towards T'akini.

Late afternoon, we pulled into T'akini amid clusters of lean-to's and tents. Most of them were getting ready for winter, by looking at the wood piles. Some had stacks of wood piled high. After we put up our tents my mother started her cooking. She had good soup and Kabubu bread and hot government coffee. After a hearty meal my mother and my father went to a meeting at Big Foot's tent so my brothers and I went down to the river and played for awhile and came to bed.[16]

On December 23, *Joseph Horn Cloud says,* I and my brother, William Horn Cloud, went down the river for some hay. When we were loading, an Indian rode up with a sweating and foaming horse and told us to hurry and get home, that some soldiers were coming to fight. We did not believe him and kept at our work and loaded up their wagon. Coming home, we met our brother Frank. He told us that a white man had come and told the Indians that a lot of troops were going to come tonight and tomorrow night. Frank said that our father had sent him to tell us to hurry home.

We hastened home as fast as we could with our hay, leaving our load of hay when we got home. We left Frank with our parents and taking White Lance, another brother, we rode over to Big Foot's, about three miles away.

There we saw the white man that Frank had told us about, his horse still wet with sweat. He was telling the Indians that the troops would come tonight or tomorrow night and that we should go to Pine Ridge, for there were more Indians there. But Big Foot refused.

This man kept on telling us to run away. We argued among ourselves; some tried to persuade Big Foot to go, saying that this white man whose Christian name was John and who they called Red Beard, was a friend to them and always had been, and he would not tell them anything but the truth.

Big Foot continued his refusal, saying that he would not leave his home. Red Beard persisted in urging them to go, telling them that he did not want to see their women and children killed. Big Foot would not yield. He said, "This is my home; this is my place; if they want to kill me—if they want to do anything to me, let them come and do as they please."

Then Red Beard spoke and said, "Red Fish," addressing one of Big Foot's men, "my friend (kola) if you want to defend yourselves, you must remember your knives and your guns; do it like a man."

Some of the Indians still wanted to go to Pine Ridge Reservation. Red Beard again spoke up: "I heard the officers agree together to bring a thousand soldiers from Fort Meade and take all the men and bring them to Fort Meade as prisoners."

He repeated this statement. He then said he was going to return to his ranch on the Belle Fourche by way of the soldiers' camp, and told the Indians not to tell on him.

Big Foot and his advisors were disturbed by this event. They realized a decision had to made, and it had to be made quickly.

After his departure, *Joseph Horn Cloud says*, we talked among ourselves, and some said we should go to Pine Ridge, while others said we should stay at our houses. Others urged that all of us should go together to the cedars in the canyon and wait there for three days, and if the soldiers did not come in that time we should all return to our homes. We were at this time at the mouth of Pass Creek, so called by the Indians, is by the whites called Deep Creek. At the mouth now stands the Pedro Post Office.

We hitched up our teams and moved up the creek to the south about six miles, then bore off on the ridge toward the east about three miles. Here we stopped and had a council and decided to go to Pine Ridge.

Big Foot still held out, but the sentiment of his people being against him, he gave in to the overwhelming pressure.

Once the decision to surrender at Pine Ridge was made, Joseph Horn Cloud says, We had to move ten miles to water; this brought us to a branch of the Bad River, where we camped for the night. Next morning, we took a southwesterly course. Going six or seven miles farther, we arrived at the big wall of the Badlands on the north side of White River.

The pass was very difficult. Wagons had been over it before, but it was now washed out. There were great gullies and holes, but the men took axes and spades and worked a passage way so that they got down and reached the White River about sundown and crossed, the rear teams getting over after dark. This day, though the sun shown brightly, was windy, raw and cold. . . . This was the 24th of December. We camped on the south side of the river.[17]

Early next morning, *Alice Ghost Horse says*, I heard my father hitching up the horses, so I got up and saddled up my own horse and was ready to go. I planned to ride all the way to Pine Ridge.

The first wagon to leave was Big Foot's wagon, followed by all his relatives. . . . We fell in about the middle of the wagon train and were headed up a long hill east side of the river. I looked back and I could see more wagons joining in and coming and many children were on horse back too. It was a sight to see. It was also exciting because we were running from the military.

We ran like this all morning without stopping. Sometimes, some riders would fall back to check on us at the request of Big Foot.

By noon, we stopped to rest, but we were not allowed to start a fire, so we ate what little mother had for us. In a short while, we were again on our way with Big Foot and his wagons still leading the way. We were trotting all the way, southerly direction, keeping to the low area, valleys and creek beds.

My younger brother sat in the back with my mother who kept an eye on me. The other brother rode up front as before. The extra horse was still tied to the side of the team.

By mid-afternoon, the going was tough but we went below Porcupine Butte still keeping in the draws and gullies. Sometimes there was not trail so the going was really rough on the wagons.[18]

THE NINTH IN THE FIELD

About their tents the Soldiers stood, awaiting one and all,
That they might hear the trumpet clear when sounding general call
Or Boot and Saddles in a rush, that each and every man
Might mount in haste, ride soon and fast to stop this devilish band
But generals great like Miles and Brooke don't do things up that way,
For they know the Indian like a book, and let him have his sway
Until they think him far enough and then to John they'll say,
"You had better stop your fooling or we'll bring our guns to play."

CHORUS:
They claimed the shirt Messiah gave, no bullet could go through,
But when the Soldiers fired at them they saw this was not true.
The medicine man supplied them with their great Messiah's grace,
And he, too, pulled his freight and swore the 7th hard to face.[19]

As Big Foot moved toward Pine Ridge, the Ninth Cavalry began an epic sweep of the Dakotas in search of stray bands of Ghost dancers. It was one of the longest marches ever made by a United States cavalry unit. According to Cyrus Townsend Brady, a historian who interviewed members of the

Ninth Cavalry, On the 24th of December Henry and the "Brunettes" were ordered out to the former's old stamping ground in the Black Hills on a scouting expedition. It was bitter cold that Christmas Eve, but, thank God! there was no blizzard. Fifty miles on the back of a trotting horse was the dose before them. They rested at four A.M. on the morning of Christmas Day.

Some of the garments the men wore were frozen stiff. They had broken through the ice of the White River in crossing it. How the men felt inside the frozen clothing may be imagined. Eight miles farther they made their camp. They did not have much of a Christmas celebration, for as soon as possible after establishing their base at Harney Springs they went on the scout.[20]

Pvt. W. H. Prather recorded his unit's cheerless Christmas in the field:

> The 9th marched out with splendid cheer the Badlands to explo'e—
> With Col. Henry at their head they never fear the foe;
> So on they rode from Christmas eve 'till dawn of Christmas day;
> The Red Skins heard the 9th was near and fled in great dismay.[21]

Theirs was a futile mission. The Lakotas they pursued were not to be found.

CHRISTMAS AT PINE RIDGE

December 24 was ration day at Pine Ridge. According to T. H. Tibbles, a correspondent for the "Omaha World Herald," in spite of government promises of more food, little food was issued to the Lakotas camped near the agency. By 9 o'clock a long line of women were standing—I should think nearly 1,000—shivering in the keen air, waiting to be served. . . . Hundreds of these women, patiently waiting hour after hour, wore nothing but a calico sack and skirt, leggings made of old flour sacks, and moccasins. The air was so keen that after standing still for a few minutes I shivered with the cold, although I wore a heavy Scotch overcoat and had the warmest underclothing I could buy in Omaha. I have been told by missionaries that in the past these women have been forced for days to stand thus in sleet and snow, waiting on the convenience of the issue clerk, and that many deaths occurred from the exposure caused by this needless cruelty. This clerk was finally dismissed on the complaint of American Horse to the General Crook Commission.

The Indian woman brings little bags into which the rations are thrown as she passes along the different parts of the long counter where the sugar, coffee, corn, bacon and flour are dealt out. Then she puts them all together into a pack and goes to her tent. Each woman has a ticket with the number of persons for whom she is entitled. I examined a great many of these packs, and some of them were brought to the Indian's house where I live.

The Indians complain that the rations are not justly divided. They say that some get more than others. The flour is not weighed, but guessed at. From the examination I made I think there are grounds for complaints. There does not seem to be sufficient force in the issue department.

The issue now is just double what it was before these troubles, and now it is barely sufficient to subsist upon. In one pack issued to three persons I found flour enough to make one ordinary baking pan of biscuit, and this was to last for seven days. In another pack issued to five persons I found what would be fair rations for that number for four days. I know what I am talking about, for I have lived in camp many years of my life and handled provisions.

In some packs I found more sugar that would make a fair ration, and in several the coffee was sufficient in quantity. The flour issued is good, the coffee and sugar very good, and the bacon of fair quality. The more I investigate, the more I wonder how these Indians managed to live at all during the last year when they only received half the amount they are receiving now. The wonder is that they did not make more of a row than they did.

I found a large number of Indians whose only clothing consisted of a sheet, used for a blanket, leggings made from old flour sacks, and moccasins. If a severe cold spell should come, many would not escape freezing to death. At least it so seems to me. The clothing issue is usually made in November, but so far this year not one article of clothing has been issued, and there is nothing here to issue.

There are camped about this agency in little canvas tipis about 6,000 Indians, many of whom have not lived in tents in years. They fled from their houses upon the order of the government, bringing nothing but the clothes upon their backs, a blanket, and a few cooking utensils. Their houses have been raided and everything they owned destroyed. They are in a desolate country . . . where no food of any kind can be obtained, except these insufficient rations. The children are dying. They shiver in the cold and patiently wait. The grass is all eaten off and the hungry ponies wander over the barren hills. And yet the government owes these people millions, some of it past debts due for more than thirty years, under the treaty of 1868.

There must be criminal negligence somewhere. Why has not the clothing to which these Indians are entitled been sent to this agency? And why—but I might ask a thousand just as pertinent questions and there would never be an answer given. The Indian system should be abolished.

In a postscript Tibbles added, Besides the rations enumerated there is one range steer issued to every sixty persons each week. It is in dividing the beef that the greatest complaints are made of unfairness. All the Indians say that they never before received rations of so good a quality as has been issued since these troubles began. Heretofore the flour was sometimes unfit to eat.[22]

Pine Ridge's teachers and ministers, realizing the hardships the Lakotas suffered, were determined to share the Christmas holiday with as many Oglalas as possible. On this same Christmas Eve, *Thisba Hutson Morgan says,* there had been set up in the little Protestant Episcopal Church at the agency, the Church of the Holy Cross, a huge cedar tree reaching to the ceiling. It was lighted by candles and a large star at the top. It was festooned with yards and yards of strung popcorn and ladies with little bags of fruit, candy, and nuts. Colorful scarves and handkerchiefs for the boys floated from the branches, and beautiful French dolls for the girls peeped like fairies from everywhere.

The two hundred pupils attending the Oglala Boarding School were having their Christmas celebration that the beautiful story of the Christ Child might be impressed upon them and the joy of Christmas be theirs. The lovely French dolls, one hundred of them, had come from the missionary-minded women of Christ Church in New Orleans. It was heartwarming to see the faces of the Indian children brighten and their eyes sparkle as they examined and caressed their gifts, never forgetting the quiet decorum so carefully instilled into them by their grandmothers that was so often mistaken by the white people for indifference or vacuity.

This was the first of a series of such services. Each day during the Christmas octave, the tree was to be redecorated and each night the Indians from the outlying districts, where the Church had sub-missions, were coming in their turn to the Mother Church for Christmas gifts. The warm heavy practical gifts of clothing for the oldsters and vestments for the Indian Catechists in charge of the sub-missions came in the most part from New York and New England.[23]

The Christmas season was fast approaching, *Charles A. Eastman writes.* The children of the Sunday Schools, and indeed all the people, look eagerly forward to the joyous feast; barrels and boxes are received and opened, candy bags made and filled, carols practiced, and churches decorated with ropes of spicy evergreen.

Anxious to relieve the tension in every way within his power, Reverend Cook and his helpers went on with their preparations upon even a larger scale than usual. Since all of the branch stations had been closed and the people called in, it was planned to keep the Christmas tree standing in the chapel for a week, and to distribute gifts to a separate congregation each evening.

I found myself pressed into the service, and passed some happy hours in the rectory. For me, at that critical time, there was inward struggle as well as the threat of outward conflict, and I could not but recall what my "white mother" had said jokingly one day, referring to my pleasant friendships with many charming Boston girls, "I know one Sioux who has not been conquered, and I shall not rest till I hear of his capture!"

I had planned to enter upon my life work unhampered by any other ties, and declared that all my love should be vested in my people and my profession. At last, however, I had met a woman whose sincerity was convincing and whose ideals seemed very like my own. . . . I do not know what unseen hand had guided me to her side, but on Christmas day of 1890, Elaine Goodale and I announced our engagement.

Three days later, we learned that Big Foot's band of Ghost dancers from the Cheyenne River reservation north of us was approaching the agency, and that Major Whitside was in command of troops with orders to intercept them.

Late that afternoon, the Seventh Cavalry under Colonel Forsyth was called to the saddle and rode off toward Wounded Knee Creek, eighteen miles away. Father Craft, a Catholic priest with some Indian blood, who knew Sitting Bull and his people, followed an hour or so later, and I was much inclined to go too, but my fiancée pointed out that my duty lay rather at home with our Indians, and I stayed.[24]

Eastman's decision to honor his bride-to-be's counsel and stay at Pine Ridge may have saved his life.

CLOSING IN ON BIG FOOT

As Christmas approached, Pvt. Walter R. Crickett's Seventh Cavalry unit, headquartered at Wounded Knee, was on patrol with Maj. Samuel M. Whitside. Well, we got to Wounded Knee about nine, *Crickett wrote.* My troop was rear guard, had to go back about eight miles to cover the trail and come back over Porcupine Creek which was a roundabout way. Crossing the creek was very bad, the ice being about eight inches thick, and as our horses stepped off the bank they went through the ice up to their quarters, some deeper, which made them plunge about, and made everything bitter.

It was so dark you couldn't see your hand in front of you, but we got over alright. The horses was cut up a bit, and some of us wet from falling off, and in less than ten minutes our clothes was frozen stiff, but we were hardened up so we didn't notice it much. We got in about twelve and pitched tents, made some coffee and turned in for the night, stayed there.

As Crickett endured life in the field, Big Foot's Band remained out of the cavalry's reach. Joseph Horn Cloud says that on Christmas day, We moved eight miles to Cedar Spring, now known as Big Foot's Spring. We had to move very slow owing to Big Foot's sickness. On the 26th, we moved again four miles to Red Water Creek. On the 27th, we moved about noon and at supper time arrived at Medicine Root Creek, about where Kyle now is.

Here Big Foot said he wanted to see the chiefs and urged his people to move on. We drove five miles farther to American Horse Creek where there was a log school house, and where there is now the regulation Day School No. 17. Big Foot was unable to proceed any farther, being a very sick man.[25]

Shortly after the escape, Dewey Beard says, Hearing from a half-breed that the general was at Pine Ridge Agency, our chieftain said we would go to Red Cloud's camp, at that place, where we could counsel with the Big Soldier [Miles]. *Miles was trusted by his old adversary as a man who kept his word.*

Dewey Beard continues, So we traveled together, coming at last to a pass in the wall of the Badlands, down which we could go to the valley of the White River. When we got there, however, we saw many white men marching below, and thereupon lay all day watching them till they went into camp at Cane Creek, to the north.

When we had passed the place wherein we hid, we went down across the valley, but the next morning, finding that Big Foot was very sick and bleeding at the nose, we went to what is now called Big Foot Springs. From there we went to Red Water Creek, but our leader became so ill he could go no farther, and we were forced to stay two nights and two days at this spot. At last he said: "We must reach Red Cloud's camp before I die."[26]

Miles, however, was not at Pine Ridge; he was at his headquarters in Rapid City. At Pine Ridge, General Brooke says, I received frequent telegrams from Division Commander Miles. In one of which, dated December 26th, and received by me at 4 P.M., he used the following language: "And I hope you will round up the whole body of them, disarm and keep them all under close guard."

To this Miles added, Big Foot is cunning and his Indians are very bad.

In a telegram Brooke received the same day at 5:50 P.M., Miles writes: It is very important to secure the men with Big Foot with as little delay as possible.

Brooke says, In another, received 6:48 P.M., of December 26th, Division Commander says: "I have no doubts your orders are all right, but I shall be exceedingly anxious till I know they are executed; whoever secures that body of Indians will be entitled to much credit. They deceived Sumner completely, and if they get a chance they will scatter through the entire Sioux camp or slip out individually."[27]

By now, Whitside, a seasoned veteran commanding the detachment from the Seventh Cavalry, was closing in on Big Foot. He wrote in his report to the Seventh Cavalry's adjutant: I left camp at Pine Ridge Agency, S.D., at 1:20 P.M., December 26, 1890, with my battalion, consisting of Troops A, I, K and B, 7th Cavalry, and two Hotchkiss guns, in command of Lieutenant H. L. Hawthorne, 2nd Artillery, and proceeded to a point on Wounded Knee Creek known as the Post Office crossing, reaching there about 5 P.M. same date. As I approached the creek my scouts reported they had seen four Indians who said they were "Sitting Bull people."

I sent Troop A, 7th Cavalry, under Captain Moylan, 7th Cavalry, forward at a gallop to try and capture them, but darkness prevented. On Captain Moylan's return, I went into camp on the creek near the crossing.[28]

At Pine Ridge, Lt. Alexander R. Piper wrote his wife, Last evening a courier came in from the Badlands with a letter from the hostiles saying the whole gang had started in. I certainly do hope it is so for then we may be able to find out what is to become of us this winter.

The news about the Indians today is quite reassuring and I feel that we can almost begin to hope for a speedy end to this performance.

He groused, About 3 o'clock the cavalry teams began coming up for forage and a rumor came around that the 7th would go to the Badlands last evening. I had my horse saddled and rode down to camp and of course found the whole thing one of the customary lies. They were simply drawing forage so as to have it on hand should anything turn up.

Preston had just gotten back so I called on him. He was disgusted and disgruntled because General Miles had relieved him of the command of the fifty scouts he took over last week. He scouted within six miles of the hostiles and saw something of the Badlands. The only news he brought was that General Miles told someone that he proposed to put an end to this thing very soon and send every one home. I am afraid it is too good to be true.

A courier came in from Colonel Henry saying he reached his post on White River at one A.M. (forty miles from here) the night he left here. He must have ridden very hard. The weather has been simply perfect for the past four or five days, but about ten minutes ago a dust storm came up and it is simply frightful now.[29]

On the morning of December 27, Brooke relayed the following order to Whitside:

> Headquarters Dept. Platte
> In the field
> Camp at Pine Ridge Agency, S.D.
> December 27th, 1890, 7:30 A.M.
>
> Major Whitside; 7th Cavalry
> Comdg Battalion in the field,
>
> Sir:
>
> I am directed by the commanding general to say that he thinks Big Foot's party must be to your front somewhere, and that you must make every effort to find him and then move on him at once and with rapidity. There must be a solution reached at the earliest possible moment. Find his trail and follow, or find his hiding place and capture him. If he fights, destroy him. Take all precautions to report promptly what you may ascertain, so that intelligence co-operation may be possible.
>
> I am, very resp'y
> Your obedient servt,
> (Sgn) Fayette W. Roe,
> 1st Lieut. 3d Infty, A.D.C.[30]

In his report Whitside writes: The following morning, December 27, 1890, I sent Lieutenant E. A. Garlington, 7th Cavalry, with twenty-one men to scout down Wounded Knee Creek and ascertain, if possible, if any Indians had crossed during the night and also to try and communicate with Major Henry, 9th Cavalry.

Lieutenant J. C. Gresham, 7th Cavalry, with twenty-one men, was sent up Wounded Knee Creek to the State Line, with instructions to thoroughly scout that country and ascertain if any Indians had crossed the creek to my south during the night.

Lieutenant Garlington returned about nine P.M. and reported he had been down Wounded Knee Creek about twenty-six miles and could find no signs either of Indians or Major Henry's command.

My Indian scouts were sent out to the east, towards Porcupine Creek, and returned about dark and reported they had seen no signs of Indians.[31]

Big Foot had vanished again.

BIG FOOT SURRENDERS

On the 28th, *Joseph Horn Cloud says*, the camp was astir early and began to march up Yellow Thunder Creek toward Porcupine Creek. By noon they had proceeded fifteen miles and as we reached the hills skirting Porcupine on the east, four Indian scouts were discovered watering their horses in the stream.

A few Indians made a dash upon them and captured two: Old Hand, who was a brother of Little Bat, and another. The other two made their escape. After the capture of the scouts, they all halted on the Porcupine for dinner.

They did not learn from their captives of the soldiers being on Wounded Knee. On the passage from White River to Porcupine, while they passed a number of houses, no person was seen, except Frank Maycock, a crazy Irishman who was guarding a house belonging to Condelario Benavidez. He told them all the Indians had gone to the agency to get annuities or to do fighting.[32]

On the morning of the 28th, *Whitside reported*, I sent a half-breed scout, known as Little Bat, who reported to me the evening before with Lieutenant Preston, Ninth Cavalry, and three Indian scouts, with instructions to scout the country about the Porcupine and try and locate Big Foot, who I felt confident was in that direction.

At eleven o'clock A.M., Little Bat came into camp and reported Big Foot on the Porcupine coming in my direction. I immediately saddled up and took the trot in the direction of the Porcupine, sending Little Bat and three scouts ahead.[33]

Paul High Back, a member of Big Foot's band, remembers, I was one of the four young men who were scouts or outriders and who rode ahead or to one side of the caravan. . . . We had just climbed the hills to get out of the Creek Valley when we saw three men coming towards us on horseback. When they came up we saw that they were Indians. Two were regular Indians and one was a mixed-blood. They had guns and we knew by their clothes that they were scouts for the white soldiers.

The mixed-blood did the talking and told us many soldiers were ahead of us a few miles, but not to be afraid. He told us the soldiers would treat us well and take us to the agency where there were many other Indians and where we would have plenty to eat. He said everything would be alright if we would go with the soldiers.[34]

By now the troops were rushing to meet Big Foot's band. Alice Ghost Horse says, Sometime later, the head wagons stopped on top of a hill and they were all looking down at something. My father went to see, and my mother came over and started to tighten my cinch and said there were some cavalry camped below on Wounded Knee Creek. She told me we might have to make a run for it and she asked me to stay close to the wagon.

My father returned and said Big Foot was very sick and laying in the back of the buggy, all bundled up. My father said they picked some men to go down and talk to the officers.[35]

Dewey Beard says, On the night before at sundown we broke camp and marched all night, coming on the second day to Yellow Thunder Creek, near Porcupine Butte. Here we saw four mounted Indian scouts, and although we called to them they spurred away as fast as they could. We continued on, but as we drew near to the Butte we discerned soldiers to the northeast. They had pack mules and were coming toward us, at which Big Foot said: "Go meet them."[36]

After an eight-mile ride, Whitside reports, Within two miles of the Porcupine the Indians were seen on the hill halted. I formed my command in double columns of fours, dismounted and formed line to the front, placing the Hotchkiss guns in the centre, then rode forward with Lieutenant Nicholson, 7th Cavalry, and met the Indians.[37]

At this time, both forces were near Pine Creek, two miles east of Porcupine Butte. Joseph Horn Cloud says, At about two P.M. Big Foot's band, having crossed the Porcupine and raised up to the top of the hill on the other side, saw a cloud of dust rising, and when they had descended on the other side, the soldiers had also come over the hills from the west, and the two columns met here on Pine Creek, the soldiers crossing it and taking a position in line of battle facing the approaching Indians who had hoisted a white flag. Four Hotchkiss cannons had been run out a few yards in front of the line of soldiers.[38]

Whitside does not mention the display of the white flag in his report.

Alice Ghost Horse continues her story: A lone rider galloped up the hill to Big Foot's wagon and they told him that the officers wanted to talk to him but his relatives said "No," that he was very sick, so the riders went back to tell them.

Some time later, a buggy was sent up with a doctor to examine the old man. The doctor said he had pneumonia. He gave him some medicine and they loaded him in the special wagon and took him down. They talked a long time and finally a lone rider came back and told them to camp along the creek on the west side.

I saw four riders riding down toward the center of the camp where they have big guns on wheels. One of the riders had a white flag, a white material tied to a stick, riding in front of the other three riders. Soon as they cross the creek, all the soldiers layed down and aimed their rifles at them but they kept on going and arrived at the big gun on wheels, where there were some soldiers and officers standing. They dismounted and they had a short talk.

When we approached they formed in line, pointing a cannon at us as though about to shoot. Big Foot had been too sick to ride a horse, so we had carried him in a wagon since leaving Red Water. He asked us to drive him toward the soldiers, which we did till an officer met us. I rode alongside, and when the man came near me, I cried: "Don't shoot! We are going to the agency. We don't want to fight."

All the Indians were frightened and thought they were going to be killed.[39]

Whitside wrote, Big Foot, who was riding in a wagon, being sick, then came to the front. I demanded the surrender of his band. In the meantime, 120 Indians, well armed, two-thirds mounted, the remainder dismounted, advanced in line. Some of the Indians tried to ride around my flanks. I ordered them to return to the band, which order they obeyed.

Dewey Beard told Ricker, We dismounted by a Hotchkiss gun and I shoved my hand into it because I was anxious to die. While I was doing this I heard the wagons coming. I saw Big Foot coming in a light wagon driven by Big Foot's nephew, a pole up at the front and a white flag . . . floating from it. Big Foot's wagon was driven right down in front of the line of soldiers and stopped there. I was in front at this moment. I saw an officer go up to Big Foot's wagon and I went up and listened to the officer talking.

Big Foot was lying in his wagon, his nose bleeding all the time; the blood had run in the wagon and the officers were standing looking at the blood. The officer opened the blanket to see Big Foot's face and spoke, "Can't you talk? Aren't you able to talk?"[40]

By now, Joseph Horn Cloud says, Big Foot's strength was failing; he spoke slowly and in faltering accents.[41]

An unnamed correspondent riding with Whitside, reported, Big Foot extended his hand in token of peace. "I am sick. My people here want peace and . . ."

Major Whitside cut him short with: "I won't nor will I have any parlaying at all; it is either unconditional surrender or fight. What is your answer, sir?"

"We surrender," said the chief. "We would have done so before, but we couldn't find you and couldn't find any soldiers to surrender to."[42]

Then the colonel asked him why he was going there. Big Foot said that he heard there was a fire likely to break out there so he was going there to try to put out the fire. He was going to make peace. Colonel Whitside said, "Big Foot do you want to fight or have peace?"

Big Foot said, "I want peace. My forefathers always had peace, and I will do the same."[43]

"I hear that you are come out from the Cheyenne River Agency," *Whitside continued*, "that you come fearful as a war party; I have been looking for you. Now I see you today. Now I want you to tell me where you expect you are going."

Big Foot answered, "I am going to see my people over on the White Clay Creek and come to the agency."[44]

Then they both shook hands.

The officer said, "I am glad to see you are peaceable. Therefore, I want you to give me twenty-five guns."

Big Foot said, "All right, but I am afraid; if I give you the twenty-five guns, I am afraid that you are going to do harm to my people in such a country. I am willing to give you twenty-five guns, but wait until we get to the agency and I will give you whatever you ask—the twenty-five guns, knives and horses."[45]

This was the first but not the last time that the cavalry demanded that Big Foot's band surrender all its weapons.

Dewey Beard says Big Foot asked, "We are ready to do that," said the chief, "but we fear something will happen to us if we do. We are friendly. Will you not wait until we get to the agency and have a chance to speak with the big general? [Miles] He will tell us everything; but now we do not understand. We are afraid. We do not know what all this means. I will go with your soldiers now, and my people will give up their guns when we reach the agency. I wish no trouble, for I am going to die."[46]

Whitside did not pursue his demand for arms. Instead, he replied, "I am glad you speak frankly to me; I had heard that you were hostile, but they lied about you."[47] *Then the major asked*, "What is the matter, Big Foot? You seem to be sick."

Big Foot said, "Yes, I have pneumonia, and I am pretty sick today on account of my jolting wagons."

The [major] answered, "I see that you are in a hard wagon, and it is pretty hard on you; I want you to ride to our camp in an easier one.[48] Now if you want to ride in my ambulance you may. That will be better for you than the rough wagon."

Big Foot replied, "If you please, I will ride in the ambulance."[49]

And when Big Foot agreed to this, *Dewey Beard says*, they brought the sick wagon, put him on some gray blankets, such as the soldiers have, and placed him in it. I grew very much afraid now, for the officers laughed when they carried Big Foot away.[50]

Then, *Joseph Horn Cloud remembers*, the [major] called some soldiers to put Big Foot into the ambulance. The soldiers then opened ranks and the ambulance going through the ranks of soldiers and on to Wounded Knee Creek, carrying white flags.[51]

Paul High Back says, Our leaders then decided to go to the agency, for there was nothing else that we could do since we could not fight them. So we came along with the soldiers.[52] *Indeed, the Miniconjous were outgunned and outmanned, and they wanted to go into Pine Ridge to receive rations.*

Crickett, who was some distance away from the negotiations, was apprehensive. While the negotiations with Big Foot went on, both sides seemed to be studying each other. At one time it looked pretty bad, *the young cavalryman says*. I thought we should of had a battle right there. They kept advancing all the time to see what our strength was. We was all dismounted and loaded ready but just as they got up to us our pack mule train came in sight, and they thought it was more troops coming up, so they came along quiet [and] got into Wounded Knee without any trouble, but I think if they had of commenced they would of made it pretty lively for us.[53]

Then, at a signal, *a correspondent reports, Big Foot's* warriors raised a white flag. In less than it takes to write it, the military had their prisoners surrounded.[54]

Once Big Foot surrendered, Whitside says, I wrote a despatch to the department commander announcing the capture, requesting that the 2nd Battalion, 7th Cavalry, be sent as reinforcement to my command to arrive before daylight the following morning to assist in the disarming of the Indians, as I did not consider it safe to make that attempt to disarm them with my command; the despatch I sent in by Lieutenants. Nicholson, 7th Cavalry, and Preston, Ninth Cavalry.[55]

I then took up my march with two troops in advance, followed by the Indians, two troops bringing up the rear, and arrived at the Wounded Knee Crossing at 2:30 P.M., and went into camp, detailing two troops, A and I, to guard the Indians during the night, which was done by placing a chain of sentinels around the camp and two Hotchkiss guns under Lieut. Hawthorne on the side of the hill overlooking the Indian village.[56]

Joseph Horn Cloud describes the journey to Wounded Knee: The Indians and soldiers were now starting for Wounded Knee about five miles away, the Indians being ahead and the ambulance containing Big Foot taking the lead. This was flanked on either side by a sergeant and a soldier mounted. There were about 40 Indians on horseback; they were flanked on each side by a line of cavalry soldiers. The rest of the soldiers were in the rear of the column. On this movement from the Cheyenne, the Indians had ridden either in wagon or on horseback.

When they crossed Wounded Knee Creek on the bridge, they passed by the door of the trader's store and some of the Indians went in and bought candles, sugar, coffee, bacon, etc. The store was kept by George E. Bartlett.[57]

Dewey Beard spoke to a soldier who said they were going to camp there overnight. He said "After you put up your tipi and get ready, we will give you rations."[58]

When Brooke received the news of Big Foot's surrender, he sent Miles a telegram at 3:45 P.M.: Major Whitside reports the capture of Big Foot, 120 men, 250 women and children. Will endeavor to make this sure. I send another battalion to reinforce him. Will send them to railroad at Gordon if you so desire. If I send them to Omaha, will send part of the 2d Infantry as guards.

To this Miles tersely replied: All right. Use force enough. Congratulations.[59]

Where Miles intended to send Big Foot's band upon their arrival in Omaha is uncertain. It would seem that Miles and Brooke had not told Whitside that his captives would not be going to Pine Ridge.

The news concerning the capture of Big Foot quickly arrived at Pine Ridge. Elaine Goodale writes, Ironically enough, there were at this moment no "hostiles" entrenched in the Badlands. The stampeding Ghost dancers had gradually yielded to persuasion and moved their camp to within some five miles of the agency.[60]

As December 28 drew to a close, the threat of an Indian war had ended. Almost all of the Ghost dancers were in government custody, and the rest were reported to be on their way to Pine Ridge.

THE CAMP AT WOUNDED KNEE

The trip to Wounded Knee was quick. Medicine Woman, a member of Big Foot's band, says, We made up our camp at Wounded Knee Creek about four o'clock in the afternoon with soldiers all around us. The soldiers brought Big Foot in an ambulance because he was sick. When we came into camp the soldiers brought him from the ambulance and put him into an army tent. After we made camp they gave us coffee, sugar, hardtack, and a small piece of breakfast bacon.[61]

When they came to Wounded Knee, *scout and translator Philip Wells says,* They were prisoners in possession of their arms. . . . Big Foot admitted the principle which Forsyth contended; namely, that the Indians should surrender their weapons, but they used evasion to avoid doing so. The Indians had delivered before the action only some inferior pieces.[62]

There is disagreement over how well Big Foot's band was armed. Civilian whites who were on the scene stated they were poorly armed and that many of their rifles were barely functional antiques. The army, however, believed Big Foot's people carried concealed weapons. This belief would become an item of contention the next morning.

As Whitside waited for reinforcements, he set up a perimeter around his captives. The section of the Hotchkiss battery was posted on a hill overlooking the camp, *he writes.* To guard against any mishap, a courier had been dispatched, when the capture was first effected, to General Brooke at the Pine Ridge Agency to join the Second Battalion of the Seventh Cavalry. The object I had in view was that, by their presence, we could overawe the Indians . . . so they would submit quietly to be disarmed.

I was convinced from the hostile demonstration of the Indians at the time of surrender, that otherwise trouble might ensue. Colonel Forsyth, with the 2d Battalion, consisting of C, D, E, and G Troops, and one section of Hotchkiss guns, under Captain Capron, First Artillery, arrived about 8:45 that night, and the colonel assumed command and went into camp, marching by a circuitous route to the rear of my battalion, and he accomplished same apparently without proclaiming their arrival to the Indians.[63]

Whitside's contention that Forsyth kept his arrival secret is hard to believe. The arrival of more than three hundred armed and mounted men accompanied by wagons and artillery into the narrow Wounded Knee Valley could not have passed without notice.

Forsyth immediately reported his arrival in a dispatch to Pine Ridge:

Hdqtrs. Camp 7th Cavalry,
Wounded Knee, S.D., December 28, 1890.
8:30 P.M.

Actg. Asst. Adjt. General,
Dept. of the Platte, in the field,
Pine Ridge Agency, So. Dak.

Sir:

I have the honor to report that I reached here with my command at 8:30 P.M.

Found everything in perfect condition. The Comdg Gen'l's orders will be carried out in the morning, or as soon thereafter as possible. I will report back to him, with the battalion I brought with me.

Rations for 400 Indians should be sent here to-morrow as early as possible, with the forage train, the general said he intended to send. I find that Major Whitside has been obliged to call in from the troops rations to feed these Indians to-day.

I trust that the rations and forage train will be pushed here rapidly to-morrow morning.

I cannot now say what time I will reach the agency on my return to-morrow, but no time will be lost.

Very respectfully,
Your obdt. servant,
(Sgn.) James W. Forsyth,
Colonel 7th Cavalry,
Commanding.[64]

Like Whitside, Forsyth thought he had been sent to Wounded Knee to escort Big Foot's band into the Pine Ridge Agency.

The army forces gathered in the Wounded Knee Valley were formidable. By now there were eight troops of cavalry, one company of scouts, and four pieces of light artillery—the dreaded rapid-fire Hotchkiss guns. This force of at least five hundred trained fighting men outnumbered Big Foot's men of fighting age—many of whom were not mounted—almost fivefold.

Among those riding in Forsyth's command was Capt. George D. Wallace, a tall gaunt man who was popular with his men and trusted by the Lakotas. According to Royer's wife, Captain Wallace was a fine man and in the habit of sending a letter to his wife every day. Before he had gone out on patrol he handed Colonel Royer a letter asking him to send it out in the mail as one went out every day at one o'clock. He said, "Royer for God's sake be careful. I have lots of trust in you but none in the Indians."[65]

It was the last letter Wallace would write.

Brig. Gen. E. D. Scott, after researching the army's part in the events, describes the Wounded Knee Valley that evening: There had been no snow that winter; the weather had been still and cold, but clear; the moon was at full on December 28. The sky may have been overcast, but even then visibility would have been good for some distance, making guard duty relatively easy.

Wounded Knee Creek . . . is small, and at the time had ice an inch thick. Its direction is northwesterly. The principal trail or road from Pine Ridge Agency to Rosebud comes from the southwest, crossing it, and then takes a more easterly direction. Near the crossing stood the trader's store, post office, and a few other buildings, and about 300 yards downstream, the church. A road passing the latter continues to the mouth of the stream. About 300 yards south of the crossing Fast Horse Road comes into the agency road from the northwest. The agency road divides a short distance south of this junction, descends by coulees into a ravine and out again, reuniting on the other side.

Between the agency road and the stream the terrain is flat and not very high above the level of the latter. West of the road the terrain rises quickly into ridges and spurs from the ridge two to three miles west that is the divide between the Wounded Knee and White Clay Creeks. The ravine above referred to heads about two miles west of the road, runs almost due east, has numerous lateral branches, especially on the north side, and all contained much brush and scrub trees. A characteristic of the prairie coulee or ravines is their sudden beginning by a vertical drop of one or several feet, directly from the prairie. Such places were made-to-order rifle pits and were so used by the Indians.

The creek itself has a border of fair-sized trees and brush, and the hills in general carried a thinly scattered growth of scrub pine and cedar.[66]

The members of Big Foot's band huddled in their cloth tipis by the banks of Wounded Knee Creek. Their camp was backed by deep gullies on one side. The main body of the Seventh Cavalry was camped a short distance to the northeast.

Troop E was on the western hillock overlooking the camp, and four Hotchkiss guns were on the east hillock. Their position allowed the troops to look directly into the Miniconjou camp and gave the artillery a direct line of fire. For Big Foot's band, neither escape nor attack was possible.

For the night, at least, the troops were separated from the Miniconjous, just as Miles had repeatedly ordered.

As the Seventh Cavalry and its captives settled into the Wounded Knee Valley, reporters began to file their stories. The "New York World" headlined "THE WAR HAS COLLAPSED" and announced, General Brooke reports that the hostiles in the Badlands have surrendered and will reach Pine Ridge on Tuesday [December 30]. Bright Eyes sends word that half the hostiles have left the Badlands and are within a few hours' march of the agency.

Short Bull, Kicking Bear, and all their followers have abandoned the Badlands and are coming in. The final movement of the troops has undoubtedly greatly influenced Short Bull in reconsidering his former determination to die rather than surrender.

It was reported from Rapid City, The news today indicates that the Indian troubles are about to be brought to a close without the sacrifice of any more lives.[67] *The Ghost Dance war seemed to be at an end.*

VISITORS FROM PINE RIDGE

Former scout and rancher James H. Cook would write, When it became known that General Miles had given orders to Colonel Forsyth to intercept Big Foot's band of Sioux Indians, who had traveled from Standing Rock Reservation and were on their way to Pine Ridge Agency to surrender, a number of civilians at the agency prepared to be on hand in order to see Big Foot and his people give themselves up.[68]

Among those rushing to Wounded Knee to cover Big Foot's surrender were reporters Charles Allen, Will Cressey, William F. Kelley, and T. H. Tibbles. Tibbles would return to Pine Ridge early the next morning; the other three remained at Wounded Knee.[69]

Father Craft, *Cook wrote,* who was well known to the Indians, also accompanied these sightseers. . . . I happened to meet him just as he was about to start off with the others. I remarked to him that he had better be careful, for it was not unlikely that lead might be drifting through the air should there be any kind of hitch in the surrendering ceremonies.

Father Craft replied that Hovering Eagle—the name given him by the Sioux people—would be in no danger from the Indians; he felt that he was both a father and a brother to them. He said a "black robe" was always safe with Indians.

I remarked to him that I had known Indian men to forget everything pertaining to the white man's religion when they were desperately angry or frightened. A white man garbed in black meant an enemy to them as much as one in the uniform of a major general of the army. He was apparently amused by my remark, for he smiled as he rolled a cigarette and took his departure for the scene of the surrender.[70]

Father Craft, known as a "warrior priest," was a colorful character often quoted in the press and much liked for his outspoken manner. Although he worked among the Lakotas, his sympathies were generally with the military.[71]

After the massacre, Craft said, I learned . . . that Indians from the Standing Rock Agency, whom I knew well were with them. By permission of General Brooke I went out to see if I could be of any service, as malicious whites on or near all agencies, during the present excitement have, by misrepresenting the intentions of the army, caused such a state of alarm and suspicion among the Indians as to make it possible for the least excitement or misunderstanding to precipitate serious trouble. I hoped to be of some service in going among the Indians and reassuring them. I reached the military camp about 11 P.M.[72]

Cook helped Cressey get to Wounded Knee even though he remembered Cressey as an object of ridicule. In the story he told, Cook nicknamed Cressey "Cola":

Cola complained quite a bit to me about the inactivity, which was about the only thing going on. One day I told him he should be thankful that matters were no worse about the agency, and that at any moment some little thing might happen which would try out the courage of us all.

When the war correspondents went out to Wounded Knee to see the surrender of Big Foot, Cola could not get a horse. There were none to be hired, and he was raring to go to see the surrender. He was in a state of despair. At last I told him that he might take my horse and saddle, as I could get along without them for a few hours. Mr. Cola was not a rider, and he gave some evidence of this fact very soon after starting. Some of the other correspondents had secured a team and a two-seated buggy for the trip. One of these gentlemen, Charles Allen, kindly gave Mr. Cola his seat in the buggy and took my saddle animal. Mr. Allen was a horseman as well as a correspondent.[73]

None of those who rode to Wounded Knee treated it as a dangerous enterprise; they viewed their trip as an outing during which they would observe the final surrender of the Ghost Dance war. The remainder of the press corps remained at Pine Ridge. There they hoped to see the surrender of Short Bull and the dancers that were coming in from the Badlands.

At nine o'clock that evening Miles telegraphed Brooke, again stating his intention to remove Big Foot and his people from the Dakotas: I send you word all right, and approve of sending them to Omaha. The only objection is it may alarm those coming in from the Badlands. It is important to secure both bodies. I can move troops forward beyond the Cheyenne line, and all can be all along the line of the White River say after tomorrow night. They have been scouting in the Badlands for the last two days. You can use the troops at Rosebud and Sanford's command at once. I will wait in the telegraph office for your reply or take any other measure you may deem advisable.[74] *It is uncertain whether Forsyth was informed of Miles's plan at this time.*

APPREHENSIONS IN THE NIGHT

After supper, *Joseph Horn Cloud says*, I went to the soldier's camp and saw a priest, Father Craft, talking with some Indians and telling them there was no danger, and not to be afraid; that Major Whitside was a good man, that we would go to Pine Ridge the next day. There were about two or three tipis of Sitting Bull's people with us.

Now about 11 o'clock Colonel Forsyth came with his troops and also some Indian scouts who went into camp southwest of us. I could not sleep at all that night, because of the noise of the arrival of the cavalry and for fear of the soldiers all around.[75]

Capt. Myles Moylan, assigned to set up the guard for the night, describes the deployment of his men: I was detailed by Major Whitside to take my Troop A and Captain Nolan's Troop . . . for the purpose of guarding the Indian village during the night of the 28th and 29th. I had four officers and eighty-one enlisted men in the guard. I established a line of sentinels around the village, covering it with twenty posts, leaving a small number of men to act as patrols during the night.

These posts were on the far side of the ravine south of the village, thence crossing the ravine west and east of the village and also extending on the north also, forming a complete chain, but especially guarding the ravine to the east and west.[76]

Crickett, assigned to Moylan's guard detail, got little rest that night. To keep Big Foot's band from escaping, he says, We formed a chain guard round them . . . with orders not to let any of the bucks through, but the squaws might go and get wood for the fires. If the bucks should attempt to pass we were told to knock them on the head, but it was easier said than done. The guard was formed into three reliefs, one on and two off. We had to sleep out in the open close to them for this was the band that got away from Colonel Sumner, and they thought they would try and serve us the same game.[77]

Alice Ghost Horse says, By sundown, we were completely surrounded by foot soldiers, all with rifles. My mother and I went down to the creek to pick up some wood and to go to the bathroom but two soldiers followed us, so we hurried back with some sticks. Everyone went to bed as they were all tired from the hectic trip.[78]

Mrs. Mosseau says, About midnight we wanted to get some water, but the soldiers refused to let us get it. After refusing to let us get water the soldiers called all the women together and let them go by twos, a soldier with a gun going behind each two women.[79]

ANOTHER QUESTION OF CONVIVIALITY

Allen and his friends, after leaving their billet, began to wander about the camp seeking old friends and possible stories. He says, We had gone but a short distance when we came to a broad opening that extended northward among the tents. Across this opening, before a well lighted tent of fair size, stood a number of men. The tent flaps were drawn back and we could see their movements in and out. A conversation of evident interest was being carried on. We approached and found that the group comprised commissioned officers of various rank, including Colonel Forsyth and Major Whitside. The tent was that of Captain Wallace, who had been in immediate charge of the captives on their way into camp.

Most of the officers we had met, and all of them we knew by sight. Soon we were of the group of listeners, but asking occasional questions. Captain Wallace's broad bed was spread on the ground in the middle of the tent, and on a nice new gray army blanket he was building with matches and explaining a diagram showing the position of the various parts of the runaway band and the troops at their time of meeting. Captain Wallace was not only an able officer but also a fine, upstanding specimen of vigorous manhood, and many times in the subsequent years we have been thankful that, while watching his little demonstration that night, Time's kindly veil had obscured the pale still face we were to gaze upon a few hours later.

We had all drifted from the tent and, as usual when a group of people feel imbued with a desire for conversation, had separated into small knots. Presently I found myself along with Colonel Forsyth, who had begun to move slowly forward as he talked. The bright moonlight and balmy breeze caused him to become reminiscent, and as we paced back and forth on the grassy walk I was unforgettably entertained with a graphic account of many incidents in his European tour with General Phil Sheridan while still on his staff after the Civil War. We finally withdrew sometime after midnight and each, wrapped with the drapery of his couch about him, lay down to "pleasant dreams."[80]

At least one local merchant capitalized on the Seventh Cavalry's arrival at Wounded Knee. Henry Cottier, who was thirteen at the time, says, The tragedy of Wounded Knee might never have happened had not one of the traders smuggled whiskey to the soldiers camped at Wounded Knee Creek the night before the battle. He saw the wagon loaded with whiskey and saw the trader offer $25 to drive the wagon to Wounded Knee.[81]

A freighter named Swigert later confessed to the Rev. James Garvey that he felt guilty all the rest of his life for taking the liquor to the soldiers the afternoon of December 28, 1890. Swigert says, "It was too bad those drunken soldiers were allowed to handle a delicate condition. I know they were all drunk. I am sorry because I feel partly responsible in hauling whisky in with the supplies. If it was not for this liquor, I don't believe this massacre of the natives by the white soldiers would have occurred."[82]

Many Miniconjous and at least one white said that the officers of the

Seventh drank heavily that evening. Allen admits there was drinking, but told Ricker, The officers were free from the influence of liquor in the morning. During the night before, there had been some conviviality. Allen was with Major Whitside, Captain Wallace and other officers that night. They were not intoxicated, but felt well.[83]

J. R. Walker, agency physician at Leech Lake from 1888 and agent from 1890, disagreed with the assertion that the officers drank moderately, stating, It should be said that the convivialities among the officers the night before was well known by enough responsible persons to leave no doubt on this point.

Mr. R. C. Stirk has told me that this pleasure was carried to a pretty high pitch and that the line officers were going from tent to tent congratulating Colonel Forsyth on his capture of the Indians. Stirk says Jim Asay, who was keeping a trader's store at the agency, was at Wounded Knee with a barrel of whiskey. Stirk says that whiskey was very abundant the night before the battle; he saw this and was invited to partake; the officers were passing from tent to tent and drinking and congratulating Forsyth on his capture of the Indians.[84]

Alice Ghost Horse says, Some of the young men stayed up all night to watch the soldiers. Some of the soldiers were drunk, saying bad things about the Lakota women.[85]

Lakota Hobart Keith Sr., whose family was there, says, Here and there was much talking and drinking well into the night. About a dozen troopers staggered over to Big Foot's tent and tried to get the dying chief outside but were stopped by the captain of the guard, Captain Moylan. The Indians couldn't sleep because of all the activity of the troopers through the night.[86]

William Horncloud, son of Joseph Horncloud, confirmed this encounter during Senate hearings in 1991. He said that even as a boy his father understood English, and that when the 7th Cavalry soldiers started drinking that night, he knew from the conversations that . . . some of these people were in the party that killed Custer.

So [my dad] told my grandfather about it and my grandfather said, "No, don't pay no attention. These are important men. They'll take us to Pine Ridge."

Then William Horncloud says that after some soldiers were very drunk, They wanted to go over and see Big Foot, but a guard turned back the soldiers. If the guards didn't turn [them] back, probably the massacre would have happened that night.[87]

Paul High Back does not mentioned any drinking, but he does say, That night we did not sleep well. Everybody was afraid. All night long the soldiers had lights and were working at something. We could hear the noise and rattle of iron being moved around and it made us all very nervous and we could not sleep. All night long soldiers walked back and forth around our camp. In the morning we found that everything had been arranged differently. There was a row of big guns set up on the side of the hill and we found that they shot bullets very fast.[88] *Paul was speaking of the Hotchkiss guns that were aimed into the Wounded Knee Valley.*

Dewey Beard says that the troops assembled some of the band's leaders for a late-night interrogation: After they ate, that's when they told Grandpa Horn Cloud to go to Big Foot's tent. Someone tapped on the tipi door. An Indian soldier peeked in. "After you get done, I want you to go to where Big Foot is staying."

I got my coat on and went out, going towards where Big Foot's tent was. On the way a white soldier started to push me around really mean. I turned around and looked up at the white soldier. Then I remembered what Big Foot had told me, to be humble.

Celene Not Help Him says that as Dewey Beard walked toward Big Foot's tent, The white soldier said something to him in English. He didn't understand and asked one of the Indian soldiers [scouts] what he said, "Don't pay any attention to him," the Indian soldier said.

He went over to Big Foot's tent and Big Foot was glad to see him. He said "Good you came over here. That's good, come and sit down."

Already Iron Eyes, Spotted Thunder and a few others were there. There were six of them altogether and they started talking.

Just then, my grandfather's little brother, Joe Horn Cloud Jr., came in. Grandmother Big Foot told Joe, "Can you go and tell one of the soldiers to fix along the bottom of the tent? It's really cold. They've got a big stove in here, but I think the tent is about two feet off the ground."

As the night progressed, the interrogations became more intense. Dewey Beard told his granddaughter, They wouldn't let us get any sleep. All night they tortured us by gun point. They asked us who all was in the Battle of the Little Big Horn, the battle with Custer. We can't tell anything—so we told them we don't know. Besides the interpreter is not that good. Maybe he tells them something else or is afraid to say anything.

One of the six men sitting there almost went to sleep. That's when the soldier poked me really hard with his gun barrel. We all looked and we didn't like how they treated him, but I said remember to be humble.[89]

Most interesting is Dewey Beard's mention of the soldiers' attempt to identify members of the band who had fought at the Little Bighorn. Nineteen officers and men in the Seventh Cavalry had been at the Little

Map 4. Wounded Knee battlefield.

From a map by Lt. T. Q. Donaldson, Seventh Cavalry, loaned to James Mooney by Dr. J. D. Glennan, U.S. Army. Reprinted from Mooney, *Fourteenth Annual Report,* 869.

A and I. Seventy-six men from A and I troops forming dismounted line of sentinels
B. Troop B dismounted and in line
C. Troop C mounted and in line
D. Troop D mounted and in line
E. Troop E mounted and in line
G. Troop G mounted and in line
K. Troop K dismounted and in line
S. Indian scouts

1. Tent from which a warrior shot two soldiers
2. Tent occupied by Big Foot and his wife and in front of which the former was killed
3. Tents put up for the use of Big Foot's band
4. Council ring in or near which were Colonel Forsyth, Major Whitside, Captain Varnum, Captain van Hoff, Captain Wallace, Doctor Glennan, Lieutenant Robinson, Lieutenant Nicholson, Lieutenant McCormick, and the reporters
5. Officers' tents, First Battalion
6. Enlisted men's tents, First Battalion
7. Bivouac of Second Battalion on night of December 28, 1890
8. Four Hotchkiss guns and detachment of First Artillery, under Captain Capron, First Artillery, and Lieutenant Hawthorne, Second Artillery.
9. Indian village
10. Indian ponies
11. Dismounted line of sentinels
12. Captains Ilsley and Moylan
13. Lieutenants Garlington and Waterman
14. Captain Godfrey and Lieutenant Tompkins
15. Captain Jackson and Lieutenant Donaldson
16. Lieutenant Taylor, Ninth Cavalry, commanding Indian scouts
17. Captain Edgerly and Lieutenant Brewer
18. Captain Nowlan and Lieutenant Gresham
19. Indian houses
20. Lieutenants Sickel and Rice

[*Note:* Just beyond the limit of the map, toward the west, the ravine forms a bend. Women, children, and a few warriors took refuge in this bend, and Lieutenant Hawthorne was shot from it. Captain Wallace was found near the center of the council circle. Big Foot was killed two or three yards in front of his tent. Father Craft was near the center of the circle when he was stabbed. The Indians broke to the west through troops B and K.]

Wounded Knee
P.O.
Wounded Knee Creek
Road
Wounded Knee P.O.
JULIUS BIEN & CO. N.Y.

Bighorn. Seven of these were officers—Capt. Winfield S. Edgerly, Capt. Edward S. Godfrey, 1st Lt. Luther R. Hare, Capt. Charles C. S. Ilsley, Capt. Myles Moylan, Capt. Charles A. Varnum, and Capt. George D. Wallace. In addition, a quartermaster, two first sergeants, six sergeants, two corporals, and one private were there. It was a small cadre of veterans in a regiment of nearly five hundred, but the men who had been with Custer held important positions of leadership, positions from which they could influence recruits and transfers.[90]

What were the Seventh Cavalry's intentions for the next morning? E. M. Keith, a minister at Pine Ridge, says, Before the battle I was passing some soldiers of the Seventh Cavalry at the agency and I heard one of them remark that if they could just get to the Indians "they would give them hell."

These Indians, Big Foot's, I have been told by another were in the Custer massacre, and these soldiers were desirous for an opportunity to square accounts with them.

I myself talked with infantry soldiers marching to the agency from Chadron who expressed to me the sentiment that all they desired was to get to the Indians and they would do them up.[91]

Man Above, a Pine Ridge Lakota, says that before he went to negotiate with Short Bull for the last time, Major Burke, Buffalo Bull's attaché, told the scouts that the soldiers were going to kill Big Foot's band when they could get them, because they were in the Custer battle; and Man Above told this to Captain Taylor, and the captain said that was true.

Man Above also says, A survivor of the Custer massacre told him that if they found Big Foot's band they were going to disarm them, and if they got angry about it they would all be killed.[92]

The ghost of Custer stalked the Dakotas during the early morning hours of December 29, 1890.

15. The Death of a People's Dream

The art of war among the white people is called strategy or tactics;
when it is practiced by the Indians it is called treachery.
—*Gen. Nelson A. Miles*

THE CAMP AWAKENS

Headquarters Dept. Platte,
In the field
Camp at Pine Ridge Agency, S.D.
December 29th, 1890.
By courier at 7 A.M.

Major S. M. Whitside, 7th Cav.,
Comdg Battalion 7th Cav., in the field,

Sir:

I am directed by the commanding general to tender you, and the officers and men of your command, his congratulations on the successful accomplishment of the capture of "Big Foot" and his band.

This capture simplified the settlement of the Indian difficulties in this section, and will aid materially in doing so.

I am, sir, very resp'y,
Your obedient servt,
(Sgn.) Fayette W. Roe,
1st Lieut. 3rd Infty, A.D.C.[1]

As a courier carried this dispatch to Wounded Knee, an apprehensive Chief Horn Cloud called his sons together and reminded them of the pacifistic nature of their newly found religion. Before the sun rose, *Dewey Beard recalls his father saying,* "I will give you advice—all my sons—Therefore, I have come. They say it is peace but I am sure there is going to be fighting today. I have been in war all my life, and I know when my heart is growing bitter that there is going to be a fight, and I have come to tell you—all my sons, what I want you to do. If one or two Indians go to start trouble, I don't want you to go with them. Don't you join them.

"Besides this, if the white people start trouble first, then you can do what you want to—you can die among your own relations in defending them. All you, my dear sons, stand together and keep yourselves sober, and all of you, if you die at once among your relations defending them, I will be satisfied. Try to die in front of your relations, the old folks and the little ones, and I will be satisfied if you die trying to help them. Don't get excited.

"When one or two under the government laws start trouble they are arrested and taken into court and put in jail, but I don't want any of you to get into such trouble, but to stand back until all the whites assail us, and then defend our people. I have come to tell you this as advice before the trouble begins. I want you to heed my warnings."[2] *Later in the morning Chief Horn Cloud's sons were obeying their father with great gallantry.*

As dawn broke in the Wounded Knee Valley, Alice Ghost Horse recalls, A bugle woke us up. I went outside, and I noticed . . . there was lot of activity at the military camp. We ate in a hurry because most of the Lakotas were loading their wagons. My father had the horses and he was saddling my horse.[3]

Many in the camp greeted the morning with optimism and good cheer. Newsman Charles W. Allen would later write, On that eventful day of December 29, 1890, we were up shortly after the sun had risen on one of God's glorified, peaceful mornings. In nearby trees the birds were singing their matins.[4]

Paddy Starr, a scout, told Judge Eli S. Ricker, The women had rations that had been issued to the Indians, and they were feeling happy and singing and it seems that they did not suspect any evil or danger.[5] *Acting Adjutant of the Second Battalion Lt. W. W. Robinson Jr., lulled by the peaceful activities within the camp, recollects,* I observed the children of all ages . . . playing among the tipis, and had commented upon it as a favorable indication, saying it was a proof to me that there was no hostile intent on the part of the Indians.[6]

Dewey Beard says that after his conference with his father, I went into Big Foot's tent. At this an Indian called and harangued all the men to come into council. The haranguer said as soon as the council is through you are going right on to the agency and they want you to hurry up.[7]

During this early morning activity, Colonel Forsyth's command received the following order from Pine Ridge:

Headquarters Dept. Platte,
In the field
Camp at Pine Ridge Agency, S.D.
December 29th, 1890.
By courier at 7 A.M.

Major S. M. Whitside, 7th Cav.,
Comdg Batt. 7th Cav.
In the field,

Sir:

The Comdg Genrl. directs that you proceed with your Battalion and the Indian prisoners to Gordon, Neb., where you will transfer the Indians to Colonel Frank Wheaton, 2d Infantry, on Dec. 30th, if possible. The ponies and wagons will not accompany the Indians further from

Gordon, and you will bring them with you on your return to this place, which will begin as soon as you transfer the Indians to Colonel Wheaton.

I am, sir, very resp'y,
Your obedient servant,
Fayette Roe,
1st Lieut. 3d Infantry, A.D.C.[8]

By now Forsyth was aware that he would be negotiating with the Miniconjous in bad faith.

THE DISPOSITION OF THE TROOPS

Forsyth planned to hold his parley with the Miniconjou men at an open circle between his main camp and the Lakota camp. As the negotiations began, Forsyth placed his troops on the alert. Troops B and K, dismounted, were to the north; Troop G was mounted and to the east. To the south was Troop A, the Indian Scouts, both mounted. Behind them were Troops C and D, also mounted. To the northwest, on a knoll that commanded the valley, were the four Hotchkiss guns, commanded by the veteran Capt. Allyn Capron. He was flanked on the right by Troop E, which was mounted, and on the left by one-third of Troops A and I, both mounted. All were within three hundred yards of the council circle.[9] In placing his troops Forsyth ignored General Miles's command that all troops should stand away from any captives. Worse still, his troops were placed opposite each other with the Miniconjou camp in between.

The disposition of the troops, Major Whitside later testified, was designed to prevent intercourse between the bucks and squaws, the latter in their tipis (the bucks had been passing to and fro against orders that had been given and seemed to be exciting the squaws), two Troops B and K, who had been in line between the camp of the troops and the Indians, were then thrown in, dismounted, into the position between the bucks and their tipis as . . . and it was decided to make a search in the tipis for missing arms. For this purpose Captain Wallace and a small detail of six or eight men were ordered to make the search, beginning at the right.[10]

Shortly before "Omaha World Herald" reporter T. H. Tibbles left for Pine Ridge, he visited Lt. Harry Hawthorne and Capt. C. S. Ilsley on Cemetery Hill and noticed Forsyth's deployment of troops. After looking into the valley, Tibbles asked Hawthorne, "Isn't that a rather strange formation of troops in case there is any trouble?"

Captain Ilsley laughed and replied, "There's no possibility of trouble that I can see. Big Foot wants to get to the agency, and we're a guard of honor to escort him."[11]

This exchange suggests that at least one of Forsyth's officers still thought the Miniconjous were going to Pine Ridge.

A few days later most of the officers in Forsyth's command insisted that the Miniconjous were packing and getting ready to flee. The Lakotas, however, insisted they had been told to pack for a journey to the Pine Ridge Agency.

Nellie Knife says, We were going to Pine Ridge to see our relations, and Big Foot was to be in a Big Council. While I was packing, a soldier from headquarters told the men and large boys to go to Big Foot's tent.

Alice Ghost Horse, who stayed in the camp, says, The women folks continued to pack their belongings in the wagons.

Seventeen-year-old Bertha Kills Close to the Lodge also says, We were issuing hardtack and we were packing ready to travel. I was standing against the wagon . . . when the men were called to the center. *Neither mentions that they intended to flee, just that they were packing and getting ready to travel.*

It is improbable that the Lakotas could have fled successfully. They were surrounded and outnumbered more than four to one. They were outgunned and well aware of the Hotchkiss guns trained on their camp. They knew that any attempt to escape would be met with armed force. Another serious impediment for flight was the presence of women and children. Lakotas never fought with their families nearby unless they were attacked.

A CALL TO PARLEY

Frog, Big Foot's brother, says, The soldiers began blowing their bugles and began to stand around us in ranks, but I thought nothing of it, as it was their natural custom to do so; and then we were told to come out and sit down at a place near the door of Big Foot's tent, which we did. Then a lot of soldiers got between us and our camp, separating us from the women and children. An officer then told us he wanted our guns, and as soon as we gave them up he would give us provisions, and we could go on our way.

We, the older men, consented willingly, and began giving them up.[12]

After interviewing surviving members of Big Foot's band, Elaine Goodale wrote, The demand for their arms was a surprise to the Indians, but the great majority chose to submit quietly.[13]

While the women broke camp, the men obediently arrived for their parley with Forsyth. At the circle was a line of Sibley tents to the south and the camp of the Indian Scouts' Troop A. To the west was the wall tent where the gravely ill Big Foot had spent the night. Forsyth, Whitside, and one or two other officers stood, waiting with two interpreters.[14] *One of these was Philip Wells, the other was John Shangrau, a Lakota scouting for the army.*

By this time, the troops were thoroughly mixed with the Lakotas, directly in disobedience to Miles's repeated orders that troops stand apart from their captives during negotiations.

Later, several officers stated that the women were mixed among the men at the council. However, Hehakawanyakapi, a member of Big Foot's band, says, Many of the cavalrymen arranged themselves in positions, while the infantrymen got between us and the women and children. All the men were thus separated from the women.

Edward Owl King confirms this, saying, We were again surrounded by another line of infantry, so that there was three lines of soldiers surrounding the men, not the women.[15]

Right down there, *Rough Feather says,* all the Indians were placed in a group and were surrounded by the soldiers. So I had a blanket on—don't know where I got it from—someone gave it to me. I covered my head up and stood there among them, and I understood that the soldiers wanted the guns. I was facing that way and I could see Big Foot. He was lying in a tent.

E. C. Swigert, a white man who had come to Wounded Knee to watch the surrender, says, Colonel Forsyth observing that the Indian boys were in the council, asked why they were there. Chief Big Foot said those boys had proved themselves brave and they had a right to be there by that reason; that when an Indian boy had proved his bravery, he was recognized of right as a warrior. Forsyth then said, "If they want them in the council, let them stay."[16]

Richard C. Stirk, a white man who ran a store in the valley, says there were sixty-three men and boys gathered for council with Forsyth.[17] *He probably underestimated the number who attended the parley. Other observers state that as many as one hundred men and boys, and a few women and children, attended the council. That would mean only a handful of the Miniconjou men and boys remained in their camp. Most who remained there were women and children.*

Years later, Wells, recollecting his part in the events that morning, admitted that he still thought the Miniconjous were going to Pine Ridge. Due to conditions at the agency, *he says,* Big Foot's band had to be disarmed. . . . The military authorities were endeavoring to obtain the arms from the hostiles, and if Big Foot's band had been allowed to come into the agency armed the effect on the hostiles would have been unfavorable, especially as the general in command made it a condition of entry into the agency that they should first deliver over their guns.[18]

The adverse "conditions at the agency" were caused by the hundreds of unarmed and nervous Lakotas who had surrendered in hope of rations.

As negotiations began, several of the Miniconjou men complained that they were told they could retain their guns until they reached the Pine Ridge Agency. Certainly, after the revelry and harassment the night before, they were most reluctant to turn in the few rifles they had left.

Even so, they were willing to negotiate. According to John Shangrau, Some of the Indians said to one another, "You go and see Big Foot. Whatever he says, we will do."

There were two Indians who went into Big Foot's tent, and I followed them in. One of the Indians said to Big Foot, "The soldiers want our guns; but we came over to ask you, and whatever you say, we will do."

Big Foot said, "This is the third time they are going to take the guns away from me. Give them some of the bad guns, but keep the good ones."

I then told Big Foot, "You better give up the guns; if you give the guns, you can get guns again—you can buy guns, but if you lose a man you cannot replace him."

Big Foot said, "No, we will keep the good guns."

These two Indians came out and I followed. When we got back the two Indians reported what Big Foot had said, and then there were seven or eight more guns given up. Then, *Shangrau says*, they would not give up any more.

Philip Wells then came over and he took my place, and the latter was ordered with ten soldiers into the Indian camp to search for guns. This composed one of the two parties. Little Bat was also ordered with ten other soldiers to do the same thing.

I started in with his party at the end of the camp toward Wounded Knee Creek. Little Bat started at the other end. I got about nine guns; Little Bat also got some.

Meantime, an Indian with a Ghost shirt on was outside the circle swinging his arms and saying, "Ha, ha, ha."[19] *This was a half-crazed Miniconjou medicine man, whose incantations would begin to fray the nerves of Forsyth and his troopers.*

As the council began, Father Craft says, Colonel Forsyth spoke very kindly to them and said he did not wish himself to take their arms, but would rather they would come forward themselves like men and lay them down. The Indians began to come forward as directed, one by one, to lay down their arms.[20]

Paul High Back says, They told us we must give up all our guns, knives, or whatever weapons we had. They said to come forward ten at a time and lay down our guns and our knives. So ten of our men went up to them but they only had one gun to lay down. The soldiers did not like this very well, but we could not put our guns down because we did not have them with us. Those of us who had guns, had left them back at our tents.

Then some soldiers went to our tents and began to look for our guns. They found quite a few and carried them out and threw them down on the ground. They did not lay them down carefully, but dumped them down in a pile, throwing them down hard. We were standing there, men, women, and children, all of us very much afraid. We were defenseless as none of us had guns. The soldiers were standing all around us holding their guns in their hands ready to shoot.[21]

First Sgt. Ragnar Theodor Ling-Vannerus, a native of Sweden, paints a less than genial picture of Forsyth, saying that upon Forsyth's request, the interpreter demanded that all guns were to be handed over against cash compensation. Not a word was replied. The demand was repeated with more determination—at the same time the speaker, now Father Craft, pointed out how useless any attempt at resistance would be and how well they had been treated.

A party of twenty warriors rose slowly from the ground and returned to their village, where the women at once began to pull down their tents. Forsyth informed the chief that fire would be opened at the camp unless the warriors did not immediately come back with their guns, and in a cold rage the men tardily reappeared. They handed over eight useless flint-locks.[22]

The Miniconjous, who were devoted to their families, approached the rest of the meeting with growing fear and apprehension.

Allen says, Some of the shrewder leaders among the Messiah-crazed band had started the rumor (utterly terrifying to them) that the government train was to take them and their possessions to Gordon, Nebraska (the nearest railroad station south of Wounded Knee), and ship them in box cars and stock cars down to Oklahoma—the hot southern climate of which was anathema to Indians of the northern plains.[23]

Did the Miniconjous hear officers talking about Miles's plan to remove them via the railroad at Gordon and transport them from the Dakotas?

As the parley began, Joseph Horn Cloud says, Big Foot was, by direction of an officer, brought out on a blanket and laid down near the eastern extremity of the half or three-quarters circle or council. On his left was his brother, on his right was Horned Cloud, my father. Just behind Big Foot stood an old man named Wounded Hand.

White Lance, Joseph Horn Cloud's older brother, adds, Big Foot was placed right in the doorway of the tent, and I stood right to his left side.

The Indians sat quietly in the circle looking at the officers, *Joseph Horn Cloud continues.* Captain Wallace was standing just behind Horned Cloud and John Shangrau, the interpreter. Captain Wallace, thinking from my costume that perhaps I belonged to the Pine Ridge Indians, asked John Shangrau who I was. Shangrau said, "You ask him. He talks English."

Wallace asked me my name and I replied, "Joseph Horned Cloud."

"Where is your father?" continued the captain.

I pointed to my father near us. . . . He was sitting at Big Foot's right with a fur cap on his head. He was smoking and passing his pipe to Wounded Hand who was standing behind him. The captain asked me if I was sure that I belonged to the outfit, meaning Big Foot's band. I said, "Yes."[24]

An officer spoke up (it must have been Major Whitside) and said to Big Foot, "Big Foot, I want twenty-five guns. Yesterday everybody had a gun. I want twenty-five of them."

Big Foot said, "All right."

He said to the people, "Bring twenty-five guns. If I was able to talk I would talk for you, but I cannot talk."

Blood was flowing from Big Foot's nose. He was stiff and weak.

The young men went into their quarters and brought out twenty-five guns and laid them down in the center of the circle. The officer then said, "I want five more."[25]

Wells confirms this, writing, The captured Indians had been ordered to give up their arms, but Big Foot replied that his people had no arms. Forsyth said to me, "Tell Big Foot he says the Indians have no arms, yet yesterday they were well armed when they surrendered. He is deceiving me. Tell him he need have no fear in giving up his arms, as I wish to treat him kindly."

Continuing, Forsyth said, "Have I not put you in an ambulance and have my doctors care for you? Did I not put you in a good tent with a stove to keep you warm and comfortable? I have sent for provisions, which I expect soon, so I can feed your people."

Big Foot replied, "They have no guns except such as you have found. I have collected all my guns at the Cheyenne River Agency and turned them in. They were all burned."

They had about a dozen old-fashioned guns tied together with strings—not a decent one in the lot.

Forsyth answered, "You are lying to me in return for my kindness."[26]

Then Joseph Horn Cloud says, The young men went again and brought forward five more guns. Then the officer demanded five more and added, "I want them all."

At this point Big Foot gave up and told his men, "Bring them all, boys."

They answered back to Big Foot, "There are no more guns."

Then the officer said, "What have you done with all the guns? I will send the soldiers to get the guns themselves."

Big Foot said, "All right. Let them do it."

The soldiers went back into the Indian camp, took sacks out of the wagons and emptied them on the ground, went into tents and everywhere examining, picked up some old shot guns, knives, tomahawks, arrows, and awls, and they searched the persons of the women.[27]

Afraid of the Enemy confirms this. He was our chief, *he says,* and we looked to him to say something but he was coughing all the time. Finally he said, "You men better give him your guns. We are not on this trip to do any fighting, but we came over here to see our relatives and to be at Red Cloud's council."

We did not like this, *Dog Chief says,* but Big Foot told us to do what the soldiers say, so the guns were piled in the center.

Stacking the guns in one place would prove to be another tactical error on Forsyth's part.

By now James Pipe on the Head had completed his errand to Big Foot. He says, The Indians were completely surrounded by both cavalry and infantry. I delivered the tobacco to the old man, and he was lying there in the center of these Indians who were called together. That is where I delivered the tobacco to him.

In the village, Bertha Kills Close to the Lodge noticed that all the soldiers were along the ridge and right in here some were loading guns. Seems as though they were taking guns on down to the center. They also came over to where I was standing and my father had a gun and they took that, we came along on the edge of the camp over to where they were stacking the arms.

At this time a detachment led by Capt. George D. Wallace started a second search of the Miniconjou camp. As they did, Big Foot's band feared that the troopers, who were loading their weapons, were preparing to go on the attack.

THE SEARCH IN THE CAMP

At the council circle, according to Ling-Vannerus, [Forsyth] was rapidly losing his patience. He ordered a detachment to search the village while the rest made a "closed square" around the unruly savages. From both flanks the dragoons penetrated the Indian camp, received by screams and cursings. Tent by tent, bundles and packages were searched, yes! even the squaws whom in most cases was sitting on top of arms or keeping them hidden under clothes or blankets. Besides some axes and clubs, the soldiers found twenty-four rifles, many of them unfit for use.[28]

Dog Chief, seated in the council circle, says, I noticed that the soldiers were moving around and they were strung around the camp. Then I saw the sergeant take some soldiers and go to where the women were getting packed up to go to Pine Ridge. They would go right into the tents and come out with bundles and tear them open. They kept this up for some time and returned to the center where we had piled the guns and they brought our axes, knives, and tent stakes and piled them near the guns.

Captain Varnum, *Whitside says,* with about the same number of men, [was] to begin on the left, and the searching was an operation tended to by me. As a result of this search about forty arms were found and taken out of the way. The squaws making every effort to conceal the same, by hiding and sitting on them and in various other ways, evincing a most sullen mien. After completing the search of the tipis it was concluded to search the bucks in the semi-circle, who sat or stood with their blankets about them."[29]

At this time, Captain Varnum says, I was ordered to take fifteen men from my right to search the north village, commencing at the north end, the end toward the hill where the cemetery is located. I commenced the search, and the first rifle I found was under a squaw who was moaning and who was so indisposed to the search that I had her displaced, and under her was a beautiful Winchester rifle.

I proceeded up the village, searching everything. I took knives, hatchets, axes, bows and arrows. I got rifles from the pockets of the tipis; and while I was searching, Captain Moylan furnished me with a detachment to help carry them off. Nearly all my stuff was carried to the battery. Everything found was so hidden that I had almost to dig for it. One gun was found under the skirts of a squaw, and we had to throw her on her back to get it.[30]

Allen, who had joined the search party, told Ricker, I went over to where the soldiers were disarming the Indians. Little Bat was there and John Shangrau. The soldiers had got about two-thirds of the way around. In front of one tent, a woman was lying on the ground. A soldier engaged in the search said, "Roll that woman over; maybe there is a gun under her."

Another turned her over, exposing a gun handsomely concealed. In another place, a girl was found covering up some kind of firearms in like manner. The soldiers were searching the bags of knives and forks and taking all the murderous weapons. The wagon that the squaws had partly or wholly loaded were unloaded and examined for arms.

While this was happening, Dewey Beard says, I stayed inside my lodge—did not go to council. I had a notion to start with the wagons. While I was in my tent, my mother came and looked in and said, "My son, some soldiers are coming and gathering all the guns and powder and axes and knives and bows and arrows and they are coming this way."

When I looked out, I saw soldiers coming loaded with guns, knives, axes, crowbars, war clubs, bows and arrows. I saw all this with my own eyes. I went inside and got my carbine gun and dug a little hole and laid my gun in and covered some dirt over it and threw the quilts and blankets over to the other side of the lodge (not over the covered gun).

A soldier came and looked in and told me to come to the council. Before doing so, I took some cartridges and buried them outside my lodge, in front of the door covering them with manure, so that if while at council trouble started, I would know where to find ammunition.

While I was going to the council with the soldier, I passed my brother Joseph who was leaving the council, and I asked Joe what he was coming out of the council for, and he replied that he was going after water—that Captain Wallace had sent him out. I went into the council and saw ten young men standing a little to one side, these had given up their guns and belts and knives.

While I was sitting in the council, my father came to me and admonished me to remember what he had said this morning. Then he asked me where my other brothers were, and I replied, "Two of them were standing over among those ten young men." Our father added that they ought all to stay together.[31]

THE MEN ARE SEARCHED

As the negotiations continued, a half-crazed medicine man walked about the circle. Hehakawanyakapi says, He was a man named Hose-Yanka, a rascally fellow. At this time he was making medicine, but I did not hear what he said. *Some say the medicine man's name was Yellow Bird.*[32]

Ling-Vannerus says, The medicine man, Yellow Bird, suddenly appeared; a grand figure of a man, with green-colored face and a yellow nose, terrifying to behold. He wore with pride his floating crown of eagle feathers, while his costume was a wonder of wild adornments. He steps forwards, turning to his brethren, and raises his arms high towards the sky, then lowers them again. He faces the sun with outstretched hands as if they were an invocation. Standing in that way silent for a couple of minutes, he then produces a small pipe of eagle bone which he incessantly blows, turning his body in all directions.

Meanwhile, the others are sitting there in unperturbed silence, but their eyes are becoming lustrous and occasional fidgets can be seen. Now he begins to circle with solemn steps round the crowd, speaking in a deep, passionate voice and wildly gesticulating. Now and then he stoops to the ground and rubs some sand on his head.[33]

Alice Ghost Horse differs, saying, During the heated discussion, a medicine man by the name of "Yellow Bird" appeared from nowhere and stood facing the east, right by the fire pit which was now covered up with fresh dirt. He was praying and crying. He was saying to the eagles that he wanted to die instead of his people. He must sense that something was going to happen. He picked up some dirt from the fire place and threw it up in the air and said this is the way he wanted to go, back to dust.

Wells interpreted the medicine man's actions in still another way. While he translated, Wells tried to overhear what the Miniconjous near the circle were saying to each other. At this time, he says, The medicine man stopped praying, and stooping down, took some dirt and rose up facing the west, raised his two hands, and still facing the west, cast the dirt with a circular motion of his hand toward the soldiers in the road. Then he walked round the circle, and when he got back to the starting point on the west side, he stopped and uttered exclamations which in Sioux signify regret, and that he had decided on a desperate course. For instance, if he has submitted to abuse, insult, or wrong with patience and fortitude, but has made up his mind to retaliate or take revenge upon the offender, he exclaims: "Haha! Haha! I have lived long enough."

Wells may have remembered that when a Lakota said, I have lived long enough, *he meant that he was ready to do battle. Wells also may have remembered that when Crazy Horse rode against Custer he said,* "It is a good day to fight, and it is a good day to die." *From this moment Wells was on the alert, juggling translating with eavesdropping on the Miniconjous around him.*

According to Dr. J. R. Walker, The father of the Horn Clouds was a doubting Thomas in the matter of the new Messiah worship. When the affair was drawing to a head in the search for arms, Horn Cloud tauntingly told the medicine man that now was the time to test and prove the efficacy of his new gospel.[34]

Then—perhaps after this taunt—Wells recalls that the medicine man turned toward the young men who were standing together and said: "Do not be afraid, and let your hearts be strong to meet what is before you; we are all well aware that there are lots of soldiers about us and that they have lots of bullets; but I have received assurance that their bullets cannot penetrate us. The prairie is large and the bullet will not go toward you, but over the large prairies, and if they do go towards you, they will not penetrate you. As you saw one throw up the dust and it floated away, so will the bullets float away harmlessly over the prairies."

After interviewing Wells, Ricker comments, Mr. Wells then stepped to Big Foot's brother-in-law to talk with him and get him to try to quiet and pacify the Indians. This brother-in-law impressed Mr. Wells by his better dress and his generally intelligent appearance as a man of more than average parts—as a rather superior Indian. Just then Colonel Forsyth called out to Wells, saying that he better get out of there for it was beginning to look dangerous. Mr. Wells answered, "In a minute, Colonel; I want to see if I can get this fellow to quiet them."

Then he addressed the Indian and said: "Friend, go in among the young men and quiet them, and talk to them as a man of your age should."

This was said to him in a low tone so that the others should not hear. He replied very loud so that all the Indians could hear his words: "Why, friend, your heart seems to beat. Why, who is talking of trouble or fighting?"

"Yes, friend, my heart beats when I see so many helpless women and children if anything should happen," replied Mr. Wells.

"Friend, it is unnecessary that your heart should beat," again said in a loud voice by the Indian.

For the moment Wells was reassured, but the scout remained alert to signs of danger. After the Indian's first reply to Wells, *Ricker says*, a powerfully built young man stepped out of the circle and came round to where the two were standing and talking, He kept taking steps slowly as though he intended to get behind Mr. Wells without his observing what he was doing. But Mr. Wells suspected his purpose and was watching him, and as the young Indian moved around, he kept turning his own body so that he did not get behind him.

At the same time, seeing that he could not persuade the older Indian, he continued to talk, attempting to change the subject. He held his rifle with both hands at the muzzle, the butt resting on the ground. The young Indian had no gun under his blanket, but Mr. Wells could not tell if he had a revolver or a knife concealed, and he was reflecting on the different modes of attack which this Indian might be contemplating—whether he would grapple and try to overpower him—whether he would strike him with a club or knife—whether he would shoot a revolver—or [however] else he would attempt to dispose of Mr. Wells and get his gun; for one of his main objects was to obtain that, as Mr. Wells saw from the way he was eyeing it.[35]

By this time there seemed to be a difference of opinion between the older and younger Miniconjous. The younger sided with the exhortations of the fanatical Yellow Bird, and the older remained loyal to Big Foot and his advisors. There also seemed to be a split between those who believed in the protective powers of the Ghost shirts and those who did not.

According to Wells, Big Foot's brother-in-law asked at the end of the conversation that the Indians be permitted to take Big Foot, who he said was dying, and continue the journey begun before the troops intercepted them.

Forsyth replied, "I can take better care of him here than you can elsewhere, as I will have my doctors attend him."

Forsyth then went to one side to give instructions elsewhere. A cavalry sergeant exclaimed, "There goes an Indian with a gun under his blanket!"

Forsyth ordered him to take the gun from the Indian, which he did.

Whitside then said to me, "Tell the Indians it is necessary that they be searched one at a time."

The old Indians assented willingly by answering, "How!" and the search began. The young warriors paid no attention to what I told them, but the old men—five or six of them—sitting next to us, passed through the lines and submitted to search. All this time, I kept watching the medicine man, who was doing the Ghost Dance, for fear he might cause trouble.[36]

Captain Varnum, who had just returned from the village, says, I also took part with a few of my men in the search of the bucks ordered by Major Whitside. I [told] him my men said that these bucks were armed with guns under their blankets. He then said we will search them when you are through with the village.

Major Whitside and I inspected about twenty Indians on the right of the circle and found no arms or ammunition. We then stood these back and commenced to pass others between us for the search. Only two or three started which we examined, and I asked Major Whitside if we should take their belts as well as their cartridges, and he told me to let them have their belts. I took a hat and emptied into it the cartridges.[37]

By this point, all but a few weapons in Big Foot's camp had been seized or surrendered. However, Forsyth persisted in demanding the surrender of more arms. According to Dewey Beard, Wells, acting on Forsyth's instructions, told the Miniconjous, "When you give all the guns and knives, you will stand in one rank right along the edge of this bank (meaning the ravine) and some number of soldiers will stand in front of you and aim the guns at your foreheads." *Forsyth added*, "The guns are unloaded."

Ricker noted, Joe [Joseph Horn Cloud] explains that the Indians were to submit to this in the nature of penance, admitting thereby that in not turning over the guns the day before, they had done wrong and would submit to this nonsense in order to wipe away their fault.

At this point in his transcription, Ricker angrily scrawled on his notepad, "Forsyth must have been drunk."[38]

By now, Dewey Beard says, My legs were trembling and my heart was thumping and I was afraid.[39] We did not understand the soldier's orders. We could not comprehend this foolishness. But this offended and angered us, and we reasoned among ourselves and said we were human beings and not cattle to be used this way. We are people in this world.

Most of us had given up our arms; there were a few standing with their guns, but the soldiers had not been to them. The knives were piled up in the center of the council; some young men had their guns and knives, but they had not been asked yet for them.[40]

Alice Ghost Horse, some distance away, says, At this time there were cavalry men all on bay horses . . . lined up on top of the hill on the north side. One officer rode down towards the center at a full gallop. He made a fast halt and shouted something to his commanding officers and retreated back up on the hill and they all drew their rifles and long knife [swords] and you can hear them load it with bullets.

In the meantime, some more cavalrymen lined up on the south side. A big gun was also aimed down towards the center and towards where we were.

Joseph Horn Cloud told Dewey Beard that after he went out to talk to his grandfather and was coming back, one of the white soldiers said, "Little boy, you're too young to be out here. Go back to your tent and stay with your mother. All these soldiers have hot stomachs."[41]

Joseph Horn Cloud identifies the concerned soldier, saying, Captain Wallace beckoned to me and told me to go and tell the women to hitch up and get out of camp because, he said, "I see we are going to have trouble. The colonel is half shot."[42]

Again the question of intoxication arises. Was Forsyth drunk that morning? Ricker states that Dr. Walker is of the opinion that intoxicants had undue effect in producing the results of the disarmament.[43]

Whether Forsyth was drunk or not, he was losing his patience; and the medicine man's repeated incantations were getting on his nerves. Wells, realizing that tensions were rising and aware of disagreement among the

Miniconjous, felt it was time to warn his superiors: I turned to Major Whitside and said, "That medicine man is making mischief," and I repeated what he had said.

Whitside replied, "Go direct to Colonel Forsyth and tell him about it," which I did.

After Wells reported to Forsyth, he says, Forsyth and I went to the circle of warriors, where he told me to tell the medicine man, who was engaged in silent maneuvers and incantations, to sit down and keep quiet. After I had translated it into the Indian language, Big Foot's brother-in-law answered, "He will sit down when he gets around the circle."

When the medicine man came to the end of the circle he squatted down.[44]

After that the situation deteriorated quickly. White Lance says, I could see that there was a commotion among the soldiers, and I saw on looking back they had their guns in position ready to fire.

John Little Finger says, I noticed that a line of infantry was standing nearby and had been commanded to load their guns and at that moment they gave us to believe that they were going to do some shooting. . . . I saw that there seems to commence some trouble.

Hehakawanyakapi agrees with White Lance and Little Finger, saying, I heard an officer say something. He must have given orders, because the soldiers began loading their guns and holding them in readiness for firing.

Alarmed, Hehakawanyakapi says, I called out and said, "Let's give up every gun."

I said it because I thought it was the best thing to do. Many were given up. I cannot say how many, but I thought all were given up. Every man among the Indians did not have a gun. I gave up my Winchester, which was all I had.

By now there were few guns left to surrender. Louis Mousseau, the owner of the trading store at Wounded Knee, says, One pile of guns was up at the foot of Cemetery Hill—twelve in this pile—the other pile with fifty-seven in it was down near the council and not far from the scouts' tent. An officer at the pile of twelve (and I was right there) called down to one down where the fifty-seven were and asked how many he had, and he answered fifty-seven, and the officer at the pile of fifty-seven asked the other how many he had, and he said twelve.[45]

If Mousseau was accurate, sixty-nine guns had been surrendered, and more may have been gathered in the camp. By this time, Stirk thinks there were not more than five or six guns in the hands of the Indians when the battle began.[46]

Joseph Black Hair claims, Anything and everything that could be used as a weapon were taken from us, even the awls that the women used to bead with were taken, what else could we have to defend ourselves with?[47]

Goodale writes, Reverend Mr. Riggs, who knew Big Foot's men intimately, believed that not more than every other man had a gun. He doubted if more than sixty, at most, were taken to Wounded Knee by the Sioux. Most of these were in fact shot-guns and old muzzle loaders, kept for hunting small game, and in a measure as the traditional badge of masculinity.[48] *This estimate coincides closely with Mousseau's count of sixty-nine surrendered rifles.*

THE FIRST SHOT

Ling-Vannerus says, A deaf warrior was on his way to the pile of weapons in front of the colonel when two soldiers intervened and brutally wrenched the loaded weapon from the young man's hands. At the same time Yellow Bird threw a handful of dust at the soldiers. Five or six braves pulled out hidden Winchesters from under their blankets, while others staggered up to their feet, helplessly pointing at the white flag.[49]

Walker insists that the medicine man's gesture was not hostile: The medicine man has been accused by the whites of throwing up dirt into the air and waving a blanket or some such emblem as a signal for action. This was only the ordinary procedure through which he went into the Ghost Dance. It happened at the moment that the searching party came to two certain young men who had Winchester rifles for which they had paid good prices, and they were not willing to give them up, though their disposition was peaceable and [they] would have surrendered their ammunition without resistance.[50]

Whatever the gesture meant, it could not have come at a worse time. The tension was unbearable and it was mounting.

Wells thought he was being stalked by an unidentified Miniconjou brave. Wells told Ricker, I dared not turn my back on the Indian who had been following me, but I began to move backwards with the intention that when I got far enough from him to walk away with safety, I would get out of the circle. By this time, I was convinced that a clash was coming. On that instant, I heard the cry to my rear and left, coming from the direction of the soldiers, "Look out! Look out!"

I threw my gun into position of "port" and turned my head quickly to the left and rear for a look at the Indians standing in a circle; one Indian near the center of the circle stood facing the soldiers with his gun pointing at an upward angle—in the last position in which a hunter holds his piece before placing it to his shoulder to fire; still holding his gun so, it was discharged—the contents going into the air, over the soldiers' heads, as the smoke indicated.

Several others say a soldier and a deaf Miniconjou warrior struggled over the possession of the warrior's rifle. Mousseau, who standing off to one side, told Ricker, At this time, three Indians with blankets were standing inside the circle at about the north and east side. Somebody went up to them (I think it was Captain Wallace) and a couple of orderlies and an interpreter with him (Wells). I opened the blanket of one who had a Winchester and the Indian turned it over to me.

Mousseau says, The second one did not have any gun that I saw. When I went up to the third, the Indian would not give his up, but he brought it up to "arms Port" and Wallace had hold of it, and they swung it first one end up and then the other and, when the muzzle was up, it was discharged. Everyone went to hollering, "Look out! Look out!" and there was quite a stampede.[51]

Dewey Beard offers a more detailed description of the struggle for the rifle. There was a deaf Indian named Black Coyote, who did not want to give up his gun; he did not understand what they were giving up their arms for. The Indians agreed among themselves that they would explain to him what the disarming meant, and then they would take his gun away from him. The Indians who had so agreed wanted to tell the officers of their plan, but the interpreter was gone just then, and Horned Cloud asked where the interpreter was.

The varied accounts of what happened after the rifle was fired provide a distorted prism of the events that followed. Crickett, who was just outside the circle, says, During the time the search was going on, the medicine man was talking to them, . . . and telling them the soldiers bullets would not hurt them. He was raving and swinging his arms about like mad, had a whistle in his mouth, making a most hideous row; but when the bucks was ordered to get up and be searched, he took up a handful of dirt and threw it in the air. I can just see him doing it now, as I wasn't fifty feet away. Then the fun began as each buck was well armed.

Crickett, like many other soldiers, claims the Miniconjous were fully armed after the shot was fired. One thing is certain: the frightened soldiers had their weapons at the ready and were ready to fire. Beard says, While the deaf man held his gun up, I could not hear all that was said on account of the confusion, but some soldiers came behind him and tried to take his gun from him. All the sergeants stepped back and yelled, "Look out! Look out!" and held their guns toward the deaf man.

While the two or three sergeants came to the deaf man and were struggling with him for possession of the gun, I heard something on the west side and looked that way and saw the Indians were all excited and afraid, their faces changed as if they were wild with fear. I saw that the guns of the soldiers were pointed at the council, a part of whom were sitting down and a few who were standing up. The old people had wrapped their blankets around their legs and were smoking.

Beard insists that the deaf warrior meant no harm, saying, If they had left him alone, he was going to put down his gun where he should. They grabbed him and spinned him in the east direction. He was still unconcerned even then. He hadn't his gun pointed at anyone. His intention was to put that gun down. They came on and grabbed the gun that he was going to put down. Right after they spun him around there was a report of a gun—it was quite loud.[52] The struggle for the gun was short; the muzzle pointed upward toward the east and the gun was discharged.

In an instant a volley followed as one shot, and the people began falling. I saw everybody was rolling and kicking on the ground.[53]

Spotted Horse insists, I was a voluntary scout at that encounter and I saw exactly what was done. . . . As soon as the first shot was fired, the Indians began drawing their knives and they were exhorted from all sides to desist, but this was not obeyed. Consequently, the firing began immediately on the part of the soldiers.[54]

The sound of the shot set off a chain reaction.

Beard says, I couldn't see anybody shot but following that was a crash. The flag of truce that we had was stuck in the ground right there where we were sitting. They fired on us anyhow.[55]

Whitside would later testify, One shot was fired by an Indian and [was] instantly followed by a volley from the west of the Indians, who had all jumped to their feet for the purpose, and thrown their blankets on the ground, and commenced firing at the two Troops B and K, formed at right angles . . . firing through these troops and their own tipis.[56]

Captain Varnum recalls, I turned to Major Whitside saying, "By God, they have broken." And the Indians faced my troop and the next thing we got a volley, and the shooting was lively. . . . They knifed some of my men immediately after the break.[57]

Neither officer says how the Lakotas could have been armed so rapidly. If they were, that means they seized the weapons that Forsyth had neatly stacked beside Big Foot's tent. It is more likely that the firing at the troops came from the officers' comrades on the opposite side of the circle.

Paul High Back admits, There were two men down at the lower end of our group who had their guns under their blankets. One of the soldiers who were walking back and forth in front of us saw the ends of those guns sticking out.

I called out to the other soldiers that these men had guns. I was standing at the upper end of the group where I could see it all and I can say that these two Indians never raised their guns or shot them but the soldiers raised their guns and fired right at us. They shot right away all us men, women and children.[58]

Wells confirms this, saying, I heard the command which sounded like Colonel Forsyth's voice: "Fire! Fire on them!"

Several Lakotas say they heard a loud voice issue a command. There were two officers in the center, *White Lance says.* The one that was standing to the left gave a command in a loud voice when we couldn't see anything for smoke. The smoke was so dense I couldn't see anything so I didn't make a move, just stood there.

Celene Not Help Them says, I heard a white man say something in excited tones, which I could not understand. . . . I looked around and saw some of the Indians throw off their blankets and raise their guns. One of the Indians fired a shot, but I did not recognize him. As I turned to run, I heard a few more shots. The firing was so fast after that, I could not tell what was happening.

Lieutenant Mann, on his deathbed a few days later, said it was he, not Forsyth, who gave the command to fire: In front of me were four bucks—three armed with rifles and one with bow and arrows. I drew my revolver and stepped through the line to my place with my detachment. The Indians raised their weapons over their heads as if in votive offering, then brought them down to bear on us, the one with the bow and arrow aiming directly at me. They seemed to wait an instant. The medicine man threw a handful of dust into the air, put on his war bonnet, and then I heard a gun fired near him. This seemed to be the signal they were waiting for, and the fire immediately began.[59] "Fire!" I shouted, and we poured it into them.[60]

Lieutenant Robinson, who had herded some men back to the circle, says that when the firing started, [the Indians] turned like a flash of lightning almost, throwing off their blankets, all of them grasping their rifles, and fired a volley into the men to the direction of the battery. The instant I saw them draw their rifles I called to the men on my right, I being the man between the men and the Indians, "Look out, men, they are going to fire."

Lieutenant Mann was on my left at this time and gave the same order about the same instant.[61]

Lt. Charles W. Taylor, commander of Troop A—the Indian scouts—

was positioned further to the rear. He offers a similar account but adds, There seemed to be a lull for a second or two, then the soldiers fired, and I saw the bucks falling fast. They broke and ran in every direction, many of them towards their village.[62]

There was a good reason for this brief delay before the firing started. Reporter Kelley says, The dismounted troops were at a great disadvantage, fearing the shooting of their own comrades. *Even so, the troopers fired and, in doing so, fired on each other.*

Harry Kills White Man, who was ordered to leave the council because he was too young, says, My father was blind at that time; so my brother-in-law, Wears Yellow Robe, went over to where the men were called and I went along with him. The soldier standing on the end motioned me back with his hand. So from there I went on to my camp where my mother was loading up the wagon. That is when I heard the volley or crash.

Several Miniconjous say that after they heard a shout in English, they heard a loud crash. One, Charley Blue Arm, insists, I did not hear a gun before the big crash came from the soldiers.

The crash may have been a volley from the troops on both sides of the council circle, or even the artillery on the knoll. John Little Finger says, I stepped out, and then I struck through their lines to try to get away. Just as I was working from this line—that moment—I heard a white man's voice at the other end, sound just like somebody calling like, "hey." When that sound was made, it was about the same time that the report of the guns came in one sound. The soldiers commenced to shoot at that moment.

Rough Feather also says he heard something like a command, Right near where Big Foot's tent was I saw a soldier. He had his gun in his hand and in a loud voice made some remarks. So I looked over at him. It may be possible that this soldier is still living. He was the one that again said something in a very loud voice. About that time I heard some noise behind me so I looked back. I saw them aim guns at us. It sounded much like the sound of tearing canvass. That was the crash. As I heard the crash I became unconscious. Something struck me.

Dog Chief recalls the same: I heard one of the white men say something but as I don't understand white man's talk, I do not know what he said. Right after that there was an awful roar as it seemed all guns fired at one time. That is all I know as I was lying on the ground when I regained my mind.

Young James Pipe on Head, after bringing tobacco to Big Foot, says, Big Foot told me that I had better go back to grandmother and to where the women folks were. Just at this moment there was a big noise; I couldn't see just what it was but it sounded like a number of gun shots together. I knew it was guns fired on us.

Alice Ghost Horse also mentions a loud noise, but says it was a big boom that came from the big gun on wheels. *If she is correct, the Hotchkiss battery fired into the valley while the troops and the Miniconjous were locked in hand-to-hand combat. While this happened, the troops were caught in their own artillery fire.*

Once the firing started, the valley exploded into a pitched firefight, most of it coming from the troops. If the Miniconjous were not armed at first, they quickly were. Mousseau says, The Indians broke for their guns in the piles. Then the soldiers fired a sudden volley. That was the dismounted cavalrymen. . . . I do not think the mounted cavalry fired; their horses were jumping and charging. After this volley, the firing was continuous and the field was soon enveloped in smoke.

A wire fence was close by and many, both whites and Indians, went through it. The horses tied at the northeast corner of the camp with ropes when the firing began got to pitching and jumping. After this gun was discharged, there was a pause of perhaps half a minute, maybe not so long, [then] two more shots were fired and I saw Wallace and the Indian fall.[63]

By then, Wells says, A general fight was raging between the soldiers and the Indians. Troop K was drawn up between the tents of the women and children and the main body of the Indians, who had been summoned to deliver their arms. The Indians began firing into Troop K to gain the canyon of Wounded Knee Creek. In doing so they exposed their women and children to their own fire.[64]

Hehakawanyakapi, who was in the circle, says, Firing followed then from all sides [and] I threw myself on the ground. Then I jumped up and run towards the Indian camp, but I was then and there shot down. I was hit in the right leg and soon after was shot in the other leg.[65]

Crickett writes, The man that stood next to me was shot down in the first discharge. I fired at the Indian at the same time but only struck him in the leg. He returned my fire and struck my revolver which knocked me down, which saved me; but if it hadn't been for the pistol I should have got it through the thigh, but he didn't go much further. Our Captain Nowlan shot him through the heart.

Whitside claims, At least fifty shots were fired by the Indians before the troops returned the fire. Some twenty-five or thirty Indians were seen to fall.[66] *It is hard to believe the Miniconjous fired fifty shots before the troopers returned fire; but Lt. W. J. Nicholson offers a similar description of the first firing*: I was about thirty yards off, in the angle between Troops K and B, and then immediately the whole lot of bucks rose, threw off their blankets, faced about and delivered a volley directed towards K Troop and their own tipis, which were surrounded or occupied by women and children. Then the mass of bucks broke through K Troop and their own tipis into the ravine accompanied by their woman and children.[67]

HAND-TO-HAND, FACE-TO-FACE

Surgeon John van Hoff, who was close to the center when the firing began, says, I turned instantly and saw these Indians breaking from their center apparently in the direction of the gap between B and K Troops, firing continuous volleys as they advanced.[68] *It is unlikely that the Lakotas went on the attack amidst the withering fire they faced.*

Paul High Back insists, We had no chance to fight back as we had no weapons. All we thought about, those of us who were still alive, was to get away. The morning was cloudy and damp and the smoke from the guns did not rise but settled right on us. From then on nothing could be seen very plain. The soldiers were rushing around shooting all of us they could see to shoot. I got shot right through the hand, the bullet entering just at the base of my thumb and coming out the base of my middle finger. Somehow I finally got down into a washout or gully south of the fight, where a lot of Indians had taken refuge and where they had been shot down. I got down among them and kind of crawled down under the dead bodies, but the soldiers kept on shooting into us whenever they saw any of us move.

Twice more I was shot, one bullet going through the fleshy part of my left forearm and a third going through the fleshy part of the calf of my leg.[69]

A few of the surviving Lakota men were capable of fighting, but very few survived the first few minutes of firing. Stirk says, The main firing, where most of the Miniconjou men were killed, did not last ten minutes.[70] *In a 1939 article Brig. Gen. E. D. Scott wrote,* There is much uncertainty as to how long this first phase lasted, estimates varying from "a few minutes" to "eight to ten minutes."[71]

It was at this time the cavalrymen, too, suffered the most casualties. One reason for this was the way Forsyth deployed his troops. According to Lt. Alexander R. Piper, The cavalry began shooting in every direction, killing not only Indians but their own comrades on the other side of the circle.[72] *This possibility was investigated, but the findings are inconclusive. Forsyth's poor deployment is best evidenced by maps that show the troops placed opposite each other. They could not have changed position when the firing began. Certainly, Forsyth had placed his men in direct disobedience of Miles's standing order that all troops remain separate from the Lakotas.*

In the first few minutes of firing, a correspondent to the "Army and Navy Journal" wrote, The soldiers, maddened by the sight of their fallen comrades, hardly awaited the command and in a moment the whole front was a sheet of fire, before which the single Indians could be seen at times flying. After the first discharge from the carbines of the troopers there were few of them left. They fell on all sides. Indians and soldiers lay together and fought on the ground. The few remaining warriors fled, turning occasionally to fire, caring more for escape than battle. Only the wounded Indians from the ground, where they had fallen, continued to fire until their ammunition was gone, or until killed by the soldiers.[73]

Accounts on both sides agree that more than two-thirds of the Miniconjou men at the council died in the first minutes, perhaps seconds, of fighting. Forsyth, in his December 31, 1890 report, listed casualties on both sides. He wrote, An accurate estimate as could be made of the dead Indians, bucks in and near the camp, was 83.[74]

If Forsyth's count is correct, fewer than thirty of Big Foot's men and boys survived the first firing. Several accounts confirm that this insignificant force did not advance as Hoff claimed. Instead, they fled into their camp, intent in getting their women and children into the ravine behind the camp. The few surviving Miniconjou fighting men took cover there and defended their families.

At this point the Seventh attacked in force.

Why did the officers urge their men to attack further? Perhaps the Seventh Cavalry feared there were more Miniconjou men, perhaps they panicked and overreacted, perhaps they were obeying the December 27 order from Miles's headquarters, If he fights, destroy him.[75]

Before the cavalrymen went on the attack through the valley, the struggle at the council circle was ferocious. The unarmed Lakota men grabbed the nearest cavalrymen, intent on securing a weapon; others fought through their enemies with bare hands, intent on reaching the stack of surrendered rifles by Big Foot's tent. Within seconds, some of the surviving Miniconjou men were armed.

According to Dewey Beard, Beard's father and Big Foot were the first to die at the council circle. One leaned sideways, the other had his face down.[76] *White Lance, Dewey Beard's brother, says,* When it cleared up a little, I was going to start to go away. When I looked to my right side, I saw Big Foot lying down with blood on his forehead and his head to the right side. I never knew that they would take advantage of a sick man. That is the first time I ever saw that happen.

Allen, who was nearby, says, When the firing began Big Foot's daughter ran toward him, and Big Foot was shot just before she reached him; she gave an outcry and stooped over him. An officer seized a gun in the hands of a soldier and shot her and she fell over her father.[77] *The killing of Big Foot's daughter was the first execution that day, but if we believe Miniconjou and white civilian testimonies, it was not the last.*

Dewey Beard, who was in the midst of the firing, says, Someone cried, "They will kill us!" and others shouted: "Get your guns and get ready!"

Shots were fired by the soldiers on both sides of us, and Black Fox and Yellow Turtle fell. The latter began his death song, then raised to his elbow and shot at the soldiers, while it appeared to me that the white men opened fire on every hand. I saw my friends sinking about me, and heard the whine of many bullets. I was not expecting this. It was like when a wagon breaks in the road.

"Get your gun," someone shouted in my ear.

I was frightened and ran. Seeing soldiers running, also, I followed but came into smoke so thick that I could see nothing.[78]

The first to fall was kindly Captain Wallace. Crickett, who was in the midst of the foray, says, Captain Wallace's brains were knocked out with the war club he took from the tipis and was swinging it about in his hand. That was the last I saw of him until he was picked up with his head smashed. His revolver was in his hand empty and four Indians dead just in front of where he laid so he must of sold his life pretty hard.

Ling-Vannerus found the violence of the moment exhilarating and rhapsodized, What a spectacle beneath the clear winter sun; the Indians' demonical war-songs, the troopers' silent but resolute killing, the injureds' groaning, the dyings' wheezing, the cracking of shots; there a skull is splintered by a terrible butt blow, there a fine-looking trooper sinks down with a knife up to the butt in his broad chest, there a white and red tumble confusedly on the grass in embraces that will come loose only in death. There, alas, my troop leader, Captain George Wallace, keeps four Indians at arm's length with his revolver but in the next moment succumbs to a club blow from a warrior attacking him from behind.[79]

Wells differs, saying, Captain Wallace was killed in the rear of his Troop K. He was struck by a bullet in the upper part of his forehead and it tore through the top of his scalp.[80]

The Miniconjous said the songs Ling-Vannerus heard were death songs, lamentations for their dead, or warriors singing because they knew they were mortally wounded and dying. Many of the wounded warriors continued to fire at the attacking soldiers.

Wells, caught at the center of the action, found himself locked in hand-

to-hand combat. Ricker says, Mr. Wells, having the Indian near him in his thoughts, turned toward him, both movements occupying only an instant of time. The Indian was already upon him with an upraised long butcher knife ground to sharp point, in the act of dealing a deadly blow. A man of surprising agility, Mr. Wells dropped to one knee, at the same time throwing up his gun with both hands as a guard, and ducking his head to avoid a blow to the face.

The Indian's wrist struck the gun, but the knife was long enough to reach his nose which was nearly severed, and hung down over his mouth, held by the skin. Before Mr. Wells could rise, the Indian renewed his attack, standing over him with the savage knife uplifted and trying to grasp his gun with his left hand. It was a desperate play between life and death and lasted but a moment.[81]

Allen says that when Wells was wounded, he was defending Father Craft: A ghost crazed Indian, actuated by some old personal grudge or the mere fact that the priest was the nearest white man, suddenly leaped at him with a drawn knife, slashing perilously close to Father Craft's throat. Serious tragedy was averted when Mr. Wells seized the wrist of the maddened man, deflecting the stroke so that the knife made only a painful gash in Craft's shoulder. But when the Indian wrenched his hand away the point of the knife swept across Mr. Wells' face, completely severing his nose.[82]

According to Ricker, Wells, holding the gun above his head, kept it in swift motion as a guard against the knife. The Indian now summoned all his strength to break down the guard with a furious blow and the weight of his body, and raising his blade higher in the air for the mighty stroke, he opened his own guard and Wells gave him a blow to the left with the muzzle of his gun, which stunned him. This gave Wells time to regain his feet.

The Indian staggered back a step or two. Wells sprang backwards. Now they were three paces apart. Wells leveled his piece at his breast; the Indian was glaring into his eyes; to escape the shot that he thought could not be withheld, he turned a quarter around and dropped on his hands and knees. Wells had saved his fire. Like a flash, the muzzle of the gun went down and the bullet entered the Indian's side below the arm; he pitched forward on his face, dead.

Then a corporal rushed up to the prostrate body and fired. About the same instant, a bullet struck him, inflicting a mortal wound from which he died in a day or two in the hospital at the agency.

Having vanquished his foe, Wells started for shelter behind the wagon close by in which some of the guns taken from the Indians had been placed. While running, he slipped on the grass and nearly fell. A young brave who, it was afterwards learned, was following him, dealt a blow with his knife from behind, intending to stab between neck and shoulder. He overreached and left a cut in the front of Wells' coat.[83]

The enraged cavalry was relentless in its attack. Fast like a prairie fire, *Ling-Vannerus exclaims*, came the response. Destroying and appalling, the bullet rain strikes the Indian mob. . . . But after the first volley we had not time to reload but used the carbines as clubs when the revolver was not resorted to. It was a fight hand-to-hand.[84]

Will Cressey, who was on Cemetery Hill when the firing began, vividly described the valley below him: The reply was immediate, however, and in an instant the draw in which the Indian camp was set looked like a sunken Vesuvius. The soldiers, maddened at the sight of their falling comrades, hardly waited for the command, and in a moment the whole front was a sheet of fire, above which the smoke rolled, obscuring the central scene from view.

Through this ghostly curtain, Indians could be seen at first flying before the fire; but after the first discharge from the carbines of the troopers, there were few of them left. They fell on all sides like grain before the scythe. Indians and soldiers lay together, and, wounded, fought on the ground. Off through the draw toward the bluffs the few remaining warriors fled, turning occasionally to fire, but now evidently caring more for escape than battle.[85]

Crickett candidly admits his confusion: They commenced firing away at us. For the minute I couldn't make out what was up, but we soon recovered and then they got it. They made a break for a ravine just where we was posted and kept up a running fire, but by the time they reached the ravine there was dozens down. Firing was in all directions. It was wild and reckless; all was confusion.

Dewey Beard tried to break away from the fight so he could find his wife and child. While he was running, *Ricker says*, he could see nothing for the smoke; through the rifts he could see the brass buttons of the uniforms. He rushed up to a soldier whose gun rested over Dewey's shoulder and was discharged when the muzzle was near his ear and it deafened him for awhile. Then he grabbed the gun and wrenched it away from the soldier. When he got the gun, he drew his knife and stabbed the soldier in the breast, but the knife did not enter deep, and the soldier was trying to seize Dewey by the throat and by his buckskin coat about the breast; as the soldier raised his left arm, Dewey stabbed him again, this time in the side close to the heart.

When the soldier fell down, he still kept struggling and tried to rise, but Dewey got astraddle his body and held his head down and then stabbed him by the kidneys till he died. The soldier was crying as loud as he could. While Dewey was on this soldier, some other soldiers were shooting at him but missed him and killed soldiers on the other side.[86]

After killing the soldier, Dewey Beard joined the Lakotas retreating into the deep ravine that cut across the valley. When I arose, *he says*, I found I was right among my comrades, so I ran back toward the ditch till I saw another group aiming at me and felt something smite me on the shoulder so heavily that I spun about and fell again. I raised my head to see a white man aiming at me but he missed, and I snapped at him with the gun I had taken from the soldier. It did not explode, however, for I had forgotten to load it, so I quickly opened the breech. As I did so, he ran away. I began to breathe hard now, while every breath hurt me greatly. I rose to my feet and tried to run, but could not, so I walked. The ground rocked and pitched like a canoe. Something warm in my throat strangled me, and when I spit it out I saw it was blood, so I knew I was shot.[87]

By this point, the fighting had spread through the valley, and the question was Who were the troopers fighting?

BEYOND THE COUNCIL CIRCLE

The initial gunfire carried across the flat plain into the village, as did some artillery fire. Bertha Kills Close to the Lodge says, The children dropped some of the hardtack and I stooped over to pick some up and just about that time, what appeared to me was a severe hail stone just rattled right under the wagon.

Frank Sits Poor, also in the village, says, As I remember it, I was sitting in a tipi and all at once it sounded to me like a crash of lighting as though wire was falling over the tipi, and I do not remember just how I got out of the tipi, but I had noticed that there was a soldier with a gun on his shoulder. I went close to him and he pointed the gun at me. I couldn't say whether he shot at me or didn't but I heard the report of a gun.

Paddy Starr says the scouts in the camp fled when the firing started and that when they reached the creek they halted, and at this point they were fired on by the soldiers, and then they moved again around behind the hill near where the Hotchkiss cannon stood.[88] *Some of the scouts who were Lakotas or mixed-bloods feared they might be killed by the rampaging cavalrymen. They wisely withdrew from the field. Later, when the firing subsided, they would persuade survivors to surrender.*

Little Bat went back into the camp amidst the rain of fire. James H. Cook, a friend of Little Bat, says the scout told him, His clothing was pierced with bullets as he tried to get to his own tent, where his weapons had been left. When he reached the place he found that the tent had been burned. A dead Indian who had been killed in the tent was lying across his gun, the stock of which was half burned away. Bat's saddle was also riddled with bullets.[89]

Captain Charles B. Ewing, assistant military surgeon, says, Lieutenant Kinsie, United States Infantry, Mr. James Asay, Indian trader at Pine Ridge Agency, and myself were seated in an open wagon within ten or fifteen feet of the end of one parallelogram of soldiers that surrounded the Miniconjou Sioux band. . . . A volley came in our direction, the bullets whistling unpleasantly about us; our horses took fright and becoming uncontrollable, ran right across the line of fire, but were turned and stopped near Louis Mousseau's store, about three hundred yards distant from the battle.

We alighted, and I was then informed by Lieutenant Kinsie that he had been shot in the foot. After examination of the same, I immediately returned to camp and busied myself in the care of the wounded. I did not think it was time for ceremony, hence dispensed with the formality of reporting for duty and went to work.[90]

Those outside the circle found the action was moving in their direction as the Miniconjous fled toward the gullies and the ravine. During the flight of the surviving Miniconjous, Lt. Sedgwick Rice says that Miniconjou women joined the fighting: One of these mounted squaws was armed and fired on our line, and one of the men said, "There is a buck."

And I said, "No, it is a squaw, don't shoot on her."

And he said, "Well, by God, Lieutenant, she is shooting at us."

"He did not fire on her."[91]

Other Seventh Cavalry units were not as judicious in their firing. Shangrau and Little Bat were searching for rifles in the Miniconjou camp when the firing started. Shangrau heard one woman say, "There is a fight!"

As soon as this was said, he heard a volley. Bat then ran down to the ravine with Big Foot's people; they all stampeded. Shangrau went on a trot toward the cannon, which were right close to the top of the hill. An Indian followed him, but was shot down before he reached John who was wondering what the Indian would do. When John got to the top of the hill, he met a lieutenant who said to John, "Scout, we got our revenge now."

And John said, "What revenge?"

"Don't you know? The Custer massacre."

John said, "Look here, Lieutenant, Custer had all their guns to protect themselves with, but they massacred him; and here you take all the guns away from them, then massacre them. You ought to be ashamed of yourself for saying such a thing!"[92]

The newsmen present immediately fled to cover, taking up positions where they could observe the action and write their dispatches. Finally, they were war correspondents.

Cook, who had loaned his horse to Cressey, later wrote, My favorite saddle horse, which I had so foolishly loaned to Mr. Cola [Cressey], had an opportunity to see the fighting on that occasion, for Mr. Allen rode him up close to the spot where the surrender was to have occurred. He had here dismounted, thrown the bridle reins on the ground, and left the horse to take care of himself knowing that most old cow horses are trained to stand when the reins are so placed.[93]

Swigert says Cressey abandoned Cook's horse and took refuge behind the creek bank when the firing began.[94] *Allen admits fleeing to safety, while Kelley remained on the knoll. By afternoon the three correspondents filed remarkably accurate reports, dispatching them to the Pine Ridge telegraph office in time for next morning's papers. The first to get his story to a telegraph office was the "Nebraska State Journal"'s Kelley.*[95]

Private Prather, far from the action, riding with the Ninth Cavalry, would compose this verse for his ballad:

> The 7th is of courage bold both officers and men,
> But bad luck seems to follow them and twice has took them in;
> They came in contact with Big Foot's warriors in their fierce might
> This chief made sure he had a chance of vantage in the fight.
>
> CHORUS:
> They claimed the shirt Messiah gave, no bullet could go through,
> But when the Soldiers fired at them they saw this was not true.
> The medicine man supplied them with their great Messiah's grace,
> And he, too, pulled his freight and swore the 7th hard to face.[96]

DEWEY BEARD LEADS THE WITHDRAWAL

Dewey Beard saw the cavalrymen attack the retreating Lakotas and recalls, I saw it was no use, and I ran back to my tipi to find my wife. There was no one there in the camp. My horses were running around. Some were still tied down and were pulling hard. I was standing there when I saw a man. He was trying to say brother-in-law [to Dewey]. He was shot and his jaw was hanging. He was trying to talk but his tongue was hanging too. He was trying to get help for his wife. I helped the man take her to the dry creek towards the west. He said he didn't know what had happened to her.[97]

After his good deed, Dewey Beard found himself surrounded by soldiers and fought his way toward the ravine. Before reaching the ditch, *he says,* other soldiers came at me and I charged toward them, thinking I would die in this way. They retreated into the smoke, and I went on, coming to a dead trooper whose belt of cartridges I cut off because mine would not fit the gun I had taken from the other man. I wished to take his gun also, but was too weak to carry it.

Then I started on. I fell for a third time, and thought I had stepped into a prairie-dog hole, till I found I could not rise. I had been shot through the leg so I sat there loading and firing as fast as I could, till my shells were nearly gone, when one broke in my gun and made it useless. I hopped toward the ditch, but whenever I stepped on my wounded leg I fell down. Through the smoke I could see nothing but dead women and children and there were dead soldiers among them.[98]

In the ravine, Dewey Beard says, I saw a woman holding up her shawl like it could be a shield against the bullets. I thought I saw a black cloth hanging in front of her, and then I realized it was her braids, shot off and . . . hanging loose in front of her.

I saw a mother with a baby in her arms. I took the baby, "Come on, let me help you."

I saw a woman; she took the baby and lay down on it and played dead. I kept on going. I saw my brother Daniel who called for me to stop. My brother was limping, I went to help him.

Celene Not Help Him says, My grandfather was shot in the back; it went through his lung in the first volley of gunfire. He was again shot in the right calf and in the hip. He was coughing blood. He had lost a lot of blood. He could hear someone singing a death song. Whenever someone moved, the soldiers shot them.

Perhaps the person he heard singing was Dewey Beard's mother. Beard says that after moving a short distance onward, I saw my mother standing and singing. She was waving a pistol. She told me to take it, she was dying. I cried and helped her sit down. I felt like I couldn't get up, I looked down and saw I had been shot again, in the lap.[99]

I was badly wounded and pretty weak too. While I was lying on my back, I looked down the ravine and saw a lot of women coming up and crying. When I saw these women, little girls, and boys coming up, I saw soldiers on both sides of the ravine shoot at them until they had killed every one of them.[100]

In later years, Brig. Gen. L. W. Colby, the Nebraska National Guard commander, bitterly wrote, The surviving Indians now started to escape to the bluffs and canons. The Hotchkiss guns were turned upon them and the battle became really a hunt on the part of the soldiers, the purpose being total extermination. All order and tactics were abandoned, the object being solely to kill Indians, regardless of age or sex. The battle was ended only when not a live Indian was in sight.[101]

The first action was brief. According to Stirk, The main firing, where most of the Miniconjou men were killed, did not last ten minutes. But scattered firing and all lasted about four hours.[102]

It has never been explained why the attack on the Miniconjous continued into the late afternoon. Against whom were the cavalrymen fighting? If we believe Forsyth's report, they were fighting against fewer than thirty men and boys, some of whom were severely wounded. In the hours ahead the gallantry of these survivors and their male children was almost beyond belief.

Somehow the Lakota men and boys held back the rampaging cavalrymen. The wounded Indians, *Cressey reported,* seemed possessed of the courage of devils. From the ground where they had fallen, they continued to fire until their ammunition was gone or until killed by the soldiers. Both sides forgot everything excepting only the loading and discharging of guns. It was only in the early part of the affray that hand-to-hand fighting was seen. The carbines were clubbed, sabers gleamed and war clubs circled in the air. But this was only for a short time. The Indians could not stand that storm from the soldiers. The remnant fled and the battle became a hunt.[103]

The blood bath at the council circle was only a prologue to the unrelenting slaughter that followed.

Of course it would have been all right if only the men were killed; we would have feel almost grateful for it. But the fact of the killing of the women and more especially the killing of the young boys and girls who are not to go to make up the future strength of the Indian people, is the saddest part of the whole affair, and we feel it very sorely.—American Horse

*

It was not a battle; just a killing.—Maj. James McLaughlin

*

Sometimes I live again the old, old days, when honor and glory were in the tipis of my tribe, and I see the faces of my people as I dream. They were good and brave and true—all but the medicine men. Those were liars, as my father said. It comes to me bitterly that perchance there was no Savior for the Sioux, or that the white man's Gods were stronger. Why else did he stand silently, with hidden face, to let His people perish?—Dewey Beard

16. On the Field of Honor

I have never felt that the action was judicious or justifiable, and have believed it could have been avoided.
—*Gen. Nelson A. Miles*

THE HUNT BEGINS

As Dewey Beard frantically hunted for his wife and child, the fighting spread across the valley. By this time, the Seventh Cavalry had suffered its worst casualties; but the death toll among the Miniconjous would triple. According to Major Whitside, The survivors then broke through the troops and their village and, followed by their squaws and their ponies, . . . left camp in a rush in three directions, the majority up the ravine, some across the same and through the chain of sentinels to the south, some up and past the mounted troop facing east.[1]

If the surviving Miniconjou men and boys were to enter their village and escort their women and children into the cover of the ravine, they would have had to storm south through K Troop or the right wing of B Troop. The fire they encountered caused more casualties, but there was no alternative route.

The mounted troops then pursued the renegades, who fought viciously and did severe execution in a most determined fight in which many were killed and wounded, *Whitside continues.* The troops were cool; and in one instance at least that came under my observation, directed a party of squaws, who showed themselves to a place of safety, guarding them through the fight.[2]

No Miniconjou survivor or white civilian mentions such an act of kindness.

First Sgt. Ling-Vannerus, like Whitside, saw the Miniconjou retreat as a disciplined withdrawal. The flight of the Indians was not panicky but took place under continuing firing, *he says.* I saw for instance one redskin, all the time coolly aiming until I at last put a bullet through his brain. Most of the warriors lie where they had fallen, with torn clothes and gaping wounds. . . . The smell of blood wraps around one, sweet and nauseating.[3]

By this time no more than twenty-five Miniconjou men and boys were alive. Once these survivors were in their village, they took up positions against the full force of the Seventh Cavalry while women and children scrambled into the ravine. For a few vital minutes, they stopped the troopers cold.

As I was standing there, *recalls Rough Feather*, I happened to look up and the smoke was awfully dense, but I could now make out a face right in front of me. As I saw him, he turned and started the other way, so I followed. As I started to follow him I saw him get in front of the soldiers and grabbed hold of one, and they both fell down together. I was right up on them, and I had to jump over them. The other soldier standing nearby struck me with his gun in the chest.[4]

Wounded, Philip Wells followed the firefight as it spread across the valley. He says, I started to pull off my nose, which hung by the skin, but Lieutenant Preston shouted, "My God, Man! Don't do that! That can be saved!" He then led me away from the scene of the trouble.[5] *Later in the morning Wells came back on the field, this time to try to persuade survivors to surrender.*

The Miniconjou men and boys joined the women and children in the ravine, where they could hold off the attacking cavalry with less risk. There they bought time for the women and children to make their way through the ravine and away from the devastating fire of the Hotchkiss guns and the rampaging troopers. Without the raw courage of this handful of Miniconjou men and boys, Big Foot's band would have been completely wiped out. By the afternoon, more than half of Big Foot's band had perished, and despite the efforts of the men, in the hours to come, even more would die. Most would be women and children.

Turning Hawk says, Those who escaped that first fire got into the ravine, and as they went along up the ravine for a long distance they were pursued on both sides by the soldiers and shot down, as the dead bodies showed afterwards.[6]

Once the fighting spread beyond the circle, Forsyth dispatched his first report:

> General Brooke:
>
> On attempting to disarm the persons of the bucks, they made a break, which resulted in a hot fight, lasting from about 9:15 to 9:45. About 15 soldiers are wounded and a few killed. The number of Indians killed and wounded not known, but believed to exceed the loss on our side. The ones who escaped have fled up the ravines to the west, pursued by three troops.
>
> Lieut. Garlington is shot through the arm—not a dangerous wound. This dispatch is indefinite but is as accurate as I can give, as we are still engaged clearing out the ravine.
>
> Very respectfully,
> Your obdt servant
> James W. Forsyth
> Colonel 7th Cavalry, Commanding.[7]

IN THE VALLEY OF DEATH

When the soldiers started to shoot, *John Little Finger says*, I ran to get away and before I could get to the deep place there was already some Indians shot and killed. A lot of them shot down and I stepped on some of them already shot down, but I kept on going until I reached the cannon this side of the store. When I reached the ravine, of course, there was a lot of Indians following up the ravine and I was with them, and on each side of this ravine soldiers were shooting down on us until we got so far . . . we couldn't go any further as a line of soldiers got in front of us so we took refuge in a big ravine.

There, Charley Blue Arm says, I was running to get in the creek. Two cannons on the hill, near where the front door of the church now is, were firing at the Indians that were trying to escape, and the bullets hit the dirt all around us and, of course, that made us run faster, for we knew that they were trying to kill all of us.

When we got a little ways up the creek where the bullets could not reach us we laid down as we were all tired out and frightened and besides we were worried about our relatives. We had to stay hid all day till the sun went down, and then the soldiers seemed to be away and we went out to hunt for our people. We knew that the women and children if not killed were hiding around somewhere and, of course, we did not want to slip away. The soldiers might shoot at us as we hunted for our wives and children.

Correspondent Kelley, watching the tragedy unfolding from the knoll above the valley, reported, Soon the mounted troops were after them, shooting them down on every hand. The engagement lasted fully an hour and a half. To the south many took refuge in a ravine, from which it was difficult to dislodge them. I should estimate the killed and wounded, from what I saw on the field and vicinity, at fifty.

Just now it is impossible to state the exact number of dead Indians. There are many more than that number killed outright. The soldiers are shooting them down wherever found, no quarter given by anyone.

The field was one of great confusion, horses running in every direction and men well-nigh frantic during the engagement, owing to the unfortunate way they were placed.[8]

Kelley was the first to notice that the disposition of Forsyth's troops had caused panic and casualties. From his view he saw chaos rather than the orderly attack reported by Forsyth and his officers.

Interpreter John Shangrau returned to the council circle once the action spread across the valley. There he found Father Craft. Ricker says, When John was coming out from among the dead, he saw Father Craft sitting on the grounds with his arms extended and his hands on the ground supporting himself. John spoke to him and said, "Father, are you shot?"

He said: "Yes."

"Can I help you?"

"Yes."

With the assistance of another we moved him a little distance away. A stretcher was brought and he was taken off the field. When he was lifted on to the stretcher, John saw that he was stabbed on one side of the spine between the shoulders; and John said to him, "Father, you are not shot; you are stabbed."

He answered: "I don't believe an Indian did that to me, I believe it was a white man."[9]

Father Craft never spoke of this possibility again. As he recovered, he praised the Seventh Cavalry for its bravery and blamed Big Foot's band for starting the fight.

The accounts of the action were becoming fragmented, mere impressions of the violence that swept through the Wounded Knee Valley. Time became a horrifying blur for the combatants and the noncombatants alike. It is evident that the troops relentlessly pressed on against an ever-diminishing force, a force whose resistance provoked the troops into even fiercer and more brutal action. The bloodlust of the Seventh Cavalry was horrifying.

James Pipe on Head, a child then, says, When these soldiers started shooting, I started to run towards the hillside over there at a distance. I came across a little boy. I took the little boy by the hand and all at once someone came on the side of me and took my hand. This woman was my mother. She had a baby on her back, my sister, but this girl that she was carrying on her back was shot. While we were running we saw on the ground dust flying. Some of the bullets struck near us. We managed to get around through the line and escape through this direction.

Louise Weasel Bear says, We tried to run but they shot us like we were buffalo. *Paddy Starr confirms this attack on women and children, stating,* When the firing began, I saw men and women and children fleeing into the ravine, some falling as shots took effect.[10]

At that time, Alice Ghost Horse says, The two cavalry groups came charging down, shooting at every one who is running and is a Lakota.

My father made it back to our wagon and my horse was trying to bolt, so he told me to jump so I got off and the horse ran for all it's worth towards the creek. We fled to the ravine, where there was lots of plum bushes and dove into the thicket. The gunfire was pretty heavy and people were hollering for their children. With children crying everywhere, my dad said he was going to go out to help the others. My mother objected but he left anyway. Pretty soon, my father came crawling back in and he was wounded below his left knee and he was bleeding. He took my youngest brother who was six years old and he said he was taking him further down the river.

Soon, he came crawling back in and said "Hunhun he, micinksi kte pelo." He had tears in his eyes so we cried a little bit because there was no time to think.

Her brother was dead.

My father said we should crawl further down, but my mother said it's better we die here together, and she told me to stand up so I did, but my father pulled me down. With a little effort, we were able to crawl to a bigger hiding place. Bullets were whistling all around us but my father went out again to help. He never came back for a long time.

Some people crawled in. They were all wounded. I recognized Phillip Black Moon and his mother. They were okay. More woman and children came crawling in. The young ones were whimpering. Groups at intervals came in. Four of the wounded died right there but there was nothing anybody can do.

Once the battle spread through the valley, Kelley says, The artillery was called into requisition. Before, the fighting was so close that the guns could not be trained without danger of death to the soldiers. Now, with the Indians fleeing, it was easier to reach them. The Gatling and Hotchkiss guns were trained, and then began a heavy firing which lasted half an hour, with frequent heavy volleys of musketry and cannon.

It was a war of extermination now with the troopers, and it was difficult to restrain them. There was only one common impulse—to kill wherever an Indian could be seen. Down into the creek and up over the bare hills they were followed by artillery and musketry fire, and the engagement went on until not a live Indian was in sight.

Charley Blue Arm, who passed through the carnage in the ravine, says, I started to the creek and on the way I saw a great number of men, women and children dead or wounded and bleeding. I went on past them down into the creek as I saw a few others running there to get protection.

Bertha Kills Close to the Lodge says, I started in a southeastern direction; and as I went on, I could see men that were shot down by the soldiers but the smoke got so severe I couldn't see much.

Medicine Woman says she fled in another direction: The women started to run toward the west, but the soldiers from both sides shot them. There was so much smoke I could not see the way. I was wounded at the first fire, but I was so scared I did not feel it. My husband was killed there and my little girl, and a little baby boy on my back was killed by a bullet which also broke my elbow, so that I dropped the body . . . the white men were so thick here like a whole pile of maggots.[11]

Perhaps the child she carried was the one James Pipe on Head recalled when he testified, Right in front of me, I saw an old woman who had been killed. As I passed her, I ran across a woman who had a girl about one year old on her back. This little girl had her head blown off.

Then they fired on us, *Medicine Woman says.* I had my brother with me. The smoke was awful thick. We were making our getaway. We had a child with us. The child was dead; my mother was packing it although it was dead. Right below here was where I was shot, right on this little bench here. All those are my relatives, my nephews and I had an uncle here.

All up and down here it looked as though something was sacked up and spread over here. There was some smoke and all of the women were headed down toward the store. My right arm was broken and I can just use my left hand now.

Celene Not Help Them laments, It was a massacre. It was nothing more than a massacre.

Frank Corn, twelve years old, saw his mother Brown Ears gunned down. She told him, "Take the Ghost shirt, put it on your back and run."

Bullets were buzzing all around him. But he ran and got away.[12]

One small boy was not as fortunate. According to anthropologist Warren K. Moorehead, One slender boy but twelve years of age, as innocent a child as ever graced the home of a fond father, be that parent white or red, while fleeing in the direction of the agency was pursued by a burly ruffian. The soldier ran swiftly after the little fellow. Upon reaching a convenient distance [he] knelt down and with cruel, deliberate aim shot the child through both hips. The boy lived long enough to be taken to the hospital at Pine Ridge and tell his story in the presence of three women, Deputy United State Marshal George Bartlett, and others.[13]

Capt. Frank J. Ives, assistant surgeon with the Seventh Cavalry, described in graphic detail the wounds he examined. Two include those received by small children:

Male baby—1 year old with mother
1 gunshot through left buttocks
2 gunshot wounds through scrotum
both wounds made by the same ball
Jan. 9—transferred to Indian camp.

Child—age 5 "Steals Running Horse"
gunshot injury over left scapular Dorsum

Left side of neck & lower floor of mouth
carrying away part of the inferior maxilla, right side.[14]

As the afternoon progressed, the Seventh Cavalry continued to attack the Miniconjous huddled in the ravine. There, Dog Chief says, I raised my head and the awful firing was going on. All the men lying around me were killed or wounded. I tried to get up and when I did, I ran toward this ravine down towards the store, and down into a coulee and there I saw women and children, some of them wounded and bleeding.

The "*Rapid City (SD) Daily Journal*" *reported,* One little boy nine or ten years old told a pitiful story as he lay wounded in the hospital. He was in Big Foot's camp when the fight commenced and hand in hand with another little fellow of about the same age; he started out at the head of the gully so often referred to as the scene of the greatest carnage. They ran to the top of the hill, when a soldier came in pursuit riding a white horse. When the trooper rode nearly up to them he dismounted, dropped to one knee and shot the narrator's companion through the head. "He then," continued the little sufferer, "fired again, the ball striking me in the leg. I fell and the solder got on his horse and rode away."

The writer editorialized, Such incidents as these are responsible for what bitterness of feeling the Indians now display toward the troops.[15]

Moorehead angrily wrote, Let me give you one other instance of the "Gallant Seventh." There were twenty-six children *under the age of thirteen* killed at Wounded Knee. There is not the slightest excuse to be offered, nor is there just cause for the shooting of these children. Women were pursued and shot down the same as if they were men. Four babies were found on the battlefield with crushed skulls, showing that they had been struck on the head with either the butt of a musket or some heavy club.[16]

In contrast to Miniconjou and civilian accounts, Capt. H. J. Nowlan, Crickett's commanding officer, insisted that the women and children were spared: Indians rushed down the ravine, up and down it; not a shot was fired at them but they were allowed to escape. But right behind them came the bucks, and the cry went up from the officers and men, "Here come the bucks, let them have it"; and our fire was returned by the bucks."[17]

Kelley's account differs, The Indian men, women, and children then ran to the south, the battery firing rapidly as they ran. Soon the dismounted troops were after them, shooting them down on every hand.[18]

The Miniconjous and several white civilians on the scene insisted there was indiscriminate firing on women and children. The cavalry officers vehemently denied this, often under oath. No one broke rank in this denial.

Elaine Goodale, after interviewing wounded survivors, was convinced there were willful attacks on women and children before and after they entered the ravine. She writes, There is no doubt that the great majority of women and children, as well as many unarmed men and youth, had no thought of anything but flight. They were pursued up the ravines and shot down indiscriminately by the soldiers. The killing of the women and children was in part unavoidable, owing to the confusion, but I think there is no doubt that it was in many cases deliberate and intentional. The Seventh Cavalry, Custer's old command, had an old grudge to repay.[19]

Miniconjou survivors support this view. Edward Owl King, then a young boy, says, All that I remember is that I was running up this ravine trying to get away. There were some ponies, women, and children shot down and scattered; and while running, I stepped on them.

John Little Finger says, In this ravine where we took refuge, most of them were women and children and, of course, defenseless and helpless; above them the soldiers just got near them and shot these people down. This was kept up until I heard a voice, an Indian voice, calling from some place in a very far distance, saying that these Indians were to come out of there because fighting was not to be continued. So some of these, not yet killed, left the big ravine of refuge, and they went up on the flat. I was not with them, because I was shot through in two places, one through my leg and my foot. So I crawled along until I got over where those that were ahead of me sat in a circle up there, and the soldiers were surrounding them. I got up on the flat, a little distance from them, and they started to shoot them again and killing them. Of course, those that were not shot tried to get away.

It was a matter of individual survival. Frank Sits Poor admits, As I started up this hill I overtook an old woman who was ahead of me. As I went past her she got hold of my hand, but I jerked away from her and went right on past her.

Among those searching the ravines was Crickett. By that time, *he writes,* lots had got away into the ravine, but we had them. There was fire in the first washout; that is a small cave. They sold their lives very hard. We had to get the Hotchkiss gun on them, but for every shot we fired, they returned it with interest. The lieutenant in charge of the gun was shot close to his gun so you see they was good shots, but they was quieted after a bit. Then some of us had to mount our horses and go after another lot. We found them in another washout farther up the ravine. We exchanged shots with them and lost one man.

Ling-Vannerus joined in the pursuit. He says, I . . . got my orders to mop up the ravine with troops K and E, who had dismounted and kept up incessant firing at the escaped redskins. We advanced in firing-line and stepped watchfully and laboriously down the almost vertical sides of the "hole." Everywhere reigned the silence of death; the destroying angel had forsooth passed here!

When the shelling started, all red women and children in the camp had immediately taken to flight. Unrestrainably, they threw themselves into carts or rushed desperately away—some up the valley to the right, others again in wild panic towards the ravine down whose sides they blindly rode, drove, or precipitated themselves, only to be massacred against the rugged rocks at the bottom or to be shot down without mercy by the skirmish line on the opposite side. Here we found them now in big heaps, piled on each other. Women, the children in their arms, young and old, horses and mules in various positions, broken carts and clothing. More scattered, the warriors lay on their faces, still clutching their weapons.

There lies a whole family, except the father, under an overturned cart body, with the horses still in the shafts; with their legs crushed, they are writhing in agony. There a papoose cries by its mother's breast which, cold and insensible, can nourish no more; there lies a young girl with her long hair sticky of blood, hiding her mutilated face—they are all lying there in death's unspeakable majesty. And here rests the beautiful young squaw whom yesterday I offered a cigarette—dying, with both her legs shot off. She lies there without wailing and greets me with a faint smile on her pale lips.[20]

As the firing subsided, Starr and others went down along the ravine and cried to the Indians that if any were living to sit up and be saved. He saw a few women sit up, all badly wounded. He looked into the ravine and saw men and women and children . . . piled up dead and dying.

After the word had been given for them to sit up and be saved, one wounded man who raised up as well as he could, bracing himself with his hands behind him, was shot dead by some soldiers coming down the ravine from above. Perhaps these soldiers had not heard the call to sit up and be saved; nevertheless, they were killing everything clean as they went.

Starr said that thirty to forty were taken prisoner and most were wounded. Most of these were taken back to the agency—but not all.[21]

There was at least one other account of a summary execution of a La-

kota. While on the battlefield, Brings It found her grandfather. His thigh was shattered, so he was laying sideways, smoking his pipe. And just then, they heard some wagons coming to load the wounded and take them to Pine Ridge. They told her grandpa to get up, but his thigh was too shattered. So the soldiers shot her grandpa.[22]

Louie Mousseau and Little Bat heard some hollering after the battle was over, down by the ravine. He heard words like these, "Shoot him again!"

A wounded woman lying in a washout right in the road and at her feet was a little baby swathed, as is their custom, and it was alive. Somebody took it . . . and it was saved; a little boy about two years old was lying against the bank, half sitting as though it was yet alive, and four soldiers were standing right above it. Louie and Little Bat went down, drawn by what they had heard, and found the woman and asked if she was hurt much, and if she could get up. She did not want to be moved, and said, "Those soldiers just now killed my two children (she thought both were dead) and I want to lie here and die with them." Bat went up to the soldiers and, in his forcible way, gave them a berating and made them go away.[23]

Richard Stirk did not see any particular barbarities committed against the Indians, but has heard of them and knows that they were true—such as rushing up on them when they were hiding down in the pockets in the ravine and killing them indiscriminately without offering to take them prisoners.[24]

DEWEY BEARD'S SEARCH

Amidst the fighting, Dewey Beard continued to look for his wife and infant son. I remained standing for some little time, *he says*, and a man came to me and I recognized him as a man known as High Hawk. He said, "Come on they have started this way, so let's go."

At last I gained the dirt creek, where an Indian gave me a carbine he had taken from a dead enemy. At that moment the fast-firing cannon began to speak, and it was so close and loud that it frightened me, so I endeavored to crawl away up the ditch. I had not gone far till I met White Face, my wife. She had been shot, the ball passing through her chin and shoulder, but she mumbled: "Let me pass. Let me pass. You go on. We will all die soon, but I must get my mother. There she is."

She crawled to where her mother lay, at the top of the bank, but as she lifted the body in her arms she fell dead, shot again.[25]

The grief-stricken Beard had no choice but to move on. So we started up this little hill; coming up this way, the soldiers started to shoot at us and as they did High Hawk was shot and fell down. I was alone so I was trying to look out for myself. They had killed my wife and baby. *He did not know his infant son was still alive.*

I saw men lying around, shot down. I went around them the best I could, got down in the ravine, then I fell down again. I was shot and wounded the first time.

I went up this ravine and could see that they were traveling in that direction. I saw women and children lying all over there. They got up to a cut bank up the ravine and there I found a great many that were in there hiding.

We were going to try and go on through the ravine but it was surrounded by the soldiers, so we just had to stay in that cut bank. Right near there was a butte with a ridge on it. They placed a cannon on it pointing in our direction and fired on us right along.

I saw one man that was shot by one of these cannons. That man's name was Hawk Feather Shooter.[26]

At this I followed up on to the prairie, for I thought I would die quickly now; but before reaching the top, an Indian pulled me back. As I fell, he was shot though the head. I took his cartridges, for they suited my carbine, and hobbled on till I met another woman coming toward me with a revolver in her hand. It was a soldier's gun which she had taken from a dead body, for she was very bloody. As she neared me, a white man peered over the bank and killed her. I fired, and he ran back.[27]

Dewey Beard's brother White Lance who was also fleeing, says, I went a little ways then. I was knocked down. I was unconscious for a little while. I was shot then and wounded and I went to this little wide cut bank and there I found that we were surrounded by soldiers.

Some were already wounded, some dead, but they continued to fire on us. There is no reason for shooting us twice. They had already shot at us. I stayed there all day with these young fellows, boys then, and since then I have been unable to use my left arm, but I struggle along. I want to say, I am not much of a storyteller.

According to Jim Mesteth, a Miniconjou, White Lance was the brave one. He had a gun and they fought him all the rest of the day.

He went up that canyon and got to the end of the canyon, but it's bank all around there under there, so he got in there. He'd peep up and shoot down one of the soldiers. That fellow killed twelve soldiers there and they never got him. They was on one side of the bank and they'd hit the opposite side, you see, when they shoot. When they do that, he gets on the other side and they shoot away above him, and when they gets through shooting, why, they send a soldier to see if he's dead. Then the soldier, one soldier, would come and peep around there. While he's peeping, he'd knock him in the head. He shot them. He killed twelve of them that way. Every time he'd shoot one down, why, they'd turn loose on him, but he'd get on the opposite side and they couldn't hit him.[28]

If Jim Mesteth was correct in saying White Lance killed twelve soldiers, then White Lance killed twelve of the twenty-five soldiers who died at Wounded Knee. Forsyth may have been writing about White Lance when he reported, One Buck held a sheltered ravine which commanded a great portion of the field, and all our efforts to dislodge or kill him failed, although half an hour was spent on the effort. He was wounded, and I thought it better to leave him than to make additional sacrifices in order to take him, which loss would certainly have followed.[29] *This was probably before White Lance was joined by his brothers.*

White Lance was aided by his dying brother Pursued. It was not long before they were joined by Dewey Beard who says, I crawled onward as fast as I could, coming to White Lance, my brother. He sat with his back against the bank, while my younger brother, Pursued, lay beside him. They were both wounded, and Pursued was dying. He said: "We will all be dead soon, my brothers. Kill as many as you can before you go."

They had three belts of cartridges which they had stripped from soldiers; and when we saw that Pursued [had died], we crawled behind a little knoll where the ditch turned, from which we could see our enemies. We fired at them many times, till they turned the fast-firing cannon at us. Then we lay down close behind the hummock. When it roared, the dirt and gravel were scattered over us by the ball.[30]

Ling-Vannerus, searching for survivors, may have encountered the sniper fire of White Lance, Dewey Beard, and Pursued. In silence we advanced at last into this valley of death without meeting any resistance, *he says,* until suddenly the sides converged and formed a narrow pass, penetrable only by a few men if they walked side by side. We were just going to slip through, pressing ourselves against the walks, when all of a sudden a couple of shots cracked—but the slugs buried into the sand on each side.

At the same time the voice of Lieutenant John C. Waterman . . . warned me against penetrating any further—the redskins lay in hiding in wash-outs ahead of us, and not the Devil could see a feather, whereas for themselves they seemed to have an advantageous survey of all visitors.

All the attempts to expel them had failed at a great loss of men. And since my casualties were bigger than I considered the whole of the Sioux nation to be worth, and I had furthermore already carried out my instructions, I in this case found discretion the better part of valor and ordered the troop to ascend the far bank of the ravine and form up at the crest.

After this had been carried out, I crawled with a comrade and worming like a snake up to the edge [in] hope of having a snap-shot at one of my opponents. Then bang, there is a crack. Zip! Zip! whistle the bullets and my cap flies without ceremony from my head, while the scorch along my scalp tells me how close I have come to visiting Valhalla. My brother-in-arms whispers calmly, "the bastard got me!" and sinks down by my side. . . . Swift as lightning I roll back . . . but only to find myself in a whole cactus family!

The troops were ordered back from the ravine; the cannons was in position, and soon shell after shell fell down in the "pit." The Indians responded with some excellent marksmanship; a couple of the gunners got wounded and the commander, Lt. Harry C. Hawthorne got a bullet in the groin. The firing was kept up for twenty minutes—the response became weaker and weaker. We advanced once again. . . . Below us we found . . . mangled and bleeding bodies, a terrible revenge for our dead comrades and brothers.[31]

Dewey Beard, desperate at the time, says, I became very sick and weak and thirsty, and could shoot no more; but I heard soldiers approaching, and saw one peep over the bank. Although I could not take aim, I fired, and they ran back, shooting the fast-firing cannon at us again, till a bullet from it cut Hawk Feather, who lay with us, almost in two. Some of the men on the hill not far from the cannon fired at me, also, with their rifles, till one bullet threw gravel in my face and I thought I was wounded again, so lay very still. After a little while they ceased.[32]

As Beard lay wounded, reporter Allen surveyed what had once been a battlefield. As rest restored normal, *he wryly admits,* I concluded that in my flight the chance of being scared to death was about equal to that of being struck by bullets. *As he wandered through the bullet-riddled camp,* the sound of rifle fire could be heard at intervals and at various places along the south front of the field. . . . Desultory rifle shots could be heard at short intervals, aimed wherever a blanket was seen to move regardless of what or who might be under it.

Gazing upon the ghastly picture before me, I felt an impulse of savagery well up and leap the faint line of demarcation between civilian and savage foes engaged in the fierce combat of a life-and-death struggle. My impulse was not so very vicious, however. I just wished to walk among the bodies and indulge in a little gloating over the fate that had overtaken the more intelligent but fanatical leaders who had brought these poor misguided people to their death.

Taking about three steps forward for this purpose, I was halted abruptly by an old friend that had rarely failed me. His name is Caution, and he whispered, "Don't do it! Some of them might be alive and welcome you with a rifle shot."

Then he describes an amazing event mentioned by no one else. Turning back, *Allen says*, I filled my pipe and was about to find a seat on one of the boxes by the road when I saw Big Foot rise to a sitting posture from the ground where he had been lying on his back with his face to the glaring sun, feigning death as long as he could endure such suffering. No sooner had he done so than—"Crack! Crack!" spoke a couple of rifles, and he fell back to earth in actual death.

Then his daughter, a woman of middle age, stoutly built and wrapped in a bright red blanket, came running from the tent where she had been nursing him. As she stooped to clasp him in her arms, another shot rang out and she fell dead at his side.

Stunned by the enormity of these two needless deaths, and feeling faint and sick, I fell back behind the ambulance and sat down on a box. After a time, however, I drew out my old pipe—a never-failing friend in such emergencies—and concluded that those boys of the Seventh Cavalry were too excited to think of anything but vengeance.[33]

Allen's account strains credulity. It is unlikely that the old chief could have survived amidst the firefight and hand-to-hand combat. Making Allen's story even more questionable is that he told Ricker an unnamed informant told him virtually the same story. Some of the Indians feigned that they were dead, *Allen says he was told.* Big Foot did so, as one of that number, or else he laid down because he was unable to sit up. At any rate, he was lying on his back. Big Foot raised up; as he did so a soldier who was standing among the other soldiers and one officer, leveled his gun at the chief and shot him in the back and he fell back dead.

Big Foot's daughter was standing by Big Foot's tent; she saw this dastardly deed and ran toward her father. As she did so, a lieutenant snatched a gun from the hands of a soldier and shot her in the back. She fell dead on the spot and her spirit kept company with that of her sire. This officer was Lieutenant Reynolds. My informant stood with this group of officers and soldiers and saw these things done.

Allen adds, The name of the officer is to be suppressed. My pledge was given never to let it be known who it was that gave me the name of the officer. It was on this condition he gave it to me. There is no mistake as to who it was. These facts are absolute and certain. My informant rode by his side to the agency after the butchery and heard him addressed by name many times. My informant is an acquaintance of twenty-two years and thoroughly trustworthy. Lieutenant Reynolds is the man.[34]

Historian Robert Utley, after researching the matter, writes that there was no officer named Reynolds at Wounded Knee.[35] *Was Big Foot executed after surviving the massacre? Allen, with his two stories, is the only person to speak of the later killing of Big Foot. All others on the scene say Big Foot died during the first fighting.*

Medicine Woman says, I hardly remember anything. I was quite excited. The soldiers followed us up and kept firing. My mother and I kept going until we got to . . . the end of the ravine. When we got there, we were charged by the army. They came in two squads. . . . If we had remained there, we probably would have been killed. I just went over those ridges.

Others also survived by fleeing to the ridges. Julia Blackfox and her mother saw the soldiers hunting and killing women. *Mrs. E. M. Keith, the wife of a Pine Ridge minister, says the women were* so frenzied . . . with fear that they fled up the western hills until they had no strength and breath to fly further; then they laid down beside a log as snugly as they could, expecting to be overtaken and slain. But they were not seen; so their lives were spared.[36]

A few Miniconjous survived through sheer ingenuity. Rough Feather, a young boy, escaped by hiding among the wounded and dead: I ran down along the flat down towards the cut bank. As I was nearing the bank it frightened me to hear some Indian calling my name. "Come," he said, "as fast as you can; it is terrible."

The man that said that was Ghost Bear who is still living. I believe that man is the cause of my living today. He said again, "There are a lot of women and men laying down over here. You had better go over and lay down."

So I went down there where they were laying and stayed there with them.[37]

Alice Ghost Horse, huddling in the ravine, says, A man named Breast Plate (Wawoslal Wanapin) came in and told us that my father was killed instantly. We all cried, but for a short while lest we would be heard. Charge in Kill and Nistuste (Back Hip) came in later, but they left again. They were brave. It seemed like eternity, but actually it didn't last that long.

The grieving and badly wounded Dewey Beard, intent on fighting to his death, says, White Lance had gone on, so I crawled after to look for him. While doing so, an Indian scout fired at me, then ran away. I felt extremely sick and wanted to die, so I wormed my way up the side of the ditch and shot at the soldiers, hoping they would kill me; but I could not stand up, and their bullets went high. Again they turned the quick-firing cannon toward me, the balls passing so close that I felt the wind lift me from the ground.

I was nearly blind and could not rise, so I lay for a long time till the firing stopped. Then I crept over the hill, coming to my brother, Yell-at-Them, and Jack La Plant. They had a horse, but I could not ride, so they held me on the pony with their arms. I begged them to leave me for I wanted to die, but they said: "We will go to the agency or die together."[38]

Dewey Beard survived the day and lived for many more years. He left several accounts of the massacre, all of which are clearly tinged by his grief, but all are remarkably free from anger or bitterness.

AT THE AGENCY

At Pine Ridge, Goodale says, A large cedar had been set up in the chapel for day to day services and distribution of gifts to the several congregations now encamped at Pine Ridge. We were filling candy-bags on the morning of the 29th of December, when swift couriers on horse-back brought sensational news of the slaughter at Wounded Knee, eighteen miles away. First reports had it that the cavalry had been cut off, leaving us at the mercy of a maddened horde of Indians.

Soon the chapel and Mission house were swamped by a crowd of sobbing, terrified women and children—church members, for the most part of mixed descent. The two Presbyterian missionary women left their more exposed cottage on the brow of the hill and joined us in the rectory, one of them carrying her pet canary in his cage. The solid outside shutters were slammed to, the oil lamps lit, and an effort made to calm the excitement with the help of hot coffee and sandwiches.[39]

Dr. Eastman writes, We were all straining our ears toward Wounded Knee, and about the middle of the forenoon, we distinctly heard the reports of the Hotchkiss guns. Two hours later, a rider was seen approaching at full speed, and in a few minutes he had dismounted from his exhausted horse and handed his message to General Brooke's orderly. The Indians were watching their own messenger, who ran on foot along the northern ridges and carried the news to the so-called "hostile" camp. It was said that he delivered his message at almost the same time as the mounted officer.[40]

Vincent Richards, a Lakota, tells a story told to him by his mother. She said, "Your grandma was at the boarding school at Pine Ridge when she heard about Wounded Knee. The soldiers were placed around the boarding school because the government thought the Indians would burn down the school like they had at Holy Rosary Mission Boarding School. My Grandmother Elizabeth Kills Enemy said, 'Some other girls and I were in the dormitory when a Lakota man with a painted face came into our room and asked in Lakota if we were all right.' The girls said they were, and he told them that they should stay there because they would be safe. He left and no one saw him go.

"The soldiers and school officials would not believe the girls, that someone could walk into the dorm and leave in the middle of the day. It was cold and snow was on the ground, and soldiers were placed just yards from one another, and still this brave Lakota man somehow came to check up on his relatives."[41]

Once she received news of the massacre, schoolteacher Thisba Hutson Morgan had to cope with the fear of her students and their families: We were sixteen miles away but news of it rapidly reached us at the school. It was the noon hour and the children were scattered over the grounds at work and at play, awaiting their call to dinner, when the first runners from the battlefield reached the agency. The children were the first to get the news and report it to us, because they could understand and interpret the sign language of the runners as they reached the knoll behind the school house, outstripping the army couriers, swift though they were. The children were panic stricken as more news came in for many of them knew that their parents must have been in the fray. A few of them escaped in their excitement although it was a rule of the school that no one, teacher or pupil, should leave the grounds, which were enclosed by a high fence, without first reporting their intention.

We hurried them into the house, battening the doors and windows, and each of the twenty or more teachers stood guard in turn while the others tried to soothe and comfort—the best we could the wailing, hysterical, fainting children who could hear those coming from the battlefield call to them to get away for they were going to shoot fire-arrows into the roof of the school house and burn it.

The teachers soon sensed that their safety depended upon keeping the children in the school house as the Indians would not set fire to it so long as their children were inside. All during that afternoon of December 29th, I could see from my classroom windows a continuous stream of Indians coming from the north, passing southward to what was known as Loafer's Camp.

An occasional shot could be heard. Mischief-makers brought tales that excited the young friendly braves. They began to counsel for immediate attack upon the agency by encircling it and striking from every side at once; but the calmer older warriors counseled for delay and the agency was saved. Chief Red Cloud and his band had remained at the agency, friendly to General John R. Brooke, then commanding, and helped to repel those counseling to destroy it.

American Horse brought his friendly band and camped on the school ground, giving valuable aid and protection.

He was a noble old savage and loyal friend of the white man. He remained near until all danger of renewed attack had passed. Now and then it became necessary for us to go into the yard for a breath of the cold crisp winter air to relieve the strain. On one such occasion, hugging the wall I ventured from the south front door of my classroom around the corner toward the west when a bullet whizzed by me less than three feet away. American Horse, who supposedly could speak no English, called, "Get back house."

I did with alacrity. Later, I recovered the bullet, which I still have. All during the days of the 29th and 30th, occasional bullets fired by hostile Indians fell in the school yard and several struck the building, leaving lasting scars on the wall.[42]

Four miles north of Pine Ridge was the Holy Rosary Mission whose father superior was aged peacemaker John Jutz. When tensions mounted at Pine Ridge, Bishop Marty gave the sisters at the Mission permission to either return to their cloister in Buffalo, New York, or join the Sisters of Mercy in Omaha; but the sisters decided to remain on duty, keeping constant vigil before the Blessed Sacrament.[43]

Wells says, From the beginnings of the difficulties, the Indians had told Father Jutz to keep within the enclosure around the Mission and he would be safe; that those precincts would be treated as sacred, and that all therein would receive protection and be exempt from danger. When it became apparent to the hostile Indians that there was a probability of fighting, the full-bloods had quietly notified their half-blood relations that, if it came, they had better go to the Mission, for there they would be safe in that place, as it was agreed among all them that the enclosed premises of the institution should not be invaded. Father Jutz had been specified as the only friend the Indians had among the whites on the reservation.[44]

Wells's wife, Teresa, a teacher at the day school, and their two young children lived near the mission. According to Ricker, at about eleven A.M. on the day of the massacre Mrs. Wells heard a commotion among the young Indians, at first the children, and then it spread to the older ones, the parents gathering at the school and talking to the children—the meaning not being apprehended by Mrs. Wells. About noon or a little after, she noticed that the young men were stripping to a war footing;

that is, were naked except the breech clout, and they were bestirring themselves and getting their ponies.

An Indian woman came and asked Mrs. Wells, who guessed from her news, to go to the Mission. Mrs. Wells tried to put her off for a little while till she could finish clearing away her dinner table, but the woman was persistent and, as Mrs. Wells seemed in no hurry to go, she caught the young child Alma in her arms and started off on the run (the child was nearly 3 years old) to the Mission, Mrs. Wells did not understand what it all meant, but she had a secret fear that the woman was kidnapping the little girl. So she grasped the boy Tommy who was between 5 and 6 years old and ran after her as hard as she could.

They reached the Mission nearly together, but when Mrs. Wells saw the woman directing her course to the Mission, she felt relieved, but she could not conjecture what all the trouble was about, though she realized that some danger was impending.

There Mrs. Wells found the mission practically emptied; there were not more than a dozen children remaining. The others had run away and the Father Superior was in the dark as to what was causing the exodus. Mrs. Wells went to Father Jutz, the Father Superior, and inquired the cause of so much commotion, but he did not know. He said he was just starting to the agency to learn the cause.

He was not gone more than half an hour when he returned and said that he had been stopped by the Indians who would not let him pass, but they told him that there was fighting going on and to go back and stay at the Mission. He advised Mrs. Wells to remain there also, and she stayed. That afternoon and night people kept coming and going, and about twenty persons from the neighborhood were there all the time. She sat up and spent the slow hours of suspense in conversation; others retired, but there was no sleep at the Holy Rosary Mission that night.[45]

AN INCIDENT AT WHITE CREEK

Capt. Edward S. Godfrey, in his sworn testimony at the Forsyth investigation, asserted, I saw no wanton destruction of non-combatants, none that could be helped, in my opinion. I told my men throughout the day not to fire on women or children. Although the Indians that we saw of Big Foot's band were at times 200 yards off, we could not discern the distinction between bucks and squaws, and firing came from the parties. No firing took place on the part of my men when other of our troops were between us and the Indians.[46]

In 1903 Godfrey described an event that another officer called an atrocity. He wrote, At the Battle of Wounded Knee, S.D. Dec. 29, 1890, my

Troop D, with Capt Jackson, Troop C, were deployed as skirmishers on one side of the Indian Encampment. In front of us and near the edge of the ravine was posted Taylor's Indian Scouts. After the fight opened and the Indians were coming toward our lines, I saw that we would be in the direct line of the fire of the Artillery and that our fire was blanked by the Scouts in our front. I explained to my men that I was going to move them to the rear and when I gave the command Rally they were to rally on a hill to our left and rear which gave us a position to command the ground in front [and] eliminated the danger of the fire from our own men following the Indians and the Artillery.

They rallied as ordered and were dismounted to fight on foot and opened fire. Soon after taking position I saw some Indians making up the ravine to our left. I cut off about half my men and ordered Lieutenant S. R. H. Tompkins, Seventh Cavalry, my lieutenant, to take them to the ravine and hold it at all hazards. This he did. After the fight in our front was over Major S. M. Whitside (now Brig. Gen'l retired) came to my position and said Captain, some Indians made their escape over the ridge on the other side of the ravine and I wish you to take your troop and go in pursuit. I said, "I have about half my men. I have sent Lieutenant Tompkins down to hold that ravine and as they have firing down there, I don't think it would be safe to take them away."

He replied, "Very well, do as you like."

I immediately mounted the men with me, between fifteen and twenty, and proceeded to find the trail of the Indians. When I got to where they had crossed the ridge, I could not discover any particular direction of the trail, and no Indians were in sight. I at once went to a valley beyond, proceeded up this valley for a distance and then went to a hill that gave a general view of the valley. I was unable to see anything of the Indians in the open so I started to scout down the valley which was pretty well covered with underbrush.

We were then about five miles from the battle ground. I followed a wagon road having my troop deployed as advanced guard. After going between two and three miles, the men called out, "There are some Indians in front, Captain."

The valley here was closed by low steep bluffs on either side. The creek bed was dry. I dismounted half my men and deployed them as skirmishers, the flankers remaining on the higher ground. I cautioned the men that they must not fire on women and children. I then called, "Hau, Cola, Squaw, Papoose, Cola! Hau cola!" and after a short interval I repeated this or something to the same effect but at no time did I get a response. 1st. Sgt. Herman Gunther, said he could see them moving a little but he could not tell what they were.

The valley was covered with bushes on which were the dead leaves. The bushes were not very thick but enough with the dead leaves to make sight uncertain. "But," he said, "if we don't open they will get the drop on us."

I told the men I wanted if possible to make sure they were not women and children. I told them to get ready and again called out, "How Cola, Squaw, papoose, Cola," and getting no response and seeing my men were getting nervous gave the orders Commence firing.

At the first volley there were screams as from women and children, and no firing coming from the Indians, I at once ordered Cease Firing. I don't think more than half a dozen shots in all were fired by my men. I said "Oh my, Oh my."

Sergt Gunther dropped his gun to an order, hung his head and said "It's too bad, Captain, but we couldn't tell what they were," or to that effect.

Expecting that other Indians were in the valley beyond, and again cautioning them about shooting squaws and papooses, I gave the command to move forward at double time down the valley, my flankers being on the higher ground outside the valley. As I passed near where the women and children were I ran over to see if they were hurt for the screams had ceased as soon as the firing ceased.

I then to my horror found a squaw and two small girls and it took but a glance to tell me they were in their death struggles, near them was a boy lying flat and motionless on his belly with his coat pulled over his head, his arms stretched out as if he had fallen and I supposed he too was dead and I was just leaving when a man named Carey who had followed me, yelled out, "This man ain't dead Captain," and I turned around and he fired, shooting the boy in the head; he was so close that he was powder burned and the coat over his head if I remember rightly was burned.

It was all over in an instant. I told him to get out of there and join the line at once as we would probably find a lot more Indians down the valley. Carey was a young recruit who had only joined the regiment the same day I did, Dec 7th. The tenseness of his voice when he called to me "this man ain't dead, Captain" and the pallor of his face was sufficient evidence to me that the man was thoroughly frightened and not malicious or wanton, and the thought that passed through my mind at the time was that he had heard of the desperation and cunning of wounded

Indians and that he did not propose to take any chances, and acted instantly on the spur of the moment, probably with that idea uppermost.

From where the skirmish line was, when I gave the command, "Commence firing," to where the squaw and children were I should judge was not less than thirty-five yards and was probably near to fifty yards. I was some yards in rear of the line and I at no time saw the Indians myself, only the skulking movement through the bushes and could not distinguish anything, only I knew they must be Indians.

These were at a point where the creek crooked, and jutted against a shouldering embankment, perhaps eight or ten feet high. I am satisfied that not a man knew they were non-combatants; that the boy was powdered burned at this time is true, but that the squaw and girls were then powder burned is not true. It was impossible at that distance for it to be done.[47] Upon my return to camp I reported to General Forsyth just what had occurred at the killing of the squaw and children.[48]

Godfrey's account was contradicted on January 21, 1891, by Capt. Frank D. Baldwin, the acting assistant inspector general, who reported that while on patrol he found the bodies of one woman, adult, two girls, eight and seven years old, and a boy of about ten years of age.

They were found in the valley of the White Horse Creek, in the brush, under a high bluff, where they had evidently been discovered and shot. Each person had been shot once, the character of which was necessarily fatal in each case. The bodies had not been plundered or molested. The shooting was done at so close a range that the person or clothing of each person was powder burned.

The location of the bodies was about three miles westward of the scene of the Wounded Knee battle. All the bodies were properly buried by the troops of my escort.

From my knowledge of the facts, I am certain that these people were killed on the day of the Wounded Knee fight, and no doubt by the troops of the Seventh Cavalry, under the command of Captain Godfrey. Tracks of horses shod with the Goodenough shoes were plainly visible and running along the road passing close by where the bodies were found.

A full brother of the dead Indian woman was present. He had been on the agency police force for several years. Considering the distressing circumstances attending the death of his sister, his demeanor was remarkably friendly. His only request was that a family of three persons, the only relatives he has living, and who were of Big Foot's band, may be allowed to remain at this agency. This I recommend be granted.[49]

Godfrey eventually paid for his part in the incident. On his retirement in 1907, the "New York Sun" reported, Godfrey was brevetted a major on February 27, 1890, for military services. He served at the Battle of Wounded Knee, and his participation in that engagement nearly cost him his life and cost him, in the estimation of many of his fellow officers, the rank of major general.

Certain alleged acts in that engagement, for which President Roosevelt held General Godfrey responsible, made the president his unsparing critic in later years, and he declared on one occasion that Godfrey should never be promoted under the Roosevelt administration. The president relented after much persuasion . . . and promoted General Godfrey from senior colonel of the line to brigadier general. This promotion was not made, however, until last January.[50]

When the aged and unrepentant Godfrey was speaking at the War College on May 29, 1931, he offered a slightly different account of the White Horse Creek incident than he had in earlier years, saying that he was ordered to pursue a small group who had escaped—over the ridge. He chased them down a partly wooded valley, calling out "squaw—papoose—cola!" apparently as an invitation to appear and make a second formal surrender! When they remained in hiding, he directed his men to fire a volley into the bushes, killing a woman and three children. A boy of about fourteen, found to be not quite dead, was finished off on the spot by a young soldier. Godfrey says he reprimanded him, but not too severely![51]

A WAR PARTY TO THE RESCUE

Shortly after the sound of gunfire was heard at Pine Ridge, the civilians took shelter and the military threw up breastworks. Once couriers began to bring news of the fighting, many of the pacified Lakotas fled to the Badlands. A number of enraged Oglalas, many quite elderly, took up arms and rode to Wounded Knee. They were intent on joining the fight. Wells says that an armed party arrived from the agency in the afternoon. The sound of battle, discharges of cannon, were heard by the Indians at the agency. They made a hurried march over the hills overlooking the battlefield from that direction. Some cavalry was dispatched to their quarter to receive them with a fire delivered over the summit by the men shielded behind the ridge. The Indians got up within range and a Pine Ridge Indian named Flying Horn was killed, and two Rosebud Indians were wounded. The hostiles then retreated.

During the preparation the sacks of grain which had been brought by the wagons that afternoon where thrown into breastworks for defense against this threatened danger, but no necessity came for their use.[52]

Godfrey's command, now escorting prisoners taken in the gullies, had a brief exchange of fire with the rescuers. Then, he says, We saw a number of Indians congregating on a hill some distance off in the direction of the agency road, between us and the agency. We were wondering who they were, when they started towards us. Several, I don't remember how many, perhaps 3 or 4, came up, said "How cola," shook hands and seemed a good deal excited; one came up to me, shook hands and gave a pretty hard pull, as I thought since, tried to pull me off my horse.

Then Captain Jackson called my attention to the other Indians deploying and advancing very rapidly. I thought they numbered 50 or 60. His lead horses were between our men and the advancing Indians, whose intentions we yet did not know; we were getting these horses back of the line when these Indians opened fire, wounding one of my men.

We returned the fire, and Captain Jackson said that we would fall back, which we did. The Indians made no effort to follow us up. Soon two other troops came up to us from the battle field, and all returned to the main command. We thought the Indians described were agency Indians; they were evidently strangers to the prisoners whom we abandoned.[53]

Crickett, who was escorting prisoners, writes, Just as we started to take them back, about three hundred of the Brulés, some of Two Strike's band came in sight and then the sixteen prisoners. We had made a break for the ravine again but they was all shot before they reached it by another troop that was waiting for them.

The officer in charge of us would not let us fire. By that time we was in a hot engagement. The last arrivals word was sent back to the main body what was going on. The colonel then gave the order for the men to build fortifications, as we expected the remainder of the Sioux would be out. Two Strike's band had to get any thing that was handy such as sacks of corn, bails of hay and boxes of biscuits, but they wasnt used, as the troops that was out drove them off. I think if they had of known our position we should have suffered a terrible loss. We waited for about two hours on the look out.[54]

Wells says that some of the rescuers met some of Big Foot's band fleeing from the battle. They united and returned to renew the battle, but were checked by Captain Henry Jackson's men. An Indian named Flying Horse, wearing a Ghost shirt, made a desperate, fanatical charge on Jackson's troop, but the soldiers cut him down. The Indians talk about this incident to this day.[55]

Forsyth reported the encounters with the rescuers as taking place sometime before 1:30 P.M., the time he wrote his second report. In this report he says Jackson, after capturing twenty-three, met five Lakotas who approached from the direction of the agency and had the appearance of belonging to the Indian police. After shaking hands with all the officers, they rode back a short distance, and evidently at a signal about 150 Indians opened fire on him, and in the running fight the captured Indians escaped.[56]

The Miniconjous who survived the day may have been saved by those who tried to rescue them. Dog Chief says, Some soldiers came and saw us and began to shoot us again so we ran up the ravine. We were being killed as we moved up toward the head of the valley. We went as fast as we could.

Two boys were with me, one is Little Finger and the other is Red Shell, but he is dead, [and] Little Finger is living and with us today. After a while some Indians on horseback came to the top of the hill, not very far from where we were hiding and these Indians had guns and were our friends that had come out to fight from Pine Ridge.

When the soldiers saw them they quit killing us and went back to where there were more soldiers. The Indians that were on horseback took all of us [who] was able to ride on behind them and we got away from the soldiers.[57]

John Little Finger says these rescuers were a number of old men, Indians, [who] came up over the hill and they were on horseback and had guns, but was some distance from us; but when the soldiers saw them they took on a run, so that shows that when the soldiers that were killing us saw that the Indians were our friends and that they might make a charge on them they lost their bravery and started to run.[58]

Among those who tried to rescue the survivors was Black Elk. He says, By now many other Lakotas, who had heard the shooting, were coming up from Pine Ridge, and we all charged on the soldiers. They ran eastward toward where the trouble began.

We followed down along the dry gulch, and what we saw was terrible. Dead and wounded women and children and little babies were scattered all along there where they had been trying to run away. The soldiers had followed along the gulch, as they ran, and murdered them in there. Sometimes they were in heaps because they had huddled together, and some were scattered all along. Sometimes bunches of them had been killed and torn to pieces where the wagon guns hit them. I saw a little baby trying to suck its mother, and she was bloody and dead. *They were probably Dewey Beard's wife and child.*

There were two little boys at one place in this gulch. They had guns and they had been killing soldiers all by themselves. We could see the soldiers they had killed. The boys were all alone there, and they were not hurt. These were very brave little boys.

When we drove the soldiers back, they dug themselves in, and we were not enough people to drive them out from there. In the evening they marched off up Wounded Knee Creek, and then we saw all that they had done there.

Men and women and children were heaped and scattered all over the flat at the bottom of the little hill where the soldiers had their wagon guns, and westward up the dry gulch all the way to the high ridge, the dead women and children and babies were scattered.

When I saw this I wished I had died too, but I was not sorry for the women and children. It was better for them to be happy in the other world, and I wanted to be there too. But before I went there I wanted to have revenge. I thought there might be a day, and we should have revenge.[59]

About going to surrender at Pine Ridge, Short Bull says, At daylight the next day we heard the firing of guns and cannon, so we started off in the direction of the firing, but before we got there we heard more firing. We met a white man who was driving in the woods after fire wood, and we asked him the cause of this firing. He told us, "It is the soldiers (of whom there were many at the agency) practicing at targets, and they shoot all the time."[60]

Short Bull rode on until he came to a Lakota village. We reached the big hill we could look down and there saw the village. Everything was in a fearful state. Further on were other Indians coming toward the village and it looked as if trouble was near.

I went into the village and was there told that Big Foot, or Spotted Elk's, band had been all killed. I saw my cousin Many Wounds who was there and confirmed this report in a measure as he himself been wounded in the shoulder. He told me that all his relatives Father, Mother, all had been killed, all of their guns were taken from them and then they were fired on and could do nothing.

He continued saying, "I do not know how it happened, I was in my lodge putting on my shirt and leggings when the firing commenced; this will make our hearts bad for a long time and we will fight the soldiers."

I told him, "It is not right even if all our relatives are killed. We will do right, they blame us when we are not to be blamed, we will now wait and see. If the soldiers continue to fire on us after three days we will try to protect ourselves and families the best we can."

I am not to blame, *Short Bull insisted.* The whites fired on us first. Twenty-three of my own relatives were killed in this fight, men, women and children. This is like butchery. Why do they kill helpless women and children? This shows the soldiers want us to all die off. When our Indians fought against an enemy of their own color, you know what kind of a man I was. I laughed and feared nothing, but now I do not want you to fight. Take care of the women and children. I am not looking for trouble, but if I am angered, I am the worst among you. I have put all badness from me and want to be a good man. I will go over to where the battle was fought in the morning and see the bodies of my relatives. When I return, if the soldiers fire on you, I will remember my old feelings, stand up and be a Soldier once more.[61]

Valentine T. McGillycuddy, Pine Ridge agent from 1879–86, wrote, Riding in from the battle that day, to agency, I was intercepted by a party of blanket Indians on a cross road in a wagon, and one of them accosted me in these words, "Little Beard, eleven years ago we made an agreement and promise with you . . . that if we would give you fifty of our young men to act as police, you would have the white soldiers taken away, the police would control, and we would have a home government. We kept our promise, and you kept yours."

Then he threw his blanket off, and showed me a bullet hole through the left arm, received that day and from which the blood was trickling, remarking, "I was one of your police. Who brought back the soldiers, and what were they brought for?"

Very reluctantly I had to reply, "I am sorry, my friend, but I am no longer your agent."[62]

RETURN TO PINE RIDGE

On the plain at Wounded Knee the Seventh Cavalry was beginning to pack and saddle up for its return to Pine Ridge. Military surgeon Charles B. Ewing says, I was on the field from 9:30 A.M. to about 4 P.M., at which hour we began our march back to the agency. Of that six and one-half hours, I am quite sure I spent two and one-half hours at the dressing station and the same length of time superintending the removal of a part of the wounded and at least three-fourth of the dead, to which must be added about three-quarters of an hour taken up in accompanying Captain Edgerly's command.[63]

We consumed about five and one-half hours on the march to the agency, which was of necessity slow, *Ewing says.* I rode a horse, kindly furnished me by a troop commander, as did also Assistant Surgeons Hoff and Glennan. I did not render any medical services on the march and think it quite unlikely that such would have been rendered efficiently as darkness came on quickly and lights were not permitted in the command.[64]

At Pine Ridge, the camp of Lakotas outside the agency had, according to Eastman, disappeared as if by magic and soon the caravans were in motion, going toward the natural fortress of the Badlands.

In the friendly camp there was almost as much turmoil, and crowds of frightened women and children poured into the agency. Big Foot's band had been wiped out by the troops, and reprisals were naturally looked for.[65]

The Pine Ridge Agency was badly situated from a military point of view. An unidentified officer writing to the "Army and Navy Journal" observed, In a deep basin, surrounded by high hills, with numerous deep canyons leading into it on all sides; it is a place easy of assault and difficult of defense.[66]

In addition to its vulnerable physical location, according to Eastman the enclosure was not barricaded in any way, and we had but a small detachment of troops for our protection. Sentinels were placed, and machine guns trained on the various approaches.

A few hot-headed braves fired on the sentinels and wounded two of them. The Indian police began by shooting at several braves who were apparently about to set fire to some outlying buildings. Every married employee was seeking a place of safety for his family.[67]

The Lakotas who had surrendered were equally frightened and took flight. Goodale writes, When the loyal Sioux learned that unarmed men, women, and children had been shot down in flight, their white camps melted away like snow-banks in April.[68] *Within hours more than four thousand "friendlies" fled into the Badlands.*[69]

Lt. Alexander R. Piper wrote his wife that the news spread like wild fire and soon our Indians were collected in groups and showed a very warlike spirit. Two Strikes and his band collected on a hill about a mile and a half off and had a big pow wow.

Suddenly the firing began in our vicinity and there was a lively fusillade for about 5 minutes. I was right in the middle of a band of scouts and friendlies when the firing began. Coming from General Brooke's presence, the Indians went in every direction and I expected a shot every minute, for one cuss rode by me shortly before waving his gun and I believe would have fired at me had not a sentinel been right in front of him. He had on a Ghost shirt and trousers and was painted up for war. Well! We formed our companies and I fixed up my battery for an attack.[70]

Just as the artillery was ready to fire back, Eastman writes, General

Brooke ran into the open shouting at the top of his voice to the police: "Stop, stop! Doctor, tell them they must not fire until ordered!"

I did so, just as the bullets whistled by us, and the general's coolness perhaps saved all our lives, for we were in no position to repel a large attacking force. Since we did not reply, the scattered shots soon ceased, but the situation remained critical for several days and nights.[71]

General Brooke, probably acting on General Miles's orders, refused to be drawn into a firefight.

Piper concludes his letter by writing: Two shots that were fired came through our camp, and one went through a 2nd Infantryman's hat, and the other took a 2nd Infantryman's finger off. Everything then quieted down but we stood on our arms until about half an hour ago. Then we stacked arms and almost immediately the firing re-commenced. The Indians have set fire to some houses near Red Cloud's and we understand old Red Cloud is a prisoner in Two Strike's hands.[72]

Indeed, Two Strike's men had taken Red Cloud prisoner and spirited him off into the Badlands. Later Red Cloud wrote T. A. Bland of the Indian Defence Association, The Brulés and others all stampeded, and the Brulés forced me to go with them. I being in danger of my life between two fires, I had to go with them and follow my family. Some would shoot their guns around me and make me go faster.

We all going down White Clay Creek, fifteen miles, and met with Short Bull, Brulés, coming in from the Badlands. There were 150 lodges. When they learned about Big Foot's people being killed, they all feel very bad. All then went in canyon and fortified, and hold council, and made a law, that no one should go back to the agency. All rather die together. I tried my best for them to let me go back, but they would not let me go, and said if I went they would kill me.[73]

Red Cloud remained a prisoner for several days. The Lakotas were ready to fight if they were attacked, and they were ready to force the "friendlies" to join them.

Civilians at Pine Ridge still made plans for escape. Eastman, who had been courting Goodale, writes, My office was full of refugees. I called one of my good friends aside and asked him to saddle my two horses and stay by them. "When general fighting begins, take them to Miss Goodale and see her to the railroad station if you can," I told him.

Then I went over to the rectory. Mrs. Cook [the missionary's wife] refused to go without her husband, and Miss Goodale would not leave while there was a chance of being of service. The house was crowded with terrified people, most of them Christian Indians, whom our friends were doing their best to pacify.[74]

Goodale, adamant, writes, Long after dark the Seventh Cavalry appeared, bringing its own numerous casualties and thirty-three severely wounded prisoners, all but six of them women and children. Mr. Cook cleared his church, ordered the pews torn out and the floor spread with hay. Quilts were brought from the house and the moaning victims lifted from the wagons and tended throughout the night by Doctor Eastman, the physician of their own blood, with such volunteer help as was available. Later one of the army surgeons came to assist, but no one wondered to see the Sioux women shrink in horror from the dreaded uniform. We made gallons of coffee, and distributed bread to as many as were able to eat. By the next day fresh beef had been requisitioned and a temporary soup kitchen and bakery set up in the rectory.[75]

When the Seventh Cavalry delivered the Miniconjou wounded to Cleveland's Episcopal Church, Eastman writes, We laid the poor creatures side by side in rows, and the night was devoted to caring for them as best we could. Many were frightfully torn to pieces by . . . shells and the suffering was terrible.

General Brooke placed me in charge and I had to do nearly all the work, for although the army surgeons were more than ready to help as soon as their own men had been cared for, the tortured Indians would scarcely allow a man in a uniform to touch them.

Mrs. Cook, Miss Goodale, and several of Mr. Cook's Indian helpers acted as volunteer nurses. In spite of all out efforts, we lost the greater part of them, but a few recovered, including several children who had lost all their relatives and who were adopted into kind Christian families.[76]

According to Ricker, Mrs. E. M. Keith says the church was filled with the suffering. She did not count the number. A good many died of their wounds, infants from a few months to tender years of age were shot in all parts of their bodies and presented pitiable spectacles.

The Keiths worked among these poor little things all that night feeding and ministering to their extreme thirst. Mrs. Keith tells me that their cries, faint from weakness and long suffering, were something never to be effaced from memory.

Mr. Keith said there was not a man in the hospital.[77]

Piper wrote, Last night while making arrangements for them, their wagons stood in front of my tent for an hour or more. I could not go to sleep with the crying and moaning and it just makes a fellow's heart ache to hear those poor little papooses cry. It was a terrible necessity which compelled the troops to shoot women as well as men, but the greater number were injured by flying bullets.[78]

IN THE EAST

The three reporters on the scene—Allen, Cressey, and Kelley—filed remarkably accurate reports. From the serious tone of their dispatches, all three realized they had witnessed a dreadful moment in American history. Their dispatches rose to the occasion. Each was empathetic to the slaughter of Big Foot's band. The "Chadron (NE) Democrat" observed that Cressey and Allen proved themselves the best rustlers, and the *Omaha Bee* and the *New York Herald* were the only papers that had a full description of the fight and a complete list of killed and wounded the next morning after the battle.[79] *These lists were complete in regard to the military casualties, but each dispatch greatly underestimated the number of Lakotas killed.*

The reporters who remained at Pine Ridge to cover the surrender of Lakotas coming in from the Badlands relied on secondhand sources. Their reports were less accurate.

Reports of a battle at Wounded Knee quickly appeared in the eastern press. It was first reported that a single troop led by Captain Wallace had been involved in the fighting. Basing his opinion on this erroneous report, the "New York World"'s reporter asked, Was the killing of Big Foot's braves on Wounded Knee Creek by Captain Wallace's troop of the Seventh Cavalry yesterday morning another massacre, like the shooting of Sitting Bull, or was it a remarkable exhibition or savage heroism on the part of the little band of desperate Indians who, finding that their guns and horses were to be taken from them, made a dash for liberty, and fought for their lives until they were either shot down by the troops or had broken through the lines of their captors and escaped?

This question has been asked more than once at the War Department today, and there is serious speculation over it in military circles here. The old Indian fighters do not hold the redskin as entitled to much consideration under any circumstances, and certainly to none at all when on the warpath, yet this is what an experienced soldier, who has fought the Indians, said to the [*New York World*] correspondent today: "There is the strongest kind of prejudice among officer and men on frontier stations against the Indians. Like General Sheridan, they believed 'the only good Indian is a dead Indian.' As compared with the white man, his life is worth almost nothing; and it is not regarded as a crime to shoot a poor red devil for a trifling offense."[80]

17. Aftershocks

I desire to express my admiration of the gallant conduct
of my command in an engagement with a band of Indians
in desperate condition and crazed by religion.
—Col. James W. Forsyth

✶

When I met Little Bat soon after the affair he told me that
the sights which he had witnessed during the killing of women
and children would never be effaced from his memory.
—James H. Cook

✶

TREACHEROUS RED DEVILS
Members of Big Foot's Band Shoot Down Soldiers
After Having Surrendered. The Troops Undertake to Disarm
the Indians, When a Fight Occurs.
One Captain and Five Soldiers Killed and a Lieutenant and
Fifteen Others Wounded.
None of the Indians Seem to Have Been Hurt, and No Report
that the Fire Was Returned.
Some of them Got Away and Further Trouble is Feared
With other Straggling
Bands—No Good Indians but Dead Ones.
—Iowa State Register, 30 December 1890.

LAKOTA FURY

Like many other "friendlies," Rosebud Agency schoolteacher Luther Standing Bear's loyalty to the whites was sorely tried when he heard about the massacre at Wounded Knee. Angry, he wrote in his memoirs, The following morning, the news arrived of the terrible slaughter of Big Foot's whole band. Men, women, and children—even babies were killed in their mothers' arms! This was done by the soldiers. According to the white man's history this was known as the "battle" of Wounded Knee, but it was not a battle—it was a slaughter, a massacre. Those soldiers had been sent to protect these men, women, and children who had not joined the Ghost dancers, but they had shot them down without even a chance to defend themselves.

When I heard of this, it made my blood boil. I was ready myself to go and fight then. There I was, doing my best to teach my people to follow in the white men's road—even trying to get them to believe in their religion—and this was my reward for it all! The very people I was following—and getting my people to follow—had no respect for motherhood, old age, or babyhood. Where was all their civilized training?[1]

Standing Bear was not alone in his anger. He did not take action, but others did. The Lakotas retaliated mainly through random sniping, small forays, and one rearguard action.

Private Crickett writes, When we got to the agency it was in confusion as all the families had left and gone on the war path. Before they left they fired into the agency and wounded several of the infantry, although there was ten companys and a battery of heavy artilly, General Brooks woundnt let them return the fire. If he had of done so it would of taken them all the winter to of buried their dead as the Lieut in charge of the guns had them sighted right on the long line of them going out. Brooks told him if he fired a shot it would cost him his commission.[2]

General Brooke continued to maintain his policy of nonretaliation.

A CALL TO ARMS

Maj. Guy V. Henry's Ninth Cavalry had been in the field since December 24. After a forty-two mile ride on December 29, they heard there had been a fight at Wounded Knee and that the Pine Ridge Agency might be under attack. They rode all night, arriving at Pine Ridge near dawn. To speed their journey, they left behind their wagon train. Henry's command had ridden eighty-five miles in twenty-four hours.

Upon their arrival, fires were kindled, horses picketed, and the exhausted men literally threw themselves on the ground for rest. They had been there but a short time when one of the men from the escort came galloping madly in with the news that the wagon-train was heavily attacked, and that succor must be sent at once.[3]

Lt. Guy Preston led his Lakota scouts to the rescue, with elements of the Seventh Cavalry not far behind. Crickett writes, Just at day break the alarm sounded and out we turned. The Ninth Cavalry's baggage train was surrounded by the red devils. It taken just about as long to turn out as it does to write, went about four miles before we came in sight of them, but no sooner than they saw us they was off, only got a few shots at them.

The "New York World" erroneously reported, The whole band [of attackers], numbering thirty-three, were killed,[4] *but the "Army and Navy Journal" would correctly state,* One man, Private Haywood, Troop D, Ninth Cavalry, having been killed, it is said by an Indian wearing a blue coat. The killed man doubtless supposed he was a scout and allowed him to come so near that his face was burned by powder.[5] *Again, a member of the press treated a minor skirmish as a full-fledged battle.*

The Lakota sharpshooters continued to fire into Pine Ridge. Henry Cotter, a Lakota, recalls, A bunch of us kids were sitting on top of the trading post at Pine Ridge. Two days before this, we heard that the soldiers had killed a lot of Indians out at Wounded Knee.

This day, we looked on as the soldiers were marching and forming ranks. On top of the hill to the east, across from where the Pine Ridge Hospital is located today, was a Lakota man. This Lakota was shooting down at the soldiers. He was shooting from a long distance, but you could see him and his horse on the hill. The soldiers would jump as the bullets would dust the ground.

We watched to see what the soldiers would do. When a bullet hit a fat sergeant in the stomach, he rolled over on his back. Us kids just started laughing because it looked so funny. The sergeant jumped up and pulled down his pants because he thought he was wounded. That looked twice as funny to us, and we laughed so hard some of us fell off the roof. "Luck was with that fat sergeant because the bullet hit his belt buckle," I was told.

You know the Indians tried to get the soldiers to chase them because, if they would have followed them into the Badlands, the soldiers would have never returned. The Lakota people were mad and angry at what the soldiers had done to their people. If the soldiers would have taken the bait and chased these warriors who were shooting at them, there would have been a different story about Wounded Knee being the last stand of the American Indian. The soldiers would have rode into glory the same way as Custer.

The Indians were wanting to get them away from Pine Ridge and then shoot their horses. The soldiers would have frozen to death just like many of the victims at Wounded Knee. But, lucky for the soldiers, the Indian people on Pine Ridge did not want to start another war. They did not want to see old people, children and women being shot again by the U.S. government. It was bad enough on the reservation because the government had already killed, cheated and stolen from the Indian people. . . . They're still doing it.[6]

AMBUSH AT DREXEL MISSION

On the morning of December 30, Philip Wells's wife, Teresa, says many straggling Indians passed the mission as they fled from Pine Ridge, four miles away. She told Judge Ricker, They stopped at the gate and were fed by the Sisters of St. Francis, Mrs. Wells herself assisting.[7]

After they passed the mission, some of the refugees set fire to nearby haystacks and a small log cabin that served as Teresa Wells's schoolhouse. The smoke from the fire could be seen from four miles away at Pine Ridge.[8] *Many there thought the mission had been attacked.*

Crickett's unit found itself quickly back in action. After rescuing the Ninth's wagon train, it returned to Pine Ridge on the morning of December 30. There, Crickett writes, We went back again to camp and was just watering our horses, when the scouts brought in word that they was burning the Mission, a large Catholic school. Out we went again and this time it was business.

The Oglalas' rear guard, a small number of young warriors, had set up defenses in a canyon just beyond Holy Rosary Mission. They waited there while their families withdrew into the Badlands. The fire they set may have been intended to lure the troopers into the field. If so, they were successful.

Midmorning, as the Seventh Cavalry rode by the mission in pursuit of the fleeing Lakotas, the troopers, too, were regaled . . . with a piece of bread and meat which each took from the baskets of the donors as each passed.[9]

The troops rode into a valley one and one-half miles wide, just beyond the burning school.[10] *Crickett writes,* Our colonel had orders only to go as far as the Mission, instead of which he went about five miles farther on where we got into a pretty fix. Had to go through a deep ravine to get on the hill opposite to see if we could see anything of them but all seemed quiet.

Forsyth, again ignoring his orders, was about to meet with carefully planned resistance.

Wells, who was scouting for the Seventh, says, We were about two miles below the Mission, where we were fired on from the hill tops near the rear of the column. The firing came from one side. Our troops formed, facing the danger, though no Indians could be seen. Then came a hostile volley from the opposite side of the column.[11] *The Seventh seemed to be surrounded and pinned down by a superior force.*

We dismounted, *Crickett writes,* four remaining mounted to take care of the horses. We than advanced about two hundred yards to the crest of the hill where we could see a few in the distance, that being their object to draw us on so as they could work round our flank. We laid there for about half an hour firing when we got the chance. We then had orders to mount but had scarcely left our position when they seemed to spring up out of the ground. The hills was alive with them, and it commenced in real earnest. Such confussion you never saw for a few minutes running in all directions.

Wells says, A disposition of some of the soldiers was made to meet the fire from this quarter. Then a fresh fire came into the column from the front. Then some more troops were wheeled into position to repel this attack. It looked as though the enemy had closed in on all sides, and the concern was that they had established themselves in the rear as well as elsewhere.[12]

Crickett admits that a few troopers panicked: Some troopers mounted their horses and galloped off, but after a bit they rallied which was their only chance. As far as I could see the only way to fight Indians is to face them and keep fighting.

After some pretty hot fighting we drove them back, and commenced a steady retreat. Half go at the time, one lot holding them in cheque while the others got through the ravine on to a bit of level ground, and then we had a good battle.

The besieged Forsyth dispatched a courier to Pine Ridge requesting reinforcements. The exhausted Ninth Cavalry was called back into action once more. Relieved, Crickett confesses, I think at one time if it hadnt of been for the 9th Cav it would of gone very hard with us as we was completely surrounded.

The man that was killed we had to leave behind as was hard pushed. When the body was recovered two days later, he was horible mutilated. His hands, ears, nose, cut off, scalp gone and eyes full of powder. It was a shocking sight to see.

Wells says, This situation lasted an hour or more until the Ninth Cavalry appeared. The situation was felt to be critical because the Indians kept out of sight and it was impossible to tell whether they were all around, nor could their numbers be conjectured. Not more than three or four could be seen at any one time.

Crickett was exaggerating when he wrote, The fury was kept up untill dark, when the colonel thought it best to get back to the agency. *Wells and others say that when the Ninth Cavalry arrived*, It made one charge . . . and the affair was done.[13]

Wells says that Lieutenant Mann, a soldier of the Seventh Cavalry, was wounded and afterwards died. Three Indians were wounded. One of these died afterwards.

Pleased to say we came out victorious, *Crickett writes*. Only lost one man and seven wounded, but two have died since. Their loss was over a hundred. *He overestimated the Lakota casualties. As a soldier in the midst of the ambush, the action must have seemed much more violent than it really was. In fact, the force the Seventh faced was quite small.*

I learned, *Wells says*, these shots came from thirty or forty young Indians who were without experience, some of whom had returned from eastern schools. They fired from one side, then ran to another place and fired, then repeated this in another place.[14]

About a month after this affair, *Ricker says*, Mr. Wells was ordered to investigate this, and he did so. He found that this force of young men had been directed by the Indians at the rendezvous not to engage the troops that might come in sight, but to get what information they could and retire before them and report, so that the main body might be put in readiness for battle.[15]

A small group of young boys, many of them students at Carlisle Indian School, brilliantly delayed the army, buying more time for their families. Now the Lakotas could contemplate their next course of action, knowing it was unlikely an apprehensive army would advance any further toward the Badlands.

General Miles, furious at Forsyth's inept performance, wrote the adjutant general on February 4, 1891, Whether this is the result of incompetency and inexperience or whether it is misconduct in the presence of the enemy, I leave to the General of the Army or higher authorities to determine.[16] *The debacle at the mission added to the growing list of grievances Miles had against Forsyth.*

By evening the weary Ninth Cavalry finally had time to rest. According to historian Cyrus Townsend Brady, In thirty-four hours of elapsed time, the Ninth Cavalry had ridden one hundred and eight miles—the actual time in the saddle being twenty-two hours. They had fought two engagements and had rested only two hours. Marvelous to relate, there wasn't a sore-backed horse in the whole regiment. One horse died under the pressure, but aside from that and their fatigue, horses and men were in excellent condition.

That was probably the most famous ride ever performed by troops in the United States. For it Henry was recommended for a further brevet, as major-general—the sixth he had received.[17]

The eastern press treated the encounter near Drexel Mission as a major battle and reported that Forsyth was helplessly outnumbered and had to be rescued at the last minute.

Major Henry, who had ridden to Forsyth's rescue, felt compelled to write Forsyth:

Camp on White River, Jan. 5, 1891.

Gen. James W. Forsyth, Col., 7th Cavalry:

General: Will you please say to your officers that my officers and myself do not feel the service rendered your regiment, during the Mission engagement, as entitled to the consideration which seems to be accorded us by the newspapers. No such catastrophe as indicated seemed imminent, and we certainly are not desirous of gaining a little glory at the expense of our comrades. The entente cordiale between the officers of the

7th and ours is perfect and we hope the newspaper statements may not change the same.

Yours truly,
Guy V. Henry, Maj., 9th Cav., Comdg. Batt.

Forsyth cordially replied the next day, admitting that the Seventh had been pinned down:

Pine Ridge Agency, S.D., Jan. 6, 1891.

My Dear Col. Henry:

Your letter of yesterday received. Please accept our thanks for the spirit of kindness and good feeling in which it was written, and receive the assurance that the same feeling is reciprocated, and has not, nor can it be changed by any newspaper article. There is no doubt, however, that your 9th Cavalry timely arrival on the 30th aided materially in the withdrawal of my troops, for that moment it was hard to tell from which direction we were to expect the strongest force.

Very sincerely,
James W. Forsyth, Colonel 7th Cavalry.[18]

Forsyth's troops spent an uneasy night at Pine Ridge as Lakota snipers continued to fire into the agency. According to Ricker, Lt. A. W. Corliss, one of the artillery commanders, went to Brooke and asked him if he might not fire on the Indians as they were over back of Red Cloud's house and he told Brooke he was tired of having them firing on his 324 Co., as they were doing without replying.

Brooke replied, "No! No! If we fire on them what will the people in the East say?"[19]

By now the army knew it had a public relations crisis on its hands. The liberal press in the East was beginning to ask questions about the Wounded Knee Massacre, and the conservative press was demanding that the army take action against the Ghost dancers who had returned to the Badlands.

INTO THE BADLANDS

A few of the massacre survivors voluntarily went to Pine Ridge, some to stay, some for medical care, and some to pick up their rations and return to the Badlands. Among those who left the agency was Alice Ghost Horse. The next morning, *she says,* we got ready to leave and found Dog Chasing with two women [who] had come in sometime during the night. The men who rode out must have sent them in. With them upping our number to sixteen, we left bright and early, the men walking ahead a little ways. Very good fortune it was, for I was again riding a horse with my little brother, and Mother, on foot, was leading the horse.

Along the way, I must have dozed off and on, half asleep, half awake. I didn't know anything for awhile. When I became clear headed again, we were heading down a hill. Down at the bottom of the valley stood a log house with even a wooden floor, and a fire place which they fired up and we rested and got warmed up. Some daylight left, we started off again, covering some miles before dark.

It started to cloud up, clouds rolling in from the west and north, cloud waves seeming to roll over the high hills and valleys like water, from misty fine drops somewhere closer to a drizzle. It started, then the wind came, some minutes later it turned into a blizzard but one of the men had steered us toward a cabin which he had spotted from a butte some miles back. This blessed haven we reached along a creek, so we stayed warm sitting out the storm. We had plenty of meat from that last butchering to keep us fed.

Later in the night, their voices woke me up, loud voices, high pitched women arguments to scatter or stay together, the calmer voices of the male, sometimes whispering as we listened. I sat up in a hurry when a new meaning came to my senses. I got scared for the first time. My heart was beating faster, my breathing becoming shorter and harder. Quickly moving closer to my mother and squirming closer to Mother's body was to me natural as a cotton tail jumping from danger into it's lair.

The noise the women thought they heard was maybe a rumbling of horse running or of buffalo stampeding, maybe even cavalrymen. But it turned out that they may have heard something then imagined their fears into loud noises. For some time we just sat there, staring at the darkness, only the occasional flickering firelight and dying embers to see by. During the night, riders went some place and later they came back and said in a low voice, "It is time to go."

No one complained. All acted on instinct to survive. It was still cloudy and dark when we left the cabin. The men loaned us their horses, so some of us rode double. Sometimes the snow would blow but we kept on moving into a deep draw, where the wind wasn't blowing that much. So, we kept to the low lands.

Finally, we stumbled into a camp of Oglalas who ran away from Pine Ridge during the shooting. They were camped in a nice place among pine trees. At the end of the camp we came across Short Bull's tent. All of the people came to welcome us in, and [the] rest of the group were all taken in to different tents and were all fed good.[20]

Alice and what was left of her family remained at this camp for three months. There they began to piece their lives together, but the scars of Wounded Knee would remain with them for the rest of their lives.

A BURIAL DETAIL

In spite of the blizzard that blew into the area on the day after the massacre, many people visited the Wounded Knee Valley. Most were Lakotas hunting for survivors. Short Bull was one of the first. The next morning with four others, *he says*, we started for the battlefield. I was looking over the dead bodies and while so doing heard cannons in the distance in the direction of Clay Creek. I found one of my uncles who had been badly shot in the leg but not dead, who told me this, "All of the Indians had their guns and knives taken from them, and as I went to my lodge to get my knife to surrender it, the firing began. I was shot in the leg and have laid here ever since. I do not know where the women and children are."

So we hitched up four of the wagons we found here and put the horses to them, picking up all that we could find who were not dead—some forty odd—taking them to a deserted house nearby on the Wounded Knee Creek. Those whom we thought fatally wounded, we left here, and with the rest we started for our camp.[21]

Dr. Eastman also visited Wounded Knee after the massacre. On the third day it cleared, *he would later write*, and the ground was covered with an inch or two of fresh snow. We had feared that some of the Indian wounded might have been left on the field, and a number of us volunteered to go and see. I was placed in charge of the expedition of about a hundred civilians, ten or fifteen of whom were white men. We were supplied with wagons in which to convey any whom we might find still alive. Of course, a photographer and several reporters were of the party.

Fully three miles from the scene of the massacre, we found the body of a woman completely covered with a blanket of snow, and from this point on we found them scattered along as they had been relentlessly hunted down and slaughtered while fleeing for their lives. Some of our people discovered relatives or friends among the dead, and there was much wailing and mourning.

Eastman was not alone in reporting killings far from the Wounded Knee Valley. No one ever explained why these Miniconjous were killed, nor was any action taken against the officers who allowed this to happen.

When we reached the spot where the Indian camp had stood, *Eastman continues*, among the fragments of burned tents and other belongings, we saw the frozen bodies lying close together or piled one upon another. I counted eighty bodies of men who had been in the council and who were almost as helpless as the women and babes when the deadly fire began, for nearly all their guns had been taken from them.

It took all of my nerve to keep my composure in the face of this spectacle, and of the excitement and grief of my Indian companions, nearly every one of whom was crying aloud or singing his death song. The white men became very nervous, but I set them to examining and uncovering every body to see if one were living. Although they had been lying untended in the snow and cold for two days and nights, a number had survived.

Among them I found a baby of about a year old warmly wrapped and entirely unhurt. I brought her in, and she was afterward adopted and educated by an army officer [General Colby]. One man who was severely wounded begged me to fill his pipe. When we brought him into the chapel he was welcomed by his wife and daughters with cries of joy, but he died a day or two later.

Under a wagon I discovered an old woman, totally blind and entirely helpless. A few had managed to crawl away to some place of shelter, and we found in a log store nearby several who were badly hurt and others who had died after reaching there. After we had dispatched several wagon loads to the agency, we observed groups of warriors watching us from adjacent buttes; probably friends of the victims who had come there for the same purpose as ourselves. A majority of our party, fearing an attack, insisted that someone ride back to the agency for an escort of soldiers, and as mine was the best horse, it fell to me to go. I covered the eighteen miles in quick time and was not interfered with in any way, although if the Indians had meant mischief they could easily have picked me off from any of the ravines and gulches.

Eastman admits, All this was a severe ordeal for one who had so lately put all his faith in the Christian love and lofty ideals of the white man. Yet I passed no hasty judgment, and was thankful that I might be of some service and relieve even a small part of the suffering. . . . We worked on.

The desolate doctor returned to Pine Ridge and continued to attend the wounded. There, he says, Bishop Hare of South Dakota visited us, and was overcome by faintness when he entered his Mission chapel, thus transformed into a rude hospital.[22]

On entering the church, *Bishop Hare says,* two sights presented themselves. On the church floor, instead of pews on either side of the aisle, two rows of bleeding, groaning, wounded men, women, and children; tending them two military surgeons and a native physician assisted by the missionary and his helpers, assiduity and tenderness marking all. Above, the Christmas green was still hanging. To one of my moods they seemed a mockery to all my faith and hope; to another they seemed an inspiration still singing, though in a minor key, "Peace, good will to men."[23]

Elaine Goodale says that in the days that followed, Most of the injuries had proved mortal. A few more wounded wandered in on foot or were picked up alive on the third day under a fall of fresh snow. But even if not crippled, nearly all of the survivors were heart-broken and apathetic.

Several orphaned children found good homes. A baby girl, taken by Dr. Eastman from her dead mother's breast, was adopted by Colonel L. W. Colby and his wife who brought up and educated her.[24]

Paddy Starr, who had been at the massacre, was hired to oversee the burial of the Miniconjou dead, a task that began on December 30. According to Ricker, Starr made his contract with General Miles and was paid two dollars for every body interred. Starr says 168 were put into the grave. Three women who were killed were pregnant. His party found seven living—five grown and two little children, infants. One of the latter was badly frozen. He thinks it lived; he handed it over to Jon Harrison, a Mexican, and told him to take it over to Red Bear's house.[25]

Anthropologist James Mooney, after interviewing many participants, angrily wrote, It is a commentary on our boasted Christian civilization that although there were two or three salaried missionaries at the agency, not one went out to say a prayer over the poor mangled bodies of these victims of war.

The Catholic priests had reasons for not being present, *Mooney concedes,* as one of them, Father Craft, was lying in the hospital with a dangerous wound received on the battlefield while bravely administering to the dying wants of the soldiers in the heat of the encounter, and the other, Father Jutz, an old man of seventy years, was at the Mission school five miles away, still attending to his little flock of a hundred children as before the trouble began, and unaware of what was transpiring at the agency. *The other priests, including Father Perrig, were hiding from sniper fire aimed at Pine Ridge.*

The burial of the dead took place on the knoll where the Hotchkiss guns had rained fire into the valley. There, Mooney says, a long trench was dug, and into it was thrown all the bodies, piled one upon another like so much cordwood, until the pit was full. When the earth was heaped over them and the funeral was complete, many of the bodies were stripped by the whites, who went out in order to get the Ghost shirts, and the frozen, bodies were thrown into the trench stiff and naked. They were only dead Indians. As one of the burial party said, "It was a thing to melt the heart of a man, if it was of stone, to see those little children, with their bodies shot to pieces, thrown naked into the pit."

The dead soldiers had already been brought in and buried decently at the agency. When the writer visited the spot the following winter, the Indians had put up a wire fence around the trench and smeared the posts with sacred red medicine paint.[26]

Reporter Charles W. Allen returned to the site of the massacre, but his intention was to hunt for souvenirs. According to the "Chadron (NE) *Democrat,"* C. W. Allen came over from the agency Sunday evening, and spent Monday in the city. He brought with him several articles taken from the dead body of an Indian brave, whose lamp of life was extinguished at Wounded Knee, Dec. 29th. These articles were placed on exhibition in the Main Street window of the Bank of Chadron, and was quite an attraction for the hundreds of people who passed the place Monday afternoon.[27]

Allen was not the only scavenger to visit the valley; the Lakotas would be fighting for years to regain lost family possessions. One of their proponents in this quest was Maj. James McLaughlin.

Luther Standing Bear felt he had to go to Wounded Knee and ignored government orders to stay at his agency. Three or four days later, *he writes,* I started over to find out how bad the reports were which we had heard about the fight. My father and mother and their family were at Pine Ridge at this time, and I had heard nothing from them. It had snowed in the meantime, and the weather was very cold. It meant a ride of thirty miles on horseback, but I had a good horse, plenty of warm clothing, and I did not mind the jaunt.

When I arrived at the place where the fight had occurred between the Indians and the soldiers, all the bodies had been removed. Here and there lay the body of a horse. The tipi poles were broken and lay scattered about in heaps. Cooking utensils were strewed around in confusion; old wagons were overturned, with the tongues broken off. Everything was confusion. It was early in the morning when I reached this place, and the silence was oppressive and terrible.

There were many little pools of water here and there, some with clear water and others red with the blood of my people. I was enraged enough at this sight to shoot anyone, but nobody was to be seen. The place of death was forsaken and forbidding. I stood there in silence for several minutes, in reverence for the dead, and then turned and rode toward the agency.[28]

As the burial of the Lakotas took place, the "Chadron Democrat"'s editorial writer jeered: For once it has occurred that more Indians than soldiers have been slain, and we doubt not but that either General Miles or Brooke will be cashiered from the service as was General Harney for such pitiless bloodshed. Nothing will be done about the poor soldiers who were slain, but the Indian department is undoubtedly already getting in its work upon some crank of a congressman to present a bill before that august and wise (?) body to investigate the cause that led to the late massacre (?) and uncalled for (?) slaughter of such dear, good

Indians as were "Tomahawk That Kills," "Moon That Steals Horses," "Scalps All," "Eagle That Skins Alive," "Hawk Burns Alive," "Gall Wants All," "Buffalo That Kills The Babe" and a host more who are now really both defacto and de jure good Indians, not made so, however, by their religious training, but by good and well-directed shots and cuts lately administered by the Seventh and Ninth Cavalry. We glory in the revenge of the Seventh, although they sustained a heavy loss, and notwithstanding there may have been but a few in the late fight left who belonged to the Seventh during Custer's life, they nevertheless belong by name to a regiment which was at one time commanded by a soldier of national reputation as an Indian fighter and who, in 1876, with his entire command was cut to atoms by Sitting Bull's warriors and probably participated in by several of the Big Foot gang who bit dust a few days ago. We predict that the killing of Big Foot and his warriors will have a telling effect on the Messiah craze, and will civilize more reds who are yet alive than all the power of God and education that has been pumped into them for the past 16 years.[29]

THE BODY COUNT

How many Miniconjous and Huṅkpapas died at Wounded Knee? There were several tallies, and none agree.

On the afternoon of December 30, Miles telegraphed General Schofield: General Brooke telegraphs as follows: Colonel Forsyth says sixty-two dead Indian men were counted on the plain where the attempt was made to disarm Big Foot's band and where the fight began. On other parts of the ground, there were eighteen more. These did not include those killed in the ravines, where dead warriors were seen but not counted. Six were brought in badly wounded and six others with a party of twenty-three men and women, which Captain Jackson had to abandon when attacked by one hundred fifty Brulé Indians from the agency. This accounts for the ninety-two killed and leaves but a few alive and unhurt.

The women and children broke for the hills when the fight commenced and comparatively few of them were hurt and few brought in. Thirty-nine are here [at Pine Ridge] of which twenty-one are wounded. Had it not been for the attack by the Brulés, an accurate account would have been made, but the ravines were not searched afterwards. The result, I think, shows very little cause for apprehension from Big Foot's band in the future.[30]

On December 31 Forsyth revised his initial estimate in a lengthy report that included the following table:

WHITES

Killed	*Wounded*
Capt. G. D. Wallace	1st Lieut. E. A. Garlington
6 noncommissioned officers	1st Lieut. J. C. Gresham
18 privates	2nd Lieut. H. L. Hawthorne
	11 noncommissioned officers
	22 privates

INDIANS

Killed	*Wounded*
83 bucks, in and near camp	8 bucks, brought to agency
7 bucks, by pursuing party	5 bucks, abandoned by pursuing party
	10 squaws and children, abandoned by pursuing party, 27 squaws and children, brought to agency

[*Note*: All of the white men killed or wounded were of the Seventh Cavalry, except 2nd Lt. H. L. Hawthorne of the Second Artillery and hospital steward Oscar Pollak.]

Source: U.S. Adjutant General, "Report of the Investigation," 111.

In his report he stated that 90 Miniconjou males were killed out of an attacking force of 125. This was 35 fewer than Miles had claimed. Forsyth lists no casualties for the women and children in Big Foot's band, again insisting, From the first instant the squaws started for the hills and it is my belief that comparatively few of them were injured.[31]

Forsyth wrote this despite knowing that nearly forty wounded Miniconjous lay dying within sight of his camp and despite allowing his officers to attack the women and children of Big Foot's band for more than four hours even though most of the men had died in the first few minutes of fighting.

On the day of the massacre, Royer telegraphed the commissioner of Indian Affairs with a more accurate count than those issued after the massacre: On Wounded Knee Creek this morning, while the soldiers were disarming Big Foot and his band after their surrender, a fight took place, which resulted in the killing of about three hundred Indians and several soldiers, including Captain Wallace, with a number wounded.[32]

The first official army body count was made on January 3. Capt. F. A. Whitney of the Eighth Cavalry writes, I have the honor to report I have examined the ground where the fight with Big Foot's band occurred and counted the number of Indians killed and wounded, also number of ponies and horses, with the following result: eighty-two bucks and one boy killed, two bucks badly wounded, forty squaws killed, one squaw wounded, one blind squaw unhurt; four small children and one papoose killed; forty bucks and seven women were killed in camp; twenty-five bucks, ten women, and two children in the canyon near and on one side of the camp; the balance were found in the hills; fifty-eight horses and ponies and one burro were found dead.

Whitney admits, The large number of dead animals suggests that the Hotchkiss and rifle fire were widespread and may not have been concentrated on specific targets. There is evidence that a great number of bodies have been removed. Since the snow, wagon tracks were made near where it is supposed dead or wounded Indians had been lying. The camp and bodies of the Indians had been more or less plundered before my command arrived here. I prohibited anything being removed from the bodies of the Indians or the camp.[33]

Whitney's count of 122 was far less than the number of bodies buried in the mass grave.

In his interview with Ricker, Joseph Horn Cloud, listing only those he knew by name, identified 185 of the dead and 103 survivors.[34] *His list is probably incomplete since it was drawn from memory.*

After interviewing a number of survivors, Dr. Melvin R. Gilmore concluded, There were about four hundred people in Big Foot's band. There were 126 men, counting boys. Of the victims there were 164 bodies buried at Wounded Knee. There were about one hundred survivors. The rest are not accounted for. They must have died in the prairie. Some of the bodies were found in Bad River, considerably more than one hundred miles away. Some of the wounded girls got back to the Cheyenne River still further away, but they afterwards died of their wounds and exposure.[35]

General Colby confirms this, stating, Most of the women and children were found killed and wounded at a distance of from a quarter to a half mile from the camp, showing they had attempted to escape after the fight began.[36]

Commissioner Morgan's statement agrees: Most of the men, including Big Foot, were killed around his tent, where he lay sick. The bodies of the women and children were scattered along a distance of two miles from the scene of the encounter.[37]

The army insisted that few women and children were killed and attempted to explain the scattering of the dead bodies by saying these were wounded Lakotas who had crawled away from the battlefield or who had been removed by relatives.

FEARS OF RETALIATION

We got back to the agency allright, *Crickett writes, after the fracas at the mission,* but it was now the work . . . to dig trenches as we expected a midnight attack. Had to bag in them night after night with a chain guard about a thousand yards in front with orders not to fire but to retreat and draw them on and then they would of got a warm reception, but Oh it was bitter cold, but they never came as they are superticious and think if they get killed at night they wont go to the happy hunting ground.

The day following, Sunday, things being a little quiet we commenced to think of the dead. A lot of us went to work and made thirty coffins (Just a pine box nailed together) as that was the number we had dead by this time. We got finished about one, the funeral being at two. It was a mournful sight to see us go to the little cemetry about half mile away from camp (mounted and well armed). What few white people that was there payed their last respects to the dead, but Oh it was a terrible day snow, rain, and sleet and as it came down it froze to our clothes, a more miserable and cold day I never experienced, but at last it was over and we marched back to camp. Evry one seemed low spirited and down hearted—the camp was like one deserted. This is the first funeral (Military) I was ever at where they did not fire three vollies over the grave. They were afraid of scaring the few friendly Indians that was on the reservation.[38]

The dead of the Seventh Cavalry were buried on December 31. Like Crickett, the "New York Times," described the scene as desolate: Amid as wild, blinding, and bitter a Winter's storm as ever swept this bleak and barren country, were laid away to their last rest thirty of the brave boys who fell with face to the foe in the bloody encounter at Wounded Knee. It was two o'clock, when the funeral cortege, with General Forsyth and Major Whitside at the head, and composed of fifteen wagons bearing the dead, followed by an escort of Companies A, K, B, I, D, and E of the noble but unfortunate Seventh Cavalry, together with an assisting squad from the Second Cavalry, wound away from the camp up to the little cemetery, situated at the crest of the hill northeast of the agency.

The graves were in rows of six, close together, in the southwest corner of the cemetery and overlooking the camp. After the reading of the burial service by Reverend Mr. Cook, the Episcopal clergyman here, aided by his assistant, the bodies were lowered into the grave. Owing to the intensely critical condition of the surroundings with hordes of the enemy flocking about the agency threatening an attack, the usual salute of guns was omitted.[39]

The army had little reason to be fearful. The Lakotas were intent on distancing themselves from the terrible firepower that destroyed Big Foot's band. Luther Standing Bear writes, Those who had not at first believed in the Ghost Dance ran away with these Indians who were bound for the Badlands. After they had seen what the soldiers did to their friends and relatives, they were not taking any more chances.

In the Badlands they had plenty of wood and water, but they needed meat. Some of the braves sneaked out in the night and rounded up all the cattle they could find and drove them into their place of retreat.

Everybody in the camp now felt safe, as they had plenty of everything to supply their needs. They could dance when they pleased, and they had no agent from whom to ask permission. They were not under obligations to the government for supplies, as they now had all they wanted. They kept two scouts posted at the entrance to the Badlands day and night, so there was no chance of interference without being seen. The soldiers did not even try to come near them. They knew better!

The troops realized that the Indians who had guns knew how to use them. Those who had bows and arrows were experts in their use. The Indians were really better armed than at the time they wiped out Custer, fourteen years previously. Had the soldiers tried at the time to enter the Badlands, there would have been many deaths on both sides.[40]

There were depredations as the Lakotas left their fortress to find food; but, according to Colby, these depredations only affected other Lakotas. The ranches of friendly Indians outside the agency were besieged and sacked by hostile bands, *the general wrote.* A friendly Indian village, a few miles distant, was totally destroyed, and an out-building at the Catholic Mission was burned.

Great excitement also prevailed among the settlers and Indians in Dakota, Nebraska and Wyoming. Homes and farms were deserted and the towns were filled with refugees. Local militia companies were organized and officered, and provided with what ammunition could be obtained. A general war, involving not only the so-called hostiles, but the friendly Indians as well, seemed imminent.[41]

The concerns over a winter war were groundless. Of the four thousand "hostiles" who had fled Pine Ridge, fewer than fifteen hundred were warriors. The army militia outnumbered the Lakotas in the Stronghold five to one. Even though the numerical odds were in the army's favor, a waiting game seemed in order. Miles did not want the army to suffer any more casualties or embarrassment.

Feeling his presence was needed at Pine Ridge, Miles left his comfortable headquarters in Rapid City. It was reported on December 31, General Miles will leave this morning by special train for Pine Ridge. The train will leave Rapid City at six o'clock. The general expects serious trouble, and in an interview with a [*Rapid City* (SD)] *Journal* reporter last night expressed it as his opinion that the willingness of the Indians to go into the agency bodes no good. He expects the Indians will make a last grand struggle at the point, and are concentrating their forces for that purpose. He proposes to be there and direct operations in person, and proposes to bring the present troubles to an immediate close, even if the Sioux nation does have to suffer.[42]

Once Miles arrived at Pine Ridge, he sent Brooke into the field with the Second Infantry and began to organize a cordon around the Ghost dancers in the Stronghold, designing his deployment so it would tighten day by day and discourage foraging parties. The objective was to starve the Ghost dancers out of the Badlands and toward Pine Ridge while he negotiated for their surrender.

ARMY CROSS FIRE

As Miles tightened his noose and negotiated, he set out to court-martial Forsyth. Wells attributed the charges Miles brought against Forsyth to a bitter feud that existed between the two men.[43] *Whether this is true or not, Miles openly and repeatedly condemned Forsyth's actions.*

On January 4 Miles relieved Forsyth of his command and ordered a court of inquiry. In issuing his order he stated he was acting "by the direction of the President." *Schofield, wanting to avoid open criticism of the army, urgently telegraphed Miles,* It was not the intention of the President to appoint a Court of Inquiry. . . . You were expected yourself first to inquire into the facts and in the event of its being disclosed that there had been unsoldierly conduct to relieve the responsible officer.[44]

In spite of Schofield's reprimand, Miles convened a court of inquiry on January 7. Presiding were Maj. J. Ford Kent, division inspector general, and Capt. Frank D. Baldwin, the acting inspector general.

The careers of Forsyth and his officers were on the line, but they had the advantage of being the only persons who were at Wounded Knee who were allowed to give testimony. No enlisted men were called to testify, and only two Lakotas—Frog and Celene Not Help Them—were asked to give testimony, and they did not appear in person. Instead, their brief testimonies were witnessed by Episcopal missionary Charles Cook and Wells. Both blamed the medicine man for inciting the first shots. Two civilians testified—Wells and Father Craft. Wells, who was in the army's employ, side-

stepped the issue of attacks on women and children. Years later, he was much more critical of what happened at Wounded Knee.

Forsyth's officers were repeatedly asked if their troops intentionally fired at women and children. Each officer asserted that his troops made every effort to avoid firing on women and children, but their testimony was contradicted again and again by the statements of Miniconjou survivors, civilians, and William Fitch Kelley.

The first to testify was Major Whitside. He was asked:

Q: What orders, if any, were given to prevent the loss of life among the non-combatants?

A: None that I know of.

Q: What efforts were made on the part of the officers, that came under your observation, to prevent the loss of life alluded to, other than you have stated?

A: Every effort was made by the officers and men to protect the women and children when they were separated from the bucks or when they were recognized.

Whitside then admitted, The first fire of the Indians themselves could not, but by a miracle, have resulted in anything else than a loss of life to women and children. After the break of the Indians many of them, men and women, got on their ponies, and it is impossible to tell buck from squaw at a little distance, when mounted.[45]

Capt. Myles Moylan swore, I think the killing of the women and children was entirely unavoidable for the reason that when the bucks broke, a large number of them made a rush for this ravine, and in order to get there they had to pass through the tipis where the women and children were. I would say, in addition, that I repeatedly heard cautions given by both officers and non-commissioned officers not to shoot squaws and children, and cautioning the men individually that such and such Indians were squaws.[46]

Lt. W. J. Nicholson of Troop I stated, I saw many instances of humanity on the part of our men, particularly towards children. I saw one trooper, with a child in his arms, going towards the women, by orders, to deliver it to a place of safety.[47]

Surgeon John van Hoff, who had joined in the attack, admitted that elsewhere during the fighting, The men, as soon as they got a glimpse of the Indians through the brush, fired about six shots. I heard the wailing of a child, and stopped the firing as quickly as possible. My men had killed one boy about sixteen or seventeen years old, a squaw and two children.[48]

Second Lt. Sedgwick Rice testified, Lieutenant Sickel, who was in command of the Troop, and myself, gave repeated orders to the Troop not to shoot at these Indians, because they were women and children, but to direct their fire on the herd of ponies. Our orders were obeyed. . . . I saw a number of killed and wounded Indians, who were principally bucks.

After the fight was over, I was ordered up with E Troop to pick up our dead. I met with two Indian scouts and showed them where the killed and wounded Indians were, as far as possible. There was one wounded squaw there, who had cut her throat and who was in the last throes of death when I went up to her; my men picked up two Indian children, who were alive, unhurt, and I turned them over to the Indian scouts with orders to turn them over to the Indian women captives.[49]

Lt. Charles W. Taylor said, One of my scouts came to me and told me that he thought there were women and children in the ravine. I spoke to Captain Jackson and Captain Edgerly, and they stopped the fire of the men.[50]

Capt. C. S. Ilsley conceded, I might say, in the general rush of the bucks, it was impossible for the men to distinguish the bucks from the squaws. After they became scattered, I heard several times men say, "Look out, don't shoot, that is a squaw."[51]

When asked what precautions he took to avoid killing women and children, the commander of C Troop, Capt. Henry Jackson, replied, I saw a party of eight or nine women and children, who kept bunched together; I saw they were women because they had their children with them; and, right there, cautioned the men not to fire on them; a party of my Troop conducted them to a place of safety.[52]

Capt. W. S. Edgerly, curtly replied to his questioner, I don't know that my men fired at a squaw. I had no occasion to caution my men.[53]

Lt. W. W. Robinson Jr., stated, During the fight at different times I heard officers several times caution their men not to fire upon women or children or in any way injure the wounded bucks, and rode down once myself and cautioned the men on that point.[54]

Lt. T. Q. Donaldson Jr. made almost the same statement, testifying, I had repeatedly ordered my men not to fire on squaws, and this order was obeyed throughout the day.[55]

Lt. S. R. H. Tompkins admitted, Generally speaking, men and women were so mingled that it was impossible to destroy the bucks without endangering the women and children. This was at the first break, but while in the ravine we took particular pains not to fire on women and children.[56]

Capt. Allyn Capron of the First Artillery, who commanded the Hotchkiss battery on Cemetery Hill, admitted, I would state in conclusion that it was impossible to prevent killing squaws, for our own protection, as the bucks were mixed up promiscuously with them. *He added*, They must have killed some of their own women and children.[57]

Capt. H. J. Nowlan stated, It came under my personal observation during that day that it was the cry all over the field, both on the part of officers and enlisted men, not to kill women or children—"Don't fire, let them go, they are squaws."[58]

What makes these testimonies suspect, aside from their marked similarity, is that the army had previously admitted that fewer than thirty Miniconjou men and boys survived the first melee. Why did Forsyth's men persist in their attack when their opposition was so small? And why were so many bodies found as far as two miles from the battlefield? Those questions have never been answered.

Also not explained—or mentioned—during the hearing was the atrocity committed by Captain Godfrey's men, even though Baldwin's report of it was attached to the hearings typescript.

The second major issue in the investigation was whether Forsyth's disposition of troops led to soldiers being killed in their own cross fire. Most of the officers denied that troops had fired on each other, but a few broke rank and disagreed with their commander's disposition of troops.

Whitside was asked:

Q: Who ordered the disposition of the Troop?

A: General Forsyth.

Q: Can you tell what necessitated such a disposition of the troops and why it was made, or what object was in mind?

A: The peaceful disarmament of the Indians.

Q: When you posted Troops D and K . . . did you take into consideration what seems to be the inevitable fact that when they might be forced to fire on the Indians, as they were in front of them, you endangered the lives of the men and animals of Troop G and some parts of Troops A and I?

A: It was not thought of by me at the time that it would endanger the lives of anyone.[59]

At the same investigation, Hoff hedged when he was asked:

Q: Do you think any of our own troops were wounded by the fire from our troops during the engagement?

A: I have not the slightest reason to know or think that any men were wounded by our own bullets. I desire to state that as a general principle it was possible that some men might have been so wounded, but there is no reason or evidence that came under my observation whatever to show that such was the case.[60]

When Captain Ilsley was asked if the troops' placement was judicious, he candidly replied:

A: I don't think it was. I think . . . the troops should have been on one side and the Indians on the other. I don't refer to the nature of the ground but the nature of the case. If General Forsyth received orders to disarm Big Foot's band right on the ground where the council was held, the flank towards G Troop left open, would have, in my opinion, made the disposition different. I think that then G Troop should not have been there.[61]

Capt. Charles B. Ewing, an army surgeon, shared Ilsley's opinion. He testified, I have every reason to believe that some of our men were killed by the fire of other of our troops. I base it from the position of the troops. The most injury was inflicted upon Captain Wallace's Troop K, and there was another troop which suffered almost as severely, I think it was Captain Varnum's Troop B. One out of every eight was wounded or killed taking the number of troops to be fifty strong each. There were about twenty-five killed from all the troops and a large number of wounded; located as the troops were and firing as they did it was impossible not to wound or kill each other.[62]

Captain Capron, whose artillery may have fired on his comrades, also hedged his testimony: I think it was unavoidable that some of our own troops should have been hurt from our own fire, but I could not swear definitely that such was the case.[63]

Even General Scott, writing years later in defense of Forsyth's command, admitted, The men of the guard were in a very precarious position should any fighting begin, and this was reflected in their losses: Troop A, five killed and five wounded; Troop I [Crickett's], four killed and six wounded.[64]

In his final report, Baldwin observed that when it appeared the women were packing for escape, Every precautionary measure should have been observed, such as securing the ponies, moving the warriors beyond the reach of their tipis and unmasking K and B Troops, who were within thirty yards of the warriors, and K Troop almost in among the tipis, also by a change of the position of the troops that would be instantly effective, either in an offensive or defensive movement or action. None of these precautions were taken.[65]

Baldwin also stated that Miles's order, "Hold them at a safe distance from your command, guard against surprise or treachery," was entirely disregarded and lost sight of by Colonel Forsyth when in the exercise of his own judgment under the firm belief that the Indians contemplated no outbreak, he placed his troops in such close proximity to the hostile camp.[66]

Despite the negative comments regarding Forsyth's disposition of troops and Baldwin's summation, on January 18 Forsyth was exonerated of all charges.

Miles was furious. On January 31 he submitted his own statement to the report. He wrote, It is in fact difficult to conceive how a worse disposition of the troops could have been made. . . . [That] a large number of the 106 warriors were without firearms when the outbreak occurred is shown by the evidence that forty-eight guns had been taken from the tipis, and that a personal search of twenty or more warriors resulted in finding them unarmed. This fact taken in conjunction with the extremely injudicious disposition of the troops, and the large number of casualties among them, constrains the belief that some of these casualties were suffered at the hands of our own men.[67]

When combined with Forsyth's count of 90 dead Lakotas at the council site, Miles's statement that there were only 106 fighting men in Big Foot's band suggests that Forsyth spent the bulk of the morning and all of the afternoon attacking women and children defended by fewer than thirty men and boys.

On February 4 Schofield wrote the secretary of war rejecting Miles's condemnation of Forsyth's disposition:

> The interests of the military service do not, in my judgment, demand any farther proceedings in this case, nor any longer continuance of Colonel Forsyth's suspension from the command of his regiment.
>
> The evidence of these papers shows that great care was taken by the officers and generally by the enlisted men to avoid unnecessary killing of Indian women and children in the affair at Wounded Knee, and shows that the conduct of the Seventh Cavalry under very trying circumstances was characterized by excellent discipline and, in many cases, by great forbearance. In my judgment the conduct of the regiment was well worthy of the commendation bestowed upon it by me in my first telegram after the engagement.
>
> J. M. Schofield
> Maj. Gen. Commanding.[68]

The criticism of Forsyth's behavior and tactics were swept under the table, and there was no further investigation of his actions. When three officers and fifteen enlisted men were awarded the Medal of Honor for their actions during the massacre, Miles's statement was further repudiated.[69]

Also ignored were the accusations of heavy drinking among the officers and enlisted men of the Seventh Cavalry, even though several Lakotas and a few whites insisted it played a part in the conduct of the troops and, especially, in the decisions Forsyth made. White civilians who claimed the men had been drinking were never called.

Were the troops disciplined for firing upon Big Foot's band? This, too, was never addressed in the inquiry. John Shangrau, who was present on the day of the massacre, observed: In the sudden breaking down of patience and restraint, the soldiers showed deficiency in discipline, the commanding officer had issued no order to fire; but the action commenced and went on in the spirit of total destruction—soldiers beyond all common decency eagerly and irregularly pursuing women and children upon the hills and shooting them to death without remorse or mercy. To say the affair was badly managed would be giving it too much dignity of description. It was not managed at all. More particularly in the beginning, and after it was underway, the men had too much freedom, for they did not seem capable of Christian impulse to spare life in cases where it ought not be taken.

Like a magazine touched off by secret means, there was an explosion; then the disaster ran its wild ungovernable rage. If men would speak afar the sodden field concerning the causes and certain of the actions, they were hushed up, and silence enjoined. That utterance in relation to some of the features that might excite inquisition was hedged about by prudential limits is not to be wondered at, for it is apparent that there was no want of necessity for caution.[70]

Who was telling the truth? Some historians accept the sworn statements of Forsyth and his officers as definitive descriptions of what happened at Wounded Knee. But in the years that followed the massacre, many Miniconjou survivors testified to their experiences in sworn statements or interviews. Even though many of the testimonies bear up under examination and cross-checking, they have never been given full credence. The Miniconjous' point of view is perhaps best expressed by the statement survivor Joseph Black Hair made during interviews conducted by James H. McGregor:

I, the man that stand here, am a God-fearing man. Therefore all things that I at this time speak of will be voiced by me in accordance with His command to me. Later when He judges the truth and that which is not the truth, I do not want Him to judge me for anything that may be untrue. I fear this.

It is our understanding that the reports of the soldiers state that we, the Indians that participated in this affair, fired the first shot and caused injury. This is understood in this country as such to this day. It is further stated that the reasons given we were fired upon was that while they were disarming us, an Indian with a blanket wrapped about him stood at the end. When they came near him, he all at once pulled out from under his blanket a gun which he kept concealed and with it killed a soldier. For this reason they fired upon those that were gathered in the center. This is the report made by soldiers and is known and repeated by others over the country.

Our relatives that were killed were all believers in God, and nearly all belonged to some church. These records are still in some of the churches they belonged to. Some of the older men [were] also at one time U.S. government scouts. I want this affair to be righted. Hereafter if you desire any survivors to make a statement of the facts he or she knows . . . let them take a sworn oath before God that they are telling the truth.

Now, I will raise my hand to God and swear that what I am telling is what I saw and what they actually done to us.[71]

OPPOSING POINTS OF VIEW

Ricker, indignant after interviewing survivors of the massacre, wrote in his notes, Suppose I say that it was an accident. Why should the soldiers have fired when no shots had been poured into them? Was there no authority and no discipline among the officers and soldiers? Could they not wait 'till the recalcitrant Indians, or Indians who forcibly refused to deliver their guns, were overcome or restrained? It is said Indians in the council arose when the first shot occurred. Was it not natural that they should do so without intention to fight? The action of the troops was over-hasty, premature, and more like a mob than trained soldiers.

Ricker goes on to compare the Battle of the Little Bighorn with the massacre at Wounded Knee, passing judgment on what he believed had happened: The whites in speaking of the two events—when the whites got the worst of it—it was a *massacre*; when the Indians got the worst of it, it was a *battle*. The Indians understand that on the Little Big Horn, they were defending themselves—their village, their property, their lives, their women, and children. They understand that at Wounded Knee, they were attacked wantonly, cruelly, brutally, and that what little fighting they did was in self-defense.[72]

After spending the last years of his life interviewing Lakotas and whites who were at the massacre, Ricker finally concluded, The affair at Wounded Knee was a drunken slaughter of white soldiers and innocent Indians—for which the white man was responsible solely.[73]

Forsyth had defenders in and out of the army, and they were equally eloquent. The "Chadron Democrat" voiced its indignation when it heard there was going to be an inquiry into Forsyth's actions, exclaiming, When the news first reached this city that Colonel Forsyth, who commanded the troops at Wounded Knee, had been suspended pending an investigation, but few people believed the report. Of course, everybody knew that the War Department, as well as the Interior Department, has been piling up errors at Pine Ridge, but no one supposed the climax would be capped with such a move as this.

Later reports, however, prove that the colonel has been suspended, the grounds being that at Wounded Knee a large number of squaws and children were killed, and that he had the cavalry drawn up in such a way that many of the boys in blue were killed by their comrades. The first is a nonsensical charge; we doubt if any army officer could distinguish a squaw from a buck at a distance of ten paces, unless it be in times of peace when the Indians are out on "dress parade." Besides, bucks, squaws and children were in the thickest of the fight, and it is a wonder that any of them got out alive.

As to the other charge, we are unable to discern how a body of men can be surrounded without the surrounding party being on all sides of them. The Indians were surrounded, when they began firing, and, of course, the soldiers either had to return the fire, or be shot down like dogs, or make a break for the agency. These soldiers were Custer's old men, and they are not built for running, unless the enemy is behind them.

We believe a very grave error was made when Colonel Forsyth was suspended, and unless he is at once reinstated it will probably prove a dampener on the balance of the officers at Pine Ridge. If every officer expects to be called upon to show cause why he killed certain Indians in battle there will probably be but few battles. It will take longer to clean out the hostiles in the way it is now being done—one at a time as they show their heads—but it may be a much better way if the officers wish to escape a court martial.[74]

The editorial writer does not ask why the Seventh Cavalry had been placed at such a disadvantage by its commander.

It was reported in the "Army and Navy Journal" that Rev. D. R. Lowell, D. D., chaplain at Fort Riley, Kas., made a most vigorous and well deserved assault in his sermon of Jan. 7 upon the newspaper critics of the noble 7th Cavalry. Not more forcibly than truthfully the reverend gentleman said: "These attacks are villainous—villainous, because so utterly unjust. The facts show that the troops acted with consummate skill and wisdom. The officers commanding these troops are gentlemen, humane and tender in all their instincts, unusually refined and cultured, the farthest removed from cruelty and inhumanity."[75]

ONE LAST ACT OF VENGEANCE

Most upsetting to the army forces was the death of popular Lt. Edward W. Casey. According to the correspondent for the "Army and Navy Journal" some Lakotas went to Casey's camp and asked him to go to their camp. On January 7, he started up with two Cheyenne scouts. He was met near the village by some Oglala and a nephew of Red Cloud, Pete, who had been sent out by Red Cloud to advise him not to come in. With this party was a Brulé, a "hostile." Lieutenant Casey started to go back when the Brulé shot him, the ball entering at the back of the head and coming out the forehead.

The Cheyenne scouts failed to avenge his death, notwithstanding their loyalty. The belt and two pistols were taken off Casey's body and offered to Cheyenne scouts, Pete, and the Brulé in succession, all declining except the latter, who took them into camp. Later the Cheyenne scouts got the body, which had not been mutilated.[76]

Lt. Alexander R. Piper relates Casey's death to Red Cloud's capture. Casey, *he wrote his wife*, I understand, is an Indian enthusiast (crank, I think) and thought he could go to the Indian camp and not be hurt. He started out with some of his scouts to go to see Red Cloud who is held by the Brulés as a prisoner.

Soon after leaving General Brooke's camp he was met by some half breeds who told him he would be shot just as sure as he went in that direction. He pooh-poohed the advice and went on; he had notified Red Cloud of his intention and Red Cloud sent his son-in-law to stop him, telling him he would be killed and also that he (Casey) would ruin his (Red Cloud's) chances of escape the very next day. This messenger also warned Casey to turn back, but like most philanthropists he was blinded by his own ideas.

When about half way to the hostiles' camp he was stopped by two Brulés, an old buck and a young fellow. They parleyed for a few minutes and then seeing his chance the young fellow shot Casey in the back. The Cheyenne scout (only one) with him did nothing as he says he would have been killed by the other had he killed either of the Brulés, more truth than fiction, but rather cowardly.

The Brulés took Casey's watch, trousers and revolver and then told the Cheyenne he could take the horse and go, which he did, leaving the body there. *Piper concludes*, This was told me by the scout who brought the telegram from General Brooke and is straight goods.[77]

Red Cloud escaped shortly after the incident. In a letter to T. A. Bland the aged chief wrote, Three nights ago [January 9] my family and He Dog and White Hawk and families, all made our escape very late at night while they all sleep, and we got right to the agency, and I reported all about it to General Miles.[78]

Grief over the death of popular Lieutenant Casey often manifested itself in anger against the Lakotas. An unidentified officer bitterly complained to the "Army and Navy Journal," Education has done much for the Sioux. A Carlisle student killed Lieutenant Casey; the Carlisle boys were at the head of those in the Badlands, and have been most active in deviltry. If a few educated ones can do so much mischief, what will be the result by a more extensive education? The ultimatum given to Indians to surrender their arms, if carried out, will result in the delivery of old pieces and hiding of the good.[79]

Frederic Remington learned of Casey's death during his return to the East. He wrote, A nasty little Brulé Sioux had made his coup, and shot away the life of a man who would have gained his stars in modern war as naturally as most of his fellows would their eagles. He had shot away the life of an accomplished man; the best friend the Indians had; a man who did not know "fear"; a young man beloved by his comrades, respected by his generals and by the Secretary of War. The squaws of another race will sing the death-song of their benefactor, and woe to the Sioux if the Northern Cheyennes get a chance to coup! "Try to avoid bloodshed," comes over the wires from Washington. "Poor savages!" comes the plaintive wail of the sentimentalist from his place of security; but who is to weep for the men who hold up a row of brass buttons for any hater of the United States to fire a gun at? Are the squaws of another race to do the mourning for American soldiers? Are the men of another race to hope for vengeance? Bah![80]

Lieutenant Casey was the last military casualty of the so-called Ghost Dance war.

THE NOOSE TIGHTENS

Some members of the press still tried to find a war to cover. The "Omaha Bee," on January 6, reported, Indications that the greatest battle in Indian history is almost at hand are increasing. The report of every scout adds new and strong support to these indications that were only emphasized by the bloody affair on Wounded Knee. General Miles believes this and has said so in strong words. The small handful of Indian employees here affirm it vehemently. Before the terrible crash comes they want to try and rescue their relatives from the enemy's camp and are now interceding with the authorities for permission, at the risk of their lives, to make the attempt.

These Indians in government employ also express the hope that they can induce many of those who were friendly before Wounded Knee battle, and were remaining here according to instructions, also to come in and be saved from the certain annihilation that awaits them within the ranks of the hostiles.

Extensive rifle pits are reported being dug twelve miles west of here by the hostiles, and the report is of such a nature that the authorities reply upon its truthfulness.[81]

On January 7, the "New York Times" reported, From the top of a high butte, near the center of their great village, the 4,000 hostiles, who are now menacing the Nebraska and South Dakota frontiers, face four divisions of soldiers which are soon to march on and destroy them if they do not surrender unconditionally. General Carr and his men are on the east, the white tents of Colonel Sumner and Captain Wells are perched to the north, and General Brooke, with the Second Infantry and Ninth Cavalry are on the west. To the south the savages can see the outlines of General Miles's breastworks, which have been thrown upon the crest of the buttes north and east of the agency buildings. The cordon has a diameter of less then eight miles, yet the fanatical Indians do not appear to fear the strength of the army, or seem to comprehend their peril.[82]

Despite the assertions in this report, the Ghost dancers certainly understood that their situation was perilous. Would the troops turn on them if they surrendered, as at Wounded Knee? Despite their fear, they negotiated with Miles. Instead of planning an attack, the Lakotas were probably planning a defense against army attacks. At Wounded Knee they saw the ruthless power of an avenging army. It was an example they could not ignore. Still, if the assurances were right they were willing to surrender once again.

On January 7 it was reported that Jack Red Cloud, Big Reed, High Horse, Lone Bear, Line Hawk, and five other Indians went into Pine Ridge to meet with Miles. Their conference was brief. During it they were told to come in and surrender, that Miles was not here to listen to their complaints, but that they would be allowed to go to Washington to make their complaints after the trouble was over.

As Miles negotiated with the Ghost dancers, he pushed for military control of the reservation system. On January 7 the five Dakota agencies were transferred from the control of the Interior Department to the control of the army.

As the transfer was taking place it was reported on January 8, The Secretary of Interior removed Royer from his position at Pine Ridge Agency at Pine Ridge and placed Captain F. E. Pierce, of the First Infantry, in charge. At the same time Pine Ridge, Rosebud, Standing Rock, Cheyenne River, and Tongue River Reservations were placed under the control of the military, with General Miles in command.[83] *Miles had finally won his political battle with the Department of Interior.*

Before the hapless Royer left Pine Ridge, Father Perrig, on January 29, 1890, wrote the ex-agent wanted to have affidavits in his favor, which Mr. Comer is collecting for him. F. Jutz could not conscientiously sign the paper prepared by Mr. Comer who said himself he would not sign the paper either. *Perrig added*, Mr. Pugh and Mr. Dyer are reinstated their former places.[84]

On January 9 General Colby wrote, In the evening, a big pow wow in the hostile camp was held at which Young-Man-Afraid-Of-His-Horses was present as a representative of the friendly Indians. Many of the Oglala, led by Little Wound and Big Road, urged their return and surrender, and after much wrangling and fighting, it was finally agreed that they should move their camp up White Clay Creek to within about five miles from the agency, near the Catholic Mission.

By this time, ranchmen and settlers in the country adjacent to the reservation recovered from their panic, and business was resumed in the outlying towns and cities. The establishment of the Nebraska National Guard at the posts indicated, and the general good conduct and discipline of the troops, very soon restored the confidence of the people; and within a few days thereafter all excitement was allayed and the settlers returned to their ranches and homes.

On the morning of January 11th, it was discovered that a large portion of the hostile Indians had moved in nearer the agency, in accordance with the resolutions of their pow-wow. . . . Little Wound, Big Road, Two Strike, Kicking Bear, Short Bull and other chiefs, with their hostile bands, were encamped on White Clay, about five miles northward from Pine Ridge Agency.[85] *The Lakotas who had fled the agencies and those who had left initially were ready to surrender, something most had done before the Wounded Knee Massacre.*

THE FINAL SURRENDER

On January 12 Colby received the following dispatch from Miles:

Pine Ridge, S.D., Jan. 12, 1891.

Gen. L. W. Colby, Rushville, Neb.

I am glad to inform you that the entire body of Indians are now encamped near here within a mile and a half. They show every disposition to comply with orders of the authorities; nothing but an accident can prevent peace being reestablished; and it will be our ambition to make it of a permanent character. I feel that the State Troops can now be withdrawn with safety, and desire through you to express to them my thanks for the confidence they have given your people in their isolated homes.

Nelson A. Miles
Maj. Gen. Commanding.

Colby immediately wrote back:

Rushville, Neb., Jan. 12, 1891.

Gen. Nelson A. Miles, Pine Ridge, S.D.,

I have the honor to acknowledge the receipt of your telegram this evening, informing me of the prospect of the immediate re-establishment of peace with the Indians at Pine Ridge Agency. I trust that no accident will intervene to prevent such a desired consummation. I assure you that the compliment expressed in your message for the State Troops under my command will be appreciated and highly esteemed by the citizen soldiers of Nebraska. I have wired the adjutant general the contents of your message, and will hold my command in its present position till I learn that peace is an accomplished fact.

L. W. Colby,
Brig. Gen. Commanding.[86]

At eleven o'clock this morning, *it was reported*, the hostiles again moved their camp, according to General Miles's order, and are now camped about one mile to the west of the agency, at the foot of the hill. *The mass surrender provided an awesome spectacle for the residents of Pine Ridge. On January 15 Kelley reported*, On the Oglalas asking permission of Miles, the Brulés were allowed to accompany them and all remain together at the camp. There were about 473 tepees by actual count, or between 5,000 and 6,000 Indians and 1,800 armed warriors and young men capable of fighting. It was a grand sight to see them slowly marching along for three hours up and down hills, and as General Miles said, a sight never again to be witnessed in Indian warfare on this continent.

Wagons driven by squaws and filled with domestic effects occupied the trail. On the hilltops above were lines of horsemen in single file, followed by lines of men on foot, in order, guarding their property in case of any attack upon them by the soldiers, as they half feared. They had out small bodies of scouts on every hill top for miles around, who have remained in their position all this morning and who doubtless will remain there for days to come.

Thousands of ponies cover the hillsides, closely herded, in anticipation of need. Kicking Bear and other chiefs are now holding a council with Miles and that they have agreed to deliver up their arms is certain, but much doubt is expressed of its taking place.[87]

Short Bull was among those who surrendered, and he admitted, During all this time my heart was bad, yet I did not want my people to fight the government. I might have done much harm but I always kept my people from it. I wanted no fighting. I wanted to do as the Messiah bid me. Some 10 days afterwards a delegation was sent out to see us from General Miles, asking us to return to the agency so as to save anymore bloodshed. General Miles sent to us several times, but we paid no attention, but now I told my people, "Pack up everything you have and we will move toward the agency, and I hope we will be allowed to live there in peace. General Miles said we shall not be fired on and I believe him."

This message I sent to General Miles: "We will surrender our guns and have peace."

So the next morning we went to the agency. We were asked to surrender our arms. I had a good Winchester Rifle which I surrendered freely and so did my people. General Miles asked me if I had any more guns. I told him, "I had an old patched up gun, the stock and barrel being wrapped with buckskin and not worth anything."

He asked me to turn it in which I done.[88]

On January 15 the Great Plains Indian wars had ended.

Crickett could write, Things now began to be quiet. The Indians was starved out and wanted to come in on the 16th. Arangments was made and they marched in. The bucks was all in single file made a line about a mile long. We was allready mounted ready for fear of any treachery, but it went off allright. Some of the chiefs came and surrendered their arms but they wasnt of much account.

AN ERA IN REVIEW

On January 21, during a gentle snowstorm, Miles held a final grand review. It was designed as a show of force, a caution to the Lakotas that they must never rise again. George H. Harries reported to the "Washington Evening Star," There passed in review this morning before General Miles what was probably the most thoroughly organized, best equipped and most efficient force of soldiers ever known in the history of the United States. Well dressed, well fed, well drilled and hardened to the life of active campaigning, it was superior to any army of equal size that has ever contended for physical superiority. The full dress uniform was not present and there was an entire absence of endeavor to put anything like polish on the men or the horses; it was a plain, practical showing of strength; the material with which war may be most advantageously be carried on.

Yesterday morning all the troops in this vicinity, with the exception of the First Infantry, moved to a long stretch of level prairie, nearly three miles from the agency, and camped there. Today the entire division was inspected and reviewed: everything from Lieutenant Taylor's Indian Scouts on the right to the unruly pack mules on the extreme left.

Snow was falling quite rapidly while the troops were being formed, and in a little while the clouds rolled away to a considerable extent and a heavy dust storm prevailed for several hours. Before the clouds of sand came up, however, the ceremony was over. Stretched out for more than a mile and a half were the soldiers, who hope to be at home within a reasonable time and who really do not care if they never have any more fighting to do. It was a magnificent sight.[89]

Years later Miles pensively recalled, The vast prairie, with its rolling undulations, was covered with the white mantle of winter. That cheerless, frigid atmosphere, with its sleet, ice, and snow, covered all the apparent life of nature. That scene was possibly the closing one that was to bury in oblivion, decay, and death that once powerful, strong, defiant, and resolute race. It was doomed to disappear, leaving behind it no evidence of its former life and power; and as the warm breezes of spring should remove the robe of winter a new life, verdure, and duty would appear.

Those prairies, *Miles rhapsodized*, would see a new civilization, happy homes, prosperous communities, and great States; and the sound of the merry bells of industrial activity and the music of progress were to take the place of the war-cry and the echoes of alarm and danger.

The scene was weird and in some respects desolate, yet it was fascinating to me—possibly on account of the jubilant spirit occasioned by the reflection that one more Indian war had been closed, and closed in the most satisfactory way, without the desolation and devastation in the settlements, as others had closed in former times. I did not even then realize that we had probably reached the close of Indian Wars in our country.

The march of the troops, fully equipped in their winter apparel, the long wagon and pack trains, the ambulance corps, were a novel and a most fitting spectacle for the closing scene of the drama. As this formidable force moved to stirring music, and with sharp cadence over the snow-clad fields, it could not but have made a strong impression upon the thousands of Indians witnessing it. They had a fair opportunity of appreciating the terrible power which they had fortunately avoided, as well as an indication to them of the advisability of remaining at peace in the future. At its close the troops moved to their various destinations, not to be reassembled again against the Indians for at least a score of years, and possibly never.

It has been more than twenty years since that time, and not a hostile shot has been fired between the government forces and the Indians. Nearly all of the great warriors have passed on to the Happy Hunting Ground, and the young men of today have ceased to know even the skill and experience of the hunter. They are not familiar with the use of firearms. Their attention has been called to peaceful pursuits. They have been taught a better way of life than that of the hunter and warrior. They have come up through the schools instead of the warpath. They have had the benefits of a life of civilization rather than the camp of Indian hostilities.[90]

Anyone who has visited the Dakota reservations knows that such an ideal world never evolved for the Lakotas. Instead of opportunity, the Lakotas have experienced poverty and continued government neglect.

Bland asserted, The good results of the invasion are mainly these. Attention was fully called to the rights and wrongs of the Sioux in such a way as to arouse public sympathy in their behalf and compel the government to redeem, in some measure, its pledges to that people. The five or six millions of dollars which the Sioux campaign cost is a large sum to spend in a few weeks on a few thousand troops. It is more than it costs to feed and clothe all the Indians in America for a whole year and more than has been spent by the government on Indian schools in four years. But it seems to be true that the people, or the government of the people, will not right great wrongs by civilized methods, until the savage method has been tried and failed.[91]

SPRING

Months after the mass surrender, Short Bull, along with other leaders of the Ghost Dance, was arrested. He testified, Some ten days afterwards General Miles asked me to go to Fort Sheridan, with "Kicking Bear" and some twenty-five others [twenty-four men and three women in all]. We started at the same time that a delegation went to Washington to hold a council with the "Great Father." When we reached Chicago we got off the train and were taken to Fort Sheridan. While there we were often visited by Genl. Miles who with all the officers there made us comfortable as could be, doing all in their power for us.

In the spring Long Hair (Colonel Wm F. Cody, Buffalo Bill) came to see us and made us a proposition to join his company across the Big Water. We said we would consider the matter, and later on Major John M. Burke came to see us. We held a council and he made us such grand offers to see the "great country beyond the water" with good salary that we all consented to go, and started with sixty of our friends and relatives from Pine Ridge Agency.

Our trip across the water made me somewhat seasick but as soon as I got on land again was in good health. Ever since I have been with the company I have been well treated and cared for, all of the promises made have been fulfilled.

Colonel Cody, Mr. Salsbury, and Major Burke as well as the entire company are our friends, and do all they can for us in every way. We get good food three times a day, good clothing, warm bedding and plenty of wood. If our people have any complaints it is fixed at once, if we do not feel well, a doctor comes and looks after us—besides we go everywhere and see all the great works of the country through which we travel. It learns us much; we see many people who are all kind to us. I like the English people but not their weather as it rains so much.[92]

Those who surrendered and chose to tour with the Wild West were spared long prison terms, deportation to distant reservations, or even federal prisons. With Cody they received generous salaries and were fed and housed during the tour. Much of their pay was banked until the end of the season, when the performers returned home. The money saved would give some Lakotas a chance to start over again. It was a better life than remaining in the Dakotas.

There was one final irony. Kelley reported on January 15 that the citizens of Northern Nebraska were raising a fund to purchase a diamond hilted sabre to be given Colonel Forsyth, the colonel of the Seventh Cavalry, for his conduct at Wounded Knee. This shows in what estimation this gallant soldier is held by the citizens in this vicinity and in what way his behavior at Wounded Knee is appreciated by all who know the facts. It is understood the board of inquiry has wholly exonerated him and submitted their report to the president for his approval.[93]

Crickett's tour of duty in the Dakotas ended. We got the order on the 23rd [of January] that we was to return to Ft. Riley, *he wrote*. We made three camping grounds between the agency and Rushville as they was afraid after we left they might break out again, got to Rushville, loaded our stock and baggage and away we went and mighty glad I was to get on board the train once more as I can tell you it was no picnic.

The first stoppage was at Fremont Nebraska. We watered and fed the stock, went on again allright untill we got within about thirty miles of the fort when we met with the railing accident, which was a shocking affair, men and horses strewn about in all directions, two killed on the spot and dozens injured, and bitter cold night into the bargain. About ten miles off was a town called Manhattan where the 7th are allways welcome and they turned out and gave all the help the could, open up their houses for us made us comfortable as the sircumstances would allow. The next day a train was run from Junction City, and took us to the fort safe.

After we got back and settled down we gave the people of Manhattan a grand banquet in our mess hall, over five hundred attended. After the supper there were lots of speeches made, and dancing up till revulle, spent a most enjoyable evening. We are invited to a picnic on the 4th of July, which is a national holiday in this country. I think this will do for the present but when I come back shall have lots more little incidents to tell you.

In his memoirs, Eastman writes, In March, all being quiet, Miss Goodale decided to send in her resignation and go East to visit her relatives, and our wedding day was set for the following June.[94] *Both Goodale and Eastman were active in advancing the cause of the Lakotas throughout their long lives.*

Alice Ghost Horse says, Soon the snow was melting and all knew it was spring. One day a rider came into the camp and said there was going to be a meeting (treaty) at Pine Ridge. Next day, early as usual, we headed for Pine Ridge again. It must be quite a ways because we camped in a deep gully.

When we started out again the next day, it was a long caravan of buggies, travois, horseback and on foot. The chiefs were walking in front, followed by young warriors on horseback.

Over the last hill we could see many tents and cavalry all over the place. Dust was flying, horses were tied to hitching posts face to face.

We made camp near the post. "Can Hahaka" (Plenty Limbs) and "Iron Thunder" came to the camp and said they came after all the Hohwoju's Cheyenne River people who were wounded or deceased, that they belonged to our band.

In Pine Ridge, my mother reluctantly signed our names as survivors, along with the rest of the family.

They pitched up three big tipis in the center where they told us to go. I remember there was Black Moon and his mother and brothers. Iron Horn and Wood Pile was there. There were many Hohwoju's that showed up at the tipi. Even some we thought had been killed. "Ashes" was a young girl then, she was there, too. I noticed other people, were "Blue Hair," "Axe," Brown Eagle, and "Can Hahaka"(Plenty Limbs).

Then, Alice Ghost Horse says, troops decided to move the survivors away from Pine Ridge: We left for Hohwoju country towards Cherry Creek. We were traveling in five wagons. One wagon was loaded with oats and hay, another one of rations, one wagon full of soldiers were leading the way as escorts, out of Pine Ridge in a different direction so we won't have to go through Wounded Knee.

Despite all these nice things being done for us, I can't forget what happened at Wounded Knee. Some nights I cried thinking about it, many months afterwards. I have never touched a white man during my life time. I just couldn't trust any white man and never will because they killed my father and brother for no reason at all.[95]

Neither Miles's nor Forsyth's careers suffered. In 1895 Miles was promoted to commander in chief of the army. He never ran for public office. In 1895 Forsyth was promoted to brigadier general and three years after that to major general. Major Sumner, who had allowed Big Foot to escape, was promoted to colonel, and he assumed command of the Seventh Cavalry. By 1920 McLaughlin had become Indian inspector.[96] *Many of the officers at Wounded Knee enjoyed long military careers and promotions.*

Years later, on March 13, 1917, Miles, addressing the commissioner of Indian Affairs, still insisted, In my opinion, the least the government can do is to make a suitable recompense to the survivors for the great injustice which was done them and the serious loss of their relatives and property.

The action of the commanding officer, in my judgment at the time, and I so reported, was most reprehensible. The disposition of the troops was such that in firing upon the warriors they fired directly toward their own lines and also into the camp of the women and children, and I have regarded the whole affair as most unjustifiable and worthy of the severest condemnation.

Since about thirty soldiers were killed and the same number wounded, the army has tried to give the impression that this was the work of the Indians, but the soldiers were killed by their own men. This is a reasonable conclusion as there were soldiers among the Indians searching for weapons and as the fire was directed at the Indians; of course, some of the soldiers would have been killed. Testimony of the Kent-Baldwin report following an investigation of the Wounded Knee Massacre is positive proof that the Indians are correct in saying that the soldiers were killed by their own bullets. It is only natural that an army of men, with revenge in their hearts, would make such an error, but to blame it on the Indians is an old trick of the white people.[97]

Miles, however, never admitted that he may have contributed to the tragedy with his own actions, such as inaccurately reporting the nature of the Ghost Dance and relentlessly dispatching troops in large numbers to the Dakotas.

A few other members of the military were outraged by what had happened at Wounded Knee. An anonymous officer told the "Washington Evening Star"'s Harries, This whole proceeding is an outrage. The government so treats these Indians that they can do nothing else than fight, and then it orders us out here to kill the victims of its duplicity. I have been fighting Indians for many years, and personally have nothing on which to base anything like affection for them, yet there are times when I feel like throwing aside the uniform that honors me with its covering and donning in its place the blanket of the savage. Then I could fight and be sure that my cause had a just foundation.[98]

Valentine McGillycuddy, giving lie to the exaggerated and false reports in the press, summed up the damage to whites in a letter to Colby, asserting, No citizen in Nebraska or Dakota has been killed, molested, or can show the scratch of a pin, and no property has been destroyed off the reservation.[99] *He added,* It was a pitiable, disgraceful affair forced on Indians and whites alike by politics, graft and bad management.[100]

Pine Ridge issue clerk Robert O. Pugh also summed up his view of the events he had witnessed: The difficulties were serious for all concerned. Ignorance and dishonesty were holding carnival. The people would make good the expense. The Indians would be blamed for the trouble. And they would be butchered, too. The whole thing was bad from the start. It wound up in the worst disgrace that has signalized our fighting for a hundred years. It seemed as though the devil had come, in capricious mood to do all the wickedness he could invent. At any rate, it was done. This is beyond controversy. Let the historic page blush with crimson color, for it is written in the blood of murder.[101]

The Miniconjous who died at Wounded Knee were finally honored by their own people. In 1930 a monument was placed over the mass grave in the cemetery above the valley of Wounded Knee. Its inscription reads:

> This monument is erected by surviving relatives and other Ogallala and Cheyenne River Sioux Indians in Memory of Chief Big Foot Massacre Dec. 29, 1890.
>
> Col. Forsyth in command of U.S. Troops. Big Foot was a great chief of the Sioux Indians. He often said "I will stand in peace till my last day comes." He did many good and brave deeds for the white man and the red man. Many innocent women and children who knew no wrong died here.
>
> June 18, 1930, the erecting of this monument is largely due to the financial assistance of Joseph Horn Cloud whose father was killed here.

Buried near this mass grave are Lakota soldiers who died in World War II, men who served a country that had ruthlessly slaughtered their ancestors. These soldiers are buried there with the bitter ironic spirit that characterizes the Lakotas' view of their tragic past.

In the years that followed, the Lakota Nation continued to subsist on government rations and the poor crops they could raise in the barren land left to them. Even today Pine Ridge is a place of intense poverty and discouragement.

What really happened at Wounded Knee?

In medicine man Black Elk's words, "A people's dream, a beautiful dream, died there in the bloody snow." [102]

My brothers, I bring to you the promise of a day in which there will be no white man to lay his hand on the bridle of the Indian's horse; when the red men of the prairie will rule the world and not be turned from the hunting grounds by any man. I bring you word from your fathers the ghosts, that they are now marching to join you, led by the Messiah who came once to live on earth with the white men, but was cast out and killed by them. I have seen the wonders of the Spirit Land, and have talked with the ghosts. I traveled far and am sent back with a message to tell you to make ready for the coming of the Messiah and return of the ghosts in the spring.

—*Kicking Bear*

Notes

PREFACE

1. Benjamin Black Elk, interview by author, August 10, 1971. Subsequent quotations in the preface refer to this interview.

2. Black Elk means his father was at Pine Ridge, not Wounded Knee, when the massacre happened. He, along with a number of other Lakotas, expected that a battle might develop and rode out to join it.

3. The government school in Pennsylvania for Native Americans.

4. Christer Lindberg includes Crickett's letter in his article "Foreigners in Action at Wounded Knee," 170–81. The undated letter Pvt. Walter R. Crickett wrote to his family in England can be accessed at the American Museum in Britain, Bath, England (© American Museum in Britain, Bath, England). Crickett's account was given to me on January 15, 1975, by G. M. Candler, then education director at Claverton Manor's American Museum in Britain. He gave me a photocopy of Crickett's remarkably detailed letter, which I quote throughout this book by permission of the museum.

1. PROLOGUE TO A TRAGEDY

1. Alice C. Fletcher, "The Indian Messiah," 57.

2. James Mooney, "The Ghost Dance Religion," 784. "The Ghost Dance Religion and the Sioux Outbreak of 1890," which is part 2 of Mooney's massive *Fourteenth Annual Report*, is a major source of information regarding the origins of the Ghost Dance and the events following its arrival in the Dakotas. It includes Mooney's observations, firsthand accounts, drawings of the Ghost Dance and the artifacts used in its rituals, and the words and music of its songs.

3. Mooney, "The Ghost Dance Religion," 765.

4. *New York Times*, November 30, 1890. Mooney writes that the name Wovoka should be translated as "Cutter." He adds that Wovoka was also called Wevokar, Wopokahte, Kwohitsauq, Cowejo, Koit-tsow, Kvit-Tsow, Quoitze, Jack Wilson, Jackson Wilson, Jack Winston, and John Johnson ("The Ghost Dance Religion," 765).

5. Mooney, "The Ghost Dance Religion," 773–74.

6. Fletcher, "Indian Messiah," 58–59.

7. Mooney, "The Ghost Dance Religion," 904.

8. Mooney, "The Ghost Dance Religion," 904.

9. Mooney, "The Ghost Dance Religion," 783.

10. Mooney, "The Ghost Dance Religion," 782.

11. Mooney, "The Ghost Dance Religion," 772.

12. Thisba Hutson Morgan, "Reminiscences of My Days in the Land of the Ogallala Sioux," 48.

13. Fletcher, "Indian Messiah," 59.

14. T. A. Bland, *A Brief History of the Late Military Invasion of the Home of the Sioux*, 8. From a conversation Bland had with Louis Richard and "other interpreters" in Washington in 1891.

15. Mooney, "The Ghost Dance Religion," 819.

16. Father Aemilius Perrig, diary, Marquette University Library (MUL), Department of Special Collections and University Archives, transcribed by John M. Carroll, 24, 49. Forty-four-year-old Perrig came to the Dakotas in 1886. He died at the Holy Rosary Mission on March 22, 1909. I have retained his telegraphic style and misspellings, except where they needed to be clarified.

17. Mooney, "The Ghost Dance Religion," 795.

18. Morgan, "Reminiscences," 48.

19. Elaine Goodale (later Elaine Goodale Eastman), "The Ghost Dance War and Wounded Knee Massacre of 1890–91," 28. New England–born, Goodale first visited the Dakota reservation system in 1885. She returned in 1886 as the first teacher at White River Camp. Eventually she became superintendent of all Lakota schools in the Dakotas.

20. Bland, *A Brief History*, 8.

21. Robert Utley, *The Last Days of the Sioux Nation*, 75.

22. Ricker notebooks (microfilm), tablet 17, Judge Eli S. Ricker Collection (hereafter ESR), Nebraksa State Historical Society (NSHS), Lincoln. Judge Ricker spent a great deal of his life interviewing whites and Native Americans regarding events leading up to the Wounded Knee Massacre and the massacre itself. Most of the firsthand accounts dealing with this event are the result of his fieldwork.

23. Short Bull's testimony, n.d., photocopy (handwritten by an unnamed translator), Buffalo Bill Memorial Museum (BBMM), Golden CO. Except where noted, all accounts attributed to Short Bull are drawn from this unpublished document. For clarity I have corrected some spelling, punctuation, and paragraphing. Otherwise, this remarkable document is intact and will be quoted in its entirety without alteration. Short Bull's account proves to be accurate when placed against events reported in newspaper stories and other accounts.

24. Mooney, "The Ghost Dance Religion," 781.

25. Short Bull's testimony, 2, BBMM.

26. Utley, *Last Days*, 61.

2. BROKEN PROMISES, BROKEN TREATIES

1. Clipping ca. late 1885, William F. Cody's scrapbooks, Buffalo Bill Historical Center, Cody WY.

2. Mooney, "The Ghost Dance Religion," 825.

3. Commissioner of Indian Affairs, "Reports of Agents (1890)," 42.

4. Commissioner of Indian Affairs, "Reports of Agents (1890)," 48.

5. Frederic Remington, "Indians as Irregular Cavalry," 61.

6. *Washington Evening Star*, January 31, 1891.

7. Mooney, "The Ghost Dance Religion," 825.

8. Joe De Barthe, *The Life and Adventures of Frank Grouard*, 469–70.

9. Stanley Vestal [Walter S. Campbell], *Sitting Bull: Champion of the Sioux*, 248.

10. Nelson A. Miles, "Report of Major General Miles," 136.

11. Miles, "Report of Major General Miles," 136.

12. U.S. Senate, *Reports of Committees*, 80–81.

13. De Barthe, *Frank Grouard*, 470–71.

14. *Washington Evening Star*, January 28, 1891.

15. Goodale, "Ghost Dance War," 27.

16. De Barthe, *Frank Grouard*, 469–70.

17. Goodale, "Ghost Dance War," 27.

18. *Cong. Rec.*, 51st Cong., 2nd Sess., 1890, 46.

19. *Washington Evening Star*, January 28, 1891.

20. DeBarthe, *Frank Grouard*, 471–42.

21. Commissioner of Indian Affairs, "Reports of Agents (1890)," 387.

22. Commissioner of Indian Affairs, "Reports of Agents (1890)," 37.

23. Commissioner of Indian Affairs, "Reports of Agents (1890)," 48–49.

24. De Barthe, *Frank Grouard*, 472.

25. Goodale, "Ghost Dance War," 29.

26. Mooney, "The Ghost Dance Religion," 840.

27. Commissioner of Indian Affairs, "Reports of Agents (1890)," 39.

28. Transcript of "An Independent Investigation of the Recent Disturbances on the Sioux Reservation, Occupying Three Months, and Made by Rev. William J. Crawford—for The Indian Rights Association," Walter S. Campbell Collection, Western History Collections, University of Oklahoma, Norman (hereafter WSC), box 110, folder 2. Throughout this book I refer to untitled documents in the Campbell collection. Most of these documents are notes Campbell wrote. They will be cited by their box and folder number.

29. "Bullets or Bread," *Army and Navy Journal*, December 6, 1890, 2–3.

30. Miles, "Report of Major General Miles," 133–34.

31. Mooney, "The Ghost Dance Religion," 841.

32. Mooney, "The Ghost Dance Religion," 840. This quote is taken from a statement American Horse made at a council at Pine Ridge Agency on November 27, 1890.

33. Miles, "Report of Major General Miles," 136.

34. Commissioner of Indian Affairs, "Reports of Agents (1890)," 49.

35. Utley, *Last Days*, 50.

36. De Barthe, *Frank Grouard*, 472.

37. De Barthe, *Frank Grouard*, 472.

38. *Chadron (NE) Democrat*, January 8, 1891, 3.

39. Mooney, "The Ghost Dance Religion," 840.

40. Mooney, "The Ghost Dance Religion," 841.

41. Commissioner of Indian Affairs, "Reports of Agents (1890)," 49.

42. Miles, "Report of Major General Miles," 140.

43. Commissioner of Indian Affairs, "Reports of Agents (1890)," 49.

44. Mooney, "The Ghost Dance Religion," 839–40.

3. THE SECOND PILGRIMAGE

1. Short Bull's testimony, 2, BBMM. Possibly another name for Mash-the-Kettle, who is believed to have been Short Bull's traveling companion.

2. No relation to the better-known Hunkpapa medicine man.

3. It is likely that Good Thunder, after making his pilgrimage a year earlier, taught the emissaries the new ritual, but there is no report of it being widespread in the Dakota reservations in 1889 and early 1890.

4. Short Bull's testimony, 2–3, BBMM.

5. Miles, "Report of Major General Miles," 141.

6. Short Bull's testimony, 3–4, BBMM.

7. Mooney, "The Ghost Dance Religion," 665, 771–72.

8. Mooney, "The Ghost Dance Religion," 820.

9. Mooney, "The Ghost Dance Religion," 795.

10. Mooney, "The Ghost Dance Religion," 797.

11. Short Bull's testimony, 6–7, BBMM.

12. Ricker notebooks, tablet 17, ESR, NSHS.

13. Mooney, "The Ghost Dance Religion," 797.

14. Mooney, "The Ghost Dance Religion," 796.

15. Short Bull's testimony, 8, BBMM.

16. Mooney, "The Ghost Dance Religion," 772–73.

17. Short Bull's testimony, 8, BBMM.

18. Mooney, "The Ghost Dance Religion," 797. Slightly edited for sequencing.

19. Perrig diary, 24–25, MUL.

20. Warren K. Moorehead, "The Indian Messiah and the Ghost Dance," 161.

21. Short Bull's testimony, 8, BBMM.

22. Luther Standing Bear, *My People the Sioux*, 217–18.

23. Commissioner of Indian Affairs, "Reports of Agents (1891)," 412.

24. Short Bull's testimony, 8–9, BBMM.

4. THE GHOST DANCE SWEEPS ACROSS THE DAKOTAS

1. Goodale, "Ghost Dance War," 29.

2. Charles A. Hyde to Secretary of Interior John W. Noble, May 29, 1890, Pierre SD, WSC, box 108.

3. Commissioner of Indian Affairs, "Reports of Agents (1890)," 127.

4. Commissioner of Indian Affairs, "Reports of Agents (1890)," 127.

5. Commissioner of Indian Affairs, "Reports of Agents (1890)," 127.

6. Goodale, "Ghost Dance War," 29.

7. The words and music for the many variants of the Ghost Dance have been recorded by field ethnologists. Mooney offers many variants, some transcribed by John Philip Sousa.

8. Moorehead, "Indian Messiah and the Ghost Dance, 162–65.

9. Charles W. Allen, "In the West That Was," 211, MS2635, NSHS. This manuscript has since been published as *From Fort Laramie to Wounded Knee: In the West That Was*, by Charles W. Allen, ed. Richard E. Jensen (Lincoln: University of Nebraska Press, 1997).

10. *Chadron (NE) Democrat*, September 25, 1890.

11. Allen, "In the West That Was," 209, MS2635, NSHS.

12. Commissioner of Indian Affairs, "Reports of Agents (1891)," 529–31.

13. Mooney, "The Ghost Dance Religion," 798.

14. Mrs. James A. Finley, "Account of the Northern Cheyennes Concerning the Messiah Superstition," 67–68. Finley was originally quoted in the *Salem MA Essex Country Mercury*, November 26, 1890.

15. James H. Cook, *Fifty Years on the Old Frontier as Cowboy, Hunter, Guide, Scout, and Ranchman*, 231–32.

16. Commissioner of Indian Affairs, "Reports of Agents (1890)," 62.

17. Charles A. Eastman, *From Deep Woods to Civilization*, 92. Eastman came to Pine Ridge on November 1, 1890.

18. Perrig diary, 36, MUL.

5. A FAILURE IN COMMUNICATIONS

1. Donald F. Danker, "The Wounded Knee Interviews of Eli S. Ricker," 176–79.

2. Rex Beach, "Wounded Knee," *Appleton's Booklovers Magazine*, June 1906, 731–36. A clipping of the article can be found in folder E83.89, B22, South Dakota State Historical Society (SDSHS), Pierre. Beach, a popular novelist of the time, probably recast an interview with Dewey Beard into his own words.

3. These numbers are based upon the army's count of Big Foot followers at Wounded Knee in December, minus the members of Sitting Bull's band who joined Big Foot in mid-December.

4. Utley, *Last Days*, 90.

5. Melvin R. Gilmore, "The Truth of the Wounded Knee Massacre," 242–43.

6. Gilmore, "Truth of the Wounded Knee Massacre," 243–44.

7. Gilmore, "Truth of the Wounded Knee Massacre," 242–43.

8. U.S. Adjutant General, "Report of the Investigation," in *Reports and Correspondence*, 65. The hearing took place on January 7, 1891.

9. Gilmore, "Truth of the Wounded Knee Massacre," 243–44.

10. Danker, "Wounded Knee Interviews," 180.

11. Eastman, *Deep Woods to Civilization*, 99–100.

12. Ricker notebooks, tablet 5, ESR, NSHS.

13. Cook, *Fifty Years*, 199–200, 233.

14. Ricker notebooks, tablet 5, ESR, NSHS.

15. Philip Wells, "Ninety-Six Years," 296.

16. Ricker notebooks, tablet 4, ESR, NSHS.

17. Commissioner of Indian Affairs, "Reports of Agents (1890)," 49.

18. Perrig diary, 26, MUL.

19. Commissioner of Indian Affairs, "Reports of Agents (1890)," 49.

20. Vestal, *New Sources of Indian History, 1850–1891*, 5.

21. Perrig diary, 28, MUL.

22. Allen, "In the West That Was," 211, MS2635, NSHS.

23. Commissioner of Indian Affairs, "Reports of Agents (1891)," 531.

24. Short Bull's testimony, 9, BBMM.

25. Commissioner of Indian Affairs, "Reports of Agents (1891)," 412.

26. Luther Standing Bear, *My People the Sioux*, 219–21.

27. Commissioner of Indian Affairs, "Reports of Agents (1891)," 411–12.

28. Commissioner of Indian Affairs, "Reports of Agents (1891)," 411–12.

29. Mooney, "The Ghost Dance Religion," 845.

30. *New York Times*, December 4, 1890.

31. For an excellent study of the press's role in the Ghost dancing crisis during the summer and fall of 1890, see Elmo Scott Watson's "The Last Indian War, 1890–91: A Study of Newspaper Jingoism." Scout and rancher James H. Cook gives an amusing account of the misadventures of *Omaha Bee* reporter Will Cressey, whom Cook nicknamed Cola.

According to Watson, the reporters based at Pine Ridge included C. C. Seymour, *Chicago Herald*; Dent H. Robert, *St. Louis Post Dispatch*; William Fitch Kelley, *Lincoln NE State Journal*; John McDonaugh, *New York World*; E. E. Clark, *Chicago Tribune*; G. F. Bailey (also a space writer), *Chicago Inter-Ocean*; Charles W. Allen, editor of the *Chadron (NE) Democrat* but also a space writer for the *New York World*; Ed O'Brien, Associated Press; Dr. Charles B. Ewing, U.S. Army; K. R. Zillucus, *Chicago Swedish Tribune*; Will Cressey, *Omaha Bee*; Alfred H. Burkholder, *New York Herald*; Boylan, *St. Paul Pioneer Press*; Irving Hawkins, *Chicago Tribune*; "Judge" Burnes (also a space writer), *Chicago Times*; and Warren K. Moorehead, *Illustrated American* (208–10). There were also a few unidentified space writers.

32. Goodale, "Ghost Dance War," 30.

33. Watson, "Last Indian War," 206.

34. L. W. Colby, "The Sioux Indian War of 1890–91," 180.

35. Colby, "Sioux Indian War," 180.

36. *Washington Evening Star*, January 28, 1891.

37. Commissioner of Indian Affairs, "Reports of Agents (1891)," 124.

38. Watson, "Last Indian War," 206.

39. Allen, "In the West That Was," 224, MS2635, NSHS.

40. Ricker notebooks, tablet 17, ESR, NSHS.

41. Danker, "Wounded Knee Interviews," 225–26.

42. "Ridin' the Range," *Rapid City (SD) Daily Journal*, March 7, 1954.

43. "Ridin' the Range," *Rapid City (SD) Daily Journal*, March 7, 1954. Bernard Gallagher's memory was in error by a few weeks. Perrig recorded in his

diary that Royer and his family arrived at Pine Ridge on September 26 (26). Indian agents were given the military title "colonel."

44. Colby, "Sioux Indian War," 179–80.

45. *Pioneer Press*, December 20, 1890.

46. Royer scrapbook, accession no. H-72.2, FB 28, John R. Brennan Family papers, SDSHS, Pierre.

47. Cook, *Fifty Years*, 232.

48. Mooney, "The Ghost Dance Religion," 93.

49. Perrig diary, 37–38, MUL.

50. Ricker notebooks, tablet 12, ESR, NSHS.

51. Colby, "Sioux Indian War," 185–90.

52. Miles, "Report of Major General Miles," 142–43.

53. Miles, "Report of Major General Miles," 144.

54. Miles, "Report of Major General Miles," 144.

55. Newspaper clipping, ca. November 7–10, 1890.

6. STANDOFF AT STANDING ROCK

1. Maj. M. F. Steele, "Buffalo Bill's Bluff," 476–77. According to Steele, who was stationed at Standing Rock in 1890, "[McLaughlin's] wife was part Sioux, a fine Christian woman who devoted her whole time and labor to the betterment of her people. She was truly a help-meet for McLaughlin in his duties of agent."

2. Box 106, notebook 54, 35, WSC.

3. Utley, *The Lance and the Shield: The Life and Times of Sitting Bull*, 249–50.

4. Vestal, *Sitting Bull*, 250.

5. Don Russell, *Lives and Legends of Buffalo Bill*, 316.

6. Vestal, *Sitting Bull*, 251.

7. For a full account of Sitting Bull's performance career with Cody, see Russell, *Lives and Legends*, 315–17.

8. Box 104, folder 5, WSC.

9. Box 104, folder 5, WSC.

10. Vestal, *New Sources*, 309–11.

11. Box 104, folder 5, WSC.

12. Vestal, *Sitting Bull*, 257–62.

13. James McLaughlin, *My Friend the Indian*, 273–80.

14. Vestal, *Sitting Bull*, 258.

15. Vestal, *Sitting Bull*, 237.

16. Vestal, *New Sources*, 309–11.

17. Vestal, *New Sources*, 309–11.

18. McLaughlin, *My Friend the Indian*, 182.

19. Commissioner of Indian Affairs, "Reports of Agents (1891)," 328–30.

20. Box 104, folder 11, WSC.

21. Vestal, *Sitting Bull*, 152.

22. Doane Robinson, "History of the Sioux War," 481.

23. De Barthe, *Frank Grouard*, 387.

24. Vestal, *New Sources*, 64.

25. McLaughlin, *My Friend the Indian*, 422–23.

26. McLaughlin, *My Friend the Indian*, 184.

27. E. G. Fechet, "The Capture of Sitting Bull," 186.

28. Miles, "Report of Major General Miles," 143.

29. McLaughlin, *My Friend the Indian*, 184.

30. McLaughlin, *My Friend the Indian*, 185.

31. Goodale, "Ghost Dance War," 30–31.

32. McLaughlin, *My Friend the Indian*, 329.

33. Vestal, *New Sources*, 340–41.

34. McLaughlin, *My Friend the Indian*, 191.

35. Commissioner of Indian Affairs, "Reports of Agents (1891)," 329.

36. McLaughlin, *My Friend the Indian*, 190–91.

37. Julia B. McGillycuddy, *Blood on the Moon: Valentine McGillycuddy and the Sioux*, 266.

38. Commissioner of Indian Affairs, "Reports of Agents (1891)," 329.

39. Commissioner of Indian Affairs, "Reports of Agents (1890)," 126.

40. Commissioner of Indian Affairs, "Reports of Agents (1890)," 127.

41. Commissioner of Indian Affairs, "Reports of Agents (1891)," 330.

42. Box 106, notebook 54, 52–53, WSC.

43. John M. Carroll, ed., *The Arrest and Killing of Sitting Bull: A Documentary*, 67–68.

44. Vestal, *New Sources*, 42–44. Actually, the horse Cody gave Sitting Bull was gray. It was one of the chief's most prized possessions. High Eagle also says, "This was the only chance I had to see the Ghost Dance. I kept this feather and every now and then they told me to throw it away. Later I went away to school and left this feather at home and my brother got to believing in the Ghost Dance and sent me the feather, telling me to wear it when the time came for the Messiah to return."

45. Box 106, notebook 34, 37, WSC.

46. Vestal, *New Sources*, 271.

47. Goodale, "Ghost Dance War," 30.

48. Commissioner of Indian Affairs, "Reports of Agents (1891)," 328–30.

49. Vestal, *New Sources*, 2.

50. Vestal, *New Sources*, 2.

51. Utley, *Last Days*, 97.

52. McLaughlin, *My Friend the Indian*, 200–201.

53. McLaughlin, *My Friend the Indian*, 201.

54. McLaughlin, *My Friend the Indian*, 201–2.

55. McLaughlin, *My Friend the Indian*, 202–4.

56. McLaughlin to Commissioner Morgan, November 19, 1890, *New York Times*, December 16, 1890.

57. McLaughlin, *My Friend the Indian*, 204–6.

58. McLaughlin to Commissioner Morgan, November 19, 1890, *New York Times*, December 16, 1890.

59. McLaughlin, *My Friend the Indian*, 207.

60. *New York Times*, December 16, 1890.

61. Goodale, "Ghost Dance War," 30.

62. McLaughlin, *My Friend the Indian*, 207–8.

63. *New York Times*, December 16, 1890.

64. McLaughlin, *My Friend the Indian*, 208–9.

65. *Chicago Tribune*, November 23, 1890. This was also reported in the *Iowa State Register*, November 23, 1890.

7. CONFRONTATION AT PINE RIDGE

1. Eastman, *Deep Woods to Civilization*, 93–95.

2. Ricker notebooks, tablet 12, ESR, NSHS. Since Ricker often veered from first person to third person as he transcribed his interviews, this interview has been cast into the first person.

3. Utley, *Last Days*, 4. The reference is to Episcopalian minister Charles Smith Cook not rancher-scout James H. Cook. According to Utley, Charles Smith Cook was "an educated Indian."

4. Eastman, *Deep Woods to Civilization*, 95–98. Eastman is in error. Royer did indeed immediately ask for troops, but they were not dispatched until a few days later.

5. Telegram, Royer to Commissioner Morgan, November 11, 1890, Royer scrapbook, John R. Brennan Family papers, SDSHS.

6. Miles, "Report of Major General Miles," 144.

7. To Brig. Gen. L. W. Colby, January 15, 1891, in Colby's "Sioux Indian War," 183.

8. Morgan, "Reminiscences," 50.

9. Telegram, Royer to Washington, November 15, Royer scrapbook, John R. Brennan Family papers, SDSHS.

10. Ricker notebooks, tablet 12, ESR, NSHS.

11. Ricker notebooks, tablet 12, ESR, NSHS.

12. *Omaha World Herald*, November 17, 1890.

13. Colby, "Sioux Indian War," 147.

14. *Iowa State Register*, November 23, 1890.

15. *Chadron (NE) Democrat*, November 20, 1890.

16. *Chadron (NE) Democrat*, November 20, 1890.

17. *New York World*, November 23, 1890.

18. *Iowa State Register*, November 23, 1890.

19. *Washington Evening Star*, November 21, 1890.

20. Gilmore, "Truth of the Wounded Knee Massacre," 241.

21. *New York World*, November 24, 1890.

22. *Omaha World Herald*, November 19, 1890.

23. *Army and Navy Journal*, November 22, 1890.

24. *Chadron (NE) Democrat*, November 20, 1890.

25. Commissioner of Indian Affairs, "Reports of Agents (1890)," 128.

26. Morgan, "Reminiscences," 50–51.

27. Eastman, *Deep Woods to Civilization*, 100–102.

28. Eastman, *Deep Woods to Civilization*, 100–102.

29. Eastman, *Deep Woods to Civilization*, 100–102.

30. Morgan, "Reminiscences," 51.

31. Standing Bear, *My People the Sioux*, 220–21.

32. Morgan, "Reminiscences," 50.

33. *Washington Evening Star*, November 21, 1890.

34. Ricker notebooks, tablet 12, ESR, NSHS.

35. Goodale, "Ghost Dance War," 33–34.

36. Gilmore, "Truth of the Wounded Knee Massacre," 241.

37. *New York World*, November 23, 1890.

38. *New York World*, November 23, 1890.

39. *New York World*, November 23, 1890.

40. *Washington Evening Star*, November 21, 1890.

41. Telegram, Miles to Schofield, November 26, 1890, in Utley, *Last Days*, 129.

42. *Iowa State Register*, November 23, 1890.

43. *Iowa State Register*, November 23, 1890.

44. *Chicago Tribune*, November 23, 1890.

45. *Omaha Bee*, November 22, 1890.

46. *Chicago Tribune*, November 23, 1890.

47. *Chicago Tribune*, November 23, 1890.

48. *Chicago Tribune*, November 23, 1890.

49. *New York World*, November 25, 1890.

50. *Chadron (NE) Democrat*, November 23, 1890.

51. *Chadron (NE) Democrat*, November 27, 1890.

52. *Chadron (NE) Democrat*, November 27, 1890.

53. *Iowa State Register*, November 23, 1890.

54. *New York World*, November 23, 1890.

55. *New York Times*, November 25, 1890.

56. *New York Times*, November 25, 1890.

57. *New York World*, November 25, 1890.

58. *New York World*, November 25, 1890.

8. RUMORS, RESTIVE TROOPS, AND A NEW INITIATIVE

1. *New York World*, November 25, 1890.

2. *New York World*, November 24, 1890.

3. *New York World*, November 24, 1890.

4. *New York Times*, November 25, 1890.

5. *New York Times*, November 25, 1890.

6. *Chadron (NE) Democrat*, November 27, 1890.
7. *Nebraska State Journal*, November 27, 1890.
8. *New York Times*, November 26, 1890.
9. *Nebraska State Journal*, November 27, 1890.
10. *New York World*, November 26, 1890.
11. U.S. Adjutant General, "Report of the Investigation," 86.
12. *New York World*, November 25, 1890.
13. *Omaha Bee*, November 24, 1890.
14. *New York World*, November 27, 1890.
15. Mooney, "The Ghost Dance Religion," 852.
16. *New York Times*, November 26, 1890.
17. *New York Herald*, November 25, 1890.
18. *New York World*, November 24, 1890.
19. Like Crickett, 1st Sgt. Ragnar Theodor Ling-Vannerus, a native of Sweden, also recorded his memories of the campaign. His words and Crickett's, including parts of Crickett's letter, are quoted in part by Christer Lindberg, ed., in "Foreigners in Action at Wounded Knee." In "Another View of Wounded Knee" Alan K. Lathrop reconstructed a badly decomposed diary of an unknown enlisted soldier. I have not used this source, however, since the letter writer is vague on some points, brags of being a confidant of officers, and is generally unreliable.
20. *Lincoln NE State Journal*, December 10, 1890.
21. Ricker notebooks, tablet 35, ESR, NSHS.
22. *Army and Navy Journal*, December 6, 1890.
23. *Chadron (NE) Democrat*, November 27, 1890.
24. *Chadron (NE) Democrat*, November 27, 1890.
25. *Chadron (NE) Democrat*, November 27, 1890.
26. *Chadron (NE) Democrat*, December 4, 1890; originally printed in the *Omaha Bee*, November 27, 1890.
27. *Chadron (NE) Democrat*, December 4, 1890; originally printed in the *Omaha Bee*, November 27, 1890.
28. Bland, *A Brief History*, 8.
29. Short Bull's testimony, 9–12, BBMM.
30. Miles, *Serving the Republic*, 240–41.
31. Perrig diary, 32, MUL.
32. Short Bull's testimony, 12–13, BBMM.
33. *Iowa State Register*, December 2, 1890.
34. *Chicago Tribune*, December 14, 1890.
35. *New York Times*, November 27, 1890.
36. *New York World*, December 2, 1890.
37. *Iowa State Register*, December 4, 1890.
38. *New York World*, December 4, 1890.
39. *New York Times*, December 1, 1890.
40. *New York Herald*, November 30, 1890.

41. *New York World*, December 1, 1890.

42. *Chadron (NE) Democrat*, December 4, 1890.

43. *New York Times*, December 1, 1890.

44. *New York Herald*, November 30, 1890; also quoted in the *Chadron (NE) Democrat*, December 4, 1890.

45. Miles, "Report of Major General Miles," 145.

46. Much has been made of this medal being rescinded several years later, but the reason for this was that authorities realized that Cody was a civilian, not a military scout. The award was reserved for military personnel. Cody's citation for bravery survives, however, as he held the rank of colonel in the Nebraska National Guard.

47. The material concerning Cody's background can be found in my article "Buffalo Bill on Stage" and in Russell's *Lives and Legends of Buffalo Bill.*

48. The card used to be on display in the Buffalo Bill Historical Center.

49. *Iowa State Register*, November 27, 1890. In his book, Utley omits Keith and adds C. W. Chadwick and "five newspaper reporters" to the party (Utley, *Last Days*, 124).

50. *New York Times*, November 29, 1890.

51. *New York Times*, November 29, 1890.

52. *Chadron (NE) Democrat*, November 27, 1890.

53. Vestal, *New Sources*, 8–9.

54. Vestal, *New Sources*, 9–10.

55. Box 72, folder 4, WSC.

56. Steele, "Buffalo Bill's Bluff," 477–78.

57. William F. Drum to assistant adjutant general, Department of Dakota, November 30, 1890, in *Prologue: The Journal of the National Archives* 1 (fall 1969): 172–73.

58. A. R. Chapin to Walter S. Campbell, November 27, 1928, box 114, folder 5, WSC.

59. McLaughlin, *My Friend the Indian*, 210.

60. Earl A. Brininstool, "How Gen. Miles Blundered in Ordering Buffalo Bill to Arrest Sitting Bull," *El Segundo (CA) Herald*, December 28, 1928, 1, 4.

61. Steele, "Buffalo Bill's Bluff," 478.

62. *Chicago Tribune*, November 30, 1890.

63. Cody (ghostwritten), *Buffalo Bill's Life Story: An Autobiography*, 310–11. While this is not an accurate source, there is a germ of truth in this account of Cody's visit to Standing Rock.

64. Steele, "Buffalo Bill's Bluff," 478.

65. Vestal, *New Sources*, 70–71.

66. *New York World*, November 30, 1890.

67. *New York Times*, November 30, 1890.

68. Steele, "Buffalo Bill's Bluff," 478–79.

69. Cody, *Life Story*, 311.

70. Cody, *Life Story*, 311.

71. Brininstool, "How Gen. Miles Blundered in Ordering Buffalo Bill to Arrest Sitting Bull," *El Segundo (CA) Herald*, December 28, 1928, 4.

72. *New York Times*, December 2, 1890.

73. Miles to Cody, n.d., Cody's scrapbooks, Buffalo Bill Historical Center, Cody, WY. This is a typed, signed letter, written on the stationery of the headquarters of the Division of the Missouri.

74. *Chicago Tribune*, December 17, 1890.

75. Miles, *Serving the Republic*, 238.

9. IN THE CORRIDORS OF POWER

1. *New York World*, December 3, 1890.
2. Utley, *Last Days*, 137.
3. *Chadron (NE) Democrat*, December 4, 1890.
4. *Cong. Rec.*, 51st Cong., 2nd Sess., 1890, 45–48 (edited).
5. *New York World*, December 4, 1890.
6. *Cong. Rec.*, 51st Cong., 2nd Sess., 1890, 70.
7. *Cong. Rec.*, 51st Cong., 2nd Sess., 1890, 70–71.
8. *Iowa State Register*, December 5, 1890.
9. *New York World*, December 3, 1890.
10. *New York World*, December 3, 1890.
11. *New York Times*, December 4, 1890.
12. *Omaha Bee*, December 4, 1890.
13. *Iowa State Register*, December 4, 1890.
14. *Iowa State Register*, December 4, 1890.
15. *New York World*, December 8, 1890.
16. *New York World*, December 8, 1890.
17. *New York World*, December 8, 1980.
18. *Cong. Rec.*, 51st Cong., 2nd Sess., 1890, 198.
19. *Cong. Rec.*, 51st Cong., 2nd Sess., 1890, 199.
20. Remington, "Indians as Irregular Cavalry," 59.
21. Remington, "Indians as Irregular Cavalry," 62–63.

10. ON AND OFF THE RESERVATION

1. Bland, *A Brief History*, 21.
2. Bland, *A Brief History*, 20.
3. Eastman, *Deep Woods to Civilization*, 104.
4. *New York World*, December 3, 1890.
5. *Army and Navy Journal*, January 24, 1891.
6. Letter to the *Army and Navy Journal*, December 18, 1890, *Army and Navy Journal*, December 27, 1890.
7. Carroll, ed., *The Unpublished Papers of the Indian Wars*, 1–19. A photocopy of 2nd Lt. Alexander R. Piper's letter to his wife, dated December 13, 1890, can also be found at the NSHS.

8. Crickett to his family in England, n.d., American Museum in Britain (signed W. R. C.).

9. *Army and Navy Journal*, December 6, 1890.

10. *Army and Navy Journal*, December 6, 1890.

11. Mooney, "The Ghost Dance Religion," 883.

12. Goodale, "Ghost Dance War," 34.

13. Perrig diary, 32, MUL.

14. Perrig diary, 35, MUL.

15. *New York World*, December 7, 1890.

16. *New York World*, December 7, 1890.

17. *New York World*, December 16, 1890.

18. *New York World*, December 8, 1890.

19. *New York World*, December 8, 1890.

20. *Lincoln (NE) State Journal*, December 9, 1890.

21. *Chadron (NE) Democrat*, December 4, 1890.

22. *Chicago Tribune*, December 12, 1890.

23. *Chicago Tribune*, December 13, 1890.

24. *Chicago Tribune*, December 13, 1890.

25. *Chadron (NE) Democrat*, December 11, 1890.

26. *Chicago Tribune*, December 12, 1890.

27. *Chicago Tribune*, December 12, 1890.

28. *Chicago Tribune*, December 14, 1890.

29. Short Bull's testimony, 13, BBMM.

30. Perrig diary, 36, MUL.

31. Chicago Tribune, December 13, 1890.

32. *Chicago Tribune*, December 13, 1890.

33. *Chicago Tribune*, December 12, 1890.

34. *Chicago Tribune*, December 14, 1890.

35. *Chicago Tribune*, December 14, 1890.

36. J. B. McCloud to Doane Robinson, n.d. The enlistment enrollment for McCloud's unit is attached to the letter. A photocopy of this letter was given to me by R. Eli Paul, from his personal files.

37. Short Bull's testimony, 14, BBMM.

38. *New York World*, December 14, 1890.

39. Short Bull's testimony, 14–15, BBMM.

40. *New York World*, December 16, 1890.

41. *Chicago Tribune*, December 14, 1890.

42. *New York World*, December 16, 1890.

43. Short Bull's testimony, 15, BBMM.

44. *Chicago Tribune*, December 15, 1890.

45. *New York World*, December 15, 1890.

46. *Chicago Tribune*, December 12, 1890.

47. *Chicago Tribune*, December 13, 1890.

48. *New York World*, December 15, 1890.

49. *Army and Navy Journal*, December 20, 1890.

50. Carroll, *Unpublished Papers*, 1.

51. *Lincoln NE State Journal*, December 15, 1890.

52. Carroll, *Unpublished Papers*, 1.

53. *Chicago Tribune*, December 15, 1890.

54. J. B. McCloud to Doane Robinson, n.d., R. Eli Paul's personal files.

55. Carroll, *Unpublished Papers*, 1.

56. *New York Herald*, December 17, 1890.

57. Margaret Lemley Warren, *The Badlands Fox*, 19.

11. A SCAPEGOAT IS SELECTED

1. Fechet, "The True Story of the Death of Sitting Bull," 180. Middle-aged Edmund Gustav Fechet, a native of Michigan, entered the army as a volunteer sergeant on June 19, 1861. He was brevetted first lieutenant for gallant and meritorious service in the Battle of Antietam. He retired with the rank of brevet colonel on July 9, 1898. He left two accounts of the encounter at Grand River as well as a written report to his superior Colonel Drum.

2. *New York World*, December 1, 1890.

3. *New York World*, December 8, 1890.

4. Vestal, *New Sources*, 67–70.

5. Robinson, "Some Sidelights on the Character of Sitting Bull," 191.

6. Vestal, *New Sources*, 67–70.

7. *New York Times*, December 12, 1890.

8. Fechet, "True Story of the Death of Sitting Bull," 180–81.

9. Vestal, *New Sources*, 12.

10. Carroll, *Arrest and Killing*, 69–70. Mrs. One Bull was also known as Four Blanket Woman.

11. Vestal, *New Sources*, 71.

12. Carroll, *Arrest and Killing*, 71.

13. Carroll, *Arrest and Killing*, 69–70.

14. Carroll, *Arrest and Killing*, 70.

15. McLaughlin, *My Friend the Indian*, 214.

16. McLaughlin, *My Friend the Indian*, 214–15.

17. *New York World*, December 18, 1890.

18. *Iowa State Register*, December 19, 1890.

19. Frank B. Zahn to Walter S. Campbell, Fort Yates, November 3, 1929, box 107, WSC.

20. McLaughlin, *My Friend the Indian*, 215–16.

21. Vestal, *Sitting Bull*, 284–85.

22. *New York World*, December 18, 1890.

23. Utley, *The Lance and the Shield*, 290.

24. McLaughlin, *My Friend the Indian*, 423–24.

25. Vestal, *New Sources*, 13–14.

26. McLaughlin, *My Friend the Indian*, 216–17.

27. McLaughlin, *My Friend the Indian*, 217–18.

28. McLaughlin, *My Friend the Indian*, 218.

29. Vestal, *New Sources*, 14–15.

30. McLaughlin, *My Friend the Indian*, 424.

31. Miles, *Serving the Republic*, 239.

32. Red Tomahawk's testimony, U.S. Court of Claims, September 8, 1923, "Sioux Tribe of Indians vs. the U.S. of A.: Evidence for the Plaintiffs," Red Tomahawk biography file D, SDSHS, Pierre. Red Tomahawk's account is interesting but self-serving.

33. Vestal, *New Sources*, 22.

34. Carroll, *Arrest and Killing*, 37–38.

35. Fechet, "Capture of Sitting Bull," 187.

36. Carroll, *Arrest and Killing*, 42.

37. *New York World*, December 18, 1890. Drum's detailed orders to Fechet read as follows (Vestal, *New Sources*, 25–26; emphasis in original):

BY ORDER OF COLONEL W. F. DRUM:
Fort Yates, N.D.
December 14, 1890.

Captain E. G. Fechet, 8th Cavalry, will proceed with *Troops "F" and "G"* 8th Cavalry, the *Hotchkiss gun* and one *Gatling gun* to the crossing of *Oak Creek* by the *Sitting Bull road* for the purpose of preventing the *escape or rescue of Sitting Bull* should the *Indian police* succeed in arresting him.

The command will move out at *12:00 o'clock midnight*, in light *marching order*, and will be supplied with *50 rounds of carbine* and *12 rounds of revolver ammunition* per man, *4000 rounds of ammunition for Gatling gun, one day's cooked rations and one days forage.*

After receiving the prisoner, Captain Fechet will return with his command to this post reporting to the Commanding Officer on arrival.

If on arrival at *Oak Creek, Captain Fechet* learns that the police are fighting or need assistance, he will push on and if necessary follow *Sitting Bull* as long as possible with his supplies, keeping the *Post Commander* informed by courier of his movements.

The march will be so regulated as to reach *Oak Creek by 6:30 o'clock, A.M.* tomorrow the 15th instant.

Should arrest be made every precaution will be taken to prevent escape or rescue.

Two Indian scouts will accompany the command.

Assistant Surgeon A. R. Chapin, Medical Department, will report to *Captain Fechet* for duty with the expedition.

First Lieutenant S. L. H. Slocum, 8th Cavalry, with Troop "F" will also report to Captain *Fechet* for orders.

Second Lieutenant H. C. Brooks, 8th Cavalry will also report to *Captain Fechet* for duty with the expedition.

One *Hospital Ambulance* with necessary supplies will accompany the expedition, the *Quartermaster* furnishing the necessary team.

By orders of
Lieutenant Colonel W. F. Drum,
E. C. Brooks,
2nd Lieut. 8th Cavalry,
Post Adjutant

The two Lakota scouts were Smell the Bear and Iron Dog; Louis Primeau, serving the Indian Department at Standing Rock Agency, was the guide and interpreter.

38. Vestal, *New Sources*, 45–47.
39. Vestal, *New Sources*, 47.
40. Fechet, "Capture of Sitting Bull," 187–88.
41. *New York World*, December 18, 1890.
42. Vestal, *New Sources*, 25–26. Also see note 37 to this chapter.
43. Carroll, *Arrest and Killing*, 61.
44. Vestal, *New Sources*, 27.
45. Box 114, folder 8, WSC.
46. Vestal, *New Sources*, 4.
47. *New York World*, December 20, 1890.
48. Vestal, *New Sources*, 2.
49. *New York World*, December 18, 1890.
50. *New York World*, December 18, 1890.

12. DAWN ON GRAND RIVER

1. Carroll, *Arrest and Killing*, 90.
2. Box 114, folder 7, WSC.
3. Johnny Baker, Cody's arena master, to Campbell, July 30, 1929, box 113, folder 2, WSC:

Sitting Bull rode a grey horse in the Buffalo Bill wild west show, season 1885. When the show closed the season, 1885, at St. Louis Mo., Col Cody presented the horse to Sitting Bull, and paid the transportation charges on the horse back to Sitting Bulls reservation in So Dakota.

No doubt this is the horse Sitting Bull wished to be saddled just before he was killed.

The horse was fairly light grey, about 16-1 in height.

Old Bull was very fond of this horse which prompted Buffalo Bill to give it to him.

Yours truly
Johnny Baker

4. *New York Herald*, December 17, 1890.

5. Handwritten affidavit signed June 21, 1930, and witnessed by Campbell and Elmer Waggoner at Keldron SD, box 104, folder 14, WSC.

6. Carroll, *Arrest and Killing*, 86.

7. Carroll, *Arrest and Killing*, 70.

8. Carroll, *Arrest and Killing*, 90.

9. Vestal, *New Sources*, 27.

10. Carroll, *Arrest and Killing*, 70.

11. McLaughlin, *My Friend the Indian*, 218–19.

12. Carroll, *Arrest and Killing*, 69.

13. Box 114, folder 7, WSC.

14. Commissioner of Indian Affairs, "Reports of Agents (1891)," 335.

15. Box 114, folder 7, WSC.

16. Carroll, *Arrest and Killing*, 68. The accounts that follow have been assembled from a number of different sources, including transcriptions made by Carroll in *Arrest and Killing*, transcriptions from WSC, boxes 100 to 116, transcriptions of some of the material in McLaughlin's report and his autobiography, dispatches by the *New York World*'s correspondent, and Vestal's *Sitting Bull* and *New Sources*. In the latter are several lengthy documents, including Colonel W. F. Drum's report (22–24), Drum's orders to Fechet (25–26), Fechet's report (26–32), various letters and reports (1–19), and a number of interviews, personal accounts, and letters (including those by Lone Man [45–55]), Robert High Eagle (42–44), and Mary Collins (61–72).

If one person provides multiple accounts, I have annotated these. For instance, Fechet's accounts are drawn from his report to Drum as well as from his articles "The Capture of Sitting Bull" and "The True Story of the Death of Sitting Bull." Vestal did not include many of the detailed short accounts in *Sitting Bull* that are included in his *New Sources*. Other documents have been separately annotated.

17. Red Tomahawk's testimony, September 8, 1923, biography file D, SDSHS.

18. *New York Times*, December 17, 1890. That Crow Foot was only twelve was reported in the *New York Herald* on the same date. In the *Iowa State Register*, December 18, 1890, it was reported that Crow Foot was "a bright young man, only twelve years old." The One Bulls are more likely to be accurate.

19. Vestal, *Sitting Bull*, 300–301. Cody bought the horse from Sitting Bull's family and featured it in his exhibition at the Chicago World's Fair.

20. Commissioner of Indian Affairs, "Reports of Agents (1891)," 336.

21. Vestal, *New Sources*, 23.

22. Sgt. George B. DuBois to Pvt. George Thomas, December 18, 1890, MS 215, box 1, Colorado Historical Society, Denver. This source was pointed out to me by R. Eli Paul, who supplied me with a photocopy of the investigation.

23. Box 105, notebook 41, 121, WSC.

24. Bland, *A Brief History*, 29–30.

25. Carroll, *Arrest and Killing*, 71.

26. Carroll, *Arrest and Killing*, 89.

27. Carroll, *Arrest and Killing*, 88.

28. Bland, *A Brief History*, 29.

29. Sgt. George B. DuBois to Pvt. George Thomas, December 18, 1890, MS 215, box 1, Colorado Historical Society.

30. Carroll, *Arrest and Killing*, 93.

31. Box 114, notebook 5, WSC.

32. Box 114, folder 8, WSC.

33. Carroll, *Arrest and Killing*, 190–92.

34. Perrig diary, 34, MUL.

35. Danker, "Wounded Knee Interviews," 99.

36. *Iowa State Register*, December 16, 1890.

37. *Lincoln NE State Journal*, December 16, 1890.

38. *New York World*, December 16, 1890.

39. *New York Herald*, December 17, 1890.

40. *New York Times*, December 16, 1890.

41. *New York Herald*, December 17, 1890.

42. Carroll, *Unpublished Papers*, 1.

43. Box 114, folder 8, WSC.

44. Fechet, "True Story of the Death of Sitting Bull," 189.

45. Carroll, *Arrest and Killing*, 65.

46. Fechet, "True Story of the Death of Sitting Bull," 189.

47. *Iowa State Register*, December 18, 1890.

48. *Iowa State Register*, December 17, 1890.

49. Several newspaper articles quoted the telegram in full. The commissioner was not as prompt in his reply to McLaughlin's report. The following is taken from Commissioner of Indian Affairs, "Report of Agents (1891)," 235.

Washington, Dec. 30, 1890

James McLaughlin
U.S. Indian Agent
Standing Rock, N.D.,

Sir:

Your communication of the 16th inst. is received wherein you report in detail the arrest and subsequent death of Sitting Bull, speak of the bravery and good judgment of your Indian police, recommend that the noble services of the survivors receive substantial recognition, that the families of those who were killed will be amply provided for, and that this department and the War Department join in an effort to obtain congressional action to that end if necessary.

In reply you are informed that this office will do all in its power to have Congress recognize and reward the praiseworthy and valuable services rendered by these men and to provide for the needs of the families of those who were killed and, in the meantime, you will see to it that they do not suffer for lack of any supplies and requisites for their sustenance and comfort, and any specific recommendation you may make in regard to them, pending legislation in their favor, will be carefully considered and promptly approved by me, if practicable and proper.

I also desire you to publicly commend in my name the bravery and fidelity of the force and inform the survivors that, while I sincerely regret that the taking of life was necessary, it is gratifying to me to know that I have such reliable assistants in my efforts to promote the welfare of these people and that their noble conduct has been highly praised wherever spoken of.

Respectfully,
T. J. Morgan
Commissioner

Years later McLaughlin published the letter of commendation in his autobiography and commented, "This sufficiently voices the sentiments of the Indian Office of that day regarding the action of the Indian police at Standing Rock" (*My Friend the Indian*, 409).

50. *New York Herald*, December 16, 1890.

51. Commissioner of Indian Affairs, "Reports of Agents (1891)," 337.

52. *New York Herald*, December 17, 1890.

53. McLaughlin, *My Friend the Indian*, 221.

13. AFTERMATH AND REPERCUSSIONS

1. *Army and Navy Journal*, December 20, 1890; also reported in *New York Times*, December 17, 1890.

2. *Columbus (NE) Sentinel*, January 1, 1891.

3. *New York Herald*, December 17, 1890.

4. Vestal, *New Sources*, 54–55.

5. McLaughlin, *My Friend the Indian*, 432–34.

6. McLaughlin, *My Friend the Indian*, 221–22.

7. Matthew Steele, "The Death of Sitting Bull: A Reminiscence," box 114, folder 8, 13, WSC.

8. Carroll, *Arrest and Killing*, 65.

9. Fechet, "Capture of Sitting Bull," 192–93.

10. *Iowa State Register*, December 17, 1890, 2.

11. *Iowa State Register*, December 17, 1890, 2.

12. McLaughlin, *My Friend the Indian*, 415.

13. McLaughlin, *My Friend the Indian*, 417.

14. Box 114, folder 6, WSC.

15. Bland, *A Brief History*, 30.

16. Letter to the *New York World*, December 21, 1890, in Bland, *A Brief History*, 25–26.

17. *Chicago Tribune*, December 17, 1890.

18. *New York Herald*, December 17, 1890.
19. Colby, "Sioux Indian War," 151.
20. McLaughlin, *My Friend the Indian*, 407.
21. *Chicago Tribune*, December 17, 1890.
22. Vestal, *New Sources*, 31–32.
23. McLaughlin, *My Friend the Indian*, 218.
24. *New York World*, December 24, 1890.
25. Bland, *A Brief History*, 27.
26. *New York Times*, December 23, 1890; emphasis in original.
27. *New York Times*, December 23, 1890.
28. *New York Times*, December 20, 1890.
29. *New York World*, December 18, 1890.
30. Vestal, *New Sources*, 79.
31. *New York World*, December 18, 1890.
32. F. F. Hodge of the Museum of the American Indian to Walter S. Campbell, September 29, 1931, box 114, folder 5, 5, WSC. The official casualty list follows:

> Number of policemen killed in the fight, four; number mortally wounded and since dead, two; number severely wounded, one. Number of hostiles killed, including Sitting Bull, eight; number of hostiles wounded, three; number of prisoners captured, two. The wounded hostiles were Bull Ghost, Brave Thunder, and Strike the Kettle. The two former are on the Reservation and the latter is at Fort Sully.
>
> Number who surrendered to the agent or police after the fight (men, women, and children), 160; number of those who, having left the Reservation, have since surrendered to the agent or police, 88, for a total of 248 surrendered (Nelson A. Miles, "Report of Major General Miles," 196–97).

1. Henry Bullhead, First Lieutenant, died 82 hours after the fight.
2. Charles Shave Head, First Sergeant, died 25 hours after the fight.
3. James Little Eagle, Fourth Sergeant, killed.
4. Paul Akicitah, Private, killed.
5. John Armstrong, Special, killed.
6. David Hawkman, Special, killed.
7. Alexander Middle, Private, killed.

1. Sitting Bull, 56 years old, killed.
2. Crow Foot (Sitting Bull's son), 17 years old, killed.
3. Black Bird, 43 years old, killed.
4. Catch the Bear, 44 years old, killed.
5. Spotted Horn Bull, 56 years old, killed.
6. Brave Thunder, 46 years old, killed.
7. Little Assiniboine, 44 years old, killed.
8. Chase Wounded, 24 years old, killed.

9. Bull Ghost, wounded; entirely recovered.
10. Brave Thunder, wounded, recovering.
11. Strike the Kettle, wounded, recovered (Commissioner of Indian Affairs, "Reports of Agents [1891]," 338).

33. *Lincoln NE State Journal*, December 17, 1890.
34. *New York Herald*, December 17, 1890.
35. *New York Herald*, December 17, 1890.
36. Eastman, *Deep Woods to Civilization*, 102.
37. Goodale, "Ghost Dance War," 34–35.
38. *New York Herald*, December 17, 1890.
39. McLaughlin, *My Friend the Indian*, 218.
40. *New York World*, December 18, 1890.
41. *New York Herald*, December 17, 1890.
42. *Lincoln NE State Journal*, December 18, 1890.
43. *Army and Navy Journal*, December 27, 1890; emphasis in original.
44. Clipping, ca. December 18, 1890, SDSHS. This is probably from a local newspaper.
45. *New York Herald*, December 17, 1890.
46. *New York Herald*, December 17, 1890.
47. *New York World*, December 18, 1890.
48. *Iowa State Register*, December 18, 1890.
49. *New York Times*, December 18, 1890.
50. *New York World*, December 18, 1890.
51. *Iowa State Register*, December 19, 1890.
52. *Chicago Tribune*, December 17, 1890.
53. Eastman, *Deep Woods to Civilization*, 102–3.
54. *Iowa State Register*, December 18, 1890.

14. SURRENDER

1. U.S. Senate, *Hearing before the Select Committee on Indian Affairs*, April 30, 1991. Alice Ghost Horse, also known as Kills the Enemy and War Bonnet, told her story to her son, John War Bonnet. He transcribed her story in Lakota. The document was kept by her family until Sidney Keit, a Lakota language instructor, translated it into English. Sam Eaglestaff, president of the Cheyenne River Wounded Knee Survivors Association, placed her testimony in the Senate hearing records. He says Keit told him, "This story sounds horrible, as it is written in the Lakota language. White men's words cannot clearly express what she is explaining." Alice Ghost Horse was born in 1878 and died in 1950. I have repunctuated and edited her commentary slightly for clarity.

2. Danker, "Wounded Knee Interviews," 164–79. Joseph Horn Cloud says he thinks it was November 17, but he probably meant December 17. His account to Ricker has been cast in the first person, since Ricker let it drift between third and first person when he recorded it in his notebooks.

3. Beach, "Wounded Knee," *Appleton's Booklover's Magazine*, June 1906, 732–33.

4. Ricker notebooks, tablet 12, ESR, NSHS.

5. *Army and Navy Journal*, December 27, 1890.

6. Short Bull's testimony, 16, BBMM.

7. Ricker notebooks, tablet 12, ESR, NSHS.

8. *Chadron (NE) Democrat*, December 25, 1890.

9. Allen, "In the West That Was," 240, MS2635, NSHS.

10. William Fitch Kelley, "The Indian Troubles and the Battle of Wounded Knee," 37.

11. Kelley, *Pine Ridge 1890*, 151–53.

12. Allen, "In the West That Was," 240, MS2635, NSHS.

13. Allen, "In the West That Was," 240, MS2635, NSHS.

14. *Chadron (NE) Democrat*, December 25, 1890.

15. Danker, "Wounded Knee Interviews," 187.

16. U.S. Senate, *Hearing before the Select Committee*, April 30, 1991, 61.

17. Danker, "Wounded Knee Interviews," 167–69.

18. U.S. Senate, *Hearing before the Select Committee*, April 30, 1991, 61–62.

19. Mooney, "The Ghost Dance Religion," 883. From a barracks ballad composed by Pvt. W. H. Prather, Ninth Cavalry, I Company.

20. Cyrus Townsend Brady, *Indian Fights and Fighters*, 352.

21. Mooney, "The Ghost Dance Religion," 883.

22. *Omaha World Herald*, December 25, 1890.

23. Morgan, "Reminiscences," 52.

24. Eastman, *Deep Woods to Civilization*, 104–7.

25. Danker, "Wounded Knee Interviews," 169.

26. Beach, "Wounded Knee," *Appleton's Booklover's Magazine*, June 1906, 733.

27. U.S. Adjutant General, "Report of the Investigation," 90.

28. Whitside's report, *Army and Navy Journal*, January 24, 1891.

29. Carroll, *Unpublished Papers*, 4. Some of Piper's letters were dated a day early, but this one seems to have been written on the 26th.

30. U.S. Adjutant General, "Report of the Investigation," 101.

31. Whitside's report, *Army and Navy Journal*, January 24, 1891.

32. Danker, "Wounded Knee Interviews," 169.

33. Whitside's report, *Army and Navy Journal*, January 24, 1891.

34. Paul High Back, "Disaster of December 29, 1890, at Wounded Knee, as told to John Williamson," *Wi-iyohi* 10, no. 3 (June 1, 1956): 2.

35. U.S. Senate, *Hearing before the Select Committee*, April 30, 1991, 62–63.

36. Beach, "Wounded Knee," *Appleton's Booklover's Magazine*, June 1906, 733.

37. Whitside's report, *Army and Navy Journal*, January 24, 1891.

38. Danker, "Wounded Knee Interviews," 169.

39. U.S. Senate, *Hearing before the Select Committee*, April 30, 1991, 63.

40. Danker, "Wounded Knee Interviews," 188–89.

41. Danker, "Wounded Knee Interviews," 170.

42. *Iowa State Register*, December 30, 1890.

43. Gilmore, "Truth of the Wounded Knee Massacre," 246.

44. Danker, "Wounded Knee Interviews," 188–89.

45. Beach, "Wounded Knee," *Appleton's Booklover's Magazine*, June 1906, 733.

46. Beach, "Wounded Knee," *Appleton's Booklover's Magazine*, June 1906, 733.

47. Danker, "Wounded Knee Interviews," 188–89.

48. Danker, "Wounded Knee Interviews," 170.

49. Gilmore, "Truth of the Wounded Knee Massacre," 246.

50. Beach, "Wounded Knee," *Appleton's Booklover's Magazine*, June 1906, 733.

51. Gilmore, "Truth of the Wounded Knee Massacre," 246.

52. High Back, "Disaster of December 29, 1890," 2.

53. Crickett, to his family in England, n.d., American Museum in Britain.

54. *Iowa State Register*, December 30, 1890.

55. Whitside's report, *Army and Navy Journal*, January 24, 1891.

56. Whitside's report, *Army and Navy Journal*, January 24, 1891.

57. Danker, "Wounded Knee Interviews," 170.

58. Celene Not Help Him, "A Descendant Relates Her Grandfather's Version," undated newspaper clipping titled "Wounded Knee Remembered," SDSHS.

59. U.S. Adjutant General, "Report of the Investigation," 91.

60. Goodale, "Ghost Dance War," 36.

61. Gilmore, "Truth of the Wounded Knee Massacre," 251.

62. U.S. Adjutant General, "Report of the Investigation," 5.

63. U.S. Adjutant General, "Report of the Investigation," 105.

64. U.S. Adjutant General, "Report of the Investigation," 105.

65. Florence Joint, quoting Mrs. Royer, January 26, 1954, John R. Brennan Family papers, SDSHS.

66. E. D. Scott, "Wounded Knee: A Look at the Record," 11. Scott's analysis of the massacre is detailed, but partisan. He bases his article mainly on the "Report of Investigation." He accepts the sworn statements of the officers involved without question, even when there are inconsistencies and deviations from logic and other accounts. The only Lakota testimony he uses is by Frog, a member of Big Foot's band. Nevertheless, his description of the landscape and the camp is accurate.

67. *New York World*, December 29, 1890.

68. Cook, *Fifty Years*, 235.

69. Cook, *Fifty Years*, 235.

70. Watson, "The Last Indian War," 214. Watson says Tibbles left before the fighting began. Tibbles apparently heard the firing as he was returning to Pine

Ridge and filed the first report of fighting at Wounded Knee. The first detailed report was filed by Kelley of the *Nebraska State Journal*. According to Watson, only one telegrapher was on duty at Pine Ridge. He writes, "Previously the correspondents at Pine Ridge had made an agreement as to the order in which this one operator should handle these daily stories." The novice reporter Kelley was first for December 29 and had his detailed account on the wire by that same evening.

71. Perrig diary, preface, MUL. Father Craft also testified for the Seventh Cavalry after the massacre.

72. U.S. Adjutant General, "Report of the Investigation," 69–70.

73. Cook, *Fifty Years*, 236–38.

74. U.S. Adjutant General, "Report of the Investigation," 91–92.

75. Gilmore, "Truth of the Wounded Knee Massacre," 246.

76. U.S. Adjutant General, "Report of the Investigation," 12–13.

77. Crickett, to his family in England, n.d, American Museum in Britain.

78. U.S. Senate, *Hearing before the Select Committee on Indian Affairs*, September 25, 1990, 63.

79. Gilmore, "Truth of the Wounded Knee Massacre," 251.

80. Allen, "In the West That Was," 262, MS2635, NSHS.

81. Bennett County Historical Society, *70 Years of Pioneer Life in Bennett County, South Dakota, 1911–1981*, 393.

82. U.S. Senate, *Hearing before the Select Committee*, September 25, 1990, 117. According to the Lakota's counselor, Mario Gonzalez, this statement is from unpublished papers held by Reverend Garvie's daughter Elaine Garvie Melior.

83. Ricker notebooks, tablet 11, ESR, NSHS.

84. Ricker notebooks, tablet 17, ESR, NSHS.

85. U.S. Senate, *Hearing before the Select Committee*, April 30, 1991, 63.

86. U.S. Senate, *Hearing before the Select Committee*, September 25, 1990, 117.

87. U.S. Senate, *Hearing before the Select Committee*, April 30, 1991, 24–25.

88. High Back, "Disaster of December 29, 1890," 3.

89. Not Help Him, "A Descendant Relates Her Grandfather's Version," undated newspaper clipping titled "Wounded Knee Remembered," SDSHS.

90. Preface, Perrig diary, MUL. The military view of what happened at Wounded Knee would be greatly influenced by the testimonies of eighteen officers, among whom were Edgerly, Godfrey, Ilsley, Moylan, and Varnum. Godfrey was involved in a proven atrocity.

91. Ricker notebooks, tablet 35, ESR, NSHS.

92. Ricker notebooks, tablet 12, ESR, NSHS.

15. THE DEATH OF A PEOPLE'S DREAM

1. U.S. Adjutant General, "Report of the Investigation," 103.

2. Danker, "Wounded Knee Interviews," 190.

3. U.S. Senate, *Hearing before the Select Committee*, April 30, 1991, 63.

4. Allen, "In the West That Was," 263–64, MS2635, NSHS.

5. Danker, "Wounded Knee Interviews," 223.

6. U.S. Adjutant General, "Report of the Investigation," 42.

7. Danker, "Wounded Knee Interviews," 191.

8. U.S. Adjutant General, "Report of the Investigation," 69–70.

9. Scott, "A Look at the Record," 11.

10. U.S. Adjutant General, "Report of the Investigation," 6–7.

11. Rex Alan Smith, *Moon of the Popping Trees*, 183–84.

12. U.S. Adjutant General, "Report of the Investigation," 65.

13. Goodale, "Ghost Dance War," 39.

14. Scott, "A Look at the Record," 11.

15. Several of the accounts that follow are drawn from James H. McGregor's *Wounded Knee Massacre*, 94–131; others came from the Ricker interviews, newspapers on anniversaries of the massacre, and separate testimonies. A few come from the proceedings of the investigation of Forsyth, but these I have approached with caution since many of the officer accounts seem self-serving and are inaccurate when juxtaposed with Lakota testimony. Crickett's letter plays a key part in the narrative that follows. From this point on, only new sources or informants that related their stories to more than one source will be annotated.

In interviews of Miniconjou survivors in 1913, McGregor took statements from Dewey Beard (longer ones are drawn from Ricker, Gilmore, and Beach and from old newspaper clippings), James Pipe on Head, Rough Feather, Louise Weasel Bear, George Running Hawk, Mrs. Mosseau, Bertha Kills Close to the Lodge, Edward Owl King, White Lance, John Little Finger, Henry Jackson or Harry Kills White Man, Alice Dog Arm or Kills Plenty, Peter Stands, Donald Blue Hair, Afraid of the Enemy, Mrs. Rough Feather, Frank Sits Poor, Richard Afraid of Hawk, Black Hair, Charles Blind Man, James High Hawk, Dog Chief, Charles Blue Arm, Annie Iron Lavatta Hakiktawin, and Nellie Knife.

16. Ricker notebooks, tablet 14, ESR, NSHS.

17. Danker, "Wounded Knee Interviews," 219.

18. Danker, "Wounded Knee Interviews," 104.

19. Ricker notebooks, tablet 27, ESR, NSHS.

20. U.S. Adjutant General, "Report of the Investigation," 71.

21. High Back, "Disaster of December 29, 1890," 3.

22. Lindberg, "Foreigners in Action at Wounded Knee," 175.

23. Allen, "In the West That Was," 266, MS2635, NSHS.

24. Danker, "Wounded Knee Interviews," 171.

25. Danker, "Wounded Knee Interviews," 171.

26. Wells, "Ninety-Six Years," 285.

27. Danker, "Wounded Knee Interviews," 170–71.

28. Lindberg, "Foreigners in Action," 175.

29. U.S. Adjutant General, "Report of the Investigation," 6–7.

30. U.S. Adjutant General, "Report of the Investigation," 15–16.

31. Danker, "Wounded Knee Interviews," 191. Gilmore recorded an almost identical account by Dewey Beard in "Truth of the Wounded Knee Massacre," 249.

> If I was not called I had a notion to stay in my tent. While I was sitting inside there was some noise, the women seemed to be excited and in fear. I looked out and saw some confusion among the women. I saw, when I looked out, that a gang of soldiers was searching the women and taking away all axes, crowbars and old guns that had been left; and they opened the women's shawls and took their awls and knives. Now when I saw this, I did not want to give up my gun, so I took my knife and dug a hole by the fireplace and hid my gun. After I had hid my gun, a sergeant opened my tent and saw me sitting there. He pointed toward a place where the men were sitting and told me to go there. While I was going to that place I saw my brother Joe coming towards our camp. When I went into that place I saw the faces of all the men changed, showing fear and excitement.

32. There is no record of a medicine man named Yellow Bird at Wounded Knee. It is a name used later by Mooney. However, it is certain that a Miniconjou medicine man played a key role in the negotiations.

33. Lindberg, "Foreigners in Action," 175–76.

34. Ricker notebooks, tablet 17, ESR, NSHS.

35. Danker, "Wounded Knee Interviews," 207–8.

36. Wells, "Ninety-Six Years," 286.

37. U.S. Adjutant General, "Report of the Investigation," 16.

38. Danker, "Wounded Knee Interviews," 191–92.

39. Gilmore, "Truth of the Wounded Knee Massacre," 249.

40. Danker, "Wounded Knee Interviews," 191.

41. Not Help Him, "A Descendant Relates Her Grandfather's Version," undated newspaper clipping titled "Wounded Knee Remembered," SDSHS.

42. Gilmore, "Truth of the Wounded Knee Massacre," 247–48.

43. Ricker, tablet 17, ESR, NSHS.

44. Wells, "Ninety-Six Years," 286.

45. Danker, "Wounded Knee Interviews," 230.

46. Danker, "Wounded Knee Interviews," 219.

47. McGregor, *Wounded Knee Massacre*, 124.

48. Goodale, "Ghost Dance War," 39.

49. Lindberg, "Foreigners in Action," 176.

50. Ricker notebooks, tablet 17, ESR, NSHS.

51. Danker, "Wounded Knee Interviews," 250.

52. McGregor, *Wounded Knee Massacre*, 97.

53. Danker, "Wounded Knee Interviews," 193.

54. Commissioner of Indian Affairs, "Reports of Agents (1891)," 180.

55. McGregor, *Wounded Knee Massacre*, 97.

56. U.S. Adjutant General, "Report of the Investigation," 7.

57. U.S. Adjutant General, "Report of the Investigation," 16.

58. High Back, "Disaster of December 29, 1890," 1–3.

59. Lt. Col. Frazer Arnold, "Ghost Dance and Wounded Knee," *Cavalry Journal* 43 (1934), 18–20.

60. Remington, "Indians as Irregular Cavalry," 67; originally quoted in *Harper's Weekly*, January 24, 1891.

61. U.S. Adjutant General, "Report of the Investigation," 41–42.

62. U.S. Adjutant General, "Report of the Investigation," 29.

63. Danker, "Wounded Knee Interviews," 230–31.

64. Wells, "Ninety-Six Years," 287.

65. Wells, "Ninety-Six Years," 293.

66. U.S. Adjutant General, "Report of the Investigation," 7–8.

67. U.S. Adjutant General, "Report of the Investigation," 18.

68. U.S. Adjutant General, "Report of the Investigation," 23.

69. High Back, "Disaster of December 29, 1890," 2–3.

70. Danker, "Wounded Knee Interviews," 219.

71. Scott, "A Look at the Record," 16.

72. Carroll, *Unpublished Papers*, 5.

73. *Army and Navy Journal*, January 3, 1891.

74. U.S. Adjutant General, "Report of the Investigation," 101.

75. U.S. Adjutant General, "Report of the Investigation," 101.

76. Not Help Him, "A Descendant Relates Her Grandfather's Version," undated newspaper clipping titled "Wounded Knee Remembered," SDSHS.

77. Ricker notebooks, tablet 17, ESR, NSHS.

78. Beach, "Wounded Knee," *Appleton's Booklover's Magazine*, June 1906, 735–36.

79. Lindberg, "Foreigners in Action," 176. Charles B. Ewing says that Wallace was hit with a bullet in the lower abdomen and received two cuts with a tomahawk or hatchet ("The Wounded of the Wounded Knee Battle Field with Remarks on Wounds Produced by Large and Small Caliber Bullets," 41). It is possible that Wallace was scalped.

80. Danker, "Wounded Knee Interviews," 209. In a much later interview, Wells says, "Captain Wallace was killed at this time while standing in front of his troops. A bullet, striking him in the forehead, plowed away the top of his head" ("Ninety-Six Years," 287).

81. Danker, "Wounded Knee Interviews," 208.

82. Allen, "In the West That Was," 286, MS2635, NSHS.

83. Danker, "Wounded Knee Interviews," 208–9.

84. Lathrop, "Another View of Wounded Knee," 256.

85. *Omaha Bee*, December 30, 1890.

86. Danker, "Wounded Knee Interviews," 193.

87. Beach, "Wounded Knee," *Appleton's Booklover's Magazine*, June 1906, 735.

88. Ricker notebooks, tablet 11, ESR, NSHS.

89. Cook, *Fifty Years*, 197–98.

90. Charles B. Ewing, "The Wounded of the Wounded Knee Battle Field," 39.

91. U.S. Adjutant General, "Report of the Investigation," 28.

92. Ricker, tablet 3, ESR, NSHS.

93. Cook, *Fifty Years*, 240.

94. Ricker notebooks, tablet 14, ESR, NSHS.

95. Watson, "Last Indian War," 209.

96. Mooney, "The Ghost Dance Religion," 883.

97. Not Help Him, "A Descendant Relates Her Grandfather's Version," undated newspaper clipping titled "Wounded Knee Remembered," SDSHS.

98. Beach, "Wounded Knee," *Appleton's Booklover's Magazine*, June 1906, 735–36.

99. Not Help Him, "A Descendant Relates Her Grandfather's Version," undated newspaper clipping titled "Wounded Knee Remembered," SDSHS.

100. Danker, "Wounded Knee Interviews," 194–95.

101. Colby, "Sioux Indian War," 156–57.

102. Danker, "Wounded Knee Interviews," 219.

103. *Omaha Bee*, December 30, 1890.

16. ON THE FIELD OF HONOR

1. U.S. Adjutant General, "Report of the Investigation," 8.

2. U.S. Adjutant General, "Report of the Investigation," 7–8.

3. Lindberg, "Foreigners in Action," 176.

4. Statements not annotated have been drawn from McGregor, *Wounded Knee Massacre*, 94–131.

5. Wells, "Ninety-Six Years," 287.

6. Commissioner of Indian Affairs, "Reports of Agents (1891)," 180.

7. U.S. Adjutant General, "Report of the Investigation," 106.

8. *Omaha Bee*, December 30, 1890.

9. Ricker notebooks, tablet 27, ESR, NSHS.

10. Danker, "Wounded Knee Interviews," 223.

11. Gilmore, "Truth of the Wounded Knee Massacre," 251; McGregor, *Wounded Knee Massacre*, 105.

12. *Argus (SD) Leader*, March 26, 1890.

13. Moorehead, "Indian Messiah and Ghost Dance," 166.

14. U.S. Senate, *Hearing before the Select Committee*, September 25, 1990, 125.

15. *Rapid City (SD) Daily Journal*, February 26, 1891.

16. Moorehead, "Indian Messiah and Ghost Dance," 166; emphasis in original.

17. U.S. Adjutant General, "Report of the Investigation," 49.

18. *Lincoln NE State Journal*, December 30, 1890.

19. Goodale, "Ghost Dance War," 39.

20. Lindberg, "Foreigners in Action," 176–77.

21. Ricker notebooks, tablet 11, ESR, NSHS.

22. *Argus (SD) Leader*, March 26, 1890.

23. Ricker notebooks, tablet 26, ESR, NSHS.

24. Danker, "Wounded Knee Interviews," 220.

25. Beach, "Wounded Knee," *Appleton's Booklover's Magazine*, June 1906, 736.

26. Gilmore, "Truth of the Wounded Knee Massacre," 249.

27. Beach, "Wounded Knee," *Appleton's Booklover's Magazine*, June 1906, 736.

28. Boyd Bosma, "An Interview with Jim Mesteth," 18.

29. *Army and Navy Journal*, January 24, 1891.

30. Beach, "Wounded Knee," *Appleton's Booklover's Magazine*, June 1906, 736.

31. Lindberg, "Foreigners in Action," 177.

32. Beach, "Wounded Knee," *Appleton's Booklover's Magazine*, June 1906, 736.

33. Allen, "In the West That Was," 276–81, MS2635, NSHS.

34. Danker, "Wounded Knee Interviews," 227.

35. Utley, *Last Days*, 213.

36. Ricker notebooks, tablet 29, ESR, NSHS.

37. McGregor, *Wounded Knee Massacre*, 100.

38. Beach, "Wounded Knee," *Appleton's Booklover's Magazine*, June 1906, 736.

39. Goodale, "Ghost Dance War," 36–37.

40. Eastman, *Deep Woods to Civilization*, 107.

41. Arthur W. Zimiga, "Stories from Past, Lessons for Future," *Rapid City (SD) Daily Journal*, December 21, 1990.

42. Morgan, "Reminiscences," 55–56.

43. Sister Mary Clement Fitzgerald, P. B. V. M., "Bishop Marty and His Sioux Missions: 1876–1896," *South Dakota Historical Collections* 20 (1940): 545.

44. Danker, "Wounded Knee Interviews," 216.

45. Danker, "Wounded Knee Interviews," 216.

46. U.S. Adjutant General, "Report of the Investigation," 27.

47. Edward S. Godfrey, "Tragedy at White Horse Creek: General Godfrey's Account of an Incident near Wounded Knee, in 1890," 3–5.

48. Godfrey, "Tragedy at White Horse Creek," 6.

49. U.S. Adjutant General, "Report of the Investigation," 80–81.

50. *New York Sun*, October 10, 1907.

51. Goodale, "Ghost Dance War," 39–40. Originally quoted in Fairfax

Downey's *Indian-Fighting Army* (1942), who in turn was quoting Godwin's personal story to the War College on May 29, 1931.

52. Ricker notebooks, tablet 5, ESR, NSHS.

53. U.S. Adjutant General, "Report of the Investigation," 25–26.

54. Crickett, to his family in England, n.d., American Museum in Britain.

55. Wells, "Ninety-Six," 304.

56. U.S. Adjutant General, "Report of the Investigation," 107.

57. McGregor, *Wounded Knee Massacre*, 126.

58. McGregor, *Wounded Knee Massacre*, 112.

59. John G. Neihart, *Black Elk Speaks, Being the Story of a Holy Man of the Ogalala Sioux*, 220–21.

60. Short Bull's testimony, 16, BBMM.

61. Short Bull's testimony, 17, BBMM.

62. Vestal, *New Sources*, 85.

63. Ewing, "Wounded of the Wounded Knee Battle Field," 40.

64. Ewing, "Wounded of the Wounded Knee Battle Field," 40–41.

65. Eastman, *Deep Woods to Civilization*, 107–10.

66. *Army and Navy Journal*, December 6, 1890.

67. Eastman, *Deep Woods to Civilization*, 107–10.

68. Goodale, "Ghost Dance War," 36.

69. Colby, "Sioux Indian War," 158.

70. Carroll, *Unpublished Papers*, 7.

71. Eastman, *Deep Woods to Civilization*, 107–10.

72. Carroll, *Unpublished Papers*, 6.

73. Bland, *A Brief History*, 21–22.

74. Eastman, *Deep Woods to Civilization*, 107–10.

75. Goodale, "Ghost Dance War," 37.

76. Eastman, *Deep Woods to Civilization*, 109–10.

77. Ricker notebooks, tablet 29, ESR, NSHS.

78. Carroll, *Unpublished Papers*, 7.

79. *Chadron (NE) Democrat*, January 8, 1891.

80. *New York World*, December 31, 1890.

17. AFTERSHOCKS

1. Standing Bear, *My People the Sioux*, 223–24.

2. Crickett, to his family in England, n.d., American Museum in Britain.

3. Brady, *Indian Fights and Fighters*, 353.

4. *New York World*, December 31, 1890.

5. *Army and Navy Journal*, January 7, 1891.

6. Zimiga, "Stories from Past, Lessons for Future," *Rapid City (SD) Daily Journal*, December 21, 1990.

7. Danker, " Wounded Knee Interviews," 216.

8. Utley, *Last Days*, 237.

9. Danker, "Wounded Knee Interviews," 216.

10. *New York Times*, January 3, 1890.

11. Danker, "Wounded Knee Interviews," 216.

12. Danker, "Wounded Knee Interviews," 216.

13. Danker, "Wounded Knee Interviews," 217.

14. Danker, "Wounded Knee Interviews," 217.

15. Danker, "Wounded Knee Interviews," 217.

16. Utley, *Last Days*, 240.

17. Brady, *Indian Fights and Fighters*, 354.

18. *Army and Navy Journal*, January 17, 1891.

19. Ricker notebooks, tablet 24, ESR, NSHS.

20. U.S. Senate, *Hearing before the Select Committee on Indian Affairs*, April 30, 1991, 67–68.

21. Short Bull's testimony, 17–18, BBMM.

22. Eastman, *Deep Woods to Civilization*, 110–14.

23. Howe, *Life and Labors of Bishop Hare*, 240, and Utley, *Last Days*, 235. Originally quoted in "The Bishop's Column," *Church News*, January 1891.

24. Goodale, "Ghost Dance War," 37. An oddly polemic account of the life of orphan Lost Bird can be found in Renée Sansom Flood's *Lost Bird of Wounded Knee* (New York: Scribner, 1995).

25. Ricker notebooks, tablet 11, ESR, NSHS.

26. Mooney, "The Ghost Dance Religion," 877–79.

27. *Chadron (NE) Democrat*, January 7, 1891. In a few days after the massacre, Agent James McLaughlin attempted to have souvenirs such as those Allen collected returned to the Lakota families.

28. Standing Bear, *My People the Sioux*, 225–26.

29. *Chadron (NE) Democrat*, January 1, 1891.

30. Colby, "Sioux Indian War," 157–58. This telegram was also printed in the *Iowa State Register*, December 31, 1890.

31. U.S. Adjutant General, "Report of the Investigation," 108–10.

32. *Iowa State Register*, December 31, 1890.

33. *Army and Navy Journal*, January 24, 1891.

34. Danker, "Wounded Knee Interviews," 176–79.

35. Gilmore, "Truth of the Wounded Knee Massacre," 248.

36. Colby, "Sioux Indian War," 159.

37. Commissioner of Indian Affairs, "Reports of Agents (1891)," 130.

38. Crickett, to his family in England, n.d., American Museum in Britain.

39. *New York Times*, January 2, 1891.

40. Standing Bear, *My People the Sioux*, 227.

41. Colby, "Sioux Indian War," 158–59.

42. *Rapid City (SD) Daily Journal*, December 31, 1990.

43. Wells, "Ninety-Six Years," 294.

44. Utley, *Last Days*, 245.

45. U.S. Adjutant General, "Report of the Investigation," 11.

46. U.S. Adjutant General, "Report of the Investigation," 14.

47. U.S. Adjutant General, "Report of the Investigation," 19.

48. U.S. Adjutant General, "Report of the Investigation," 28.

49. U.S. Adjutant General, "Report of the Investigation," 28–29.

50. U.S. Adjutant General, "Report of the Investigation," 30–31.

51. U.S. Adjutant General, "Report of the Investigation," 33.

52. U.S. Adjutant General, "Report of the Investigation," 35.

53. U.S. Adjutant General, "Report of the Investigation," 39.

54. U.S. Adjutant General, "Report of the Investigation," 42–43.

55. U.S. Adjutant General, "Report of the Investigation," 44.

56. U.S. Adjutant General, "Report of the Investigation," 45–46.

57. U.S. Adjutant General, "Report of the Investigation," 46–47.

58. U.S. Adjutant General, "Report of the Investigation," 49.

59. U.S. Adjutant General, "Report of the Investigation," 9.

60. U.S. Adjutant General, "Report of the Investigation," 21.

61. U.S. Adjutant General, "Report of the Investigation," 34.

62. U.S. Adjutant General, "Report of the Investigation," 87.

63. U.S. Adjutant General, "Report of the Investigation," 47.

64. Scott, "A Look at the Record," 11.

65. U.S. Adjutant General, "Report of the Investigation," 76.

66. Capt. Frank D. Baldwin's January 17, 1891, report. The report is attached to a February 5, 1876, letter from the acting secretary of the Department of the Interior to Senator James O. Eastland, NSHS.

67. U.S. Adjutant General, "Report of the Investigation," 115.

68. U.S. Adjutant General, "Report of the Investigation," 116.

69. Scott, "A Look at the Record," 6. Listed are William G. Austin, Sgt., Cav.; John E. Clancy, musician, Art.; Ernest A Garlington, 1st Lt., Art.; John C. Gresham, 1st Lt., Cav.; Matthew H. Hamilton, Pvt., Cav.; Joshua B. Hertzog, Pvt., Art.; Harry L. Hawthorne, 2nd Lt., Art.; Marvin C. Hillock, Pvt., Cav.; George Hobday, Pvt., Cav.; George Loyd, Sgt., Cav.; Albert W. McMillan, Sgt., Cav.; Frederick E. Toy, 1st Sgt., Cav.; Jacob Trautman, 1st Sgt., Cav.; James Ward, Sgt., Cav.; Paul H. Weinert, Cpl., Art.; and Herman Ziegman, Pvt., Cav.

70. Ricker notebooks, tablet 3, ESR, NSHS.

71. McGregor, *Wounded Knee Massacre*, 124. McGregor affirms, "The Indians tell a straight story with but few inconsistencies and is free from exaggeration and prejudice as you would reasonably expect, considering the lapse of time and the enormity of the offense" (92).

72. Ricker notebooks, tablet 11, ESR, NSHS; emphasis in original.

73. Ricker notebooks, tablet 22, ESR, NSHS.

74. *Chadron (NE) Democrat*, January 8, 1891.

75. *Army and Navy Journal*, January 17, 1891.

76. *Army and Navy Journal*, January 17, 1891.

77. Carroll, *Unpublished Papers*, 11–12.

78. Bland, *A Brief History*, 22.

79. *Army and Navy Journal*, January 24, 1891.

80. Remington, "Indians as Irregular Cavalry," 77; originally quoted in *Harper's Weekly*, January 31, 1891.

81. *Omaha Bee* and *New York Times*, January 5, 1991.

82. *New York Times*, January 7, 1891.

83. Colby, "Sioux Indian War," 165.

84. Perrig diary, 53, MUL. McGillycuddy later wrote Campbell, "That fellow Royer was a speciman, he is a resident of Orange Co., Cal. now practicing medicine, he was suspended about a year ago by the State Medical Board, for indulging in drugs, but begged off on his trial, stating that the habit was acquired by reason of the Terrible exposure and hardships he went through in trying to civilize and save the poor Indians" (box 107, folder 7, WSC).

85. Colby, "Sioux Indian War," 167.

86. Colby, "Sioux Indian War," 158–59.

87. Kelley, *Pine Ridge 1890*, 253–54.

88. Short Bull's Testimony, 19, BBMM.

89. *Washington Evening Star*, January 29, 1891.

90. Miles, *Serving the Republic*, 245–47.

91. Bland, *A Brief History*, 30–31.

92. Short Bull's Testimony, 19, BBMM.

93. Kelley, *Pine Ridge 1890*, 256.

94. Eastman, *Deep Woods to Civilization*, 114–15.

95. U.S. Senate, *Hearing before the Select Committee*, April 30, 1991, 66.

96. Utley, *Last Days*, 249.

97. Letter photocopy, personal files of R. Eli Paul.

98. Bland, *A Brief History*, 24.

99. Colby, "Sioux Indian War," 180.

100. Box 107, folder 7, WSC.

101. Danker, "Wounded Knee Interviews," 226.

102. Black Elk, interview by author, August 10, 1971.

Bibliography

LIBRARIES AND COLLECTIONS

Buffalo Bill Historical Center, Cody WY

Buffalo Bill Memorial Museum (BBMM), Golden CO

Colorado Historical Society, Denver CO

Denver Public Library, Western Section, Denver CO

Iowa State Historical Society, Des Moines IA

Marquette University Library (MUL), Milwaukee WI, especially the Father Aemilius Perrig diary

Nebraska State Historical Society (NSHS), Lincoln NE, especially the Judge Eli S. Ricker Collection

South Dakota State Historical Society (SDSHS), Pierre SD, especially the John R. Brennan Family papers

University of Oklahoma Library, Western History Collection, Norman OK, especially the Walter S. Campbell Collection

NEWSPAPERS AND PERIODICALS

Most of the newspapers and periodicals I consulted date from 1889 to 1891. Some of the articles I perused in clippings collections were unpaginated, and some clippings included neither the newspaper name nor the date.

Army and Navy Journal

Chadron (NE) Democrat

Chicago Tribune

Columbus (NE) Sentinel

Custer (SD) Chronicle

Denver Post

El Segundo Herald

Harpers Weekly

Iowa State Register

Lincoln (NE) State Journal

Nebraska State Journal

New York Herald

New York Sun

New York Times

New York World

Omaha Bee

Omaha World Herald

Pioneer Press

Rapid City (SD) Daily Journal

Sioux Falls (SD) Argus Leader

Washington Evening Star

BOOKS, ARTICLES, AND INTERVIEWS

Adams, Alexander B. *Sitting Bull: An Epic of the Plains.* New York: G. P. Putnam's Sons, 1973.

Arnold, Frazer. "Ghost Dance and Wounded Knee." *Cavalry Journal* 43 (1934): 18–20.

Bennett County Historical Society. *70 Years of Pioneer Life in Bennett County, South Dakota, 1911–1981.* Pierre SD: State Publishing, 1971.

Black Elk, Benjamin. Interview by author. South Dakota, August 10, 1971.

Bland, T. A. *A Brief History of the Late Military Invasion of the Home of the Sioux.* Washington DC: National Indian Defence Association, 1891.

Bosma, Boyd. "An Interview with Jim Mesteth." *The Indian Historian* 11 (1978): 18–21.

Brady, Cyrus Townsend. *Indian Fights and Fighters.* 1904. Reprint, Lincoln: University of Nebraska Press, 1971.

Carroll, John M., ed. *The Arrest and Killing of Sitting Bull: A Documentary.* Glendale CA: Arthur H. Clark, 1986.

———. "Extracts from Letters Written by Lieutenant Alexander R. Piper . . . during the Sioux Campaign, 1890–1891." In vol. 10 of *The Unpublished Papers of the Order of Indian Wars Book,* 1–19. New Brunswick NJ: n.p., 1977.

Cody, William F. (ghostwritten) *Buffalo Bill's Life Story: An Autobiography.* New York: Rinehart and Company, 1920.

Colby, L. W. "The Sioux Indian War of 1890–91." *Transactions and Reports of the Nebraska State Historical Society* 3 (1892): 144–90.

———. "Wanagi Olowan kin (The Ghost Songs of the Dakotas)." *Proceedings and Collections of the Nebraska State Historical Society* 2nd ser., 1 (1895), 131–50.

Coleman, William S. E. "Buffalo Bill on Stage." *Players* 47 (1972): 80–91.

Commissioner of Indian Affairs. "Reports of Agents." In *Fifty-Ninth Annual Report of the Commissioner of Indian Affairs to the Secretary of the Interior.* Washington DC: GPO, 1890.

Commissioner of Indian Affairs. "Reports of Agents." In *Sixtieth Annual Report of the Commissioner of Indian Affairs to the Secretary of the Interior.* Washington DC: GPO, 1891.

Congressional Record. 51st Cong., 2nd sess., 1890.

Cook, James H. *Fifty Years on the Old Frontier as Cowboy, Hunter, Guide, Scout, and Ranchman.* New Haven: Yale University Press, 1925.

Danker, Donald F. "The Wounded Knee Interviews of Eli S. Ricker." *Nebraska History* 62 (1981): 151–243.

De Barthe, Joe. *The Life and Adventures of Frank Grouard.* St. Joseph MO: Combe Printing, 1894.

Eastman, Charles A. *From Deep Woods to Civilization.* 1916. Reprint, Lincoln: University of Nebraska Press, 1977.

———. "Plain Words on the Indian Question." *New England Magazine* 2 (1890): 147–48.

Ewing, Charles B. "The Wounded of the Wounded Knee Battle Field with Remarks on Wounds Produced by Large and Small Caliber Bullets." *Second Annual Meeting of the Association of Military Surgeons*. St. Louis MO: Becktold and Co., 1892.

Fechet, E. G. "The Capture of Sitting Bull." *South Dakota Historical Collections* 4 (1908): 185–93.

———. "The True Story of the Death of Sitting Bull." *Proceedings and Collections of the Nebraska State Historical Society* 2nd ser., 2 (1898), 179–91.

Finley, Mrs. James A. "Account of the Northern Cheyennes Concerning the Messiah Superstition." *Journal of American Folk-lore* 4 (1891): 66–68. Originally published in the *Salem MA Essex Country Mercury*, November 26, 1890.

Fitzgerald, Mary Clement. "Bishop Marty and His Sioux Missions: 1876–1896." *South Dakota Historical Collections* 20 (1940): 545.

Fletcher, Alice C. "The Indian Messiah." *Journal of American Folk-lore* 4 (1891): 57–60.

Gilmore, Melvin R. "The Truth of the Wounded Knee Massacre." *American Indian* 5 (1917): 240–52.

Godfrey, Edward S. *Tragedy at White Horse Creek: Edward S. Godfrey's Unpublished Account of an Incident Near Wounded Knee*. With notes and introduction by Barry C. Johnson. Brand Book series, no. 9. London: The English Westerners' Society, 1977.

Goodale (Eastman), Elaine. "The Ghost Dance War and Wounded Knee Massacre of 1890–91." *Nebraska History* 26 (1945): 26–42.

High Back, Paul. "Disaster of December 29, 1890, at Wounded Knee, as told to John Williamson." *Wi-iyohi: Monthly Bulletin of the South Dakota Historical Society* 10, no. 3 (1 June 1956): 1–3.

Howe, M. A. DeWolfe. *Life and Labors of Bishop Hare: Apostle to the Sioux*. New York: Sturgis & Walton Co., 1911.

Hyde, George E. *A Sioux Chronicle*. Norman: University of Oklahoma Press, 1956.

Jensen, Richard, R. Eli Paul, and John E. Carter. *Eyewitness at Wounded Knee*. Lincoln: University of Nebraska Press, 1991.

Kelley, William Fitch. "The Indian Troubles and the Battle of Wounded Knee." *Transactions and Reports of the Nebraska State Historical Society* 4 (1892): 30–42.

———. *Pine Ridge 1890*. San Francisco: Pierre Bovis, 1971.

Lathrop, Alan K. "Another View of Wounded Knee." *South Dakota History* 16 (1986): 249–68.

Lee, Robert. "Messiah Craze: Wounded Knee." *Wi-iyohi: Monthly Bulletin of the South Dakota Historical Society* 9 (1955): 1–12.

Lindberg, Christer. "Foreigners in Action at Wounded Knee." *Nebraska History* 71 (1990): 170–81.

McGillycuddy, Julia B. *Blood on the Moon: Valentine McGillycuddy and the Sioux*. 1941. Reprint, Lincoln: University of Nebraska Press, Bison Books, 1990.

McGregor, James H. *The Wounded Knee Massacre*. 1940. Reprint, Rapid City SD: Fenwyn Press, 1969.

McLaughlin, James. *My Friend the Indian*. 1910. Reprint, Lincoln: University of Nebraska Press, 1989.

Miles, Nelson A. "The Future of the Indian Question." *North American Review* 152 (1891): 1–11.

———. "Report of Major General Miles." In U.S. War Department, *Report of the Secretary of War*. 52nd Cong., 1st sess. Washington DC: GPO, 1892.

———. *Serving the Republic*. New York: Harper and Bros., 1911.

Mooney, James. "The Ghost-Dance Religion and the Sioux Outbreak of 1890." Part 2 of the *Fourteenth Annual Report of the Bureau of Ethnology to the Secretary of the Smithsonian Institution, 1892–93*. Washington DC: GPO, 1896. Reprinted as *The Ghost Dance Religion and the Sioux Outbreak of 1890* (Lincoln: University of Nebraska Press, Bison Books, 1991).

Moorehead, Warren K. "The Indian Messiah and the Ghost Dance." *American Antiquarian and Oriental Journal* 12 (1891): 161–67.

Morgan, Thisba Hutson. "Reminiscences of My Days in the Land of the Ogallala Sioux." *South Dakota Historical Collections and Report* 29 (1958): 21–62.

Neihardt, John G, ed. *Black Elk Speaks, Being the Story of a Holy Man of the Ogalala Sioux*. Lincoln: University of Nebraska Press, 1979.

Potomac Corral of the Westerners. *Great Western Indian Fights*. Garden City NY: Doubleday and Company, 1960.

Prologue: The Journal of the National Archives 1 (fall 1969): 172–73.

Remington, Frederic. "Indians as Irregular Cavalry." In *The Collected Writings of Frederic Remington*, ed. Peggy and Harold Samuels. Garden City NY: Doubleday and Company, 1979.

Robinson, Doane. *A History of the Dakota or Sioux Indians*. Minneapolis: Ross and Haines, 1967.

———. "History of the Sioux War." *South Dakota Historical Collections* 2 (1904): 459–508.

———. "Some Sidelights on the Character of Sitting Bull." *South Dakota Historical Collections* 5 (1910): 187–92.

Russell, Don. *The Lives and Legends of Buffalo Bill*. Norman: University of Oklahoma Press, 1960.

Scott, E. D. "Wounded Knee: A Look at the Record." *The Field Artillery Journal* 29 (1939): 5–24.

Smith, Rex Alan. *Moon of Popping Trees*. Lincoln: University of Nebraska Press, 1975.

Standing Bear, Luther. *My People the Sioux*. Lincoln: University of Nebraska Press, 1975.

Steele, M. F. "Buffalo Bill's Bluff." *South Dakota Historical Collections* 9 (1918): 475–85.

"The Truth of the Wounded Knee Massacre." *American Indian* 5 (1917).

U.S. Adjutant General. "Report of the Investigation." In *Reports and Correspondence Relating to the Army Investigations of the Battle of Wounded Knee and to the Sioux Campaign of 1890–91*. Washington DC: National Archives, 1974. Microfilm.

U.S. Senate. *Hearing before the Select Committee of Indian Affairs*, 101st Cong., 2nd sess., September 25, 1990. Washington DC: GPO, 1990.

U.S. Senate. *Hearing before the Select Committee of Indian Affairs*, 102nd Cong., 1st sess., April 30, 1991. Washington DC: GPO, 1991.

U.S. Senate. *Reports of Committees*. 48th Cong., 1st sess. Vol. 1, 1883–84. Washington DC: GPO, 1884.

Utley, Robert M. *The Lance and the Shield: The Life and Times of Sitting Bull*. New York: Henry Holt and Company, 1993.

———. *The Last Days of the Sioux Nation*. New Haven: Yale University Press, 1963.

Vanderworth, W. C., comp. *Indian Oratory*. 1971. Reprint, New York: Ballantine Books, 1975.

Vestal, Stanley [Walter S. Campbell]. *New Sources of Indian History, 1850–1891*. Norman: University of Oklahoma Press, 1934.

———. *Sitting Bull: Champion of the Sioux. A Biography*. 1932. Reprint, Norman: University of Oklahoma Press, 1957.

Warren, Margaret Lemley. *The Badlands Fox*. Hermosa SD: privately printed, 1991.

Watson, Elmo Scott. "The Last Indian War, 1890–91: A Study of Newspaper Jingoism." *Journalism Quarterly* 20 (1943): 205–19.

Wells, Philip. "Ninety-Six Years among the Indians of the Northwest—Adventures and Reminiscences of an Indian Scout and Interpreter in the Dakotas." *North Dakota History* 15 (1948): 265–312.

Wetmore, Helen Cody. *Last of the Great Scouts; The Life Story of Colonel William F. Cody*. 1899. Reprint, Lincoln: University of Nebraska Press: 1989.

Index